Reflections on International Tourism

Expressions of Culture, Identity and Meaning in Tourism

edited by

**Mike Robinson
Philip Long
Nigel Evans
Richard Sharpley
John Swarbrooke**

UNIVERSITY *of* *at* NEWCASTLE   *Sheffield Hallam University*

2000

©The Centre for Travel & Tourism, Centre for Tourism and the Authors

ISBN 1 871916 45 3

First published 2000

Cover Design by Tim Murphy Creative Solutions

Published in Great Britain by
the Centre for Travel and Tourism in association with
Business Education Publishers Ltd.,
The Teleport,
Doxford International,
Sunderland   SR3 3XD

Tel: 0191 525 2400
Fax: 0191 520 1815

British Cataloguing-in-Publications Data
A catalogue record for this book is available from the British Library

Printed in Great Britain by Athenaeum Press, Gateshead

Preface

Tourism continues to reach out in to space and time. Implicit within the trite phrase of 'tourism is the world's largest industry', it *appears* that everyone is either a tourist or a potential tourist, everywhere is someone's destination and no human activity is immune from the fleeting glimpses of transient eyes. Appearances, of course, can be deceptive.

Ironically, change, movement, development and growth are the norms that characterise a phenomenon that many still see as an opportunity to slow down, relax and do little. The new millennium will undoubtedly see more tourists, more tourism, more travel, more impacts, more to market, more to manage. Core human traits of creativity and curiosity, desires to consume and commune, along with the need to survive, remain as the fundamental, and often conflicting, drivers for this thing we label tourism. Tourism is an important subject of academic inquiry *precisely* because it is an extension of our humanity and the cultures we inhabit, and because of the rapidity of change and growth that now typifies it.

This series of six volumes arose out of a major international conference held at Sheffield Hallam University, UK, in September 2000. Organised by the Centre for Travel and Tourism, University of Northumbria and the Centre for Tourism Sheffield Hallam University, **Tourism 2000: Time for Celebration?** was designed to reflect on, evaluate and anticipate the growth and development of tourism from its roots in pilgrimage and exploration, to its present and future role as a vast and complex social and cultural activity, a diverse international industry, and a focus for academic discourse. The conference attracted tremendous interest from academics, policy makers and practitioners from across the world and in itself was a touristic experience. These books contain 173 of nearly 200 papers presented at the conference.

The importance of this series lies in its diversity as well as its dimensions. We believe it to be important that authors from differing disciplines, perspectives, nationalities and cultures are able to reflect on the many facets of tourism. With diversity, however, comes problems of categorisation and hard editorial decisions. We trust that in the main we have managed to produce a reasoned and manageable breakdown of papers.

The production of one book can generate a plethora of problems. Not surprisingly the production of six volumes involving so many contributors and from such a diversity of locations has not been without anguish. Differing interpretations of the word 'deadline' is a common source of editorial angst! Technology too, though we are indebted to it, has frequently been the object of derision – the email delivery failure, the server that is down, the lost file, the scrambled text, and the ever popular 'pressing the wrong button.'

Fortunately there are those amongst us that appear to take problems in their stride and who sail on through the waves of worry. Thanks must go to Richard Shipway for his help in chasing the most elusive of authors. Thanks also to Jill Pomfret for her help in the editing process and to Amanda Miller for her assistance. Central to this bout of thanks are the staff at Business Education Publishers Ltd (BEP), who have been down this road with us many times now and continue to deliver a service second to none. Without the professionalism, commitment and good humour of Andrea Murphy, Moira Page and everyone who has worked on this series at BEP, you would not be reading this.

Finally our thanks go, as ever, to all the contributors to the series. Reflections on International Tourism provides a home for over 200 researchers, thinkers, critics and practitioners from nearly forty countries who have been through the processes of contemplation and reflection – those precious intellectual spaces between doing and being.

The important thing that all our authors now offer us through the work contained in these pages, is an invitation for you, the reader, to engage in your own process of reflection.

Mike Robinson
Sheffield, 2000

Introduction

Travelling and participating in tourist activity plays an important part in the cultural and social lives of millions of people world-wide. At the same time, the ways in which tourism develops is strongly influenced by social and cultural conditions and changes in areas that both generate and receive tourists. The emergence and development of new and adapted forms of tourism products, and changes in consumer demand for these products can all be examined (and arguably explained) in relation to cultural conditions and influences that operate at global, national and local levels.

The nature of social and cultural 'impacts' of tourism as an agent of change on 'hosts' and 'guests' has been of longstanding interest to academics and policy makers and to some elements of the tourism industry. Identity, both in the sense of the representation of places as visitor destinations, and in existentialist terms reflected in the meanings that people ascribe to their tourist experiences and their effects on (inter-) personal life, are also of substantial research interest. However, 'culture', 'identity' and 'meaning' are all complex terms with many alternative, competing and complementary interpretations and definitions. They can all be conceptualised and studied from several academic disciplinary perspectives. This volume includes state-of-the-art work that addresses some of these different perspectives and the ways in which they might be applied to an understanding of tourism in past, present and future society.

There are many reasons for the growing interest in studying the relationships between tourism and culture, identity and meaning. Forms of tourism such as; 'mass-', 'package-', 'eco-', rural-, urban-, health-, and 'sustainable-' have all emerged and developed (and in some cases, declined) over time, and vary in nature from place to place. Different forms of tourism may usefully be examined in relation to their social and cultural contexts. There is also a practical need for the tourism industry, policy-makers and 'host' communities to understand *tourist* cultures and the meanings that people bring to and take away from their travel experiences. Such an understanding is important in marketing, management and quality terms.

While the relationships between culture and tourism are receiving increasing attention from academics, they arguably remain inadequately understood by the tourism industry, politicians, agencies and authorities involved in the development of tourism. The tourism industry in some cases also needs to develop a better understanding of the cultural identities of 'host' communities in tourist destinations. A better level of understanding may, for example, foster improved 'host-guest' relations and result in the development of tourism policies and products that reflect and promote unique and distinctive characteristics and place identities.

The elusive concept of the 'cultural tourist' is also explored in this volume. Cultural tourists, albeit sometimes inadequately defined, are widely claimed by the tourism industry as being a valuable and desirable market segment (or segments). They are commonly represented as being civilised, tasteful, high spending, discerning travellers (as opposed to 'tourists'), who read literature about the destination prior to and during their visit. They are seen to be respectful of indigenous cultural tradition (or at least those traditions that are publicised). Cultural tourists, it is suggested, buy locally produced arts and crafts and patronise museums, exhibitions and concerts. They are knowledgeable about and consume local cuisine and they stay in locally owned accommodation. Cultural tourists may also assist in the fostering of civic and local pride by their valuing the distinctiveness of places and by their appreciation of a community's history, landscapes, traditions and art-forms.

However, cultural tourism, in this conception is controversial. It may be seen as being elitist and conservative in reinforcing the precedence of the mainly north European and North American urban middle classes in determining value and defining taste. Some may also argue that governments' attention to the development of cultural tourism is a distraction from more serious social and economic concerns and that public spending in this area is effectively a subsidy for the interests of the urban middle classes. Furthermore, the priorities of the cultural and arts sectors, which are not exclusively market-driven, may not ultimately be reconciled with the needs of tourists and the tourism industry.

There are a number of research strands in this complex and contentious field. There are, for example, continuing efforts to understand the role and meaning of tourism within contemporary (and past) societies. Such studies include analyses of the ways in which tourism has been organised as a social system, including attention to industry structure and organisational cultures as well as the motivations, attitudes and behaviours of both individuals and groups of tourists and of communities in destinations, and their interactions. The connections between tourism and wider social changes are also the subject of research. This involves study of the effects that the tourism industry and tourist behaviour may have on changes and developments in societies in both generating and destination areas. Conversely, research attention may also be focussed on the possible consequences *for* tourism of social changes in origin and destination regions.

Explanations of tourism as a form of ritual and quasi-religious pilgrimage have also been presented and developed over the past thirty years or so. For some theorists, people are actively seeking levels of authenticity and meaning through travelling that are lacking in their everyday lives. Other writers argue that, on the contrary, tourists are, increasingly knowingly, participating in inauthentic, pseudo-experiences. This anthropological strand of tourism research has also included analyses of the part that tourism plays in the development of myths and symbols about places and people.

Expressions of culture via the film and literary, broadcast and print media, and their direct and indirect relationships with tourism are receiving growing research attention. The media is, after all, a major phenomenon and industry in contemporary society. However, and in spite of this, literary critical and media studies approaches are still comparatively under-represented in the tourism literature. The literary *genre* of 'travel writing', for example, is now hugely successful, with many authors in this field regularly leading best-seller lists, and most book-shops in the UK, Europe and North America now contain well stocked 'Travel' sections.

There is scope for tourism researchers to undertake further studies in this, and other literary and broader areas of the media. Such research might, for example, examine; the narrative form (or story line) of literary texts, the style of writing and the language used by authors, the gendered nature of texts in terms of distinctions between male and female, gay, lesbian and heterosexual authors, the ways in which opinions, prejudices and positions held by authors are revealed in texts, how authors represent the 'other' in terms of the landscapes, cultural practices and people encountered during a journey, how itineraries and sites are mapped and evaluated by authors, and whether a guide to conduct for travellers to the destination(s) featured in the text is included and what this might comprise.

There are many other key research issues in the expressions of culture, identity and meaning in tourism. Examples include the connections between culture, tourism and political economy through the expression of policies and plans for cultural tourism (or culture *and* tourism), and their links with area-based regeneration programmes. The relationships between tourism and the 'creative industries' in the 'cultural quarters' of cities is a particular focus of such policy and economic development based work, as are the connections between tourism and other expressions of urban culture, for example, sport, shopping and entertainment in the 'twenty-four hour city.'

The chapters presented in this volume contribute perspectives on these and many other critical issues that are associated with the expressions of culture, identity and meaning in tourism.

Table of Contents

Cultural tourism activity as stimulus to revitalisation: Old Banten, Java

Akmalia K Arif

Bandung Institute of Technology, Indonesia

Abstract

When a cultural asset has a very deep historical meaning, it becomes an important evidence of the history of human being, and that means the object has becomes an unrenewable resource. An effort for preservation and conservation is needed, because documents and photos will never be enough to represent the essences of historical objects. By conserving an environment that has a historical meaning, we give opportunity for every human to get a kind of psychological comfort through touching, seeing, and feeling physical evidence in its tradition.

In efforts to conserve built heritages, a strategy that can be attempted is by assign it as a tourist attraction and cultural recreation. In much of the world, cultural tourism is linked closely to built heritage, and is seen as a stimulus to urban economies and revitalisation. Not only the built heritages become self-afforded, but also it can increase regional --even national-- income.

Old Banten once achieved high civilisation in the past. With more than nine- century life span (approximately 9th-18th century), Old Banten left many valuable heritages, specially the archaeological urban site with its architectures. According to the Monumenten Ordonantie issued by Netherlands Indische Government, this built environment has been designated as National Heritage since 1914. Much later, in 1992 the free Indonesia Government arranged a set of regulations to protect national built heritages and cultural objects.

This paper will propose a methodology for ensuring that the cultural heritages of Old Banten, as contained within the many historic layers of surviving documentation and physical remains, are both conserved and made intelligible to the wider community.

Introduction

Indonesia, with its area stretching from Sabang to Merauke has a wealth of cultural remains. Chronologically they represents remains from the oldest evidence, that is when the early man appeared in Java about 1.5 million years ago, until the period with remains of the arrival of the Europeans in the archipelago since 1602 up to the 19th century.

Since the opening of Borobudur and Prambanan temple as a major historical site and tourist destination in 1983, the Indonesian government has given more attention to efforts to conserve built heritage. Developing cultural-heritage sites as tourist attractions is expected to be a stimulus to urban economies and revitalisation. Another purposes are making the built heritages become self-afforded and increasing regional - even national - income.

Banten, formerly known as Bantam, is now an abandoned seaport on the north-west coast of the Island of Java, and 60 miles west Jakarta. At the present time, Old Banten town is administratively part of Banten village. It is located about 10 km on the north of Serang -- one of regencies in West Java - and surrounded by several industrial centres. This Location can be reached easily from Jakarta by varied modes of transportation, including toll-ways, railways, and sea transport.

Most of the current residents of Banten village are outlanders coming from other regencies of West Java, from Sumatra, and from South Sulawesi. The major religion is Islam, which affects the cultural arts of Banten. Their social and economic lives are very modest, with agriculture and the sea as their means of livelihood.

Old Banten has a very unique and potent setting, compared to other places doesn't. The most significant asset that should bring this place to a new life is the cultural heritages, including the archaeological sites, the cultural patterns, local arts and crafts, traditional economic activities, cultural festive, and the residents' perceptive character.

Approach to cultural tourism

In approach to Old Banten master plan, we combine historic site management and interpretation with new opportunities for overnight accommodation, conference and education activities, landscape management and casual recreation.

In the planning process, the first step is assessing significant objects of the place, then comprehending their cultural meanings. The next step is deciding conservation treatments for each single object, considering its significance, location, physical condition, integrity, authenticity, and impacts to surrounding environment/community.

After assigning locations for tourism activity, we have to create an integrative linkage system between them. Destination points, visitors' spatial patterns, kinds of activity, and kinds of facility provided will affect the scenario's level of success.

Other thing should be done is looking for the most optimal alternatives of tourism scenario, which could 'sell' Old Banten. The tourism concepts not only contain preservation and revitalisation aspects, but also integrated 'selling' strategies such as exhibitions, demonstrations, animations, and other interpretive techniques.

Besides those factors, there are other considerations: ownership, visitors' character, local population, cost and financing. Therefore, special studies on institutions involved and suitable return of investment is needed.

Historical background of Banten

Once the capital of Muslim sultanate, Banten was developed as a Portuguese trading station in mid of 16th century. As Michrob (1993) found, historic data suggests that Old Banten's historical development can be divided into five broad phases:

Banten prior to the 14th century: pre-Islamic Sundanese period

Reports of historical sources on Banten from the period prior to the 16th century are not to be found, but at least between the 12th to the 15th centuries Banten was already a harbour for the kingdom of Sunda. In the near of Pajajaran, capital of the kingdom of Sunda, were found two land routes connecting the coast to the capital. The rivers flowing from the interior down to the north coast of Java were already used as connecting routes between the interior and the coastal area. One of the land-routes was the road from Pajajaran via Jasinga, turning northwards Rangkasbitung, ending at Banten Girang, about 3 kilometres south of the present town of Serang (some 13 kilometres from Old Banten). Considering the name Banten Girang (upstream Banten), we may assume the possibility of the existence of downstream Banten. But was there indeed such a town by that, and if so, could it perhaps be identified with the present town of Old Banten?

In 1513, there was an insignificant harbour, though already mentioned as being the second largest harbour of the kingdom of Sunda, after Sunda Kelapa. A lively trade between Banten and Sunda was already existing. Vessels from all over the country were anchoring at Banten. At that time, Banten had already exported rice, foodstuffs and pepper from that harbour. Banten became an important harbour in 1522, when the kingdom of Sunda exported 1000 *bahar* of pepper annually.

Banten in the 16th century: early Islamic fluorescence

When the Islamic kingdom of Banten was founded, the centre of power originally in Banten Girang, was moved to the town of Surosowan on the coast. From the economic point of view, this shift was meant to facilitate the connection between the north coast of Java and the coast of Sumatra, by way of Strait Sunda and the Indian Ocean. This situation was caused by the political conditions in Southeast Asia at that time, when Malacca had already fallen under suzerainty of Portugal, so that the merchants who were averse of dealing with the Portuguese moved their trade-route to Strait Sunda.

The town of Surosowan was made capital of the kingdom of Banten ad decreed by the first Moslem ruler of Banten. The arrival of the Moslem ruler at Banten occurred circa 1524-1525, when Banten was still under the suzerainty of Sunda. According to local tradition, the last ruler of Sunda at Banten Girang was Prabu (King) Pucuk Umum, son of Prabu Seda.

Sunan Gunung Jati or Syeikh Syarif Hidayatullah who became the first Moslem ruler of Banten was not crowned as its first King, but put his son, Maulana Hasanuddin in charge of the kingdom. When he founded the town Surosowan in the area of what is now known as Old Banten, Sunan Gunung Jati ordered not to move the Watu Gilang (ceremonial stone) in front of the palace, as its removal may cause destruction. Hasanuddin, who in 1526 married the daughter of Sultan Trenggana, ascended the throne of Banten in 1552. Besides ordering the construction of the Surosowan palace, Hasanuddin built also two mosques in the area of Old Banten. The first one is the building on the West Side of alun-alun (square).

Maulana Jusuf succeeded Hasanuddin as Banten's second ruler (1570-1580). He expanded the territory of the kingdom of Banten, reaching far into the interior, which had been originally under the suzerainty of Sunda and even successfully occupied the capital of the kingdom at Pakuwan. According to the tradition, Maulana Jusuf enlarged the Great Mosque by adding a gallery and built another mosque at Kasunyatan (South Old Banten).

When Maulana Jusuf died, Prince Muhammad the rightful heir was to ascend the throne, but as he was still a child, a regent was appointed: Prince Aria Japara. One important event during the reign of Prince Muhammad was the arrival of Dutch ships in 1596, which anchored in the harbour of Banten under command of Cornelis de Houtman. The written notes left by the Dutch guests are valuable source of information on Banten. In a note of Jan Kerel Jansz, dated August 6, 1959 was mentioned that foreign ships, which anchored in Banten, could only do so after obtaining consent of the Syahbandar. In order to enter the town from the harbour one had to go through the *tolhuis* (tollgate) of the customs office.

Banten in the 17th centuries: The period of fluctuating fortunes

One characteristic of the political and social condition of Banten in the 17th century was the beginning of the impact of the Dutch on the administration and trade in royal circles. Observing the list of sultans who ruled Banten, Banten was on its peak of prosperity and progress in the 17th century.

Banten in the 17th - 18th centuries: Dutch overlord-ship period

The major construction at this period was Fortress of Speelwijk. The Dutch built canals on the perimeters of Surosowan palace, the fort, and connected to the seaport.

Banten in the 19th centuries: The decline and fall of Old Banten

In this period, Surosowan Palace was burnt in fire and the kingdom moved to Kaibon Palace near Cibanten River. The Dutch built Anyer-Panarukan way and railways across Banten. At the end of this period, the Dutch ended their economic activity in Banten and this town left by the residents.

Archaeological remains of Old Banten

Compound of Surosowan Palace

The whole compound is now in ruins, with only the surrounding wall and some of its parts left. The remains consist of foundations and parts of the ruined walls of the rooms in the palace, remains of a bathing place and a pond with a floating pavilion. The surrounding (fortress) wall measuring 0.5-2 meters in height is still preserved with an approximate with of five meters. In some parts, in particular in the south and east, one can see that the whole wall has vanished.

The palace compound is oblong in plan and about three hectares large. The entrance is the large gate on the north side, facing the alun-alun (square). According to old maps and drawings, there used to be a door on the East Side, now invisible, as it is buried in the soil. The four corners of the surrounding wall form bastions, being protruding parts of that wall. Meanwhile, inside of these bastions was found four entrance doors leading to former halls. According to old maps, one can see that this compound was formerly surrounded by canal, constructed for defence purpose. Part of this canal now no longer exists. Only the southern and western parts are left.

According to historical data, this Surosowan palace compound, also named Kedaton Pakuwan, was built during the reign of Maulana Hasanuddin (1552-1570). Later Maulana Jusuf (1570-1580) built the fortress wall and the gate constructed from bricks and rocks.

Figure 1   The Surosowan Wall and the Canalisation

Compound of the great mosque

This compound consists of the mosque with galleries on the left and right, the Tiyamah, the tower, and the cemetery north of the mosque.

(a) The Great Mosque was built during the reign of Maulana Hasanuddin. Similar to Surosowan Palace, this mosque is located in the middle of Old Banten. Currently a destination point for pilgrims, the Great Mosque of Banten is in quite good condition.

The ground plan is square, with five tiers supporting one big roof. The galleries on the left and right of the building were built in a later period. On the left (north) gallery are the tombs of several Banten kings and their relatives: among others are Maulana Hasanuddin and his wife, Sultan Ageng Tirtayasa and Sultan Abu Nasr Abdul Qahhar. Meanwhile on the right gallery are the tombs of Sultan Muhammad, Sultan Zainul Abidin, and others.

(b) The Tiyamah is a two-storey additional building in the south of the Great Mosque. The style is Old Dutch -- according to tradition, this building was built by a Dutch Architect named Lucas Cardeel -- the Tiyamah was formerly used as a meeting place, particularly for discussing religious matters.

(c) The Tower (minaret) stands in front of the compound. According to tradition, it was also built by Lucas Cardeel. The age of this building is not certain, but Cornelis de Houtman's Map of Banten, 1598 had showed this minaret.

(d) Several old graves were found in the cemetery on the northern side of the compound.

Figure 2   The Great Mosque of Old Banten

The Canon Ki Amuk

This canon, originally standing in Karangantu, is now placed on the corner of the Alun-alun, in front of the Surosowan compound. On the canon are three inscriptions in Arabic, using Arab characters. According to KC Crucq, this inscription is a chronogram, meaning 1450 Saka (AD 1528/1529).

The Pacinan Tinggi Mosque

In the Kampong Pacinan (Chinese Lodging), exist ruins of an old mosque. Besides the remains of the main building, there also part of the wall of the *mihrab*. In the left of the mosque are remains of the minaret which oblong in ground plan. The minaret itself is constructed of brick, while rocks were used for its foundation and base. According to tradition, the mosque and the minaret already existed before the Great Mosque of Banten was built.

Figure 3　Pacinan Tinggi Minaret

Compound of the Kaibon Palace

Kaibon Palace is located in the kampong of Kroya. This palace is said to be residence of Ratu (Queen) Asiyah, mother of Sultan Safiuddin. The Dutch Colonial Government in 1832 destroyed the buildings. What is left now are all in ruins with only the foundations and part of the surrounding walls and the gates.

Figure 4a. and 4b.   Ruins of The Kaibon Palace

The Koja Mosque

What is left is only a ruin on the southern bank side of the road leading from Fortress of Speelwijk to Karangantu. Around this mosque was the settlement of Koja community (residents from Moslem Countries).

The fortress of Speelwijk

This fortress is located in the kampong of Pamarican, near Kampong Pabean. It is now a ruin, but part of its wall is still standing in one piece, in particular those on the north side. The Dutch built the fortress in 1685, on the ruins of the northern part of the surrounding wall of the town of Old Banten. Outside this fortress is the canal, while on the east is the cemetery of European residents.

Figure 5   Part of Fortress Speelwijk

The Chinese Temple

This temple stands on the west of the Fortress of Speelwijk. There used to be another at the kampong of Pacinan, built by the local Chinese. It is not known for sure when this temple was built, but according to tradition, the building of this temple took place in the early days of the Banten sultanate.

Figure 6   The Chinese Temple

The Watu Gilang

There are two Watu Gilangs on the Alun-alun, one in front of the Surosowan Palace and another on the north side of the Alun-alun. These are square-shaped stone with a level surface. These two Watu Gilangs were formerly used in case of enthronement of the Sultans of Banten.

Karangantu Port and Market

Old map created by Cornelis de Houtman at 1598 shows the town of Banten, including Karangantu Port and Market, surrounded by origin's lodgings.

Figure 7a. and 7b.   Activities at Karangantu: Port and Fish Market

The Tasik Ardi Pond

Figure 8   Tasik Ardi Pond

This pond was an important part of water-supply system of Old Banten town. It is located outside the town, about 2 kilometres in the south-east of Surosowan Palace. The area is approximately 5 hectares, and the base paved with bricks. Tasik Ardi supplied clean water for Surosowan Palace, while watering the field rice around the town. In the middle of the pond was the king's bathing garden, constructed on a 500m² small island.

Tourism components analysis

Access and linkage

The means of transportation to the location are varied -- two highways, railways, river, and two seaports -- but it does not guarantee that Old Banten could be reached easily. The obstacle is the lack of proper public transport.

Foreign visitors arrived at Cengkareng International Airport could not reach this place by public bus. Trains from Jakarta that pass through Old Banten provide only economic class. One of the two seaports has been abandoned for a long time. The other one occupied by fishermen's boat and wood freighters -- almost never by passenger ships.

Although Old Banten is located between Jakarta and Anyer (main tourist destination of West Java), no proper linkage is available to bring tourists to the location. In the location itself, the destination point is not clearly assigned and the parking area is not sufficient.

Infrastructures

Because Old Banten had been deteriorating for a long period, this location is no longer an urban site, but an abandoned village. The opening Old Banten to wider community will need a totally new infrastructure development programme.

Institutional components

The status of Old Banten as a cultural heritage site attracts many parties with many interests. This brings a misunderstanding about who is the most responsible to develop and maintain the historic site of Old Banten. Another issue is that the people of Banten from the larger area are now attempting to join their regencies into a new province.

Accommodation facilities

There is no accommodation facility around the area. The nearest facility centre is in Serang, 10 km from Old Banten. In fact, the topography and the beautiful landscape of the location have great potential to become resort areas.

Visitor facilities

There are several points of crowd that facilitated by small vendors. Unfortunately, the vendors are not well arranged and they have no sense of tidiness. Most of the goods offered are souvenirs, whereas visitors also need other kinds of goods.

Tourist attractions and activities

The possible main theme for tourism in Old Banten is pilgrimage tourism. All cultural remains of Old Banten are very potential to be main tourist attractions. That will be supported by recreational activities such as maritime tourist recreation, art and cultural park, agriculture recreation, and sightseeing.

Historic-based interpretation

According to Miksic (1986), the pre-Islamic Sundanese period could be an introduction leading to a second set of displays which would depict the Sundanese port which Chinese merchants may have known about during the late Song Dynasty, and which Tom Pires described in its last years. The general distribution of remains from that period which have been discovered could be shown by a map of the site, a diorama could be constructed to provide a concept of the size of the port, its architecture, and distribution of activities. Another two cases could be devoted to artefacts from this period, such as the Nandi statue and fragment of black stone image, and the Chinese, Thai, and Vietnamese ceramics found on the site which date from earlier than sixteenth century.

It would also be worthwhile to add a case describing the Kingdom of Pajajaran, with a map depicting its approximate sphere of control, the location of its capital at Bogor, the port at

Sunda Kelapa, and the overland route, which connected Pakuwan Pajajaran with Banten. In the future, it would be worthwhile contemplating some restoration work in Bogor, and the construction of an interpretative centre, to accommodate those who might find that site of intersect after visiting Old Banten.

A major difficulty in presenting illustrative material from Old Banten's pre-Islamic period is that we do not yet have a clear idea of what the local pottery may have looked like. To fill in this gap, some shards from Banten Girang may be shown. In future, cataloguing and further excavation at Old Banten may furnish a chronology for the local pottery, which we don't yet process.

Early Islamic period perhaps the most important phase in Banten's history, and deserves the greatest amount of displays space. Unfortunately, the amount of artefacts firmly dated to this period is small. Much will have to be depicted by means of maps, dioramas, and other reconstruction and other reconstruction rather than by physical remains. There is a large amount of pictorial and narrative material dating from 1596 onward, however, and this can be used to supplement the artefacts largely.

Special attention can also be given to interpreting the architecture and gravestone, which dated from this period, the Watu Gilang and Watu Sinayaksa and the large canon, Ki Amuk. Here visitors to the site can be given both historical information about early mosques, graves, stone thrones, and 16th century artillery, and information about the specific examples found at Old Banten site before they view these objects. Again, if a chronology for local ceramics can be formulated, these can be integrated into the displays.

Exhibits of this phase should be designed to illuminate the significance of the present appearance of the Surosowan palace and the Tiyamah. The stages in the constructions of the Surosowan wall in it self are worth a display. In future, perhaps the area within the Surosowan wall also is thoroughly described in the museum by means of diagrams, maps, and displays of artefacts connected to various stages of its existence. Studies of the areas already excavated could yield conclusions regarding the foundations, which dated from the period before intense Dutch influence in 1682. Among the ceramics, the Japanese Imari were dated from this period. The map of settlement produced by Francois Valentijn probably dated from this period, and could be used to depict the division of space within the city. The types of houses used by the population, and the structure of the various kampongs into which the city was divided could be portrayed.

Most of the Chinese ceramics found at the site dated from the period of the Dutch overlord-ship. The major new construction at this time was the fort Speelwijk. Displays should be designed to depict the relations existing at this time between the Dutch and the local inhabitants; the distribution of activities in and around the fort; corresponding development in the Surosowan; and the changes in the plan of the city and its residential sectors could also be displayed.

The fate of the city wall could also be explored at this point, from its construction sometime before 1596, through to its decay in the 18th century. The small portion of it, which remains, beneath Speelwijk, can be pointed out here as an architectural remnant worthy of note, and as an example of how remains of different periods came to be superimposed here.

For the period of the decline and fall, the effects of Napoleonic wars can be introduced, including the revolt and its suppression. The invasion by the English, the removal of the centre of Sultanate to Serang and the subsequent abdication of the ruler, and the ultimate intentional destruction of the palace by Dutch also can be shown.

Summary

There have been several studies about Banten, undertaking historical documentary and physical research of the place. They help to establish a good understanding of the heritage significance of the area, and how it relates to the overall history of Islamic Kingdoms in Indonesia. Other research attempts to identify the physical remains from each layer of history and possibly divide the area into precincts or zones, each of which may be conserved and developed in different ways

In the making of the master plan for Old Banten site, the next step is to establish what the physical requirements are for the conservation of the surviving remains and artefacts on the area. Identify the interest groups that may wish to participate in the planning of the area and its future. In particular work with the key management authority is to establish their expectations for the future. Due to the lack of access, possible methods of access to the area should be explored extensively. Appropriate services and facilities for visitors should be provided, and any possible opportunities for generating revenue from such operations should be explored.

Overall, as an archaeological site with many cultural heritages, Old Banten is very interesting to explore, attracting researchers to make further studies, especially to find the best methodology for conserving, as well as making it intelligible to the wider community.

References

Ambary, H. Michrob, M. and Miksik, J. (1988), *Katalogus Koleksi Data Arkeologi Banten*, Direktorat Perlindungan dan Pembinaan Peninggalan Sejarah dan Purbakala, Jakarta.

The Australia ICOMOS Charter for The Conservation of Places of Cultural Significance, 1981.

Inskeep, E. (1991), *Tourism Planning: An Integrated and Sustainable Development Approach*, Van Nostrand Reinhold, New York NY.

Michrob, H. (1993), *Sejarah Perkembangan Arsitektur Kota Islam Banten, Suatu Kajian Arsitektural Kota Lama Banten Menjelang Abad XVI sampai dengan Abad XX*, Yayasan Baluwarti, Jakarta.

Undang - Undang Republik Indonesia no. 4/Th. 1992 tentang Benda Cagar Budaya.

Bibliography

Attoe, W. *"Historic Preservation"* dalam Catanese, Anthony and James Snyder, (1983), *Introduction to Urban Planning*, Van Nostrand Reinhold Company, New York NY.

Austin, R. L. (1988), *Adaptive Reuse : Issues and Case Studies in Building Preservation*, Van Nostrand Reinhold Company, New York NY.

Bacon, E. N. (1969), *Design of Cities*, Thames and Hudson, London UK.

Batubara, B., Saringendyatnti, E. and Adyawardhina, R. (1988*), Manfaat pemugaran Situs Arkeologi Banten Lama bagi Perkembangan Ilmu Sejarah serta Dampaknya terhadap Kehidupan Masyarakat di Sekitarnya*, Laporan Penelitian Fakultas Sastra UNPAD, Bandung.

Budihardjo, E. (1997), *Arsitektur, Pembangunan dan Konservasi*, Penerbit Djambatan, Jakarta.

Budihardjo, E. (1997), *Arsitektur sebagai Warisan Budaya*, Penerbit Djambatan, Jakarta.

Burns, J. A., et. al (1989), *Recording Historic Structures*, The American Institute of Architects Press, New York, NY.

Djajadiningrat, H. (1983), *Tinjauan Kritis tentang Sejarah Banten*, Penerbit PT Djambatan, Jakarta.

Galion, A. B. and Eisner, S. (1980), *The Urban Pattern,* Fourth Edition, D. Van Nostrand Company, New York NY.

Garnham, H. L. (1987), *Maintaining the Spirit of Place*, PDA Publishers, Mesa, Arizona AZ.

Journal of Southeast Asian Architecture, vol.1, September 1996, Inaugural Issue, School of Architecture, NUS, Singapore.

Kotler, P., Haider, D. and Rein, I. (1993), *Marketing Places*, The Free Press, New York NY.

Lawson, F. and Baud-Bovy, M. (1977*), Tourism and Recreation Development : A Handbook of Physical Planning*, The Architectural Press Ltd., London UK

Rossi, A. (1982), *The Architecture of The City*, MIT Press, Cambridge, Massachusetts MA.

Sanoff, H. (1991), *Visual Research Methods in Design*, Van Nostrand Reinhold Company, New York NY.

Sevcenko, M. B. ed. (1984), *Continuity and Change: Design Strategies for Largescale Urban Development*, The Aga Khan Program for Islamic Architecture, Harvard University and MIT, Cambridge, Massachusetts.

Trancik, R. (1986), *Finding Lost Space, The Theory of Urban Design*, Van Nostrand Reinhold Company, New York NY.

Uzzel, D. (1992), Heritage Interpretation Vol. 2 : *A Visitor Experience*, Belhaven Press, London UK.

Williams Jr., Norman and Edmund H. Kellog (1983*), Readings in Historic Preservation : Why? What? How?*, Centre of Urban Policy Research, New Brunswik NJ.

Wiryomartono, A Bagoes P. (1995), *Seni Bangunan dan Seni Binakota di Indonesia*, PT Gramedia, Jakarta.

Two museums devoted to one writer: The Danish writer, Karen Blixen/Isak Dinesen (1885-1962)

Marianne Wirenfeldt Asmussen

The Karen Blixen Museum, Denmark

I wrote this paper just as we had put Christmas well behind us and I was tempted to say "thank God for that".

That expression – "thank God for that" – is perhaps as clinched and as far removed from its origins, as is the Christmas we now celebrate. There was a time when we would praise God but it is much more in keeping with the spirit of our age *to price goods* than to *praise gods*. And it is not simply a question of the price tags we find on the many goods we shop for at Christmas. We have, in a more general sense, put a trade price on Christmas as such. We shop till we drop and we use our purchases as a means of compensating for things we left undone over the year. We buy absolution, succumbing to the lessons taught to us through tasteless, materialistic market promotions. The phrase, praise God has had its meaning worn away, it no longer fits. But where does that leave us?

Karen Armstrong, a Danish-born author, now resident in London, and a former nun, has written a book entitled *The History of God*, about the history of the three monotheist religions – about God, Allah and Jahve. Karen Armstrong gave up being a nun after seven years and now considers herself to be an atheist – and yet in her own opinion religious now than she was then. Life in the monastery made her – as I suppose it does others – so egocentric in her search for her faith, her God, that she forgot her love for her fellow human being, she forgot her humanism. She goes as far as to say we have lost God in Western Europe because at some time in the nineteenth century we insisted on saying that he had really existed, we spoke of him as a historic person, demanded rational explanations for his deeds. This is Karen Armstrong's conclusion: "God must be understood as an art form, must be considered not as fact but like a piece of music or a poem describing love or despair, it touches you for a split second, shows you that there is an ulterior purpose to life."

Christmas is a time for us to reflect on the great issues which we are constantly trying to understand or fit into a philosophical system. And what has all this to do with museums? What struck me was that there is a parallel here to the work we do in our institutions. If we accept the idea of the art form as opposed to fact, then that is indeed what we have been asked to take care of in museums. The immeasurable, the irrational, that is the very essence of our work. That is our FAITH. That is what we try to get across, we are not dealing with some product to be taken to market. Of course our daily lives in museums are almost completely taken up with pragmatic and financial tasks, but we must not forget that we are distinct from the commercial world exactly because we stand for something irrational. If we do not keep making this point ourselves, nobody will.

Today museums are repopulated at the same rate as churches are depopulated. Museums fill a gap, so to speak, they satisfy a demand for system of faith. That is a heavy legacy to take on, it is a great responsibility. It was discussed at a recent ICOM conference in Australia. Here, several colleagues from different parts of the world said that museums are where modern people go to find anchor points for their identities. And that means that the work we have taken upon ourselves becomes an even greater obligation. It means that we have to take an even clearer stand in relation to the tourist industry, which sees us as entertainment attractions – cultured entertainment for a Sunday afternoon. From their point of view we can be seen as products in the market place, goods to stick a price label on! We must constantly be prepared to discuss the role we have to play, be humble before the literary body of work, the art that is entrusted to us, and we must make that humility obvious, as an inspiration to our visitors.

Christmas and the New Year are also a time for thinking about our hopes for the future. In our field – literary museums – Weimar's position as Capital of Culture 1999 is a very exiting event. Never in the history of cultural capitals has a city been better suited for that task of being a place where culture, as a fundamental condition of life, in the true meaning of life and death, can be followed through history. This is a place where we can now be confronted, on the one hand, by world literature, as Goethe was the first to see literature, as something universal, an art without borders – and on the other hand we see that same culture, distorted, perverted, twisted in the interests of Nazi propaganda, we even meet it taken to its most repulsive extreme in the shape of the Buchenwald concentration camp, only a few miles from the very Weimar where Goethe sat in his aesthetically pleasing, yellow rococo house, contemplating Greek antiquity and Plato. And it is the intention of the German European Capital of Culture committee to put this contrast on display, no matter now painful it is.

Literary museums uphold the Word. Goethe's house in Weimar is such a museum. The role played by that house, through the ages, and the role played by the European Capital of Culture in our own time, can serve as an inspiration to us all. It illustrates important our work is, how much care we must take in looking after our literary sites. We must not allow ourselves to be misused or seduced in any way. Lively debates must always be part of the lives of our museums, our houses must not be single-track places of worship, redolent with the melancholy of a life that ended long ago. Henrik Wivel puts it eloquently in his article in *Berlingske Tidende* (January 2nd 1999), "Weimar – city of pacts with the Devil": "Nobody should be asked to live their lives in a preserved museum landscape like that of Weimar or in a crime such as Buchenwald" – in other words we are obliged to present people with the truth regardless of the pain it may cause, and this is where our institutions have a particularly important role to play. We must offer more than a cultured entertainment on a Sunday afternoon, although of course there is a place for that, too – our museums are deadly serious and essential places in our own time and in our societies, places where we put forward cognitive interpretations that just may have the status of the spiritualism of our times. Spaces, open in an intellectual sense, that can counterbalance the alternative religious movements of our age, which risk becoming as self-centred and narrow-minded as is all fundamentalism.

Goethe sat and wrote in a green room, that same green colour which in his colour system is seen as suitable for concentration. Many authors have concentrated in green rooms – Karen Blixen did so, too, at her Danish home, Rungstedlund. Her green room has the same shade of green on the walls as you see in the park outside her windows and this is where she liked to sit when the wind blew too strongly from the east and she could not keep warm in the Danish poet Ewald's room, which faces the east and the sea. This was her preferred room and its walls are a cool greenish blue, harmonising with the water and the sky outside. She was conscious that interior and exterior spaces must harmonise. Ewald's room is evidence of conscious Blixen's self-staging. Until 1958 when central heating was installed at Rungstedlund, that room looked different. The walls were covered in subtle wallpaper and a variety of bookcases and cabinets stood around the room. There were small tables to put things down on and larger ones to sit and work at.

The writing desk which her father had used before her is, however, still in its original place, as when Boganis, the pseudonym used by her father, sat working in his "office". Up until 1958 the room had a rather more bourgeois, uninteresting atmosphere and these were the surroundings in which Karen Blixen wrote all her books. This also makes the house more interesting in general, because this is where everything was created, in this physical framework. Along with the fame she earned towards the end of her life may have come a stronger wish to stage the crime scene, her study, which she herself created in its surviving form. The African weapons on the walls are gifts – although she leant heavily on the man who gave them to her, her brother Thomas Dinesen, who took them off his own wall at Leebaek and put them up in the same way on the walls of her sister's study. African objects, a small stool, a map of the entire farm in Africa, a small set of scales, a casket and first and foremost her own paintings from Africa surrounded her in there – surrounded her **reputation**. As we well know, Africa was the beginning and the end of that author's work. The last book she wrote was *Shadows in the Grass* where African motifs are reconsidered from the light of passing years, across a span of thirty years. Karen Blixen's Danish house, her childhood home, her home as an author and also the place where she died, like all homes it this one has presented changing faces over the years.

•

This is what Karen Blixen said about her house: "I do not think that the house itself was ever planned or designed by any architect, in a manner of speaking it grew of its own accord and has been embellished in line with the changing tastes of the generations. It is constantly falling on my head and I am constantly propping it up. The Danish Professor of Architecture, Steen Eiler Rasmussen, who is my neighbour in Rungsted and who has taken a particularly delightful interest in Rungstedlund, explains to me this or that detail dates to 1800 or 1850. When suddenly a ceiling collapsed and a primitive type of reconstruction was revealed behind it, the Professor told me that that was the way they built houses during the period of National Bankruptcy in 1813 and I could well imagine that. Seen with modern eyes the house is impractical in the extreme, having as much "no man's land" – corridors and stairs and butler's pantries – as it has rooms for living in. And yet Rungstedlund must have retained some of its summer sweetness and winter cosiness of its one hundred year life." (From "Rungstedlund – a Radio Essay", in *Collected Essays*).

When Karen Blixen had to return from Africa to Denmark in 1931, she was met by her mother with whom she shared a home until 1939, the year when her mother died. Only then, at the age of 54, could she make her personal imprint on the house, which she wanted to be "a little grander than a vicarage but not as grand as a manor house". She would probably have liked it to be a manor house but as this was not possible she invented a style in between the two. It is a typical Karen Blixen remark, she had a peculiar talent for making a virtue of necessity so that it took on a conscious life all of its own. The small doilies vanished from the tables and Karen Blixen arranged her home in a slightly simpler style than her mother, adding only a few pieces of furniture, as she had sold most of her belongings in Africa. Only furniture that held a personal value were brought back to Denmark. The rooms which we can enter today have not been arranged to be like they were at the moment of her death in 1962, frozen in time. Rather, they represent a cross-section of styles throughout her lifetime and only a few things have been changed in order to accommodate the museum visitor. Thus the small room which originally served as a playroom and, in the 40s and 50s, as a linen room, has now been turned into a small gallery, where visitors can view Karen Blixen's own works, her drawings and paintings. But you will find no pencils or sheets of paper lying around in an artistic chaos, nor is there ash in the ash trays as if the Baroness had just left the room. We have avoided that particular style of theatrical exhibition. The only changing traces of the life as lived by the author are seen in the fresh flower arrangements in the vases, which we have been able to reconstruct as they were in Karen Blixen's time, using Professor Steen Eiler Rasmussen's many photographs.

In its style and appearance, this house is as Danish as her house in Ngong Hills is African in its form and construction. Two houses, each one in its own very different geographical surroundings. Yet both frame the life and work of one author. Although Karen Blixen only really began to write after her return to Denmark, she draws on her African life, experience and insight. That it why it makes complete sense for both houses to serve as museums to her, commemorating her artistic work. Like the two houses, the curatorial interpretation of her professional role is contrasting in the two museums. At first I saw it as a weakness that the African museum pays so little attention to the presentation of the author's work. Now I see it more as an interesting insight into museum history when you compare those two museums both associated with the same person. The understanding of history differs in the two countries. We in Denmark stress historical correctness, and perhaps our view of reality as we see it is a little narrower, we are afraid of adding to creatively to that reality. There – in Africa – they still love a good story – and there the story about the film of *Out of Africa* really is a good story, which bears being told time and time again. Which reality is truer: theirs or ours?

"As long as man could speak, stories have been told, and without stories mankind would have withered and died, as it would have foundered without water" are the words which Karen Blixen makes cardinal Salvati speak *in The Cardinal's First Story*", from *Last Stories*. Storytelling is something Karen Blixen knew about, she had many radio listeners of her own, and she had and still has an even larger readership. More than 500,000 people have visited the Karen Blixen Museum since its opening in May of 1991. At the museum we deliberate, long and hard, the stories which WE tell the visitors and the way we tell them. We value the legacy that has been placed in our care, price it highly but do not offer it for sale. A literary museum mediates the word, the free word, and that is something we have to protect and preserve with the greatest care.

Karen Blixen was a bilingual writer (Danish / English) who during her lifetime published the following books: Seven Gothic Tales, 1934; Out of Africa, 1937; Winter's Tales, 1942; The Angelic Avengers, 1946; Last Tales, 1957; Anecdotes of Destiny, 1958'; Shadows on the grass, 1960.

The power to define: Meanings and values in cultural tourism

Alan Clarke

University of Derby, UK

Abstract

This paper will address the important issues of political economy which underpin our understanding of the touristic system and in particular the shaping of the development of cultural tourism packages. The paper is organised an exploration of four key concepts: culture, commodification, consumption and power. The first three offer stages through which the discussion of tourism can be managed, whilst power offers a necessary motif to inform the critical understanding of the phenomenon.

Beginning with an examination of how the offer has been structured, the paper will explore the rationales for these niches and the definitions of culture which are inherent within them. Drawing on a theoretical framework from cultural studies - using Williams, Hall and Bourdieu - the paper will critically contextualise the notion of culture and the linkages which have been formed with tourism. The construction of cultural tourism as a series of commodities will be unpacked and the constituent elements re-evaluated.

The notion of local cultures as objects of consumption will be debated and contrasted with the notion of cultures as every day life, to be enjoyed through participation rather than consumption. Cultural production necessarily involves production and consumption in one moment - cultural tourism seeks to separate out production and consumption both spatially and temporally. The concept of cultural capital will be introduced and used to explore the levels of value and meaning involved in cultural tourism. Exchange values and legitimacy will also be addressed in an attempt to understand what is recognised as cultural within tourism and therefore what is deemed to have value.

The analysis will consider examples of specific cultural tourism offers and also look at the ways in which culture is offered within other forms of the touristic experience.

Introduction

Here we seek to establish the complexities of the 'other' term in the construction of cultural tourism - that of 'culture' itself. It is a word which has come to take on many meanings in popular usage, from defining a range of activities to representing the well bred or the noble (and this applies not only to people but also to racehorses and footballers who are often described as cultured when we mean that they are graceful). It is our contention that the development of cultural tourism has been premised upon a restricted and exclusive definition of culture and that the future development of cultural tourism must challenge that definition if it is move forward and fully exploit the potential of cultural rather than cultured tourism. Therefore this paper will take you through a range of definitions - theoretical and practical - of what culture has represented and what it could mean to arrive at an inclusive definition of culture for tourism.

The cultures of tourism

The aim of this paper is to look critically at the ways in which cultures have been constructed and represented in tourism. Not only has cultural tourism been seen by many as a panacea for the future of tourism development, but cultures have been melded to the needs of tourism along the way. This paper will suggest that these approaches to cultural tourism have taken an overly simplistic approach to the role of culture within cultural tourism. It has assumed that culture can be packaged and consumed without any significant impact upon the local people or the local culture itself. In deed it will become apparent that even referring to the local culture is in itself too simple as the local people will have a diverse variety of local cultures and traditions which will be shared differentially between the different sections of the local peoples. Moreover the paper will argue that what is presented as cultural tourism is a commodified form of culture, developed and packaged for the consumption of the tourists. The role of the tourists must also be seen culturally, as the tourists are developing a complex of patterns of behaviour which can be referred to as a touristic culture.

We must begin to ask questions about the sense in which culture is being used within this debate. The idea of culture as a set of established rituals and practices, expressed through performance, art works and buildings is one which has been readily accepted within the tourism industry. It is precisely these elements of culture which can be packaged and presented (and re-presented on a regular and repeatable basis) for the delight of the touristic customers. If we are to remain true to the principles of cultural development, we must strive to ensure that the determination of the local culture is in the hands, minds and practices of the local people. The ownership of culture should not be something which is transferred out of the local, despite the global pressures to do so.

Tourism is a phenomenon that is shared by large numbers of people throughout the world. This commonality, which is found in groups, does not necessarily imply uniformity as the motivations and behaviours of the group members vary considerably (Cohen, A, 1985) Moreover the discriminatory use of culture within the construction of cultural tourism by the European Union has led to a series of packages that are based upon exclusion rather than inclusion of cultural products . We must now address the questions of what is culture and whose culture it is that is being referred to within cultural tourism.

> *"The dominant European linguistic convention equates 'culture' largely with the idea of 'civilisation'; they are regarded as synonymous. Both ideas may be used interchangeably with integrity in opposition to notions of that which is vulgar, backward, ignorant, or retrogressive"* (Jenks, 1993: 9).

Williams (1981) also notes that culture can be used to describe the active cultivation of the mind. For Arnold (1869) this culture was set as 'high culture'. "Culture which is the study of perfection, leads us ... to conceive of true human perfection, as a harmonious perfection." (cited in Jenks, 1993: 21) Although Arnold's philosophy was similar to that of Plato, Arnold insisted that culture "had become transformed into the post-enlightenment forms of industrialisation, it had become 'external' and 'mechanical'.... Arnold's work can be heard as polemical and it certainly bears a literary style that Williams refers to as 'soured romanticism'." (Jenks, 1993: 22) It is an attempt to put forward a view of the culture as rooted in the glories of the past and suggests that true enlightenment can be found only in the understanding of our classical heritage. This is a view of culture which was found in some of the earliest forms of tourism - the pilgrimages and the Grand Tour - and still inspires the packaging of the cultural past in the cultural tourism brochures of companies offering guided trips to understand our past. In these terms, culture can be seen as a core part of the Civilising Process. Culture is seen as the entry to the treasures of civilisation, the jewels of the past. These glories are found in the appreciation of the 'high arts' - classical music, classical architecture, opera, ballet, and classical art forms of representational art.

Williams (1981: 11) outlines a range of definitions of culture, including:

- a developed state of mind - as in a person of culture, a cultured person;

- the process of this development - as in cultural interests, cultural activities;

- the means of these processes - as in culture as 'the arts' and humane intellectu works.

He continues by distinguishing two main kinds of culture, these include "(a) an emphasis on the 'informing spirit' of a whole way of life, which is manifest over the whole range of social activities but is most evident in specifically 'cultural activities' - a language, styles of art, kinds of intellectual work; and (b) an emphasis on 'a social order' within which a specifiable culture in styles of art and kinds of intellectual work, is seen as the direct or indirect product of an order primarily constituted by other social activities." (Williams, 1981: 12) Although Williams' views of culture is classless, his work was primarily defined in relation to the art, language and literature, which in turn are largely products resulting from society as a whole. As a Marxist, he saw 'working class' culture as a contribution to the common culture of the whole of society. The products of art language and literature are too narrow and represent the binary opposition between the real and idealised in cultural forms.

Raymond Williams described the search for culture as the quest for the cement that held social life together, a lived reality that constituted a shared process. In the search for our cultural identity, he argues:

> *"we find here a particular sense of life, a particular community of experience hardly needing expression, through which the characteristics of our way of life that an external analyst would describe are in some way passed, giving them a particular and characteristic colour."* (Williams, 1965:57)

This belief in culture as a lived reality is re-emphasised by Hall (1990) who argued that culture is "not a practice; nor is it simply the descriptive sum of the 'mores and folkways' of societies .... It is threaded through all social practice, and is the sum of their interrelationship." (Hall, 1990:22) Here we see culture used more broadly as lived reality.

Culture is seen as including the cultural activities of everyday life. It celebrates high art forms equally alongside the valuing of popular cultural forms. It is the characteristic colour of a living society. In this definition the power to define has been diffused.

Wallerstein distinguished two usages of the term culture. In usage 1, he refers to culture as "a way of summarising the ways in which groups distinguish themselves from other groups. It represents what is shared within the group, and presumably simultaneously not shared (or not entirely shared) outside it." (1994: 31-2). He continues by posing the question "Who or what has such a culture?" It seems that 'groups' have (ibid:33) Although this seems to be an accurate analysis, the term 'groups' in itself is still not sufficiently precise for further analysis. Landis (1986: 75) for example uses society rather than 'groups'. He refers to society as a 'an organised, independent, continuing number of people living in a specific area and culture as a "a complex set of learned beliefs, customs skills, habits, traditions and knowledge shared by members of a society." In other words culture is a result of people coming together in a group in the format of a society.

Culture in the context of tourism can be seen in two ways when referring to usage 1 in Wallerstein's terminology. Firstly it is the tourist who is part of a commonality. They accept and yet reject behaviour within a society indicating that commonality need not be uniformity and that certain cultural codes overlap but need not replicate. In this way the tourist is the carrier of symbols and symbolic values that are shared by the culture form which the tourist emerges. Second the society of the destination will also have a culture of commonality. In fact this society may have a set of learned beliefs, customs, skills, habits, traditions and knowledge which is primarily what motivates the tourists to see them as interesting.

> *Culture in usage 2 is used, according to Wallerstein (1990: 32): "to signify not the totality of the specificity of one group against another but instead certain characteristics within the group..... We use culture to refer the 'higher arts as opposed to popular or everyday practice.... 'superstructural' as opposed to what is 'base'.. 'symbolic' as opposed to that which is 'material'. These various binary distinctions are not identical, although they all seem to go in the direction of the ancient philosophical distinctions between the 'ideal and the 'real', or between the 'mind' and 'body'."*

Extending this, culture in this usage is then used as a reference point to distinguish between right and wrong, paralleling a distinction between high culture and low culture as being the acceptable and unacceptable forms of culture within a society. By doing so it means that certain forms of culture are valued and others are at the same time and through the same cultural accreditation processes are not valued and therefore are effectively devalued. Thus cultural practices become reified and are therefore products which not only serve to produce a cultural identity of a society but also serve to differentiate within that society.

Cultural capital and cultural consumption

Bourdieu (1984) has articulated a theory of cultural capital to explain the processes involved in the valuation and revaluation of culture. He traces the value of certain forms back through patterns of ownership and patronage to their inscription in dominant education patterns to demonstrate why certain forms have value and others do not. Bourdieu argued against simply 'reading off' economic and cultural practices, first wanting to understand the articulation which takes place between cultural and economic capital. However the same principle of accumulation underpins both cultural and economic practices. It has to be understood that the process of accumulation can only make sense in a condition where the framework of exchange value already exists, that is to say where there are accepted patterns of what is accepted as valuable and what is not. If all elements of the cultural world were seen as equivalents, the accumulation process would consist of nothing more than simply adding another experience to your 'account'. What Bourdieu insists upon is that culture can described in terms of different denominations, where certain cultural forms are gilt edged securities, whilst others are counted in pennies. As Featherstone (1987: 62) points out; "To attempt to map taste purely in terms of income is to miss the dual principles in operation, for cultural capital has its own structure of value, which amounts to convertibility into social power, independent of income or money."

These ideas are taken forward by Bourdieu but not in terms of culture, which he uses as a given construct of particular social orders. He introduces the notion of habitus to his analysis to provide the link between determinism and voluntarism. In his own words: "The habitus is by necessity internalised and converted into a disposition that generates meaningful practices and meaning - giving perception; it is a general, transposible disposition which carries out a systematic, universal application - beyond the limits of what has been directly learnt - of necessity inherent in the learning conditions." (Bourdieu, 1984:170) This allows people to read their situations creatively without any sense of strict obedience to a given regulations, yet still operating within the framework of given cultural paradigms

It is within this notion of habitus that it is possible to 'read' the distinguishable levels of cultural capital. Many accounts of cultural capital have been presented , this summary indicates the nuances of the concept very clearly: "This transposible disposition, armed with a set of perceptual and evaluative schemes that are available for general application, inclines its owner towards other cultural experiences and enables him to perceive, classify and memorise them differently. Where some only see 'a Western starring Burt Lancaster', others discover 'an early John Sturgess' or the 'latest Sam Peckinpah'. In identifying what is worthy of being seen and the right way to see it, they are aided by the whole of their social group .... and by the whole corporation of critics mandated by the group to produce legitimate classifications and the discourse necessarily accompanying any artistic enjoyment worthy of the name."(Bourdieu, 1984: 28)

Bourdieu has written on the notion of cultural capital within French society, locating cultural practices alongside categories of social worth, documenting the high value of ruling class patterns of cultural practices. These are the same cultural patterns and artefacts which we noted could easily be conflated into the definition of heritage and certainly are contained within the definition of European heritage. We have been applying this notion of cultural capital to the critical review of cultural tourism (Smeding and Clarke, 1994; Smeding, 1998) and have mapped the role of dominant cultures in Europe in creating a map of valued cultural tourism events and locations. This work needs to be developed by further study of the value system of tourists. However it is possible to argue for the emergence of a touristic culture - in Wallerstein's usage 1, where there is an expression of a set of practices, rituals and expectations which establish a framework within which the distinctive practices of particular tourists can be understood.

What can be seen in the consumption of culture is the way in which this framework contextualises and constrains the appreciation of the visited culture. Cultures are viewed - only very rarely can they be participated in actively in a way which has meaning for the host as well as the guest - as objects of interest. They have a value in the touristic culture because they resonate with the expectations of the cultures of the tourist and the expectations of those tourists. The theoretical assumption that authenticity is an important element for all tourists is clearly not borne out by the numbers of tourists who are willing to consume artificial and staged forms of the visited culture. Authenticity holds an appeal for one section of the touristic market but not for all. Equally the authenticity is usually of a fixed version of the culture rather than an authentic feel for the living cultures of the places visited. Far better to see an authentic recreation of a tribal dance than the modern forms of dance being produced and performed in here and now of people's every day lives - if that is what you have paid to visit. Again when you are dealing with a commodified form, you know it is safe to tell your friends and they are then able to go back and see the same performance next month or next year - the commodity form has the advantage of being packaged and repeatable and hence tourism can develop through the recollections of the satisfied tourists and the expectations of the audiences for their reminiscences.

Within this process of consumption, we must remember that the relationship is never reducible to a simple economic model of supply and demand but it will also be an experience based on exchange. Part of the exchange will be economic and part will be cultural. Within the process of exchange, there has to be a notion of and the possibility of a valuation taking place. However this valuation will be occurring on both sides of the transaction and reflecting on the value of the specific experience and on the touristic exchange overall. The participants in the exchange will be cognisant of a part of the cultural registers involved n the exchange but not of all of the cultural significances and values. This creates a problem for the exchange relationship as it is not, and can never be, based on a perfect equivalence of exchange.

There is a danger in writing about culture from a European perspective that the term becomes conflated with and sometimes is even taken as synonymous with heritage. This results in two particular concerns for the debate here. Firstly the European heritage is already present, it exists. The ruins of former civilisations the masterpieces of past creativity are the defining elements of the received culture which we 'know' as Europe. However although it is presented as a fixed and 'given' construct, it is possible to debate what it is and what is actually included within the definitions. At what point do the Beatles gain access to the classical canon? This results in cultural itineraries following ancient routes, take for example the two major routes to Santiago de Compostela and the Magna Grecia pathway through Greece and Italy. What we are witnessing is the recognition and recreation of the old civilisations' patterns of trade and belief. We are seeing nothing of the new Europe and the practices and systems of the new Europeans. We are seeing, yet again, the representation of the accepted old forms of high culture.

Although this process is normally described as a valuing of cultural practices and products, we must be alert to the possibility that the process carries with it of the devaluation of the cultural practices and products involved in the exchange. This can come from the touristic consumers who see the experience as just one more manufactured event - slightly more or less exotic than the last trip, but still less exciting as the exotic becomes normalised within the boundaries of their expectations. More significantly is the possibility of the devaluation which can be engendered in the local people as they see their own cultures - or versions of them- trivialised and popularised for the entertainment of the tourists. If this is seen only as a characteristic of the spectacle, the consequences for the lived cultures may be contained within the touristic transactions. However if the devaluation is transferred in to the every day worlds of local people, two things happen. Firstly the sense of importance in local cultures is diminished and secondly, but simultaneously, the importance of the 'other' cultural practices is increased.

The cultural framework

As Appadurai (1990:295) states: "The central problem of today's global interactions is the tension between cultural homogenisation and cultural heterogenisation. ... Most often, the homogenisation argument subspeciates into either an argument about Americanisation, or an argument about 'commodotisation' and very often the two arguments are closely linked." This in itself is not surprising given the impact of the distinct cultural identity of the many American people, which is enhanced by its social and political system. The influences of Disney and McDonalds are felt throughout the world (Eisner/Ritzer) but the powers of global culture are more complicated and will be explored in a subsequent paper.

Indeed, culture and more specifically cultural identity can be divided into several categories, which are both individual and shared by larger groupings (Wallerstein, 1990) Some argue that: "There is now a world culture ... which is marked by an organisation of diversity rather than by a replication of uniformity. No total homogenisation of systems of meaning and expression has occurred, nor does it appear likely that there will be one any time soon. But the world has become one network of social relationships, and between its different regions there is a flow of meanings as well as of people and goods." (Hannerz, 1990:237) The largest possible culture would be a 'Global Culture'. Featherstone (1990) has argued that we can only think of a global culture if we move away from a notion of the static polarity of nation states writ large and try to employ a broader definition to think the processes of cultural development through. Hannerz claims that there is already a world culture which manifest through the "increasing interconnectedness of varied local cultures, as well as through the development of cultures without a clear anchorage in any one territory. These are all becoming sub-cultures, as it were, within the wider whole... "(Hannerz, 1990:237). A world culture which is primarily based upon values of the capitalist west is largely manifest in media such as newspapers, television and films, although the fast food and financial service industries are also important contributors. On a political level the work of the non-governmental agencies also help to foster this world culture, the interventions of NATO and the IMF being prime examples of such cultural influences. This analysis suggests that there are a number of cultures which flow from this world culture. These sub-cultures are expressed as continental and inter-continental cultures, national and inter-national cultures, trans-cosmopolitan cultures and regional and inter-regional cultures.

The European Union has a programme to construct and promote a European culture and a European cultural identity. What we must ask here is what is 'European culture'. We must question first its diversity (in terms of ethnic backgrounds, language, customs, food and drink, religion, etc.) and its heritage, both elements could be used to argue for differentiation and conflict rather than unity and commonality. Indeed as a result of the conflicts between imperial powers and nation states over the centuries, only a few states could claim cultural significance rather than Europe itself. As a new construct in socio-cultural terms, the geographical definition pre exists the formation of the Union, this cultural identity programme outlines a number of the key issues which underpin the critique of the concept of culture within this book. Europe is a custom made homogeneous body, which is unlike America as it is less united in terms of language, legal framework and so forth. By imposing policies and measures to create a European cultural identity it is imposing policies which create a fear of cultural imperialism, absorption and eradication amongst minority cultural groupings within Europe. As Appadurai (1990:235) points out: "One man's imagined community (Anderson, 1983) is another man's political prison." Whilst condemning the gendered nature of this comment, the principle Appadurai is emphasising is very important. On e of the prime purposes for cultural identification is to identify those who share the culture and also identify those who do not. It is therefore essential that a definition of culture is used which values many forms of culture, not just those forms of culture espoused by the ruling elites of the 'imagined community'.

Culture can be used a signifier of binary distinctions between the ideal and the real, and between the mind and the body. This has resulted in a way of seeing tourism in which cultural tourism has evolved as distinct from other forms of sun, sand and sea type tourism. As a culture is a result of people, or more specifically people acting together in society, one should not be ignorant of its dynamics. Culture is anything but static and it is precisely this dynamic which makes the concept of culture so difficult to grasp . Moreover it is also probably why the culture which appears in cultural tourism is packaged and commodified, presented to the tourist as a static an idealisation rather than the presenting the complex dynamics of the 'real'.

Anthropological perspectives

The 'real' or lived local cultures have provided the setting for the study of anthropologists. Critical accounts have been provided by anthropologists about the cultural dynamics of a given society, by seeking to examine the particularities of local practices. Ever since the emergence of mass tourism, of which a critical account was presented by Turner and Ash (1975), the content, if not the focus, of the studies of many anthropologists should have changed given the impact of tourists on the host societies. As Crick (1995) has pointed out: "Despite this ubiquity of tourism however, anthropologists are still prone to producing monographs about societies as if the international tourism industry did not exist." (Crick,1995:207) Crick makes the interesting comparison of the tourist with the early anthropologists, arguing that tourists are distant relatives of the anthropologists, especially those who are keen to take an interest in the cultures of their destinations.

He uses the word 'ludic' to describe the playful, fun loving and sometimes ignorant tourists and poses this category against the 'liminoid' who he pictures as the serious culturally integrated anthropologist. The ludic tourists take photos, videos, collect souvenirs and other things they rate as having value in the host culture which constitute symbolic capital which they transform into status and cultural capital back home in their own societies.

Tradition, modernisation and authenticity

Culture is perhaps the most controversial term used within the social sciences. The study of tourism as a relatively new discipline within the social sciences system, has rightly paid attention to culture as part of its studies. However the application of culture within tourism has often been discussed in general terms rather than with due attention being paid to its specific values for both the tourists and the host communities. Within modernisation theory, tradition is often used as signifier for culture. "As Myron Weiner (1969) has noted, modernisation theorists tended to confuse two separate concepts of tradition: one defined analytically as the opposite to modernity and one defined empirically, as what ever is handed down from the past. Early modernisation theorists clearly tended to equate the two. Traditional culture in third world countries thus formed a radical contrast to modernity, More than this traditional culture and society was seen as having great staying power, requiring a powerful antidote." (Wood,1992: 2) This construction of culture as tradition and through that linkage culture as difference we see the establishment of one of the cornerstones of the definition of culture for cultural tourism.

Although culture within tourism studies has led to an ever increasing awareness by researchers of the sensitivity with which the concept must be used, the ways in which the concepts of culture still differ quite significantly between the developed and the lesser developed destinations, often being used to support discourses of the exotic around the lesser developed regions. This has been take as a given when looking at these regions. " The folklorist Ben-Amos has observed that 'tradition' has generally been a term we have thought with, rather than about" (Ben-Amos 1984: 97 cited in Wood 1990: 9). This quote could easily apply to the concept of culture.

There is a debate, following MacCannell (1976) and Urry (1990), as to the role of authenticity in the touristic experience. MacCannell introduced the notion of 'staged authenticity' (1976: 91 -107) as a way of negotiating the difference between the tourist experience and the lived realities of society in the destination. However, as Selwyn observes, "we need to add that such authenticity has two aspects, one of which has to do with feeling, the other with knowledge. In yet other words, the tourist is after both authentic social relations and sociability (which would certainly include an authentically 'good time') as well as some sort of knowledge about the nature and society of the chosen destination" (1996: 7-8). These two dimensions become very important in understanding the elaboration of the critical approach to cultural tourism developed here.

We can see the power of this argument if we look at the levels of state funding and state support for the culture which underpins the cultural tourism packages. The power structures support the 'high arts' and put little, if any, support behind popular cultural forms. The high cultural forms receive the most support because they are the most valued and their significance as being the most valuable is reinforce by the amount of support they are seen to receive.

What you see on a visit to anywhere can only ever be a superficial glimpse of the place and this is even more true of the culture. When culture is studied within an area, what is revealed is a multifaceted and multidimensional set of cultures which interact and overlay one another. Within this patterning, it is observable that certain forms of cultural expression come to have a dominance and a currency. This recognition of the 'dominant culture' is not to deny other cultures which contest and challenge the dominant view but it is precisely to recognise and value those differences. In Europe we live with a dominant culture which derives from the great civilisations of ancient Greek and Rome - which in turn borrowed from the cultures of the lands which became their empires. We have a tradition of great music (symphonies and opera), great art (the Old Masters) and great theatre (Shakespeare) which draws upon an amalgamation of cultures from across Europe which have been sponsored, directly paid for and bought up by the ruling classes of those societies for generations. This oversimplified view of 'high culture' in Europe does stand up to some critical tests - it is the culture that inspired the Grand Tour and it is the culture which cultural tourists seek to visit and value now (Smeding, 1998). What it is important for us to recognise here is that it is also a different tradition of high culture to that celebrated outside Europe - for instance here in South East Asia different forms of landscape representation are found in high art than in Europe, different types of theatre, dance and so forth.

This cannot be read as heritage, despite the attempts of some commentators to use this term interchangeably with culture. The focus on heritage emphasises the fixed and given remnants of previous civilisations and previous lives. It directs our attention to the relics and remnants of those social orders. We are called to the archaeology of past civilisations rather than to its anthropology. The fallen stones and the ruined edifices are made the attractions for the masses and cater for the core niche in the cultural tourism market place. These tangible returns are there and demand touristic attention. They are easier to place and to understand than the intangibles of the lived cultures of those civilisations. We can admire the size and scale of the buildings more easily than we can begin to understand the complexities of the religious practices. However if we are to approach an understanding of the cultures of host societies we have to understand the social relations and cultural practices which helped to produce the edifices that confront us on our touristic visits. Moreover the 'heritage' is not confined to the past as it continues to influence the present relations. The strong traditions of the 'high arts' still influence the agenda and perceptions of the cultural policy decision makers in Europe. In other ethnic dominant cultures we can see the living impact of the relevant historical traditions still affecting the current approaches to perspective and content of contemporary local cultures. The picture of cultural development is overwritten by the underpinning high arts which support the dominant forces of globalisation. The drive of Western capitalism and Oriental capitalism is supported on an appreciation of the cultural forms of the dominant classes.

The question here must be about who owns the local culture, who takes it and develops it for the local people themselves and similarly who takes it and develops it for the touristic consumption by strangers. How far does the culture become formalised, packaged and removed from the lived existence of the local people in order for it to be presented and received in an enjoyable fashion by the tourists? The answers will be different for every section of every population- some may be left undisturbed as their practices are not thought to appeal to the sense of enjoyment of the tourists but for others they will find that life has changed as they dance to the tune of their new visitors. The clearest example of this tendency in Europe can be found in Spain where a rich and diverse set of local cultures comes together in one form of dance for the tourists - flamenco. Flamenco belongs to one part of Spain but is now performed for the benefit of the tourists (and therefore the tour operators and the tour promoters) throughout Spain. It is even possible to see flamenco being performed in the Canary islands, where the locals see it as one form of domination from the capital of mainland Spain but where the tourists see it as a high point of their holiday experience.

This distancing of culture from its original sources has other implications as it must by definition also distance it from its original meanings for its original practitioners. We have heard similar tales of dislocation from the tribal dancers forced to perform to the arrival of the tour bus rather than the summer solstice, of artists carving animals they have never seen because they would look good in the homes of the tourists - there are even touristic centres offering to capture the experience of Greek culture in one night. It should be made clear that this is the Greek culture of drinking large amounts of local wine, eating copious amounts of food and attempting to dance in a Greek way, whilst possibly spending some of your Greek holiday money on Greek souvenirs to help you remember your Greek evening. Outside these developments there seems to rather more to Greek culture and the Greek way of life - not to mention the influences on European civilisation to be found in Greek history. There is no mention of philosophy in these new Greek centres. They are cultural theme parks, operating with a stereotypical and narrowly focused view of the culture which they are offering to display for the delectation and benefit of the tourist. This removes us from the moral high ground of the cultural tourism promoters and returns us firmly to the hedonistic base of the pleasure periphery.

There must be a time when we reflect on this and on Wood's argument (1984) that the policies towards tourism in South East Asia being adopted by the state governments at the time were going to have just as significant an impact on defining - and redefining - traditions as they were on introducing and reinforcing notions of modernity. These arguments apply no less in Europe, Africa and the Americas than they do in South East Asia. We are reinventing our cultural histories in order to sell the packaged creation to the tourists and as a consequence to the next generations of our own societies.

Costs and compromises - the local impacts

There are many examples of such cultural developments taking place around the world at the moment, but the important lesson of those developments is that they have to be controlled by the local people and not imposed or enforced upon them. The development of cultural tourism must be handled sensitively and yet positively, within the framework of global, national, regional and local factors outlined in this paper. For the policy makers and the tourism promoters, culture offers an area of great interest and considerable potential but the implications from the variety of projects is that culture cannot simply be seen as a gimmick to attract more tourists. Cultural forms have become commodities to be traded in the global cause of tourism development. However they carry meanings far beyond this touristic exchange and these meanings, locally generated and locally developed have to be recognised in the way in which the cultural forms become encapsulated within the wider touristic systems. As tourists, tourism developers and tourism analysts, we must ensure that these local meanings are not lost in debate about the economic commodification of the touristic experience and the cultures involved in those interactions. Cultures are as precious and precarious as ecosystems and must be promoted just a s vigorously.

Promoting cultural and heritage tourism

There is nothing new about the ideas of cultural tourism. Some of the earliest forms of tourism - religious pilgrimages and the Grand Tour in Europe - depended upon highly developed notions of culture. However what we saw in the development of tourism along the pleasure periphery was a marginalisation of such serious concerns as culture in favour of a new holy trinity - sun, sand and sex. This repositioning of the tourist market has led to one commentator being able to suggest that the premises of sex tourism in Thailand can now be visited as a form of heritage tourism (Peleggi, 1996). What we have seen in the recent attempts to establish cultural tourism is a concerted effort to re-establish the high moral codes of the pilgrimages. By extending the visits to the relics of the saints to the modern extensions of those 'high' cultures we can see a positive moral spirit enthusing a new aspect of the rhetoric of touristic development. The reality of the package we are offered as cultural tourism may well be different - and we shall argue later that it is significantly different - but the rhetoric appeals to our finer senses as the tour promoters offer us a taste of history and culture amongst the remains of former civilisations. Recently Sicily and Spain have both offered to show us the culture of our lives. The television advertisement for Turkey shown in the United Kingdom in 1996 offered us the image of a boy diving amongst the ruins of the ancient civilisations - without any hint of contradiction about the choices to be made between exploitation and conservation. What we are seeing in the current promotions of heritage and culture is a desire to maximise the numbers of tourists and to maximise the number of tourists who are likely to be interested in culture and heritage because they are the highest spending sectors of the touristic market. There is a simple and crucial economic motive to reaching out for this niche of the market. Significantly the way of tapping this market most fully is to commodify the culture which is the centre of the touristic activity.

Conclusions

We have presented a critical account of the definition of culture, moving away from the simple definitions of culture being represented as a repertoire of arts, skills and knowledge to a position where the culture is seen as the lived reality of people engaged in everyday life. This definitional shift means that culture should no longer be seen as an exclusive concept but as an inclusive one. It is inclusive because all forms of activity can be valued as capital as long as the old register of cultural values are challenged and the dominant definitions of the high arts broken apart.

Wallerstein's model of two usages has allowed a space to be created in which culture can be re-examined. When this space is used to analysis the ideas of commodification and of cultural capital, it is possible to develop a strong critique of cultural values as received traditions. This then means that the significance of cultural tourism for the development of local cultures can be explored. We have taken a challenging view of concepts such as 'tradition' and heritage', seeking to explore how these terms are constructed and then help to construct particular definitions of culture. It has been necessary to unpack the notion of power and power relations in order to expose this process of construction of cultures. We have exemplified this by looking at the practices of culture within Europe and have looked at how these can be questioned if a local reading of the culture is taken.

References

Allen, C. et al (1988), 'The Impact of Tourism Development On Residents' Perceptions of Community Life' in *Journal of Travel Research* Vol. 27 No.1 pp 16 –21.

Anderson, B. (1983), *Imagined Communities*, Verso, London.

Ap, J. (1990), 'Residents' Perceptions Research on the Social Impacts of Tourism' in *Annals of Tourism Research* Vol. 17 No. 4 pp 610 –616.

Appadurai, A. (1990), Disjuncture and Difference in the Global Cultural Economy. In: Featherstone, M. (Ed) *Global Culture - Nationalism, Globalization and Modernity*, Sage Publications, London, pp.295-310.

Archer, B. and Cooper, C. (1994), 'The positive and negative impacts of tourism' in Theobald, W. (Ed) (1994) *Global Tourism: the next decade* (Butterworth Heinemann).

Bourdieu, P. (1984), *Distinction: A Social Critique of the Judgement of Taste*, Routledge, London.

Chaney, D (1996), *The Cultural turn* (Routledge).

Cohen, A. P. (1985), *The Symbolic Construction of Community*, Ellis Horwood Ltd., Chichester.

Craik, J. (1995), 'Are there cultural limits to tourism?' in *Journal of Sustainable Tourism* Vol. 3 No. 2 pp 87 – 98.

Hannerz, U. (1990), Cosmopolitans and Locals in World Culture. In: Featherstone, M. (Ed.) *Global Culture - Nationalism, Globalization and Modernity*, Sage Publications Ltd, London, pp. 237-253.

Husbands, W. and Harrison, L. C. (1996), 'Practising Responsible Tourism: Understanding Tourism Today to Prepare for Tomorrow' in Harrison, L. C. and Husbands, W. (Eds) (1994) *Practising Responsible Tourism* (John Wiley).

Jenks, C. (1993), *Culture*, Routledge: London

Lee, M. J (1993), *Consumer Culture Reborn* (Routledge).

MacCannell, D. (1976), *The Tourist: A New Theory of the Leisure Class,* Schocken Books: New York.

Peleggi, M. (1996), 'National Heritage and Global tourism in Thailand' in *Annals of Tourism Research* Vol. 23 No. 2 pp 432 – 448.

Selwyn, T., ed., (1996), *The Tourist Image - Myths and Myth Making in Tourism*, John Wiley, Chichester

Smeding, S. and Clarke, A. (1994), 'Whose culture is it any way?' in Munroe, J. (Ed) (1994) *Cultural Tourism* (Gateway Publications, Hull).

Smeding, S (forthcoming), *Conceptualising Cultural Tourism in Europe* (unpublished PhD thesis, University of North London).

Turner, L. and Ash, J. (1975), *The Golden Hordes*, Constable, London.

Urry, J. (1990), *The Tourist Gaze: Leisure and Travel in Contemporary Society*, Sage Publications Ltd., London

Wallerstein, I. (1990,) Culture as the Ideological Battleground of the Modern World-System. In: Featherstone, M. (Ed.) *Global Culture - Nationalism, Globalization and Modernity*, Sage Publications Ltd, London, pp.31-57.

Williams, R. (1981), *Culture*, Fontana: London

Wood, R. E. (1984), 'Ethnic Tourism, the State and Cultural change in South East Asia' in *Annals of Tourism Research* Vol. 11 No. 2 pp 353 – 374.

Searching for genuineness and rituality: Dance celebrations and tourism

Anne Décoret

Université Lyon II, France

This paper intends to deal with dance as a tourist component. If tourism gives the opportunity to discover monuments and sites, it proceeds above all from meeting with the cultural otherness. In this framework, dance holds a particular place which results from its very nature. Whatever it could be: an aesthetical, a symbolic or a ritual expression, dance is achieved, within the tourist setting, under a performing order. Thereby, cultural otherness is grasped according to a performing term. In that way, dance appears to be a component particularly attractive that travel agencies are keen to exploit including it in their travel offers. This paper is thus concerned with the discourse regarding dance that travel agencies convey through their leaflets. Which place does dance make up in the tourist journey? What reflections concerning cultural otherness is it related to? Set as a performance given for an outside audience who does not belong to the same culture, dance is becoming a tourist and cultural product. This new status alters the relations between a culture and its own folk patrimony. Tourism then brings in changes which I am going to draw some of the aspects and results.

Since the end of the nineteenth century, a large French audience was given the chance, for the very first time, in its own country, to attend dances coming from faraway lands. What was just known through travel literature and explorer's accounts then could be really encountered. These dances were firstly performed in the set of Universal and Colonial exhibitions before being billed in music-hall and theatres. The meeting with an exotic cultural form gave rise to a discourse that renders the reflections of a time regarding cultural otherness[1]. Analysing this discourse, I have realised that it still remains notably in travel agencies leaflets. Thus an historical view may be helpful as well as relevant to tackle the matter of dance and tourism. Admittedly, it is about two different situations. In the first one, spectators were not tourists. They didn't achieve any journey, they didn't cross any sea. They were just discovering, at home, some dances completely different from their own ones, that is western ones. The dancers were rather travellers. In the tourist set, it is exactly the opposite. Nevertheless, in both cases, the confrontation with cultural otherness through a spectacular bodiliness is in question. In that extent, knowing the discourse that was running at the early century allows to assess nowadays reflections and to pick out continuations and severances of the French speech regarding the Other and its cultural expressions. History then appears to be a useful knowledge in the sense that not only it helps to get acquainted with our past but it contributes to stand ourselves with this past as well as to understand what determines our topical understanding of things and people surrounding us. This paper is going to analyse the discourse conveyed today by the travel agencies[2] at the prospects of the discourse that resulted from the discovery of the first exotic dances in France, during the first part of the twentieth century.

Dance and travel literature

Until the first foreign dancers performed in France and more generally in Europe, the only available knowledge concerning exotic dance was due to the exotic literature and accounts written by travellers or explorers. Literary exoticism offers to readers descriptions of the strange habits that are practised at the other side of the world. Dance is high up amongst these habits. In travel accounts, describing a event, a celebration where dance takes place makes up a compelled episode. Accounting this moment gives the writer the opportunity of a difficult literary exercise that prompt them to retranscribe with the Word a beauty scene combining colours, rhythms and movements. The dance episode appears to be a particular moment in the discover of the otherness. In the nineteenth century, travelling to the Orient was a kind of initiation path for writers who considered it as an area of pleasure. In Gérard de Nerval's, dance descriptions give birth to colourful scenes. In his writings, "dance is firstly a curiosity. It is, with music from which it can't be split up, the gist of the crossed countries". In *Voyages d'Orient*, he describes the dancing dervishes. "Dance then takes on, in opposition to Europe, a holy character, a major face of the Orient according to Gérard de Nerval"[3]. Théophile Gautier, very keen on dance and famous for his ballet libretto dropped many lines about dance, on the occasion of his journeys in Spain, Algeria and Egypt. With realist writers, such as Gustave Flaubert, exoticism is rendered through a writing of the spectacularness which pays attention to the strangest aspects of the otherness. Exoticism is notably based on dividing up the reality in rainbow-coloured and comical elements and on a spectacularisation and a theatricalisation of the Other[4]. Thereby, the description of a dance celebration appears to be very suitable. Exotic literature has build a exotic imaginary which is used in travel agencies leaflets.

In the Twenties and the Thirties, travel accounts wrote this time by dancers and dance amateurs were often published in the press or in books. They gave detailed descriptions of dance celebrations they had attend. The American dancer Ted Shawn wrote many articles after he had toured in India with his company, the Denishawn. The famous Anna Pavlova's partners brought back many accounts of their journeys in the Orient where they had the opportunity of discovering other dancers. Published in the specialised or the daily press, these reports stirred up the deep inquisitiveness yet existing towards these foreign dances. A new trend of tourism is sketching out after under the cover of dancers. Journey adventure had found a new interest. The recent spring of a very new form of tourism combining dance training and tourist paths may be considered as one of the consequences.

Dance as the emblematic element of the cultural otherness

French spectators discovered the first exotic dances within universal and colonial exhibitions. Firstly they aimed to present the fruits of industrial progress and new technologies, these events were the chance for the great nations to state their omnipotence and their domination over the rest of the world. The architectural frame was based on a line of pavilions build by each participating country. Some "walk-on" people requested to play their own part enlivened pavilions. The exhibition then became a "festival of national representations"[5]. France and other colonial empires also conferred a pavilion to their colonies because "their folk display helps to reinforce the national prestige and thus the consistency of the country"[6]. Then, pavilions turned out to be the expression of a country's identity, of a people as well as a colony. "How easy one may identifies a people's character at the first sight just entering its pavilion" wrote Gaston Bergeret about the 1900 exhibition[7]. The great success won by national and colonial pavilions had progressively transferred the visitor's interest from technological sights, window of the industrial progress, to the folk and exotic restorations. Very soon, the exhibition get into the charge of disorientation. Fulfil a journey all around the world became the main illusion brought by the exhibition. Besides, 1931 Colonial Exhibition's advertisement was: "Touring the world in one day". One goes to the exhibition to take a change of scenery, to discover very closely the Other.

To drain the largest audience and to arouse its inquisitiveness, the exhibition ruling authorities granted a significant place to dance, as they were aware of its impact. Bringing in displays within pavilions partook of a folkisation process, consequence of the search for exoticism. In 1900, organisers privileged so much dance displays amongst side-shows that visitors fulfilled, as André Warnod wrote, a "dancing trip around the world"[8]. Exhibitions dance displays are a "wonderful godsend for the passive traveller and the chamber explorer"![9] It was a vivid experience. Meant to entertain and to give the audience a rest, exotic displays numbered among the most valued side-shows. At the 1889 Universal Exhibition of Paris, the Javanese dancers, allowed by the Sultan of Solo to perform in France, had such a triumphant success that they remained for the visitors the most unforgettable souvenir. In the "Cairo Street", sensual hip swaying of the oriental female dancers performing the "belly dance" exhilarated gentlemen. In 1900, the Japanese dancer-actor Sada Yacco won a triumph. Six years later, the Royal Ballet of Cambodia was such successful at the Marseille Colonial Exhibition that the Minister of the Colonies organised a party in the Elysée garden where Parisian people could attend both of their performances. In 1931, African dancers from Dahomey, Soudan, Guinea amazed the audience as they were parading between reconstructed huts of the French Western Africa's pavilions. Balinese dancers ravished a stupefied audience with their hieratic gestures and movements. The varied exhibitions which took place in France from the end of the nineteenth century to the Forties have broadly contributed towards the discovery of exotic dances and have allowed to enlarge the choreographic viewpoint.

If organisers of exhibitions granted a significant place to dances, it was not only in order to give visitors entertainment and a resting time. This choice also partook of a reflection according to which the remarkableness of a people stands through its dances. Dance is considered as the most liable form to express people peculiarity. One of the most brilliant and famous dance critics of the two-world-war, André Levinson asserted that "When one has seen an indigenous dancing, one has almost visited its country". He added, "there is nothing like dance and its dionysiac appeal to come back up to the surface the secrets of its people"[10]. Hence, within exhibitions and its lines of reconstructed pavilions, dance appears to be one of the most relevant elements trough which visitors achieved a meeting with the cultural otherness. *Le Monde Colonial Illustré* stated : "it is throughout dance that a people's soul is best expressed, above all when it is question of our black African and Asian possessions who mostly have kept their primitives traditions"[11]. Considered as the emblematic folk expression of colonised peoples, dance is thereby given an important place within exhibitions.

Exhibitions were built on a scenic appliance in which the exotic Other became a performing subject. In travel agency literature I have noticed that the Other, now met in its natural environment, is the subject of a folkisation process as well. Because of its physical difference, its habits, its ritual observances, it gives rise to a change of scenery as well as landscapes and monuments. As within exhibitions, the display of the Other is reinforced by the mean of a spectacularisation which stresses the sensation of queerness. This spectacularisation is based on the most spectacular aspects belonging to the Other, that is dance, which creates entertainment and amazement thanks to its costumes, its music, its movements. It also proceeds from the recursive conception according to which the peculiarity of a culture is the deepest expressed in its dances and songs. Other elements of the social life, less apparent, "more" complex and above all less colourful remains neglected. That is what is shown through travel leaflets. Beneath a picture where five Senegalese women, dressed traditionally, aligned between huts made in earth are executing dance movements, for the obvious sake of the photograph is very significant : "Songs and dances are the village soul"[12]. The Donatello agency proposes to meet Zulus from Zululand and states that "their traditions, their dances make this area a compulsory rendezvous for the traveller who aims to face the ancestral spirit of the true Africa"[13]. In other words, when attending the dances of a people, one is sure of discovering its "soul", its "spirit".

Topical travel brochures almost systematically include dance display. Most of the time, they are given on the occasion of a dinner, in one of the stop hotels of the tour. It can be seen in all travel agencies catalogues, drawn up in different forms : "local dances show", "dinner with traditional dances show", "diner with folk show". Sometimes, the ethnic belonging is given : "dinner with a show of Burmese dances and songs", "dinner with a show of traditional Khmer dances", "dinner with entertainments of Bhil tribal dances" (In Northern India), "dinner with a show of Zulu dances", "dinner with a show of traditional dances of the mountain tribes of Siam".. When taking place in a hotel setting, the display aims to entertain. Dances are transplanted outside of their observance place for the sake of the tourist. Ritual, symbolic, religious or social functions with which these dances are invested disappear even though they are simulated so as since the finality of the display has now changed and become the tourists' entertainment. Dance displays may also take place in a "natural" setting, on the occasion of a village visit. Rev'Afrique's south African tour includes a "lunch in a Zulu Kraal where you will attend songs, dances and varied craft and war activities". The indigenous display responds to the nature display. Victoria Falls are a "display that warrant to cross the continent". This visit is followed by a "traditional dances display" in which "Shoba, Ndebele and other ethnic groups will sing you their customs in a picturesque display". In Accor tours', on the occasion of a stop at a Masaï village, the traveller could "get familiar with some Masaï traditions and dances". Here, even though dances are performed in the corresponding context, all is verging on display and entertainment. The village visit is scheduled and so are the dances. Costumed dancers are probably waiting for the tourists bus stops to start dancing. The performance is ordered by the tourist passing. Only the lightening differs but all the situation is planned or reconstructed. Besides, Jets Tours points out as to warrant its genuineness that the traditional Zulu Kraal is "entirely reconstructed". As Brown (1999) said, here is a case of a "genuine forgery". Every thing is false because it is reconstructed but the sensation of genuineness blossoms precisely because the building is an exact reconstruction. At last, in the hostelry setting, dances could be danced in a way that bestows an other style, not devoid of a sort of tribal feature. In Donatello's, dinner is served aside a camp fire where Zulu dancers are performing around.

Within the tourist tour, dance celebrations are considered as a density moment which grant the tour all its interest. Inserts trimming travel agencies' catalogues attest of it as they put to the fore the advantages of the journey proposed. Dance always appears. It makes up the high point of the tourist tour because it gives an exacerbated situation of disorientation where the exoticism feeling increases. Through costumes, colours, rhythms, gestures, tourists can weight the cultural difference that divide him from the dancers, that difference remaining one of the major motivations of the journey. Dance display is a moment of exoticism exuberance. Besides, colour numbers among the tourist selling points precisely because it is opposed to the gloomy dullness of the daily that tourists want to back out of. The word "colour", whatever it applies to landscapes, costumes or encountered people paved travel agencies leaflets. In Burma, there are "tribes more coloured one another". The landscapes draw a "coloured symphony". Vietnam is full of "villages with multicoloured costumes"[14]. In Bali, "women achieved to preserve their coloured costumes". In South Africa, "the social fabric is variegated". Jet Tours does not even dare to use pleonasm when talking of the "coloured colours of the local costumes" of Peru's peoples. Colour, rhythms and dances are requisite ingredients for a successful journey.

Searching for novelty, genuineness and rituality

Exhibitions displays have gained an audience searching for novelty and eager for exoticism. In 1921, Raymond Escolier wrote : "we need something new, something original, extraordinary, extravagant and, if possible, something savage"[15]. Spectators take delight in watching "savages" and "beastly" African dances. They are dazed by the hieratic Asian dances. They are convinced of the genuineness of these dances even though these ones are adapted at the sake for a western audience, in a cultural context different from the one they are belonging to. Beyond the peculiarity and the originality of the display, its so-called genuineness bestows all its value and interest. In the 1900 Parisian exhibition "people went to the Asian Theatre in order to see genuine dances with strange movements and varied exercises"[16]. Emile Dermenghem reported that the "colonial displays have made us known the genuine dances of Africa"[17]. The sensation of exoticism is reinforced by the feeling of genuineness. "There is nothing tastier than the indigenous dances, especially when they are indeed genuine"[18]. Genuineness thus frames the advertisement plot used by exhibitions and theatres directors as well, who started to bill exotic dances at the beginning of the twentieth century and more intensively in the Thirties. The official guide of the 1931 Colonial Exhibition, Paris, stated with regard to the Javanese and Balinese dancers : "their costumes are authentic and the origin of their instruments is perfectly pure"[19]. Genuineness appears to be a criterion which always needs to be capped. Every new exhibition will claim a more genuine genuineness comparing to the former ones. Exotic dances posters condemn the "false genuine dances" performed before in order to legitimise the genuineness of the show they praise.

The comments that the discover of exotic daces have given rise to underline primitivism reflections regarding exotic dances that are in keeping with the allegorical conception of genuineness. Not only spectators were convinced of the genuineness of the show but they do think that what is performed in front of them is part of an ancestral tradition. They grasped the cultures these dances are belonging to as a permanence, an immutability and in a lack of temporality. Therein, they denied the historicity misled by changes that every social pattern is subjected to. They believed that these dances did not have an history. At the 1925 Decorative Arts Exhibition, Paris, the Singhalese and Hindu dancers were "perpetuating the oldest Asian traditions"[20]. According to Edouard de Keyser, Javanese dances "transport us through time"[21] Hindu female dancers "remain true to their ancestral rituals"[22]. The ritual and ceremonial feature of the Asian dancers fascinated. Ritual is discerned as the sign of an ancestrality, as the continuation of a tradition whose decline is the consequence of the "civilisation". "Exotic dances have kept their holy feature" wrote Claude Valmont who explained that "the more people become civilised and the more dance parts with the religious worship until to become a desecrated entertainment"[23]. Regarding African Dances, they are considered as "the highest expression of the tribal life". The tribal life is the sign of a primitivness, of a near state to the nature where the man is not submitted to an social pressure. By of their religious character, their immutability or their tribality, exotic dances became the antinomic image of the western dances. While watching them, the visitors of the exhibition take the leaves of the worries due to the modern civilisation and the progress. It is what Edouart de Keyser expresses: "In our feverish life, amongst worries, crisis, disasters and revolutions that surrounds us as many gulfs, we took a rest one moment and watched dancing". Holy dances and savages dances come up to the ardent boom that takes hold of mind marks destroyed by a four dreadful war which have proved one of the morbid finalities the modern civilisation and the progress could lead to. On one hand, exotic dances represented an expected novelty. On the other hand, because they were sacred or wild, stemmed from ancestral cultures which had not been penetrated by modernity and its harmful consequences shown in the Great War, exotic dances brought in a benefactress lease, some values and a peacefulness that the civilisation lost

The same primitivist discourse appears in travel agency brochures. Admittedly, it is not only directly related with dance displays but as dance constitutes one of the lures of the proposed travel tour, it comes within the same reflections pattern. Tourist countries are shown as immutable cultural lands where ancestral traditions, ritual and religious practices still remain alive in spite of the modern world. Ethnic groups' way of life did not yielded to the Western stressful frenzy an to the infernal race of the progress. The nearness to nature and the faithfulness to traditions warrant their genuineness, the word recovered with a striking recurrence[24]. Moreover, their immutability set them free from any time submission. These people are considered as devoid of temporality and history. In Burma, Asia ads that "you will discover the out of the time tribes way of life". In Saint Louis, Senegal, "life flows out outside the time". Madagascar is an "continent outside of the time" and Africa a continent "out of the time and history". Ancestrality, immutability and genuineness are the master words of the travel agencies selling points. Asia intends to discover "a genuine and cordial

Indochina", an "immutable India", "a Tibetan people with unaltered traditions", a Vietnam "where peasants have not forsaken their traditions". Fishermen of the Mekong's shores are living "in full respect of ancestral craft techniques and in a gentle way of life". Genuineness gives credit to the journey. Jet Tours states that Eastern Bali is "the most interesting part of the island because of its genuineness". These tourist countries seem to be protected[25], perfectly intact, and keeping on living just like their forebear. Proceeding from ancestrality, rituality as well as religiosity thus appear to be subject of the tourist inquisitiveness, as it is presented by travel agencies. In Philippines, the Ifugao are a "ethnic group keeping millennial animist traditions". In Bali, "life is still rhythmed by impressive animist celebrations". "Tribes with spectacular rites are living" in Sumatra. In Thailand, Yao and Akhan ethnic groups have "rites, costumes and customs out of the time". In India, peasant's life is running according to "the rhythm of seasons and religious celebrations". Asia even dares to state that India spirituality is genetic since "India is spiritual by atavism". Travelling to these area of immutability, ancestrality and rituality suit to the tourist who wishes a change of scenery as well as resting. What is offered to him is a resourcefulness moment in favour with cultures which have achieved to keep the essential. What is proposed to him is to isolate himself from his hectic life, to recover harmony that the modern civilisation destroyed. Donatello's editorial speaks for itself, going to Africa means "coming across the lost sources of the dawn of the world".

Theatricalisation and artistic acknowledgement

In the context of universal and colonial exhibitions as well as in the tourist pattern, cultural otherness is submitted to a folkloration process that fulfil exoticism and spectacularness expectations. More than the knowledge about the Other, it is its display that is searched for. Much more than any other cultural expression, dance thus appears to be most appropriate element. Within exhibitions, the mise en scène of the Other asserted the imperialistic and colonial propaganda. In the tourist situation, it reinforces the exotic imaginary. It responds to the quest of spectacularness and disorientation. The permanence of the reflexions regarding the Other proves that mentalities hardly changed, in spite of geopolitical overturning. These reflexions have an importance on the artistic recognition that can be assigned to non-western dances, recognition which has political and economic consequences.

The context in which a dance, proceeding from social, ritual or symbolic functions is performed changes its initial purpose. Their performing for the sake for a outside audience to the culture they belong to implies a theatricalisation of its content and functional modes. That theatricalisation had been done by the first exotic dancers when they went to perform on French and European stages their folk patrimony. The same theatricalisation is achieved when Zulu dancers dance in front of an audience of tourists that have stopped in their villages, at one time of their tour. In these conditions, does the genuineness remain possible? Of course not, but this is not harmful. Theatricalisation doesn't reduce the oddness of a dance. It provides conditions of a cultural recognition and artistic as well. In the Twenties and the Thirties, as they were spurred on by the western's craze, exotic dancers undertook an exploration of their folk heritage, adapted it for the stage and performed it on numerous European and Western theatres. Thereby, they contributed to spread it beyond its cultural area of adherence and to make reach it the choreographic world rank. The primitivist speech keen on genuineness but carrier of a inner contradiction however since the spectacularisation prevent from any authenticity, doesn't grant any artistic recognition to adapted dances and keeps on considering them as folk demonstrations. In that way, amongst exotic dances performed in France during the two world war, some were considered as documentary displays coming under an ethnological interest (such as African, Oceanian, Amerindian dances), and some were appreciated as real artistic performances (such as Asian, Indian and Japanese dances). The dancer was considered either as a simple folk performer or as a choreographic artist. However, any adapting or transposition, so minute it could be, needs the dancer's creativity as he is elaborating a scenic product. This creativity bestows *ipso facto* the quality of artist. Besides, conceiving a culture as unchangeable means reproving all kind of dance experimentations on behalf of their members. In the Thirties, two African dancers, Féral Benga and Habib Benglia performed dances of their own creation using a gesture language stemmed from their culture as well as the western classical dance. They were both blamed for not being "wild" enough and for being corrupted by the civilisation. Nowadays, the colour of the skin and the cultural origin determines the spectator's judgment. French dancers trained in a Indian classical style of dance complain about the unfavourable preconceptions of which they are subjected to. Yet, are the tourists attending a Bharata Natyam performance in Southern India able to decide of the quality of the show?

The western craze for exotic dances in the beginning of the twentieth century as well as the interest they still arouse have given birth to a new cultural product for the tourist economy. Liable to attract customers, made-up dance celebrations and displays are now sometimes created. One example is the Ladakh festival in Nepal[26]. The complexity of certain kind of dances prompt some tourist countries to adapt their folk patrimony so that it could be more accessible. In Bali, "the arrival of tourists has greatly stimulated the advent of dance celebrations called "free" dances (*Tari lepas*) in the sense that they are detached of any ritual or dramatic natures links. Some have been extracted from their original context to be transformed in dances for soloist, others have been conceived originally at the sake for foreign audience, while others are abridged and simplified versions of court dances or recent creations"[27]. The tourist affluence have modified relations between a culture and its folk patrimony, which proves, if need be, that these cultures are not unchangeable as travel catalogues state. As cultural products, dance displays are also liable to be sold abroad. Since about a decade, French theatres and festivals regularly bill foreign "companies" which perform danced rituals on stage. In that way, it was recently possible to attend displays of Dogon dancers from Mali, of dancing Dervishes from Konya and monk dancers of Tibet. Performing such sacred or ritual dances in a theatre, floodlighted, before an outside audience renews the matter of the ritual and worshipness spectacularisation and theatricalisation. Are the dancers considered as fully artist? What are their motivations and their incentives? What does profitability implies in terms of arrangements ?

Finally, the new relations between a culture and its dances can be seen through the recent emergence of a new kind of tourism. A new tourist market including dance training has appeared. "African dance" teachers who give classes in France also organise training courses in Africa. It is notably the case in Senegal. These practising-journeys provide to this new tourist the opportunity to learn a singular dance within the very country where it is usually practiced. Generally, the journey includes a few daily hours of training and the rest of the day or the week is dedicated to visits of the surrounding sites[28]. Modes of learning are mainly modelled on those common in France. If the cultural otherness is here approached differently, it is nevertheless according to a cognitive process belonging to the tourist culture and not the one of the country. This new trend of tourism leads to another matter concerning now the changes misled by tourism within the relations between a culture and the transmission of its cultural knowledge.

Endnotes

1. Décoret (1998).

2. The corpus used in this paper is based on different travel agencies catalogues (spring - summer 2000) such as Donatello, Jet Tours, Rev'Afrique, Club Mediterannée, Asia.

3. Auraix-Jonchière (1998 : 226). All French translations are mine.

4. Mourra (1992 : 78).

5. Ory (1982 : 94).

6. Ory (1992 : 100).

7. Bergeret (1901 : 47).

8. Warnod (1937 : 89).

9. Levinson (1931).

10. Levinson (1929 : 281).

11. 26.09.1931.

12. Jet Tours catalogue.

13. Donatello

14. Asia.

15. Escholier (1921).

16. Dupays (1939: 113).

17. Dermenghem (1936).

18. Franck (1934).

19. Demaison (1931)

20. Charensol (1925).

21. De Keyser E. (1931).

22. Lejay (1926).

23. Valmont (1933).

24. Accor Tours' travels are even entitled: "Genuine Senegal", "Genuine Zimbabwe".

25. Jet Tours proposes "A new approach of Thailand and Southern China, which gives the chance to discover minorities still preserved".

26. Shackley (1999 : 28-29).

27. Picart (1992 : 158).

28. The Senegalese travel agency Nio Ko Bokk proposes staying including tourist visits as well as craft and artistic activities such as dance.

References

Auraix-Jonchière, P. (1998), De la tradition au mythe : la danse comme figure-prétexte chez Gérard de Nerval, in Montandon A (Editor), *Sociopoétique de la danse*, Anthropos, Paris.

Bergeret, G. (1901), *Journal d'un nègre à l'Exposition*, Librairie Conquet, Paris.

Brown, D. (1999), Des faux authentiques. Tourisme versus pélerinage, in *Terrain*, 33, 09.1999, pp. 41-56.

Cadilhac, P. E. (1931), L'heure du ballet, in *L'Illustration*, 22.08.1931.

Charensol, (1925), Les attractions, in *Exposition Internationale des Arts Décoratifs*, Librairie Larousse.

Coast, J. (1954), *Dancing Out of Bali*, Faber and Faber, London.

Décoret, A. (1998), Les danses exotiques en France, 1900 - 1940, Thèse de Doctorat dirigée par Remi Hess et Philippe Tancelin, Université Paris VIII.

Demaison, A. (1931), *Guide officiel de l'Exposition Coloniale*, Editions Mayeux, Paris.

Dermenghem, E. (1936), *Cahiers du Sud*, mars 1936.

Dupays P. (1939)*Vie prestigieuse des Expositions*, Henri Didier, Paris.

Escholier, R. (1921), *La Danse*, 03.1921.

Franck, A. (1934), *L'Intransigeant*, 03.07.1934.

De Keyser, E., "La danse à l'exposition coloniale", in *Lectures pour tous*, 09.1931.

Lejay, C., *Paris Music-Hall*, 01.05.1926.

Levinson, A. (1929), *La danse d'aujourd'hui*, Editions Duchartre, Paris.

Levinson, A. (1931), Le spectacle exotique à l'Exposition Coloniale, *L'Art Vivant*, 08.1931.

Mourra, J. M. (1992), *Lire l'exotisme*, Dunod, Paris.

Ory p. , (1982), *Les expositions universelles de Paris*, Ramsay, Paris.

Picart, M. (1992), *Bali. Tourisme culturel et culture touristique*, L'Harmattan, Paris.

Shackley, M., Himalaya (1999), jeux de masques pour tous, in *Courrier de l'Unesco*, juillet-août, pp. 28-29.

Warnod, A. (1937), *Exposition 1937. La vie flamboyante des expositions universelles*, Editions de France, Paris.

Valmont, C. (1933), Danses sacrées, in *Sourire*, 26.01.1933.

Approaching tourism policy making through multiculturalism

Rob Dodson and Alan Clarke

University of Derby, UK

The study of tourism has advanced from its early roots in economics and business subjects. At this time, there was no pressure for governments to seek to control what was largely seen more as an industry than as an overall phenomenon. Therefore it is perhaps not surprising that the politics of tourism and tourism policy making are areas of study which have been neglected. This paper proposes to demonstrate that rather than being ignored policy making and the politics which surrounds it should be taken more seriously by academics, practitioners and all interested parties.

In order to appreciate the complexity of the evolution of tourism aspects of historical background are offered. This is followed by an examination of some of the more significant academic papers relating to international tourism and policy. Approaches through institutional solutions to policy making are given using the U.K. and Thailand as examples.

The main purpose of this paper is to consider Multiculturalism as a way of approaching international tourism policymaking. This aims to adopt a critical perspective regarding the development, operation and management of tourism. Using a broadbased philosophy derived from engagement it is possible to get underneath differences of existing knowledge and develop a greater understanding which will assist analysis. In this case, the analysis is directed towards government policy relating to international tourists.

It is accepted that tourism policy making does not lie exclusively with national government institutions, however it is recognised that government is a key player. It is therefore within government policy making that this paper will be confined. The focus will be on the approach to international tourism policy making. These will be dealt within the three sections of the paper: Research origins, Approaches to Policy Making for Tourism, Multiculturalism.

Research origins

This introductory part of the paper begins by looking at the temporal dimension and sketches the history of tourism as it appears to apply here. The history and development of tourism up to the post war period is undoubtedly extensive but like many matters relating to tourism, not yet well documented. For this reason and also because of the need to be brief, this section and the others will be constrained. There is plenty of room for research over all periods of time and throughout all parts of the world (Dodson,1998). The phenomenon of tourism, as well as international politics, has not emerged in isolation. Whilst both may be regarded as recent fields of study in terms of attracting the attention of the academic, they are rooted in the development of the study of humans as represented by social science. History is one valuable database.

Nationalism is one powerful ideology on which to draw. One might ask what has nationalism got to do with tourism? It would seem that the most obvious answer, is that the international tourist cannot exist without national borders to cross. The nation, as expressed through the nation state, is the central feature of the contemporary international tourism phenomenon. International tourists primarily visit the nation state(s), not continents, regions or cities. The National Tourist Office (NTO) was the source of tourist information. However, lying behind the nation, and the force behind it, is nationalism and the national identity it creates. Both host and guest are familiar with such feelings in any encounter they may have. Nevertheless in some places this is breaking down.

The literature on nationalism is quite extensive and much of it emanates from international political and historical studies (Carr,1945; Holsti,1972; Kedouri,1966; Reynolds,1973; Waltz,1979). Carr, an historian widely recognised for his scholarship in international politics, divides the modern period of international history into "three partly overlapping periods marked by widely differing views of the nation as political entity" (1945:1). [Of course, he is writing from a British perspective, largely about Europe, immediately, following the Second World War]

His three periods are:

1. The gradual dissolution of the pre-international order of the mediaeval unity of empire and church and the establishment of the national state and the national church. This period was terminated by the French Revolution (1789) and the Napoleonic Wars, which lead to the Congress of Vienna;

2. This second period was the product of the French Revolution and lasted until the start of the First World War in 1914 with the Treaty of Versailles as its outcome; and,

3. The third period began in 1870 and reached its culmination between 1914 and 1939.

Following on from this there is a fourth period, about which Carr speculates (1945:34-37), but with which we are now more familiar. This is clearly the contemporary period in which the mass international tourist emerges. Nevertheless, it is argued this development can only be understood by drawing on previous periods.

Towner's (1985) study of the European Grand Tour falls mainly into the first period, but also extends into the second period. He concludes his study in 1840 when many of the European states we now know today did not exist , for example Italy and Germany. The ideas of nationalism were only beginning to germinate in Europe. This was a long way away from the establishment of many nation states, and from the creation of national institutions such as national tourist organisations (NTOs).

For present purposes, the second and the third periods may be combined. For much of the period, conflict chiefly originating from national self-determination ravaged Europe, spilling over into Asia and Africa in the Second World War. There was a brief respite favouring travel and tourism, after some recovery in the interwar period. "An important step towards opening up this activity to the wider population came during the 1930s when annual paid holidays were introduced for the first time in the industrialised countries of Europe and beyond" (Davidson,1992). However, for the masses this was reflected in modest domestic tourism of day trips and visits to relatives. Urry (1996), gives a clear account of this mass phenomenon in his description of the rise and fall of the seaside resort in Britain.

The international tourism of the elite, affected as it was by the depression in the 1930s, came to an abrupt end towards the close of the decade with the outbreak of war. The Second World War was unique in that nearly all parts of the globe were engaged in the conflict or affected by it. Two obvious similarities between tourism and war are mass participation and international awareness. These two features are significant if one believes that the origins of this war are rooted in nationalism and expectations of self-determination. They are also significant in the development of contemporary mass tourism in the wealthier, western countries. What we are therefore suggesting is that the early mass movements of international tourists are post war and that they are mainly within Europe.

Resources for research are greater within European and North American countries, therefore it is not surprising that these sources contribute a substantial amount of the literature on the subject of tourism. "Pioneer papers can be traced from the 1930's or even earlier but it has only been since the late 1960's that a significant and substantial body of literature has started to emerge" (Pearce and Butler,1993:1).

One is tempted to ask why? Certainly the 1960's was a time of substantial growth in the liberal arts and the social sciences. Indeed, it has been observed that "the field of tourism was discovered by social scientists in the early 1970's"(Dann, Nash and Pearce,1988). This would coincide with the foundation of tourism's premier academic journal, the Annals of Tourism Research (ATR) in 1973. Surprisingly, in view of comments about lack of research in the politics of tourism (Richter,1983; Hall,1991), writers in the early volumes of this journal were preoccupied with politics.

It was the period during which the intergovernmental World Tourism Organisation was established (Jafari,1975) and this marked the demise of the International Union of Official Tourist Organisations (IUOTO,1975). Nevertheless, as we shall see, analysis of international politics and policy has been subsumed by other issues which have preoccupied the journal's contributors. In many respects while these issues may not have been addressed directly from a political dimension by the academic community, we can assume that the formulation of policy and its subsequent implementation or non-implementation have been quietly bubbling away.

Britton sums up these 'other issues' in his review of Harry. G. Matthews' book (1978), when he wrote that "many in the industry choose to believe that tourism is somehow above politics" (Britton, 1979). Certainly, by Volume 3, 1975-6, contributions to the ATR appear to have moved away from concern with the reporting of the activity of international organisations. However, there is more to politics than the recording of the deliberations of international political fora.

Approaches to policy making for international tourism

As is generally accepted, the advent of cheap charter flights and package holidays revolutionised international tourism and made it a really mass activity for citizens of wealthy nations. However, before the late-1960's, only relatively small numbers of people travelled to Southeast Asia, principally from the wealthy industrialised countries of Western Europe, the United States and Australasia, and consisting of those social groups which could afford the not inconsiderable cost of sea- and later airborne travel the Far East (Hitchcock et al, 1993:2). Therefore the extra decade meant that it was as late as the 1970's before long-haul Asian destinations experienced international tourism on a mass scale. Generally, it was only at this point that it became a concern for policy makers and managers.

There is evidence that tourism has been harnessed to solve problems, generally of an economic nature, as the examples given below indicate. Economic recovery, sometimes assisted by substantial aid, paved the way for a growth in international tourist arrivals and receipts. According to the WTO figures (World Tourism Organisation, 1987), there were around 45 million international tourist arrivals in 1950 and this grew to slightly more than 330 million arrivals by 1985. Of those in 1985, 67.41% arrived in Europe whilst.11.1% arrived in the East Asia and the Pacific region. When spread over so many countries and over the complete year, the total number of arrivals in any one state outside Europe is small and not surprisingly did not attract political attention in some countries.

In the United Kingdom, for example, it was not until 1969 that tourism legislation was passed. The Development of Tourism Act of that year was formulated primarily to help to solve two domestic issues and not really to facilitate international incoming tourism. At the time, there were balance of payments problems and secondly there was a need to placate nationalist sentiment in Scotland and Wales. (Dodson, 1991) Since then ministerial responsibility for tourism in the UK has been passed from Trade to Employment to National Heritage to the present location in the Department for Culture, Media and Sport.

Thailand's tourism initiatives provide a good example from outside Europe. A special publicity section for visitors was set up by the Royal State Railway of Siam as early as 1924. In B.E. 2502 (1959), a national tourist office was set up, called the Tourist Organisation. It was renamed the Tourist Organisation of Thailand in 1963, replaced by the creation of the Tourism Authority of Thailand (TAT) in 1979 (Dodson, 1994). The TAT was therefore well placed to exploit the growing market.

Policy and management in both examples appear to reflect the belief in NTO's and the projection of the destination in nationalistic terms. However, nationalism has frequently been all absorbing, monocultural, and simplistic in integrating the land, the idea and the people. Now the tourist, policy maker and host are aware of greater diversity. This stems from an awareness of differing views of international tourism.

The task here is to indicate which literature has something to offer for, in a sense, all writings about tourism are political contributions. They reflect the values and beliefs of the author(s). Frequently, they may also be documents supportive of specific tourism industry proposals or national tourism plans.

There is a continuing debate about values. It is quite topical currently in parts of Asia, particularly the Asean countries, where the promotion of 'Asian values' is very real. One article, which concisely sums up this debate, concludes:

> *"to say that one set of values is both distinct and superior, owing nothing to outside forces, is self-defeating. There is a constant interchange between different cultures-in the long run, values will be adapted and shaped to the needs of each society. The ability to respect and understand differences of emphasis on global human values-providing they do not violate international norms-is one lesson of history that we should never forget"* (Owen and Roberts:1997).

The short article, from which the extract above is taken, opens with a discussion of values from a religious, economic, political and cultural perspective, making a comparison with the West. In the conclusion, there is little that one would challenge, except the phrase in the last sentence. Nowhere in the article is it clear what international norms are, let alone who decides what they are. However, the authors are advocating a position similar to multiculturalism to which we will return.

But, before this, given that we have stressed the importance of declaring values, a personal outline is now made. With a privileged, rural, western European, academic background, it would be unusual not to be in favour of the status quo both locally and globally. Nevertheless, early exposure to people from countries outside England has fostered a continuing interest in things foreign. This has resulted in an awareness of a range of religious and secular thinking, whilst retaining Quaker convincement. Keynesian economic thought has been influential, however it is recognised that economic policy must be left to the various national governments on behalf of their people. The political and cultural perspectives will emerge through this interpretation of multiculturalism.

Multiculturalism

Looking at the literature, (for example: Bennett, 1998; Goldberg, 1994; Willett, 1998), it is clear that the word Multiculturalism has a variety of interpretations. Time does not permit an extensive debate here but it must be said that multiculturalism is an inquiring approach and of course a dynamic one. 'Mining thoughts' is a much loved phase of Fay (1996) and it is his thoughts I am mining here. Some further expansion is required in order to adopt a multicultural perspective to the literature and hopefully to the remainder of the paper. In the interplay of thinking between atomistic and holistic viewpoints, and indeed many viewpoints in between, Fay suggests that because of various problems with the concepts of respect and acceptance multiculturalism is better defined by means of the concept of engagement. By this he points out that; "engagement suggests that mere acceptance of differences is insufficient. Social science sensitive to the demands of living in a multicultural world is devoted to understanding the nature of these differences; it seeks to learn why people differ and how these differences sprang up over time and in what manner they relate to us" (1996:240)

Using the tenets of multiculturalism, as advocated by Fay, is an appropriate starting point for an approach to tourism policy and management. They are as follows:

1. Beware of dichotomies. Avoid pernicious dualisms;

2. Don't think of others as Other. Conceive of similarity and difference as relative terms which presuppose each other;

3. Transend the false choice between universalism and particularism, assimilation and separation. Instead of trying to overcome the differences or hardening them, interact with those who differ by means of these differences with an eye towards ongoing mutual learning and growth;

4. Think processurally, not substantively;

5. Insist on the agency of those being studied;

6. Recognise that agents are agents only because they are situated within systems which simultaneously empower and limit;

7. Expect more light from whatever human act or product you are trying to understand;

8. Do not conceive of societies as integral monads isolated from one another, or others simply as members of a particular culture or group;

9. Acknowledge the past's role in empowering you. But recognise the ways you make the past what it is;

10. Attend to the historical and cultural embeddedness of social scientific knowledge. Expect that what we know today will be outmoded by conceptual and other changes in our own lives as well as the lives of those we study;

11. Don't hide behind an illusory facade of neutrality to convince yourself or others that you are objective......Seek out the criticism of others. (A welcome purpose of this paper); and,

12. Acceptance or celebration is not enough. Engage others. (Fay, 1996:241-245).

The twelve theses give advice on how to engage in interaction and growth which are the ends of social science understood from a multicultural perspective. As a social science, there is a multicultural perspective to tourism including its policy and management. In their broadest sense the latter two may be difficult to separate. Hall and Jenkins (1995), for example suggest this in relation to policy formulation and implementation, which may be equated to policy and management in the context of this study. Nevertheless, we will separate the two to begin with and start with tourism policy.

"The role of government is an important and complex aspect of tourism, involving policies and political philosophies" (Lickorish and Jenkins, 1997:182). Whatever political philosophy is pre-eminent within a state, it seems clear that those holding power decide who gets what, when and how. In the past, as we have illustrated, in the early stages of international tourism governments appear to have no policy. This is because if there are no perceived benefits then there is nothing to distribute. Policies then emerge to divide up the spoils. Those tourism interests closely involved with a nation state's government will generally play a role in policy and management. These interests are initially economic.

We are assuming that the politics of tourism is no different from politics in any other arena: that politics is about power and therefore it is about who gets what, when and how. We would also argue that any international policy is strongly influenced by domestic policy. In the era of globalisation, we are also arguing that in an international context a multiculturalist approach is not only most suitable, it is inevitable.

Now, tourism policy in many countries stretches beyond economic considerations. The debates about sustainability have placed environmental issues high up the agenda. This policy issue is not exclusively within the boundaries of the state but in many instances requires international collaboration. Policy is responding to global pressure as well as the perceived tourist image of the country. Sustainability in the context of tourism is not achieved, if it is achievable, by responding to just to global and national issues. Local interests of a sociocultural nature also should contribute. Indeed, it must be argued that diversity is unlikely to be maintained or sustainability recognised without the local dimension. Stakeholders in tourism are now clearly recognised at national, international and local levels. Currently the degree of power is uneven and depends on the different influences these levels have over policy and management.

'Engagement', as we noted earlier, demands an understanding of the nature of differences. Can a concept like power be construed differently in different societies and cultures? Understanding the idea the 'all powerful' in a Buddhist culture, like Thailand, may be very different from the supreme being as understood in Christendom or under Islam. Moreover, differences extend beyond religious belief into the very roots of the culture. For these reasons an awareness of the nature of differences is a cornerstone of multiculturalism.

Early tourism appears to have presented great diversity of experience to guests and hosts. The economic exchange was likely to have been greater and the environmental damage was minimal. With the advent of international mass tourism in Europe in the 1960's and in Southeast Asia from the 1970's a monocultural experience was offered. The tourist industry which developed for the mass international tourist tended to offer a standardised package, stamped with the name of the country as the only distinguishing mark. Turning a country into a commodity inevitably gave rise to environmental problems as well as the 'manufacturing of culture'. As we know this still continues today. These challenges are compounded by the need for diversity in tourism. Further standardisation or 'branding' will not provide a dynamic approach in policy or its management long term. Western writing about the business of tourism, at most accepts differences but frequently does little more than impose a western perspective of how something should be done. The so-called 'best practice' model usually comes from richer, western generating countries. They dominate the supply of international tourists so it is assumed western practice and thinking is the best model. "Best practice" can be formulated with the host, but appropriate to the destination. This involves awareness of the international, national and local. This approach is a multicultural one where all participants to tourism "engage, question and learn". The perception of tourism then becomes a phenomenological process rather than merely a commodity. Sustainability too becomes a constant issue with policy implications. International tourism policy making can be improved overall by drawing on the lessons of multiculturalism.

References

Annals of Tourism Research (1991), Tourism Social Science, Special Issue, *Annals of Tourism Research*, 18 (1).

Bennett, D., Ed (1998), *Multicultural States: Rethinking Difference and Identity*, London, Routledge.

Britton, R. A.(1979), Book Review of International Tourism; A Political and Social Analysis, *Annals of Tourism Research*, 6 (2): 205-206.

Carr, E. H. (1945), *Nationalism and After*, London, Macmillan, 1968 ed.

Dann, G., Nash, D. and Pearce, P. L. (1988), Methodology in Tourism Research, *Annals of Tourism Research*, 15:1.

Davidson, R. (1992), *Tourism in Europe*, London, Pitman Publishing.

Dodson, R. C. (1991), International Incoming Tourism Policies-A Study of the United Kingdom of Great Britain and Northern Ireland, Unpublished M.Soc.Sc thesis University of Birmingham, U.K.

Dodson, R. C. (1995), British Tourism Policy, *Bangkok Post*, February 6, !995.

Dodson, R. C. (1998), Towards a Multicultural View of Tourism Politics, *ABAC Journal*, 18:1, 38-54, Assumption University, Bangkok 10240, Thailand.

Dodson, R. and Courtney, J. J. (1996), *Ticket to Thailand: A Study of Tourism*, Bangkok, Assumption University Press.

Fay, B. (1996), *Contemporary Philosophy of Social Science*, Oxford, Blackwell.

Goldberg, D. T., Ed (1994), *Multiculturalism: A Critical Reader*, Cambridge USA, Blackwell.

Hitchcock, M., King, V. T. and Parnwell, M. (1993), *Tourism in Southeast Asia*, London, Routledge.

Holsti, K. J. (1972), *International Politics: A Framework for Analysis*, London, Prentice-Hall Int.

IUOTO. (1975), IUOTO Transformed: Aspects and Prospects, *Annals of Tourism Research*, 2 (5): 250-260

Jafari, J.(1975), Creation of the Inter-governmental World Tourism Organisation, *Annals of Tourism Research*, 2(5):237-245.

Kedouri, E. (1966), *Nationalism*, London, Hutchinson.

Klosters, M. (1984), The Deficiencies of Tourism Science Without Political Science-Comment on Richter, *Annals of Tourism Research* 610-612.

Krippendorf, J.(1987), *The Holiday Makers*, Oxford, Butterworth-Heinemann.

Lasswell, H. D.(1936), reprinted (1950), *Politics: Who Gets What, When, How*, New York, Peter Smith.

Lickorish, L. and Jenkins, C. (1997), *An Introduction to Tourism*, Oxford, Butterworth-Heinemann.

Lukes, S. (1974), *Power: A Radical View*, London, MacMillan.

Matthews, H. G. (1975), International Tourism and Political Science Research, *Annals of Tourism Research* 2 (4): 195-203.

Matthews, H. G. (1978), *International Tourism: A Social and Political Analysis*, Cambridge, Schenkman.

Owen, N. G. and Roberts, E. V.(1997), Value Judgements, *Asia Magazine*, December 5-7:23, Hong Kong: Asia Magazines.

Pearce, D. G. and Butler, R. W.(1993), *Tourism Research: Critiques and Challenges*, London, Routledge.

Reynolds, C. (1973), *Theory and Explanation in International Politics*, London, Martin Robertson.

Richter, L. K. (1983), Tourism Politics and Political Science: A Case of Not So Benign Neglect, *Annals of Tourism Research* 10:313-335.

Richter, L. K. (1989), *The Politics of Tourism in Asia*, Honolulu, University of Hawaii Press.

Ritchie, J. R. B. and *Goeldner, C. R. (1994), Travel, Tourism and Hospitality Research;* A Handbook for Managers, 2nd Ed, New York, John Wiley.

Towner, J.(1985), The European Grand Tour, circa 1550-1840: A Study of its Role in the History of Tourism, unpublished doctoral dissertation, University of Birmingham, U.K.

Urry, J.(1996), *The Tourist Gaze: Leisure and Travel in Contemporary Societies*, London, Sage.

Waltz, K. N. (1979), *Theory of International Politics*, U.S.A., Addison-Wesley Publishing Company.

Willett, C. ed. (1998), *Theorising Multiculturalism: A Guide to the Current Debate*, Oxford, Blackwell.

Wilson, R. and Dissanyake, W. (1996*), Global/Local: Cultural Production and the Transnational Imaginary*, Durham and London, Duke University Press.

World Tourism Organisation (WTO), (1987), *World Tourism Statistics*, Madrid, WTO.

Tourism and popular arts: The Talavera of Puebla

Elena de la Calleja and Guadalupe Revilla

Universidad de las Americas Puebla, México

Introduction

Over thousands of years, many cultures have been settled in the Puebla Valley, where the City of Puebla of Zaragoza (Puebla of the Angels, before), the capital of the state with the same name in Central Mexico, is now located. (González Pozo, 1998). The heart of this metropolis is its historic centre, one of the largest, richest and best conserved monumental zones of Latin America, named World Heritage Site in 1987 (UNESCO, 1998). In this city is produced a fine pottery named talavera, mostly for sale to tourists.

Of the thin glazed earthenware made in colonial Spanish America, the variety known as Talavera Poblana is perhaps the most important. It has enjoyed the longest continuos tradition and is still manufactured today. It was also the pottery that achieved the widest distribution in America, precisely because it was one of the most important products in the trade established between colonies (Castro, 1995). It is very significant that the talavera from Puebla had a strong influence on the ceramic ware in other parts of Mexico.

The talavera had an enormous influence on the civil and religious architecture of Puebla City and Mexico City. In Puebla City, the most outstanding feature was that it gave to the façades a strong Moorish or Mudejar accent. It is an inspired combination of red brick and tiles featuring a blue and white glaze which were used to cover many church cupolas, façades, and their prism-shaped pediments. Tiles were so popular that they could be found in palaces, houses, corridors, stairwalls and kitchens (Tercero, 1995). The sacred and the profane gestures of a community were concentrated in the talavera of churches and convents, house façades and kitchens.

The eighteenth century chronicler Fernández de Echeverría y Veytia claimed that Talavera was the finest pottery produced in the City of Puebla, and wrote that the design of the pieces was just as good as any imported into Mexico from Europe (Velázquez Thierry, 1995). Puebla's pottery workshops were held in special high esteem and their production included objects of every day use , as well as ornamental pieces of particular artistic value (Castro, 1995). There were produced large vases, pitchers, planting pots, tiles, bowls, plates, tableware, lebrillos and religious sculpture (Sánchez Navarro, 1995).

Purpose of the study

Talavera is today the most traditional, recognised and sought after popular art of Puebla City. For many tourists who visit the city, it is very important to buy a talavera piece, as part of the enjoyment of their trip, to take home and to give to family and friends. There are talavera factories open to the public, with guided visits which are very popular as tourist places. The local market of crafts and souvenirs is full of small shops that sell talavera products to tourists. Many studies (Cohen, 1993; Graburn, 1969, 1976; Littrell, Anderson and Brown, 1993; Popelka and Littrell, 1991) describe the effects of tourism in popular and fourth world arts. The purpose of this study is to explore the process of artistic change, as it was stated by Graburn (1969) and Cohen (1993), of a traditional pottery, the Talavera Poblana, and the effect in that process of the tourism and the Mexican legal norms.

Literature review

The process of artistic change

It is necessary to understand the marketing system of popular art. Successful modifications of traditional art depends upon this understanding. Graburn and Jules Rosette (cited by Popelka and Littrell, 1991) have examined changes in products intended for tourist and producers, who also sell the products. As Graburn (1976) stated, the art of the dominated people could be made for the external world. This art is then called tourist or airport art, and suffers a process of artistic change, from extinction to assimilated fine art and popular art, as the art market pass from the native people to the external people, and if the arts are made purely according traditional criteria or with the traditions of the dominant society, as it is showed in table 1.

Table 1   The process of artistic change

Intended audience	Source of tradition		
	Minority society	Novel/Synthetic	Dominant Society
Minority	Functional	Reintegrated	Popular
	Traditional		
External	Commercial	Souvenir	Assimilated
	Fine	Novelty	Fine

Source: Graburn 1976, p. 8

The functional or traditional arts should suffer some changes in technique and form, but these changes do not disturb the transmission of symbolic meaning. The commercial or pseudo traditional arts are made with sale in mind, they adhere to culturally embedded aesthetic and formal standards. The reintegrated arts are those which take some ideas, materials or techniques from the industrial society and apply them in new ways to the needs of indigenous people. The souvenirs are elaborated to satisfy the external consumer, these objects are commonly standardised or simplified, and the symbolic content is much reduced. The popular arts are assimilated arts, the content of which express the feelings of the culture of the minority. The assimilated fine arts are so influenced that compete directly with the art in the dominant society (Graburn, 1976).

Many art forms fit more than one category at the same time, as they are multifunctional (Graburn, 1976). The different aspects of an ethnic art do not necessary change to the same extent as they are adapted to the tourism market; production techniques may remain virtually unchanged, even as the products suffer a considerable heterogeneization (Cohen, 1993).

Contacts with foreign peoples, education, literacy, travel and modern media produce cultural changes. The market itself is the most powerful source of change, this change can be in size, simplification, standardisation, naturalism, grotesquery, novelty and archaism (Graburn, 1976). The persistence of traditional arts and crafts depends on: a continued demand; the existence of traditional materials; availability of the work force; knowledge, prestige for the producers; and the role of the product in the life of the community (Graburn, 1976).

Tourism and shopping

Tourism is a fragmented industry with many parts and activities. McIntosh and Goeldner (1986), mentioned shopping as one of the most important elements in tourism and one of the most important tourist activities. Shopping is becoming an increasingly important element in trips which are primarily of a leisure or tourism nature. This trend reflects the increasing emphasis on consumption in modern society and the importance which the acquisition of material goods has assumed in many peoples' lives (Timothy and Butler, 1995). Many people view shopping as a way of fulfilling part of their need for leisure and tourism, this type of activity is becoming a form of recreation and provides enjoyment and relaxation (Timothy and Butler, 1995). In many tourism destinations, shopping is the preferred activity and tourists often expend more money on shopping than on food, lodging, and other entertainment. Shopping opportunities can also function as a tourism attraction (Timothy and Butler, 1995; Ngamsom, 1999).

The production and marketing of tourist arts is a growing and increasingly important branch of the tourism industry (Cohen, 1993a). To satisfy tourist, gifts and souvenirs offered for sale should be crafted or manufactured in the country or region where the purchase is made. The most important single element in shopping is the authenticity of the products offered for sale as they relate to the local area (McIntosh and Goeldner, 1986).

The commercialisation of the art crafts can appear under diverse local conditions. Sometimes, local crafts are still viable whereas elsewhere they are declining and in danger of disappearing. Cohen (1993b) distinguished four types of commercialisation of art crafts with different dynamic:

1. complementary commercialisation, the spontaneous production of a viable craft, used by the local client;

2. substitutive commercialisation, the spontaneous reorientation to the external market of declining craft;

3. encroaching commercialisation, the sponsored (there is not contact between producers and consumers) reorientation of a still locally viable craft to an external market; and

4. rehabilitative commercialisation, the sponsored revival of a declining craft for an external market.

Tourist arts often experience a period of creative innovation, immediately following their commercialisation for an external public. However, after some time, as the market for the new arts products becomes established, routinisation tends to set in, as products become standardised and mass produced (Cohen, 1993a). Standardisation and routinasation seems to be "specially pronounced once a tourist art becomes oriented to the export market, with the accompanying publications of catalogues" (Cohen, 1993a, p. 4). Tourists tend to acquire some expensive items for themselves and smaller ones as presents for friends.

In the production of tourist arts, natural, locally prepared materials are typically substituted for industrial raw ones, and functional objects are often changed into decorative ones. There also exists a contrary trend towards the production of new kinds of functional objects, adapted to the needs and lifestyle of the tourist audience (Cohen, 1993a). It is very common that the original and traditional styles and products do not enjoy legal protection and can be imitated by anyone who has the resources to do so.

The talavera productive process

Today, tin-glazed pottery from Puebla is still referred as Talavera, and the techniques involving in its production have hardly changed at all since colonial times. The city talavera potters association was trying to establish a legal norm whereby only the ceramic ware produced in Puebla City could have the name Talavera.

To produce talavera, potters used two kinds of clay: a black variety extracted from deposits on the hills near the city, and a pink clay found in a near small village, Totimehuacán. Once the clays had been sifted to get rid of all foreign matter, they were mixed and then left in water tanks to rot (Velázquez Thierry, 1995).

Before the potter could work the clay, he had to remove all excess water. He then began to wedge the clay by placing it on a brick floor in a covered area were it was treaded barefoot to achieve an even consistency. The wedging was finished off by hand, and the clay was then divided into lumps of different sizes. The potter worked the smaller lumps on the wheel to create numerous objects and use moulds for making tiles. Once the pieces were completed, they were left in a closed room for a long period of time to ensure that they dried evenly. They were then fired in a wood-fuelled kiln. After this firing, which lasted from ten to twelve hours, each piece was examined carefully in order to separate the good pieces from those with imperfections or those that have been fired unevenly. They were then covered with a white glaze, made of a tin and lead base, which gave the enamel finish to each piece. Once the glaze had dried, pieces were decorated with different designs. The range of colours was designated by the seventeenth century Ordinances, and would vary depending on the quality of the ceramic piece. Pieces were then ready for the last firing which would take up to forty hours (Velázquez Thierry, 1995).

Talavera is the synthesis of various influences. In the first place, it assumes its heritage of craftsmanship, imagination and quality from the pre-Hispanic culture which flourished in Puebla Valley; but it also bears the mark of Islam, Spain, Italy and China, which really implies a five-fold cultural cross-breeding (Gamboa, cited by Tercero, 1995).

Methodology

Initial approaches were made to 24 talavera potters in the City of Puebla, based on the Yellow Pages Directory and in the Directory of the Council of Popular Art of the City of Puebla. Three of these potters did not exist anymore. Each one of the rest was contacted and invited to participate in the study, and only 16 agreed. A administered questionnaire with open and fixed questions was developed based on the process described by McDaniel and Gates (1991) with the purpose of facilitate the data recollection. The survey took place in the winter of 1999 and all the potters who agree to participate were visited in their offices or their factories. The questionnaire took no more than two hours and a half to complete. The talavera potters were interviewed about the production and design of talavera, the sales and the clients, the interactions with the clients, and the legal norms to be considered in the talavera production.

The completed interviews were examined and the content analysed. For the open ended questions, the responses were analysed for common themes and ideas and placed in categories, as described by Bogdan and Biklen (1992). Because the themes were easily identified, the responses naturally fell into the various categories listed in the result section.

Results

Potters characteristics

Half of the potters interviewed had from six to ten years producing Talavera, only two had less than six years, and only four had more than 30 years. Half of them started to produce Talavera to have their own business, only five produced talavera as a familiar tradition.

Nine potters had 30 employees or less, and only two had more than 50 employees. Almost all the potters made an average of 16 pieces per day. Twelve potters started to produce plates and tableware, two started producing tiles, and one started producing an innovating product: decanter bases.

The market

Fourteen potters mentioned that they sell to external clients (tourists), the American and European tourists regarded as the most important clients, but also they sold to Brazilian and Argentines. The potters perceived that tourists usually go shopping in groups, and are young adults. The potters indicated that tourists mostly buy plates and large vases, the potters believed for decorative purpose. Six potters perceived their tourist prefer traditional designs, and two potters mentioned they received demands from the American tourist for more innovative designs. Only two potters sold to foreign collectionist their own designs. Seven potters exported in regular form, mostly to United States of America, but also to Europe and South America.

Fifteen potters mentioned the local market as important. This market is composed, in a large part, by institutions, like universities, banks, hotels, and restaurants, who use the talavera pieces as decorative objects, and they buy plates, large vases, tiles and tableware, by order and with special designs. The local market is also composed of families who buy talavera for utilitarian purposes, but the potters said these clients are fewer, because the talavera pottery is a very expensive product for them. For only one potter, the only one who produced with a almost totally mechanised process, the local market was the most important one, and he sold mostly utilitarian products.

In general terms, the potters did not perceive changes in the preferences of the market, they did not use market research, and almost all (twelve) did not use intermediaries. Only one mentioned the client is more demanding now than in the past, two potters mentioned the clients seek less expensive products.

Marketing

Twelve potters did not have distributors, and always made direct sales. All potters had their own retail store, and only few potters had more than one store in the city. The potters or their employees, who did not have more than medium education, made the sales. Only one potter hired bachelor graduates as sales persons. Six potters usually go to commercial fairs. Almost all of them work with commercial orders.

Nine potters have a product catalogue, and they prepared the catalogue when they started to sell to external clients. Five potters used Internet sites. Eight potters mentioned they did not receive any product information from the client, eight potters mentioned as their only client information available, the data contained in the sale ticket.

The product

Three different kinds of Talavera pottery were found: traditional, white and "taladura", almost all potters produced the traditional pottery, only one produced "taladura". Only one potter acquired the clay from deposits on the hills near the city, as was traditional, most of them acquired the clay from concrete producers. Five potters used colours that were not the traditional, because the tourists ask for more colour; the rest used the five traditional colours: blue, black, yellow, green and orange. The traditional productive process had been simplified, and it is almost the same; only in one case, the "taladura case", it had been almost totally mechanised.

Nine potters mentioned they produced smaller products to sell more. All the potters mentioned the best sold products are the plates, the tableware and the large vases. Only two potters produced tiles, and they mentioned these pieces are not for tourists. Eight potters made mostly ornamental pieces, and eight potters made utilitary pieces. Nine of them produce innovations, as decanter bases, lamps, tequila cups, and ash trays, to satisfy market demand.

Ten potters mentioned they make personal designs, almost all with flowers, mostly based on the market demand, whilst only two potters make the traditional designs. Two potters mentioned they produced more simplistic design, because is less expensive. Seven potters mentioned they produced "modern" designs, and six potters mentioned they had been reproduced classic pieces.

Six potters mentioned they worked according the new legal norm, and seven of them mentioned it was good for the talavera production, because the production was going to be protected nationally and internationally. Five potters mentioned the legal norm probably was going to change the tradition, and it was only in interest of few potters, the largest ones.

Conclusions

After interviewing the talavera potters, it was found that there had been an artistic change in the talavera production. Many talavera potters sold their products mostly to tourists, and depended on this external market to survive and to make the talavera art viable as commercial product, because it was expensive to local market. The market orientation of the talavera ceramic stated what the potters produced and sold. The Talavera Poblana fitted more than one Graburn's category of artistic change at the same time, depending on the market the product is sold and its use.

As the talavera ceramic had been sold to the local market, it fitted the category of functional or traditional art, because the products had the same symbolic meaning that they had in the past. For example, talavera tiles are still used in buildings façades and houses façades and kitchens in Puebla City. Also, the talavera fitted the category of reintegrated art, as new talavera products that respond to new habits, new activities of the community and new uses, as tequila cups and decanter bases had been introduced to the local market. The case of the decanter bases is an example of an existing utilitary product that is spontaneously produced by one potter, with a non-traditional material to this product: the talavera, that had some vantages over traditional materials, as durability and resistance. The large sales of this product motivated other potters to produce it.

As the market changed from the local market to the external market, the talavera also fitted another two Graburn's categories: 1) commercial fine arts, because the designs, colours and even the products had lost their symbolic meaning and they were produced in the form that they can be sold faster, and in better conditions to tourists; and 2) souvenirs, because the talavera products had been changed in size, to be cheaper, and the designs had been simplified, in forms and colours, trying to satisfy the tourist demands.

The talavera marketing system had two of the four types of commercialisation stated by Cohen: 1) the complementary commercialisation, because some talavera potters started to produce talavera very few years ago, to the local market, without intermediaries, producing, as it was demanding, tiles, plates and tableware; and 2) the substitutive commercialisation, because the potters started to offer to tourist and foreign collectionist their products, without intermediaries, and after that, they started to innovate and to export the talavera. Some talavera potters used a very innovative distributing system, the Internet, to sell to external clients.

The talavera potters had simplified the productive process, and substituted the materials for industrial raw ones. They changed the traditional designs, because these designs were very complicated. As Cohen observed in his study (1993b), functional talavera objects, as plates, large vases, and cups, had changed to decorative ones. One significant part of the local market only bought talavera products as decorative ones, and the tourist made the same. As long as these decorative objects had been demanded, the talavera ceramic could remain as a viable form of popular art.

Although the talavera potters successfully identified their market, they did not recollect market information in a systematic way, and the changes in designs and forms many times are produced to simplified the designs and reduce in size the pieces, as it was mentioned previously. The talavera potters did the changes in the talavera artistic designs they believed the tourist market was looking for, and many times some potters just copied the changes introduced for another potter, without market information, but these new design were produced again if they were demanded. The government and a potter association were looking for the introduction of a legal norm that intended to protect the ceramic production of Puebla City, from the competitors of other parts of the country. This norm tended to reduce the artistic changes and innovations, because the elements of the design and the production is going to be protected by a original denomination. At the same time, the government and the association intended to make the talavera factories an international tourist attraction

As Octavio Paz (1995. p.10) mentioned *"made by hand, the craft object bears the fingerprints, real or metaphorical, of the person who fashioned it"*. The popular arts are one of the most significant elements of the culture, and had to be preserved. The talavera poblana is one example of a popular art with a long past that could remain in our daily lives, as the ceramic production is directed to the tourist and some large local clients.

References

Bogdan, R. C., and Biklen, S. K. (1992), *Qualitative research for education*. Needham Heights, MA: Allyn and Bacon.

Castro, E. (1995), Puebla y la talavera a través de los siglos. *Artes de México*, 3, 20-29.

Cohen, E. (1993a). Introduction. Investigating tourist arts. *Annals of Tourism Research*, 20, 1-8.

Cohen, E. (1993b). The heterogeneization of a tourist art. *Annals of Tourism Research*, 20, 138-163.

González Pozo, A. (1998), Centro Histórico de Puebla de Zaragoza en Patrimonio de la Humanidad en México. México: Fondo Editorial de la Plástica Mexicana.

Graburn, N. H. H. (1969), Art and acculturative processes. *International Social Science Journal*, 21, 457-468.

Graburn, N. H. H. (1976), Introduction, in Graburn, N. H. H., ed. Ethnic and Tourist Arts. Cultural expressions of the Fourth World. Berkeley: University of California Press.

Littrell, M. A., Anderson, L. F., and Brown, P. J. (1993), What makes a craft souvenir authentic? *Annals of Tourism Research*, 20, 197-215.

McDaniel, C. and Gates, R. (1991), *Contemporary Marketing Research*. St. Paul: West Publishing Company.

McIntosh, R. W. and Goeldner, C. R. (1986), *Tourism, principles, practices, philosophies*. New York: Wiley and Sons, Inc.

Ngamsom, B. (1999), Shopping tourism: An alternative for Thailand tourist destination development. *Advances in Hospitality and Tourism Research*, 4, 219-228.

Paz, O. (1995), La artesanía, entre el uso y la contemplación. *Artes de México*, 3, 10-14.

Popelka, C. A. and Littrell, M. A. (1991), Influence of tourism on handcraft evolution. *Annals of Tourism Research*, 18, 392-413.

Sánchez Navarro, B. (1995), La Talavera en los museos mexicanos. *Artes de México*, 3, 57-61.

Tercero, M. (1995), De la talavera y otras cerámicas. *Artes de México*, 3, 68-71.

Timothy, D. J. and Butler, R. W. (1995), Cross border shopping. A North American perspective. *Annals of Tourism Research*, 22, 16-34.

UNESCO, (1998), Historic center of Puebla. www.unesco.org/whc/sites/416.htm

Velázquez, Thierry, L. (1995), Fabricación de la Talavera y origen del término. *Artes de México*, 3, 16-19.

Cultural sensitivity and planned responses - A spectrum of initiatives to meet the expectations of different visitor types, whilst 'protecting' the cultural resources

Michael Fagence

University of Queensland, Australia

Abstract

This paper explores an aspect of 'the tourist gaze' in which particular cultural groups attract a high degree of vulnerability because of their exposure to the 'outside' world as special tourist attractions in a generally well-resourced tourism region. This paper will argue that there are other reasons why the particular geographical area in which 'interesting' cultural groups live and work are attractive for the purposes of tourism. The challenge for tourism planning is to develop and implement multi-focus strategies which meet the various requirements of a wide spectrum of visitors, whilst both providing for that segment which has a particular interest in the cultural groups and offering reasonable protection of the culture of those groups. Using the Anabaptist communities of the Amish (in Pennsylvania) and Mennonites (in Ontario) as case studies, this paper will examine ways and means of planning for the sustainability of these particular cultures in a context of general regional tourism attraction.

Introduction

There is an uneven-ness in the study of the interaction with their host environments of small communities and groups which have sensitive and particularly vulnerable cultures. Much of the published research focuses on the sensitivity of remote and mainly indigenous groups, especially in developing countries (see, for example, *Cultural Survival Quarterly,* 1990; Hinch and Butler, 1996). Whilst there has been some companion research into aspects of special interest in some of the culturally-distinct communities in parts of Europe (see, for example, the collection in Boissevain, 1996), a less well-researched perspective has been on the interaction of special cultural groups in developed countries which have struggled to sustain their cultural individuality in part to meet the expectations of the 'tourist gaze'. Embedded in this perspective are studies of indigenous groups such as the Aborigines in Australia (Altman and Finlayson, 1991; Hollinshead, 1996) and the American Indians in various parts of USA (Lew, 1995, 1996). The Anabaptist groups (Amish and Mennonite), which form the basis of the case studies presented in this paper, have attracted research which tends to focus on the potential damage which could be inflicted by the insistent 'gaze' of tourists (see, for example, Fagence, forthcoming; Kreps, et al, 1997; Luthy, 1994). However, there is companion research on these groups which suggests that the impact of tourist inquisitiveness may not be detrimental in every case, especially if it is carefully channelled or focused on particular aspects of the culture and its environment (see, for example, Fagence, 1999A; Hovinen, 1995).

The tourism attractiveness of a region with a distinctive culture may extend beyond that culture to some of the more conventional tourism attractions and activities. For example, in the special cases reported in this paper, there are at least four purposes which stimulate tourist interest in and access to Amish and Mennonite groups. These four purposes are:

- conventional mass tourism, with a diversity of 'things to see and do', with the cultural groups and their working environment providing only one focal point or catalyst for tourist interest within a region which has an extensive range of attractions;

- special interest in the particular culture, and its various manifestations of dress, work practices, crafts, behaviour, beliefs;

- recreational day trips, from a busy metropolitan area into the surrounding countryside in which the cultural groups are almost coincidental to the general recreational purpose;

- access to particular retail opportunities at designer-label shopping malls, outlet malls, craft villages and 'tourist shopping villages'

The two case study regions used in this paper have locational, cultural, commercial and recreational characteristics which tend to obfuscate the principal rationale for the tourist visits; for example:

- they are within easy travelling distance of major metropolitan centres

- they are located close to major transport corridors

- they have a peculiar heritage of development

- they are 'different'

- they have a reputation for quality of production and service

- they offer a wide range of serious and recreational shopping activities

- they provide a range of spectacular entertainment

- they are within regions which have a diversity of recreational opportunities

- they have become targeted by major entrepreneurial development and management

Despite these similarities, there are distinct differences in the way they have been approached in terms of planning and management. It is these differences which have contributed to the spectrum of initiatives to respond to the expectations of different visitor types, and to the capacities and intentions of the principal stakeholder groups. These are matters which are considered later in this paper.

It is the purpose of this paper to use interpretations of the experiences in tourism regions where Amish and Mennonite groups live and work to explore tourism planning strategies which may meet the general touristic requirements of different visitor types whilst affording reasonable protection to these vulnerable cultural groups. In the next section the focus is on some of the significant product-consumer mix issues. There is a brief review of some of the purposes of accessing regions for tourist purposes, and then a comment on the suitability of generalising and specialising a region's attractiveness. That section is followed by one which provides background information on the Amish and Mennonite groups and which interprets the previous general review of tourism resources into the specific contexts of Pennsylvania and Ontario. The focus is then sharpened to a consideration of some of the stakeholder responses to the particular interest of tourists in the special Anabaptist cultural groups. A concluding interpretation section is preceded by a brief assessment of fourteen strategies disbursed across a planning spectrum according to their response to stakeholder interests.

The product-consumer mix: types of tourism and tourism attraction

There are particular planning and management challenges in tourism regions which have both a specific cultural heritage which provides a focus of tourist attention, and which, at the same time, offer an extensive range of touristic opportunities with appeal to a diverse scope of visitor types. Attention in much of contemporary tourism planning practice tends to cater either for generalized 'mass tourism' or for the more particularized 'special interest tourism' (Gunn, 1993; Pearce and Butler, 1993; Weiler and Hall, 1992) with much less conspicuous attention to the likely scenario of multi-faceted and multi-interest tourism. One of the outcomes of this polarized circumstance is a 'battleground' in which there are occasional skirmishes involving the host communities and their environments, the tourism industry, particular interest groups, government and public agencies, and the tourists. The outcome of these skirmishes is often determined more by the relative strength of the forces brought to bear on the issues, and the ability of those forces to dominate the decision-making process, than to calm, rationalised thought and the use of 'textbook' solutions (Hall, 2000).

The published literature on motivation for tourism, and the factors which influence the decision-making of individual tourists, suggests that the potential attractiveness of a destination region is conditioned by the degree to which special and general interests can be met, with the range of 'things to see and do' an important determinant of relative attractiveness. One of the first steps is to identify the range of attractions available to potential tourists.

A simple categorisation

Many tourism planners have formulated categorisations of tourism attractions (see, for example, Gunn, 1993). For the purposes of the subsequent examination conducted in this paper it is sufficient to develop a simple categorisation. The attributes of destination regions (or places) which can be expected to stimulate visits, whether for general recreational or specific reasons, are likely to include the following touristic purposes:

Outdoor recreation:

- targeted for active pursuits (such as picnic locations, sports fields, stretches of river for fishing or boating)

- for passive pursuits (such as scenic backdrops, landscape and vistas)

- for relaxation and contemplation

- for touring and driving for pleasure

Cultural development and understanding:

- for access to and encounters with particular cultural groups, witnessing their activities, learning of their heritage, participating in some of the conspicuous aspects of their lifestyle

- for studying built environment heritage

- for education and information

Shopping:

- for examining and acquiring crafts of the particular cultural groups

- for conventional shopping in major shopping centres, enclosed or strip malls

- for special retailing in designer-label and factory outlet malls

- for 'country collectibles' in tourist shopping villages

- for food and produce shopping

Entertainment:

- for sporting events, including golf tournaments,

- for live commercial entertainment, including theatre, music hall, concerts and other performing arts

- for 'commercial attractions', theme-parks

- activity zones

- cinemas

In order to retain competitiveness, targeted destination regions and places need to match the supply of localised tourism products and services with those purposes which they can most easily satisfy. A summary of the purposes listed here would indicate that tourists seek to maximise their experience of outdoor recreation, cultural understanding, shopping, and entertainment taking into account, for example:

- the journey length and duration to the targeted region or place

- the costs of preparing for the journey

- the costs of that journey

- the costs incurred at the destination

- the economic advantage of having made the effort (the perceived benefits)

- the psychological satisfaction in terms of personal 'improvement' and education

- asset accumulation (such as goods bought)

- the physical benefits gained

- the independent and/or family benefit derived – the 'feel good' factor

- the suitability of companion servicing (such as, and where necessary, accommodation, food and beverage outlets, support services - such as filling stations, personal services, public services)

Some of these issues are addressed in market segment targeting. Whereas that targeting may be relatively straightforward for a tightly focused destination region or place, it is less easy where the region or place has a diversity of potential attractions and experiences to offer. One of the outcomes from a simplistic assessment of target markets may be a commitment to a strategy of either tourism specialisation, or of generalisation. This polarised approach is unlikely to be satisfactory in terms of realising the region's potential, the interests of the stakeholders and the planning instruments which can be used to achieve a multi-faceted strategy. This is the particular circumstance faced in the two case study regions, where a potential commitment to a specialised cultural strategy would overlook the optimum use of a broad range of tourism resources, or where a commitment to a generalised tourism strategy may not provide the necessary protection for vulnerable communities, cultures and environments.

The challenge for tourism planning is to develop a strategy which can achieve a product-consumer mix which is sensitive to the peculiar circumstances of the tourism region and responsive to the expectations of the various visitor types. These issues are considered in a sharpened geographical and cultural focus in the next section.

Case study: the touristic circumstances

In the tourist visits which target the regions in which there are significant concentrations of Anabaptist communities (Amish in USA and Mennonites in Canada) there is a mixture of purposes. Although there have been no studies which can verify the following statements with any quantitative assurance, there would seem to be:

- some inquisitiveness about the culturally-different community groups which exhibit a markedly distinct lifestyle

- a predominance of general visitation to countryside areas, such as driving along directed trails, visiting nature reserves

- opportunities taken to indulge in shopping expeditions, in both major malls and in tourist villages.

In the Anabaptist regions there seems to be an overlap of motivations for tourist visits, and even the taking up of more than one touristic opportunity whilst in the region. A brief statement about the origins of the Anabaptist communities is appropriate at this point.

The Anabaptist communities: a brief history

The diffuse groups which are referred to generically as Anabaptist, comprise the Amish, the Mennonites, the Hutterites and a few other sub-groups; these are readily identifiable by their particular social and religious codes and behaviour (see, for example, Hostetler, 1968; Kraybill, 1989). These groups emerged in the period of social and religious chaos in the seventeenth century in Europe. They developed unique ideas about the church, the state, the family and the person, and this development contributed to the creation of a particular code of behaviour regarding dress, conduct, association with people outside of their community, the maintenance of a peculiar language, and led the groups to high levels of skill and self-sufficiency in rural crafts and production. It also contributed to a fortress mentality of separation from 'mainstream' society. The various groups of Anabaptists migrated across Europe in the eighteenth century seeking a safe haven for their practices, some eventually travelling to North America with several arrival points on the east coast of USA and Canada. Since the early arrivals in the eighteenth century the Anabaptists have spread out across the continent, with distinct concentrations in, for example, Pennsylvania and Ohio in north-eastern USA, and Ontario and Manitoba in Canada. The tendency for these groups to have concentrated in rural areas which now lie within a few hours drive of major urban centres has contributed to them becoming a legitimate target for visitor interest.

Interest in the Anabaptists as cultural 'attractions'

The special character of the people themselves seems to act as a magnet for the inquisitive tourist. One of the first points to be made is that the Anabaptist groups are not homogeneous in life-style and commitment to underlying religious beliefs. One of many complicating issues in unravelling the impact of visitor interest in the Anabaptist communities is the existence of many different 'orders' or congregations. The Anabaptist communities are not uniform in their lifestyle and modus operandi. In the case of the Canadian Mennonites, for example, there are possibly as many as fourteen identifiably different groups (Redekop, 1988). However, the highest level of tourist interest is focussed on the conspicuously different 'Old Order' Anabaptist people who have adopted and maintained a rigorous lifestyle based upon their religious code. To the mass tourist, most subtleties of difference between the 'orders' are of little consequence.

A second point to be made is that the independence, self-sufficiency and particularly the commitment to strongly held beliefs of the 'Old Order' groups causes them to eschew the use of services and technology (such as electricity) which modern society considers indispensable. This tends to increase the admiration of the tourists for the quality and diversity of the craft production of the Anabaptist communities. Some of the less strict orders of these communities have become involved in cottage industries and services (activities which have been described as a potential Trojan horse for Amish society – see Olshan, 1994). The manifestations of this relaxation include the farmer's markets (especially, but not exclusively for food products and crafts), the roadside stalls of Amish quilts, maple syrup and other products, the living museums of Amish farms, and the visitor centres which purport to exhibit authentic evidence of Amish and Mennonite history, lifestyles, crafts and production. These are some of the trappings to which the recreational tourist is attracted.

In summary, the special features of touristic interest include, for example:

- the sombre dress code of plain colours, free of decoration and embellishment, with a style which is reminiscent of the puritanical forms of the seventeenth century;

- the horse and buggy transport;

- the focus on agrarian, and agrarian-related skills;

- the pursuit of simple agricultural practices (such as the use of horse-drawn farm machinery, and the avoidance of chemical fertilisers);

- the simple architectural forms for farm buildings (sometime described as the Dutch barn) and houses, with the readily identifiable additions to farm-house structures to accommodate an increase in family members and especially the grandparents;

- the communal telephone boxes, the lack of electrical power cables, and sometimes ingenious substitute engineering devices to generate power, distribute water and so on;

- the range of quilts and other furnishings, wood and other craft items;

- the ranges of quality garden and farm produce available in local stores and restaurants;

- the peculiar language.

With this potential scope of touristic interest it is hardly surprising that "it is safe to say that any sizeable Amish settlement within several hours driving time of large cities is being affected by tourism" (Luthy, 1994, p. 129).

General touristic interest in the Anabaptist regions

Despite this clear focus of touristic attraction, there are clearly other purposes for which visitors travel to and stay in the two case study regions. Comprehensive inventories of tourism resources in some of these case study Anabaptist regions would include the following categories:

- general, nature-based recreation environments

- general, built environment

- shopping opportunities

- entertainment

Each of these is considered briefly here.

General, nature-based recreation environments and the built environment

This category includes, for example, national and state parks, forest reservations, river banks and other water courses, for both general recreation and for fishing and boating, rural landscapes exhibiting particular farming styles and operations, and farm buildings, small town and village communities with distinct historical associations, heritage buildings, sites and trails, museums and galleries exhibiting local products, and refurbished buildings (a re-use of previous commercial and industrial premises). Some districts of southern Ontario offer spectacular geomorphologic features (such as the Niagara region) and fruit-farming areas.

The location and distribution of many of these resources may frustrate their inclusion in a tidy geographical strategy, so that they remain as isolated entities in a loosely-drawn structure. Some of the natural locations are not easily accessed, and local regulations on the use of waterways may preclude their incorporation into strategies of active recreation. The gradual realisation of the historical and heritage significance of the regions has led to some of the resources being included in heritage strategies. This diversity of natural and built environment attractions provides the 'pull factors' for aggregate day-travel populations of up to 50 million in the case of Pennsylvania (the mega-metropolitan region including Boston, New York, Philadelphia, Baltimore and Washington DC), and up to 5 million in the case of southern Ontario (focusing on Toronto and the Niagara Falls region). Both regions have general rural tourism resources.

Shopping resources

There is increasing world-wide evidence that shopping expeditions, either with an intent to make a particular purchase or to browse through a range of retail outlets is a common use of leisure time. There are significant opportunities to indulge in shopping expeditions in the two case study regions. Although not exceptional, the range of options include the following:

- designer-label outlet malls, with 'up-market' shops retailing fashion clothes, jewelry, white goods, fashion home accessories and appliances in both open and enclosed malls and precincts;

- factory outlet malls, with direct retailing from the manufacturer to the customer;

- fresh farm produce, through 'farmer's markets', with both conventional stalls in enclosed buildings, and open-air stalls, with some retailing directly from farmer's vehicles;

- artisan crafts, particularly made from fabrics (such as quilts and other domestic furnishings), wooden furniture and toys, garden furniture and appliances;

- curiosity, craft and antique shops, mostly retailing domestic items which have regional and heritage significance, particularly made from fabrics, precious metals, and wood;

- artist galleries, with examples of most of the visual art forms, often (but not exclusively) in exhibitions of parochial scenes and episodes of local history, and made from locally-available materials.

The particular relevance of these various types of shopping opportunity has been considered in the special case of the Ontario examples. For example, Mitchell et al (1993) have referred to 'recreational shopping villages' which "provide specialised goods or services for the travelling public ....with ......establishments specializing in country collectibles" (p.16). Although one of the features of attraction is the association of some of these small townships with the local Mennonite population, the entrepreneurial community has attempted to 'generalise' the attractiveness of "small town ambience and 'old-fashioned' hospitality" (p.22). Getz (1993) has taken this type of study further, referring to the phenomenon as a 'tourist shopping village'. In both Anabaptist regions shopping is clearly one of the principal attractions, whether or not it includes the culture-based outlets. Getz has posed the question whether the activity of recreational or tourist shopping is (or could be) an independent strategy in a tourist region, or whether it is (or should be) merely complementary to (or even a viable alternative to) other types of tourist attraction. The opportunities for shopping to make a significant contribution to the regional tourism strategy are based on the existence of, for example, a stable population base for conventional convenience and fashion shopping, and qualities of quaintness and local idiosyncrasy which can appeal to both a localized and more distant tourist clientele.

Despite the potential contribution which shopping can make to the touristic attractiveness of the two case study regions, there is little 'hard data' on which to base firm judgements.

Entertainment resources

In the two case study regions, the entertainment focal points include:

- the ubiquitous theme parks (some, as with the Dutch Wonderland experience in Lancaster, excessively commercialized and almost incongruous),

- major theatres for drama and experiential extravaganzas (including the Shaw theatre at Niagara, the Imax theatre at Lancaster, the Sight and Sound Millenium theatre at Strasburg),

- purpose-designed music halls (such as the American Music Theatre at Lancaster),

- locale-specific museums and information centres, including exhibits of crafts, products, dress, transport,

- special interest museums, such as the Steam Railway museum to Strasburg.

Commentary

This kaleidoscope of attractions has the potential to meet many of the purposes of touristic travel to these (and other) regions, and to meet the expectations of the various types of visitors - day visitors/excursionists, the week-end and short stay visitors, the touring visitors, and even the long-stay vacationists. It is necessary to return to the cultural features of the case study regions and to interpret the planning initiatives which are necessary to effect a composite strategy which, whilst achieving a full expression of the touristic opportunities, provides evidence of the ways and means of affording reasonable protection to the vulnerable cultural resources.

Planning responses to touristic interest: the spectrum of initiatives

The emergence of a set of cooperative strategies

As was mentioned in an earlier section, it is the relative ease of access to these tourism regions from major urban concentrations which stimulates the demand for a diversity of tourism resources and touristic opportunities. However, it is unlikely that it is proximity alone which is responsible for the remarkable success the two case study regions have in continuing to attract tourist business. Another factor which seems to underpin the attractiveness is the 'different' cultural group which provides a counterpoint to the lifestyle of most visitors. Yet this still does not 'explain' the ongoing attractiveness, and particularly the underpinning interest in non-Anabaptist facilities and services. Some recent attempts (Fagence 1999A, 1999B) to discover the rationale for the approaches to tourism planning in both of the case study regions have drawn attention to the significance and influence of the various principal stakeholder groups. In summary there are three principal groups; these include:

Amish and Mennonites - the focal point of the culture interest:

- the 'custodians of the culture', being the most conservative and orthodox members of the Old Orders, both Amish and Mennonite;

- the more liberal Amish and Mennonites who have decided to work within relaxed parameters of behaviour and interaction with tourists and touristic activity, and who have chosen to become involved indirectly with tourism activity through servicing the accommodation, restaurant, furnishing and other domestic retail activities;

- the most 'relaxed' members of these groups who have chosen to become closely involved directly with tourism, in staffing information centres, both staffing and servicing outlets which retail Amish and Mennonite-made goods (especially foodstuffs and crafts), and in operating businesses which provide some insight into Anabaptist culture (such as country tours, buggy-rides, farm tours).

Non-Anabaptist community

- the entrepreneurial business-people who use the touristic interest in the Anabaptist culture to promote and offer the rationale for their own tourist-related businesses, including, for example, retail outlets, accommodation and tour packages which refer explicitly to the Anabaptists especially by the use of the cultural symbolism;

- other entrepreneurs who extend the range of tourism attractiveness in the creation and development of the complementary facilities including theme parks, cinemas, sports grounds (especially golf course), theatres, museums;

- major entrepreneurial groups who complement the local business community with franchised hotels/motels and restaurants, factory and fashion outlet shopping malls.

Government and quasi-government agencies; public interest groups

- the various government agencies (departments, units, centres, bureaux) at State/Province, regional/County and local which pursue a range of interests which impinge on the sustainability of local culture as a factor of touristic attraction (see later);

- the public interest groups concerned about the sustainability of local culture, communities and rural practices.

These various groups have become 'fused' into a cooperative working relationship so that their independent strategies contribute positively to sustaining one of the principal purposes - visits to the Anabaptist communities - which attract visitors from the local area, the region, and from overseas. What has emerged in the circumstances of both case study regions is a loose, almost coincidental planning and development strategy which has the potential to sustain the respective attractiveness. Attention is turned now from the groups of strategists to the initiatives and strategies.

A spectrum of initiatives

Although the various initiatives of each of these groups of stakeholders in the two case study areas have been implemented with some differences, there is a sufficiently high degree of similarity for a 'generic' list to be presented and considered. The initiatives, in summary, include the following:

1. *Creation of a touristic critical mass and network*

    One of the geographically-extensive initiatives has been the creation and implementation of a region-wide tourism strategy, with input from both the tourism industry and government at various levels. The particular contribution of this initiative has been to provide a spatial strategy in which the nodal points of touristic critical mass interest have been deployed in a rural setting close to metropolitan areas so that the multi-faceted needs of the potential visitors can be addressed (if not met) to degrees which would provide a satisfactory touristic experience

2. *Creation of precinct-specific strategies*

    As a sub-component of the region-wide strategies, but not necessarily derived from them, there have been district or precinct-specific strategies composed essentially by groups of local entrepreneurs. A noticeable outcome has been the development of complementing tourism shopping villages (sometimes as entire villages, but most often defined precincts within villages) with some evidence of locational specialization. This specialization has taken distinctive forms, including retailing of Anabaptist crafts (especially woodwork and fabric crafts), agricultural produce, and even concentrations of accommodation and restaurants. Other forms of precinctization have included heritage buildings and settings, and commercial entertainment.

3. *Land consolidation*

In the case of many of the precinct-specific strategies, the opportunity to achieve a consolidated planning approach has been facilitated by land amalgamation and consolidation programs pursued, in the main, by major local entrepreneurs. This concentration of ownership has empowered the entrepreneurs to establish both a recognizable physical/spatial entity, and a distinctive marketing unit which has heightened visibility.

4. *Nucleated shopping malls*

A companion form of precinctization has included nucleated concentrations of fashion retail malls, most often linked to regional distributor roads (see also 11 and 12).

5. *Planning regulations*

These forms of precinct and district development have been facilitated by the formulation of planning regulations which have set guidelines for various forms of touristic activity. These regulations have most commonly been set at the level of local government (at district or township level), after having been endorsed at the 'higher' level of administration – the counties. General characteristics of this regulatory base include little or no specific reference to the Anabaptist communities and their activities, and the absorption of tourism within a category of commercial development. This, in particular, has contributed to some of the concern expressed in the case of Lancaster County, where the most disturbing visual and aesthetic landscape of tourism has been created in a commercial land use zone where tourism-related activity is a permitted land use.

6. *Specialist cultural retail precincts*

Some entrepreneurial initiative has been invoked to create specialist retail precincts within villages which focus attention, at a small scale, on the products of the Anabaptist culture.

7. *Farmer's markets*

Local planning regulations have provided for the 'isolated' development of farmer's produce markets, which tend to concentrate on or near major highway linkages, or at urban peripheral locations (where they function, in part, as regular provisioning centres – similar to the 'out-of-town shopping malls)

8. *Regulations to achieve cultural protection*

Some small townships, in consultation with 'higher' levels of county government, have introduced particular land use regulations which provide for the protection of cultural resources and their landscapes. The difficulties of formulating and implementing legislative provisions which are clearly discriminatory (even positively) have caused some regulations to be expressed so that there is no specific and explicit mention of Anabaptist groups, their culture, or their rural and commercial activities. However, given the primary characteristics of the Anabaptist lifestyle, there should not be too much doubt about the group being referenced in the following policy statement:

"In order to preserve and support the historic social, economic and cultural needs of a unique segment of the Region's existing rural community which rely on horse drawn vehicles as their sole means of transportation..." (Regional Municipality of Waterloo, 1996, p.89)

9. Supportive functional groups

These land use initiatives, especially in so far as they lead to the protection of farmland, have been supported by farming and environmental groups.

10. Diversionary strategy

In some instances, the creation of a strategy has been fortuitous. For example, as an outcome of the change of emphasis in the Pennsylvania-wide State strategy for tourism, a conscious decision was made to generalize the tourism potential and attractiveness of the region which includes the Anabaptist communities in Lancaster County. This generalization was to focus on the historic and heritage potential, not only of the Anabaptist groups, but also many of the other cultural groups which have contributed to the special identity of the region. This has been referred to as a 'diversionary strategy', and has the consequence of lessening the symbolism of the Anabaptists and their lifestyle, by directing attention to many other groups which migrated into the region since the eighteenth century, and which have contributed to the diversification of the rural (and small-scale urban) environment. In addition, and in the case of south-east Pennsylvania, the opportunity has been taken to highlight the contribution of this region to the period of the Civil War in USA and the role of the districts in providing transit routes for slaves escaping from the southern states.

11. Loosened interpretations of 'commercial development'

As part of the 'diversionary' process and strategy land use regulations and region-wide policies have been devised which can accommodate, most often within general commercial zones, facilities and amenities for major entertainment venues. The rationale for this loosened interpretation of 'commercial' development has included an assessment that the regions need a complementary range of 'things to see and do' so as to attract a broadened spectrum of market segments, both for first time and repeat visitation. Thus, these regions now include conventional theatres, music halls, spectacular venues for mammoth theatrical productions, museums, theme parks, water-slides and water parks.

12. Retail malls

In recognition of the special locational qualities of the two case study regions, planning regulations have been supportive (also in the general commercial zones) of the fashion and factory outlet malls. These take one of three forms: one form is the isolated shopping mall at a critical location adjoining a major highway; a second form is the establishment of a major mall as part of commercial strip development, also with frontage to a major highway; the third form is the establishment of an 'intimate' shopping precinct within a refurbished heritage building.

13. Heritage trails

Another aspect of the 'diversionary' strategy has included the creation of heritage trails, and the establishment of heritage-relevant sites and settings.

14. Backcountry 'zones'

There is evidence that the Old Orders have decided to 'retire' into 'backcountry' locations, behind boundaries of tourism-related developments (and other conventional urban development), so as to continue to practice their particular lifestyle relatively free from intrusion.

Although none of these is intrinsically remarkable, it is the combination and integration of them which provides the distinctiveness for tourism planning in the two case study regions.

Interpretation

One of the interesting facets of planning for tourism in the two case study regions is the apparent unconscious adoption of a cooperative multi-faceted strategy which provides opportunities for various tourist expectations to be met. Whereas a reasonable preliminary expectation would have been that, given the conspicuous cultural attraction, the regions would have become sharply differentiated as 'special interest' tourism destinations, the reality has been that the regions have provided a more diverse range of tourism opportunities. In so doing, the regions have been able to afford some protection to the cultural resources, in part by distracting attention from them. A number of deductions may be drawn from the Lancaster and Waterloo experiences:

- the different products and services have their own clientele of visitors, and serve to satisfy particular touristic purposes;

- it is the range and diversity of touristic opportunity which stimulates the economic fortunes of the regions;

- the attractiveness of the regions for a range of touristic visits is derived from their proximity to and ease of access from major metropolitan areas which have a need for adjacent areas for recreation of various kinds;

- it is this range and diversity of potential touristic experiences which, perhaps coincidentally, serves to afford the cultural groups and their culture a measure of protection from the 'tourist gaze';

- the loose cooperative arrangements between the principal stakeholder groups combine to form a multi-faceted coincidental strategy which provides opportunities to gain different touristic experiences without any one resource group becoming overloaded with attention;

- the adoption of a generic heritage and historical sub-strategy relieves the targeted cultural group of intrusive tourist behaviour;

- a relaxation of interpretation of planning ordinances provides the context for a mixed-use commercial zone, which, whilst attracting some opprobrium because of its aesthetic untidyness, facilitates a conventional busy environment for mass tourism activities.

The scale of tourism development in the two case study regions is significantly different. However, it may be suggested that there are two important conclusions which may be transferable to other regions experiencing pressure on their cultural resources:

- the first is that pressure can only be contained or relieved if the region can offer complementary attractiveness in other aspects of tourism, especially in the realm of mass visitation;

- the second is that for a strategy to be workable it is incumbent upon the various stakeholder groups to pursue complementary initiatives across a spectrum which contributes positively to sustaining the resources of tourism attractiveness.

There is evidence in the two case study regions that much of the required complementarity is in place, and that the spectrum of initiatives is undergoing constant appraisal and revision so that the tourism opportunities retain their attractiveness and, thereby, avoid the decline phase foreshadowed in Butler's cycle of evolution for tourist destinations (Butler, 1980). This is further evidence to support the contention of Hovinen (1982) that Lancaster County, in particular, has the breadth of resources to forestall decline. In summary, the solution to relieving touristic pressure on sensitive cultures is to create and work within a spectrum of complementary strategies forged to meet the special requirements of different market segments and tourist types.

Note: the field research contained in this paper was conducted in the period 1996 to 1999, and was supported by research grants from The University of Queensland and Wilfred Laurier University (Waterloo).

References

Altman, J. Finlayson, J. (1991), *Aborigines and tourism: an issues paper,* Canberra, Centre for Aboriginal Economic Policy Research, Australian National University.

Boissevain, J. (editor) (1996), *Coping with tourists,* Providence, RI, Berghahn Books.

Butler, R. (1980), The concept of a tourism area cycle of evolution, *The Canadian Geographer, 24 (1), 5-12.*

Cultural Survival Quarterly (1990), Note: Two-part investigation: "Breaking out of the tourist trap" Vol 14, 1 and 2.

Fagence, M. (forthcoming), Tourism as a protective barrier for Old Order Amish, In Smith, V. and Brent, M. (editors) *Hosts and Guests Revisited*, Elmsford, NY, Cognizant Communications Corporation.

Fagence, M. (1999A). Sustaining cultures in the face of tourism, Paper to TEI Symposium, Jyvaskyla, Finland, September 1999.

Fagence, M. (1999B), Entrepreneurism and partnerships in rural communities, Paper to Sustaining Rural Environments Conference, Flagstaff, Arizona, October 1999.

Getz, D. (1993), Tourist shopping villages, *Tourism Management,* 14 (1), 15-26.

Gunn, C. (1993), *Tourism Planning,* Washington DC, Taylor and Francis.

Hall, C. M. (2000), *Tourism Planning,* Harlow, Prentice Hall.

Hinch, T. and Butler, R. (1996), Indigenous tourism: a common ground for discussion, In Butler, R. and Hinch, T. (editors), *Tourism and Indigenous Peoples,* London, Thomson International Business Press, Chapter 1.

Hollinshead, K. (1996), Marketing and metaphysical realism: the dis-identification of Aboriginal life and traditions through tourism, In Butler, R. and Hinch, T. (editors), *Tourism and Indigenous Peoples,* London, Thomason International Business Press, Chapter 13.

Hostetler, D. (1968), *Amish Society,* Baltimore, Johns Hopkins Press.

Hovinen, G. (1982), Visitor cycles: outlook for tourism in Lancaster County, *Annals of Tourism Research,* Vol 9, 565-83.

Hovinen, G. (1995), Heritage issues in urban tourism, *Tourism Management,* 16(5), 381-88.

Kraybill, D. (1989), *The Riddle of Amish Culture,* Baltimore, Johns Hopkins Press.

Kreps, G., Donnermeyer, J., Hurst, C., Blair, Kreps, M. (1997), The impact of tourism on the Amish sub-culture: a case study, *Community Development Journal,* 32 (4), 354-67.

Lew, A. (1995), American Indian reservation tourism in Arizona, in Merrill, H. (editor), *American Indian Relationships in a modern Arizona economy,* Tucson, University of Arizona.

Lew, A. (1996), Tourism management on American Indian lands in the USA, *Tourism Management,* 17 (5), 355-65.

Luthy, D. (1994), The origin and growth of Amish tourism, In Kraybill, D. and Olshan, M. (editors), *The Amish struggle with modernity,* Hanover, University Press of New England, pp 113-29.

Mitchell, C., Nolan, R. and Hohol, F. (1993), Tourism and community economic development: a case study of St Jacobs, Ontario, In Bruce, D. and Whitla, M. (editors), *Tourism strategies for rural development,* Sackville, NB, Rural and Small town Research and Studies program, Mount Allison University, pp 16-25.

Olshan, M, (1994), Amish cottage industries as Trojan Horse, In Kraybill, D. and Olshan, M. (editors), *The Amish struggle with modernity,* Hanover, University Press of new England, pp 133-46.

Pearce, D. Butler, R.(editors) (1993), *Tourism Research,* London, Routledge.

Redekop, C. (editor), *Mennonite Identity,* Latham, MD, University of America Press.

Regional Municipality of Waterloo (1996), *Planning for a sustainable community: Regional Official Policies Plan,* Kitchener, Ontario.

Weiler, B., Hall, C. M. (editors) (1992), *Special Interest Tourism,* London, Belhaven Press.

The future of hallmark events: Spectacular or specious?

Joe Goldblatt

The George Washington University, USA

Introduction

A hallmark event is defined by Getz as (1991) "an event that gives a destination a high profile or provides the tourism theme for the destination; the event and its host community possess mutually reinforcing attractiveness." Often times this definition is used interchangeably with the term mega-event. However, Getz expands the definition by adding (1991) "a mega-event is a popular expression describing the largest and most visible of events, such as world's fairs and the Olympics. In the context of event tourism, they are events that attract the largest number of tourists or a proportion of tourists substantially higher than other events, or have a major impact on the image of the destination."

During the recent century, beginning with numerous world fairs and major sport events and concluding with the ubiquitous millennium festivities, the tourism industry has seen a significant increase in the size, scope, length and visibility of these unique ventures. However, there continues to be little empirical evidence that validates the social, political, ecological and economic benefits of these projects.

Therefore, in this paper the investigator will examine a wide range of events that are classified by the organisers as hallmark and/or mega-events as well as provide an in depth review of the failed Tonga Millennium celebration to explore the following questions.

- What change phenomena have driven the development of these events?

- How can the planners and organisers of these events objectively and systematically analyze the potential positive and negative impacts of these events to make an informed decision prior to bidding and development?

- What alternatives exist to the development of a hallmark or mega-event that will produce the same or better impacts without the high degree of risk (and subsequent losses) incurred by earlier events?

Lofgren asks (1999) "Do we live in a age obsessed by having great experiences? An age in which places like Freemont Street in Las Vegas are malled in a re-designed as "the Freemont Street Experience," following the popular trend of tourist architecture as event?"

In fact, in recent years one could reasonably argue that the term "event" has been used to define that which is extraordinary in popular culture. For example, the popular U.S. television program entitled "Who Wants to Be a Millionaire" has been labelled by the popular media as 'event' television.

Robert F. Jani, the first director of public relations at Disneyland amusement park in Anaheim, California described the Main Street Electric Parade as "a special event" in 1954 and, pressed for a definition by the media, he further explained, "I suppose it is that which is different from a normal day of living." (Goldblatt, 1990). Regardless of what definition you accept, it is a reasonable assumption that planned events have significantly changed in volume, size, scope and quality during the past half century since Jani issued the definition.

Why the event sector is growing

The event sector is actually not one but many sectors. Brian Losourdo (1997) conducted a study of two dozen professional trade associations whose members derive revenue from professional events. According to Losourdo (1997), the aggregate revenue derived from these sectors exceeds 800 billion dollars per year. Supporting this statistic is evidence from the International Events Group in Chicago stating that commercial sponsorship has grown globally from 6.5 billion dollars in 1996 to over 9 billion dollars in 1998. What has fuelled this rapid growth?

The first theory I will advance is that as the earth's population ages there is significantly more to celebrate and events provide the forum for these celebrations. For example, during the next decade in the United States over 70 million people will turn fifty years of age. Few will mark this personal milestone quietly. Rather, they will organise events (or they will be organised on their behalf) to chronicle this "day that is different from a normal day of living".

Another theory is that, with the advance of technology, individuals are seeking more high touch experiences to balance the high tech influences in their lives. Events remain the single most effective means of providing a high touch experience. Pine and Gilmore (1999) acknowledge this trend in their book "The Experience Economy." They cite numerous examples of corporations and other organisations who have used events to heighten the experience of the moment. Describing a bi-centennial celebration, they write "The Cleveland Bicentennial Commission spent $4 million to illuminate eight automobile and railroad bridges over the Cuyahoga River near a nightspot called the Flats. No one pays a toll to view or even cross these illuminated bridges, but the dramatically lighted structures are a prop that city managers now use to attract tourist dollars by making a trip downtown to Cleveland a more memorable night-time experience." (Pine and Gilmore, 1999)

The second highly noticeable change is the shift toward technology both in work and leisure. John Naisbitt in his book *Megatrends 2000* (1990) describes a high tech and high touch world and it appears that as individuals in developed and developing countries rush toward a virtual world (the internet) they collectively wish to preserve their humanness through personal interaction through live events. America On Line (AOL) has stated that while trial members initially connected for the purposes of accessing free information (such as travel education, and entertainment), they agreed to *pay for their membership* when they discovered people of similar interests within the seemingly infinite number of chat rooms and discussion areas. The on-line introduction and connection with people of similar interests may have forged the creation of numerous live face to face events.

A third shift that may have fuelled the demand for bigger and better events is the growth in the U.S. economy, especially in the leisure and recreation sector. According to the Travel Industry Association in Washington, DC (TIA), over one fifth of the U.S. adult population attended a festival while on a trip of 100 or more miles away from home in 1998. Nearly one third of this group attend arts or music festival events. According to the International Festivals and Events Association, there are approximately 40,000 festivals held annually in the United States. These events range from food festivals to those for religious purposes. In other studies, festival goers have repeatedly identified "value" as the primary reason for motivating their attendance at the event. Live events serve as a value added investment for individuals, couples as well as families with children as evidenced by TIA in their 1998 study.

The fourth and final change was first identified by Faith Popcorn in her book "The Popcorn Report". She reported that Americans are increasingly time poor and will make investments based upon the need for convenience and accessibility. In fact, what has occurred is time shifting wherein individuals actually blur the distinction between work and leisure. Historically leisure activities has been defined as that which is the absence of work. However, in recent years this clear definition has changed as more and more individuals work harder and play harder. Evidence of this shift is best documented in the reduction in the length of vacations as more and more individuals opt for shorter and more frequent holidays versus the annual two week grand tour that was popular in previous years.

These four changes: ageing, technology, income, and time have dramatically increased the demand for a wide variety of events both the U.S. and throughout the world.

These factors are summarised in the model shown in figure (1).

Figure 1   The Four Factors Influencing Event Growth

1. Demographic Shifts (Youth to Ageing)
2. Technological Shifts (Low Tech to High Tech)
3. Disposable Income Shifts (Limited to Limitless)
4. Time Shifts (Defined time to Undefined Time)
∧
Demand for High Touch Experiences
∧
Supply Increases to Satisfy Demand

Objective and systematic impact assessment

McDonnel, Allen, and O'Toole describe the typical impacts resulting from events in Australia in their book "Festival and Special Event Management" (1999). The list the possible event impacts include increasing visitation during the shoulder or off season; enhancing the overall tourism experience; acting as a catalyst for development; promoting economic benefits, providing a cost-benefit analysis; and, finally, a means of promoting the long term impacts within destinations.

Whether or not all events achieve each of these objectives is questionable. Events Corp, the organisation in Australia charged with developing, managing, and assessing significant local events, is currently working to develop a uniform tool to objectively and systematically measure these impacts. Currently each destination uses a different methodology and formula to describe the outcome of the event. Therefore it is difficult for event organisers to compare apples to oranges as they attempt to benchmark their event operations and outcomes against others.

Donald Getz and this investigator favour a comprehensive assessment scheme that embodies a wide range of factors rather than limiting impacts to only short term economic performance. However, according to Getz (2000), the majority of event stakeholders still select economic performance as the leading indicator of event success.

Additional impact factors that should be evaluated in addition to the short term economic performance should include capital, ecological, media, political and stakeholder benefits.

Capital impacts

From the re-development of San Antonio, Texas (following Hemisphere) to the major transformation of New Orleans, Louisiana (following the World's Fair), there are innumerable examples of how the capital projects initiated during hallmark events have produced positive impacts for tourism destinations. In San Antonio the historic Riverwalk area was cleaned up and is now touted as a major tourism attraction (in fact some would say the new heart of the city) in this destination. Simultaneously, the 1985 World's Fair in New Orleans resulted in the construction of exhibit hall A of the Ernest A. Morial Convention Centre. As a result of this economic catalyst New Orleans is now one of the top five convention destinations in the United States. Most major hallmark events are now designed first and foremost with the concept of re-use. Lisbon, Portugal's former Expo site has become a major tourism attraction with exhibit space, an aquarium and other valuable assets to provide ongoing benefits to the local economy long after the event has ended.

Economic impacts

Historically, event economic impact measurement has focused upon visitor spending as well as multipliers that extend this spending to other sectors of the economy. Multipliers may be linked to income or job creation, however, due to the inconsistency in formulas, event organisations have faced difficulties in comparing and their events performance against those of others. Due to this inconsistency in reporting and collection of data, this information has been flawed and often results in under or over reporting which may produce future problems for those assessing the suitability of developing or bidding upon a future event. One example is the World Cup games held in the United States in 1995. Hotels projected high occupancy based upon studies of previous games held in other destinations and were sorely disappointed and economically distressed when demand did not meet the expectations projected by flawed studies. As a result of lack of standardisation, according to Getz and others, economic impact studies continue to be misleading and should be viewed in proper balance with other impact assessments.

Ecological impacts

Tourism destinations always seek to mitigate the negative environmental impacts resulting from visitors and maximise the positive ecological outcomes through leaving the destination's ecosystems in better condition that before the event occurred. For example, Sydney, Australia has an elaborate plan in place to achieve this type of balance in terms of ecological impact. However, numerous news media reports have questioned whether or not the Sydney Organising Committee for the Olympic Games (SOCOG) can achieve or afford all of the ecological measures they promised when bidding on the games. The U.S. Environmental Protection Agency (EPA) awarded a grant in 1998 to The George Washington University Event Management Program for the purpose of exploring the development of a green event certification program that would be developed and operated by non governmental organisations. According to the EPA (1998) the focus on positive environmental impacts resulting from events will grow exponentially as the events sector increases in size and scope in the years to come.

Media impacts

Although it may be argued that the internet has had the same profound influence on global communication as Guttenberg's printing press, the ubiquity of television's Cable News Network (CNN) has literally accelerated the role of news dissemination into that of light speed. As a result of this development even the smallest most inconsequential occurrence in a third world country can quickly become major news due to the global reach of CNN. Therefore, a mass casualty at a soccer game or the major scandal recently affecting the International Olympic Committee not only becomes a major story but one that endures through repetitive broadcasting on CNN. CNN has literally become the global campfire where the human tribe gathers to receive today's news. Increasingly, this news reporting involves feature stories about events ranging from recent millennium celebrations to the Academy Awards. As a result of this power, event organisers must now consider the media impact of even the slightest event.

While teaching in Bethlehem, Palestine, this investigator was asked by the event organisation, Bethlehem 2000, how to find doves to release on New Year's eve in manger square. The organisers wished to use doves to symbolise peace and fireworks to symbolise celebration. The investigator cautioned the organisers not to use doves as they could not be released into the wild and survive (ecological impacts) and the resulting media outcry would be disastrous for the event. Instead, the investigator recommended using homing pigeons that would be released and return or even latex shaped doves filled with helium. The organisers ignored these suggestions and released live doves which subsequently flew directly into the exploding fireworks. The results of this intersection were seen on CNN over and over again and regrettably the enduring image of the Bethlehem 2000 millennium celebration is this disastrous outcome.

Political impacts

When considering the political impacts from a hallmark event organisers often limit their scope to elected politicians. In fact, the term politics is derived from the greek term meaning "city". Within the city that is hosting the event there are innumerable political considerations. Perhaps chief among these considerations is that of where is the power centred and is it hierarchical (concentrated at the top) or level (equally distributed) among the stakeholders. By identifying the power brokers and decision makers, the event organisers may assess the challenges that will confront the approval process and determine how to re-distribute the power to incorporate the inputs of all event stakeholders. Additionally, it is important for the organisers to determine what political outcomes the stakeholders desire as a result of the event activity. For example, perhaps the power has historically been concentrated around the event founder and one goal of the event is to democratise the event planning and operations process. Moving toward this outcome will in fact improve the impact of the event.

Stakeholder benefits

The multitude of stakeholders who comprise the event organisation may range from politicians (see political impacts), volunteers, vendors, regulatory officials, government officials, media representatives and a host of others too numerous to name. Therefore, it is essential that the event organisers determine early in the process how to produce more stakeholder benefits rather than deficits. In order to achieve this, the event organiser must invest time in research to determine the key benefits each stakeholder expects from their involvement in the event. According to Silvers (1999), most event volunteers participate due to three primary motivations. First, they wish to make a contribution to the cause or event organisation. Second, they desire to be recognised for their contribution. Third, and finally, they want to be part of a community, albeit perhaps temporal, to work toward a mutual goal. To achieve positive impacts the event organiser must assess the stakeholder's motivations and then meet or exceed these desires during the event process.

Figure two summarises the major impacts the investigator theorises may be objectively quantitatively and qualitatively measures through event impact evaluation measures.

Figure 2   Key Informant Pre-Post Event Suitability/Impact Scale (SIS)

Instructions: The event organiser will identify ten (10) event key informants who will complete the following instrument. Each key informant will select the numerical value that represents the pre-event suitability level as well as the post event assessment for each factor listed below.			
1. Capital impacts:			
Pre: 1	2	3	4
Post: 1	2	3	4
Unsuccessful	Marginal Success	Successful	Very Successful
2. Ecological impacts:			
Pre: 1	2	3	4
Post: 1	2	3	4
Unsuccessful	Marginal	Successful	Very Successful
3. Economic impacts:			
Pre: 1	2	3	4
Post: 1	2	3	4
Unsuccessful	Marginal	Successful	Very Successful
4. Media impacts:			
Pre: 1	2	3	4
Post: 1	2	3	4
Unsuccessful	Marginal	Successful	Very Successful
5. Political impacts:			
Pre: 1	2	3	4
Post: 1	2	3	4
Unsuccessful	Marginal	Successful	Very Successful
6. Stakeholder impacts:			
Pre: 1	2	3	4
Post: 1	2	3	4
Unsuccessful	Marginal	Successful	Very Successful
Tabulation: The event organiser will tabulate the comprehensive suitability/impact assessment in two ways. First, the event organiser will compare the pre versus post event scores to determine the size of the gap between the forecast or desired outcome and the actual evaluation. Next, the organiser will add all pre and post scores and divide by the number of key informants. to identify the mean cumulative score. The mean cumulative score will assess the comprehensive impact of the event as scored by the key informants.			

Copyright, Joe Goldblatt 2000

Viable alternatives to hallmark events

If a destination's key informants determine after careful analysis that a hallmark event is marginal or unsuitable, there may be alternative ways in which to generate similar benefits with minimal negative impacts. Often times the best part of the research phase in event development is the opportunity to literally apply the brakes on event growth by promoting alternative programming.

The investigator was once queried by a student in Ashland, Oregon about the concept of bigger being better in event design. The mature student, who owned a bed and breakfast business and conference centre, asked, "Why does every new event need to be bigger and better than the last one?" The investigator paused to consider the question and then asked one in return. "Are you suggesting that some events should be downsized?" The student replied, "Perhaps the better term is 'right-sized' to ensure that the destination and the event achieve a perfect fit."

The student is absolutely correct. Event tourism researchers have seen numerous examples of destinations who have promoted events that are inappropriate due to the carrying capacity of the destination. One recent example of this misstep is the 1998 Woodstock rock festival in upstate New York.

One alternative to a traditional hallmark event includes developing local neighbourhood or sector events that are small in scale but large in local involvement. These events may be stretched out over a period of months producing longer and better economic injections for the host community versus the short or limited duration hallmark event.

Another alternative may be the incorporation of technology such as the internet or video teleconferencing to create a broadcasting event in place of the major capital investment required for a traditional hallmark event. Technology may create many virtual events to supplement or support the actual event and therefore drive more direct benefits through the use of e-commerce to sell tickets, merchandise, and other event products and services.

Finally, the event organisation may wish to use the pre- or post-Broadway approach to theatrical release and develop a miniature version of the event for export to other destinations. The kingdom of Saudi Arabia successfully used this approach in 1998 when they developed and implement a tour of North American cities to expose citizens in the U.S. to the art and culture of Saudi Arabia. Using centrally located convention centre venues in major U.S. destinations such as Washington, D.C. and Dallas, Texas, the miniature Saudi Arabian festival promoted products, services, and tourism as well as the image of the country without requiring major long term capital investment within their country. Therefore, one alternative to hallmark events in the future may be the opportunity to try out the event in other cities before hosting the smaller version in the sponsoring destination or to export the event following a successful run in the host destination.

Tonga's millennium celebration: a case study

In 1998 a group of business professionals led by Hussein Khashoggi (see figure 3) investigated the possibility of organising a major millennium celebration in the south sea Kingdom of Tonga. Tonga is a series of small Islands near Figi and Australia (see figure 4) that holds the distinction of geographically being located directly on the international date line. Tonga's location provided tourists with the opportunity of being the first to celebrate the dawn of the new millennium.

Figure 3   Organisational Structure

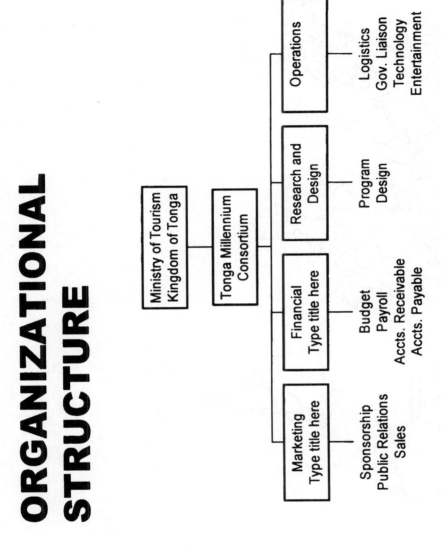

Figure 4   Locations of Worldwide Millennium Celebrations

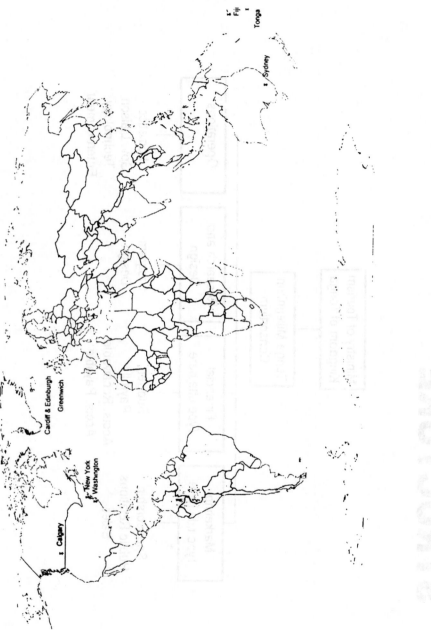

Khashoggi provided a grant to The George Washington University Event Management Program to conduct a needs assessment and feasibility study that would result in a business plan to develop and promote this event. The University conducted an extensive comprehensive literature review of millennium and hallmark celebrations: and interviewed dozens of key informants including Tongan government officials as well as potential guests. The investigators then drafted a preliminary business plan.

This research revealed three very interesting findings. First, it is difficult to transform what is typically a friends and family event (New Years eve) into a mass tourism hallmark event. Culturally, most individuals mark the coming of the new year surrounded by familiar faces. They do not invest hundreds or even thousands of dollars to join strangers in exotic destinations. Although there continues to be a market for high ticket New Year's celebrations it is not a mass market for the reasons stated above. Second, the Y2K concerns would prevent many individuals both in the U.S. and abroad from travelling during the new years eve period. Third, and finally, the destination of Tonga, though exotic and fantastic, was unknown to many potential tourists and they did not want to experiment with a new destination during this critical event: the 2000 new years celebration.

Although there is a growing market for adventure tourism it continues to be a small segment as compared to traditional package tours. The millennium celebration in Tonga would require identification of not only adventurists but those adventurists who are also extremely wealthy and able to invest in this type of exotic excursion.

Khashoggi envisioned a luxury cruise ship (or several) (see figure 5) filled with wealthy passengers who would sail from Hawaii to Tonga arriving in time for the new years celebration. He further imagined that major entertainers would perform on the cruise ship before, during, and after the new year's eve festivities.

To ensure exclusivity, the investigators recommended, and Khashoggi concurred, that his organisation should be given sole rights to market the millennium celebration in the Kingdom of Tonga. The Kingdom of Tonga ministry of tourism and culture provided the investors with a writ of exclusivity that would expire during a fixed period of time if the organisers could not secure financing for their event.

The Khashoggi group attempted to identify prospective investors through corporate sponsors and financiers. However, they were routinely rejected due to the unpredictability of the outcome. Therefore, it became even more essential to provide the investors with research to help convince others of the viability of this event.

The investigators developed a series of scenarios to propose to potential guests. However, when these concepts were tested with potential customers the reaction ranged from disinterest to no interest. The vast majority of the persons surveyed stated that they wanted to "wait and see" what other opportunities would be available for celebrating the new year.

In fact, many cruise ships which sailed during this period held major sales deeply discounting their published fares during the final weeks approaching New Year as they could not reach capacity through traditional marketing hype. In addition, many expensive millennium events were cancelled at the last minute when ticket sales fell below desired profitability for the organisers.

Figure 5   Map of Cruise Ship Itineraries as of April 6, 1998

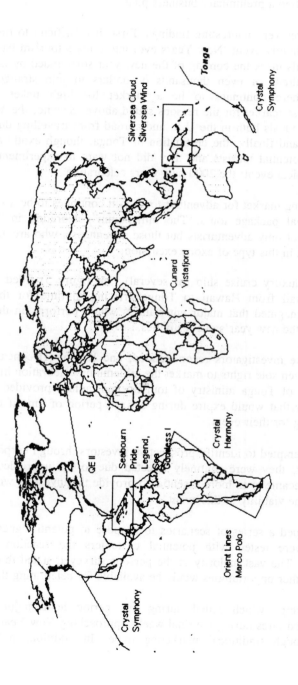

Map of Cruise Ship Itineraries as of April 6, 1998:

Free, public events, such as the new years celebrations in Times Square (New York City) and The Eiffel Tower (Paris, France) fared significantly better and attracted large crowds of tourists seemingly hungry for a historic experience. However, overwhelmingly the expensive private events promoted heavily prior to the millennium celebration systematically failed to deliver the ticket sales required to achieve even minimal success.

The investigators who examined the Tonga Millennium celebration recommended that Mr. Khashoggi and his fellow investors organise a local event on the main island of Tonga and link this event to the rest of the world through the Internet. Furthermore, the investigators recommended that the Tonga event be cause related and result in improving the infrastructure for tourism in Tonga. The addition of a well known cause such as UNICEF would soften the focus from a strictly narcissistic celebration conducted by and for extremely wealthy people in a destination inhabited by largely poor people.

As a result of the investigation, the investors decline to proceed with the development of the event as they could not identify the proper return on investment they required. Furthermore, the Kingdom of Tonga proceeded with holding a small, modest local celebration that achieved little media interest.

Findings, conclusions

Numerous hallmark events such as the Tonga Millennium celebration are considered each year by individuals or groups without sufficient research to confirm their feasibility, viability, and sustainability. The factors influencing event growth and the suitability and impact factors must be closely examined to ensure a goodness of fit between the event and the destination.

As societies age and technology increases their may be greater demand for large scale human celebration through hallmark events. However, event organisers may capture the same or more benefits through developing alternatives to hallmark events such as grass roots (neighbourhood, sector) celebrations, technology mediated events, and/or exporting event products to other destinations.

According to The Wall Street Journal (2000), even Broadway theatres are turning legitimate musicals into "events" by inviting the audience to "get up and dance" in the aisles after the actors have taken their bows. In a society that increasingly is turning toward experiential enterprises it behoves event strategists to carefully consider the suitability and impacts of major events before further development. The spectacular may appear specious if event organisers fail to systematically and thoroughly evaluate alternatives to the development of hallmark events. However, as event tourism moves rapidly into the 21st century it is obvious that there will be much more to celebrate and as a result event tourism specialists must be ever vigil in assessing, selecting, and evaluating the most feasible, viable and sustainable options. A wise historian once wrote that those who do not examine the past are doomed to repeat it. The future of event tourism may begin with a careful examination of that which was designed to be spectacular yet, through negative impacts, become specious. This self examination and application of new models such as those suggested in this study may ensure a future filled with appropriately sized events resulting in better outcomes for the destinations that host them.

The term event is derived from the latine "e" and "venire" which literally translated means "out come". The purpose of every event should be to create a positive outcome. Hallmark or mega-events may achieve this outcome in the future with careful consideration of alternatives that will better benefit the destinations that host them.

References

Clarke, R. (2000), Environmental Protection Agency, Interview.

Getz, D. (1991), *Festivals, Special Events and Tourism*, Van Nostrand Reinhold: New York, NY.

Getz, D. (2000), Interview.

Ukman, J. (2000), Interview.

Lofgren, O. (1999), *On Holiday, A History of Vacationing*, University of California Press, Berkley: California.

Losourdo, B. (1997), Interview.

McDonnell, I., Allen J. and O'Toole, W. (1999), *Festival and Special Event Management*, Jacaranda Wiley Limited: Sydney, Australia.

Naisbitt, J. (1990), *Megatrends 2000* William Morrow: New York, NY.

Pine, B. J. II, Gilmore, J. H. (1999), Harvard Business School Press: Boston, Massachusetts.

Silvers Rutherford, J. (2000), Interview.

Travel Industry Association (2000), *Tourism Works for America 2000*, Travel Industry Association: Washington, DC.

The redefinition of time and space in the global village: Impacts on tourism

Meg Hart

University of Las Palmas de Gran Canaria, Spain

Media: time and space

Marshall McLuhan and Quentin Fiore, in their book *The Medium is the Massage* (1967) wrote:

> *"Electric circuitry has overthrown the regime of 'time' and 'space' and pours upon us instantly and continuously the concerns of all other men. It has reconstituted dialogue on a global scale. Its message is Total Change, ending psychic, social, economic, and political parochialism. The old civic, state, and national groupings have become unworkable. Nothing can be further from the spirit of the new technology than ' a place for everything and everything in its place.'*[1]

The media alter our perceptions of the world and our behaviour. Time and space in the 21st century are no longer what they were for, say, George Orwell when he wrote 1984, and far less what they represented for HG Wells when he wrote The Time Machine. Time and Space will very soon not even be what they were for Kubrick in 2001: The Space Odyssey. Time can be real or virtual, can be managed, or 'quality' in the 21st century. We all live 'time-compressed' existences according to the sociologists. Time, therefore, is perhaps the single most valued commodity in a Society which is 'downsizing', or paying time managers to bully them into organisation in order to achieve more of the same.

Space is usually Outer, or cyber-, outside the Global Village where all frontiers have been gradually erased, even the frontier of different currencies with the advent of the Euro and the world-dominance of the dollar. Emigration and immigration, often due to major political conflicts, have all but erased traditional spatial identities in many parts of the world. Private space can be invaded thanks to the video-camera and computers as the film The Truman Show demonstrated. Reality shows (which are the opposite of what?) allow us to enter the intimate spaces of others, without scruples. Location identities become more and more difficult to establish as the world becomes Disneyfied or McDonaldsised. The same franchises exist the world over only with different hours of daily sunshine, with marketing concepts and images pared to the bare essentials to guarantee the assurance of homogeneity of standards and to make them as 'user friendly' as possible, as spatially accessible as possible, to the mixed populations, in the enormous urban settlements the world over.

Even capital cities are no longer the capital cities of their nation but are Cultural Capitals of Europe. The atlases of the world's distribution have to be constantly updated as frontiers and even names of places change overnight, as the result of political developments. People's national identities or spaces are no longer easy to define either, with political conflicts causing all kinds of international confrontations, not all of which are quite as anecdotal as the type Clinton/Castro-Elian. Whole nations' identities have changed, much as there may be movements, such as in the US or Austria to try and turn back the tide. Like it or not, for example, the Americans have to recognise (as the Presidential candidate, Bush, has, principally because he is married to one) that the Hispanics are a force to be reckoned with, and that Spanish is probably the first language (although not necessarily the language of preference) of the majority of the population in the States at present. After all, the product most immediately associated with the States i.e. Walt Disney was Hispanic.

From the point of view of personal time on this planet, things have changed radically over the last half of the century. The population has moved, in the First World, from the Baby Boom of the 40s and a dramatic increase in birth rates in the Allied countries, to the dominance of the baby boomers in the 21st century (now representing some 52% of the population) and a drastic decrease in birth rates in all but the so-called developing countries. With pensions and retirement ages still calculated to coincide with useful life span (useful in the economic sense), and gender now playing havoc with the predictions, as women filter more and more into the active workforce, the whole structure of the Welfare State or solidarity between generations has been radically altered. Nuclear families are now a thing of the Past with growing divorce rates the world over and more and more single parent families or alternative family arrangements. Extended families are even less common than nuclear families, reducing parallel to the increase of insertion of women into the workforce, above all, in the countries which were traditionally considered stalwarts, on account of their religious faith, such as Spain, Greece or Italy. Recent figures have suggested that Spain now has the lowest birth rate in the whole of Europe and that difficulties will very soon be encountered in providing coverage for the elderly who live beyond the raised (probably due to gender differences again) retirement age of 75. In other words, Spain has fallen dramatically below replacement rate since Democracy. France, Italy and Japan have already raised the retirement age and the possibilities are that this will be the general tonic in the twenty countries which produce international tourists. Thus, people will be living, working and playing longer and with demographic patterns as they stand, the gender profile of tourism will alter, with a lot more economically independent older women travelling in the Future.

The baby boomers are a complex community, of the new type of communities which have historical memory in common, such as 'Where were you when they shot JFK?' or 'What about Woodstock?' They were the rebels of the post May 68, the hippies and the yuppies. They are now facing middle age in a totally different way from any other group before them. On the one hand, they enjoy the maturity of experience and the prowess achieved over the years, but they resist ageing with a vengeance, investigating all kinds of possibilities from antioxidants through to Genetic Engineering to stave off the ravages of Time. On the one hand, they have fought hard to get to the top of the ladder in their various businesses, to carve out their niche, their Space and on the other, they want to cash out while they can, while they're still on top, Bill Gates style, to do something more 'creative', more 'quality' with their time. They want adventure and enterprise, like Richard Branson, but they also require a certain degree of security and comfort.

These 'baby boomers' who are going to be 'sixteen until they die' are crowding out the next generation, the fated Generation X. The greatest sector of unemployed in the EU is youth and this will continue to be the picture for quite some time, despite the Union policies designed to correct the imbalances. The crisis in the education system is common to all the European countries. A study carried out by the London-based group, Research International and quoted in the newspaper The European described Generation X as united by their underlying desire for conformity. Their key aim in life was found to be financial security and their passwords 'disengagement, cynicism and detachment' (which is why, presumably, Benetton and its controversial publicity campaigns originally worked well with this sector). However, in the next twenty years, according to the World Bank predictions, the total number of young adults and children in Europe will drop by 12 million from 28% to 24%, whereas the 20s-40s will suffer an even more dramatic decrease in numbers, dropping by 16.5 million, from 30% to 24%. The logical conclusion to be reached, then, is that the baby boomers, who are in the executive posts in the businesses all over the world and, thus, dictating trends, will continue to control business and leisure through to, at least, the year 2020.

Tourism: time and space

These are difficult times because ... we approach the new with the psychological conditioning and sensory responses of the old and ... attempt to do a job demanded by the new environment with the tools of the old (McLuhan and Fiore, 1967. Op.cit.).

As far as tourism is concerned, and tourism research, in particular, this has significant implications. First, since most of the major academics in the field are baby boomers, the research has reflected, up until now, the general concerns in all areas of Society of this sector of the population with respect to Time and Space. First, the preoccupation with sustainability, of leaving heritage for the future generations to enjoy, which is a consideration only broached by people reaching a mid-century of existence on the Planet, and broadly in line with the environmental concerns displayed on a world wide level. The Internet and international television, or activists such as Geldof and Sting, both of whom are baby boomers, have brought home to their socially conscious fellow boomers that all things are inter-related and inter-dependent in the Global Village. Second, the inter-connected concern with 'quality' tourism runs parallel to the trends of 'downsizing' and 'cashing out' in order to achieve 'quality' time, or streamlining in one's personal life, via Feng Shui or 'clanning', the 21st century's revamped edition of the hippy commune. The present concern with distinguishing between 'tourists' (nostalgia) and 'travellers'(soft eco-tourism), authenticity and staged authenticity are other baby boomer constructs, as is the factoring in of the host population and the tourism 'advocacy' and 'cautionary' platforms with respect to erosion of 'traditional'(ethnic) values by the onslaught of 'modernity'(globalisation).

All of these arguments are based on outdated premises of Time and Space. Communities are considered to be bounded by social, cultural and geographical realities but this is, by no means, the case in the Global Village of the 21st century, not even on islands (Giddens, 1991)[2]. Location 'identities', with 'identity' referring to the immediate associations evoked by the place, have changed radically in all places apart from those whose major tourist attractions are their built heritage. The only real spatial divisions which exist in the 21st century are between the North (civilisation) and the South (the noble savage), or between Western and Eastern Europe, with the bulk of the tourists proceeding from the former. In spatial terms, tourism is still Western with a strong divide between North (cultural, eco-tourism, hence the 'traveller' or 'discerning client') and the South (hedonist, 3'S' tourism, hence the 'tourist' or 'indiscriminate consumer'). The game of providing tourism or the grounds for tourism is directed more and more towards developing countries (mainly in the South), in order to make it more select, exclusive and expensive but the investment still comes from the same 20 countries (largely in the North) which provide the tourists and who have a vested interest in offering what they know is going to be the demand: 17 European countries, with Germany and the UK way up front, plus the States, Canada and Japan. This, according to the WTO forecasts, is the way things are going to be through to the year 2020 when there will be a calculated 1.5 billion tourists circulating internationally, most of whom will be travelling from these same countries.

Bell (1994)[3] argues that the Western Europeans have always travelled in search of the 'exotic Other', to witness what Bruner (1991)[4] describes as 'primitive peoples' living in a place 'untouched by Western ways'. In our times, it is hardly necessary to travel abroad to come into contact with the exotic Other, who is possibly living on your very doorstep or working with you, although 'exotic' is an adjective difficult to define in times when the media allow easy access to information of any kind from all parts of the world. 'Primitive peoples' or the slightly more positive definition of 'noble savages' are, indeed, difficult to find, above all, where tourism has made any kind of inroads. The 'Bahianas' in Salvador, Brazil or the Tuareg now charge for tourist demands, in the former case, for allowing to be photographed in the Pelourinho and in the latter, for their 'traditional' hospitality of offering refreshment to their guests. To find any place unsullied by Western ways is, indeed, complicated. The Kentucky Fried Chicken has made it to the Great Wall of China and Benetton is in Havanna. Is it not the case that once the host population has been introduced to Western ways and has the wherewithal to decide, that it is they themselves who demand these products and would feel culturally inferior and deprived were they not to have them? As Elizabeth Jack commented (2000) with respect to the community project of Kangaroo Island, TOMM, they do not have a McDonald's yet but that does not mean that the community will not demand one in the near future. Is it necessarily unsustainable, within the spatial and temporal references of the Global Village, in the wide environmental sense now embraced by researchers in general, when the representative for the development of the Great Baikal Trail Project in Siberia, Andrey Suknev[5] has drawn upon experiences as diverse as Bed and Breakfast circuits in Scotland (similar albeit in climate) and the Amazonia projects (quite the contrary) to put together a formula for rural tourism in a region as remote as Lake Baikal (which, nevertheless, already boasts a Holiday Inn)? Is standardisation and acculturation not something imposed by the baby boomer themselves, in their former search for safety and standards of quality? After all, who is going to go to Siberia to sleep in a log cabin or, worse still, a tent?

However, Time and Space are still essentially the two main components which dictate the choice of travel, if 'choice' is still something we can talk about in an industry dominated by a handful of tour operators and airline consortia. How you spend your time 11 months of the year ('business' is '*negocio* in Spanish, i.e. the negation of leisure, '*ocio*') and in what kind of space, i.e. in the North, in a city, essentially dictates how you will try to break with that routine in the time devoted to leisure, and where. It should be borne in mind that the former time spent travelling in their youths has preconditioned the baby boomer of the 21st century, moreover, to look for guarantees of safe space, exclusive space, prime time and quality experiences. The traditional 3 'S' resorts, now standardised, can offer none of these: the up and coming developing resorts can only offer exclusivity with none of the rest, and certainly not the quality or the comfort levels required by these discerning, experienced tourists. For example, Cape Verde, which is one of the areas suffering most pressure from the tourist developers at present, and most in need of development via tourism, can 'only' offer its unique ecosystems, its beaches, flora and fauna to the visitors since there is no widespread basic sanitation at present. No matter how 'primitive' the people may be, and unsullied by Western practices, it is doubtful that the value-for-money conscious baby boomer from any part of the world apart, perhaps, from the truly Green sector of Germany, will be attracted to the area. In their search for soft eco-tourism, the baby boomers impose the very standardisation they reject (chain hotels, bars such as Hard Rock Café and a long etcetera).

With this profile of Time, Space and Society in the 21st century, to continue using the same definitions (which have never been clearly defined) and the same parameters as we used in tourism in the Past, or to talk about sustainability at any level, is somewhat lacking in substance. The product is not the same and the people using it are also radically different. In any case, to talk about 'sustainability' has always depended largely upon from where you are viewing 'sustainability'. It is all very well for us to talk about 'sustainable development', in our space, in First World developed economies, where tourism is part of the accepted lifestyle, and many resorts are looking towards alternative, more environmentally conscious types of tourism as a means of revitalising attractions at the near end of their life cycle. However, 'sustainable development' means quite another thing when seen from the viewpoint of a Third World developing economy. Even the economic parameters have lost all reasonable proportions in this changing world when we consider that Mitsubishi was higher up the scales than Indonesia at the zenith of the latter nation's economic boom. To talk about sustainable tourism, then, from the point of view of protection of the physical and socio-cultural environment together with the safeguarding of the material interests of the resident population on a long-scale basis is, at best, foolhardy and, at worst, cynical, when a developing country has to attract hard European investment to 'improve' its economic situation and cover the demands of the discerning consumer of the 21st century, 55% of which income, at least, will leak back to the countries of origin, in the North, who control the infrastructure and who dictate the product (Mann, 2000).[6] All of this, whilst providing the smiling hospitality required of the executive baby boomer.

Time and space: The great north-south divide

The great North-South divide tends also to be a mirror reflection of the Haves and the Have-Nots, the First World versus the Third World, the developed and the developing countries (Featherstone, 1990).[7] Therefore, the 'primitive' peoples which attract the Europeans and the

West, in general, are unsophisticated in that they belong to largely agricultural, semi-subsistence economies. This 'lack of sophistication' produces a certain subservience on the part of the host population in attending the perceived (and unperceived) needs of the tourist, offering levels of intensive service such as will not be found, for example, in Paris or London. The baby boomer of the Western world, therefore, is looking for the kind of personalised service which was to be found in Colonial days and is certainly not on offer in the stressful, competitive world of the large metropoles, or for that matter in the long-established three 'S' resorts (where most of the service staff are now clients themselves of the tourism trade and on an economic par with their guests).

The South is where all living creatures migrate to in search of warmer climes. The traditional concept is that the further South you travel, the warmer the people of the area are, although this, like many other commonly held myths, is probably no longer true in the Global Village. What is true is that Life moves at a different rhythm in the South and that the dietetic needs, plus the timetables of meals, are radically different from those of the North. Thus, when choosing a holiday, the person will generally opt for a break with their normal climate, the normal rhythm of their daily life. If even the Spaniards and the Italians head South, what can be expected of the rest of the Europeans who will continue to represent the bulk of international tourism over the next twenty years?

When we talk about 'alternative' or eco-tourism, we give the impression that the mainstream mass tourism package, 3 'S' tourism, preferred, as Chris Ryan (1994)[8, 9] has indicated, by over 80% of the tourist population for their main holiday, is no longer valid which, quite clearly, is simply not the case. Mass 3 'S' tourism is unsustainable for resorts, such as Gran Canaria, Benidorm, Torremolinos, Tenerife and Menorca, because these resorts depend solely on their infrastructure and human resources for their appeal (together, very obviously, with their climate). It is unsustainable because the needs of the host population have been covered thanks to years of exposure to tourism: ie. they now have the hospitals, roads, air transport and communication networks that were not in existence when tourism first hit their coastlines. However, they have the attendant problems of tourism ever more apparent: exorbitant taxes due to the need for waste disposal, and an extremely high cost of living, above all, of housing, even more apparent on island territories where land (i.e. their space) is at a premium. Plus the fact that they are crowded off their beaches or excluded from the same, thus producing 'ghetto' beaches for the locals, which are not normally the best and which, at peak periods, are forced far beyond their carrying capacity thus leading to protection via privatisation.

Added to this, there is the spin-off stress and modification of rhythms of life and work (time),caused by an increase in traffic (again more noticeable on islands) and changed timetables (above all, for eating, with the Germans dining, at the latest, at 19.30 and the Spanish natives, at the earliest, at 21.30). Moreover, in places where the tourism is not affected by seasonal deadlock, such as the Canary Archipelago, where work is guaranteed all year round in the travel business, the host population has seen the security of their employment affected by the negotiating power of the tour-operators and the need for the bosses to cut overheads (read, human resources) plus the surplus supply of cheap immigrant labour.[10] 3 'S' tourism, at the end of a resort's life cycle, where the perceived benefits of tourism are few but the dependence on tourism is total, and the control of tourism is external, is unsustainable because it simply cannot adapt to the market demand for the fourth and fifth 'S'es i.e. Specialised and Specialist Service.

Centring the arguments of tourism around the host population are not so obtuse as they might seem because it is the host population which most suffers the adverse effects of invasion of Time and Space in the 21st century. It is the host population who has had to make sacrifices for a 'sustainable' future, in the main 3 'S' centres, who are now turning their backs on a tourism to which they feel economically equal and socially (and morally) superior.[11] The host population of any successful 3 'S' resort is, twenty or thirty years down the road of mass tourism, a multi-racial centre, with most of the tourist services provided by natives of other countries who market the 'typical' products of a culture which is not their own and which they value the more for that very reason. The more prosperous of the locals, meanwhile, aspire to the culture/s which have been imported.

For the North, the South is a hedonist holiday world, frivolous, lacking in substance, artificial, a Paradise 'construct' to be consumed. As Selwyn (1993)[12] comments: ".. they are centres of physical and emotional sensation from which temporal and spatial continuities have been abolished." The Dutch Centre Park complexes are a direct spin-off from this idea. These areas are tourist *non plus ultra*, islands above all, and no promotional campaign will be able to move them from the romantic associations which surround them, mainly created in literature (Robinson Crusoe, Treasure Island, The Swiss Family Robinson among others) and film. In the Past, seafarers celebrated the discovery of an island, something which Disney has used to its advantage in its development of cruise tourism with the creation of artificial islands and sunken treasures. (Cruise tourism will be the big product in the Future, marking the cop-out from Time and Space. You can always count on Disney to lead the way.) And islands, above all, are deserted - or if there are natives, they oscillate between being extremely hostile, as they have been known to be, for example, in Jamaica, or overwhelmingly servile, Hawaii style. On islands, the shipwrecked or the seafarers behaved in ways completely alien to their normal habits in their home countries. *Tout ça change, tout c'est la même chose*.

The major move towards eco-tourism and rural tourism in the South, where such would appear to be irrelevant, redundant or unnecessary, from the point of view of sustainability - we must bear in mind, for example, that the Canary Islands enjoy a 90% occupancy rate almost all year round- is an attempt to stave off emigration and to make the younger generation value something which the native baby boomer generation of the resort would seem not to value or not to have valued sufficiently: the roots of any location identity. It is a last desperate attempt to stave off total acculturation and commoditisation, an attempt to regenerate pride in national difference and to celebrate the community of the same. Urry (1992)[13] affirms that 'social identities emerge out of imagined communities, out of particular structures that bind together three elements - of space, of time and of memory - often partly in opposition to an imagined 'other', such as the neighbouring country': but warned that 'spaces of a neighbourhood, town or region may become overwhelmed by visitors, so that locals no longer feel it is their space/place any more ... Visitors are viewed as the polluting 'other'.

If, in the Global Village, tourism is not to be seen as a destructive force and xenophobia is not to arise as the result of prolonged 'intrusion' of the 'Other' then efforts must be made towards the retrieval and evaluation of 'traditional' values of any one location, in order to allow them to gain the sense of community which will lead to a renewed control over their product. This retrieval of the 'traditional' values is designed at giving purpose and motivation to the Generation X for them to create businesses in the sector of 're-creation' and for them to feel a greater pride in their home area.

Conclusions

Tourism has, and will continue to be, a positive development for many new, and less than new, territories if and when it is not directed monolithically towards serving the perceived needs of any given group or time, thus obviating the possibility of response to change. Although the baby boomers will continue to be the major consumer group, occupying the major Space at all levels in the Global Village, which is their design and their 'baby, over the next twenty years, sustainability is based on more than such a short-term prospect in Time. To be able to retrieve location identities without political or civil conflict, the implication and commitment of the younger generations is a necessity, above all when it comes to providing SMEs offering the specialist and specialised services for the pampered baby boomers which the large multi-nationals cannot or will not. At some point, some space has to be left open for the initiative of the younger generations if sustainability (be it eco-, heritage, mainstream, adventure or rural) is not to be a mere topic for textbook study.

Endnotes

1. McLuhan, Marshall and Fiore, Quentin (1967), The Medium is the Massage. Renewed (1996) Jerome Agel, Hardwired, Singapore.

2. Giddens, A. (1991), The Consequences of Modernity. Polity Press, Cambridge.

3. Bell, M. (1994), Images, Myths and Alternative Geographies of the Third World. In D. Gregory, R. Martin and G. Smith (eds). Human Geography: Society, Space and Social Science. Macmillan, London.

4. Bruner, E. (1991), Transformation of Self in Tourism, Annals of Tourism Research, 18.

5. Jack, Elizabeth (2000), talking about the TOMM project on Kangaroo Island, Australia and Suknev, Andrey (2000) talking about the Great Baikal Trail in Siberia during the proceedings of World Ecotour 2000 held in Salvador de Bahía, Brazil between the 5-8th April.

6. Mann, Mark for Tourism Concern (2000), The Community Tourism Guide. Earthscan Publications Ltd, London.

7. Featherstone, M. (ed) (1990), Global Culture: Nationalism, Globalisation and Modernity. Sage, London.

8. Ryan, Chris (1994), Leisure and tourism - the application of leisure concepts to tourist behaviour - a proposed model. In Seaton, A. V.(ed) (1994), Tourism: The State of the Art, John Wiley and Sons, Chichester, UK.

9. Selwyn, Tom (1993), Peter Pan in South East Asia: Views from the Brochures. In Hitchcock, M., King, V. T. and Parnwell, M. J. G. (eds). (1993), Tourism in South-East Asia, Routledge, London.

10. See everything written on the subject by Bianchi, Raoul (2000), University of North London, UK.

11. Urbain, Jean-Didier (1993), L'Idiot du Voyage, Librairie Plon, Paris.

12. Urry, J. (1992), Europe, Tourism and the Nation-State. In C. Cooper and A. Lockwood (eds.)

13. Progress in Tourism, Recreation and Holiday Research, 5, Wiley, Chichester.

The elusive cultural tourist

Howard L Hughes

Manchester Metropolitan University, UK

Introduction

There is a view that the mass tourism market for sun, sea and sand has matured and there is a search by tourists for new experiences. 'Cultural tourism is one of the growth sectors of the West European tourism industry' (Bywater 1993: 30). 'In the twentieth century ever-increasing numbers of people are participating in arts and heritage based forms of cultural tourism' (Zeppel and Hall 1992: 49). In this paper it is argued that the concept of cultural tourism is such that it is difficult to determine trends and results in some confusion for the development of strategies. It is suggested that it may not be productive to consider cultural tourism as a single entity given the diversity of activities within it. It may be more productive, at least initially, to isolate components of cultural tourism for the purposes of study. Using the performing arts as a case, a simple classification of the tourist in audiences is proposed. In this way issues which are specific to the performing arts may emerge.

The relationship between culture and tourism is widely believed to be mutually beneficial. There has, as a consequence, been an increase of interest in the relationship from organisations in, for instance, the arts and tourism and the relationship is one that is actively encouraged. The Arts Council of Great Britain (ACGB) has long identified the importance of the arts as a tourist attraction (ACGB 1985). The London-based Society of West End Theatres (now Society of London Theatres) claimed, way back in 1982, that 'if it were not for the overseas visitors to London it is doubtful whether West End theatres could remain open during the summer' (Society of West End Theatres 1982). The tourist boards have similarly recognised the link for many years (see for instance British Tourist Authority 1983). More recently the British Tourist Authority (BTA) and English Tourist Board (ETB) have actively fostered the relationship and links with arts managers through publications and seminars (ETB 1993) and through promotions such as the Festival of Arts and Culture 1995.

There has been a great deal of academic interest in 'cultural tourism' including Weiler and Hall (1992), Richards (1996), Robinson, Evans and Callaghan (1996), Gilbert and Lizotte (1998), McDougall (1998), Foo and Rossetto (1998), Dodd and van Hemel (1999). Despite this 'very little is known about the cultural tourism market in Europe' (Richards 1999, p.18). It is evident however that an interest in culture by tourists has always been present (Towner 1996; Feifer 1985). The spectacular growth of beach related holidays has overshadowed this continuing presence of cultural tourism. The conclusion of the European-wide studies undertaken by the European Association for Tourism and Leisure Education (ATLAS) was that there was little new about the convergence of culture and tourism and it was likely that recent cultural tourism in Europe had grown no faster than tourism in general (Richards 1996). The influence of culture on the appeal of tourist destinations may appear to have become greater if only because culture has been increasingly used as an important marketing tool (Zeppel and Hall 1992). Unfortunately there is little evidence that demonstrates clearly whether cultural tourism has been growing. The way in which statistics on tourism are recorded does not enable patterns in cultural (or any other type of) tourism to be determined. The undoubted popularity of short breaks and city breaks provides some indirect evidence for believing that culture is an increasing focus for tourism (Gratton and Taylor 1992).

The lack of information about cultural tourism is not made easier by two features of current research and data collection: the definition of cultural tourism and the failure to adequately consider tourist motivations.

Definitions

'The existing tourism literature has not yet settled upon a generally accepted single definition of the heritage and cultural tourism concepts' (Alzua et al 1998: 3) and it becomes difficult therefore to discuss its size or growth or to explain why it occurs. The term 'cultural tourism' is used to cover several different (but related) activities:

> *'universal' cultural tourism. The word 'culture' itself has different meanings; in the widest sense of its use it is 'a complex of values, ideas, attitudes and other meaningful symbols' which binds people into groups and imparts group character so that a distinct way of life results - a different culture such as German, English or Mexican (Williams 1988). Most international tourism is 'cultural' in this sense because it usually involves some exposure to aspects of other cultures.

> *'wide' cultural tourism. Some tourists will set out with the purpose of experiencing a different culture, in the widest sense, of a destination visited: the arts, crafts, work, religion, language, traditions, food and dress. Walle (1998) uses the term cultural tourism to refer solely to the culture of 'ethnic groups and hinterland peoples' living usually in small scale societies that are relatively untouched by western values.

> *'narrow' cultural tourism. 'Cultural tourism' is most widely used in this narrower sense: tourism which includes visits to experience the 'artistic and intellectual activities' of a society (Williams 1988) rather than the whole different way of life of a society. It includes visits to historic buildings and sites (castles, churches, battle fields, etc), museums and art galleries and to theatres and concert halls (to attend the performing arts)

> *'sectorised' cultural tourism. The components of cultural tourism identified above may be distinguished individually so that visits under museums and historic houses may be classed as 'historical' or 'heritage tourism' and visits to the theatre or concert hall or arena as 'arts tourism'.

The terms 'arts tourism', 'cultural tourism' and 'heritage tourism' have however been used interchangeably to refer to tourism which includes visits to historic buildings and sites, museum and art galleries, visits to view contemporary paintings or sculpture or to attend the performing arts and visits to a variety of other attractions (see for instance Ashworth 1993; Prentice 1993, Leader-Elliott 1996). A Canadian study defined cultural tourism to include all of these as well as visits to festivals and fairs, zoos and national parks and viewing wildlife or birds and attending aboriginal or native cultural events (McDougall 1998). Aboriginal sites and cultural displays were also included in an Australian study (Foo and Rossetto 1998). The term 'arts tourism' has been used by Myerscough (1988) to cover museums and art galleries and theatre. The terms 'historical tourism' (Smith 1989) and 'heritage tourism' have been used to include visits to view modern paintings or sculptures. Prentice (1993) also uses the term 'heritage tourism' to include natural history attractions (including zoos) and the performing arts. Heritage tourism is used by Zeppel and Hall (1992) to include local cultural traditions. Zeppel and Hall 1992 include in arts tourism 'the visitor experience of paintings, sculpture... and all other creative forms of human expression and endeavour' (p48). Gratton and Taylor (1992) use a time dimension to distinguish arts tourism ('consumption of contemporary culture') from heritage tourism ('consumption of historical culture') though clearly this also is too simplistic.

Studies that focus on the arts tend to focus on the 'high arts' and it is rare for any to include 'entertainment' even though this may be a significant attraction and form of activity for many tourists (Hughes and Benn 1997).

Motivation

The term 'cultural tourism' (however defined) is applied to tourists regardless of motivation or interest in culture and this can inflate its significance. All who visit a relevant site, building or event are frequently classified under that heading. McDougall (1998) defined cultural tourism trips in Canada as any which included participation in any of the activities or visits to any of the sites specified. Similarly a cultural tourist to Australia was defined as 'an inbound visitor who attends at least one of the... cultural attractions during his or her stay' (Foo and Rossetto 1998: 1). Alzua et al (1998) focused on cultural tourists outbound from the UK; they were also distinguished as those who had participated in at least one of the specified cultural activities. Arts-tourists were widely defined in the Policy Studies Institute (PSI) study of the economic importance of the arts as any who attended or visited any of the arts (widely defined), regardless of motivation (Myerscough 1988). Using this criterion, at least three-quarters of foreign visitors to Britain are cultural visitors (i.e. those who visited historic buildings or castles: BTA and ETB 1996).

In a few studies though, motivation is featured. In the ATLAS research project any tourist who visited a museum, art gallery or heritage site was classified as a 'cultural tourist' regardless of motivation but the report did acknowledge a distinction between 'specific cultural tourists' (those with a focused cultural intent to tourism) and other visitors to cultural sites. Specific cultural tourists were '9% of tourists visiting the cultural attractions' (Richards 1996: 314). Prentice (1993) also acknowledged two broad types of 'heritage tourists': any who made a visit to a heritage site and those who visited as 'their principal or sole holiday activity' (p51). Like Richards he concluded that those visitors with a specific interest were in a minority. Demand for cultural tourism was segmented by Bywater (1993) into three, though the dimensions of each was not estimated: culturally-motivated or culturally-inspired or culturally-attracted. The first of these were those who chose a holiday on the basis of the cultural opportunities and was likely to be a very small proportion of the market.

Alzua et al (1998) classified tourists as 'cultural' on the basis of at least one cultural visit and, on this basis, 69% of the long haul visitors out of the UK that they surveyed, were cultural tourists. A number of 'types' of cultural tourist were distinguished however and for two out of the five cultural tourist clusters identified, culture and educational benefits were particularly important when choosing a destination. These two clusters accounted for 40% of the cultural tourists surveyed. (The study did not indicate how important these had actually been in the choice of a particular destination). It was concluded on the basis of identifying five tourist clusters that cultural tourists were obviously not a broad mass but a differentiated market with different needs and characteristics.

Silberberg (1995), in a study of museums identified four categories of cultural tourist. The 'greatly motivated' travel specifically to see a museum and were estimated at 15% of out-of-province visitors (Ontario, Canada). There are also tourists whose cultural motives as important as other reasons for visiting; these are motivated 'in part' and were 30% of out-of-province visitors. Silberberg's 'adjunct' tourists are those with a cultural motive that is secondary to some other (20% of visitors) and the 'accidental' are those for whom culture does not feature at all in the destination choice (20% of out-of-province visitors).

A different approach was taken in a study of foreign visitors to Australia. The criteria for distinguishing 'specific cultural visitors' from 'general cultural visitors' were motivations for visiting the cultural attraction itself (not the reason for visiting the country). Specific cultural visitors were those 'whose primary motivation for travel to a cultural attraction is based on a specific desire to experience a particular aspect of Australian culture' (Foo and Rossetto 1998, p.55). For 'general cultural visitors' culture is a secondary motivation. The respective percentages for each were 28% and 72% of all cultural visitors to Australia.

Regardless of how cultural tourists are defined, it would appear that significant proportions of people do visit cultural facilities or attend cultural events whilst tourists. Culture can also have a significant ability to draw tourists to a destination especially (but not solely) inland and historic towns and cities (Hughes and Benn 1995; Hughes and Benn 1997; Hughes 1998).

Many of those who visit cultural attractions may, though, be more satisfactorily categorised as 'mass tourists' rather than as 'cultural-tourists'. Nonetheless the blanket term 'cultural tourism' continues to be widely applied to less-specifically motivated visits and statistics require careful interpretation.

A clarification

The following consideration may assist in clarifying the nature of the cultural tourist. As a first step it is suggested that there is a need to focus cultural tourism studies more than has been evident to date. Apart from the confusion of terms, there has been a tendency to treat cultural tourism as a single entity. Studies do not usually address one particular aspect of 'culture' such as the performing arts or museums. It may be at the level of individual cultural forms (such as drama performances) or events that the tourism significance lies rather than at the level of 'culture'. There is a need to identify the market more closely by focusing cultural tourism studies to a greater degree: for instance, to individual art and entertainment forms and to individual events. For the remainder of this paper the focus will be the performing arts: drama, comedy, music etc performed for an audience in theatres, concert halls, arenas and other venues.

The motivation of different segments of audiences will differ and tourists may be classified by degrees of interest and intent in the arts. These will range from trips where the performing arts are the prime motivation and main activity through to trips where they are an incidental motivation and a secondary activity and no more than an entertaining holiday diversion.

In any audience there may be tourists classified according to (i) the role the arts play in being at the destination (ii) the nature of the visit: holiday or non-holiday.

(i)   role of the arts

> *arts core: a person has chosen to travel in order to see a performance. He or she has primary intent and is a 'primary' arts-related tourist whose main purpose in travelling to the destination is to see a show.*

> *non arts core: a person will be away from home primarily for other reasons such as business, visiting relatives or being on holiday. He or she has incidental or accidental intent.*

> *The 'incidental' arts-related tourist has a main reason for visiting the destination which is something other than theatre but a desire to see the show is a secondary reason for the visit.*

> *The 'accidental' arts-related tourist is in the audience but theatre does not feature at all in the decision to visit the destination.*

The arts-tourist by a strict definition is limited to the situation where the arts are the primary intent even though there may be a combination of all other tourists in an audience. This form of categorisation applies to all of the variations of cultural tourism - whether to theatres, museums, art galleries, or historic houses.

In the first case (arts core) the decision is equivalent to any decision to attend a performance but with an extra time and distance dimension included. Theatres and live performances are widespread but they are not found everywhere. Large towns and cities, in particular, usually have a high concentration of theatres and of the arts performed in them such as drama, comedy plays, musicals, opera and ballet. These are resources that small towns and rural areas may not have and it will be necessary for the people who live in them to travel. There will also be people who do live in large towns and cities which are well-endowed with theatres and concert halls but certain productions or performers are not being presented in these; to see them, people will have to travel. Finally, seeing productions away from home may occur because standards are better or because the theatre itself is preferable or because there is an opportunity to do other things as well - shopping, eating out, etc. The decision here is less of a necessity than it is in the other two cases.

For the non-arts core audiences it is not the production that is the decisive factor in being away, it is other reasons such as holiday or business. The opportunity to see a performance in the theatre may be an important part of that time however, especially as part of the holiday experience. It will probably be secondary to the main 'purpose' of the trip. It would appear nonetheless that many holiday-makers visit the theatre during their stay in the tourist destination (Hughes and Benn 1995; Hughes and Benn 1997; Hughes 1998).

(ii)   holiday or non-holiday

The primary tourist may or may not consider the visit to be a holiday. Some arts core persons could consider the trip to be a holiday; others would not. What is or is not a holiday is essentially a personal internal construct. In the other, non-arts core cases they could be holiday visits or business or visiting friends. Nearly half (48%) of the tourists in opera audiences at the Buxton Festival classified themselves as being non-holiday. Nearly all of both non-holiday and holiday tourists in those opera audiences were arts core.

Tourists who attend or visit cultural events or places can therefore be categorised in a matrix of arts core or non-arts core and holiday or non-holiday. Arts-core (primary intent) classification cuts across both holiday and non-holiday categories; similarly there are non-arts core tourists in both holiday and non-holiday categories.

The arts perspective

Much of the current discussion is about attracting tourists to the arts audiences with particular emphasis on foreign tourists. Associated with that, though to a lesser extent, is the issue of the arts and domestic tourists. These perspectives are probably of greatest significance to tourist boards and the tourist industry in a strategy to determine new tourism opportunities.

In the arts world there may be little concern about whether audiences are tourists or holidaymakers (Leader-Elliott 1996). There may, though, be a desire to extend the catchment area for audiences. The tourist market may be only one of several they choose to explore and exploit in order to catch the more 'distant' market. The approach will be to develop and encourage arts that will appeal to a wide geographical area (perhaps by being distinctive) and to have promotional strategies that will reach such a wide audience. Some may, if considered appropriate, be more purposefully aimed to appeal to tourist and holiday audiences.

The live performing arts are, like most services, only consumable at the point of production. The consumer needs to travel to the theatre or concert hall in order to consume the product. With a few significant exceptions the audiences of most theatres are 'local'. Each theatre has a local geographical threshold from within which most of their audience comes. For most audiences a visit to the theatre is 'a night out' and similar to many other forms of localised leisure including eating-out, clubbing and drinking. Even the West End and Broadway have sizeable 'local' audience cores: respectively, 70% from London and South East England (MORI 1998) and 54% from New York city and suburbs (Hauser and Roth 1998).

For those outside the threshold any perceived benefit from seeing a production will be outweighed by the extra cost of seeing it: cost in the form of time, effort, cost of travel, perceived distance and so on. The aim of an arts manager will be to raise the level of perceived benefit. This may mean 'adding-value' by promoting its special qualities (star performer, the only production, etc) or offering as a holiday package. It may simply be a matter of drawing the attention of the potential audience to the existence of the production. An alternative strategy is to reduce costs.

The desire on the part of arts managers to attract tourists into audiences does not usually arise from some particular attribute of the tourist but simply as part of the desire to maximise sales. The effort and cost involved in attracting non-locals may, however, be high relative to that of attracting a more local audience. By definition the non-local audience will not only be geographically distant but also widely dispersed; the channels for distributing the marketing message are therefore less obvious. Potentially such audience segments could be resident anywhere and be exposed to a great variety of message transmitters.

The arts-tourism relationship is not of significance to all in the arts and tourism. For some arts organisations a local audience may be sufficient to fill seats. In other cases there is little opportunity because not all towns and cities or arts products have significant potential for attracting long distance audiences or for holiday tourists. There are also many in the arts who would regard it as undesirable to target tourists. There is a reluctance on the part of some to regard themselves as a tourist attraction (Canadian Tourism Commission 1997).

The effort involved in determining who is in the audience in such a way as to identify these market segments and in targeting those segments may be beyond the capabilities of many individual arts organisations and the pay-off may not be worth the effort. This suggests a case for some form of joint activity with others in both the arts and tourism. Similarly, each tourist market segment may not be large enough nor readily identifiable nor reachable in a cost-effective way.

Implications

The arts are basically regarded by tourism as a potential part of the tourist product. For hotels, tour operators, travel agents, tourist boards and city marketing boards it is largely a case of using the arts product for their own purposes. The arts however are the outcome of the artistic community for whom tourism considerations are not particularly important (Canadian Tourism Commission 1997; Leader-Elliott 1996; ACGB 1991).

In the search for audiences any art organisation may well seek to draw from a distance. Once convinced that there is potential then an individual arts organisation may adopt one or both of two broad approaches. The first is product development - the development of a new product or modification of an existing arts product so that it is more likely to attract audiences from outside the locality. This implies the production of something distinctive. The alternative or complementary approach is promotion. The product may well have tourist appeal (whether holiday or non-holiday) and the appropriate strategy may lie more in the promotion of such an existing arts product that has unexploited tourism potential.

Campaigns directed at the non-local target segments may take several forms including promotion of the arts to markets outside the destination and promotion inside the destination to tourists already there. There is also a case for involvement in promotion of the destination itself.

Some of strategies go beyond the individual efforts of any theatre, concert hall or arena. Some require working with others in the arts and some require a relationship with sectors of the tourism industry. Much of the advice by bodies such as the BTA and ACE focuses on the benefits to be achieved through working with others (ETB 1993) or, at the least, through the achievement of a greater understanding by each of the other's objectives and interests (Austwick 1991). Implicit throughout is the view that each sector can benefit from the other. Much of the practical advice centres on how the two sectors may be enabled to reach a greater understanding and a greater degree of co-operation in order to facilitate a mutually beneficial development. The two activities - the arts and tourism - are characterised by business philosophies that are, in some cases, quite radically different. As a simple distinction one sector has been driven by artistic and creative considerations whereas the other has had a much more commercial approach.

For the tourist industry the need for improved communication and consultation therefore obviously applies. Direct links for the opportunity to negotiate with the arts about use of mailing lists, packages and the selling of theatre tickets should be encouraged. It does also however make sense for tourism to develop indirect links in the sense of encouraging - through financial support or appropriate lobbying - the development of the arts and entertainment. It would appear relevant to encourage development that might be particularly successful in attracting non-local audiences. The tourism industry might advise on how such audiences could be targeted successfully. The relevant promotional bodies in tourism should also, where appropriate, recognise the role of arts and entertainment in destination choice and use this in promotion campaigns.

There are certain strategies that seem especially relevant in being able to 'capture' a particular cultural tourist market segment. If each segment is a small or not easily identifiable one then it would, of course, not be cost-effective to apply a different approach to each.

For the arts core tourist (whether holiday or not) a distinctive product will be a necessary provision. This will be less so for the non-arts core. The arts core may be encouraged additionally by offering the arts with other productions (and with other attractions) and being offered in a pleasant 'holiday' place. The provision of packages, especially short duration, may be especially relevant to the non-holiday segment. It is the product rather than the destination which has priority in the promotion process.

For the non-arts core, those on holiday (whether seaside or city), will probably be looking for 'entertainment' rather than the arts in the sense of the 'high arts'. Theatre would be promoted as part of the holiday experience. The destination promotion would be first, followed by the production promotion. It is possible, though, that destination choice may be influenced by theatre and its productions in which case it is a parallel rather than two-step process.

A non-arts core person on a business trip or visiting friends may also look for entertainment. Much of the promotional activity will be centred on consumers when they are in the destination and could include targeting local hotels and also local firms who are known to have regular visitors and targeting local conference and exhibition venues. Destination promotion would be first in the case of conferences in particular followed by the production promotion. For business and friends trips it would be important to promote to 'locals' - residents, hotels and other key informants.

Conclusions

This paper has focused on one part of the culture-tourism relationship, that relating to the performing arts. For this one sector it is suggested that there are several segments that can be distinguished, classified by arts core or non-arts core, by holiday or non-holiday. It is likely that many people classified as cultural tourists are holidaymakers who, as part of that holiday experience, require entertainment in the evening almost as an appendage to the main daily activities of heritage or beach. It might be difficult to justify classifying these 'theatre' tourists as cultural tourists; the performing arts and tourism relationship may need to treated separately. This may not, of course, be so true in the case of visitors to museums or historic houses. It should be recognised too that many of those who go to the theatre as part of a holiday are often not included in the discussion of cultural tourism at all. Data is frequently collected through audience and site visitor surveys - usually at theatres in cities and at museums, art galleries and historic sites - rather than through general tourist surveys. The tourist who visits the theatre when on holiday at a coastal destination does not often feature in the data-collection but theatre and entertainment in other places and other forms is a significant part of the holiday experience.

In addition, however, there are tourists in audiences who are drawn entirely by the arts with no concept, for them, of holiday (or tourism) surrounding the visit. Although technically tourists they are not in the same category as the arts-core holidaymaker in whom the tourist industry is interested if only because of the likelihood of greater expenditure.

These distinctions are not evident when cultural tourism is regarded as an entity. There is justification therefore for examining the components of culture separately. This does not, however, detract from the idea that the influence of any one cultural component may be joint with the others and with non-cultural resources of a destination.

It is likely that much of the discussion explaining cultural tourism or special interest tourism - in terms of 'learning' in particular - does not readily explain tourists' interest in the performing arts. It is doubtful whether the continuance in the West End of 'the Mousetrap' since 1952, 'Cats' since 1981 and 'Les Miserables' since 1985 can be explained by anything other than a desire for 'a good night out'.

The initial suggestion was that the components of culture should be separated out for analysis. In the case of the performing arts this has identified a rather more complex situation than was evident when it was subsumed under the category of cultural tourism.

References

Alzua, A., O'Leary, J. and Morrison, A. (1998). 'Cultural and heritage tourism: identifying niches for international travellers' *Journal of Tourism Studies* 9 (2) 2-13.

Arts Council of Great Britain (1985), '*A great British success story*' London: Arts Council of Great Britain.

Ashworth, G. (1993), 'Culture and tourism: conflict or symbiosis in Europe?' in W Pompl and P Lavery (eds) *'Tourism in Europe: structures and developments'*. Oxford: CAB International.

Austwick, D. (1991), '*Summary and conclusions' in Arts Council of Great Britain 'Today's arts, tomorrow's tourists: report on a seminar on the arts and tourism'* London: ACGB with the Museums and Galleries Commission.

British Tourist Authority (1983), '*The arts as an attraction for overseas visitors to Brit*ain' London: British Tourist Authority.

British Tourist Authority and English Tourist Board (1996). '*Overseas visitor survey 1995*' London: British Tourist Authority and English Tourist Board.

Bywater, M. (1993), 'The market for cultural tourism in Europe'. *Travel and Tourism Analyst* No 6, 30-46.

Canadian Travel Commission (1997), '*Fulfilling the promise: a report on six regional round tables on cultural and heritage tourism'*. Ottawa: CTC.

Dodd, D. and van Hemel, A. (eds) (1999), '*Planning cultural tourism in Europe: a presentation of theories and cases'* Amsterdam: Boekman Foundation and Ministry of Education, Culture and Science.

English Tourist Board (1993), '*The arts tourism marketing handbook'* London: ETB.

Feifer, M. (1985), '*Going places: the ways of the tourist from Imperial Rome to the present day'* London: Macmillan.

Foo, L. and Rossetto, A. (1998), 'Cultural tourism in Australia: characteristics and motivations. *BTR occasional paper no 27'* Canberra: Bureau of Tourism Research.

Gilbert, D. and Lizotte, M. (1998), 'Tourism and the performing arts' *Travel and Tourism Analyst* 1: 82-96.

Gratton, C. and Taylor, P. (1992), '*Cultural tourism in European cities: a case study of Edinburgh'*, Vrijetijd en Samenleving 10 (2/3): 29-43.

Hauser, K. and Roth, S. (1998) '*Who goes to Broadway? A demographic study of the Broadway audience 1997*' New York: the League of American Theaters and Producers Inc.

Hughes, H. (1998), 'Theatre in London and the inter-relationship with tourism' Tourism Management 19 (5) 445-452.

Hughes, H. and Benn, D. (1995), 'Entertainment: its role in the tourist experience' in D Leslie (ed) 'Tourism and leisure: perspectives on provision' Eastbourne: *Leisure Studies Association*: 11-21.

Hughes, H. and Benn, D. (1997), 'Entertainment in tourism: a study of visitors to Blackpool' *Managing Leisure: an International Journal* 2 (2): 110-126.

Leader-Elliott, L. (1996), *'Cultural tourism opportunities for South Australia'* Adelaide: South Australian Tourism Commission and the Department for the Arts and Cultural Development.

McDougall, L. (1998), *'A close-up of culture/heritage travel in Canada'* Focus on Culture (Summer). Statistics Canada.

MORI (1998), *'The West End theatre audience'*: a research study conducted for the Society of London Theatre 1996-97' London: Society of London Theatre.

Myerscough, J. (1988), *'The economic importance of the arts in Britain"*. London: Policy Studies Institute.

Prentice, R. (1993), *'Tourism and heritage attractions'* London: Routledge.

Richards, G. (ed) (1996), 'Cultural tourism in Europe' Wallingford. CAB International.

Richards, G. (1999). 'European cultural tourism: patterns and prospects' in D. Dodd, and A. van Hemel. (eds) (1999). *'Planning cultural tourism in Europe: a presentation of theories and cases'* Amsterdam: Boekman Foundation and Ministry of Education, Culture and Science. 16-32.

Robinson, M. Evans, N. and Callaghan, P. (eds) (1996), *'Tourism and culture'* conference *proceedings* (4 volumes). Newcastle: the Centre for Travel and Tourism, University of Northumbria with Business Education Publishers.

Silberberg, T. (1995), 'Cultural tourism and business: opportunities for museums and heritage sites' *Tourism Management* 16 (5) 361-365.

Smith, V. (1989), *'Hosts and guests: the anthropology of tourism'* Philadelphia: University of Pennsylvania Press.

Society of West End Theatre, (1982), *'Britain at its best: overseas tourism and the West End theatre'*. London: Society of West End Theatres.

Towner, J. (1996), *'An historical geography of recreation and tourism in the western world 1540-1940'* Chichester: Wiley.

Walle, A. (1998), *'Cultural tourism: a strategic focus'* Boulder: Westview Press.

Weiler, B. and Hall, C. (eds) *'Special interest tourism'* London: Belhaven.

Williams, R. (1988), *'Keywords: a vocabulary of culture and society'*. London: Fontana.

Zeppel, H. and Hall, C. (1992), 'Arts and heritage tourism' in B. Weiler, and C. Hall, (eds) *'Special interest tourism'* London: Belhaven.

A 'Trojan Horse' at the opera

Jane James

Flinders University of South Australia, Australia

Abstract

Ch6.

Over the past few years a research program at Flinders University has been involved with the assessment of the visitor experience at a number of festivals and events in South Australia. The researchers utilised Unobtrusive Observational - or 'Trojan Horse' - Visitor Surveys as well as face to face visitor surveys at Opera In The Outback, the Victor Harbour Folk Festival and at 'Tasting Australia', to evaluate the success of these events.

At each of these events the surveyors found that there was a dilemma, in that the visitors were best surveyed at the conclusion of the event, or certainly towards the end of it. The dilemma was that at the end of the event most visitors were keen to leave and less inclined to want to complete questionnaires about the various aspects of the festival, event or performances. To survey earlier in the event meant that performances were not complete and visitor's perceptions of the event, not finalised.

Seaton in 1997 experienced similar dilemmas when conducting visitor surveys at the Eastwood Festival, south west of Glasgow, in Scotland. He used an Unobtrusive Observational Visitor Survey method to gain additional information that could be used in conjunction with the face to face surveys that were conducted at the festival.

This method of Unobtrusive Observational Visitor Survey involves having surveyors in the audience at these events and for them to record the audiences response to the event or festival. Visitors are not asked questions, rather their behaviour, comments and attitudes are recorded by the surveyor, without the visitor being aware that they are being surveyed.

These 'Trojan Horse' surveys have been used in conjunction with face to face visitor surveys at a number of outdoor events in Australia. All of the events are cultural and have been held over a number of days in diverse natural environments, including the outback of the Flinders Ranges, the Botanic Park and Gardens of a capital city and at a coastal resort town. All have included a disparate number and variety of performances, shows and small events as part of the larger overall festival. Each of the events or festivals has attracted a wide variety of clients with all age groups, genders and socio-economic classes with a range of cultural backgrounds represented.

The results of these 'Trojan Horse' surveys have been used in conjunction with more quantitative face to face surveys to evaluate the success of these festivals and events, and offer an alternative methodology for festival/event evaluation. The 'Trojan Horse' results have contributed significantly to the information available for the Opera In The Outback, Victor Harbour Folk Festival and 'Tasting Australia' events.

Introduction

Over the past two decades, South Australia, the Festival State, has built up its Calendar of Festivals and Events to over 330 per year. Nationally, Australia holds over 1500 similar festivals and events annually.

Many, if not all, of these festivals and events are tourism opportunities, as recognised by Getz (1991), Mayfield and Crompton (1995a and b) and, specifically in Australia, by McDonnell, Allen and O'Toole (1999). Often it is only major events that prompt evaluation of their contribution to the tourism economy, or generate a measure of visitor or client satisfaction with either the festival or the event.

In South Australia one, if not the, major festival, the Adelaide Festival, has been evaluated for its economic impact, and the South Australian Tourism Commission (SATC 1996) recognises the benefits to the State of having a broad range of festivals and events for both locals and visitors. In its Corporate Plan for 1998-2003, the Commission acknowledges the need to 'attract and develop Major Events' and to 'encourage regional development' (SATC 1998).

As a consequence, numerous events, both 'major' and 'minor', are now part of the South Australian events calendar, and many have both a regional location, within the state, and a community focus in terms of being public sector led festivals.

Consumer response to festivals and events would be of enormous use to festival organisers, but only limited research in this area has been carried out. Mayfield and Crompton (1995a) site examples from the United States, and Seaton (1997) sites evidence from research in the UK.

Most festival evaluation is still conducted using face-to-face survey questionnaires, for example the Adelaide Festival (SATC 1996), the Barossa Valley Vintage Festival (Tourism South Australia 1991), Opera in the Outback (SATC 1997), Scottish Folk Festivals (Scottish Tourist Board and Highlands and Islands Development Board), the 1990-91 Edinburgh Festivals (Scotinform), and the 1995 Eastwood Festival (Seaton 1997).

This article describes the results of unobtrusive observational visitor surveys at a number of festivals in South Australia. The results are compared with the results received from utilising more conventional face to face survey questionnaires. The information gathered provides useful data which can be, and has been, utilised by festival organisers for future events.

The method of using unobtrusive observational surveys was commented on by Seaton (1997), when he reported on the dilemma facing surveyors at the eight day Easter Arts

Festival in Eastwood, Scotland, where traditional survey methods were less than successful in evaluating performances and events with fast exit rates.

Unobtrusive observational - or Trojan Horse - surveys were used at a number of events in South Australia, to provide supplementary information to the evaluation process. The objectives of the surveys were to:

- provide information on visitors to create a visitor profile.

- evaluate the reception of each overall festival.

- provide data on the level of satisfaction of people attending the events within the festival.

A range of festivals have been utilised in this research, three of which are reported on here - Opera in the Outback in 1997, the Victor Harbour Folk Festival in 1998 and Tasting Australia in 1999.

These festivals have several commonalities. Each festival ranged over a number of days, consisted of more than 6 separate events - including stage performances, children's events, indoor and outdoor activities, music events and associated food happenings - and attracted both locals, interstate and overseas visitors. Two of the three events took place in rural South Australia (Opera in the Outback and the Victor Harbour Folk Festival) and one in the city of Adelaide (Tasting Australia).

Opera in the outback

Opera in the Outback was held over four days in the Flinders Ranges in South Australia's arid Outback. It featured Dame Kiri Te Kanawa and the Adelaide Symphony Orchestra in an operatic concert in the remote Yalkarhina Gorge at sundown, and included an appearance of the Adnyamathanha Women's Choir, who are all members of the traditional Aboriginal landowners of the Flinders Ranges. Other events over the four days included an elite Athlete's Run, historic steam train rides, horses in action featuring camp draft and cutting demonstrations, fine art exhibitions, country and western concerts and a bush dance at the historic Arkaba woolshed.

The event was held over a distance of some 160 km through the Flinders Ranges, beginning in the south at Quorn with the Great Country Concert in Warren Gorge, and culminating, after the operatic concert in Yalkarhina Gorge on Saturday night, with a picnic race meeting at Beltana on Sunday.

An unpredictable feature of the Opera in the Outback event was the highest rainfall in 36 years at Warren Gorge, on the day of the Great Country Concert, which provided a challenge for both festival organisers, visitors and visitor surveyors alike, and produced some interesting results from both the traditional and Trojan Horse Surveys.

Victor Harbour Folk Festival

The Victor Harbour Folk Festival, presented by the Folk Federation of South Australia, was promoted as 'Eight Festivals in One' as the program of events included Celtic music, Blues, World Music, Acapella, Dance, Spoken Word, Country and Bluegrass, Acoustic and Contemporary Folk and children's culture. The festival presented 130 different acts on ten stages over the four days.

The Folk Festival combined community and grassroots forms of folk culture with professional and high profile folk artists. It included acts from both overseas and Australia with programming run on four levels with overseas, interstate, South Australian and community events.

The festival site is located in Victor Harbour, a seaside country town, approximately 100 km south of Adelaide. The Folk Festival takes place over a holiday long weekend, from Friday to Monday, with most acts and performances at the festival site, but with a number of acts occurring in and around the town, in a variety of venues.

Tasting Australia

The inaugural Tasting Australia Festival, as a festival of food and wine, was introduced to Australia in 1997. The second Tasting Australia Festival was held in South Australia over 8 days, in October 1999. There were a number of events including the World Food Media Awards, the Australian Regional Culinary Competition and a Food and Wine Writers Festival. The week culminated in the City of Adelaide's Feast for the Senses in Botanic Park over two days. This Feast for the Senses event included an Australian Regional Food and Wine Expo, a Wine Tunnel, a Waiter's Race, the 'Get into Cooking' Competition, an Aussie BBQ Challenge and Australian Petanque Tournament.

Survey methods

Face-to-face Surveys

A 26 item multiple choice questionnaire survey was designed as the principal research method for face to face visitor surveys. It included questions aimed at establishing a visitor profile (age, gender, state/country of origin, party size and composition), motivations, activities, transport and accommodation, source information about the event, spending and satisfaction. The questionnaire was conducted as a face-to-face survey by trained interviewers, to a random sample of visitors at each festival. The survey was modified to accommodate the individual characteristics of each of the three festivals, but the basic survey questions were consistent.

The survey questions identified both the main events and/or performances and a number of smaller ones, that took place over the days of a particular festival, so that visitor attendance at specific events could be identified and their satisfaction levels documented and recorded.

The number of events identified and monitored at the various festivals is listed below:

    (a)   Opera in the Outback   19 events

    (b)   Victor Harbor Folk Festival   15 events

    (c)   Tasting Australia   8 events

The program at each of the festivals was complex, with two, Tasting Australia and the Victor Harbour Folk Festival, being held in a fixed location, and the third, Opera in the Outback, being a "moveable feast". There were also events running concurrently at each festival, at different locations within the various "festival sites".

Surveyors worked in groups of 4 - 6, so that surveys were conducted both during and after main features on the festival programs. Each research project was managed, on site, over the entire duration of each festival.

Trojan Horse surveys

The "Trojan Horse" survey method was developed to accommodate the "unobtrusive measures" referred to by Webb et al (1966) and in line with methods used in Mass Observation (Madge and Harrison, 1939). Mass observation techniques were utilised by Madge and Harrison to explore the anthropology of everyday life, i.e. the activities and experiences of people in Britain in 1937.

This mass observation survey technique was used at the Coronation Day Festival of May 12, 1937, where a national survey was conducted, using anthropological observation methods to study British leisure behaviour. Similar methods were used during World War II, under government sponsorship, to monitor morale and public opinion in wartime Britain (Seaton 1997).

These techniques have also been used subsequently to research popular culture (Calder and Sheridan, 1984) and movie visitation (Richards and Sheridan, 1987). Participant observation research has also been discussed by Ryan (1995) in his book 'Researching Tourist Satisfaction' as a method of evaluating tourists experiences.

In the light of UK research at the Eastwood Festival reported by Seaton (1997) and in anticipation of the complexity of the initial event, Opera In The Outback, a qualitative Trojan Horse survey was developed prior to this, and subsequent, festivals. It asked the observers to be aware of both verbal and non-verbal reactions.

Members of the research survey team at each of the events at a particular festival, took it in turns to be part of the audience. They were instructed to observe the audience and record information that was indicative of audience reaction to a particular performance or event, notably reactions that indicated the event's success or failure, and the level of visitor satisfaction, and reasons for it.

The survey team were issued with Trojan Horse survey forms which enabled them to list or identify a particular event, to record the observational characteristics that implied satisfaction or otherwise, and to record audience verbal and non-verbal indicators. Importantly, the surveyors were asked to be discreet in their completion of the Trojan Horse surveys, so as to maintain the level of "unobtrusive" evaluation that was required.

As a result, surveyors were able to record estimates of audience numbers, unsolicited audience comments and descriptions of audience behaviour, both individual and collective.

Those people conducting face-to-face surveys were also briefed to record, where possible, spontaneous comments pertaining to specific events, and to keep supplementary notes, as well as recording responses to the formal survey questions.

At the end of each day a collective debriefing was held where comments and observations were compared and discussed. As a result of this debriefing, notes from each of the events at a particular festival were collected and collated, and compared with the results of the face-to-face interview survey.

A second debriefing took place at the end of each festival and, following discussion, qualitative summary notes were produced.

Results

The Trojan Horse survey results from South Australia, confirm many of those produced at the Eastwood Festival by Seaton (1997), and were found to augment the face to face surveys by providing additional information, detailed explanations of comments made and confirming conclusions from the face to face surveys.

(a) Additional information

Valuable information was gained by surveyors utilising Trojan Horse observational methods from being at the festival site for the whole duration of each of the festivals. Much of the documented, unsolicited material was gained from casual conversations and by listening to visitors comments. Information was gained on audience profiles and numbers, event scheduling and organisation, performer perceptions of the events and festival organisation generally and site management.

Audience Data: All three festivals had a significant number of people who were WFRs (Seaton 1997) - those people who were *'watching friends or relatives'* perform. This was especially true at children's events at both the Victor Harbour Folk Festival and Tasting Australia, where there were clearly identified children's activities, but less so at Opera In The Outback where the program was targeting a specifically adult audience.

The *WFRs* were also obvious at the Great Country concert at Opera In The Outback, where groups of local pastoralists were a clear entity amongst the participants.

This feature was emphasised by the fact that much of the face to face surveying of the event took place on the track that led to the concert site. Many of the survey results from this location suggested that many clients were so affected by the weather - the highest rainfall in the area for 36 years (Advertiser, 1997) - that they turned away from the event or only stayed for a short period of time, preferring instead to return to the relative comfort of their accommodation. Media reports of the Great Country concert suggested that it was both literally and metaphorically 'a wash out', whilst in fact it was truly successful. Trojan Horse surveys that continued at the concert venue, within Warren Gorge, noted that the participants at this particular event couldn't have been happier, expressing this joy at both the concert and the turn in the weather, by dancing in the aisles, on the chairs and comparing the agricultural bounty that would flow - quite literally - from such a downpour. There was also a clear correlation between satisfaction of this particular concert event and the demographic characteristics of a large section of the audience – i.e. local people with a common interest in country music, able to both withstand and appreciate the inclemency of the situation.

From this, event organisers may be well advised to consider including both local and 'outside' performers, so as to continue to attract significant local support to regional festivals.

Sponsor/VIP groups: Another observation made by the Trojan Horse observers was both of, and towards, sponsors and VIPs at the various festivals. Sponsors clearly had a vested interest in seeing the event and/or festival succeed, and administrative and political participants clearly were observed to be expecting preferential treatment. This preferential treatment included separate seating areas, receptions adjacent to major events within the festival, often generating noise that then detracted from the event for non-VIPs, and allowances made for late arrivals that were not always afforded to others in the audience. As with the Seaton Eastwood festival in the UK the Trojan Horse survey was able to record the annoyance and frustration of the general audience on a number of occasions, in quite different situations at all three festivals under review.

Visitor numbers and behaviour: Estimations of visitor numbers were gathered from ticket sales both before and after each festival, but the Trojan Horse surveys enabled surveyors to estimate and comment on the numbers attending specific events or performances within a particular festival site. Ticket sales offered a good method of ascertaining total numbers at the festival, but not the numbers at specific events, nor the comments that were recorded about the scheduling of events so that visitors are able to go to a variety of events that were on at a variety of times over the program period.

Information of this type gathered at each of the festivals will have ramifications for the program design, the use of concurrent sessions and the venues within a particular festival site where different events are held.

The occasion arose at the Victor Harbour Folk Festival where one particular folk group, performing in a marquee, decided part way through their performance that the chairs for spectators were redundant, as most people wanted to dance. So they organised a rapid furniture removal session by the spectators themselves, as part of a bizarre dance routine. Then, when other festival goers stopped to see what was going on, they too became part of the audience, and this particular performance became an impromptu outside event as they had outgrown the confines of the marquee where they started. Much of the unsolicited comment from visitors at this time was directed either at the enjoyment from being part of the whole audience-removalists-dancers cohort, to comments from other festival goers who complained about having the external space given over to other activities at the festival being invaded by the unwelcome audience-removalists-dancers. Little or none of this experience would have been caught by traditional survey methods.

Event and site management: The face to face surveys elicited information about the site and facilities (car parking, catering, toilets) for visitors. It did not cater for comments about environmental impact on the site, nor the effects of this impact on visitors. The Trojan Horse surveys noted impact at all three festival sites.

At Opera In The Outback the environmental impact ranged from the damage caused to dirt roads that rapidly became impassable for the majority of festival traffic (coaches, cars and all but the hardiest of 4WD vehicles) following the heavy rains; to the dust clouds that were generated in the northern parts of the Flinders Ranges that hosted the latter parts of the festival, that did not receive the same rainfall that was experienced at the southern sites. *Greening Australia* and *Landcare* organisations who were using the high numbers of visitors to the Flinders Ranges region for the Opera event, to raise awareness of the fragility of the outback, and the need to both conserve and preserve the native vegetation, were able to utilise to their advantage, real and current situations to illustrate their environmental message. Visitors verbal and non-verbal reactions to the obvious detrimental environmental impact were recorded by the Trojan Horse surveys.

Similarly it was possible for similar observations at the Victor Harbour Folk Festival and Tasting Australia to reveal other limitations and benefits of both festival sites.

The Victor Harbour Folk Festival experienced both bad and good site management with:

- poor acoustics at some concerts, especially those where venues were in close proximity, with one performing loudly and the other quietly (causing annoyance and frustration to patrons and performers alike);

- poor display of on site information about individual events and insufficient on site staff and/or volunteers with adequate information about the program (many knew specifically about an individual event, but few knew about the overall program);

- limited food and beverage options for visitors;

- inadequate rubbish bins, infrequently emptied, especially those adjacent to the food areas, which were soon over flowing, creating both a visual eyesore and a potential health hazard;

but:

- excellent security arrangements (fencing, security patrols) that were essential for a festival that was aimed at a range of socio-demographic visitors, and with both a day time and evening program of performances;

- clearly signposted entrances for both visitors and performers;

- adequate staff to deal with the diverse range of performers and their varied storage requirements for instruments, equipment etc;

- appropriate pricing structure that enabled visitors to access as much, or as little, of the festival that they required, with benefits proportional to greater participation.

The Tasting Australia Festival had similar experiences in site management with:

- promotional material that assumed knowledge about the location of the Botanic Park, which was particularly frustrating for interstate and international visitors;

- inadequate parking;

- inadequately signposted entrances for visitors;

- little orientation available once at the site to clarify the layout relative to which entrance was used;

- a lack of maps at the Tasting Australia site caused confusion and frustration for visitors trying to ascertain the location of events within a particular time frame;

- a loudspeaker system that competed with the one being used at events already running within the festival and which did not give directions to wherever the next event was to be held;

- an inaccurate map within the festival program (which in itself was poorly promoted and distributed, despite the fact that it was free as part of the entry cost) which resulted in a significant part of the events available at the festival being by-passed by a large number of visitors;

but:

- a diverse range of Australian regional producers of both food and wine represented;

- a clear identification of local - South Australian - regions and their produce;

- a broad variety of both active (Petanque, Waiter's race), passive (Aussie BBQ Challenge), observational (decorative body art using local produce) and experiential (food and wine tasting) activities for visitors;

- an ideal location and setting that favourably show-cased Australia's position in the food and wine industry;

- a broad range of participants involved (trade shows, school children, chefs and wine makers, olive growers and bee keepers).

(b) Explanatory data

Unsolicited comments from visitors provided information about how each of the festivals was received by the public and why some elements of each worked better than others.

Face to face, quantitative surveys elicited a generally high level of overall satisfaction with each of the three festivals - Opera In The Outback, the Victor Harbour Folk Festival and Tasting Australia, with significant percentages of people indicating that they would consider attending a similar event in the future (75% for Opera In The Outback, 52% for the Victor Harbour Folk Festival and 93% for Tasting Australia).

The Trojan Horse surveys suggested reasons for the level of satisfaction, with all three festivals eliciting comments about the festival being 'good for the area/region' and the contribution that was made by and to the local community.

Opera In The Outback was seen as successful because of its naturally spectacular location in the Flinders Ranges. Nature turned on a magnificent sunset and the sulphur crested cockatoos that wheeled above the stage as the Adelaide Symphony Orchestra began its first overture could not possibly have been stage managed. The initial frustration and potential anger at the delay that was felt by many of the participants as they had to queue for the restricted access to the operatic concert site was dispelled, when word passed down the line (at this stage almost 1 km long) that the local State football team had won and progressed to the national finals. The euphoria that followed this news was a significant factor in the enjoyment of the ensuing concert - a feeling that was recognised by one member of the orchestra as he waved the winning team's scarf above his head during the orchestra's warm up, much to the delight of the waiting audience.

A similar euphoria contributed to the success of the Great Country Concert event when drought breaking rains, which caused such headaches for the festival organisers, provided farmers with a much needed break in the season and the potential for a brighter future for the local community that was hosting the Opera In The Outback festival.

A lasting impact of Opera In The Outback has been the raising of awareness of the regions historic and cultural diversity and enabled both Aboriginal and non-indigenous tourism operators to demonstrate 'their patch' to future potential clients.

The *Victor Harbour Folk Festival* was perceived a success because it provided a focus for special interest visitors and for the broader community who were in the region because it was a long weekend. It was also apparent to the survey team that many people who attended the various events did so because they were in the *WFR* category, and this influenced the other type of performances that they went to watch, usually concentrating on similar shows or waiting until their 'own' performer was due to do their next spot. More adequate information at each marquee or venue within the festival site listing the acts/shows over the course of the day might have encouraged further participation from this particular group.

However many seemed to be happy to stay in the one venue and simply watch whatever act appeared there next.

It was clear that visitors to the festival made use of, and appreciated, the multiple entry scheme that was in place, allowing them to come and go from the (fenced) festival site over the duration of their ticket, i.e. anywhere between 1 and 4 days.

Despite the clearly inadequate use of signs within Victor Harbour showing the direction to the festival site, it became clear to observers that many people were drawn to the festival from passing traffic. This was confirmed from results in the face to face surveys. Many people were heard to remark on the relaxed and 'laid back' atmosphere at the festival, which was facilitated by the nature of the festival site and partly by the composition of the audience. Family groups were observed enjoying performances as both groups and as individuals, with the compact nature of the venue adding a sense of security and a 'village like' ambience. This may be due in part to the large numbers of volunteers involved (supported by the quantitative data) who clearly felt an ownership of the festival, and/or of the town in which it was held.

One of the visibly successful aspects of the festival was the workshops that allowed festival goers the opportunity to be guided by the artists in their particular aspect of music, dance or spoken word. The interactive nature of these occasions prompted a great deal of audience participation and resulted in, again, a feeling of ownership amongst the festival goers themselves. The face to face surveys did not adequately survey this activity, partly because this aspect of the festival was not clearly identified on the program, partly because it was not requested as part of the quantitative survey by the Folk Federation of South Australia, but mostly because many of the workshops were an impromptu development that stemmed from a demand from participating audiences. It obviously was an aspect of the Victor Harbour Folk Festival that would not have been recorded in the face to face surveys, but contributed significantly to the success of the event. This workshop aspect of the festival was also seen to be an on-going tradition at the festival, as comments from people referred to what they had 'learnt or discovered last year', and is something that could perhaps be better promoted for future events.

The Feast for the Senses at *Tasting Australia* was successful for a number of reasons. The general ambience of the Botanic Gardens and the beautiful spring weather was conducive to people spending significant amounts of time sitting in the central pavilion areas. These areas were provided with tables and chairs, were shaded by large open sided awnings and were clearly in the 'centre of the action'. Observers noticed that many groups spent only a cursory amount of time visiting the various displays in the first instance, but rather found themselves a table and settled themselves for several hours whilst various members of the party were either sent as runners to return with 'goodies and supplies' (where part of the enjoyment was to see what they would return with) or as individuals they would wander for a while before returning with their own choices of produce.

This attitude to the festival was clearly a more comfortable option than that envisaged by the festival organisers of people standing in marquees balancing their food and drink. It lent significantly to the relaxed and 'lazy afternoon' atmosphere, but probably meant that some of the events that were located away from the main circuit were completely missed by some festival goers.

It appeared to the observers that festival participants either walked around the festival site with a more or less cursory look at the displays and events on offer, or formed part of the 'sit and runners' contingent. Both groups enjoyed different aspects of the program that was available, but the former group is probably the one that the festival organisers were targeting with the festival whilst the second group may well provide an opportunity for the provision of strolling goods and produce at future festivals.

(c) Confirming conclusions from the face to face surveys

Much of the quantitative data received from the face to face surveys was corroborated by the information gathered from Trojan horse surveys, notably in the following areas:

Audience profiles. The socio-demographic data for each of the three festivals was supported by observational data. At Opera In the Outback there was a correlation between the high class make or model of cars parked in the parking area, especially at the operatic concert, and the dress standard of the participants. Even though this event was definitely an 'outback' event many of this group of the audience emerged from their vehicles in either full evening dress or with walking boots to go with dinner jacket and tie, or evening gown, gloves and tiara, as a concession to the environment. This was in contrast to the (perhaps?) more appropriately dressed jean clad component of the audience that emerged from less well heeled vehicles or from the campsite along the road.

Observational assessment of gender and age of the participants, matched survey results at all three festivals.

Facilities and catering. Generally the observational data supported the findings of the face to face surveys. There were some instances where toilet facilities seemed to be over utilised, with queues a familiar site, but most comments overheard were understanding of the fact that these facilities would necessarily be busy at times when performances ended and before the next ones began. Most people were sympathetic to the reason and patient about the need to wait. Correlations did not indicate otherwise from the quantitative data from any of the festivals.

The majority of observational comments about catering were either about the lack of variety of food (e.g. little or no vegetarian catering at the Opera In The Outback); the cost and suitability of food available, especially for children (e.g. at Tasting Australia where the point of the festival was the provision of high quality and variety of different produce and wines); or the times that food was/wasn't available (e. g. at the Victor Harbour Folk Festival where some food outlets did not open until the middle of the day despite the fact that performances began mid-morning). Either way, the majority of these comments were recorded in the quantitative data from the face to face surveys.

Satisfaction. Trojan Horse observations based on people's unsolicited comments and conversations and non-verbal actions and behaviour matched satisfaction responses from the face to face surveys.

Non-verbal responses included body language and facial expressions, animated discussions and participation or bored attitudes and sleep, fidgeting, early departure as opposed to aggressive entry to already overcrowded venues, volume and length of applause and demand for encores.

Verbal responses included overheard comments and conversations that indicated either complaint or approval, unsolicited comments to members (identifiable and otherwise) of the survey team and recommendations made between festival goers on 'what was worth seeing/doing'.

The festivals success overall was also evaluated from an observational point of view by the comments and behaviour of the audience in relation to facilities, signs and costing where it was possible to do so, not just to activities and performances that were part of a particular festival program.

Conclusions

Whilst it is difficult to maintain a consistent approach to the methodology of Unobtrusive Observational - or Trojan Horse - visitor surveys at festivals and events, it is still clear that this method of surveying can contribute to the data available about audience participation in, and enjoyment of, festivals. The difficulties inherent in surveying festivals with fast exit rates, in a variety of physical locations and over a number of days, will also remain as issues that need to be addressed in the use of quantitative surveying. The usefulness of employing both types of survey, resulting in both quantitative and qualitative data is apparent. The data produced, correlated and compared for all three festivals cited in this case study - Opera In the Outback, the Victor Harbour Folk Festival and Tasting Australia - has already proved useful and viable for the festival organisers involved. Both of these survey methods have recognised limitations and neither is new.

On the other hand, festivals and events on either a major or minor scale, held in a variety of locations and offering a multitude of diverse events within any given festival, are an integral part of both community and tourism life. Evaluation of the benefit that they bring to, and the impact on, host communities, festival organisers and the visitors and festival goers themselves, is clearly a desirable outcome. Not to attempt to do so would be foolish. This researcher endorses categorically the comments of Seaton (1997) which stated that 'diverse audience effects can never be fully caught by the diligent analysis ... of responses to ... questions, preselected long before the event, by those who have little way of knowing the half of what is going to happen before it does.'

The case studies presented in this paper demonstrate the value of the Trojan Horse, which like its reference in the Odyssey, (Askin, 1999) was used to achieve an outcome without alerting the audience. In this case the outcome was a better evaluation of the satisfaction levels of visitors and the success overall of a number of multi-faceted festivals in South Australia.

References

Advertiser (1997), *Deluge at the Opera,* Advertiser Newspapers, Adelaide, South Australia.

Askin, M. (1999), *A Revised Edition - Troy,* Keskin Color Kartpostalcilik Ltd., Sti. Matbaasi, Turkey.

Calder, A. and Sheridan, D. (1984), *Speak for Yourself: A Mass Observation Anthology 1937-1949.* Jonathan Cape, London.

Getz, D. (1991), *Festivals, Special Events and Tourism.* Van Nostrand Reinhold, New York.

Madge, C. and Harrison, T. (1939), *Britain by Mass Observation,* Penguin, London.

Mayfield, T. L. and Crompton, J. L. (1995a), The Status of the Marketing Concept among Festival Organisers, *Journal of Travel Research,* 33 (Spring), pp 14-22.

Mayfield, T. L. and Crompton, J. L. (1995b), Development of an Instrument for Identifying Community Reasons for Staging a Festival, *Journal of Travel Research,* 33 (Winter), pp 37-44.

McDonnell, J., Allen, J. and O'Toole, W. (1999), *Festival and Special Event Management,* John Wiley and Sons Australia, Ltd., Brisbane.

Richards, J. and Sheridan, D., (1987), *Mass Observations at the Movies,* Routledge and Kegan Paul, London and New York.

Ryan, C. (1995), *Researching Tourist Satisfaction,* Routledge, London and New York.

Scotinform Ltd., (1992), *Edinburgh Festivals Study 1990-1991*, Scottish Tourist Board, Lothian and Edinburgh Enterprise, Lothian Regional Council and Edinburgh District Council.

Scottish Tourist Board and Highlands and Islands Development Board, (1990), *Survey of Scottish Folk Festivals,* Edinburgh: Scottish Tourist Board and Highlands and Islands Development Board.

Seaton, A. V. (1997), Unobtrusive Observational Measures as a Qualitative Extension of Visitor Surveys at Festivals and Events: Mass Observation Revisited, *Journal of Travel Research,* Spring, pp 25-30.

South Australian Tourism Commission., (1996), *1996 Adelaide Festival: An Economic Impact Study,* Market Equity SA Pty. Ltd, South Australia.

South Australian Tourism Commission., (1997), *Opera in the Outback: An Economic Impact Study,* South Australian Tourism Commission, Adelaide, South Australia.

South Australian Tourism Commission., (1998), *Corporate Plan 1998 - 2003*, South Australian Tourism Commission, Adelaide, South Australia.

Tourism South Australia, (1991), *Barossa Valley Vintage Festival Visitor Survey, April 1991*. Adelaide, South Australia.

Webb, E. J., Campbell, D. T. Schwartz, R. D. and Sechrest, L. (1996), *Unobtrusive measures: Non-reactive Research in the Social Sciences*. Rand McNally, Chicago.

Tourists on the mother road and the information superhighway

Marjorie Kibby

The University of Newcastle, Australia

Introduction

Cultural tourism is a high growth area of the travel and recreation industries. Consumer participation in cultural tourism suggests increasing interest among the 'baby boomer' generation in their cultural roots, particularly in travel to an 'authentic' destination that represents a mythologised aspect of popular culture.

But these tourists are becoming increasingly sophisticated, looking for more than a "Elvis slept here" sign - they want to relive a moment in history. To maximise their cultural experience, these tourists are demanding detailed information, and the opportunity to share their pop culture pilgrimage with fellow travellers. More and more they are looking to the Internet for both the information and the community.

Route 66, Steinbeck's Mother Road that stretched across the USA from Chicago to Los Angeles, is an example of cultural mythology as tourist destination. It is also an example of the way that travellers are looking to the 'information superhighway' for specific information on the out-of-the-way locations and honest-to-goodness events that will authenticate the experience, and for the community of fellow travellers and would-be travellers that confirm the experience as mythological.

Cultural tourism

Cultural tourism is one of the growth sectors within the tourism market of the 21st century (Jansen-Verbeke 1996:6), as contemporary leisure travel is increasingly directed towards experiencing the special quality of a place in a novel and informative way. The increased interest in cultural tourism is in accord with other trends within the tourism market, such as 'added value' tourism associated with 'quality' leisure experiences; 'consumption' tourism, and the search for new products and experiences; and 'sustainable' tourism as a way of providing for the ongoing viability of an attraction. The growth in cultural tourism is also an effect of a range of social changes which have served to re-position tourist practices so that "tourism is no longer a differentiated set of social practices with its own distinct rules, times and spaces" (Urry 1994:234). Contemporary tourism is likely to form part of broader practices of consumption, leisure and social activity, in an "intertwining of tourist practices and cultural texts in contemporary societies" (Urry 1994:233), exemplified by modern pilgrimages to the setting of *Heartbeat* and the re-enactment of movie moments such as the *Stone* funeral procession. Tourism is increasingly linked to social activities, recreational pursuits and popular-culture consumption.

Cultural tourism has many dimensions including arts, history, architecture, nature, events, and lifestyles, but it is ultimately about experiencing the unique character of a place and its cultural resources. Heritage tourism is a type of cultural tourism that is directed towards engaging with the cultural tradition of a particular location. Heritage tourism represents a way of recuperating the past for contemporary travellers, and is part of a wider nostalgia for traditional social values, and an appreciation of the way things were, or at least are perceived to have been. Heritage is, by definition, something of value that has been passed on from previous generations, something that is under threat (Hewison 1987:137). Heritage tourism offers opportunities to, if not recover the past, then to recruit it to meet present needs. Heritage tourism "provides an infinite time and space in which the past can be experienced through the prism of the endless possibilities of their own sense of historic places to create their individual journeys of self discovery" (Nuryanti 1996:251). Heritage experiences assist in the formation of self identity, through identification with specific cultural archetypes and values.

Collective nostalgia acts to restore a belief in the superiority of traditional social arrangements and practices, while at the same time facilitating the adoption of new ways and beliefs (Kibby 1998:). Jameson (1989) describes this as a "nostalgia for the present," an expression of desires for the present, rather than of fond remembrances of the past. Collective nostalgia is usually based on a reconstructed or mis-remembered social past; on an idealised or romanticised history. Davis (1979) points out that the nostalgia of the last decades of the twentieth century was not for a personal past, but for the past of the popular media – of film, television and music. The interest in pop-culture history marks "a culture trying desperately to rope off, sanction, and harden its myths into an intellectual iconography" (Graham 1984 p350). Trotter argues that "nostalgia is a natural ally for tourism: both offer a means of 'escape'; one to another time, the other to another place" and that "heritage tourism unites both escape routes" (Trotter 1999:22). But heritage tourism offers more than an escape from the present. It provides a commodification of pastness. Heritage tourism offers an authentic version of a mythologised history that can be appropriated within the present.

In the search for the authentic, the heritage tourist is increasingly demanding to understand the significance of a site. Heritage tourists require more than simple information - an "Elvis slept here" sign - they recognise that the meanings of a site can only be derived if the circumstances surrounding the site can be interpreted. Heritage sites possess "historical values and meaning derived from the settings in which they occur and the societal values that ascribe worth to them (Nuryanti 1996:252). In seeking an authentic experience of cultural heritage, contemporary tourists are searching out encounters that go beyond the provision of "physical facts and tangible elements" (Nuryanti 1996:253). They are looking for sites that "are in essence experiential products facilitating feelings, emotions, imagination and knowledge" (McIntosh and Prentice 1999:607). Heritage sites are very much social spaces where collective memories and private experiences combine, in a meshing of public symbols and private spaces. Meanings are created which incorporate the dynamic social relations of the setting, and the various experiences which imbue it with cultural value (Wearing and Wearing 1996). To maximise their effective participation, heritage tourists require detailed information that allows them to incorporate their personal experiences in a collective mythology.

Moscardo (1996) draws on an educational psychology term, mindfulness, in saying that tourists at heritage attractions can be seen as 'mindful' in how they respond to the experience. Mindful visitors see "learning, self-discovery, and exploration as motives for, and activities in, tourism" (Moscardo 1996:377). Mindful tourists are generally those who are well informed about the attraction and its historical and cultural context, and are able to connect the site with their personal and social values and the experiences of themselves and their peers. The process of cultural interpretation is more than the internalisation of facts. It is a holistic process that is both individual and collective. It involves thinking and feeling, exchanging opinions, and interpreting private experiences as part of a cultural system.

An essential part of a mindful tourist experience is contact with others with whom to share the experience. "People to people contact facilitates learning experiences and increases understanding" and "people to people contact is a key feature of cultural tourism" (Reisinger 1994:24). Tourist experiences are governed by social relationships; by networks of relatives and friends, fellow travellers, and chance acquaintances. Tourist behaviours are established through collective social networks, and tourist practices ordered by interactions with peers. Tourists also depend on social networks for travel information with studies finding that visitors gather information on travel destinations from close connections, such as family and friends, while distant social networks provide general information like area attractions and activities (Stokowski 1992).

In summary, tourists in search of a heritage experience are likely to incorporate their tourist activities in their broader social practices; they are in all likelihood motivated by a nostalgia for a popular-culture past; they will presumably require information that goes beyond simple facts; and they will probably be looking for people to people interaction as part of the experience.

Studying Historic Route 66 as an example of a heritage tourism destination, I found the World Wide Web playing an important role in providing these elements of the cultural heritage experience. I analysed Route 66 Web-sites, both commercial and personal, monitored Route 66 discussion forums, and talked to travellers and business operators on Route 66 Arizona, and discovered that the Web was becoming an increasingly important link between visitors and the heritage experience.

Tourism and the Web

Recent surveys show that the online travel market is expanding rapidly. Worldwide, Internet users spent US$5 billion at online travel sites in 1999 and this is expected to increase to US$30 billion by the end of 2001 (Cyber Atlas 2000:1). "Three quarters of Internet users visit travel sites to research timetables, flight options, prices and special deals. This represents a four hundred percent increase on 1998"(Gartner Group 2000:1). The survey identified the top three online travel firms currently as Expedia, Travelocity and Preview

Travel, sites that offer comprehensive services. It is reported that, during 1999, 70% of all air travel in the US had some connection with the Internet (Edwards 1999:89), with travellers logging on to get information about destinations, to check availability of dates, and to compare fares and rates.

While statistics on online travel sales are more readily available, there are indicators that tourists are increasingly using the Internet for a range of travel related activities other than purchasing travel items. A number of print travel guides are now available online, including Fodors, Rough Guide and Lonely Planet. The online guides offer a range of services impossible to provide in the print versions such as weekly updates, customisable mini-guides, personalised travel maps, individual advice from experts, reviews from fellow travellers, and the opportunity to share travel experiences and opinions.

Another growth area is that of 'travel community' sites such as Great Outdoor Recreation Pages and Virtual Tourist. While these provide goods such as books and maps, and trip planning and reservation services, their primary commodities are information and interaction. On the travel community sites tourist have access to 'expert' advice and opinion, but the major feature is the exchange between travellers. For example Virtual Tourist says "What to do on Virtual Tourist:

1.   Build your travel page and create your personalised travel maps and share your experiences easily and for free.

2.   Explore more than 1700 destinations and other members travel pages to research your next trip.

3.   Interact with 46432 other members by free web email, instant messages, forums, and chat."

Virtual Tourist was one of the first online travel communities, and is an example of a 'general' site catering for all travel interests. GORP targets those interested in outdoor activities such as hiking, skiing and fishing, or in natural heritage destinations such as National Parks and walking trails. A third type of travel community is that organised around a specific destination. An example of this is the Route 66 Web Ring, a collection of linked web sites that provide services, goods, information and the exchange of viewpoints on all aspects of Route 66.

Route 66

By the beginning of the 1920s in the USA most cities and towns had paved roads that extended to the limit of the urban area, and rarely beyond. The rural areas were criss-crossed by local roads that connected one town to the next, but these had developed through use rather than forethought and both routing and maintenance were haphazard at best. With the growth of the automobile age it became apparent that these roads were unsuited for mechanised traffic, and many groups lobbied for the creation of a system of roads which would be suitable for automobiles. One such lobbyist was Oklahoma's Cyrus Stevens Avery.

Largely as a result of Avery's agitation the American Association of State Highway Officials agreed in 1924 on the principles for the establishment of a national road running from the mid-west to the California coast (Wallis 1990:7). This road would become Route 66 in 1926. The Route began in Chicago, headed south to Texas, then south-west to Los Angeles and the Pacific Ocean. Crossing eight states, it was constructed out of existing local roads, so it followed the contours of the land; meandering alongside rivers, skirting hills and following natural boundaries. Route 66 was dominated by the environment, unlike modern highways which seem to be imposed upon the environment. Route 66 was 'America's Main Street', running through the downtown of every city and hamlet it passed from St Louis and Albuquerque, to Oatman and Pontiac.

A two lane road stretching 2,500 miles, Route 66 was the highway of choice for 1930s migrants, 1940s returned soldiers, and 1950s families and tourists. From 1926 to the late 1950s, Route 66 was the symbol of the 'road trip', of relocation, pioneering and adventuring. In response to the large numbers of travellers and their diverse needs, alongside the Route grew up a landscape of motels, restaurants, gas stations, recreational activities and tourist attractions - built by entrepreneurs who anticipated that drivers passing at 35 mph would be enticed by quirky and colourful signage and pull off the road. Driving Route 66 was an adventure, celebrated in popular culture with songs like Bobby Troup's *Get Your Kicks on Route 66*, and the television series *Route 66*.

Then, in 1956, President Dwight Eisenhower, inspired by the autobahns that he saw in Germany during World War II , launched the Interstate Highway system - a limited access, multi-lane, road system that carved a high speed path past towns, through hills and over valleys. In the south-west states it was I - 40. Each year another segment was opened until 1984 when the last town (Williams, Arizona) was bypassed, and in 1985 Route 66 was officially decommissioned. Traffic slowed to a trickle, businesses closed, buildings decayed.

In 1999 Congress allocated over US$10 million "to preserve the cultural resources" of the Route 66 corridor (US Congress 1999:1). Today preservationists are at work all along the highway; tourists are returning as baby boomers look to discover their cultural roots; and small business owners are finding it viable to resurrect their 1930s era gas station, diner or motel.

Route 66 on the Web

Route 66 Web sites can be broadly categorised although there is significant overlap between the categories in terms of the nature of the information provided. The first group is that of sites published by associations and organisations. Examples of these include National Historic Route 66 Federation, the Northern Arizona University, and Pitzer College. The Federation site provides brief information, links to other Route 66 sites, news, events listings and a photo gallery, and offers further benefits to those who join the Federation, such as Route 66 trip consultations, quarterly magazines, and a range of products including memorabilia, maps, books, and video documentaries. Sean Evans, who is Reference librarian at the Cline Library of Northern Arizona University maintains a collection of material from both federal and Arizona state governments published about Route 66. His web site also includes a brief history of the road, and a guide to assist those doing research into the route. Although the focus is academic, the collection includes popular guide books, cookbooks and folk histories. The Pitzer College site is an elaborate class project arising out of a semester of studying Route 66, and includes a descriptive travelogue, photo gallery and links to information sources.

The next grouping of sites are those promoting Route 66 businesses, attractions and personalities. The Route 66 Place not only publicises its 50s soda fountain in Williams, Arizona, it offers information for tourists visiting Williams and the surrounding district, or travelling Route 66, and sells a wide range of 66 memorabilia via its online catalogue. Similarly the Route 66 Giftshop not only offers its products via online sales, but also provides a history of the Route, and information on events and attractions along the Route through Seligman. The Giftshop is run by one of the Route's major characters and one of the primary advocates for its restoration, Angel Delgadillo. Angel no longer cuts hair, but a stop at the Delgadillo Barber Shop is an essential part of the Route 66 experience. Angel's brother Juan, runs the nearby Snow-Cap Drive In. Online discussion forums warn first time travellers of his trick door knobs and squirting mustard bottles. The Giftshop site goes partway to explain Route 66's contemporary appeal as a cultural heritage destination.

> *"The people of Seligman will say the interstates ignore a sunshine America - a land where motel guests still talk to each other. Where the gas station bathroom doesn't require a key. Where the road promises adventure and rampant, irrepressible, entrepreneurial individuality.*
>
> *Maybe that land never existed. Maybe it doesn't matter. It will exist now, if people along the Route have anything to say."*

The heritage of Route 66 is part fact, part media fiction, and part contemporary expressions of a nostalgia for a way of life that is largely unremembered. This heritage is constructed through the articulation of individual experiences of collective values, and as such is dependent on communication and interaction. To keep the mythology alive it is necessary to share the stories.

Another of the Route's 'personalities' was Lucille, the 'Mother of the Mother Road'. Her daughter, Cheryl Nowka, maintains Lucille's General Store Web site, a huge site featuring life histories, anecdotes, Route 66 myths and many photographs of Lucille and other Route 66 characters such at Tattoo Kenny and his motorcycle trailer made from a coffin. Cheryl believes firmly that Route 66 businesses need a Web presence, because tourists and collectors are searching the Web for goods and information related to the Route. The site is dedicated to the people who own businesses on Route 66, and has an extensive list of links to business sites. For those Route 66 businesses that are not online, she offers to create and host a web page, giving phone and fax contacts, stressing that travellers are looking to the Web "to get info and even buy merchandise."

The third category of Route 66 Web sites are the personal Web pages maintained by interested individuals. Some of these are diaries of road trips, and collections of personal photographs, others are 'gateway' sites offering links to the wealth of information on Route 66 that is on the Web. Some of these sites represent significant investments of time, at least, on the part of the site maintainer, and reflect a strong commitment to sharing information on the personal experience of a cultural heritage. While Route 66 has a special place in

American mythology, it is part of a global cultural heritage. Many of the personal Route 66 pages are international in origin. The Route 66 Photo Lounge records a Japanese tourist's pop-culture pilgrimage. Belgian Swa Frantzen's huge gateway site describes the Route both from Chicago to Los Angeles, and in reverse, "because many International visitors want to start from LA." Ma Route 66 is in French, but appears to contain trip descriptions and links to other Route 66 information.

Many of the personal sites feature a detailed description of an individuals journey along the Route. One of these road trip reports is xroad.diary, the traveller posting a description of the day's experiences each night to the Web. On Friday May 30th, the diary reads

> *"I slept very late this morning, but it took me until almost one to get yesterday's report written. It was close to eleven when I finally made it onto the road. ... Just up the road and south of Hydro is Lucille's General Store, one of the Famous Route 66 Stops. She's been living and working right there for fifty years, and if given a chance she'll tell you about every one of them. Twice. ... I passed through what I guess was Bridgeport. If it was, then I finally did see a ghost town. ... The Big 8 Motel in El Reno has "Amarillo's Finest" on its neon sign. This is not a mistake: its an addition made when the motel was used in the movie 'Rainman'."*

. Dr Voyager, not only describes his trip down "Highway 66, the route of legend and romance," he also provides advice on how to do the trip by bus or train, following the tracks of the old Santa Fe Super Chief. Jamie Jensen's Roadtrip USA, is an online version of a Moon Travel Handbook, and gives detailed information on the Route, state by state, including Freeway exit numbers, distances, attractions and mythology.

> *"One of the most demanding, desolate, and awesomely satisfying stretches of the old road climbs from I-40 along the Colorado River, beginning just east of the California border and rejoining the freeway at Kingman. ... Oatman looks like a Wild West stage set, but it's the real thing ... the Oatman Hotel was where Clark Gable and Carole Lombard spent their first night after getting married in Kingman in 1939."*

The Exmachina site is another roadtrip that has also been published in print form. Both book and web site are rich with photographs and snippets of history, as well as touring tips and personal anecdotes. The Web page is headed by a quote:

> *"Every land has its own special rhythm and unless the traveller takes the time to learn the rhythm he or she will remain an outsider there always - Juliette de Bairchi Levy."*

In a way, this is what travellers are attempting to do with Route 66 via the Web. Unable to spend sufficient time on the road absorbing the rhythm, they are hoping to soak up its special atmosphere through the shared experiences of other travellers, and to thereby maximise the authenticity of their own experience. They are using the Web as a source of information, in order to plan their travel experience, and they are looking to the Web to connect them with other travellers, both as a source of 'authentic' information and as a community with whom they can share experiences.

It is the forum or community that makes up the fourth type of Route 66 web site. A major example of this category is the Route 66 mailing list. Members can receive email from each other as posted, or as a daily digest, or they can read a weekly archive of messages on the Web site. As its site says, the list has become "the place" on the Internet for discussing anything and everything involving Historic Route 66. While members discuss the authenticity or otherwise of Route 66 memorabilia offered for sale elsewhere, and similar topics, the majority of the exchanges are concerned with travelling the Route, or visiting one or other destination along the Route. Typical exchanges asked for, or gave tourist information.

> *"I am planning to drive Route 66 < Chi - LA > in late summer or fall of 2000. I have read a lot about this trip and I have purchased 3 books to guide me: Route 66: The Illustrated Guidebook to the Mother Road (Moore) The Route 66 Travelers Guide and Roadside Companion (Snyder) A Guide Book to Highway 66 (Rittenhouse) My goal is to drive as much of the Old Route 66 as possible....does any of these offer the most information, or is there another book that I can use?"*

> *"Hi! Can you members give me the titles and authors of books dealing with different adventures of driving on Route 66? Have long dreamed of setting out in my motor home (with my two indoor-only cats) and following 66 wherever it still exists."*

> *"My family travelled to California via route 66. About the only remembrance I have is the Petrified Forest. We are headed that way this summer and to the Grand Canyon. I would love to hear other members favourite sites along that stretch of the route."*

> *"Spend a night at the Blue Swallow in Tucumcari - incredible place! (the owners of the motel, the Bakke's are on the list) Also, go to the abandoned Painted Desert Trading Post in AZ. A little hard to get to, but well worth the drive."*

> *"Boy, did you come to the right place! Before you know it, you will have your entire trip all planned! There are so many people on this one-list that have travelled the very roads you are soon to explore! They will be more places, people, and things suggested to you to "not miss" that you will have to plan many more trips just to see them all!! Ok, folks! Let's give them the "scoop" on what "not to miss"! Me first! My favourite Route 66 attraction is the Blue Whale in Catoosa, OK! It is on the east of Tulsa! You must make plans to stop there!!"*

> *"Sleep in a wigwam at the Wigwam Motel in Holbrook. The kids will love it."*

The information that tourists seem to be getting from the Web is not available anywhere else. While travel agencies and tour companies do promote Route 66 as one 'Discover America' option, they are less able to provide the wealth of detail that supports the mythology; the first hand experience that authenticates the pop-culture heritage of the Route; and the opportunity to share a cultural experience with others.

The other dimension that the Route 66 Web sites add to the heritage tourism experience is the opportunity to expand the tour into other aspects of life. Tourists return from their trip, and until the next vacation and beyond they can post their photographs on Web sites for others to admire; debate the merits of one location or attraction over another; follow the restoration, modernisation, or deterioration of a landmark; shop for collectibles and memorabilia; and advise travellers just setting out on where to find those out-of-the-way locations and honest-to-goodness events that will validate their pilgrimage.

2001 marks the 75th anniversary of the designation of Route 66, and coupled with the availability of Federal funds this has provided an impetus for the development of the Route as a major tourist destination. For example, the state of New Mexico announced that it "recognises the benefit of developing heritage tourism, which promotes local commitment to historic preservation and conservation of historic Route 66; and wishes to capitalise on the national celebration, the legend and the mythology by enhancing and marketing its Route 66 assets" (Legislature, State of New Mexico, 1999). This initial study suggests that the Internet is playing an important role in the development of Route 66 as a heritage tourism destination, by providing access to information that goes beyond facts to include social mythology, and by allowing the formation of a community where the cultural legacy represented by the Route can be explored and shared.

References

Congress of the United States of America (1999), *An Act to Preserve the Cultural Resources of the Route 66 Corridor* [H.R.66] 6/1/99.

Cyber Atlas (2000), Online Travel Market Continues Surge http://cyberatlas.internet.com/ [Feb 4].

Davis, F. (1979), *Yearning for Yesterday: A Sociology of Nostalgia,* New York, The Free Press.

Edwards, H. (1999), Traveller Logs on and Saves the Hassle, *The Sun-Herald,* November 28, p89.

Gartner Group (2000), Online Travel Market Expanding Rapidly, *Nua Internet Surveys,* http://www.nua.ie [Jan 7].

Graham, A. (1984), History and Nostalgia and the Criminality of Popular Culture, *Georgia Review* 38 (2), Summer pp.348-364.

Hewison, R. (1987), The Heritage Industry: Britain in a Climate of Decline, London, Methuen.

Jameson, F. (1989), Nostalgia for the Present, *South Atlantic Quarterly,* 88 (2): 517-537.

Jansen-Verbeke, M. (1996), Cultural Tourism in the 21st Century, *World Leisure and Recreation*, 38 (1): 6-11.

Kibby, M. (1998), Nostalgia for the Masculine: Onward to the Past in the Sports Films of the Eighties, *Canadian Review of Film Studies,* 7 (1): 16-28.

Legislature, State of New Mexico (1999), Requesting the Tourism Department to Work with the New Mexico Route 66 Association, Communities, Indian Nations, Tribes And Pueblos Along Historic Route 66 to Develop, Promote and Market New Mexico's Historic Route 66 in Preparation for the Upcoming Celebration of the Seventy-fifth Anniversary of Former United States Route 66. *NM Route 66 Association Newsletter*, Spring. http://www.rt66nm.org/NEWSLETT/99sprin3.html

McIntosh, A. J. and Prentice, R. C. (1999), Affirming Authenticity: Consuming Cultural Heritage, *Annals of Tourism Research,* 26 (3): 589-612.

Moscardo, G. (1996), Mindful Visitors, Heritage and Tourism, *Annals of Tourism Research*, 23 (2): 376-397.

Nuryanti, W. (1996), Heritage and Postmodern Tourism, *Annals of Tourism Research*, 23 (2): 249-260.

Reisinger, Y. (1994), Tourist-host Contact As a Part of Cultural Tourism, *World Leisure and Recreation,* 36 (2): 24-28.

Stokowski, P. A. (1992), Social Networks and Tourist Behaviour, *American Behavioural Scientist*, 36 (2): 212-222.

Trotter, R. (1999), Nostalgia and the Construction of an Australian Dreaming, *Journal of Australian Studies,* Dec, pp.19-25.

Urry, J. (1994), Cultural Change and Contemporary Tourism, *Leisure Studies*, 13, pp. 233-238.

Wallis, M. (1990), *Route 66: The Mother Road*, St Martin's Press, New York, NY.

Wearing, B. and Wearing, S. (1996), Refocusing the Tourist Experience: the Flaneur and the Choraster, *Leisure Studies*, 15, pp.229-243.

Web Sites

Dr Voyager http://drvoyager.com/route66.html

Exmachina http://route66.exmachina.net

Expedia http://www.expedia.com/

Frank Maloney's Route 66 Satellite Photos http://astro4.ast.vill.edu/66/satmig.htm

Fodors http://www.fodors.com/

Great Outdoor Recreation Pages http://www.gorp.com/

Lucille's General Store http://www.route66clicks.com/index.html

National Historic Route 66 Federation http://www.national66.com

Northern Arizona University http://jan.ucc.nua.edu/ ~ rse/route66.htm

Pitzer College http://www.pitzer.edu/Route_66/index.html

Preview Travel http://www.previewtravel.com/

Roadtrip USA http://www.moon.com/road_trip/us66/arizona.html

Rough Guides http://travel.roughguides.com/index.htm

Route 66 Gift Shop http://www.route66giftshop.com

Route 66 Mailing List http://members.tripod.com/ ~ greglaxton/66list.html

Route 66 Place http://www.pitzer.edu/Route_66/index.html

Swa Frantzen's Route 66 http://route66.netvision.be

Travelocity http://www.travelocity.com/

Virtual Tourist http://www.vtourist.com/

Xroad Diary http://www.thom.org/xroad/southwest/053097.html

Tourism pioneers and racing heroes: The influence of ski tourism and consumer culture on local life in the Tirolean Alps

Jacqueline McGibbon

Southern Cross University, Australia

Introduction

In recent years in the field of anthropology, there has been a growing interest in how local communities in Europe have been responding to and coping with the developments of mass tourism (e.g. Boissevain, 1996). This paper examines some of the new patterns of social organisation and new cultural identities and lifestyles generated in one European community in the context of international mass tourism. Specifically, the paper explores how mass tourism and the ski and leisure industries have become integral parts of local life and culture in the ski resort of St. Anton am Arlberg in Western Austria.

Ski tourism has a long history in the region and has influenced diverse aspects of local society including village composition, communal life, gender and familial relations, patterns of land use, modes of production and consumption, and regimes of labour. Today, most residents are dependent on ski tourism for employment and income. Further, most are consumers, as well as producers, of the facilities and products of the ski tourism industry, and leisure consumption has become a central aspect of local society, altering local activities, spending patterns and status hierarchies. Thus ski tourism now provides a framework for everyday life, at least for part of each year, with local identity often forged around the industry. In addition, ski tourism, in combination with other social developments, has incorporated this once remote and impoverished farming village into the ultra-modern worlds of global consumer culture, competitive sport, travel, advertising and fashion.

The changes stimulated by ski tourism are on-going. Over the years, ski tourism itself has changed (and continues to change) in form, and each form is associated with different practices and ideas and has generated different interactions between locals and tourists. As Boissevain notes "Host communities are often portrayed as passive victims of acculturation and the affluence and lifestyle of mass tourists" (1996, p.21). In the case of St. Anton however, members of the local community have responded creatively to the challenges and opportunities brought by tourism, actively pioneering and promoting ski tourism and generating new social forms.

The paper begins by tracing the history of ski tourism in the village, whereby some residents played instrumental roles in the development of the new sport of alpine skiing and St. Anton became one of the first alpine ski resorts. Then it examines the role and significance of ski tourism in contemporary local life, addressing how locals are socialised into ski culture, the central role of the ski school and ski instructor in the community, and the role ski tourism and ski racing play in local and national identities. Using the example of snowboarding, the paper demonstrates how a new transnational winter sport and the dynamics of consumer culture can become involved in local identity formation and inter-generational struggles. Finally, it describes how some local residents become embodied advertisements for the ski tourism industry, particularly in the figure of the ski racer. The commercialisation and professionalisation of ski racing however, means that the lives of ski racers are increasingly shaped by the demands of the global media and corporate sponsorship.

A history of ski tourism in St. Anton

In the past, most residents of St. Anton were mountain farmers who had to labour intensely to wrest a living from the hostile mountainous terrain. The extremely poor conditions for agriculture combined with population pressures meant that income from farming often had to be supplemented by waged labour and temporary migrations away from the home. Even children as young as six years old regularly travelled to Schwabia in Germany to find work on farms for the summer (the *Schwabenkinder*) (Spiss, 1993). It was against this backdrop of rural poverty and outward migration that in the mid-1800s tourism began to develop in the region.

Early guests were wealthy travellers and Alpinists, who came in the summer for weeks at a time to enjoy the spectacular landscapes and mountain air, and to climb the mountain peaks. The development of Alpinism marked a radical change in attitudes towards mountains among Europe's elite. In the seventeenth century, the Alps were predominantly perceived as terrible, treacherous and inhospitable environments. By the end of the eighteenth century however, they had been "discovered" and re-evaluated as aesthetically pleasing, restful and refreshing (Oelschlaeger, 1991).[1] Local residents quickly adapted to the needs of Alpinists, providing accommodation and transforming themselves into mountain guides.

Winter tourism began around the turn of the century with the development of modern alpine skiing. Forms of skiing, used for transportation and warfare, had existed since prehistoric times, at least in Nordic lands. Although there are sporadic mentions of skiing in the Alps dating back to 1689, it was not until the Norwegian, Fridtjof Nansen, wrote a book in 1890 about his journey across Greenland on snowshoes that skiing rapidly began to attract attention in Central Europe (Pfeifer, 1934). In the 1890s, a series of ski clubs were established (e.g. the Austrian Skiclub in 1892) and an array of books about skiing were published.

Skiing rapidly reached St. Anton and in 1901, a group of enthusiastic skiers, including the village's first hotelier and the local doctor, founded the Ski Club Arlberg (SCA) in order to promote the "noble pleasures" of skiing and ski racing. In 1903, the club held its first ski race, and by 1907, it had 155 members. The professionalisation of skiing followed rapidly and by 1910, six of the village's mountain guides were also ski guides (Thöni, 1990, p.33).

The shift from Nordic lands to the Alps, where slopes were steeper, required the development of new skiing techniques and more controllable skis. Several residents of St. Anton were involved in these developments. One such resident was Hannes Schneider. Born in 1890, Schneider taught himself to ski, developing his own method - a method that was to form the basis of the world-renowned Arlberg Technique.[2] Schneider became a successful ski racer and ski jumper, and at the age of 17 was hired as a full-time instructor by the village's first hotel.

World War One brought a temporary halt to tourism in St. Anton, with Schneider and other locals conscripted to train alpine divisions in the Austrian and German armies. The time between the wars is often described as the village's "Golden Era" of tourism, the time when St. Anton established its reputation as an international ski resort. The new medium of film was central in promoting both skiing and the village. Between 1920 and 1931, the renowned German director Arnold Fanck made nine movies in the region starring Schneider and featuring many other locals, culminating in 1931 with the acclaimed *Der weisse Rausch* (The White Rush), which also starred the controversial Leni Riefensthal.[3] These films were immensely popular and had an international impact. The premier of *Der weisse Rausch* was shown simultaneously in 180 cinemas across Germany, while a book with the same name as Fanck and Schneider's first film, *Wunder des Schneeschuhes* (The Miracle of the Snowshoes), sold 25,000 copies in German and was translated into English, French and Japanese (Thöni, 1990, pp.55-65).

St. Anton's reputation was further enhanced when Schneider established the Ski School Arlberg in 1922, the first of its kind in the world. Then in 1928, the village became the focus of an international sporting event, the Arlberg Kandahar ski race, and numerous successful ski racers emerged from the context of the Ski Club Arlberg. Schneider also promoted the region when he gave a series of lectures and demonstrations of skiing in Japan in 1930. Schneider received a royal reception and over 3,500 people attended his first lecture in Tokyo (Thöni,1990, p.72).

Early ski tourism remained an elite preserve, attracting mainly wealthy urban professionals and industrialists, and the discourses and practices associated with the new and fashionable sport of skiing, were intertwined with the discourses and practices of Alpinism and athleticism.[4] At this time, there were no devices for transporting skiers uphill and skiing involved challenging climbs, day long tours and the exploration of previously inaccessible mountain environments. In the course of the twentieth century however, skiing was industrialised, commercialised and incorporated into the realm of consumer culture. One factor in the commercialisation of skiing was the introduction of cable-cars. St. Anton's first cable-car was built in 1937, only the fifth of its kind in Austria. Another factor was the rising standards of living and rapid expansion of tourism in Europe in the post-World War Two era.

Skiing is now a highly commercialised, mass sport. A maze of rapid chair-lifts and cable-cars carry thousands of people around the mountains each hour, and a ski pass is required to access the clearly marked, often artificially prepared ski runs.[5] Large restaurant complexes have been constructed in the mountains and a mass of shops, bars, and other facilities have emerged to cater to the needs of ski consumers. Currently, each winter the village's 2,500 residents cater to some 130,000 guests and the village is transformed into a site of intense consumption organised around just a few commodities – skiing facilities, equipment and accessories, accommodation, entertainment, food and alcohol.

This brief history has outlined the transformation of St. Anton from farming village to ski resort and drawn attention to the active roles that residents like Hannes Schneider played in pioneering ski tourism and attracting guests to the village. It has also illustrated the shifting nature of ski tourism, which in the last 100 years changed from an exclusive sport requiring little specialised infrastructure, to a mass sport with an elaborate infrastructure extending far into the mountains. The next section turns to the contemporary situation in the village.

The influence of ski tourism on contemporary local life

As well as attracting tourists to the village, skiing is significant to many local residents. In part, this is because skiing is a major source of employment and income. Locals make a living by providing guests with accommodation, meals and entertainment during their ski holidays, by selling ski equipment and by teaching them to ski. But skiing is also an important individual, social and communal activity in the village and it can play a major role in the formation of local identity. In Austria, skiing has even become part of the national imaginary.

One way in which skiing has become part of local identity is through local engagement with consumer culture. In the modern world, the consumption of consumer goods, including the products of the sport, leisure and tourism industries, plays a central role in identity formation. Local residents (like tourists) use their strategies of consumption both to mark their belonging to particular social groups (such as generations, ethnic groups, class fractions and sub-cultures), and to distinguish themselves from others and shape their individual personas. Further, in the context of consumer culture, participating in sporting activities is also a type of consumption, a means of creating a lifestyle and a mechanism of individual and group expression. Here the work of Bourdieu (1984), who argues that people's choice and appropriation of symbolic goods and lifestyles are the processes by which they accumulate cultural capital and locate themselves in the social hierarchy, has been most influential.

The shift to consuming sport and leisure is part of a wider trend in Austria, not confined to tourist resorts. Austrian families now spend an average of one fifth of their budgets on the pursuit of leisure (excluding holidays) and since the end of the 80's the leisure industry has been the fastest growing branch of the Austrian economy (see Graber and Grubelnik, 1994). Nevertheless, tourism has undoubtedly promoted these changes in rural regions, as a comparison of villages with high levels of tourism to those with less tourism clearly indicates.

"Here, children are born wearing skis"

Villagers are drawn into the world of skiing at a young age. Most children get a pair of skis before they reach school age and are taught to ski by their parents. By the age of ten, most are good skiers who spend much of their free time in winter skiing and socialising with their friends on the mountains. Thus for many youths the ski slopes serve as a giant winter playground. An integral part of learning to ski is learning how to take part in races. Local ski clubs and ambitious parents alike seek out particularly talented children and encourage them to compete in the vast network of local, regional and national ski races. Schools also promote skiing, with over 200,000 children taking part in school ski courses in Austria annually (*Profil*, 6/2/94, p.60).

Skiing is further promoted in local life by village ski races. These are important community events. Villagers come together to compete in the races or to watch others compete and to socialise. The races bring together all age groups, with race categories ranging from 3 to 60 years. Both men and women take part in the races, although the number of female competitors drops dramatically after they reach adulthood. After the race, a celebration and an award ceremony is held in a local inn. The high point of the evening is the presentation of the outwardly spectacular (though inexpensive and somewhat kitsch) winners' trophies. Although the dominant process in the races is to rank villagers according to their skiing ability, rewarding the fastest among them, this process is partly counter-balanced by the sociality of the event, the presentation of multiple trophies and the oft repeated assertion that "*dabei ist alles*" (taking part is all that matters).

Currently, a large proportion of the adult population in St. Anton ski and purchase ski passes and equipment each winter. Many not only ski, but engage in a range of mountain activities, such as hiking, mountaineering and mountain biking. Indeed, some locals fashion themselves into experts in various sports and mountain activities, into veritable "mountain men", taking pleasure in these activities in their free time, mountaineering or skiing in other parts of the world during the off-seasons. Some engage in expensive equipment fetishes, purchasing the most modern equipment for a complex of mountain activities: including skis (downhill, cross-country and telemark skis), mountain bikes, trail bikes, climbing ropes, kayaks, paragliders and all the accompanying gadgets. I say "mountain *men*" here advisably, since it is particularly, though not exclusively, men who become mountain experts. Girls and young women engage in mountain activities too, but most reduce their participation as they get older and take on family commitments. The diverse range of mountain sports means that locals can participate in them in various ways – developing different interests and personas within the same broad symbolic field (for example, as ski racers, mountaineers, extreme skiers or rebel snowboarders – see below). Locals also use the facilities of the village's hospitality industry, such as bars, nightclubs and restaurants, and in the off-seasons they frequently become tourists and travellers to other destinations.

In many local homes and guest-houses, skiing regalia features prominently. Ski racing trophies are proudly displayed in interior public spaces, such as hallways, breakfast rooms and lounges. The homes of particularly keen skiers are often bedecked with literally hundreds of trophies, ranging up to half a metre in size. Other popular items of display are examples of early skiing equipment and framed photographs of local instructors alongside their prominent guests. Further, skiing and the mountains are popular topics of conversation among hosts as well as tourists – in particular, the snow and weather conditions, the state of the ski runs, the results of recent ski races, and accidents and avalanches.

The role skiing plays in local identity already has considerable historical depth. Some families have produced generations of ski racers and/or instructors, and have reputations as great "skiing families". People recount how their fathers and grandfathers were pioneers and experts in many facets of the ski industry: in the development of skiing techniques and equipment, in the promotion of ski tourism and in the organisation of bureaucratic structures for ski instructing and racing. In St. Anton, the local heroes who are honoured in the village museum and in narrations of local history are those who pioneered ski tourism, Olympic medallists and other successful ski racers.

Skiing for a living

While locals, like tourists, often ski as a hobby, for pleasure or exercise, many also become professional skiers, either as ski instructors or racers. Most professional skiers in the village work in the Ski School Arlberg. The ski school is one of the largest employers in the region, engaging some 280 instructors each winter, including about 200 locals. Tourists draw on the services of the ski school to teach them how to ski, to improve their technique and to guide them around the mountains.

The ski school is considered a central community organisation. Unlike many ski schools, the Ski School Arlberg is not a privately owned company, but a share company in which the local ski instructors are shareholders. At the end of the season, the school's annual profits are distributed among these shareholders, according to how much they worked and their level of qualifications. Uniformed instructors are considered village representatives, who are expected to meet certain standards of behaviour and attire and to work voluntarily in mountain rescues and at community events. Practically every family in the village has at least one member in the ski school in any season. Thus the ski school and ski slopes are also meeting places for locals, sites where information and gossip are exchanged, as well as sites for social control and arenas in which locals observe each others' behaviour.

Since 1927, ski instructor qualifications in Austria have been standardised by the state. The only way to become a qualified instructor is to attend a series of expensive, time-consuming and challenging state-run ski courses and exams. These courses are conducted in state-owned, boarding schools with students required to live in for two to six weeks at a time, and it costs around fifteen thousand US dollars to become a fully qualified instructor. Not only do these courses teach the predominantly male students how to instruct skiing, but they are sites of ideological instruction and male bonding. Women too can work as ski instructors, however there are few highly qualified female instructors, Further, since women are considered better with children, female instructors are persistently burdened with children's groups.

The profession of ski instructor is well accepted in the village and instructors play prominent roles in the local community, occupying senior positions in village administration. Qualified ski instructors are officially self-employed, a valued status in Tirolean society and instructing is an active and sociable job with relatively short hours and good pay. Instructors work largely independently, as experts and guides, touring the slopes with their classes, and there is considerable scope for instructors to develop particular teaching styles and increase their earnings with tips. Instructing carries considerable responsibility, since instructors must ensure the safety of their students, often in difficult and dangerous weather conditions, and it requires extensive knowledge of the mountains. Further, the ability to ski is a skill that gives locals the opportunity to travel overseas and work at ski resorts around the world.

A ski instructor is also expected to be an *Animateur*, animating guests to enjoy their holidays (see Pompl, 1983). This is not new: a prospectus from the 1930s stated that while St. Anton's instructors teach skiing during the week, on the weekends they "celebrate" with their guests (Sonnewend, 1986, p.120). Today, there are often considerable pressures on instructors to socialise with guests and consume alcohol with them into the evening. Although this is often fun for young instructors, it can wear thin when each week new guests arrive with similar demands. This aspect of ski instructing often leads to alcoholism and marital stresses. Finally, although ski instructors are frequently admired and envied by their guests for their skiing abilities and life-styles, they are still engaged in a service job, catering to wealthy elites on holiday.[6] While older locals often combine the professions of ski instructor and farmer, younger locals are more likely to travel and work overseas in the off-seasons.

Ski racing and the nation-state

As well as being significant to local communities like St. Anton, skiing is important to the Austrian nation-state. Indeed, in Austria skiing has been described as a "state prescribed program" (Christoph et al., 1994). As outlined above, the state promotes skiing in schools and controls ski instructor qualifications. In addition, it is also a major sponsor of boarding schools for ski racers, and of regional and national ski teams.

It is not surprising that the state promotes ski racing, since international competitive sport plays a major role in "structuring modern nations, cultures and societies" (Mangan, 1995, p.8). Sport is often "a mechanism of national solidarity, promoting a sense of identity, unity, status and esteem" (Ibid., p.1). In particular, sporting heroes are often regarded as symbols or representatives of national, regional and local communities. Holt & Mangan (1996) describe sporting heroes as "vessels" into which are poured "all manner of gender, class and patriotic expectation", and some argue that "emotional investment in national sporting heroes is the most significant source of national pride in the modern world" (pp.1-2). Competitive sport offers an international stage upon which nations compete for status. Yet while sport promotes "tribal identities" and competition between nations, it also links players and spectators across national boundaries in shared activities and events.

Historically, alpine skiing and its associated technologies played significant roles in the construction of an Austrian national mythology and identity, both in the First and Second Republics. After World War One, the mountains took on a special role in rebuilding the defeated German *Volk* (Tschofen, 1993; Lipp, 1993). Although they had lost the war, in the Austrian/German imaginary the mountain regiments remained undefeated. Thus pre-war associations of the Alps and alpine sports with the heroic were undiminished by the war. Rather, the heroic aspects of war and of skiing were compounded into a "heroism of the mountains", and after the war there was an explosion of interest in mountain sports. Further, drawing on the technological advances made during the war, an increasing number of cable-cars were built in the post-war era. For the nation, these cable-cars and other challenging technological constructions, such as mountain roads and dams, became symbols of modernity and progress, against the backdrop of a bitter recession.[7] A 1925 brochure promoting one of the first cable-cars in Austria commented that:

> *Already in a few months, the first cable-cars will float silently up to the heights, and will offer new proof abroad, that Austria is leaving no stone unturned to rise up again using its own power* (quoted in Tschofen, 1993, p.226).

Similarly, skiing played an important role in the post-World War Two re-birth of Austrian self worth and a sense of modern national identity (Christoph et al., 1994). After the defeat, suffering and shame of the war, victory at the 1956 winter Olympic games at Cortina, Italy (with 9 of the 18 Olympic medals in alpine disciplines going to Austrians) meant that one could again be proud to be Austrian.[8]

Today, skiing is one of the most popular sports in Austria and successful ski racers become national, as well as local heroes. The successes and failures of ski racers are given intimate coverage in the media, and Austrians have turned out in the thousands to show support for skiing heroes. In 1994, the funeral of the popular Austrian women's champion ski racer, Ulli Maier, who died during a downhill race in Germany, was televised live and a time of national mourning. More recently, Hermann Maier, the winner of several medals at the 1998 Winter Olympics has been hailed as the new "people's hero" and has captured the imagination of a huge national following. St. Anton has also produced numerous successful racers, including Karl Schranz, giving the village an important place in Austrian ski history.

Having outlined the central position of skiing in contemporary local life and in processes of local and national identity formation, I now turn to how on-going developments in consumer culture can become inter-twined with generational struggles in the village.

Snowboarding: on-going processes of identity formation in the context of consumer culture

While Bourdieu (1984) explores how people actively shape their identities and locate themselves in the social hierarchy with their strategies of consumption, he emphasises cultural reproduction in identity formation. Bourdieu focuses on how people perceive a constructed social order as natural or given, and how they shape their identities appropriate to this naturalised *habitus*. In contrast, other theorists focus on how new groups, such as class fractions and generations, employ new goods and distinctive strategies of consumption to differentiate themselves from other groups (Featherstone, 1987; Urry, 1988; Friedman, 1990; Munt, 1994). Featherstone for example, examines how struggles between generations often take the form of struggles over the relative evaluation of different patterns of consumption. While new groups, and especially new generations, often try to differentiate themselves from mainstream culture and the mass market, over time their alternative strategies of consumption generally become incorporated into consumer culture as a new market niche, with a range of products designed specifically to cater to their needs. The combination of these social struggles and the "market dynamic to sell new commodities leads to a constant search for new images, symbols, fashions and life-styles" (Featherstone, 1987, p.131). In the context of globalising cultures and markets, this generates particularly dense, open-ended, unstable symbolic fields, that not only draw their material from diverse sources, traditions and cultures, but which also alter or discard fashions with rapidity (Ibid., p.126).

The relatively new phenomenon of snowboarding offers a useful example of how a new form of sport and the dynamics of consumer culture can become factors in identity formation and generational struggles. Snowboarding originated in the late 1970s, when surfers in the US started to adapt their surfboards to winter conditions. Since the 1990s, snowboarding has been enthusiastically taken up in St. Anton by young locals and tourists alike (particularly teenagers). In the media, some articles estimate that around 80 percent of the under-fourteen year old winter sports market in Austria now prefer to snowboard than ski. And it is not difficult to understand why snowboarding appeals to young people, as it has been cleverly marketed as the "rebel" snow sport for today's youth. Snowboarding culture is a blend of surfing, skateboarding and skiing cultures, as well as of the aesthetisied US "street culture" as presented in popular music videos and sports/fashion advertisements alike (a good example being Nike). In the words of one devotee: "Snowboarders, we have a kind of attitude.... Everyone tries to be a kind of rebel, like skateboarders. I love it, we're like the outlaws of the slopes" (Parisi, 1992).

These various cultural influences are evident in the design and decoration of snowboarding equipment (clothing and boards), the organisation of competitive events, the Americanised jargon that has emerged around the sport, and the advertising images used to promote snowboarding. Snowboarding fashions include headscarves, oversized trousers and sweatshirts, and a combination of the dark colours and checks of US "street" clothes, and the primary colours and expensive fabrics of ski fashions. Although snowboarding fashions draw on images of "street" life, they are actually expensive, designer clothes, created for middle-class, high disposable incomes. Village snowboard competitions, which exclusively attract young people, blast out contemporary "grunge" rock bands (Pearl Jam, Nirvana, Sonic Youth), instead of the usual Tirolean style *Volksmusik* played at all other local events. The term snowboarding has no German translation, and a hybrid language surrounds the sport in German speaking lands, with terms such as *"Freestyle-Bewerb"* (free-style competition), *"Halfpipe-Weltmeister"* (half-pipe world champion). Snowboarding culture offers an alternative to skiing within the same context and broad symbolic field.

Initially, older generations and ski and tourism officials in Austria were wary of snowboarding and its sub-culture, so popular amongst the nation's youth – no doubt reinforcing its image as a rebel sport. Many places attempted to ban snowboarding from their ski slopes, seeing it as a threat to the established traditions of ski tourism. In the media, snowboarders were stereotyped as dangerous and anti-social youths, and as long-haired, drug-users, most likely to cause avalanches.[9] In the early 90s, officials in St. Anton were reluctant to provide special facilities for snowboarders. More recently however, some locals have recognised that snowboarding is an important commercial market and the preferred sport of what will be the next generation of winter tourists. Therefore, they have attempted to incorporate snowboarding into official structures and include it as part of the village's tourist-leisure offer. They have hired young snowboarders to work as snowboard instructors in the ski school, opened up snowboard shops and introduced a snowboard class in village races. As a result, what was once considered a rebel sport is rapidly becoming just another niche market in the broad palette of winter sports.

Competitive sport as spectacle: locals as embodied advertisements for ski tourism

Like most sports in the last few decades, competitive skiing has been professionalised and commercialised. Professional ski racers now compete for substantial prize money, lucrative advertising contracts and media fame, via a network of spectacular international competitions. In 1993, the successful racer Mark Giardelli secured advertising contracts alone worth $US 1.6 million (*Sportsmagazin,* 1994, 3). The professionalisation of ski racing has re-shaped the sport to create more marketable products. This has had major consequences for the lives of racers, who have become a form of embodied advertising for ski tourism and ski products.

Today, professional ski races are media events. They are sensationalised, mass-produced spectacles, which celebrate risk-taking, the "cult of winning", an "aggrandised masculinity" and "tribal" struggle (such as between regions or nations) (Alt, 1983, p.103). In Austria, ski races are also colourful events staged against a backdrop of beer tents, flowing alcohol, Tirolean music and television cameras, and drawing large crowds of fans and spectators. Although women too can become successful ski racers, it is men who represent the highest achievers in the sport, attracting the most media coverage and spectators and the largest prizes.

Many organisations, both state and private, recognise the advertising opportunities and economic benefits associated with these media events. Powerful players in the ski tourism industry acknowledge the importance of ski racers for glamorising and promoting the sport of skiing, by setting equipment fashions and goals in skiing ability. Ski equipment companies are major sponsors of individual ski racers, offering large contracts for successful skiers and sponsorship for rising skiers. Other companies and state bodies also recognise the value of ski racing to the Austrian tourism industry. In 1977 for example, five state bodies founded an organisation called *Skipool Tirol* to support young Tirolean ski racers. The Skipool encourages companies to invest in young racers, for the stated reason that "the sport of ski racing in Tirol is an advertisement for the state" (Annual Report, 1988). The Skipool now has over 300 sponsoring members including numerous ski schools, ski companies, cable-car companies, sports shops, travel agents, tourist offices and hotels, but also banks and insurance companies. Thus competitors resemble billboards, each prominently displaying a range of brand names on their clothing and accessories.

Ski resorts also consider ski races as promotional events, and given that they receive extensive media coverage, as a type of "free" advertising. Since inception, ski races have been viewed as promotional events in St. Anton, and much of the village's contemporary appeal stems from its renowned skiing heroes. Staging international events also helps ski resorts obtain government funding. Recently, St. Anton won the right to hold the World Skiing Championships in 2001, and has since obtained large sums of funding from the national and regional governments to improve and expand village infrastructure (the rail line, roads and village facilities).

Ironically, although ski racers are used to promote ski tourism using images of the powerful, skilled, fit, and healthy body, in ski racing, as in many other professional competitive sports, "the athletic ideal of fitness has become a sham" (Alt, 1983, p.104). In order to win a portion of the $US 3.2 million annual prize money on offer, ski racers must compete in the physically exhausting ski circuit with an intensity and seriousness reaching the ferocious. Ski racers have rationalised, rigorous, highly disciplined, training programs often conducted in special institutions (Staudinger, 1994). Their bodies and performances are carefully monitored and managed by a bevy of sport trainers, medical professionals, and national officials, to the extent that they are virtually "removed from effective control over [their] athletic labour" (Alt, 1983, p.103). As a result, a ski racer's:

> *injury potential has increased while his working life has decreased .... it is common knowledge that the average athlete is probably less physically healthy than a normal person his age, and considers himself lucky to finish his career without permanent physical and mental damage* (Alt, 1983, p.104).

Indeed, ski racing is a particularly dangerous sport. Annually, twenty percent of the Austrian ski team have to stop or pause from skiing because of injuries, including broken bones, ripped tendons and ligaments, and internal bleeding. Damage can be permanent, with only two members of the Austrian women's ski team still possessing healthy knees (*Profil*, 7/2/94). There is also the occasional death: two Austrian skiers have died racing since 1990 (Gernot Reinstadler in 1991 at Wängen and Ulli Maier in 1994 at Garmisch). To quote one article, "world cup leaders are mostly sport cripples before they reach the top" (Christoph et al., 1994, Ortlieb, 1994).

Competition is now so intense that to become professional ski racers, children must start competing in races by the age of 9 to 12 years old. Once involved in racing, skiing monopolises their time and injuries damage their health, particularly since they are still growing and their bones are not yet fully formed. Ski racing is also costly for the family of the budding skier (coaches, equipment, ski schools, transportation to races). Given that young racers spend four to five hours a day training on the slopes, most leave ski high schools not only as unsuccessful racers with physical injuries (since as in any sport only a small minority are successful), but also with poor educations, although some find employment as coaches or in the ski bureaucracy. Local newspapers place considerable pressure on young skiing talent to do well, not just for themselves, but as representatives of their regions.

The demands of the media and the consumers of ski racing force competitors to take further risks. Given that the more dangerous and spectacular races draw the largest crowds of spectators and television viewers, some courses have been made *more* difficult and dangerous in recent years. Unlike in the past when it was relatively easy to cancel or re-schedule a race if weather conditions rendered racing dangerous, today there are so many vested interests and expenses involved in world cup ski races (the media, multi-million dollar sponsors), that organisers are reluctant to cancel them and incur financial losses. Occasionally, competitors have united to complain about race track or weather conditions. For the most part however, solidarity among racers is undermined by their status as competitors and rivals. Some report having been threatened with removal from the highly competitive national teams if they refuse to ski. Ulli Maier for example, reportedly complained about the condition of the track on which she was killed shortly before the race began. To sum up, the international ski racing circuit, which taps into the dreams of success of local youths, via a network of regional and national ski clubs, is run according to the needs of the global media, big business and corporate sponsorship. These youths, some of whom also achieve wealth and fame, become embodied advertisements for ski tourism, often at the cost of their own health.

Conclusion

Two decades ago, Lanfant suggested that one task of tourism research should be to examine the "new cultural identities formed under the pressure of international tourism", or to examine how tourism "embodies itself in [the] actual host environments" (1980). Yet even today, this subject has received only limited attention from tourism researchers. This paper focused on some of the new social and cultural forms that have emerged in the village of St. Anton in the Tirolean Alps, through villagers' engagement with ski tourism and consumer culture. In St. Anton, international ski tourism has become an integral aspect of contemporary local society. Many of the activities and events associated with ski tourism have become a part of local culture and inform processes of local identity formation. Increasingly within the village, producers in the ski and tourism industries are also consumers of the facilities and products of these industries. Villagers have enthusiastically taken up skiing and other sports, as well as the consumption of leisure and luxury goods (e.g. designer clothes, sports equipment, holidays) originally associated with tourists. Hosts, as well as guests, now work within the contours of consumer culture, and engage in the choice and appropriation of consumer goods and cultural capitol to fashion their lifestyles and identities, to mark their belonging to particular social groups, and to locate themselves in the social hierarchy.

Although tourism is only one of the factors influencing changing lifestyles in Austria, it has been particularly influential in rural farming villages, which over the course of the last century have become dependent on ski tourism. Previously rural regions were considered backward and were often neglected by urban cores and nation-states. Tourism however, has rendered them desirable sites for experiencing nature, local colour, recuperation, sport and leisure. Thus tourism has brought large flows of people into the village, particularly people from urban centres in Europe, with all their different beliefs, values, and ways of behaving, and it has also re-directed core wealth to the region.

But local residents have not simply been the passive recipients of new cultural forms invented elsewhere. Rather, they have been actively involved in shaping these new cultural forms. Yet much of the tourist literature continues to assign the motor of change in local societies to tourists and tourism industries, denying the important role played by local actors in pioneering, promoting, and managing, but also in challenging and resisting, tourism development. For example, the expression often used to describe the influence of tourists on host societies – "the demonstration effect" – suggests the passive uptake or simple copying of tourist behaviour by their hosts. Villagers however, do not participate equally in shaping tourism and the new cultural forms in their communities, as my references to particular individuals, different generations, and gendered subjects indicates.

This paper is based on research undertaken by the author for her doctoral thesis in anthropology, completed in 1998 for Macquarie University, Sydney, Australia. A more detailed treatment of the subject can be found in her book entitled *The Business of Alpine*

Tourism in a Globalising World: An Anthropological Study of International Ski Tourism in the Village of St. Anton am Arlberg in the Tirolean Alps (1999).

Endnotes

1. Several writers argue that it only became possible for the upper and middle classes to view wild nature as an aesthetic object when they were no longer dependent on agricultural production and natural processes for survival (see Bätzing, 1991, p.138). The romanticisation of the mountains was a phenomenon of educated urban classes, not of mountain farmers trying to wrest a living from the Alps, who in contrast valued land according to its fertility. In the movie *Der Berg Ruft* (1937) for example, about the first ascent of the Matterhorn, villagers regard the early mountaineers and the few local enthusiasts, and their desire to climb mountains, as somewhat mad. One villager asks the local mountain guide what he is looking for up there where there is only stone, ice and snow and "where nothing grows", while the valley is green, beautiful and safe. Gradually, rural attitudes have changed, and today many villagers also romanticise mountains as aesthetic objects. For a more detailed treatment of this subject see McGibbon, 1999, pp.76-9.

2. Schneider was born in the nearby village of Stuben, but he settled in St. Anton and in 1928 he received honorary villager status (*Ehrenbürger*). Schneider did not invent alpine skiing single handedly. Rather as various people in Central Europe wrestled with similar problems induced by the steep alpine slopes, they simultaneously devised parallel solutions. Other important names in the history of alpine skiing are Matthais Zdarsky (Upper Austria), Captain Bilgeri and Viktor Sohm (Vorarlberg) and Eduard Capiti (Switzerland).

3. Riefensthal was a popular ballet dancer, actress, and film director who became associated with the National Socialist regime when she directed a series of films (1933-1936) for Hitler and the Nazi Party. Since the war, Riefensthal has lived in the US and worked as a photographer and film maker, though largely ostracised by the artistic community (see Nowotny, 1981; Sontag, 1983, pp.73-105; Riefensthal, 1987).

4. The discourses and practices of Alpinism and skiing shared a romanticisation of "wild nature" and a pioneering spirit, with the mountains conceptualised as realm of struggle between man (specifically men) and nature. In addition, Alpinism and skiing shared a focus on athleticism. The phenomenon of athleticism emerged in Britain in the second half of the nineteenth century (Hargreaves, 1987; Robbins, 1987). Athleticism emphasised the necessity of amateur competitive sport, particularly for men, for the cultivation of health, fitness and physical skills, and for the cultivation of mental health and moral qualities, such as leadership skills, sportsmanship, courage and self-discipline. At this time, athleticism played a central role in the formation of dominant classes and was also deployed by these classes in sport and leisure programs designed to "improve" subordinate classes in Britain, the US and on the Continent and on both the right and left of the political spectrum. In the early years of skiing, the attire of male tourists, competitors and local instructors echoed the dress of the English upper classes most associated with athleticism: that is, plus-fours, neck ties, caps and patterned sweaters, complete with a pipe.

5. A ski pass purchased in St. Anton provides access to some 84 transportation devices, 260 kilometres of prepared runs and 180 kilometres of unprepared runs. In order to create suitable ski runs, cable-car companies have cut down trees and substantially re-arranged parts of the mountains (e.g. blasting rocky outcrops). Each night these runs are "groomed' by heavy vehicles to make skiing easier the next day, and when possible, artificial snow is manufactured to cover any bare patches.

6. Local residents are often envied and admired by their wealthy, well-educated, urban guests for their superior skiing skills and knowledge of the mountains. Peter Ritchie, the chairman of McDonalds Australia and a director of Channel Seven, Westpac and Tabcorp, was quoted in answer to the question of "What job do you most covet in the world?" as saying "Heli-skiing guide in Canada" (Sydney Morning Herald, 9/9/95). Ski instructors describe how their uniforms (a sign they are accomplished skiers) make people behave differently towards them: they find they are constantly being given seats and bought drinks in bars, picked up whenever they hitchhike, and paid more sexual attentions by guests.

7. This can be compared to the building of the Harbour Bridge in Sydney during the depression years.

8. One could draw a parallel here with South Africa's win of the Rugby Union World Cup in June 1995, which after the shame of apartheid and years of international sanctions, gave a boost to national pride.

9. These stereotypes were reinforced by events at the 1998 Winter Olympics in Japan when a gold medallist in a snowboarding discipline tested positive to cannabis. After initially being stripped of his gold medal, the snowboarder in question successfully appealed to have it restored, arguing firstly that he had not used cannabis, but had inhaled it through passive smoking at a party held in his honour, and secondly, that cannabis is not a performance enhancing drug. The Olympic officials decision to restore the medal is interesting in that cannabis is still considered an illegal drug.

References

Alt, J. (1983), Sport and Cultural Reification: From Ritual to Mass Consumption, *Theory, Culture and Society*, 1 (3): 93-107.

Bätzing, W. (1991), *Die Alpen: Entstehung und Gefärdung einer europäischen Kulturlandshaft*, C. H. Beck, München.

Boissevain, J. (Editor) (1996), *Coping With Tourists: European Reactions to Mass Tourism*, Berghahn, Providence and Oxford.

Bourdieu, P. (1984), *Distinction: A Social Critique of the Judgement of Taste*, Trans. Richard Nice, Harvard University Press, Cambridge.

Christoph, H., Huber, M., and Tanzer, O. (1994), Hölle Ski Himmel: Dem Tod von Ulli Maier folgten Trauer und Tränen, *Profil*, 6, 7/2/94, pp. 60-4.

Featherstone, M. (1987), Leisure, symbolic power and the life course, in Horne, J., Jary, D. and Tomlinson, A. (Editors), *Sport, Leisure and Social Relations*, Routledge and Kegan Paul, London, pp. 113-138.

Friedman, J. (1990), Being in the World: Globalization and Localization, in Featherstone, M. (Editor), *Global Culture: Nationalism, Globalisation and Modernity*, Sage, London, pp. 311-328.

Graber, R. and Grubelnik, K. (1994), Die Verkaufte Freizeit, *Profil*, 28, 11/7/94, pp. 40-45.

Hargreaves, J. (1987), The body, sport and power relations, in Horne, J., Jary, D. and Tomlinson, A. (Editors), *Sport, Leisure and Social Relations*, Routledge and Kegan Paul, London, pp. 139-159.

Holt, R. and Mangan, J. A. (1996), Prologue: Heroes of a European Past, and, Epilogue: Heroes for a European Future, *The International Journal of the History of Sport*, 13 (1): 1-13, 169-175.

Lanfant, M. (1980), Introduction: Tourism in the Process of Internationalisation, *International Social Science Journal*, 32 (1): 14-43.

Lipp, W. (1993), Alpenregion und Fremdenverkehr. Zur Geschichte und Soziologie kultureller Begegnung in Europa, besonders am Beispiel des Salzkammerguts, *Zeitschrift für Volkskunde*, 89, pp. 49-62.

Mangan, J. A. (1995), Introduction, *The International Journal of the History of Sport*, 12 (2): 1-9.

McGibbon, J. (1999), *The Business of Alpine Tourism in a Globalising World: An Anthropological Study of International Ski Tourism in the Village of St. Anton am Arlberg in the Tirolean Alps*, Vetterling Druck, Rosenheim.

Munt, I. (1994), The 'Other' Postmodern Tourism: Culture, Travel and the New Middle Classes, *Theory, Culture and Society*, 11, pp. 101-23.

Nowotny, P. (1981), *Leni Riefensthals 'Triumph des Willens' zur Kritik dokumentarischer Filmarbeit im NS-Faschismus*, Arbeitshefte zur Medientheorie und Medienpraxis, Band 3, Dortmund.

Oelschlaeger, M. (1991), *The Idea of Wilderness: From Prehistory to the Age of Ecology*, Yale University Press, New Haven and London.

Ortlieb, P. (1994), Die Abfahrt lebt von den Stürzen, *Profil*, 6, 7/2/94, pp. 64-6.

Parisi, M. (1992), Rebels of the Slopes: A Snowboarder's Attitude, *Insider*, 9 (3): 9.

Pfeifer, E. (1934), *Hannes Schneiders hohe Schule des Skilaufens, St. Anton am Arlberg*, Alpensportverlag, Innsbruck.

Pompl, W. (1983), The Concept of Animation: Aspects of Tourist Services, *Tourism Management*, 4, pp. 3-11.

Riefensthal, L. (1987), *Memoiren*, Albrecht Knaus, München.

Robbins, D. (1987), Sport, Hegemony and the Middle Class: the Victorian Mountaineers, *Theory, Culture and Society*, 4, Sage, London, pp. 579-601.

Sonnewend, T. (1986), *Das Tiroler Volksbild in Plakaten und Prospekten des 20 Jahrhunderts*, Doktor Dissertation, Universität von Innsbruck.

Sontag, S. (1983), Fascinating Fascism, *Under the Sign of Saturn*, Writers and Readers Publishing Cooperative, pp. 73-105.

Spiss, R. (1993*), Saisonwanderer, Schwabenkinder, und Landfahrer: die 'gute alte Zeit' im Stanzertal*, Universitätsverlag Wagner, Innsbruck.

Staudinger, K. (1994), Stams - ein Zentrum des alpinen Skirennsports, *Austria Ski*, 3, p. 8.

Thöni, H. (1990), *Hannes Schneider: zum 100. Geburtstag des Skipioniers und Begründers der Arlberg-Technik*, Verlaganstalt Tyrolia, Innsbruck.

Tschofen, B. (1993), Aufstiege - Auswege. Skizzen zu einer Symbolgeschichte des Berges im 20. Jahrhundert, *Zeitschrift für Volkskunde*, 89, pp. 213-231.

Urry, J. (1988), Cultural Change and Contemporary Holiday Making, Theory, Culture and Society, 5, pp. 35-55.

Family business: Commercial hospitality in the domestic realm in an international ski resort in the Tirolean Alps

Jacqueline McGibbon

Southern Cross University, Australia

Introduction

In the tourism dependent ski resort of St. Anton am Arlberg in the Tirolean Alps in western Austria, tourism businesses (hotels and pensions) are typically small to medium-sized family enterprises located in the home and reliant on familial as well as seasonal labour. Generally, these businesses are run by the woman of the household, while men find employment beyond the home. In rural Tirol, commercial hospitality or the accommodation and care of tourists has largely been incorporated into a woman's "traditional" domain of responsibility: that is, into the domestic realm as an extension of her roles as wife and mother. Within the region, the tourism boom and the industry's decentralised structure have intersected with traditional ideologies of gender and the household to create a situation whereby the "private" domestic sphere has become substantially harnessed into direct commercial production, with complex and often contradictory consequences for differently placed gendered subjects and families.

This paper examines the gendered division of labour in these family businesses, as well as women's participation in other spheres of local life. In so doing, it explores how tourism has influenced gender and familial relations in one particular local context. In addition, the paper offers another perspective on the theoretical dichotomies and conceptual categories of public/private, employment/housework and work/leisure, concepts that have played a prominent role in debates about gender and the family in recent decades.

Theoretical concerns: gender relations, the family and tourism

An influential line of research in family theory has argued that the pressures of modernisation and industrialisation have re-shaped the "traditional" extended family by promoting the smaller nuclear family, by removing productive tasks from the realm of the household, and by differentiating between "a private sphere of interpersonal closeness, and a public sphere of employment and state power" (Cheal, 1991, p.82; see also Parsons, 1951, 1955). Theories about the public/private divide have also been influential in understanding gender inequality. In the 1970s for example, Rosaldo argued that in most societies women are primarily associated with the domestic sphere, engaged in domestic reproduction and consumption, and responsible for the home, family and children, while men are primarily involved in the public spheres of external employment, social institutions and political hierarchies (1974, pp.23ff.). Further, she argued that this division of responsibilities partly explains what she saw as women's cross-cultural inferior status, economic dependence, and lack of formal political power. Since women's time is monopolised by reproductive tasks and domestic life, their access to wealth and power structures is limited, and since many cultures accord more importance and value to male, rather than female, activities and roles, women can achieve little status or recognition in the public realm (Ibid., p.19).

More recent research has shown that both evolutionary models, which view the extended family as the precursor of the contemporary nuclear family, and economic deterministic models, which pair the nuclear family with industrialisation and capitalist production, have to be re-thought, and the diversity of actual lived familial and household forms throughout different historical periods and forms of production recognised. Not only is it the case that "in some places nuclear family living in fact preceded industrialisation" (Cheal, 1991, p.86; also Laslett, 1972), but also the extended family can "fit" with commercial, profit-motivated production, as the family businesses in St. Anton demonstrate. Similarly, the limitations of the public/private dichotomy have received substantial critical attention. Critics argue that the degree of separation generated by the public/private divide has been over-estimated and overlooks the "multitude of overlapping and interdependent contexts for social interactions" shared by men and women (Cheal, 1991, pp.111ff.). Indeed, often the private family is more of a cultural ideal than a lived reality, since not only are the public and private intertwined in complex ways, but also the boundaries of the private family are breached by such things as the state and mass media (Ibid., pp.84, 106-112).[1]

Despite the recognition at the theoretical level of the diversity of familial forms and the limitations of the public/private dichotomy, studies of contemporary European family life often pay little attention to families engaged in domestic production. Boh et al. for example, in a study of fourteen eastern and western European societies, focus specifically on the "transfer of productive tasks from families to enterprise" and on the increasing "division of functions between the family and work" (1989, pp.2,41). Similarly, the Austrian literature has given little attention to commercial production in the domestic realm, despite the centrality of family businesses in the Austrian tourism industry and the widespread significance of tourism in Austria more generally.[2] The influential family historian Michael Mitterauer comments that agriculture is the last sector of modern European society that has retained the unity between the family and economic production, the home and the work place, once so common in pre-industrial times (1992, p.32). I argue however, that tourism is another sector of modern society where the family, the home and economic production often substantially overlap.[3]

The concepts of public and private remain useful tools for thinking about gender and the family in specific locations. In the context of Tirolean tourist resorts however, where the "private" domestic sphere (the home) is simultaneously a public sphere (a hotel or guest-house), and where women engage in substantial commercial production in the home alongside their tasks of reproduction and consumption, these concepts are inadequate when used in isolation. Family tourism businesses offer a fascinating case where the household continues to be a major site of production and where the boundaries between the public and private, employment and housework, and work and leisure, are particularly unclear - and particularly for women.

St. Anton: from mountain farming to international ski tourism

Although St. Anton is a small village nestled in the Alps at an altitude of 1,300 metres and with less than 2,500 residents, it is also a thriving international tourist resort, attracting over 160,000 guests and almost a million overnight stays a year. Tourism in the village dates back to the mid-1800s, when wealthy travellers and early Alpinists began to visit the region in the summer months to enjoy the mountain landscapes and benefit from the reputed health giving properties of mountain air. Winter tourism began around the turn of the century with the emergence of Alpine skiing. With the explosive expansion of tourism in Europe in the post-war period, the village became a site of mass tourism, drawn largely from urban centres in north-western Europe, and it now has an elaborate infrastructure of accommodation, sport, and entertainment facilities that extends into the mountains.

Over eighty percent of the village's overnight stays are recorded in the winter months, with tourists coming to St. Anton to participate in winter sports and in the flourishing night life. The summer season is shorter and quieter, with guests mainly attracted for the purposes of recuperation, hiking and enjoying the natural scenery. The complex flows of people, capital, ideas and images associated with tourism have re-fashioned multiple aspects of local life, including regimes of land use, levels of wealth, and the size and composition of the village. The economic opportunities offered by the industry have attracted a range of migrants, including many young women, who married local men and found employment in family businesses.

Prior to the development of tourism, residents were mostly mountain farmers and the *Bauernhof* or family farm was the basic unit of production, consumption and reproduction, proudly handed down through the generations, and run according to a gendered division of labour. While the farmer was responsible for the farm and represented the household in communal politics, the farmer's wife was responsible for the three K's *Kinder, Kuche und Kirche* (children, kitchen and church), although she also assisted with the farm (with the harvest, planting, weeding and care of small animals). The *Bauernhof*, which accommodated and drew on the labour of the extended family, including grandparents, dependent children and unmarried siblings, aimed for self-sufficiency. The extremely poor conditions for agriculture however, combined with population pressures caused by high birth rates and the practice of partible inheritance, meant the income of the family farm frequently had to be supplemented by waged labour and temporary migrations away from home.

When tourism began in the region, many women, seeing an opportunity to increase the household income, rented out a couple of rooms to guests. Since women were considered responsible for the domestic sphere the additional work of accommodating and caring for tourists was treated as an extension of their existing duties. Guests were incorporated into daily family life and the money earned from renting rooms was absorbed into the household budget, which women generally controlled (Preglau et al., 1985, p.15). Although men often became mountain guides or ski instructors, they rarely catered to the guests staying in their homes. In an account of his childhood spent in the village of Bad Ischgl, Wolfgang Reiter recalls how his grandfather would have nothing to do with renting rooms as it was considered *Frauen Sache* (women's business) (1984). In 1906, a travel writer commented that in Tirol:

> *...the landlady almost always plays the main role. Often a man is nowhere to be seen; he is more of an assistant, helping out with masculine tasks, he hammers in nails, looks after the luggage, gives out directions, keeps the building in order, produces foodstuffs and looks after the cows. But the pension is almost exclusively the domain of the woman* (quoted in Köfler and Forcher, 1986, p.100).

Today, the family hotel or pension has replaced the family farm as the central unit of production and consumption.[4] These businesses have been built upon the ideological foundations of the *Bauernhof*. The family hotel is also expected to accommodate and provide for the extended family, and is usually a large, solid, expensive construction designed to be passed down through the generations. Although most families no longer have a couple of guest-rooms, but rather substantial businesses with between 10 and 80 beds, these businesses retain a gendered division of labour. The accommodation and care of tourists continues to be primarily the responsibility of women, alongside their responsibility for the household and family. With the exception of families that own large, five- and four-star hotels, employing both the man and woman of the household, the income of home-based businesses is usually supplemented by men, who work beyond the home in a range of professions and trades (e.g., as ski instructors or public servants), or in another family business (e.g. a sports shop or taxi company). While men may help in the home-based business or with the care of children, they rarely take primary responsibility for them. Family businesses continue to draw on the unpaid and paid labour of other family members, such as grandparents, school children and students who "help out", and adult offspring and other relatives who work for a wage.

There are a number of ways that this gendered division of labour is promoted in Austrian society. Dominant ideologies present these gender roles as the appropriate behaviour for gendered subjects, particularly in rural regions. It is widely accepted that women will want to stay home to raise their children and care for their family, just as it is accepted that men will want to pursue a career and other activities in the public sphere. The policies and payments of the Austrian State also encourage women to return to the domestic sphere when they have children. Regardless of their income, women are entitled to two years of child support (*Karenzgeld*) after the birth of each child, and labour laws require that a woman's position be held open for her, should she decide to return to work after the period of a year.

A gendered division of labour: different rhythms of life

The well-established, gendered division of labour in local tourism businesses generates quite different rhythms of life for women and men. Before describing these different rhythms, it is important to note that gender categories are not uniformly experienced by "men" and "women". Rather, they are cross-cut by other social divisions and identities, such as class, ethnicity and generation. In St. Anton, the exact tenor of both men's *and* women's lives depends on a range of factors including the size and composition of the family, the origin of family members, the type and size of the family business, the wealth of the family and extent of its debts, and the specific relationship between various family members (e.g. between husband and wife).

During the winter season, women running hotels or pensions have intense regimes of work centred on the home - homes that are simultaneously public domains and sites of commercial enterprise. Within these private/public domains, women's multiple tasks of running a business, catering to guests, doing housework and raising children are fully intertwined. Typically, women are the first members of the household to rise in the morning and the last to bed. Their working day begins around six when they fetch fresh bread and prepare breakfast for their family, guests and staff. As they get their children ready for school, they simultaneously serve the guests breakfast and perform the important work of *Gästebetreuung*, or chatting with guests and answering their questions. Once guests and family members have gone out for the day, women either do the housework associated with the family and the business, such as cleaning rooms, washing, ironing, mending and shopping, or they supervise their staff in these tasks. Since lunch is the main meal of the day, with school children and husbands returning home to eat, women also prepare the mid-day meal. After lunch they do any paperwork associated with the business, as well as supervising their children with homework and at play. From mid-afternoon into the evening, they greet guests returning after a day's activities, catering to their needs, and in the meantime, serve the family supper.

In small guest-houses, women often work excessively long hours to reduce the cost of personnel: for example, working the so-called *Leerlaufzeiten* (empty runs of time) or times when there is little to do but answer the telephone. Larger hotels with restaurants or bars have different demands. Although hotels employ more staff, women running them often help in the restaurant or bar late into the night, only to rise at six again the next day. These work routines run seven days a week for the duration of the season, which lasts between 100 and 120 days.

During the winter season, many women become tied to the family business and experience both a "lack of time" and little clearly delineated "free time". Often women do not eat meals with their families, but rather cook for and serve other family members, while still attending to guests and other tasks. Women describe how they run on a deficit of sleep in the winter months and only manage to snatch time for personal and social activities, between their various tasks and responsibilities. Given their busy schedules, arranging to meet these women was difficult, and when we met, our discussions were usually repeatedly interrupted as they were intermittently called away to answer the telephone, speak with a guest, or respond to the inquiries of children or staff. Women's lack of leisure time is striking in a village that predominantly caters to the leisure needs of others.

The dual roles of mother and hotel manager often compete for time and have quite contradictory demands. In the words of one woman: "Children need time, but so do guests. At eight o'clock in the morning when the guest wants breakfast, I can't explain to him that I need to find my son's socks". Running a business at home is particularly stressful when children are young, which often coincides with when couples are building up their business.

The constant presence of tourists in the home can also disrupt family life. During the season families have little private space. In small pensions, the traditional family living space - the *Stube* - becomes part of the guests' living space, and family life is displaced to the kitchen. Although a pension or hotel is usually sub-divided into public and private areas, tourists often fail to respect "Private" signs and barge into the little private space a family might have. Given that tourism businesses are always open, it is difficult for the family to spend time together: to arrange shared meals, days out, or annual celebrations like birthdays or Christmas. When the season begins, family routines can change drastically. Children may have to be quiet around guests, modify their behaviour or spend long periods of time in the care a nanny, and some have to vacate their bedrooms for guests, moving into less attractive rooms in the basement.

Mothers frequently express concern about the effects of having tourists in the home on their children. Children are surrounded by tourists engaging in the consumption of leisure, which often involves the consumption of alcohol. Tourists appear free from the intense routines of labour that constrain their parents, concentrating instead on pleasurable activities and spending money. They also appear to have a higher status than locals: they get the best rooms and while children have to be well-behaved in front of them, tourists are frequently badly behaved (drunk, rude, loud all night) without censure. Although mothers often try to impress upon their children that being a tourist is an exceptional status, children learn that tourist behaviour is tolerated because they are paying guests, and come to identify money as a source of freedom (see Burgmann, 1982, pp.126,135).

The new regimes of labour and patterns of spatial organisation accompanying tourism tend to atomise women in their home businesses. One woman recounted how:

> *Before, when the children were small, we always sat in the sun in the afternoons, and the children played together, and we did our knitting ... But that has totally gone now ... now everyone has to do their own work and it's always getting narrower here and the houses bigger ... Now in winter we sometimes don't see our neighbours for weeks because everyone is in their own home and has to wait for the telephone.*

But despite their busy, home-based routines, women are not completely isolated from society. The telephone becomes an important tool of communication between women during the season. Women also meet briefly and chat in the supermarket, outside the school and in the doctor's waiting room. Many hear village gossip through their husbands and older children, and women who are religious meet at church. Women in harmonious extended families are more able to organise time away from the business, drawing on the assistance of their mothers, mothers-in-law, and sisters. The many women who married into the village however, often have limited support networks of relatives and friends to draw on for assistance.

Men also have busy routines during the winter. Ski instructors for example, work six days a week (Sunday to Friday) from nine to four, often socialising and drinking with their ski groups into the evening. On Saturdays, or "change-over-day" when guests traditionally leave and arrive, many men assist at home, typically concentrating on "outside" tasks, such as the care of buildings, snow shovelling, garbage disposal, recycling and carrying heavy loads.

Nevertheless, men tend to have more varied and differentiated work, social and leisure routines with distinct working hours and "free time". Although they live in a hotel or guest-house, they are rarely confined to it on a daily basis. Rather, they move between the home, place of employment, and various public spheres, such as political meetings, voluntary associations and the local *Gasthof* (inn). Further, men do not allow their free time at home to be eroded by guests or routine housework, as the following description by one woman of what her husband does in the family guest-house illustrates:

> *My husband does not work at all in the house. He is actually an electrician and sometimes he should repair something, but mostly I have to get a tradesman in. He regularly does the garden ... and in winter he shovels the snow. I don't have to say anything about that. He does it in an orderly fashion. But in the house, nothing, unfortunately. He does nothing for the guests. Mostly he doesn't even answer the door or the telephone.*

Men sometimes disassociate themselves from the daily business of the guest-house to the extent they know little about it: unsure of the cost of rooms, if rooms are occupied, or how to operate the telephone switchboard. Some men want little to do with the guests staying in their homes, although most work with tourists beyond the home. Men who work alongside their wives in large hotels are often responsible for the office and more visible socialising with guests, while women deal with the guests, staff and running of the hotel on a routine basis. According to one local: "Even in big hotels the men are the ones who socialise and sit with the guests and the women are the ones who really do the work".

Men and women's starkly different routines can sometimes come between them, and the atmosphere of the ski resort can place additional strains on marriages. A ski holiday is marketed with glamour and sexuality, particularly through the figure of the ski instructor. When tourists visit St. Anton, they break from "normal" routines and may have dreams and fantasies of romance. While husbands are engaged in the "glamorous" job of ski instructing, with all its sexual tensions, intensified by alcohol, wives routinely work long hours each day in the home business, cleaning, cooking, and catering to the needs of others. As one villager observed:

> *A lot of men are ski instructors and the women are slaving away in their houses and domestic things don't make you a beautiful glamorous woman, and your husband is out teaching beautiful and glamorous women to ski.*

The extensive use of alcohol, generally considered harmless in social and public circles, also creates marital problems, and recent studies have established that there are both high levels of alcoholism in Tirolean tourist resorts and high levels of estrangement between married couples in the tourism industry (see Juffinger, 1993; Schönberger, 1994; Kurz, 1995). Prevented from seeking divorce by highly indebted houses and economic interdependence, many women, tied to the home and children, burdened with high work loads, and more subject to local censorship, invest their energy and love into their children, while men, who spend more time away from the confines of the family business, are more likely to have affairs.

In summer, work routines are less intense for both men and women. In between catering to guests, women find time to spend with their children, go for walks or to the swimming pool. In the off-seasons, men and women have time for a range of activities, such as going on holiday, engaging in hobbies and obtaining qualifications. One tourist official therefore argued that the division between public and private life in a ski resort is temporal rather than spatial:

> *Everyone working in winter sports surely has to know that for five months he [sic] has lots of work, and therefore must forget his private life and put it to one side, but in return, he has seven months where he can do everything. The ski instructor has to shut down his private life and be there for the guests, and then he has seven months holiday again.*

It is debatable if it is possible to "shut down" one's private and family life for five months each year. Further, frequently the promise of recuperation in the off-seasons is not met. The abrupt changes induced by the season's end bring their own stresses: with the guests gone and the facade of happiness no longer required, frustration, anger and depression can burst forth (Schönberger, 1994, p.141).

Issues of autonomy, status and power

Notwithstanding their demanding routines and the difficulties of melding home and business life, women often highly value running the family guest-house – precisely because it does not involve a strict separation between the home and workplace and because it enables them to generate an income, while staying at home to care for their families. Women often express a dislike of both working beyond the home and of "just" being a housewife. Many value the autonomy that accompanies running a business: they need not worry about unreasonable bosses, commuting, day-care, or leaving sick children at home. Women generally use the wealth they generate to improve the lives of family members, reinvesting the bulk of their profits into foodstuffs, clothes, children's educations and consumer goods. Men's disinterest in "women's work" and the daily operation of the guest-house gives women scope to put money aside from the business for their own priorities. Some women also enjoy working with people and the acquaintances they form with guests. Many women closely identify with the gendered division of labour and roles of wife, mother and home manager. Such women consider themselves responsible for providing home comforts for their families and for running the family business, and take great pride in managing their diverse tasks.

The autonomy women gain from running family businesses however, tends to be undermined by other aspects of local society. Men often retain a controlling role in the business. It is men who deal with official institutions like the bank, take out loans, and make the final decisions about when to extend or renovate the house, and often it is men's first and second names that grace the external walls of the family hotel, rendering women's immense contributions to it all but invisible. Frequently, women are not legally recognised as "owners" of these businesses. In part, this situation arose because so many women migrated into the region, and although they married into a local family, they were not customarily made part owners of the family business.[5]

The organisation of social security payments in Austria unintentionally exacerbates this situation. Since social benefits, such as unemployment money and health insurance, are only available to dependants, disadvantaged groups and employees, women often prefer to work as employees in their own (officially their husbands') businesses. Often these women work as unpaid employees: though they live from the family business, they do not actually receive a wage. Women's employee status brings short-term financial gains and probably causes few problems in solid relationships. In the case of divorce however, these women do not have equal rights to the fruits of their own labour and often "face economic ruin" (Kurz, 1995, pp.63,131).[6]

Although women engage in commercial production within the home, since their commercial tasks are seen as an extension of their domestic duties, they are still associated with the undervalued activities of domesticity. Women's roles are also naturalised: women are considered "naturally" suited to domestic labour and childcare. A common perception is that these tasks are simply easier for women. Another is that they are not really "work. Thus women's abilities are considered innate, rather than achieved, and they are not congratulated for a job well done or for their special learned skills. In contrast, men generally have professions and trades, which are considered achieved and which contribute to their social standing.

While the home business is primarily considered a female domain, the public arenas of political institutions, tourism committees, and voluntary associations are primarily considered male domains. Together these organisations direct village affairs, make up the fabric of communal life, and help stage the tourist experience. Many men *and* women in the village consider these organisations beyond the realm of responsibility of women, and indeed inappropriate for them. Some voluntary associations do not permit women to join or strictly limit the ways they can participate (e.g. the Mountain Rescue Service). Women's participation in these spheres is also limited because their multiple duties in the home leave little time to attend meetings. In addition, women rarely spend time at the *Stammtisch* or the regular's table in the local guest-house, where men routinely meet to socialise and practice politics (debate issues, express grievances, develop verbal skills and cultivate social bonds).

One consequence of women's absence from these public domains is that although men often know little about the daily operation of the family guest-house, they exercise greater influence in the organisation of tourism in the village and tend to consider themselves the "experts" in all matters tourism. Further, since these public domains are contexts in which community members compete for and achieve social standing and prestige, another consequence is that women are less likely to become prominent community figures, garner social status, or have their names and deeds recorded for posterity.

Narrations of local history typically prioritise masculine activities and male figures. These narrations, repeated in most texts about the area including the village museum, documents commemorating local events, and the mass of books and brochures designed for tourists, focus on the transformation of St. Anton from a bitterly poor farming community to a prosperous cosmopolitan tourist resort, and on those who promoted ski tourism. The central characters of these narrations are the pioneers of ski techniques and equipment, prominent hoteliers and successful ski racers - practically all of whom were men. These narrations leave out women's substantial contributions to the development of tourism, such as the labour they have invested in generating tourism businesses, catering to guests' daily needs, and shaping tourist experiences, as well as the particular contributions of a few exceptional women.

In Tirol, a potent combination of masculine ideologies and practices have coagulated around the mountains and snow sports, and dominate the public sphere. Historic notions of Tirol as a *Starkes Land* (strong land) of courageous and independent mountain farmers, have consolidated with the highly masculine discourses of Alpinism, athleticism, war heroism, and competitive sport, generating a region dominated by masculine images of place and identity (McGibbon, 1999, pp.57,98-101). Like many sports, since its inception skiing has been male dominated. Although both men and women can become ski racers, men represent the highest achievers in the sport, attracting the most media coverage and spectators, and the largest prizes, and the honouring of successful ski racers throughout Austria typically takes the form of a celebration of manliness. While theoretically men and women have equal opportunities in the ski school, there are few highly qualified female instructors (with higher qualifications translating into better wages and working conditions), and since women are considered better with children, female instructors are persistently burdened with children's groups.

Advertising images of local life also gender the region as masculine. The mountains are portrayed as rugged and hard and the central figures glamorising Tirol are the strong masculine persona of the ski instructor, ski racer and mountain climber. In contrast, local women tend to be presented in the background, at work "in service", dressed modestly in traditional costume. In Tirol, it is local men, rather than local women, particularly in the guise of the ski instructor, who have been sexualised and presented as part of the attraction of a ski holiday.[7]

Future directions: the contestation of gender roles

It is unclear how long the situation described here will continue. Attitudes to the family and family business are changing among younger generations and young women are questioning traditional gender ideologies and roles. Many women now wish to pursue an education and career, rather than marry at a young age and establish a family and guest-house. Like young men, young women increasingly lead more cosmopolitan lives - working as ski instructors or in night-clubs in the winter, socialising with travellers and seasonal workers, learning various sports, travelling overseas in the summer, and engaging in the consumption of leisure and fashioning of a life-style. Some youths (both male and female) are rejecting the family business altogether, seeing the high debts incurred in constructing, maintaining, and modernising them as a burden in this increasingly mobile world.

Yet traditional ideologies of motherhood remain strong in the village, and young women often express ambivalence towards the position of women, as the following comment illustrates:

> *Now women simply want to make more of their own lives. Today, women travel the world together. Before, they were always seen as the little mother behind the stove, always there for the children. Although, I also find that good. If one has*

children one should stay at home as long as they are small. My mother was always at home and I have a very warm relationship with her.

Further, for those who wish to continue living in St. Anton, employment opportunities beyond the tourism industry are limited. But even if young women do take on a family business they often attempt to disengage from the intense form of tourism that until now has dominated in the village. They may renovate the guest-house to create more private living space or adapt the business to reduce their workloads (e.g. converting guest rooms into self-catering apartments or closing bar facilities so guests go out in the evening). Young women often have a different philosophy of how a tourism business should be run from their mothers' or mothers'-in-law. One woman explained:

I would like to run the pension completely differently from my step-mother. She has another attitude. She thinks one has to sit and talk for hours with the guests. I just don't think it is necessary.

Some use symbolic gestures to alter the perceived hierarchy between locals and guests: for example, shifting family living space to the best part of the house and relegating guest-rooms to the basement. Others consciously take more time for their own needs and a few have become involved in local politics. It is easier however, for those who inherit well-established businesses with fewer debts, or whose husband's have professional jobs and high incomes, to successfully disengage with intense forms of tourism.

By providing new sources of income, ideas, role models, relationships, and experiences, tourism can profoundly alter the traditional ideologies and practices of gender and the family in local communities. Similarly, the images of gendered subjects used to promote tourism not only speak to and generate the desires of tourists, but also influence local identities and expectations. In part, St. Anton is marketed with images of young attractive men, women and families engaging in active and glamorous sport holidays. The desire of businesses and resorts to tap into the female tourist market promotes an equality between the sexes in some advertising, with women pictured joyfully skiing, rock climbing, parachuting, and socialising alongside men. The encroaching European Union may also influence gender relations and familial patterns in the region. The creation of a monetary union is putting intense pressure on member states to meet tight fiscal policies of low inflation and low national debt. This is encouraging governments to reduce their spending, largely through the dismantling of the welfare system (see Judt, 1996, p.25). Changing social security payments like child support and unemployment benefits may affect people's strategies of family formation and organisation.

Conclusion

At one level, this case study of women's work and gender relations in an Austrian ski resort has examined some of the on-going social, cultural and economic transformations influenced by tourism in one local context. At another level, it has offered another perspective on the highly debated dichotomies of public/private, employment/housework and work/leisure. Rural Tirolean tourist resorts like St. Anton offer an interesting case whereby the domestic sphere (the home) is also a public sphere (a hotel or guest-house) and a site of intense commercial production, for at least part of each year. Within these home-based, family businesses, women engage in a complex mix of activities that blur the boundaries of these theoretical dichotomies. Nevertheless, although these women operate in realms that cannot be defined as strictly "private" or "domestic", their commercial tasks are conceptualised as an extension of their duties as wife, mother and home-maker, and women continue to be associated in local thinking with the "private" sphere of the family and the undervalued tasks of domesticity. This, combined with their rigorous labour routines centred on the home, and their limited participation in other public spheres, such as local politics, voluntary associations and sport, tends to limit women's influence in the wider community, as well as marginalise them in the telling of local history.

Thus while the boundary between the public and private is largely "fictional", it is used to ideologically constrain women to the less valued, private domestic realm, demonstrating that "the construction of the boundary between the public and the private is a political act in itself" (Yuval-Davis, 1997, pp.2-6,80). In the context of tourism in St. Anton, local men are often considered to have been empowered by the industry as tourism pioneers, mountain experts and racing heroes, while women have simultaneously been relegated to background, supportive, labouring roles, as the providers of everyday care for their husbands, children, families and guests.

This paper is based on research undertaken by the author for her doctoral thesis in anthropology, completed in 1998 for Macquarie University, Sydney, Australia. A more detailed treatment of the subject can be found in her book entitled *The Business of Alpine Tourism in a Globalising World: An Anthropological Study of International Ski Tourism in the Village of St. Anton am Arlberg in the Tirolean Alps* (1999).

Endnotes

1. Due to limitations of space, I am unable to discuss these critiques in any detail. For a more comprehensive discussion see McGibbon, 1999, pp.142-145.

2. Austria is one of the most concentrated sites of tourism in the world. Although it only has a population of 8 million, Austria has approximately 5.5 percent of the world tourism market, and tourism accounts for around 9 percent of Austria's GNP (Knoll, 1992, p.30). For a sense of the dimensions of the Austrian tourism industry consider that it has 1.25 million guest beds and that in 1993, 24.9 million guests spent a total of 127.6 million nights in the country (Zimmermann, 1991; Jochum, 1994). Further, the Austrian tourism industry has a particularly localised and decentralised structure, dominated by small to medium-sized family businesses (see endnote 4). Yet, the central contribution women make in managing and running tourism businesses, and the effects of home production on family life, have not been analysed in any depth (though see Burgmann 1982, Preglau et al., 1985; Juffinger, 1993; Kurz, 1995).

3. This phenomenon is not restricted to Austria. For discussions of family, home-based tourism businesses in Greece, see Kousis (1989), Herzfeld (1991) and Galaní-Moutáfi (1993, 1994); in Portugal, see Mendonsa (1983); in the UK, see Ireland (1993); and in Ireland, see Breathnach et al. (1994).

4. Unlike many tourist destinations, which are dominated by foreign capital, international hotels and restaurant chains, in Austria the industry consists mainly of small to medium-sized family businesses, built up from localised capital (savings and bank loans). One reason for this is that after World War Two the Austrian state nationalised many of the country's industries and major banks, developing a state controlled market economy with an extensive social welfare system, and restricting the flow of foreign investment and multi-national capital into the economy (März and Szecsi, 1988, pp.31-3). Another reason is that the state actively encouraged small pensions and the renting out of private rooms by providing inexpensive credit for tourist enterprises and by making businesses with under 10 beds tax and license free. In particular, the distribution of the substantial funds of the post-war European Recovery Programs (ERP) in the form of small loans allowed the number of private beds to grow rapidly, peaking in 1976 at 470,000, a figure representing 40 percent of the total tourist beds in Austria (Zimmermann, 1991, p.163).

5. Similarly in the past, when a woman married into a family she generally did not become a legal owner of the family farm. Thus even though a woman often ran her husband's farm after his death or during his absence (e.g., when he was engaged in seasonal employment or drafted into war), she did not have rights of ownership or disposal in it. Rather she worked it in trust for her children until they all came of age, at which time the property would be inherited by the appropriate heir/s (Köfler and Forcher, 1986, pp.79-81). Locally born women could however, inherit parcels of land from their parents as their *Erbteil* (share of inheritance), although sons were more likely to inherit their parents' farmhouse and the bulk of the farm land.

6. Certainly, in the case of divorce, a woman is entitled to a portion of her husband's property, which she can contest in court. Successfully contesting a portion of the property however, depends on her being able to demonstrate her input into the family business. This is often difficult given that most women do not record or even know how many hours they work in the business, largely because their work and domestic chores are so intertwined. In contrast, if the woman was an equal owner, then in the case of divorce she would automatically be entitled to half the property. Similarly, as a co-owner of the property, on the death of her husband a woman would probably inherit it automatically. But since most women are not owners, they often have to contest for a share of the property with other relatives, such as their adult children and husband's parents.

7. Contrast this with the situation in many "exotic", non-European tourist destinations such as Thailand and the Philippines, where the sexuality of local women has been commodified and marketed as a major attraction. See Edensor and Kothari (1994) for another example of a tourist site that has been gendered as masculine (Stirling in the Scottish Highlands).

References

Boh, K., Bak, M., Clason, C., Pankratova, M., Qvortrup, J., Sgritta, G. B., and Waerness, K. (Editors) (1989), *Changing Patterns of European Family Life: A Comparative Analysis of Fourteen European Countries*, Routledge, London.

Breathnach, P., Henry, M., Drea, S. and O'Flaherty, M. (1994), Gender in Irish Tourism Employment, in Kinnaird, V. and Hall, D. (Editors), *Tourism: A Gender Analysis*, John Wiley and Sons, Chichester, pp. 52-73.

Burgmann in Baumgärtner, W. (1982), *Fremdenverkehr und Familie: Einfluss des Fremdenverkehrs auf familiale Kommunikationsstruktur dargestellt am Beispiel Naturns*, Doktor Dissertation, Universität von Innsbruck, Innsbruck.

Cheal, D. (1991), *The Family and the State of Theory*, Harvester, New York.

Edensor, T. and Kothari, U. (1994), The masculinisation of Stirling's heritage, in Kinnaird, V. and Hall, D. (Editors), *Tourism: A Gender Analysis*, John Wiley and Sons, Chichester, pp. 164-187.

Galaní-Moutáfi, V. (1993), From Agriculture to Tourism: Property, Labor, Gender, Kinship in a Greek Island Village, Part One, *Journal of Modern Greek Studies*, 11, pp. 241-270.

Galaní-Moutáfi, V. (1994), From Agriculture to Tourism: Property, Labor, Gender, Kinship in a Greek Island Village, Part Two, *Journal of Modern Greek Studies*, 12, pp. 113-131.

Herzfeld, M. (1991), *A Place in History*, Princeton University Press, New Jersey.

Ireland, M. (1993), Gender and Class Relations in Tourism Employment, *Annals of Tourism Research*, 20, (4), pp. 666-684.

Jochum, B. (1994), Tourismus in Tirol: Bedeutung, Struktur, Probleme, Aufgaben und Ziele der Tirol Werbung, Tirol Werbung, Unpublished Paper.

Judt, T. (1996), Austria and the Ghost of the New Europe, *The New York Review of Books*, 15/2/96, pp. 22-25.

Juffinger, S. (1993), Lust am Frust: Die vergessenen Frauen im Tourismus, in *Informationen für die Frau in Tirol*, 4/93, Aug/Sept., Herausgegeben vom Frauenreferat des Landes Tirol, Innsbruck.

Knoll, A. (1992), *Diese Arbeit macht Krank: der Versuch einer epidemiologischen Untersuchung im Hotel und Gastgewerbe*, Verlag des Österreichischen Gewerkshaftsbundes, Wien.

Köfler, G. and Forcher, M. (1986), *Die Frau in der Geschichte Tirols*, Haymon-Verlag, Innsbruck.

Kousis, M. (1989), Tourism and the Family in a Rural Cretan Community, *Annals of Tourism Research*, 16, (3), pp. 318-332.

Kurz, B. (1995), *Die Rolle der Gastwirtin im Bezirk Landeck: Spitzenmanagerin oder Mädchen für Alles*, Diplomarbeit, Institut fur Allg. Soziologie und Wirtschaftssoziologie an der Wirtschaftsuniversität, Wien.

Laslett, P. (1972), *Household and Family in Past Time,* Cambridge University Press, Cambridge.

März, E. and Szecsi, M. (1988), Austria's Economic Development 1945-85, in Steiner, K. (Editor), *Modern Austria*, Sposs Inc., Palo Alton, pp. 123-140.

McGibbon, J. (1999), *The Business of Alpine Tourism in a Globalising World: An Anthropological Study of International Ski Tourism in the Village of St. Anton am Arlberg in the Tirolean Alps*, Vetterling Druck, Rosenheim.

Mendonsa, E. L. (1983), Tourism and Income Strategies in Nazare, Portugal, *Annals of Tourism Research*, 10 (2): 213-238.

Mitterauer, M. (1992), *Familie und Arbeitsteilung*, Böhlau, Wien.

Parsons, T. (1951), *The Social System*, Routledge and Keegan Paul, London.

Parsons, T. (1955), The American Family: its Relations to Personality and to the Social Structure, in Parsons, T. and Bales, R. F., *Family, Socialisation and Interaction Process*, Free Press, New York, pp. 3-33.

Preglau, M., Meleghy, T., Frantz, K., and Tafertshofer, A. (1985), *Fremdenverquer: Kosten und Nutzen des Tourismus am Beispiel Obergurgl*, Gaismair, Innsbruck.

Reiter, W. (1984), Ischler Herzen, in Schuh, F. (Editor), *Kritische Texte über den Tourismus*, Ritter Verlag, Wien, pp. 16-19.

Rosaldo, M. (1974), Women, Culture and Society: A Theoretical Overview, in Rosaldo, M. and Lamphere, L. (Editors), *Women, Culture and Society*, Stanford University Press, Stanford, pp. 17-42.

Schönberger, A. (1994), *Alm-Rausch: Die Alltagstragödie hinter der Freizeitmaschinerie*, Überreuter, Wien.

Yuval-Davis, N. (1997), *Gender and Nation*, Sage, London.

Zimmermann, F. (1991), Austria: contrasting tourist seasons and contrasting regions, in Williams, A. M. and Shaw, G. (Editors), *Tourism and Economic Development: Western European Experiences* (2nd edition), Belhaven Press, London, pp. 153-173.

Tourism and cultural heritage: Controversy on key tourist destinations in Zimbabwe

Munyaradzi Manyanga

University of Zimbabwe, Zimbabwe

Introduction

Zimbabwe has a rich cultural heritage which has become a major tourist attraction over the years. Key among these is prehistoric rock art, the stone walled Zimbabwe tradition monuments, colonial monuments and national shrines of which the later are associated with strong living traditions. While a lot of marketing has been done to promote these sites for tourism, sites like Great Zimbabwe and Rhodes's Grave in the Matopos have been able to publicise themselves through debates, political interpretation and emotions that are associated with such heritage. This paper focuses on Great Zimbabwe and the legacy of political interpretation, the cultural and colonial heritage of the Matopos and the tourism potentials of national shrines such as Njelele and *NtabazikaMambo* (Manyanga 1996). It will also review the management, emotions and discord that arose in the interpretations and presentation of such heritage.

Great Zimbabwe and the legacy of political interpretation

Great Zimbabwe is a dry stone walled monument which is located in south central Zimbabwe. It is one of the most outstanding man made monuments in the world and has World Heritage status. With its high conical tower, long curved stone walls and cosmopolitan artefacts, Great Zimbabwe attests to the existence of a thriving city-state that dominated trade and culture throughout Southern Africa between the 12th and the 17th century. The country Zimbabwe derives its name from this site and other related sites, which are scattered throughout the country. Debates on whether Great Zimbabwe was built by local indigenous populations or by a foreign group of people dominated debate since the 1890s. Successive governments, civic groups and associations have used the site since the 1980s to gain political mileage. The use of the site for political ends by the successive governments of Zimbabwe since 1890 is known world wide as the Zimbabwean controversy (Sinamai, 1998). The colonial government took much interest on the site such that it instituted research to unearth the mystery of Great Zimbabwe. Today the site has become a national icon on national television and currency. The politicisation of the site has had a great impact in the way the site has been managed, researched and presented as a tourist attraction.

The political manipulation of Great Zimbabwe began early with such people as Cecil John Rhodes, who wanted to popularise the colonial conquest of the Region as an attempt to revive the Aryan civilisations of Phoenicia (Hall, 1905). The colonial government then instituted archaeological research which sought to prove the foreign origins of the Zimbabwe culture (Bent, 1892; Hall, 1905). Subsequent work by Randal-McIver (1905), Caton Tompson (1931) and Robinson and Summers in the 1960s demonstrated that the site was of African origin, a suggestion that was hardly acceptable to the colonial establishment. The African response to the Zimbabwean controversy was very minimal, as the indigenous populations were marginalised in the interpretation of the heritage (Sinamai, 1998). However the indigenous people's use of the Zimbabwe heritage was to be seen on the political arena where culture was seen as the only way to enrich the life of the Africans, instil dignity and foster national unity (Bhebe, 1989). During the formative years of nationalist party building, the name Zimbabwe became enshrined in the names of many political parties and the future state was to assume the name Zimbabwe. During the armed struggle, Great Zimbabwe became an important centre of spiritual inspiration for those who were fighting the colonial system. The use of the site by nationalist movements called for a heavy censorship of research, literature and museum displays that advanced the indigenous origins of Great Zimbabwe (Mahachi and Ndoro, 1997).

Today the debate on the origins of Great Zimbabwe is considered a dead issue. Despite the numerous testimonies which advance the indigenous origin of the Zimbabwe tradition sites, old hypotheses about the origins of Great Zimbabwe still find publishers and a wide range of readers (Mahachi and Ndoro, 1997). Because of the wide distribution of this literature and the legacy of colonial interpretation, Great Zimbabwe is still seen as a mystery in the eyes of many tourists. This had a negative impact on the domestic tourist, who viewed the colonial interpretation as a deliberate exercise to expropriate the African past. The monument had also been alienated from the indigenous people in two ways. Firstly, their association with the monument used to be functional, relating mostly to religious consultation and ceremonies. Even those who advanced the indigenous origins of the site did not fulfil the wishes of the people as the site was only of symbolic value. Pointing out that the site relates to one's past achievements without any functional value is not adequate to the indigenous people. The site and others representing the Zimbabwe tradition were physically alienated from the people as these sites fall in either commercial farm land or state land (Ranger, 1987). The site was and is still alienated from the local people and this has adversely affected the domestic visitorship to the site. The use of the site as a national icon in post independent Zimbabwe has not helped the situation as people's relationship with the site is still symbolic. Functional relationships with the site have been limited to a few selected groups. It is no wonder that the highest number of local people visiting the site today are school groups. As much as propaganda, both colonial and post independence has highlighted the achievements and grandeur of Great Zimbabwe, this politicisation has perpetuated the Zimbabwean controversy, with negative responses from the local tourists. Mahachi and Ndoro (1997) have noted that despite the fall of the Rhodesian colonial system and a change in national policy towards archaeological research, many myths about Great Zimbabwe have continued to exist. This has resulted in patronising tourists at Great Zimbabwe, who wish to see the site presented in a way that suits their political, racial, religious or social orientation at the expense of scientific truths.

Contested management and emotional history: The Matopos cultural landscape

The Matopo hills which are characterised by large numbers of natural overhangs, balancing rock boulders, shelters and caves encloses a large number of archaeological, historical, ritual and scenic places. Most of the heritage is now enclosed in a National Park, while others are in the adjourning communal areas. This scenario brought in 3 interested government institutions in the management of the area namely National Parks and Wildlife Management (Natural heritage), National Museums and Monuments of Zimbabwe (NMMZ) (Cultural, natural and historical heritage) and the Department of Local Government and Rural Development (Administration and Development). While these institutions pursue different goals, the distribution and collection of the income that derives from the heritage of the area has created discord in the management of the area and unwelcome frustration to the tourist. Controversy also surrounds the status of Rhodes's grave, a listed monument in the park. The grave, together with many colonial forts and memorials has been a centre of debate which revolves on their relevance as national heritage.

The Matopo cultural Landscape is located 35 km south of the modern city of Bulawayo, in the south-western part of Zimbabwe. The area mainly consists of the Matopo National Park, commercial farms and part of the Matopo, Khumalo and Gulati communal areas. The present park was established in 1965 through proclamation No 42 and the area is currently administered under the National Parks and Wild life Act. The National Park is clearly demarcated on the ground by a security fence to prevent grazing and animal poaching from the surrounding communal areas. As a geographic unit, the cultural landscape is dominated by spectacular granite hills. The scenic and captivating geological formations characterised by balancing rocks, dwalas, castle kopjes and caves which are punctuated by alluvial valleys cut by streams provide the Matopo hills with one of the most picturesque landscape in the whole country. The environment supports a diverse fauna and flora. The Matopos area is a unique cultural landscape with a dense diverse cultural and natural heritage such that it has been nominated as a landscape deserving World Heritage Status.

Weathering and erosion are continuously modifying this physical environment. The decomposition of the granite has yielded course-grained sandy soils, which characterise the area and has influenced human settlement in the area. The rich and varied flora of the Matopo means that there is a wide range of plants with commercial and medicinal value. The combination of the topography and climate has always attracted human settlement in the area. With the creation of the Park a rich fauna and flora has also been part of the landscape.

In terms of archaeological research, the Matopos area is one of the most extensively researched areas in Zimbabwe yielding more than 3 000 recorded sites out of a present country database of 14,000. The research has largely focused on the Stone Age and the interpretation of rock art panels (see Cooke, 1963; Walker, 1995; Walker and Thorp, 1997; Ranger 1999). Apart from the archaeology, the Matopo hills document the country's history from the time of the arrival of the Ndebele, to colonisation and later to the liberation struggle. Some of the major historical events witnessed in the Matopos were like the signing of the Rudd Concession of 1888, which gave the country to Rhodes. The Matopo hills are probably one of the most important cultural places for the Shona and Ndebele people today (Ranger, 1999).

The Matopo area is well known for its rich rock art sites, which has been described and researched by many scholars for many years (See Cooke, 1963, Garlake, 1987, Walker, 1995). There are more than 300 rock art sites known to exist in the National Park alone. The Matopo hills probably possess one of the highest concentrations of rock paintings in sub-Saharan Africa. The hills contain a wide range of paintings, most of which seem to have been executed by the hunter-gatherer communities of the Late Stone Age. The Iron Age communities executed some of the painting, although these are not many and seem not to have attracted the attention of most of the researchers who worked in the Matopo hills (Taruvinga, 2000).

Walker (1995) suggests that some of the paintings could be 8000-10000 years old. It appears the most common colour used by the prehistoric artists in the Matopos area was red, derived from red ochre or hematite. The ochre occurs in a variety of shades; brown to yellow, orange and purple. The famous sites in the area include Bambata, Nswatugi, Pomongwe, Silozwani, Gulumbawe and White Rhino.

There is an abundance of sites that represent the Stone Age period in the Matopo hills area. Some of these sites are associated with rock paintings. The sites are mostly found in the hemispherical caves and other forms of rock shelters (Muringaniza, 1995). One of the important sites is Bambata Cave, which has yielded one of the oldest painted piece of stone. The site also yielded early pottery associated with Stone Age communities. Equally important is the Nswatugi Cave. The site is associated with the oldest skeleton discovered in Zimbabwe and evidence of occupation during the Middle Stone Age dating to about 42 000 years BP (Walker, 1995). The paintings at Nswatugi have been described as the most varied and colourful in the Matopos area (Garlake, 1987). Research at Pomongwe Cave has yielded artefacts associated with Middle and Later Stone Age occupation. Several sites represent the Iron Age in the Matopo area including stone walled sites of the Khami phase and the later Zimbabwe period sites.

A range of historical sites are represented with the earliest sites occupied by the Ndebele being perhaps of high significance for example the capital of the Lobengula and Mzilikazi's grave. It was also in the Matopo hills that some of the fiercest battles of resistance to colonisation were fought between 1893 to 1897 (Ranger, 1999). The Matopos also witnessed the subsequent negotiations and eventual occupation of the area by white settler communities. The Matopo hills as Ranger (1999) shows, has been a landscape which has been contested by various groups because of its favourable climatic and environmental conditions. Apart from this the battles on land acquisition and the subsequent liberation war have all left an imprint on the cultural landscape.

Several legal instruments apply to various parts of the Matopo hills. The National Parks and Wildlife Department under the Ministry of Environment and Tourism (*National Parks and Wildlife Act 1975*) administer the Park. The department is tasked with the responsibility of managing the natural and physical environment of the Park. The *National Museums and*

Monuments Act 25-11 empowers National Museums and Monuments to protect, document and present all cultural and historical heritage in the country. The diverse cultural heritage in the Matopos all falls under the control of National Museums and Monuments. The commercial farms and communal areas around the Matopos National Park fall under the jurisdiction of Matobo Rural District Council which is empowered by *the District Councils Act* (Ministry of Local Government, Rural and Urban Development). The different legal instruments are meant to complement each other in the main goal of preserving, conserving and presenting the cultural and natural heritage in the park. This has however resulted in contested management plans in the face of decreasing government funding. National Museums and Monuments and National Parks and Wildlife can not agree on a uniform fee for access to the park. The situation that stands now is that of a dual payment system were National Parks and National Museums services are charged separately much to the inconvenience of the tourist. The situation in the Matopos demonstrates the problems associated with managing archaeological and historical sites which do not incorporate the landscape as part of the heritage. National Museums and Monuments are managing 'islands' in the Matopos area, where much of the natural physical structures are managed by National Parks. It has been shown that the Matopos area was continuously occupied by prehistoric and historic people. Since the past communities habitually exploited the area, this therefore qualifies much of the Matopos area as a cultural landscape that calls for conservation. The expertise possessed by both National Museums and National Parks should be seen as crucial in the management and conservation of the Matopos area. Both institutions' respective roles should not be seen as contradictory but complimentary in the ultimate goal that seeks to see a total conservation of an area that is so rich in both cultural and natural heritage. The discord that one might notice in the management of the Matopos area has nothing to do with management ethics but has to do with the distribution of the rewards that emanate from the heritage. A single entry fee and a combined marketing strategy would certainly bring rewards for all those interested in the conservation and presentation of the natural and cultural heritage of the Matopos area. Although different parties in the Matopos area have different terms of reference, these can certainly be reconciled for the sake of the heritage and for tourism development.

The Matopos is also home to Cecil Rhodes's Grave. Rhodes, the founder of Rhodesia (1890-1980) is buried in the Matopos, having stated his intention of being buried there. He did not only show his interest in the Matopos by simply selecting a burial place, but he also owned a summerhouse and a horse stable both of which are national monuments (Muringaniza 1999). The status of Cecil John Rhodes's grave which now form part of the Matopos cultural landscape has been the centre of debate in Zimbabwe in the past few years. There have been calls for the exhumation of Rhodes's remains from pressure groups like *Sangano Munhutapa*, *Vukani Mahlavezulu* and *Imbovane Yamahlabezulu* (Muringaniza 1999). Their arguments for the removal of Rhodes's remains are based on the view that the grave is on a revered shrine where pre-colonial kings were buried (Chronicle 19/2/98). The controversy associated with Rhodes's grave has to do with the fact that the grave represents minority heritage which conflicts with the values of post-colonial majority rule (Turnbridge and Ashworth, 1996: pp.123). The legal custodians of the site, NMMZ, have vowed to protect the site from such vandalism by the pressure groups and would only yield to their demands when the site loses those qualities that it was accorded a national monument (Muringaniza, 1999: pp.7). The underlying issue here is that Rhodes's Grave and all colonial heritage in Zimbabwe, although associated with past injustices of colonial rule, are now part and parcel of the country's past. This past has had a significant impact on the past and present generations. It is also important to note that Zimbabwe is a multi-cultural society and the vestiges of these past societies should make Zimbabwe's presented past. The World View has assumed a new economic value as it is one of the most popular tourist destination in Zimbabwe. A visitor survey by NMMZ between 1997 and 1998 shows that the view of the world, whose main attraction is Rhodes' Grave and other colonial memorials contributes significantly to the tourism industry in Zimbabwe (Table 1).

Table 1

	Locals		Non Residents		Free Admission		
Period	Adults	Minors	Adults	Minors	Adults	Minor	Totals
July-Dec 1997	9 251	6 091	17 207	1 060	5 266	470	39 345
Jan-June 1998	7 784	1 695	11 388	443	952	323	22 585
July-Dec 1998	1 8866	6 090	28 623	1 423	19	598	53 619

(NMMZ Annual Reports 1998)

It must however be noted that the burial of Rhodes in the Matopos is still viewed as a tremendous challenge to the African concept of the Matopo landscape despite the acknowledgement that it has become part of the country's history together with its contribution to the tourism industry. The present impasse has to do with the unbalanced presentation of the World View. Visitors visit Rhodes's grave and other colonial places in the Matopos without any knowledge of the African history and cosmology of the hills (Ranger, 1999). The demands of international tourism have insured that the park presents much of the same symbolic face that it did under settler rule. The easily marketable Rhodes' Grave has remained the key attraction at the site at the expense of local history and culture. The indigenous people's past associated with the World's View is not part of the current presentation, and talk of a colonial museum at the site would possibly incorporate this in future presentations. The biggest criticisms in the presentation of the Matopos area has been that the area is now connected with conservation and international tourism and less and less focus has been put on the local history (Ranger, 1999). It is becoming more and more important that the presentation in the Matopos Park must re-instate culture and history into nature.

Another bone of contention has to do with the present imbalance on those sites accorded national monument status in Zimbabwe. The national monuments register of Zimbabwe is still dominated with colonial heritage. This is a legacy of colonialism where few sites associated with local communities were given national monuments status. Muringaniza (1999) noted that in the Bulawayo area, 6 sites associated with Rhodes (Rhodes' Grave, View of the World Farm, Rhodes's Summerhouse, Rhodes's Stable, Rhodes's Indaba site and Rhodes's Hut at the Bulawayo state house) are national monuments. This compares unfavourably with only four in the whole of Matebeleland that are associated with the Ndebele (Mzilikazi's Grave, Mzilikazi Memorial, Old Bulawayo and Lobengula's Grave).

Turnbridge and Ashworth (1996) noted that colonialism brought two conflicting heritage values that relate to the coloniser's value of conquest and exploitation and the indigenous values of subjugation and resistance. With decolonisation the colonial heritage, which naturally is associated with the injustices of the colonial administration, has become the burden of the indigenous communities. While Rhodes's grave is an inspiration to the local white population, it is a symbol of colonial conquest and exploitation in the eyes of the local inhabitants. These controversies, although fragmenting the tourists, appear to have strengthened the popularity of such sites as tourist destinations. This can be noted from the increase in visitorship at Rhodes grave in 1998 despite the emotionally charged debate on Rhodes grave as national heritage (Table 1)

Living traditions and tourism: The case of Njelele and Ntabazikamambo national shrines

The Matopo hills have always and are still playing an important role in the spiritual life of the Shona and Ndebele people of Zimbabwe. The most important site for Shona and Ndebele religion is the site of Njelele. A similar site related to Njelele, is the site of *NtabazikaMambo* (Manyanga 1996). National shrines such as Njelele and *Ntabazikamambo* (Manyanga 1996) have always received local and regional pilgrimages relating to rain making ceremonies. Sites associated with the living traditions in Zimbabwe are numerous and heritage managers have been pondering on what could be made of these sites. These sites present a new impetus to the growth of cultural tourism as these sites have the potential of becoming major attractions to both local and international tourists.

As indicated the Matopo hills have always and are still playing an important spiritual role to the Shona and Ndebele people. Rain making and cleansing rituals have been performed in the Matopos including at some of the rock art sites like Silozwane. However, the most important site for the Shona and Ndebele religion is the site of Njelele. The Shrine of Njelele is not only important to people in Zimbabwe but also the Kalanga in Botswana and Venda in South Africa. People from these two countries are known to pay annual pilgrimages to this site. Even early white settlers to Zimbabwe were quick to note the religious significance of the Matopo Hills. Rhodes's idea of being buried at the Matopos had to do with the belief that he was to become the leading deity of the land, and his spirit was to quicken the control of land in Zimbabwe (Ranger, 1987). It is therefore not surprising that Rhodes's grave has become a place of pilgrimage for white settlers.

Another site that is related to the *Mwari* shrines of the Matopos is *NtabazikaMambo* (Manyanga 1996) National Monument. The shrine is located in the Mambo hills, which are now form part of a commercial ranch. The Mambo hills form a natural fortification which resemble the Matopo Hills. The monument, which is located in a commercial farm and administered by National Museums and Monuments, has become the focal point of regular ritual prayer groups. Heritage managers (legal custodians) have condemned the activities of these groups as an archaeological disaster and a distortion of the cultural landscape. On the other hand the ritual groups (traditional custodians) view the national monument as their rightful heritage, which they need to utilise for their well being as dictated by their ancestors. Similar conflicts in heritage management that relates to these living sites have occurred elsewhere in Zimbabwe and heritage managers have been left pondering on what use they can make of such sites (Munjeri, 1995; Manyanga, 1996).

Despite the obvious negative impact on the archaeology of *NtabazikaMambo*, it should be noted that the revival of these living traditions at the site has enhanced the value of the site. Its utilisation by people who claim a direct link with the builders of the site has brought the site back into focus and the activities of the loyal traditional custodians can be viewed as offering an extra attraction at the site. While it is not implied here that the site has benefited from the activities of the ritual consultation, it is a possibility that with some flexibility, the activities and involvement of the traditional groups can be put to the good of both archaeology, culture and tourism development. It is argued here that if the traditional ceremonies at the shrines become archaeologically sensitive, regular and adopt a regular calendar, they may become major attractions for both local and international tourists. Benefits can be harvested by both the legal and traditional custodians in the manner CAMPFIRE (Communal Areas Management Programme for Indigenous Resources) projects have been run in the management of wildlife resources in parts of Zimbabwe, where a percentage of the proceeds goes towards development projects which benefit the local communities.

International conservation bodies like ICOMOS are advocating for such sites like Njelele and *NtabazikaMambo* to be accorded World Heritage status and to be promoted for cultural tourism. National Museums and Monuments of Zimbabwe's master plan for cultural resource conservation and development also stresses the need to develop and utilise the archaeological and cultural sites as a tourist resource. It is apparent that modern management of cultural sites stresses the need to integrate the material heritage into tourism and development as the mere conservation of monuments without tourism and development is seen as a liability (Munjeri, 1998). However the idea to promote shrines for tourism development has been viewed by others as the root cause of heritage distortion and inauthentic presentations as ceremonies with a ritual significance to the locals might be carried out for the benefit of the tourist (Boniface and Fowler, 1993; Munjeri, 1998). In the case of the living traditions, the rituals that are carried out at the site are an uplifting process to the locals and drama to the tourist. The mere presence of outsiders during a ceremony minimises the ritual act of the locals (Munjeri, 1998). These observations should be viewed as challenges of a potentially marketable cultural resource, whose benefits are not only economic, but will increase inter cultural understanding. The world-wide trend in the tourism industry today is the growing appetite for indigenous cultural experiences by the tourist (Zeppel, 1998). This scenario presents a situation where local communities can derive income from such sites as Njelele and *NtabazikaMambo*. However, a wider involvement of indigenous communities into the tourism industry entails striking a balance between the tourist needs and maintaining environmental, social and cultural integrity of the indigenous communities (Zeppel, 1998). The Tourism Industry is the fastest growing industry and the second most contributor of foreign currency earnings in Zimbabwe. It is therefore imperative that the resource base of the industry be broadened to incorporate national shrines and cultural components of Zimbabwe' s heritage whose potential has always been underplayed for a long time.

Conclusion

An overview of some of Zimbabwes' key tourist attractions has shown that heritage can be an actual or potential political instrument (Turnbridge and Ashworth, 1996). The controversies associated with the Zimbabwe culture and Rhodes's Grave have helped publicise the sites with both positive and negative impacts. The Zimbabwean controversy has perpetuated the mystery associated with the Zimbabwean culture while Rhodes Grave has worsened the delicate racial relations in Zimbabwe. The threat to repatriate Rhodes's remains by some pressure groups can also be seen as a political statement, that relates to the relatively weak relations between England and Zimbabwe in recent years. Heritage in Zimbabwe once again, gets entangled in the political game with detrimental effects for international tourism in the long term. The living sites like Njelele and *NtabazikaMambo* present a lively heritage and offer an opportunity to broaden the resource base of the tourism industry in the 21st century. This however needs to be sustainable and I agree with Zeppel (1998) that this need to balance three variables which include the maintenance of social and cultural integrity, maintaining the physical environment and commercial success.

References

Ashcwaden, H. (1990), *Karanga Mythology*, Mambo, Gweru.

Baker, H. and Stead, W. T. (1977), *Cecil Rhodes: The man and his dreams*, Books of Rhodesia, Bulawayo.

Bent, J. T. (1892), *The Ruined Cities of Mashonaland*. Longman Green, London.

Boniface, P. and Fowler, P. J. (1993), *Heritage and Tourism in the Global Village*. Routledge, London.

Bhebe, N. (1978), The Ndebele and *Mwari* before 1893: a religious conquest of the conquerors by the vanquished, in Schoffeleers J. M. (editor), *Guardians of the land: Essays on central African territorial cults*, Mambo Press, Gweru, pp. 287-294.

Bhebe, N. (1989), The Nationalist Struggle 1957-62, In Banana, C. S. (Editor), *Turmoil and Tenacity: Zimbabwe 1890-1990*, College Press, Harare pp. 50-109.

Caton-Thompson, G. (1931), *The Zimbabwe Culture: Ruins and Reaction*, Claredon Press, Oxford.

Chronicle, 19 February 1998.

Clarke, M. F. (1996), '*A miniature Matopos' The Mambo Hills of Matebeleland North: Their religious and historical significance*, Discussion Paper, Oxford.

Cooke, C. K. (1963), Report on excavations at Pomongwe and Tshangula caves, Matopo Hills, Southern Rhodesia, *South African Archaeological Bulletin*, 18, pp. 73-151.

Daniel, M. L. (1970), *The God of the Matopo Hills,* Mouton, Hague.

Garlake, P. (1987), *The Painted Caves*, Modus, Harare.

Hall, R. N. (1905), *Great Zimbabwe*, Metheun and Co, London.

Mahachi, G. and Ndoro, W. (1997), The Socio-Political Context of Southern African Iron Age Studies with Special Reference to Great Zimbabwe, in Pwiti, G. (Editor), *Caves, Monuments and Texts*, Uppsala University, Uppsala. pp. 89-107.

Manyanga, M. (1996), What use can be made of the living Traditions? The case of NtabazikaMambo. *NAMMO Bulletin*, 1, pp. 1-2.

Munjeri, D. (1995), *Spirit of the people, nerve of heritage, African cultural heritage and the World Heritage Convention, National Museums and Monuments of Zimbabwe*, pp.52-58.

Munjeri, D. (1998), Cultural Tourism, in Chiwome, E. M. and Gambahaya Z. (Editors), *Culture and Development*, Mond Books, Harare, pp. 81-84.

Muringaniza, J. (1999), The heritage that hurts: The case of the grave of Cecil John Rhodes in the Matopos National Park of Zimbabwe, *Paper presented at the World Archaeological Congress* 4, Cape Town, 10-16 January 1999.

NMMZ Act Chapter 25-11, Government of Zimbabwe, Harare.

NMMZ, (1998), *Annual Report* 1998. NMMZ, Harare.

Pwiti, G. and Ndoro, W. (1999), The legacy of colonialism: perceptions of the cultural heritage in Southern Africa, with specific reference to Zimbabwe, *Antiquity*, 16, (3), pp. 143-153.

Ranger, T. O. (1987), *Holy places and pilgrimages in Zimbabwe, Past and Present*, pp. 158-194.

Ranger, T. O. (1999). *Voices from the Rocks: Nature, culture and history in the Matopos Hills of Zimbabwe*, Baobab Books, Harare.

Sinamai, A. (1998), Heritage in Politics: Great Zimbabwe in the struggle for self-determination, in Chiwome, E. M. and Gambahaya, Z, (Editors), *Culture and Development, Harare*: Mond Books, pp. 93-98.

Taruvinga, P. (2000), *Geographic Information Systems and Rock Art studies in the Matopos area*, Paper presented at the Human Responses and Contributions to Environmental Change Workshop, Bagamoyo 9-17 February 2000.

Turnbridge, J. E. and Ashworth G. J. (1996), *Dissonant Heritage: The management of the past as a resource in conflict*, John Wiley and Sons, Chichester.

Walker, N. (1995), Late Pleistocene and Holocene Hunter-Gatherers of the Matopos: An archaeological study of change and continuity in Zimbabwe, *Societas Archaeologica Uppsaliensis*, Uppsala.

Zeppel, H. (1998), Land and Culture: sustainable tourism and indigenous peoples. In Hall, C. M. and A. A. Lew (Editors), *Sustainable Tourism, A Geographical Perspective*, Longman, London. pp. 60-74.

Tourism: Towards a global cultural economy?

Kevin Meethan

University of Plymouth, UK

Introduction: tourism and globalisation

What I wish to address here are certain themes I outlined elsewhere (Meethan forthcoming) relating to the ways in which culture and cultural change have been approached within many analyses of tourism. It will be argued that the conceptual underpinning of these approaches needs to be rethought in the light of recent theoretical and empirical work in both anthropology and sociology. In turn, this needs to be seen in the context of the changing nature of social, political, economic and cultural relations brought about by the processes of globalisation.

At a base level, globalisation refers to the interconnections - economic, social and cultural - that now exist across space and time, and are also impinging more and more into the daily lives of people across the world. In this sense such interconnections, particularly in the field of international trade, are not a new phenomena. Globalisation though is not merely the sum of all international or, if you prefer, transnational connections between places but rather implies a different order of relationships structured across space and time. There are a number of theoretical models which attempt to account for this (Held et al., 1999), and despite the differences of emphasis they place on various aspects of globalisation, what tends to focus on are a set of concerns which involve the apparent decline of the nation state, the rise of transnational corporations, and the spread of new technologies and electronic broadcast media. To this list we also need to add the emergence of a global deregulated capitalist economy, increasing labour migration and changes to the global distribution of manufacturing production. Such changes are also leading to a fundamental reordering of the ways in which economic political and cultural relations are both conceptualised and consequently organised on a global basis, rather than within the confines of the nation state.

Yet globalisation is, at least in the surface, a rather contradictory state. First, it is uneven in both its spread and effects. Secondly, it is not simply an economic phenomena. One of the dominant features of globalisation is that of mass migration (Held, et al., 1999). This movement of people also leads to situations where people live both between and across cultures (Hearn and Roseniel, 1999 p 4) and also, within the global flows of commodities, cultural influences seem to move freely from one place to another. Yet for most people, the experiences of life are rooted in particular localities. The significance of globalisation lies in the ways that such localities are transformed through what Tomlinson (1999) refers to as deterritorialisation. This term describes the weakening of the connection between culture as everyday lived experience and its territorial location '...involving the simultaneous penetration of local worlds by distant forces, and the dislodging of everyday meanings from their 'anchors' in the local environment' (p 29). To put it another way, the assumption that culture and location are necessarily linked can no longer be taken for granted.

Arguably then, it is not only people that travel, but also their ideas, beliefs and values, in this sense cultures are also more mobile than they have ever been. Tourism, as a form of leisure migration (Böröcz 1996) which often involves forms of culture contact can also be seen as one aspect of these globalising tendencies (see also Pizam 1999). Globalisation then is both complex and multi dimensional and needs to be conceptualised, at a basic level, as a case of 'flows' of people, money, commodities and cultural practices across national boundaries (Appadurai, 1990; Hannerz, 1996; Schudson, 1994) as much as within (Eade, 1997; Gillespie, 1995) to the extent that notions of centre – periphery, first second and third world are no longer sufficient to account for the contemporary situation (Hoogvelt, 1997; Crow 1997).

Within this context here are two themes to be addressed. The first concerns the role of tourism in terms of cultural change, especially since it is often seen as the vector for the introduction of 'alien' values, or the means by which 'western' patterns of both taste and behaviour are incorporated into 'other' cultures. The second concerns what Appadurai terms the 'central problem of today's global interactions' (1990 p 295) which is the tension between cultural homogeneity and heterogeneity, or convergence and divergence (Pizam 1999). What is being referred to here is whether or not globalisation is leading to the creation of an homogenous world which in effect flattens out cultural differences, or by contrast, is leading to the development of more distinct and localised forms of cultural identity. But before these can be properly addressed, it is necessary to come to some definition as to what 'culture' is in the first place.

Culture

The first distinction that needs to be made is that between culture in tourism, or cultural tourism, and culture as an analytical concept. In terms of the former, culture tends to be loosely associated with what may be described as the arts. In the developed economies, these are further subdivided into high and low, or elite and mass culture, despite claims that post-modernism has erased this distinction. Cultural tourism tends to emphasise the high arts and heritage, but can also include customs, rituals and performances and is often seen as a form of niche marketing (Fladmark, 1994; Richards, 1996a,1996b; Robinson and Boniface, 1999; Zukin, 1995).

Within such analyses culture tends to be seen as an economic resource, but also one that is often contrasted to mass tourism, as if pursuing 'culture' is a kind of 'improving' or 'educational' activity as opposed to the apparently more mindless pleasures of idling on sun filled beaches. In the less developed economies culture for tourism tends to be regarded in terms of ethnic arts and customs or ethnicity itself. In such cases we are dealing with both material culture and certain activities as the visible and concrete expression of differences.

Such forms of tourism tend to be based on some notion of culture as a primordial attachment to place, underpinned by three assumptions. First, cultures are socially homogenous, secondly, they are delimited in terms of ethnicity, thirdly, they are delimited in respect to other cultures. (Welsch, 1999 pp194/5). In this way, nations as much as more discrete locations within them are often defined in part through the possession of a distinct culture (Schudson, 1994) an idea rooted in Enlightenment ideals of self determination and cultural cohesiveness (Callinicos, 1999). To have a culture is not only to belong, but also to be different from others (Dann, 1996; Van den Berghe, 1994; Selwyn 1993). Cultures are then viewed as being not only differentiated vis-à-vis each other in terms of their 'authentic' material and social forms, as well as being spatially delimited and, especially when dealing with less technologically developed cultures, timeless and unchanging. In may cases this also results in a misplaced romanticism which views modernity as a negative condition in which a presumed lack of social cohesion is contrasted to the presumed social homogeneity within other more 'primitive' cultures (MacCannell, 1976).

The use of culture as an analytical category, at least in tourism research, tends to see as an adjunct to both the economic or the social, and is often added as what appears to be a concession to issues of change, and the 'impacts' or 'effects' wrought by tourism development (Archer and Cooper, 1996; Shaw and Williams, 1994). The distinction between the social and the cultural is often vague and difficult to grasp (Brunt and Courtney, 1999) and the two terms are sometimes bracketed to become socio-cultural. At the risk of over generalisation though, it is possible to see the social or society as referring to institutional forms generally associated with nation states (Crow, 1997 pp 13 – 17) and culture to the set of values and beliefs that underpins such forms, often associated with differences attributed to nationality (Pizam, 1999). Culture is thus confined to the status of a residual category, what remains after other factors, most notably economic and political, are taken into account. To do so is to reduce culture to a form of collective consciousness comprising of idealised essential attributes, often viewed as being inherent, timeless and unchanging which exists above and beyond the actions of individuals as some form of external objective reality. (Barth, 1992; Kuper, 1992, 1999).

However, there is another way of viewing culture which views it as comprising of both material and symbolic production (Abram (et al) 1997, Abram and Waldren, 1998; Boissevain, 1996; Hitchcock (et al), 1993; Lavie, (et al) 1993; Kuper, 1999; Lanfant (et al), 1995; Nash, 1996; Smith, 1989). Martinez for example argues that in this sense, what we should examine are the relationships between the production of material goods and the symbolic meanings that these may carry (1998 pp 3-4). Culture is then conceptualised as a symbolic system by which and through which people create and recreate shared meanings which inform their actions, a formulation which has much in common with that employed within cultural studies (Bocock, 1992; du Gay, 1997; Storey, 1999; Tomlinson, 1999). Culture in the sense that it is used here is seen in terms of processes and practices, rooted in forms of knowledge and symbolic production, which encapsulate common values and act as general guiding principles for action. It is through these forms of knowledge that distinctions are created and maintained, so that for example, one culture is marked off as different from another.

To conceptualise culture in this way is to see it as an active process of generating meaningful practices, and moves us away from the simplistic conception of cultures as a collection of essential attributes found within spatially bound entities. This latter assumption is no longer tenable as nation states are now more multi-cultural and more internally differentiated in terms of gender and socio-economic status than they have been in the past. Further to assume that cultures are ethnically bound, that is, associated with particular ideas of race assumes there is little contact between different cultures which in turn implies exclusivity and in its most extreme form racial purity. As Featherstone and Lash (1999 p 1) argue, 'It is no longer adequate to conceptualise culture as an integrated whole'.

Changing culture

The processes of commodification are often taken as evidence that tourism has eradicated cultural differences. The most naïve form of this is known as the demonstration effect, which assumes that host populations will simply mimic the behaviour and values of the guests, and by doing so introduce some form of distortion into their own culture. (Bleasdale and Tapsell, 1999; Burns and Holden, 1995; Cooper et al, 1998; de Kadt, 1979; McMinn and Cater, 1998; Moore, 1995; Pearce, 1989; Williams, 1998; Youell, 1998).

As de Kadt (1979) put it, the demonstration effect is best regarded as '...changes in attitudes, values, or behaviour which can result from [the hosts] merely observing tourists' (p 65). As Pearce writes, the residents of tourist areas may then aspire to obtain the 'material goods so casually displayed by him' (1989 p 223). For example Bleasdale and Tapsell single out the wearing of 'western' clothes by young Tunisian males as evidence of cultural change caused by tourism (but see Poirier 1995 on the same subject). Patterns of behaviour can also be viewed in this way, so that

both McMinn and Cater (1998) and Moore (1995) point to changes in local patterns of alcohol consumption caused by tourism. Williams states that the concept of demonstration effects is '...particularly attractive in explaining tourism impacts where contact between the hosts and guests are typically superficial and transitory' (1998 p 153). What is being singled out in these accounts are two interrelated factors. First, the assumption that western commodities are at worst unsuitable or at best incongruous for 'others'. Second, changes to patterns of social interaction which are seen as a direct consequence of tourism. Now the influence of outside factors in relation to the processes of change associated with tourism cannot be denied. Although a focus on local level or micro processes of change is necessary, the immediate question here is how such changes are to be apprehended and analysed, and whether or not the demonstration effect provides an adequate conceptual tool for explaining cultural change.

The first problem is the overwhelmingly negative valuations ascribed to the demonstration effect. This is the result, I would suggest, of the fact that assessments couched in terms of the demonstration effect are both normative and prescriptive as it is implied that 'they' should not presume to behave like 'us', as 'they' have their own set of cultural beliefs and ways of acting, how else could they be 'other'? In this sense it is deeply patronising.

A further problem is that of methodological as much as conceptual naivety. Proof of the demonstration effect relies on observations which are not adequately contextualised, as if causal relationships can simply be inferred from the presence of certain items of material culture or superficial similarities in ways of acting. Such explanations are not sufficient in terms of establishing either cause or meaning. As both Gamradt (1995) and Wall (1997) argue, explanations of changes in behaviour require gaining knowledge of 'insiders' as much as 'outsiders' understandings in context, which is a methodological as much as a theoretical necessity for understanding cultural change (Decrop, 1999).

The demonstration effect is also predicated on the assumption that cultures are bounded, self contained entities. In turn, this assumes that change is caused by external rather than internal factors. As Böröcz (1996 p 16) points out, people are thus being regarded as passive recipients, not capable of exercising agency or engaging with the processes of change. Yet traditions and rituals, those prime markers of cultural distinctiveness whose commodification is often bewailed, can go through a series of transformations in both form and content whether or not they are performed for tourists (Macdonald 1997 pp 108-111) or for internal consumption (Gore, 1998; Paerregaard, 1997 pp 203-228). Or to put it simply, cultures are not static. Finally, such approaches make the a priori assumption that 'cultures' existed in some pristine or uncontaminated state of authenticity before the intrusions of tourism, otherwise its 'effects' could not be observed, which in turn means treating culture in terms of '...homogeneity and authenticity in a world of inauthentic and unrooted global influences' (Amin and Thrift 1994 p 9). Such models and their variants are therefore predicated on concepts of essentialism, which also denies the possibility that people are capable of re-interpreting and using commodities in novel ways, as much as creating new forms of social interaction to fit new circumstances.

Although the above criticisms relate specifically to one formulation of change, many can be equally applied to other forms of analysis such as the concept of acculturation. Nuñez describes this as follows: '...when two cultures come into contact of any duration, each becomes something like the other through a process of borrowing' (1989 p 266). Similarly, Williams views acculturation as a form of convergence which occurs with prolonged contact, as opposed to the transitory contacts resulting in the demonstration effect (1998 p 153). The notion of acculturation has a superficial appeal, but also contains a number of problems. First is the assumption that there is a linear process of change by which cultures will converge, even if this is somewhat asymmetrical (ibid). Secondly, the other assumption is that cultures are the entities which 'contact' rather than people. We also need to consider as well what may happen if the hosts receive guests from a variety of different cultures - which would have the greater influence? Once more the problems of internal change are glossed over in favour of seeing external factors, acting in a simple in a simple cause - effect model, as the agents of change. In this regard, both the demonstration effect and acculturation have much in common with other forms of impact analysis many of which, as Wall (1997) argues, '...conjures up images of negative change' (p 7) and do so because of their implicit conceptual underpinnings of essentialism.

So far, the examples used have been confined to what we might term tourist – host encounters and reactions to them. As noted above, one of the factors often associated with the demonstration effect relates to the introduction of new commodity forms. If we accept that cultures are dynamic systems of meaning construction, the question then arises as how we are to account for the apparent 'transplanting' of commodities from one cultural context to another other than resorting to the demonstration effect or seeing them as evidence of convergence. One of the sub themes to run through the literature described above is the ambiguous relationship between culture and commerce, in which the commodification of culture, either in terms of material or ritualised performances, is seen to render them inauthentic. Cultures and indeed objects and commodities travel, yet it should not be assumed that meanings associated with both actions and objects is somehow fixed and essential and therefore travel too. Indeed the ethnographic record indicates that people are more capable of reinterpreting meanings according to their particular situations and needs than is sometimes allowed for, even if this is in a form that may appear strange or incongruous to the casual observer (see for example Friedman 1994; pp 102-116 and Clifford, (1997) pp 156).

One example which we should all be familiar with can be seen in the spread of karaoke which as Kelly points out, is a rare example of a Japanese leisure activity that has been distributed globally. Yet as he points out, it is '...*the object* - the karaoke machine – and *not so much the culture*, as defined by its use in a particular social context, which has been exported' (1998 p 76 emphasis added). The phenomenon of karaoke is defined depending on the context in which it is located. The object has no intrinsic meaning in itself, it is localised practices which define its cultural meaning. Gurnah for example, in a fascinating account of his Zanzibari childhood in the 1950s, recalls that the indigenous culture was not only composed of Islamic, African and European colonial elements, but also more recent 'foreign' cultural influences which '...once absorbed ... became 'ours', as much as they were once located elsewhere' (1997 p121). So if we are then to reject the simple cause – effect models implied in both the demonstration effect and acculturation, and see the changes associated with tourism as one factor of change, does this mean that we are dealing with the emergence of new and different cultural forms, as the example of karaoke suggests?

Hybrid or travelling cultures?

The term hybridity is often used to describe changes which combine elements from a number of sources (Hannerz, 1996; Nederveen – Pieterse, 1995). To take such an approach means focussing on the ways in which cultural influences are adapted, borrowed and reinterpreted for more localised forms of consumption. However the notion of hybridity itself has been criticised by, for example, Albrow et al. (1997) and Friedman (1999) in that it presupposes some notion cultural essence or purity to begin with. As such, hybridisation is often seen as a matter of '...regret and loss - loss of purity, wholeness, authenticity' (Nederveen - Pieterse 1995, pp 54-55). Perhaps the concept of 'travelling cultures', first coined as far as I can tell by Clifford (1992, 1997, but see also Howell, 1995) can offer a conceptual outline for explaining the changes associated with tourism. Taking up this idea, Rojek and Urry (1997) note that cultures do not exist in a pure state, and are continuously being made and remade, and that travel itself is an integral part of this process (ibid pp 10-12). As they comment, cultures are '...impure and being constantly reinvented' (ibid p 11). Despite the reservations I have concerning the use of the term 'impure', which implies a notion of 'authentic purity' somewhere along the line (see also Wood, 1993) the basic idea that cultures are engaged in a continuous process of invention and reinvention is one approach that moves us away from the notion of culture as a collection of essential attributes located within a given locality or nation state, as if what occurs beyond our boundaries is simply what 'they' do 'over there' (Featherstone and Lash, 1999; Hannerz, 1996; Lovell, 1998). This also requires us to focus on the macro processes of globalisation as much as the micro processes of cultural change within specific localities (Cohen, 1996; Fardon, 1995; Howes, 1996; Martinez, 1998; Watson, 1997).

Although this looks promising, Tomlinson warns that simply replacing the 'roots' implied by essentialist notions of cultures with the 'routes' of travelling cultures does not actually solve the problem (1999 p29). Having freed culture from its essentialist moorings does not mean that everything is therefore a globalised free for all of post-modern simulacra (Urry, 1990 p 85). Despite the processes of deterritorialisation and the greater movement of people as a consequence of globalisation, cultures are still created and maintained by practical actions at a mundane and local level. However, it must be acknowledged that as a consequence of global change, both the physical and conceptual boundaries of localities cannot be accepted as given. Although these concepts need careful qualification, overall it follows that forms of behaviour, as well as the ways in which commodities are consumed adapted and changed, cannot be simply be inferred from the cultural context in which they were originally produced but need to be seen in the context in which they are used, adapted and changed (Kopytoff, 1986; Gell, 1986; Hendrickson, 1996; Linnekin, 1997). To ignore this latter point is to privilege form over content (Abu-Lughod, 1991; Wilk, 1995) and to conflate the production of both meanings and commodities with their consumption.

A clear example of such conflation in terms of cultural change relates to the spread of broadcast media. The idea of the 'global village' (Boniface and Fowler 1993) or whatever phrase is used to imply global connectivity leading to homogeneity is often, as Tomlinson (1999) points out, the result of equating the spread of technology with the assumption that this inevitably results in the spread of western values. Technology thus becomes another demonised vector for outside influences. To see the spread of technology *per se* as leading to cultural homogeneity ignores the role of indigenous broadcast media (Mattelart et al, 1984 p102) and its adaptation, interpretation and uses in terms of localised conditions (Barker, 1999; Bredin, 1996; Gore, 1998; Gurnah, 1997; Hughes-Freeland, 1999), for as Howell comments, the 'cultural supremacy' of the west is often over estimated (1995 p 171). It also ignores the ways in which 'mainstream' media in the west can be reinterpreted in terms of both diasporic and emerging ethnicities (Gillespie, 1995). The increasing flow of media images across borders resulting from globalisation is subject to mediation at a number of levels just as much as the flows of commodities and indeed people. Yet there is an important issue here that needs to be addressed, and that is whether or not cultural changes are caused in part by the creation and manipulation of images, representations and discourses, which given the processes of deterritorialisation outlined above, are located beyond the immediate micro level experience of the tourist – host encounter.

Politics, culture and representation

The global spread of media may also be portrayed as a form of ideological domination, an attempt to assert cultural hegemony through symbolic forms of representation and discourse. For example, Hall (1994) argues that the creation of tourist representations, or 'gazes' to use Urry's (1990) terminology, is linked to both politics and economics which in turn transforms social realities through the processes of commodification (pp 176-177). Although Hall is certainly correct to draw attention to the relationship between culture, economy and politics (see also Street, 1997; McGuigan, 1996), the problem here lies in assuming that social reality is primarily a matter of representations, that it can be treated solely as if it were a text or discourse to be decoded as ideological dominance or resistance to such domination. Such approaches, derived largely from post-structuralist theory, focus on the contested nature of social reality and in particular the importance of language or discourse, and representations (for example see Dann 1996a).

Now there are clearly a number of important issues here concerning control over representations. For example, tourism marketing often relies on western romanticised notions of the 'other' in selling an imaginary world of leisure (Dann, 1996b; Rojek and Urry, 1997; Selwyn, 1993; Urry, 1990). Yet the danger here lies in privileging the production of imagery over and above other factors and also seeing the discourse of tourism commodification as resulting in some form of distorted, contrived or inauthentic reality (see Dann 1996a pp 4-29). Although it must be acknowledged that struggles over the representation of people and cultures are matters of concern, such representations and discourses are not free floating entities which exist over and above the material conditions out of which they are constructed, and have no autonomy in themselves (Finlayson, 1999b p58).

Control over representations can involve issues of national and ethnic identity which may need to be maintained against other conflicting claims (Bovin, 1998; Jamison, 1999; Robinson and Boniface, 1999; Zukin, 1995). For example critiques of tourism as a form of cultural contamination are often voiced by internal groups as much as external analysts (Abram and Waldren, 1998; Picard, 1996; Poirier, 1995; Wilson 1997). Yet this should not be taken as *prima facie* evidence of cultural loss or contamination. Although such criticisms must be treated with the seriousness they deserve, if they are evidence of anything, it is the ways in which cultures need to be constantly made and remade in the face of both internal and external factors of change as culture is always '...fitted to new circumstances' (Hannerz, 1996 p 5). One example is the way in which the people of Bali have been able to reinvent and recreate elements of their traditional culture for both internal as much as touristic consumption (Picard, 1993, 1996; Wall, 1997). Hobart observes that what '...people in a particular part of Bali previously just did is coming increasingly to be constituted self consciously as 'culture'. In part a response to tourism, but also as a result of government policy' (1995 p 64).

The arguments I have outlined above relating to the malleable nature of commodities can also be extended to representations. Analysing their production in the way suggested by Hall will inform us of their contextual utilisation as policy or marketing instruments, but this is not the same as analysing their consumption (Dann, 1996b p 79). There is no guarantee that they will be 'read' or 'decoded' in the manner intended as we cannot assume that 'sending' and 'receiving' cultures are internally homogenous (Kiely, 1998 p 14), that people are simply caught in a web of textual significations or signs and symbols to which they can only passively respond. As Finlayson cautions, '...we should not overestimate the power and importance of the text' (1999a p147). To treat cultures solely as 'texts' or 'discourses' to be decoded abstracts and objectifies the practical actions whereby meanings are attributed (Friedman, 1994). Representations do not have power in and of themselves, their importance lies their utilisation as a means to gain access to resources, entry to the global tourist market, as attempts to create some notion of shared identity, or to pursue a political agenda. Such uses are not mutually exclusive which can be seen in cases where both culture and tourism policies have been used instrumentally for economic purposes as much as creating and asserting regional (see European Union 1998) or localised identities. One example of the latter can be seen in Sjöberg's ethnographic study of the Ainu, an indigenous ethnic group in

Hokkaido, Japan, where tourism commodification is used both as a means of generating income and as a means of asserting ethnic identity: '...the stress on cultural factors is an indispensable means of unequivocally defining their own position in the context of the larger society' (1993 p 187).

Tourism, change and the cultural economy

To view cultural change in terms of the simple before and after models outlined earlier is to perform an unwarranted act of reductionism which, coupled with the essentialist fallacy which assumes a static pre-existing state of cultural stability and internal homogeneity, can only lead to sterile and misplaced accounts of cause and effect. Culture, in the sense defined here, is an emergent quality of interactive processes, not a steady state. As Wall (1997) has argued, what is required is a much broader conceptualisation of change which accounts for internal as much as external factors, or to be more precise, the dynamic nature of cultural change.

The first requirement here is for models of cultural change to be grounded in the macro processes of globalisation, as these are clearly leading to new forms of economic, cultural and political organisation. As I mentioned above, one of the central features of globalisation is that of mass migration, for both economic and leisure purposes which results in a situation where cultural influences are more mobile than at any previous time. In turn, this leads to the situation where it is no longer feasible to consider cultures as confined to specific localities.

I have also argued against other implicit assumptions concerning the presumed homogenising tendencies of both tourism and globalisation. As the empirical material indicates, both commodities and less tangible forms of symbolic representation are more malleable than they may first appear. Cultural forms may be appropriated or changed by tourism but also cross boundaries and are indigenised whether or not tourism is present as they have no intrinsic or essential meaning in themselves, but are defined by context and use. Such changes then cannot be seen as effects solely attributable to tourism, rather they are an integral part of the processual nature of cultural change itself, which arguably has been accelerated through the global flows of capital, people, commodities and symbolic representations. Culture is both used and reproduced though practical actions, it is not something that people respond to, but something they engage with.

The crucial difference between the formulation offered here and the earlier approaches outlined lies in rejecting the notion that cultures as sets of inherent essential characteristics confined within spatial boundaries, and seeing them as being actively constituted as dynamic systems, in which people are continuously engaged in creating and recreating their social worlds. However this is not to perform a simple inversion, and argue that the cultural should therefore take precedence over the economic or the political, rather it means seeing the relationship between the economic, the cultural and other factors as mutually constructive, comprising of the attribution of meaning which is socially situated.

One way of approaching this is in terms of what du Gay terms the cultural economy (1997 p 3). As he notes, the use of this term not only intended to draw attention to the relationship between the cultural and the economic, as outlined above, but also to the increasing aestheticisation of commodities which are sold '...in terms of particular clusters of meaning' (ibid p 5, see also Featherstone 1991 pp 87-94). Frow writes that this '...is realised as a practice of differentiation of commodities and of places ... with place now increasingly marketed as a commodity on the basis of its specific difference/or its 'authenticity'' (1997 p 48). What is sold in this sense is a world of fantasy, of dreams, of images and representations. This commodification of place and people on which tourism relies on differentiating people and place, and also underlines the interdependence, within the global economy, of cultural meanings and their economic utilisation. This situation applies as much to the developed as the less developed economies (Featherstone, 1991; Chang, 1997; Judd and Fainstein, 1999; Hannigan, 1998; Held et al, 1999; Picard, 1996; Zukin, 1995, 1996).

We cannot therefore simply reduce culture to an effect of economics (du Gay, 1997) nor consider it as a fixed autonomous sphere, as if it were something external or objective that people simply respond to (Friedman, 1994 p 211; Tomlinson, 1999 p 24). Neither can we view economics as being simply and only about the maximisation of profit, for like culture, economics does not exist as an autonomous or neutral sphere, but is related to patterns of social life and the ways in which human activity is conceptualised and acted upon (Appadurai, 1986; Sahlins, 1976). Economic as much as cultural processes depend on the generation of meanings (duGay, 1997; Featherstone, 1991; Zukin, 1995, 1996) and their realisation in practical and mundane actions. The symbolic and representational forms of culture cannot then be simply separated from material and economic conditions out of which they are fashioned (Zukin, 1995, 1996). To view culture in these terms should not be seen as a reason to invoke the spectre of inauthenticity. To commodify and use culture for economic means does not devalue it or render it false, or necessarily lead to loss, contamination or despoliation (Bruner, 1996). As the examples have shown, there is no easy fit between the production and consumption of meanings, there is always scope for reinterpretation at a number of levels. For example, there is a need to account for the ways in which culture is used as a policy instrument not only for economic growth but also as a means of creating or asserting forms of identity, culture itself is a contested and political realm in which the currency of symbolic meanings also acts as a currency of social identity (Zukin, 1995).

Yet there is an apparent paradox here. On the one hand both theoretical developments and empirical evidence point us in the direction of accepting that cultures are not bounded entities composed of unchanging essential elements, and that they are more mobile than before, while on the other hand, we have people attempting to define their culture by asserting essential characteristics, often bound to place, as the basis for their unique authentic identity. In order to account for this we need to draw a distinction between the *commodification* and *analysis* of culture. Both tourism and forms of identity can draw on the same cultural repertoire of images and representations which reduce complexity to a recognisable formula, in this sense representations or symbolic forms act as metaphors for the culture as a whole.

What tourism commodification adds is a new, if somewhat complex, dimension as it relies on the same process, so that the analysis of the relationship between tourism and culture requires us to account for commodification, but without reducing culture to the commodified form – the representation – itself. Representational forms whether for internal or external consumption need to be seen as means, not ends. Analysing their role and significance requires a focus on the deployment and uses of culture, and the ways in which commodification both interpenetrates cultures, while also acting as a means by which local forms of cultural identity are changed and maintained.

If we take the cultural economy as the point of enquiry, rather than split the economic from the cultural, then a different and more dynamic framework for analysis presents itself. The focus then changes from accounting for impacts, effects or whatever to assessing processes and practices, and the ways in which the production and reproduction of cultural forms involves both internally oriented patterns of values as much as those that are externally oriented. This also requires taking account of the cultural forms and influences that are incorporated into localised practices and indigenised. There is therefore a need to account for the dynamics of change in terms of both generation of cultural meanings, for internal consumption as much as those produced for external consumption, to see culture as forms of practical action which need to be understood in terms of their context and use. This requires analyses of the changes that emerge from the interaction between micro level, localised practices, set in the context of macro analyses of the global political economy of tourism.

References

Abram, S. and Waldren, J. (1998), (Editors) *Anthropological Perspectives on Local Development: Knowledge and sentiments in conflict*. Routledge: London.

Abram, S., Waldren, J. and MacLeod, D. V. (Editors) (1997), *Tourists and Tourism: identifying with people and places*. Berg: Oxford.

Abu-Lughod, J. (1991), Going beyond Global Babble. In King, A. D. (Editor) *Culture, Globalisation and the World System: Contemporary conditions for the representation of identity*. Macmillan: Basingstoke, pp. 131-137.

Albrow, M., Eade, J., Dürrschmidt, J., and Washbourne, N. (1997), The Impact of Globalisation on Sociological Concepts: Community, culture and milieu. In Eade, J. (Editor) *Living the Global City*. Routledge: London, pp. 20-36.

Amin, A. and Thrift, N. (1994), Living in the Global. In Amin, N. and Thrift, N. (Editors) *Globalisation, Institutions and Regional Development in Europe*. Oxford University Press: Oxford, pp. 1-22.

Appadurai, A. (1986), Introduction: Commodities and the politics of value. In Appadurai, A. (Editor) *The Social Life of Things: Commodities in cultural perspective*. Cambridge University Press: Cambridge, pp. 3-63.

Appadurai, A. (1990), Disjuncture and Difference in the Global Cultural Economy. In Featherstone, M. (Editor) *Global Culture: Nationalism, Globalisation and Modernity*. Sage: London, pp. 295-310.

Archer, B. and Cooper, C. (1996), The Positive and Negative Effects of Tourism. In Theobald, W. (Editor, 2nd edition) *Global Tourism*. Butterworth - Heinemann: Oxford, pp 63-81.

Barker, C. (1999), *Television, Globalisation and Cultural Identities*. Open University Press: Buckingham.

Barth, F. (1992), Towards greater Naturalism in Conceptualising Societies. In Kuper, A. (Editor) *Conceptualising Society*. Routledge: London, pp. 17-33.

Bleasdale, S, and Tapsell, S. (1999), Social and Cultural Impacts of Tourism Policy in Tunisia. In Robinson, M. and Boniface, P. (Editors) *Tourism and Cultural Conflicts*. CABI Publishing: Wallingford, pp.181-204.

Bocock, R. (1992), Consumption and Lifestyles. In Bocock, R. and Thompson, K. (Editors) *Social and Cultural Forms of Modernity*. Polity: Cambridge, pp. 119-168.

Boissevain, J. (Editor) (1996), *Coping With Tourists: European reactions to mass tourism*. Oxford: Berghahn Books.

Böröcz, J. (1996), *Leisure Migration: A sociological Study*. Pergamon Press: Oxford.

Boniface, P. and Fowler, P. J. (1993*), Heritage and Tourism in the 'global village'*. Routledge: London.

Bovin, M. (1998), Nomadic Performance – Peculiar Culture? 'Exotic' ethnic performances of the WoDaaBe nomads of Niger. In Hughes-Freeland, M. and Crain, M. (Editors) *Recasting Ritual: Performance, Media, Identity*. Routledge: London, pp. 93-112.

Bredin, M. (1996), Transforming Images: Communication technologies and cultural identity in Nishnawbe-Aski. In Howes, D. (Editor) *Cross – Cultural Consumption: Global markets, local realities*. Routledge: London, pp.161-177.

Bruner, E. (1996), Abraham Lincoln as Authentic Reproduction: A critique of postmodernism. *American Anthropologist,* 96, (2), pp.397 – 415.

Brunt, P. and Courtney, P. (1999) Host Perceptions of Sociocultural Impacts. *Annals of Tourism Research* 26 (3): 493 - 515.

Burns, P. and Holden, A. (1995), *Tourism: A new perspective*. Prentice Hall: London.

Callinicos, A. (1999), *Social Theory: A historical introduction*. Polity Press: Cambridge.

Chang, T. C. (1997), Heritage as a Tourism Commodity: Traversing the tourist - local divide. *Singapore Journal of Tropical Geography*, 18 (1): 46 - 68.

Clifford, J. (1992), Travelling Cultures. In Grossberg, L., Nelson, C. and Treichler, P. (Editors) *Cultural Studies*. Routledge: New York, pp. 96-116

Clifford, J. (1997), *Routes: Travel and translation in the late twentieth century*. Harvard University Press: Cambridge, MA.

Cohen, E. (1996), The Sociology of Tourism. In Apostopolous, Y., Leivadi, S. and Yiannikis, A. (Editors) *The Sociology of Tourism: Theoretical and empirical investigations*. Routledge: London, pp. 51-74.

Cooper, C., Fletcher, J., Gilbert, D. and Wanhill, S. (1998 2nd edition), *Tourism Principles and Practice*. Longman: Harlow.

Crow, G. (1997), *Comparative Sociology and Social Theory: Beyond the three worlds*. Macmillan: Basingstoke.

Dann, G. (1996a), *The Language of Tourism: A sociolinguistic perspective*. CAB International: Wallingford.

Dann, G. (1996b), The People of Tourist Brochures. In Selwyn, T. (Editor) *The Tourist Image: Myths and myth making in tourism*. Wiley: Chichester, pp. 61-82.

Decrop, A. (1999), Qualitative Research Methods for the Study of Tourist Behaviour. In Pizam, A. and Mansfeld, Y. (Editors) *Consumer Behaviour in Travel and Tourism*. Haworth Hospitality Press: New York, pp. 335-366.

de Kadt, E. (1979), *Tourism: Passport to Development?* Oxford University Press: Oxford.

du Gay, P. (Editor) (1997), *Production of Culture/Cultures of Production*. Sage: London.

Eade, J. (1997), (Editor) *Living the Global City*. Routledge: London.

European Union (1998), *Investing in Culture: An asset for all regions*. Office for the Official Publications of the European Communities: Luxembourg.

Fardon, R. (Editor) (1995), *Counterworks: Managing the diversity of knowledge*. Routledge: London

Featherstone, M. (1991), *Consumer Culture and Postmodernism*. Sage: London

Featherstone, M. and Lash, S. (1999), Introduction. In Featherstone, M. and Lash, S.(Editors) *Spaces of Culture: City, Nation, World*. Sage: London, pp. 1-13.

Finlayson, A. (1999a) Culture. In Ashe, F., Finlayson, A., Lloyd, M., MacKenzie, I., Martin, J. and O'Neill. *Contemporary Social and Political Theory*. Open University Press: Buckingham, pp. 131-154.

Finlayson, A. (1999b), Language. In Ashe, F., Finlayson, A., Lloyd, M., MacKenzie, I., Martin, J. and O'Neill. *Contemporary Social and Political Theory*. Open University Press: Buckingham, pp. 47-68.

Fladmark, J. M (Editor) (1994), *Cultural Tourism*. Donhead: London.

Friedman, J. (1994), *Cultural Identity and Global Process*. Sage: London.

Friedman, J. (1999), The Hybridisation of Roots and the Abhorrence of the Bush. In Featherstone, M. and Lash, S, (Editors) *Spaces of Culture: City, nation, world*. Sage: London.

Gamradt, J. (1995), Jamaican Children's Representations of Tourism. *Annals of Tourism Research*, 22 (4): 735-762.

Gell, A. (1986), Newcomers to the World of Goods: The Muria Gonds. In Appadurai, A. (Editor) *The Social Life of Things: Commodities in cultural perspective*. Cambridge University Press: Cambridge, pp.110 – 138.

Gillespie, M. (1995), *Television, Ethnicity and Cultural Change*. Routledge: London.

Gore, C. (1998), Ritual, Performance and Media in Urban Contemporary Shrine Configurations in Benin City, Nigeria. In Hughes-Freeland, F. (Editor) *Ritual, Performance, Media*. Routledge: London, pp.66-84.

Gurnah, A. (1997), Elvis in Zanzibar. In Scott, A. (ed) *The Limits of Globalisation*. Routledge: London, pp.116-142.

Hall, C. M. (1994), *Tourism and Politics: Policy, power and place*. Wiley: Chichester

Hannerz, U. (1996), *Transnational Connections: Culture, people, places*. Routledge: London.

Hannigan, J. (1998), *Fantasy City: Pleasure and profit in the post-modern metropolis*. Routledge: London.

Hearn, J. and Roseneil, S. (Editors) (1999), *Consuming Cultures: Power and resistance*. Macmillan: Basingstoke.

Hendrickson, C. (1996), Selling Gautemala: Maya export products in US mail-order catalogues. In Howes, D. (Editor) *Cross – Cultural Consumption: Global markets, local realities*. Routledge: London, pp.106-124.

Held, D., McGrew, A. Goldblatt, D. and Perraton, J. (1999), *Global Transformations: Politics, economics and culture*. Polity Press: Cambridge.

Hitchcock, M., King, V. T and Parnwell, M. J. G (Editors) (1993), *Tourism in South East Asia*. Routledge: London.

Hobart, M. (1995), As I Lay Laughing: Encountering global knowledge in Bali. In Fardon, R. (Editor) *Counterworks: Managing the diversity of knowledge*. Routledge: London, pp. 49-72.

Hoogvelt, A. (1997), *Globalisation and the Postcolonial World: The new political economy of development*. Macmillan: Basingstoke.

Howell, S. (1995), Whose Knowledge and Whose Power?: A new perspective on cultural diffusion. In Fardon, R. (Editor) *Counterworks: Managing the diversity of knowledge*. Routledge: London, pp.161-181.

Hughes-Freeland, F (1999), Balinese on Television: Representations and response. In Banks, M. and Morphy, H. (Editors) *Rethinking Visual Anthropology*. Yale University Press: New Haven, pp.120-138.

Jamison, D. (1999), Tourism and Ethnicity: The Brotherhood of coconuts. *Annals of Tourism Research* 26 (4): 944-967.

Judd, D. R. and Fainstein, S. S. (Editors) (1999), *The Tourist City*. Yale University Press: New Haven and London.

Kelly, B. (1998), Japan's Empty Orchestras: Echoes of Japanese culture in the performance of karaoke. In Martinez, D. P. (Editor) *The Worlds of Japanese Popular Culture: gender, shifting boundaries and global cultures*. Cambridge University Press: Cambridge, pp.75-90.

Kiely, R. (1998), Introduction: Globalisation (post)modernity and the Third World. In Keily, R. and Marfleet, P. (Editors) Globalisation and the Third World. Routledge: London, pp.1-34.

Kopytoff, I. (1986), The Cultural Biography of things: Commoditisation as process. In Appadurai, A. (Editor) *The Social Life of Things: Commodities in cultural perspective*. Cambridge University Press: Cambridge, pp.65-94.

Kuper, A. (1992), Introduction. In Kuper, A. (Editor) *Conceptualising Society*. Routledge: London, pp.1-16.

Kuper, A. (1999), *Culture: The anthropologists' account*. Harvard University Press: Cambridge, MA.

Lanfant, M. F., Allcock, J. B. and Bruner, E. M. (Editors) (1995), *International Tourism: Identity and Change*. Sage: London.

Lavie, S., Narayan, K. and Rosaldo, (Editors), *Creativity/Anthropology*. Cornell University Press: Ithica.

Linnekin, J. (1997), Consuming Cultures: Tourism and the commoditisation of cultural identity in the island Pacific. In Picard, M. and Wood, R. E. (Editors) (1997) *Tourism, Ethnicity and the State in Asian and Pacific Societies*. University of Hawi'i Press: Honolulu, pp. 215-250.

Lovell, N. (Editor) (1998), *Locality and Belonging*. Routledge: London.

MacCannell, D. (1976), *The Tourist: A new theory of the leisure class*. Schocken Books: New York.

Macdonald, S. (1997), *Reimagining Culture: Histories, identities and the Gaelic renaissance*. Berg: Oxford.

Martinez, D. P. (Editor) (1998), *The Worlds of Japanese Popular Culture: Gender, shifting boundaries and global cultures*. Cambridge University Press: Cambridge.

Mattelart, A., Delcourt, X. and Mattelart, M. (1984), *International Image Markets: In search of an alternative perspective*. Comedia: London.

McGuigan, J. (1996), *Culture and the Public Sphere*. Routledge: London.

McMinn, S. and Cater, E. (1998), Tourist Typology: Observations form Belize. *Annals of Tourism Research* 25 (3): 675 – 699.

Meethan, K. (forthcoming), *Tourism in Modern Society: Place, culture and consumption*. Macmillan: Basingstoke.

Moore, R. (1995), Gender and Alcohol Use in a Greek Tourist Town. *Annals of Tourism Research*, 22 (2): 300 – 313.

Nash, D. (1996), *Anthropology of Tourism*. Pergamon Press: Oxford.

Nederveen - Pieterse, J. (1995), Globalisation as Hybridisation. In Featherstone, M., Lash, S. and Robertson, R. (Editors) *Global Modernities*. Sage: London, pp. 45-68.

Nuñez, (1989), Touristic Studies in Anthropological Perspective. In Smith, V. L. (Editor, 2nd edition), *Hosts and Guests: The anthropology of tourism*. University of Pennsylvania Press: Philadelphia, pp. 265-280.

Paerregaard, K. (1997), *Linking Separate Worlds: Urban migrants and rural lives in Peru*. Berg: Oxford.

Pearce, D. (1989, 2nd edition), *Tourist Development*. Longman: Harlow.

Pearce, P. (1998), The Relationship Between Residents and Tourists: The research literature and management directions. In Theobald, W. (Editor, 2nd edition) *Global Tourism*. Butterworth - Heinemann: Oxford, pp.,129-149.

Picard, M. (1993), 'Cultural Tourism' in Bali: National integration and regional differentiation. In Hitchcock, M., King, V.T and Parnwell, M.J.G (Editors) (1993) *Tourism in South East Asia*. Routledge: London, pp.71-98.

Picard, M. (1996), *Bali: Cultural Tourism and Touristic Culture*. Archipelago Press: Singapore.

Pizam, A. (1999), Cross-Cultural Tourist Behaviour. In Pizam, A. and Mansfeld, Y. (Editors) *Consumer Behaviour in Travel and Tourism*. Haworth Hospitality Press: New York, pp.393-407.

Poirier, R. (1995), Tourism in Tunisia. *Annals of Tourism Research*, 22 (1): 157 – 171.

Richards, G. (1996a), Production and Consumption of European Cultural Tourism. *Annals of Tourism Research*, 23 (2): 261 - 283.

Richards, G. (Editor) (1996b), *Cultural Tourism in Europe*. CAB International: Wallingford

Robertson, J. (1998), It Takes a Village: Internationalisation and nostalgia in post-war Japan. In Vlastos, S. (Editor) (1998) *Mirror of Modernity: Invented traditions of modern Japan*. University of California Press: Berkeley, pp.110-129.

Robertson, R. (1992), *Globalisation: Social theory and global culture*. Sage: London.

Robinson, M. and Boniface, P. (Editors) (1999), *Tourism and Cultural Conflicts*. CABI Publishing: Wallingford.

Rojek, C. and Urry, J. (1997), Transformations of Travel and Theory. In Rojek, C. and Urry, J. (Editors) *Touring Cultures: Transformations of travel and theory*. Routledge: London, pp. 1-19.

Sahlins, M. (1976), *Culture and Practical Reason*. University of Chicago Press: Chicago.

Schudson, M. (1994), The Integration of National Societies. In Crane, D. (Editor) *The Sociology of Culture*. Blackwell: Oxford, pp. 21-44.

Selwyn, T. (1993), Peter Pan in South East Asia: Views from the brochures. In Hitchcock, M., King, V. T. and Parnwell, M. J. G (Editors) *Tourism in South East Asia*. Routledge: London, pp. 117-137.

Shaw, G. and Williams, A. (1994), *Critical Issues in Tourism: A geographical perspective*. Blackwell: London.

Sjöberg, K. (1993), *The Return of the Ainu: Cultural mobilisation and the practice of ethnicity in Japan*. Harwood Academic: Chur.

Smith, V. L. (Editor) (1989 2nd edition), *Hosts and Guests: The anthropology of tourism*. University of Pennsylvania Press: Philadelphia.

Storey, J. (1999) *Cultural Consumption and Everyday Life*. Arnold: London.

Street, J. (1997), 'Across the Universe': The limits of global popular culture. In Scott, A. (Editor) *The Limits of Globalisation: Cases and arguments*. Routledge: London, pp. 75-89.

Tomlinson (1999), *Globalisation and Culture*. Polity Press: Cambridge.

Urry, J. (1990), *The Tourist Gaze: Leisure and travel in contemporary societies*. Sage: London.

Van Den Berghe, P. L. (1994), *The Quest for the Other: Ethnic tourism in San Cristóbal, Mexico*. University of Washington Press: Seattle and London.

Wall, G. (1997), Rethinking Impacts of Tourism. In Cooper, C. and Wanhill, S. (Editors) *Tourism Development: Environmental and Community Issues*. Wiley: Chichester, pp.,1-10.

Watson, J .L. (Editor) (1997), *Golden Arches East: McDonald's in East Asia*. Stanford University Press: Stanford.

Welsch, W. (1999), Transculturality: The puzzling form of cultures today. In Featherstone, M. and Lash, S.(Editors) *Spaces of Culture: City, Nation, World*. Sage: London, pp. 194-213.

Wilk, R. (1995), Learning to be Local in Belize. In Miller, D. (Editor) *Worlds Apart: Modernity through the prism of the local*. Routledge: London, pp. 110-133.

Wilson, D. (1997), Paradoxes of Tourism in Goa. *Annals of Tourism Research*, 24 (1): 52 – 75.

Williams, S. (1998), *Tourism Geography*. Routledge: London.

Wood, R. E. (1993), Tourism, Culture and the Sociology of Development. In Hitchcock, M., King, V. T and Parnwell, M. J. G (Editors), *Tourism in South East Asia*. Routledge: London, pp.48-70.

Youell, R. (1998), *Tourism: An introduction*. Longman: Harlow.

Zukin, S. (1995), *The Cultures of Cities*. Blackwell: Oxford.

Zukin, S. (1996), Space and Symbols in an Age of Decline. In King, A. D. (Editor) *Re-presenting the City: Ethnicity, capital and culture in the 21st century metropolis*. Macmillan: Basingstoke, pp.43-59.

Tourism and cultural changes: The crafts of Chiang Mai

Ploysri Porananond

Chiang Mai University, Thailand

Abstract

Chiang Mai is a city with a seven hundred year long history. The crafts of Chiang Mai can therefore be traced back hundreds of years. These crafts are representative of the daily lives of the rural people who made them. They hand crafted useful tools for every day living from agriculture, such as: wooden utensils, woven products and earthenware pottery. The crafts of Chiang Mai were further influenced and enriched by Buddhist philosophy and symbolism. One such example, is the wooden carving of the Vihara, which is located in the main hall in many Buddhist temples.

As Chiang Mai has changed over time, so too have the crafts of its people. In the late 1970s Chiang Mai was officially developed and promoted internationally as the *'Rose of the North'* and tourism centre of Northern Thailand. Tourist demand for local crafts was high and many crafts were developed and adapted to capitalise on this growing lucrative market.

The increasing numbers of foreign tourists to Chiang Mai has affected both the quantity and the design of crafts produced. Many of the original production techniques, patterns and styles, for example, have been lost to easier designs and production methods more suited to mass production. The use and meaning of the crafts for the local people have also changed. Rather than representing local beliefs and culture, today they have value only in their ability to attract the tourist dollar in souvenir shops. There is no longer any meaning or function of these crafts to the local community of Chiang Mai.

Many factors regarding the impact of commercial tourism on the crafts of Chiang Mai will be discussed. In particular, how the local craftspeople have adapted their trade to the tourist market; the loss of local knowledge of traditional craft design and production techniques; and the loss of value and meaning of the crafts for the local community.

Introduction

Chiang Mai, with a population of 1,420,000, is located in northern Thailand. This city covers an area of 20,107 square kilometres, and its rich history dates back 700 years, beginning with several different ethnic groups.

King Mungrai was the first king who unified the different towns and villages into what came to be known as the Lanna Kingdom. Chiang Mai became the centre of this Kingdom which later expanded to cover much of Northern Thailand. There followed sporadic warfare for several generations, and Chiang Mai fell several times to both the Burmese and to a powerful kingdom to the south that was centred around the Choa Phraya Basin. In the end, Chiang Mai was claimed by Krung Thon Buri, then the capital of Thailand, and under the fifth Rama, the city officially became a part of Thailand.

For centuries, Chiang Mai has been the centre of religious activity in Northern Thailand. During the Lanna Kingdom, Buddhism was the main religion that flourished and grew. Evidence of this is seen in many ancient temples in Chiang Mai today. Currently, there are 1,255 temples in Chiang Mai with 5,977 monks and 5,977 novices.

Legend of traditional crafts of Chiang Mai

The city of Chiang Mai has a history rich in local crafts made from natural resources. The Buddhist faith has been the foundation of most of the crafts and art-styles of the local people. Their love of beautiful art has resulted in many branches of folk arts in Chiang Mai crafts. The unique folk art of different groups can be observed in the many artistic tools and utensils produced for their daily work, religious ceremonies, and rituals.

Some examples of Chiang Mai art, will be discussed in detail of role and function of traditional crafts of Chiang Mai.

Wood carving

Chiang Mai has a very interesting history of wood carving. Since, in the beginning, as religious beliefs and social customs dictated, carving wood was traditionally used to decorate the *"temples"* and *"Kum"* (the residential buildings of the ruling class). In the former, time wood carving was considered only appropriate for a 'holy place' such as a temple or a 'high place' such as a residential building for the Prince.

At that time, houses decorated with such wood carvings were limited to only the ruling class. These wood carvings served as a symbol to distinguish and reinforce the difference in status of the ruling class from the common people.

For the houses of the ordinary people, only wood carvings based on spiritual beliefs were allowed in the houses . For example; a *"Ham Yon"*, which was a square piece of carved wood, was commonly placed over the door of the house, under the belief that it would protect the house from bad spirits. Another wood carving of the ordinary people, was the elephant figure, which was carved on a long piece of wood that attached at the back of the farmer's oxen-cart.

Wood carvings, such as those that decorated the vihara in many temples, were made by the local craftsmen to accrue merit. They believed that producing crafts for a holy place was the best work that they could do in their lives, and would bring the greatest rewards, 'merit' to them.

In the beginning, there is no historical evidence that wood carvings were produced to meet *"market"* demand. About a hundred years ago, however, the carving of wood for religious beliefs and to distinguish personal status, changed to production for the *"market"*.

From this time to the present day, market driven production has meant that the wood carvings of Chiang Mai have lost their meanings and the transfer of wood carving skills from generation to generation has disappeared from the community.

For example, the wood carvings of elephants has become a very popular souvenir for tourists to Chiang Mai. The tourist demand for elephant carvings began in 1927, when Dr. Cheek, an ex-American missionary, who then turned to the logging business, developed his interest in a local craft, an elephant wood carving at the back of a farmer's oxen-cart. He asked his craftsman to carve a replica in a whole body of an elephant. When he saw his craftsman could produce an elephant in a whole body, he created the idea to carve figures of elephants at work, which included elephants using their trunks to push and pull logs in the forest.

Since then, elephant wood carvings have been extremely popular as an image of Chiang Mai, particularly for tourists. Thus, wood carvings have been produced mainly for the tourist market.

In the years 1957 to 1977, the wood carvings of Chiang Mai were actively promoted as souvenirs from Chiang Mai. At the same time, wood carving shops were opened in the city using hired craftsmen to work in their shops. Some of these craftsmen were from *Ban Ta Wai*, a village located about 15 kilometres south of the city.

Originally, four to five men from *Ban Ta Wai* village worked on carving wood for many years in one shop in the city. Later, the increase in market demand enabled them to work from home, and produce their carvings under the order of the middle men. This system also enabled other farmers in the village to learn and develop these crafting skills, and the numbers of craftsmen in Ban Ta Wai gradually increased.

Further, as tourists like to buy souvenirs directly from the local people, villagers have opened small shops in the village. Today, *Ban Ta Wai,* once a farming village, is now famous as the wood carving centre of Chiang Mai.

A major result of this however is that the majority of carvings produced in *Ban Ta Wai* are now designed to meet tourist demand. Even though some carvings have retained the traditional styles, but the traditional function of these carvings has changed.

Silk weaving

San Kam Paeng, a district located east of the city of Chiang Mai, has been the weaving center of the city for hundreds of years. This area is comprised of many minority groups and each group is skilled in traditional methods of cloth weaving by loom which had been passed on through the generations. They wove cotton clothes for ordinary people, such as *Pa Sin* (woman costume), *Sarong* (man costume), *"Tung"* (a cloth used in religious ceremonies) and other household materials.

Originally, silk clothes were neither worn nor woven by ordinary people. The reasons for this were not only the costly price, but also the status symbol that silk gave to people at that time. Silk was regarded as a symbol of the ruling class, since only those people dressed in silk costumes. Silk clothing and products were also made only in *"Kum"*, the residences of the ruling class. This was because the silk weaving process was considerably more difficult and expensive than cotton weaving. The labour, however, was free, as craftsmen worked under the slavery system of that time.

Silk weaving in *San Kampaeng* was started by the wealthy *Promchana and Peinkusol* families and later by the *Chinawat* family. The weaving began when the wives of these families originally began to weave silk products for themselves, creating their own styles, patterns and colours.

Silk weaving in *San Kampaeng* became commercialised between 1910-1911, when capital was invested in a hired-workforce of weavers. The first development of a new weaving system began when the *Promchana, Peinkusol and Chinawat* families (the local San Kampaeng investors) hired the local villagers as weavers. These villagers were divided into groups based upon different stages of the weaving process. This meant that each stage of the weaving process such as the weaving raw yarn, or creating the colour designs and patterns, were the responsibility of a group of villagers.

The woven silk products were then collected by the investors who sold them in Burma. At that time, the family leaders of the local investors had to travel to Burma by themselves to buy the raw silk and sell the silk products. The weavers of San Kampaeng silk were the *"Lue"* tribe of people and they did not want to kill silk worms because killing animals was forbidden by the Buddhist faith. So, the raw silk had to be bought in Burma and brought to the Sankampaeng village for weaving.

In former times, Chiang Mai was the commercial centre of silk trade, as it was located between Yunan in the south of China and Moulmein in Burma. In the Report on Trade and Commerce of the United Kingdom in the year 1908, the Consular District of Chiang Mai reported that silk products were sent from Chiang Mai to Moulmein in Burma.

The report showed the relationship between Chiang Mai and Burma at that time. It is suggested that those silk products which were sent to Burma at that time might be made in the *"Kum"* of Chiang Mai. Burma became the main market of San Kampaeng silk products between 1911 to 1935.

Later, Bangkok also became an important market for Chiang Mai silk with the development of the railway from Bangkok to Chiang Mai in 1921. The main products sent to Bangkok were the *Pa Sin* and *Sarong* in solid colours, and striped and checked designs.

In 1931, many silk weaving shops opened in the city of Chiang Mai to cater to the increase in demand for San Kampaeng silk. In San Kampaeng there were the weaving silk shops of *Shinawat, Peinkusol* and *Promchana* families in the Ban Kad village.

In 1935, the *Shinawat* family brought in a new commercial loom with the flying shuttle that enabled weavers to produce a greater quantity of products of the same quality. Home-weaving had thus made the full transition into factory weaving, and weavers were paid by the amount of the cloth they made each day.

After 1974, the hired-weavers in the village gradually disappeared along with old local patterns of silk.

In 1953, the traditional eating style of the Lanna local people which used *Khan Tok* (a low round wooden table) to put food on, was adapted to serve as the dinner style for the guests of Chiang Mai. This dinner style which is called *"Khan Tok Dinner"* requires the women to wear costumes made of San Kampaeng silk. The ceremonial *"Khan Tok Dinner"* brought more demand for woven San Kampaeng silk.

In 1960, a demand for the silk in international markets arose as a result of the visit to the western countries by King Bhumipol and Queen Sirikit. The beautiful traditional costume in Thai silk worn by the Queen attracted great interest from the western ladies.

In 1965, when Apasara Hongsakul won Miss Universe, her traditional Thai dress also made Thai silk more popular to the westerners. It also brought San Kampaeng silk to international markets.

In 1967, silk shops in *San Kampaeng* were asked by to demonstrate the process of silk production from silk worm to the finished silk products for visiting tourists.

During 1943-1981, silk shirts, neckties, ready-made cloth, and various silk accessories were added to production. *Pa Sin* designs and colours changed and the *Sarong* disappeared from the market as men adopted wearing trousers.

After 1981, the expanding domestic and international markets resulted in further modernisation of products to meet a more sophisticated market. After that stripe *Pa Sin* gradually disappeared from the local market of Chiang Mai.

In 1977, Chiang Mai was promoted as the 'Tourist Centre of the North'. This influenced San Kampaeng silk products to change their patterns and styles to complete for the tourist market. To enable mass production and in order to be competitive, these products were produced using easier processing techniques and made in smaller sizes to be easier for tourists to carry back home. These cheaper made silk products also enabled them to be sold at a more attractive price for the tourist market.

Muang Kung Pottery

Muang Kung is a village located in Hang Dong district, about 5 kilometres south of the city of Chiang Mai. It is thought that the ancestors of these villagers were forcible relocated from Kengtung in Burma to Chiang Mai. In 1804, during the reign of Phra Chao Kavira, Prince of Chiang Mai, many people from Burma and southern China were forcibly relocated to Chiang Mai. The reason for this was that at that time Chiang Mai needed more inhabitants and skilled labourers. Most of these relocated people were skilled craftsmen. Some of these craftsmen worked on the properties owned by the ruling class.

Today, the old villagers tell of how their ancestors worked in rice fields around the village, owned by Princess Dararatsamee. In their free time, these villagers always made pottery from the village soil. This skill in making pottery was then passed down through the generations. The majority of pottery made were *"Mor Nam"*, water containers. These *Mor Nam* were used to store drinking water in the house. *"Nam Ton"* was another pottery water container served for guests. People in Lanna always used these pottery containers to hold water, because it was believed that these containers could keep water cool and give the drinking water a good earthy smell.

Mor Nam and *Nam Ton* from the Muang Kung village were then sold to all villages of Chiang Mai. The advent of the refrigerators, however, resulted in a decline in their popularity in the villages. Nowadays, the *Mor Nam* or *Nam Ton* are sold only in the rural villages around Chiang Mai. These rural villagers not only use these products daily but also offer them to the temples to gain merit. These two factors might be sufficient to sustain the tradition of old-style Chiang Mai water containers.

Today, the villagers of Muang Kung are still producing pottery like their ancestors, however the design, pattern and style of the pottery have been adapted to suit the tourist market. *Mor Nam* and *Nam Ton* are also sold in the tourist market in Chiang Mai but their functions are changed from use as water containers, to be decorative products of Lanna culture. Other pottery products are also produced such as vases, fire-work containers, cigarette ashtrays, Buddhist monk bowls, jugs, lamps, lanterns and flowerpots. Each of these products has many varying patterns and styles created for tourists.

The main market for Muang Kung pottery today is tourism and they have changed to suit this new and lucrative market.

Borsang umbrella

The village of Borsang, which is located in the San Kampaeng district, about nine kilometres east of Chiang Mai, has been engaged in the handicraft of umbrella making for over two centuries. When the art of umbrella making came about or why it was embraced by this particular village, however, remains a mystery. There is at least one story, however, that has been told from time to time. It is said that a local Buddhist monk learned about umbrella making during a long pilgrimage through the upper region of old Lanna, parts of Burma and Sibsong Panna, (an area which currently lies within the boundaries in Yunan province of southern China).

Regardless of how the art was first conceived, this type of handicraft represents a most significant advancement in technology. An umbrella is a device used for protection against the sun and rain. The world derives from the Latin 'umbra', meaning shade. Incidentally, the word of umbrella, *"Rom"*, in the Thai language means *'shade'* also.

In the beginning, the Borsang villagers, like other craft villagers of Chiang Mai, made the umbrellas during their free time or the off season for rice farm work. The umbrellas of Borsang were made for use by the villagers themselves or for selling in other parts of the region.

The larger umbrellas were called 'ceremonial umbrellas' as they were used in various feasts and religious ceremonies, such as *Suppathon,* which is the name for the umbrella used in important ceremonies. It always has a metal frame and an elegant silk fabric cover. In addition to the silk fabric covering, the umbrella has a long handle. The *suppathon* is used in ceremonial processions where it is carried by a porter to provide shade to royal personages and persons of rank while walking. The *suppathon* is also an embellishment required in many Buddhist processions, especially when a Buddha statue is moved from one place to another. Suppathon is also used during Buddhist ordination processions where a young man is about to become a monk. During the time of ordination, the young man represents an elevated person who gives up the material life for a spiritual life. In this particular instance, the umbrella represents an unnecessary object for pampering oneself and is symbolically discarded.

"Sa" paper, which is still handmade from the bark of mulberry trees, has been used to cover the part of umbrella.

When the tourists came, they wanted to buy the umbrellas and watch demonstrations of the umbrella making process. This encouraged the umbrellas to be made in the factory bringing in villagers who used to make umbrellas in their free time, to be full-time workers demonstrating umbrella making for the tourists.

Nowadays most Bor sang umbrellas are produced for the tourist market of Chiang Mai. At the same time, these umbrellas are rarely used as protection from the sun and rain. They are always used for decorating rooms or halls in hotels, restaurants or at the airport. The function of Bor Sang umbrella has changed from its initial use in the daily life of the local people, to be a decorative ornament of Lanna culture.

Woa Lai Lacquer ware

Lacquer ware, or *"Kruang Kern"*, are special containers made of wood, bamboo or clay and beautifully vanished and inlaid with pigments, dyes, mother of pearl, gold or silver-leaves and lacquer juice called *Yang Rak*. This process is used to create household items and also much bigger items such as the doors of temples and the thrones.

It is believed that the lacquer work originated from the southern part of China. The art has been passed on from Yunan, Chiang Rung, Chiang Tung, and then to Chiang Mai. The word *"Kruang Kern"*, is derived from the tribe *"Thai Kern"* in Chiang Tung. This tribe was forcibly relocated to Chiang Mai from Burma during the reign of Prince Kavira. These people settled in a sub-district, in the south of the city at *Hai Ya,* and came to be known as *Ban Kern* which literally means 'the village of the Kern people'.

Formerly, lacquer ware made in Chiang Mai was used to make household utensils. About 80 years ago, trays and bowls of lacquer ware were made for serving food in various temples. Many households also used tobacco-boxes, cigarette-cases, betel-trays, wash-bowls, and trays coated with lacquer. The subsequent introduction of ceramics, enamelware, aluminium-ware, and plastic goods, however, has resulted in their gradual decline in popularity.

Unfortunately, with the advent of modern times, the profession of making lacquer ware has almost ceased to exist. Today, a few craftsmen exist who know the production process intimately enough to pass it to the younger generations. The products of *Kruang Kern* of the Thai Kern style have thus almost completely disappeared. The Kruang Kern found in Chiang Mai's markets today are poor imitations of the original crafts. The lacquer ware products found in Chiang Mai now have rough patterns that are easily and quickly produced for the tourist market.

Therefore, today most lacquer ware is purchased as gift items, souvenirs or as decoration. They are no longer used for household utensils or when offering food to the monks. The function of lacquer ware can therefore be seen to have considerably changed from being a practical part of every day life of the local people to attractive souvenirs for tourists.

Tung: An expression of belief

> *"Belief is the magnificent birth-place and beginning of a culture. It is the sculptor that chisels and defines the shape of each civilisation."* (Trip Info, 1994 Vol.1 No.12)

The culture of the people of Lanna Kingdom has been created mostly from their deeply embedded beliefs in Buddhism. Thai people have bona fide convictions about such issues as : sin, the law of destiny, hell, heaven, and even of the after-life, which they believe is determined by one's past deeds. These unique convictions, on these prolific issues, draw a very definite sketch on the distinct traits of the Lanna kingdom. This can be clearly seen from the "tung", which is a direct result of the Lanna people's devotion to Buddhism.

"Tung" of Northern Thai, can be literally translated to mean flag. The *"tung"* resembles a normal flag in that it is a rectangular piece of cloth attached on the shorter side to a pole. The *"tung"* is made from either from wood, cloth, paper or brass.

There are many different appearances and uses for the *"tung"*. Every Buddhist-related ceremony would not be considered complete without a "tung".

Normally, a *"tung"* is offered as a sacrifice to images of Buddha and to the deceased. To make merit for the deceased in the world to come, the living relatives often make a *"tung"* which has a wooden ladder and is believed to lead up to the highest heaven. People believe that making the "tung" will allow the deceased to escape from the sin's they may have committed, and allow them to be reborn into the human world with prosperity and high status.

Besides being used as sacrifices and offerings, a *"tung"* is often used to eliminate all evil and freak accidents that may occur as a result of sin or deceiving spirits.

The *"tungs"* that can be seen around homes and Buddhist temples are used as decorations and adornments for religious ceremonies and celebrations. During celebrations of making merit at local temples, *"tungs"* are hung in the front of and inside the sanctuaries. In the "Poy Luang" ceremony, which is the commemoration of the construction of certain rooms in the temples such as the stupa and vihara rooms, *"tung"* are hung from the bamboo poles and placed around the construction areas, as if to declare to all who pass by, that there is a fiesta occurring inside the monastery. The *"tungs"* are placed like toy soldiers in rows leading up to the temple.

"Tungs" that are used are varied and many. The names of certain types of "tungs" depend upon the definite characteristics of the *"tung"* and the rite that it is to be used in. There are three *"tungs"* most common used in merit-making ceremonies; *"Tung Jai"*, *"Tung Yai"* and *"Tung Lao"*.

The *"Tung Jai"* is made from a lengthy piece of cloth, for it is believed that the longer the cloth the more the merit that will be received. The cloth used is often silk or cotton spun into fine, elaborate patterns, in which each shining strand is distinct. *"Tung Jai"* are used in the making of merit for a deceased ancestor.

The *"Tung Yai"* is made from silky strands bound together delicately like a spider's web. White yarn is tied or knitted into different shapes using bamboo as a structural form. This "tung" is then decorated with flowers or frills. It often has ascending steps, which are believed to lead up to heaven. The smallest of these *"tungs"* is the *"Tung Lao"*. It is made from colourful pieces of paper, often in a triangular or rectangular shape. The *"Tung Lao"* is habitually hung lengthwise from a string in the hall for sermons in a monastery.

"Tung Sarm Hang", which literally means 'the three-tailed tung", when seen in Northern Thailand signifies a funeral . It is carried in front of the casket, containing the body on its way, into the designated cemetery. This "tung" can be recognised by a rounded top that resembles a human head. It is made from filmy, white material, and decorated on the bottom in various patterns of gold or silver paper. This type of *"tung"* solely signifies the death of a Buddhist person. If the body being cremated has no *"tung"* in front of it, it is generally accepted that the deceased was not a Buddhist, and probably of another ethnic group.

The *"tung"* that is most commonly seen is the triangular shaped *"tung"* called the *"Tung Jaw"*. Ceremonies in which certain types of *"Tung Jaw"* are used in the Songkran Festival, where the *"Jaw-Noi"* is used. The *"Jaw-Noi"* is made of triangular shaped pieces of coloured paper, stuck onto a bamboo pole, and then placed on top of a sand pagoda. It is also believed to bring luck in villages and towns.

There is also the *"Jaw-Chang"*, which is made from different shades of silk, with intricate hand-stitching on it. The *"Tung Sai Moo"* is another feature stupa-like shape which has a distinctive. This *"tung"* is made from hundreds of interwoven pieces of paper that scrunch up and stretch out lengthwise.

Thus these mysterious emblems of belief can be found sacredly collected in Buddhist temples.

Nowadays, many of these types of *"tungs"* are used for decorative purposes without meaning, and can be found in the hotels and restaurants in the city of Chiang Mai, as a symbols of Lanna culture.

Crafts, functions and changes

There is no historical evidence that Chiang Mai's traditional crafts were originally produced to meet *"market"* demand, especially a tourist market, as is seen today. Crafts at that time always had meanings and functions related to the life style of the local people. They were made as "holy Buddhist symbols", or functioned as utensils of daily life or ritual articles of the local people.

It is found that traditional crafts were created with a functional purpose and meaning for the local culture. Today, even though they might be made in the same pattern or design, the meanings and functions of these crafts have changed. It is also found that their process of production, patterns and designs, have changed. Some of these crafts, which disappeared from the local community, have lately reappeared in the tourist market in new styles and patterns. The cause of these changes, are the demands of the tourist market, as they are now produced to satisfy people outside the local culture.

Another example are the intricate wood carvings which were once powerful symbols of religion, and functioned as a highly revered crafts, given a holy or high place, such as the main hall in temples, and "Kum", a residential building of the ruling class. The value of the original wood carvings were also considerable as they depicted the higher art and culture of the local people. The craftsmen who made wood carvings to decorate the main halls of temples did so to accrue merit for the rebirth in the next life. Further, the meaning of the wood carving of the "Kum", was to distinguish the difference in status of ruling class from the common people.

When the wood carvings became popular souvenirs for tourists visiting Chiang Mai, the wood carving industry became popular too. This also encouraged the problem of deforestation in the area around Chiang Mai to feed the wood carving industry. It is said that even the old trees in the rice fields, which gave shade to generations of farmers, were sacrificed to this industry.

Further, a law that restricts logging concession in Thailand has created a shortage of raw material for the wood carving industry. As a result, many traditional wooden utensils once a part of the daily lives of local people such as: a mortar, a grinding utensil used to take rice-grain skin; the wooden water tube, used for carrying water from the stream into the household; wooden trays, used for preparing sticky rice; or even the oxen-cart, are now being used as raw wooden carving material. Today, remaining traditional utensils can be seen in huge piles in the wood carving villages of Chiang Mai, waiting to be changed into tourist souvenirs.

At present, in *Ban Tawai,* a carving wood center of Chiang Mai, there are many wooden products that are made in replication of the same traditional patterns and designs. Some are made in new designs, such as cowboy figures, elephants, frogs, naked ladies and even Buddha statues, angels and so forth to suit the tourist demand. These wooden crafts are always bought by tourists as souvenirs and decorative objects.

The woven silk products of Chiang Mai have changed considerably in their role in the local community. Originally, a symbol of status for the ruling class, they later became costumes for the ordinary local people, such as silk *Pa Sin* (silk tube skirt for women), or silk *Salong* (silk tube skirt for men).

Nowadays, these quality silk P*a Sin* and S*along* have all but disappeared from the local society. They might be seen in performances of traditional dance on stage for tourists, but they are not normally used as normal costume any more. They have also been replaced by smaller and cheaper silk products that function as tourist souvenirs. Silk neckties, silk scarfs, silk shirts and silk handkerchiefs are all examples of new silk products catering for the new tourist market. Nowadays, it can be seen that silk is not part of the life style of the local people of Chiang Mai anymore. Thus 99 percent of silk products nowadays are produced to serve only the tourist market.

Yet another example are the earthen ware pottery crafts of Muang Kung village. This village used to be a well known earthen water-pot making village for households in the villages of the region, such as *Mor Nam, a* water container for the household and *Nam Ton,* water container for monks or guests. Nowadays, Mor Nam and Nam Ton function as water containers only in the rural villages. Despite their continued production in Muang Kung village, they are no longer used as water containers in the city of Chiang Mai. Today, they are used as decorative objects depicting Lanna culture in hotels or restaurants. Sometimes they are used as vases, not water containers.

In addition to adaptation of earthen ware crafts from Muang Kung to supply the tourist souvenir market, other 'foreign' products are now created, such as earthen vases, ashtrays, tea pots and earthen home ornaments.

Likewise, the traditional umbrellas of Bor Sang, were made to provide shade from the sun and rain. The larger umbrellas were used in various feasts and religious ceremonies. The *Suppathon* used in important ceremonies, such as in the Buddhist processions when a Buddha statue is moved from one place to another, or in the ordination procession where a young man is about to become a monk.

Nowadays the function of the umbrellas has changed. The larger umbrellas, such as the Suppathon, have retained their size and design, but they now have a purely decorative function in the hotels or restaurants to represent traditional Lanna culture. They are also seen in performances for tourists to show Lanna culture, and lack the original meaning of both the performance and the umbrellas themselves. Further, they vary in size from key-rings to huge sizes appropriate for a home or hotel ornament to attract the tourists demand.

The products of lacquer ware or *Kruang Kern* of the Thai Kern style have almost completely disappeared. The Kruang Kern found in Chiang Mai's markets today are poor imitations of the original crafts. *Kruang Kern* were originally used as trays and bowls for serving food in various temples, or household utensils such as tobacco-boxes, cigarette-cases, betel-trays, wash-bowls, and sometimes in the bigger items such as the doors of temples and Buddhist thrones for the monks in the temples. There were many steps in the original production process and each item took a long time to be made. The lacquer ware products found in Chiang Mai now have rough patterns that are easily and quickly produced for the tourist market.

Therefore, today most lacquer ware is purchased as gift items, souvenirs or as decoration. These lacquer ware products are also never used for their original purpose, for household utensils or when offering food to the monks. The function of lacquer ware can therefore be seen to be considerably changed, from being a practical part of every day life of the local people to attractive souvenirs for tourists.

Also, the *"tung"* is a direct result of the Lanna people's devotion to Buddhism, normally offered as a sacrifice to images of Buddha and to the deceased. It has been believed that to make a *"tung"* meant to make merit for the deceased in the world to come. A *"tung"* would function as a wooden ladder to lead the deceased up to the highest heaven. People believed that the *"tung"* would enable them to be reborn into the human world with prosperity and high status. Besides being used as sacrifices and offerings, a *"tung"* is often used to eliminate all evil and freak accidents that may occur as results of sin or deceiving spirits.

Nowadays, *"tungs"* are also used as decorative ornaments for hotels or restaurants. They are also used in many parades at ceremonies or festivals for tourists. There is no meaning of the *"tung"* in this way, they are used just as a symbol of Lanna culture for the tourists.

Conclusion

It can be therefore concluded that the crafts of Chiang Mai have changed considerably in both functions and meanings for local people. Traditional crafts of Chiang Mai which once served practical and religious functions in everyday life, now cater to the tourist market. Several main factors contributing to these changes can be identified.

Tourism Promotion is the main factor contributing to the changes in traditional crafts. In 1977, Chiang Mai was promoted as the tourist centre of the north. This was part of a policy to use tourism as a tool to gain more revenue for economic development of the country. This resulted Chiang Mai becoming the craft centre with many functioning as tourist souvenirs. The increase in demand for traditional crafts caused cost saving and mass production techniques, which altered the original patterns and styles of the crafts.

Tourism Organisations is the second factor. Both government and private tourist organisations in Chiang Mai have actively encouraged the local people to bring their traditional utensils or articles for belief to the tourist market. Much of the traditional culture has been taken from the local communities and adapted to the tourist market. For example, the government tourist organisation, Tourism Authority of Thailand (TAT), assists the private business sector in Chiang Mai to conduct crafts festivals, such as the Rom Bor Sang or Ban Ta Wai wood carving festival. The main purpose of these festivals is to promote umbrellas and wood carving to the tourists. Previously, such support was given for festivals that were based on Buddhism beliefs and functioned to strengthen the local community, not just to promote the market products. It appears that attracting the tourist dollar has taken priority over what necessarily benefits local people of Chiang Mai.

Tourist Demand is another main factor contributing to the changing of traditional crafts to meet the satisfaction of the foreign tourists. Today, the craft market of Chiang Mai exist as a huge souvenir market. Tourist demand has not only brought a change in patterns and styles of traditional crafts but has also encouraged the local people to bring more traditional crafts to the tourist markets and sell them as antique crafts or replica crafts.

The system effort to prolong the traditional skill. The problem of the loss of authentic traditional patterns and styles of Chiang Mai crafts can be linked to the art and culture prolongation system of the government of Thailand. The Thai government preserves traditional arts and crafts by keeping them in museums. As a result, the craftsmanship skills are lost to new generations. In Thailand, there are many prizes to praise the traditional artists. However, these prizes aim to increase the profiles of these artists and do not encourage them to transfer these skills to younger generations. Thus, such prizes encourage the craftsmen to keep their skills to themselves more than the producing process to the society.

Tourism should not be the main factor to lessen the high value of local crafts as they used to in the past or weaken the community by bringing those crafts from the local community to the tourist market. Tourism should act to strengthen the local community by retaining the original meanings and functions of the crafts.

References

English language sources

Chambers, E. (1997), *Tourism and Culture: An Applied Perspective*. New York : State University of New York Press.

Hargreave, O. (1998), *Exploring Chiang Mai*. Chiang Mai : Within Books.

Netherlands Institute of Tourism Development Consultants and SGV-Na Thalang and Co., Ltd. (1976), *National Plan on Tourism development* Bangkok: TDC.

Rojek, C. and Urry, J. (1997), *Touring Cultures: Transformations of Travel and Theory*. London : Routledge.

Smith, V. L. (1978), *Hosts and Guests: The Anthropology of Tourism*. Oxford: Basil Blackwell.

Surber, J. P. (1998), *Culture and Critique*. Oxford : Westview Press.

Tettoni, Luca Invernizzi. (1989), *A Guide to Chiang Mai and Northern Thailand*. Bangkok : Asia Books.

Thai language sources

Tourism Authority of Thailand. (1977), *Seminar for Tourism Leaders in Thailand*. Bangkok: TAT.

The Office of Industry Promotion. (1978), *Lacqueware*. Bangkok.

Faculty of Social Science and Humanities, Chiang Mai Teachers College (1987), *Historical Attractions in Chiang Mai*. Chiang Mai: CTC.

Chaleaw Piyachon.(1989), *Galae House*. Chiang Mai University: Centre for the Promotion of Arts and Culture.

Narumon Srikitkarn. (1983), *Silk Weaving at Ban Kad, San Kampaeng District, Chiang Mai*. Research Report, Bangkok: The National Culture Commission.

Nithi Iewsriwong. (1999), *Alternative Tourism*. Bangkok: Weekly Mathichon.

Tourism and Bon Bung Fai or Rocket Festival in Esarn, (1993), Bangkok: Mathichon Publishing House.

Tourism Industry and Cultural Impact, (1995), Bangkok: Mathichon Publishing House.

Tourism and Community Culture, (1995), Chiang Mai: Social Research Institute.

Boonserm Satrapai. (1996), *Chiang Mai in Yesterday*. Bangkok: Art and Culture Magazine, 17:17, 104-112.

Ploysri Porananond. (1996), *Chiang Mai and the Impacts of Tourism*. Research Report, Bangkok: Thailand Research Fund.

Chiang Mai : The Wilted Orchid, (1996), Chiang Mai: The Sixth International Conference on Thai Studies.

Two Cities of Cultural Tourism: Chiang Mai and Kyoto, (1996), Chiang Mai and Kyoto: Cultural Renewal of the Two Cities, Chiang Mai: Centre for the Promotion of Arts and Culture.

Paitoon Promvijit. (1996), *The Residence of the Chiang Mai Ruling Prince*. Art and Culture Magazine :17:7, 122-123.

Faculty of Education, Chiang Mai University. (1985), *The Production of Earthernware in Muang Kung Village*. Chiang Mai University.

Department of Informal Education. (1994), *Lacqueware*. Bangkok: Ministry of Education.

Chiang Mai Cultural Centre. (1993), *Lanna Studies: History and Archeology*. Chiang Mai: Chiang Mai Teachers College.

Saratsavadee Ongsakul. (1986), *History of Lanna*. Chiang Mai: Centre for the Promotion of Arts and Culture.

Singkaew Manopet. (1996), *Legend and History of Tung (Flags)*. Northern Bank Magazine, 97-103.

Suree Bunyanupong and Surasak Pomthongkam. (publication date unknown), *Traditions for Tourism: Turning Point of Social Relation System*. Chiang Mai: Social Research Institute.

Attachak Sattayanurak. (1994), *The Changes in Production Process of Wood Carving for Sale. Art and* Culture Magazine, 15:12, 76-94.

"Frizzling in the sun": Robert Graves and the development of mass tourism in the Balearic Islands

John W Presley

Oswego State University of New York, USA

In a letter to W. K. T. Barrett, Robert Graves was quite dilatory about his choice of Majorca as his place to live and work:

> ". . . we live here in perhaps the best place anywhere - these are the Classical Hesperides where it never freezes and never gets too hot and where it costs nothing to live if one is content to go native, and where the population is the most hospitable, quiet, sensible and well-being that you can imagine. We are near the sea and Palma a big town, is within reach for any European necessities . . . We tried France and Germany first but of course though we knew the best parts it was no use; (the Germans are too serious and the French too false) it was just to confirm our previous choice of this island." (Graves, R. 1997. p. 34)

This was May 20, 1930. Graves, even at that early date, ended his letter with a warning:

> "Don't advertise Majorca! You might want to come out here yourself some day. It's not overrun yet" (Graves, R. 1997. p. 35).

But for contemporary Europeans, the Balearic Islands, including Mallorca and Ibiza, form the paradigmatic case study of mass tourism attacking landscape, culture, and economy, transforming an agricultural society into a service-based, much more urbanised culture. One of the most complete of many analyses and descriptions of the tourist "boom" in the Balearics may be found in R. J. Buswell's essay, "Tourism in the Balearic Islands," (Barke, 1996). Among the hundreds of statistics Buswell uses to illustrate the rapidity of change brought on by tourism in the Balearics, only a few are necessary to imagine the effects of commercial air travel and package tourism on the fragile resources of an arid island: in 1935, there were 43,000 mostly Spanish visitors to the islands, yet the number of visitors had risen to 3.6 million by 1973. At one point in 1964 a new hotel was being opened every 53 hours. In 1992, the Palma de Mallorca airport alone recorded 11,867,370 passengers arriving - up from 63,676 air passengers in 1960 - these were, of course, in addition to all those arriving by boat and ferry.

From 1929 until his death in 1985, Robert Graves lived in Mallorca, except for the years of World War II and the Spanish Civil War. Though never a travel writer *per se*, Graves did write essays about his experience living in Mallorca (in which he explicitly deals with the subject of increasing tourism), short stories with Mallorcan characters, poems describing the behaviour of certain types of tourists, and he even edited the early and infamous tourist report *A Winter in Mallorca* by George Sand. But in addition to his role as an early critic and witness of the tourism phenomenon, Graves was actually a participant or precipitating cause in the rise of Balearic tourism, however ambivalent or contradictory his participation may seem. In the 1930's, Graves and Laura Riding may have been the most famous literary couple in the world, drawing American and British writers, artists, musicians and like-minded intellectuals into a salon that did much to make the little village of Deya an international literary landmark. After World War II, that salon grew until it began to attract large numbers of rather unsavoury types drawn by what they had understood of *The White Goddess*. Moreover, though Graves was honoured for his work to preserve the northern coastline of Mallorca, he was also honoured for having brought so many tourists to Deya, and at various times in his long stay on the island, he too was even a speculator and at the least, a would-be developer.

So, the case of Robert Graves offers a rare opportunity to study a writer working in close observation of history's most notorious development of mass tourism.

Mallorca was famous as a destination well before the invention of the package tour. Thomas Cook's first advertised Mallorca in 1903, as one stop for an organised tour of the Balearics. Clients were advised that "the climate of Palma rivals that of Malaga and Algiers." The sights listed included the Palma Cathedral, the bullring, La Lonja, the casino, and "quaint 16th century houses." Again in 1905 the island was promoted as one of the best viewing spots for the eclipse of the sun in August of that year (*Passport*, 1995, p. 12).

Though wealthy travellers came to Mallorca in small numbers in the late 1800's, it was not until the years after World War II that tourists came in hordes. About this phenomenon, Robert Graves sounded a worried note: "Around 1951, British, French, and American travellers accepted the fantasy of Majorca as the Isle of Love, the Isle of Tranquillity, the Paradise where the sun always shines and where one can live like a fighting cock on a dollar a day, drinks included" (quoted in *Passport* 1995, p. 16). During this period, Palma Nova and Magaluf, west of Palma, developed into the "concrete jungle" - high rise apartment and hotel blocks, restaurants, bars, souvenir shops - that "still attracts a raucous element." Despite Mallorca's reputation as resort for celebrities - film stars and royalty vacation or own property on the island - it has a parallel reputation as the habitat of the *gamberros Ingleses* (English hooligans) and the classic tourist "wearing an oversize sombrero, carrying a donkey, and trailing a family of bad children. The place they are headed is a turbulent ocean of pink flesh and grey concrete" (Robert Elms, quoted in *Passport* 1995, p. 26).

Even now, the figure of Robert Graves himself has become a sort of tourist attraction - just as before his death, he attracted artists (and later artistes) to the island. The Passport/Thomas Cook guide to Mallorca includes, in its brief section on Deià, a paragraph of biography for Graves, noting that the village and the writer "will be forever associated." The guide goes on to say that "Graves strove hard to stop Deià being ruined by the encroaching

developments, and the town's unified and natural appearance is its greatest attraction."
However,

> *Today the town lives in thrall to La Residencia, an idyllic mansion turned hotel that is partly owned by the British entrepreneur Richard Branson and attracts arty types from around the world. As the author Robert Elms puts it, "Everything in Deià is taken slowly, except your money"* (Passport, 1995, p. 68).

Other attractions listed include "several restaurants, a couple of art galleries, and a narrow, twisting road that leads down to the sea at Cala de Deià" (*Passport,* 1995: p. 68).

Of course, other artists and writers have made Mallorca their residence. Joan Miró kept his studio outside Palma; his wife and mother were Mallorcan. Miró was very conscious of Mallorca's influence on this work. "As a child I loved to watch the always changing Mallorcan sky. At night I would get carried away by the writing in the sky of the shooting stars, and the lights of the fireflies. The sea, day and night, was always blue. It was here that I received the first creative seeds which became my work."

The most famous artists, before Graves, to remain in Mallorca were George Sand and Chopin, who spent the winter at Valldemossa in 1838-1839. Their experiences were not entirely pleasant, but Sand gave Mallorca credit for the maturity and sublimity of Chopin's *Preludes*. In editing Sand's *Winter in Majorca*, Graves' notes are a frequent counterpoint to Sand's scandalous references to Majorcans as thieves, monkeys, and Polynesian savages. On her side of the argument, the locals had ostracised Chopin on the rumour of his tuberculosis, and Sand since she was a "cigarette-smoking, trouser-wearing pioneer-feminist." The "lugubrious rain" and poor food didn't help matters any, but Sand later commented that things might have gone differently "had they bothered to attend Mass" (*Passport,* 1995: pp. 70, 78-79).

In his translation of *Winter in Majorca* Graves takes great pains in his notes and introduction to point out that Sand, the most well-known and vociferous critic of Majorca (until the tourist explosions of the 1960's) was entirely at fault in her relations with the Mallorcans. Typical is Graves' quotation from an 1839 traveller who reports that the local priest was "mortified."

> *"This French lady must indeed be a strange person! Just think of it: she never speaks to a living soul, never leaves the Cartuja and never shows her face in church, even on Sundays, and goodness knows how many mortal sins she is amassing! Furthermore, I have it from the apothecary, who also lives in the Cartuja, that la señora makes cigarettes like nothing on earth, drinks coffee all hours, sleeps by day, and does nothing but smoke and write all night. I beg you, dear sir, since you know her, to tell us what she has come to do here in midwinter"* (Graves, 1956: p. 116).

At the end of her stay on the island, as Sand was leaving on the French ship Meleager "surrounded by intelligent, pleasant faces," she cries "Vive La France" and summarises her stay in Mallorca, "We felt as if we had been round the world, and come back to civilisation after a long stay among the savages of Polynesia." Graves' annotation is direct, contradictory, and based on his loyalty to the Mallorcans - and his antipathy to the French: "This remark will read most ironically to anyone who has studied the story of nineteenth-century French colonial enterprise among the noble Polynesians; even if he has not had the privilege of living among the generous, honest, and lovable Majorcans" (Graves, 1956: p. 165).

Graves treats Sand's account of her winter on the island as yet another of his Gravesian puzzles. "I find it difficult to square this account of the winter with Chopin's letters" (Graves, 1956: p. 175). If Chopin felt "poetic" in Mallorca, and was working productively, why was Sand so miserable? Graves imagines that the villagers "will have described him [Chopin] among themselves proverbially as 'a man who expects you to doff your hat from three leagues away.'" They would describe Sand as "a shameless one who leaps out in anger like a stone from a crushed cherry." As for Sand's children, Maurice "hotly championed his mother," and his "precocious sketches made the Valldemosans uneasy, "especially the Monastic Orgy, pinned up in the cell." Solange comes in for a special bit of characterisation; she "offended their [Mallorcans'] sense of propriety by wearing trousers and playing the tomboy, instead of busying herself with the needle, the catechism, and other useful tasks." And of course, Chopin's consumption was a physical threat to the villagers, consumption then being incurable. The Mallorcans believed, "as they still do, that sickness is a divine punishment for ill-doing." The Mallorcans would have considered Sand "wicked" for exposing her children to consumption. "They would think the same today," Graves writes, "and with reason unless strict sanitary precautions were taken" (Graves, 1956: p. 178).

Solange was "no more than eight years old . . . known only as rebellious, arrogant, lazy and a domestic tyrant who relied on violent displays of temper for getting her own way." Graves, in fact, blames Solange for much of the misery of Sand and Chopin's visit. "George spoilt and idolised Solange. . . Solange repaid George with the cruelty, deceit and greed that [her father] had bequeathed to her" (Graves, 1956: p. 179). Graves assumes that Chopin's obsession with the haunting of his cell by the ghosts of the original monks was intensified by Solange's stories of spectres in the cloisters. With little evidence but his own surmise, Graves solves this puzzle by imputing virtually all the mischief - spilled milk, fleas in bed and at table - to eight-year-old Solange, including serving even as her mother's conduit for learning the village gossip! Graves imagines that the villagers would have "felt it their duty to enlighten Solange on the seriousness of her position" and would "never have spoken directly to her mother or to Chopin on these subjects." Moreover, Luis Ripolis' *Chopin: Su Invierno en Mallorca* "supported [Graves'] theory by referring to a letter of Solange's" in which "she gleefully describes how the chambermaid, presumably the *niña*, and herself dressed up in monk's habits, which they found in the monastery, and frightened Chopin out of his wits by creeping into the cell at dusk" (Graves, 1956: p. 182).

George Sand blamed the villagers, Graves says, for Chopin's return to "orthodox morality," and she "revenged herself in this book on the Valldemossan villagers."

> *"She called them uncharitable, superstitious wretches, monkeys, cannibals, thieves and (most significant of the way in which her mind was working) the bastard children of lascivious and hypocritical Carthusian fathers, whose main pleasure lay in seducing the married women who came to their confessionals"* (Graves, 1956: p. 185).

Graves skewers Sand for her factual errors:

". . . she devotes two chapters to denouncing the inhuman cruelties of the vanished Dominican Fathers, and extolling the noble rage of the people who had risen up and destroyed their monastery, though she is aware that this was the work of a demolitions contractor. Nobody could mistake hers for sober historical criticism" (Graves, 1956: pp. 183-184).

Graves gives the penultimate word to J. M. Quadrado, whose "To George Sand: A Refutation" appeared in *La Palma: A Weekly Journal of History and Literature* in May of 1841. Quadrado refutes Sand's "doctrine" by the character of "its evangelist." After quoting Sand's "verdict"

that "the Majorcan is a savage who cheats, extorts, lies, abuses and plunders to his heart's content, and would eat his fellowman without a qualm were that the local custom; but who, despite his vices, is no more to be hated than an ox or a sheep because, like theirs, his spirit is lulled in animal innocence,"

Quadrado's retort, "George Sand is the most unmoral of writers, and Mme. Dudevant the most obscene of women!" is weak, frankly, as is Graves' observation that "the original manuscript of *Un Hiver a Majorque* is even cruder than the version published" (Graves, 1956: p. 200).

The essay central to understanding Graves' own attachment and loyalty to the island is an essay written for *Harper's Bazaar* in 1953, "Why I Live in Majorca" (collected in Graves, 1965). It reads almost as a sentimental farewell to the island Graves first saw in the 1920's.

He chose Mallorca, Graves writes, "because its climate had the reputation of being better than any other in Europe . . . I should be able to live there on a quarter of the income needed in England . . . it was large enough, some 1,300 square miles, not to make me feel claustrophobic." Graves chose Deià, then a fishing and olive-farming village, because the village offered everything he needed as a writer: "sun, sea, mountains, spring-water, shady trees, no politics. . .electric light and a bus service to Palma, the capital. Ever pragmatic, he does not fail to note "it was also fairly mosquito free, being some 400 feet above sea level." Other "desiderata" used to make his choice included "good wine, good neighbours, and not too great a distance from the Greenwich meridian" (Graves, 1965: p. 7).

Graves always claimed real affection and respect for his "good neighbours," the Mallorcan people themselves. He described them as "excessively honest and friendly." Indeed, during his ten-year "exile" from Mallorca, he certainly had reason to note these two qualities. During the Spanish Civil War and World War II, Graves could send neither money nor letters to Deià from Galmpton, England. Yet when he returned, on what, ominously, was the first-ever charter flight to Palma, he found the house he had built (on the best site for miles around Deià), "unplundered" by either side and, in fact, Graves was grateful to see that "everything I had left behind had been looked after, linen, silver, books and documents . . . and if I felt so inclined, could have sat down at my table, taken a sheet of paper from the drawer and started work again straight away" (Graves, 1965: p. 21).

In his own first seven years in Deià, Graves' life was, by English standards, primitive, but rewarding. "Beef, butter and cow's milk were not easily obtained; but there was plenty of fresh fruit throughout the year." Graves provides a list of the fruits, by season: "oranges, loquats, cherries, apricots, peaches, plums, strawberries, apples, pears, first figs, grapes, pomegranates and oranges again." The necessities were there, and were cheap. "So with black coffee and cheap black tobacco, and a very sound heady wine from the village of Binisalem, and brandy at three pesetas a bottle, all was well" (Graves, 1965: p. 9).

Even though Deià was a place where "nothing of importance had ever happened . . . no hunting, no racing, no yachting . . . no ancient monuments . . . not even village politics," the little fishing village had for years drawn a certain type of tourist, most of whom probably came for the same reason Graves came. His catalogue of the visitors during his first seven years in Deià includes "painters, professors of literature, dipsomaniacs, pianists, perverts, priests, geologists, Buddhists, run-away couples, vegetarians, Seventh Day Adventists." There were, according to Graves, seldom less than two painters renting cottages or staying at the inn "during the season" (Graves, 1965: pp. 11-13).

For three years after World War II, "the flow of tourists remained negligible." Spain suffered under severe rationing of food, and a depressed economy. The slow increase in tourism was welcomed. "There is this to say for tourists: their arrival in bulk tends to relax police regulations, encourage amenities in food and household utensils, and decrease unemployment." In 1953, Graves was aware of the dangers that increased tourism presented, but felt that the island was little-spoiled except for the "Golden Mile" west of Palma. "And though an excess of visitors sends up prices and wages and fills the towns with ugly advertisements, souvenir shops, cheap-jacks, and shady adventurers from everywhere - and at the peak season can actually wear down the tempers of so patient and long-suffering a people as the Majorcans - still, the island has not yet been spoiled even by the massive influx of the recent 'Majorca, Island of Love' period." Graves perhaps reasonably did not fear for the island, because "few Majorcan roads are capable of taking buses and taxis, so tourist traffic is canalised along a narrow grid" (Graves, 1965: pp. 21-22). (One could hardly have predicted that six buses at once might be parked at the first tiny restaurant outside Deià, or that on occasion one bus may have to squeeze off Deià's main street to allow two others to pass.)

Typically, Graves insists that previous writers on Majorca hadn't got it quite right. The flawed description of his predecessors Graves blames on "the strange, hallucinatory power that Deià exerts on foreign visitors." Writing in 1719, one such visitor named Campbell described "the church and the country houses, but did not see the village; his successors saw the village, but neither the church nor the country houses." Campbell describes a broad plain, but at Deià "there is only a steeply terraced valley with nowhere a broad enough level place for a tennis court" (though one can see tennis courts now in Valldemosa, on the way to Deià). Writers after Campbell describe the "trilling of wild canaries, there are none on the island, festooned barren precipices with foliage, crowned them with eagles' eyries, and credited the houses of Deià with non-existent gardens." Without providing specifics, Graves claims that "Germans have written more extravagantly about the place," and since Deià is built on the site of a Moon-goddess shrine, Graves is willing to consider their "derangement" the result of the Deià moonlight, so bright "one can even match colours by it" (Graves, 1965: p. 13).

Nor did the painters get it quite right. "The painters splashed their canvasses with cobalt, viridian, vermilion, and a dirty olive-green, though the prevailing colours of the landscape are grey, smoke-blue, a translucent grey-green, blue-black, biscuit and rust; and the sea is never cobalt." His severest criticism Graves saves for the painters who, for lack of attention, do not paint what is before them. "They painted the crooked olive trees as though they were elms; and the harsh rocks as though they were cakes of castile soap" (Graves, 1965: pp. 13-14).

Graves describes Deià as "a spectacular but not really beautiful place." During his exile in England, Graves says he longed for "the fruit in my garden, the smell of olive-wood fires; the chatter of card-players in the village cafe; the buoyant green waters of the cove; the sun-blistered rocks of the Teix mountain; my quiet whitewashed study; the night noises of sheep bells, owls, nightingales, frogs and the distant surf" (Graves, 1965: pp. 10, 11).

In two graceful, central paragraphs of "Why I Live in Majorca" Graves describes his village. Deià is evoked in specific, sensuous detail; typically, Graves' description is based firmly in the spatial, or geographical, arrangement of detail:

> *"But what was Deià really like? A village of some 400 inhabitants, and some 200 solid stone houses, most of them built on the landward side of a rocky hill which occupied the centre of a great fold of mountains. The coast-road encircled Deià but touched the outlying houses only. A church with a squat tower and a small cypressed cemetery crowned the hill; no houses at all were built between it and the sea, half-a-mile away. A torrent, dry during the summer, ran halfway round the village and down in a narrow gorge until it emptied into a cove, with a beach of sand and pebbles. Apart from the small port of Soller, six miles up the coast, this was one of the very few inlets along the island's ironbound north-western coast. No car could get down to the cove from the village, and the fisherman's path was a rough one indeed: a 400 foot descent from the coast-road, first through olive groves and then through a scrub of lentiscus, spurge, asphodel, caper and wild asparagus"* (Graves, 1965: p. 14).

The open vowels, repeated *I* sounds, the specificity of the diction describing both the landscape and the flora of northern Mallorca complement the purposeful syntax. Though the sentence patterns are quite varied, the sentences are dominated by nominals, absolutes, noun complements and by compound subjects and their modifiers. All in all, with the noun series which ends the paragraph, Graves uses very graceful, and standard, structures to pack a great deal of specific detail into these few sentences.

The attention to Mallorca's distinctive flora continues in the second of these paragraphs:

> *"The fisherman's huts in the cove were used only in the summer months. No refreshments could be obtained there and one got very hot climbing back after a swim. The mountains had been laboriously terraced all the way up from sea-level to about 900 feet. There were lemon and orange groves where irrigation was possible; but only three springs in the village ran all the year round, and the soil was everywhere poor and stony; apart from a few carob trees that provided wholesome fodder for mules, all the rest was olive orchard. And the olives were*

> *not the well-behaved, bushy-topped, stately variety that one finds in Italy,*
> *France, and California, but twisted, bossed, hacked-about grotesques, often*
> *growing from cracks in the live rock, never watered, never manured, once a year*
> *scratched around with a primitive mule-plough, and every seven years trimmed of*
> *their biggest branches. They were almost indestructible; a good many had been*
> *planted by the Moors, more than 700 years before. "Pamper an olive tree," the*
> *villagers used to say, "and spoil the fruit." In the spring some of the olive*
> *terraces could be persuaded to raise a sparse crop of broad beans. These, with*
> *figs, served to feed the black pigs which were ceremoniously killed at Martinmas,*
> *and turned into red and black sausage; each household had its pig and the*
> *sausage must last until the following Martinmas. Above the olive-trees rose an*
> *unterraced belt of stunted evergreen oak, where charcoal-burners worked all*
> *summer, pigs rooted in the autumn, wild peonies flowered at Easter. And wild*
> *cats, martens, and civets maintained a precarious existence. Above that, towered*
> *sheer precipices streaked with rusty ochre, and above those the bald limestone*
> *brow of the Teix"* (Graves, 1965: pp. 14, 17).

Here Graves displays in a beautifully organised paragraph (up the mountainsides from the cove to the "brow of the Teix") the same attention to phonology and syntax as in paragraph one, and again, the specification is done with a profusion of nouns, note that only three colours are specified in this very lengthy passage. The overall effect is of a great tension between what should be a sparse, barren landscape and the profusion of crops which in fact the Mallorcan villagers can force the rocky landscape to bear. And with his two asides about the cultivation of pigs and olives, Graves indicates that he both shares and respects the villagers' knowledge of agriculture, wresting a life from stony mountainside.

Graves' regard for the Mallorcan people continued to remain high. "I have now lived here under the Dictatorship, the Republic, and the present regime, but the people do not change." Mallorcans, according to Graves, "have always been liberty-loving, though staunchly conservative; highly moral, though confirmed sceptics of ecclesiastical doctrine; with a rooted dislike of physical violence, drunkenness, or any breach of good manners." And Graves was particularly grateful that "money-grubbing" was considered a breach of good manners. "In the villages, bills are presented neither weekly, nor monthly, nor quarterly, but at the end of the year" (Graves, 1965: p. 22). Graves was noted for presenting his Deià baker with a cigar each time he paid his annual bill.

In his fiction, however, Graves is much less charitable about his adopted fellow citizens. All the stories of Mallorcan characters are replete with business swindles, family squabbles, death by witchcraft, even plagiarism.

In his "Majorcan Stories," a separate section of the *Collected Short Stories* (1968), there is little evidence that Robert Graves thought highly of the Mallorcan national character. Perhaps for dramatic reasons, each of the stories revolves around a situation in which a Mallorcan behaves less than honestly ("The Whittaker Negroes," a non-story of which the less said the better, has no Mallorcan characters). In "6 Valiant Bulls 6," the plot depends on a failed conspiracy to supply unenergetic bulls for the *corrida*. "A Bicycle in Majorca" begins with a lesson on bringing an English bicycle into Spain without paying import duties, then proceeds by theft and re-theft of the imported bicycle, with an attempted suicide thrown in. "Evidence of Affluence" exposes the ways in which Mallorcans are careful not to look too affluent, in order to avoid taxation. The most complex and most entertaining of the Mallorcan stories is "The Viscountess and the Short-haired Girl," a tale of peasants conning a con. This story depends upon Mallorcan peasants willing to pretend to believe that a "Bulgarian heretic" has kidnapped a "short haired girl" long enough to testify about her presence in the village; the joke around which the story revolves is that the peasants know as well as the lawyer and detective that the short haired girl is having an affair with the Bulgarian and is not the niece of the Viscountess who will pay them to testify, but is in fact married to the Viscountess' lover - rather than a kidnapping trial, it is a divorce trial at which the peasants will testify. But first, they run up enormous expense accounts and squeeze the Viscountess for more and more pesetas in exchange for their testimony.

In "To Minorca!" (Collected in *Food for Centaurs*, 1960) Robert Graves heaps criticism on the customs, food, architecture, even the climate of that neighbouring Balearic island. Little escapes his eye: "Minorcans lack the enterprise of their Majorcan cousins," so they have never returned to olive growing. Their vineyards were destroyed by *phylloxer*, "so that their staple drink is no longer wine, but gin, a word and habit borrowed from the British." It is their British-derived customs Graves decries most, but he finds little about Minorca to recommend it, with the possible exception of their fresh seafood. The shopkeepers are complacent and far from accommodating: "In these islands, storekeepers always believe that customers are trying to get rid of their money, it doesn't matter on what. You need a hammer; they haven't got one in stock, so they say brightly: 'It will have to be a saw.'" Indeed, almost the entire essay is a catalogue of the extreme nonchalance of the Minorcans: when told that the Pope has died, the confectioners' clerk shrugs, "Indeed? I feel it deeply. So he has left us! But patience! What can we do? All things pass" (Graves, 1960: pp. 212, 214, 221).

Ironically, Graves may have had a model close at hand for the conniving and subtle Balearic businessmen of his fiction. At least one Mallorcan native may not have been so scrupulously honest as he appeared. Juan Marroig Mas, known locally as Gelat, became Graves' local adviser. It was Gelat who convinced Graves that he should buy 36,000 square meters of land to foil the building of a German tourist hotel between Graves' home and the sea. (He also convinced Graves to place his property in Gelat's name, since foreigners could not own land within five kilometres of the beach). To pay for this purchase, Graves should build a road from his home to the cala, and recoup his investment by selling the road to the government. The road could be financed by selling plots of the 36,000 square meters to Graves' rich English friends. In the summer of 1931, Graves considered devoting the land, by then called "Luna Land," to a university which would teach Laura Riding's views on life and society. Graves mortgaged his home to buy the land, eventually; this debt was a major factor in his decision to undertake the writing of *I, Claudius* (Seymour 1995, pp. 204-205, 210-211). In September 1933, a rainstorm washed the new road away, and none of the land had been sold; in the fall of 1935 Graves was forced to explain the purpose of the road and to "produce the appropriate authorisations" that would clear him of rumours of spying; sale to the government was impossible (Seymour 1995, pp. 219, 237).

In 1947, after his return from exile in England during the war years, Graves was anxious to settle ownership issues with Laura Riding, who had returned to America in 1939. Riding gave Gelat power of attorney, and the properties were transferred; Gelat would farm the land, providing olives and wood to Graves in rent payment. None of the transfers were legal, however; Graves was still a foreigner and still prohibited from owning land so near the beach. In fact, when Gelat died in 1949, he passed the properties on to his son. It was not until 1959 that Graves, finally realising the duplicity, had a friend arrange for the village of Deya to "annex" the property so his claim would be legal. He then had to repurchase his own properties from a trusted Mallorcan emigre, Ricardo Sicre, who acted as negotiator and go-between (Seymour, 1995: pp. 325, 327). In fact, we know that Graves later based at least one conniving Mallorcan character on Gelat: on December 4, 1957 in a letter to James Reeves, Graves mentioned that "a light story, as pleadingly asked for *New Yorker*" was based on "Old Gelat and the Lady Carnarvon divorce case" (Graves, 1988: p. 172). This "light story" eventually became "The Viscountess and the Short Haired Girl."

Mallorcan society and geography were being transformed rapidly in the years after Graves' return to the island. Before the Spanish Civil War, Mallorca had been the medically prescribed holiday for a "rest in the sun." With recently discovered penicillin, these visitors no longer came, and winter holidays in the sun went out of fashion" (Graves, 1995: p. 135). After the war, in the early 1950's, the Mallorcan Board of Tourism began advertising the island as a honeymoon destination; then the Ministry of Tourism in Madrid, a Franco project to develop the economy, took up the program. State controls on room rates and the development of commercial airline routes made Mallorca cheap and convenient. "Tourist complexes developed with little infrastructure and no consideration for the landscape. Planning permission in supposedly protected areas could be obtained, provided a high enough bribe was paid in the right place" (Graves, W. 1995: p. 135).

When "Why I Live in Majorca" was reprinted in *Majorca Observed* in 1965, it was accompanied by a "Postscript." In this late addition,

Robert Graves brought his earlier ideas into the context of "the brand-new phenomenon of mass-tourism." By 1965, there were "5,000 planes a month" bringing tourists to "over 1,000 new hotels." Graves derides the worship of sun tanning, "a new idea derived from D. H. Lawrence's German-inspired sun-cult." Graves voices the criticisms of tourists which have by now become *de rigeur*, if not *passe*: food, behaviour, ignorance of geography or customs, guided tours of the Mallorcan countryside with bored and uninformed guides. "Majorca is fortunate in its lack of exploitable historical attractions; mass tourism and individual travel need not get confused" (Graves, 1965: p. 47). Graves then goes on to list the ways in which organised tours must exaggerate local history - such as Sand's visit to Valldemosa, or Archduke Ludwig Salvator's love life, simply to give tourists something to look at and think about, other than getting "frizzled" on a beach. Already Graves was quoting the authorities' worries about the effect of "the daily exhalation of carbon dioxide from the lungs of several hundred tourists. . .rapidly flaking off the colours" (Graves, 1965: p. 50) of not only the Mallorcan caves, but caves in Spain or France.

In 1965, Deiá seemed relatively untouched in contrast to Palma, where "the old Palma has long ceased to exist; its centre eaten away by restaurants, bars, souvenir shops, travel agencies and the like." But, in contrast "fortunately the rocks from which we swim at Deyá are inaccessible to the mass-tourist, nor is the village exploitable . . ." Graves, correctly as it turned out, predicted that Deyá would remain relatively untouched as long as the roads were bad, "but the still unexploited Majorcan hinterland is constantly shrinking as the roads improve." Deiá was, even in 1965, already touched by tourism of a different manner: ". . . of course, the usual German colonists have bought up the more spectacular sites on the coast nearby, and built houses in their own familiar domestic style" (Graves, 1965: p. 51).

Graves' attitude may have become like that of the Count of Deia, a character in "She Landed Yesterday," one of Graves' Mallorcan stories. The Count of Deia is heir to the family seat, the Palacio Deia in Palma, but chooses instead to live in the village of Deia, to take "refuge from the enemy, here in the mountains." When asked "what enemy?" he replies,

> *"Those who smoke blond tobacco; those who strew our quiet Majorcan beaches with pink, peeling human flesh; those who roar around our island in foreign cars ten metres long; those who prefer aluminium to earthenware, and plastics to glass; those who demolish the old quarters of Palma and erect travel agencies, souvenir shops, and tall barrack-like hotels on the ruins; those who keep their radios bawling incessantly along the street at siesta-time; those who swill Caca-Loco and bottled beer!"* (Graves, 1968: p. 277).

If this series of characteristics attributed to tourists by the Count of Deia seems to come easily and be heartfelt, consider that for the Count "the last straw came with the closing of the Café Figaro, which everyone of character in Palma used to frequent and the conversion of its premises into palatial offices for Messrs Thomas Cook and Son" (Graves, 1968: p. 277). The Figaro was Graves' favourite cafe/bar in Palma.

William Graves' memoir, *Wild Olives* (1995), is the story of his attempts to find a way both to earn an adult living (his original career was that of petroleum engineer) and to remain in Deia. His final chapter is an evocation of the changes that were wrought in Deia by tourist development between 1946 and the mid-1980's:

> *". . . the village we returned to was not the one I grew up in . . .There were now two luxury hotels . . . an up market restaurant with its own swimming pool . . . one could no longer walk to Canellún without being passed by a steady stream of cars and buses. Even Laura and Father's road to the Cala had been blacktopped by the Deyá Town Hall. The metamorphosis was complete. Deyá was an up-market holiday resort . . . no longer did the fishwives bring the morning catch to the village; no longer did one hear the rattle of the carob beans being knocked down; no longer was the cafe filled with smoke and the cries of the* **Truc** *players on a Sunday morning"* (Graves, W. 1995: pp. 258- 259).

A horrible irony of this transformation is that, for five years, William Graves was himself a hotel-keeper in Deyá, the solution to his career dilemma being one of the causes of Deiá's move "up market."

When Bill Waldren, a friend of Graves' son, successfully remodelled an old mill in Deya to serve as a museum for his archaeological discoveries, Robert Graves bought two houses opposite the new museum and converted them into an apartment, a library, and a laboratory. Thus, William became co-director of the "Archaeological Study Centre" in Deia. In its last incarnation, it became known as the "Deya Archaeological Museum, Library and Gallery Teix." There were even plans to "add a shop to the complex, to sell paintings, sculpture, photographs, ceramics and jewellery produced by *estrangers*" (Graves, W. 1995: pp. 178-207).

Robert Graves was recognised by the Mallorcan government in the spring of 1967 with a plaque honouring his contribution to the island. That same March, William Graves and his wife Elena opened their hotel Ca'n Quet for its second season. The first season had not been particularly successful but things changed in the second year.

> "We were now listed as one of the special hotels in the Erna Low Travel brochure, and our clientele included doctors, architects, TV producers and writers. We were written up in glossy magazines such as **Cosmopolitan** and **Nova**. On my desk I found a flood of letters to answer and, by mid-June, we were fully booked. Erna Low charged £50 a fortnight, full board, including the flight; we had become the "in" place to be. Girls wearing the latest Carnaby Street mini-skirts and white knee-high boots graced our **terraza** . . . When Father was interviewed by the BBC, the crew stayed at Ca'n Quet . . . We were discovered by young British actors . . . Some even managed to pick up work on films being shot on the island" (Graves, W. 1995: pp. 233-234).

In 1962, Robert Graves had been instrumental, almost solely, in the decision to declare the north-west coast of Mallorca a National Park, with no high-rise hotels allowed. He suggested this solution to Don Manuel Fraga, the Minister of Tourism (who had once been dispatched by Franco to visit Graves) as a way of halting a planned hotel and villa complex on the Deia cala. After this rather high-handed intervention on Graves' part, Deia and the other coastal villages were regulated by new building codes, and all new building had to win the approval of the Fine Arts Council in Palma. Many Deia villagers were angered both by this new restriction and by the loss of jobs that the hotel would have generated. Older villagers remembered that Graves had built the road to the beach, had planned a university campus between his home and the beach, and had even at one time considered building his own hotel on this land. "The *senyor* plainly had double standards" (Graves, W. 1995: p. 165).

By 1968, when Robert Graves was made an "adoptive son of Deya," among the accomplishments for which the Mayor thanked Graves were his role in bringing electricity to Deya and for "attracting so many *turistas*" (Graves, W. 1995: p. 242).

One biographer, Miranda Seymour, believes that by the 1960's, Graves was in fact tiring of village life in Deia, and especially of his role as a counter culture guru for an alarming band of bohemians, "hippies," and would-be artists, these last an element whom Graves satirised in his poem "Wigs and Beards."

After a first stanza describing how the "bewigged country Squire" of the past would not pay his debts except for gambling losses, "horsewhipped his tenantry" as he "urged his pack through standing grain," how he "snorted at the arts," "blasphemed," and "set fashions of pluperfect slovenliness," Graves introduces the modern version, the "Beards", who,

"Latter-day bastards of that famous stock,
They never rode a nag, nor gaffed a trout,
Nor winged a pheasant, nor went soldiering,
But remain true to the same hell-fire code
In all available particulars
And scorn to pay their debts even at cards.

At least the "bewigged Squire"

Shot, angled. . .
And claimed siegneurial rights over all women
who slept, imprudently, under the same roof.

In contrast, the modern, loutish "Beards" are first seen

Hurling their empties through the cafe window
and belching loud as they proceed downstairs.

. . . Moreunder (which is to subtract, not add),
Their ancestors called themselves gentlemen
As they, in the same sense, call themselves artists. "
(Graves, 1977: p. 270)

In a graceful and laudatory article in the June 1996 *Gravesiana*, Joan M. Fiol points out this essential contradiction. After Graves was duped into buying the land from his home to the cala, to forestall, Fiol maintains, the building of a German tourist hotel next to Graves' house, he built the famous road and attempted to sell plots along it.

"The image of a land developer clashes noisily with that of the poet who so intensely loved that countryside and who later forcefully defended it against any danger of being spoilt. However, in those days the concept of balearization was not even an issue (Balearization is a word coined by French geographers to describe the systematic destruction of the coastline by indiscriminate and excessive building). Sadly, the scheme failed . . . " (Fiol, 1966: p. 65).

Fiol points out that the failure of the scheme at least led to Graves' writing the Claudius novels to climb out of bankruptcy. Yet the road also led to rumours that Graves was a spy - who else would need a road to the water? (And his evacuation from the island by a British destroyer in 1934 kept this rumour alive well into the 1950's, even after an official inquiry cleared Graves.) In fact in 1967, the road was "the sole point in the agenda of a special meeting held by the Town Council . . . when the poet was about to be named Adoptive Son of Deià." The Mayor's final remarks about "Mr. Graves" and his interest "in matters related to his village, history, customs, folklore, etc . . ." contain this sentence: "In 1934 he built at his own expense a road leading to the cove." Finally in 1976 the local administration made the road public after repairing and paving it. Even Fiol writes, "A happy end for an embarrassing business" (Fiol, 1966: p. 66).

Fiol can be more direct. Of Graves' mistakes about the Mallorcan language, his debunking of local legends used to "attract tourists to his neighbourhood," balanced with his debunking of Chopin's and Sand's harsh criticism in *Winter in Majorca*, Fiol says "This is just another example of Graves' two different, sometimes contradictory, levels of expression when dealing with Majorcan matters" (Fiol, 1966: p. 71).

Nowadays, though Mallorca has its share of bohemians, artists, and artistes, Ibiza is becoming the holiday destination for the bohemian class. Still, the Mallorcan tourism that led to the creation of the word *balèariser*, to describe the Mallorcan transformation from paradise to tourist development, (a transformation copied around the Mediterranean and a word not meant as a compliment) continues. Now, with the University of the Balearics running a degree program in tourism, and with a private Escuela de Turismo in Palma, the Mallorcan government is consciously, however, following a strategy to move "up market and green" with new beaches, hotels, and roads (*Passport*, 1995: pp. 16-17, 26, 56). The government is now following a policy of destroying hotels in order to re-establish "greenbelts" around some of the larger hotel complexes, but all this may be too late. With a polluted and depleted aquifer, Mallorca now is brought potable drinking water by daily tankers that unload in Palma. Still, perhaps the enigmatic figure of Robert Graves, that so contradicts his works about the island he loved, can play a role in helping to develop a more sustainable tourism for Mallorca and the other Balearic Islands.

References

Barke, M., et al, eds. (1966), *Tourism in Spain: Critical Issues*. Wallingford, UK: CAB International.

Fiol, Joan. (June 1996), "The perfect guest: the poet and the island, a lasting affair." *Gravesiana: The Journal of the Robert Graves Society* 63-74.

Graves, Robert. (1960), *Food for Centaurs*. New York: Doubleday.

Graves, Robert. (1965), "Why I Live in Majorca," *Majorca Observed*. London: Cassell.

Graves, Robert. (1968), *Collected Short Stories*. London: Penguin.

Graves, Robert. (1977), *New Collected Poems*. New York: Doubleday.

Graves, Robert. (1988), *Between Moon and Moon: Selected Letters of Robert Graves*. Paul O'Prey, ed. London: Moyer Bell.

Graves, Robert. (1997), *Letters to Ken*. Harvey Sarner, ed. Cathedral City, CA: Brunswick Press.

Graves, William. (1995), *Wild Olives*. London: Hutchinson.

Passport Illustrated Travel Guide to Mallorca. (1995), Chicago: Passport Books and Thomas Cook Group Ltd.

Sand, George. (1956), *Winter in Majorca*. Robert Graves, translator and editor. London: Cassell.

Seymour, Miranda. (1995), *Robert Graves: Life on the Edge*. London: Doubleday.

Ways of seeing 'them' and 'us': Tourism representation, race and identity

Annette Pritchard

University of Wales Institute, UK

Abstract

This paper attempts to contribute to the development of a critical analysis of tourism representations, arguing that the influence of repressive and liberating historical, political and cultural discourses can be discerned in contemporary marketing. The paper adapts and develops a content analysis technique which facilitates the quantitative analysis of racialised tourism representations and qualitatively evaluates representations of destinations in the Caribbean, Africa and Asia within a discursive framework. A case study of a range of UK tour operators' brochures forms the basis for a discussion of the relationship between race, discourse, tourism representations and destination marketing. The value and limitations of the content analysis research tool are discussed, as is its further applicability as a measurement of representations in tourism marketing.

Introduction

This paper contends that tourism processes are part of a much wider discursive framework grounded in complex, multi-dimensional, cultural, social and historical systems. In particular, it attempts to contribute to the development of critical analyses of tourism representations, arguing that the nature and the use of tourism representations is constrained by historical, political and cultural discourses. Powerful discourses shape our ways of seeing the world (Berger 1983, Hall 1997) - a process from which tourism is by no means immune since historical, political and cultural discourses influence how peoples and places are seen and represented in contemporary marketing. Thus, for instance, whilst colonialism may have been rejected economically, it continues to exert cultural power by defining how tourism marketing constructs certain peoples and places (Britton 1979; MacCannell 1984: 377; Silver 1993).

Studies have analysed how the identities of peoples in Asia (Said 1978, 1991), the Southern States of America (Fredrikson 1987, Mellinger 1994) and Africa (McClintock 1995) have been shaped by powerful discourses which '...intersect, so that certain identities are constituted as more powerful and more valuable than others' (Rose 1993: 6). Notwithstanding the contributions of such studies, there remains little recognition that repressive and liberating discourses are reflected in today's marketing of tourism destinations - and almost no recognition that racial and ethnic discourses shape marketing representations of communities and countries. In part this reflects the continuing lack of critical analyses of image representation in tourism (Mellinger 1994), but it is also symptomatic of tourism research's attachment to positivist paradigms which have defined 'appropriate' research agendas (Morgan and Pritchard 1999: 2) and marginalised analyses of social exclusion and the peripheralisation of peoples and places.

Analyses of tourism representations must begin to incorporate discussion of the relationship between tourism marketing and ideology. To date, however, these ideological aspects have received little attention, resulting in an incomplete analysis of what is a powerful political and cultural phenomenon: despite its importance, 'discussions of the ideological dimensions of tourism have been virtually non-existent' (Hall 1994: 11). Recognising this, we need to re-examine the interplay between power, culture and history if we are to fully understand contemporary tourism processes (Foucault 1980: 187). Tourism representations do not exist in isolation but are inexorably intertwined in 'a circuit of culture' (Hall 1997: 1) whereby representations utilise and reflect identity and in which images are continuously produced and consumed. The following case-study-based discussion focuses on the socio-cultural and racial construction of tourism processes through a critical examination of tourism marketing. First, however, it demonstrates how historically and culturally certain destinations and their peoples have been constructed as 'Other' - a process conceptualised by Rose (1993: 116) as othering - 'defining where you belong through a contrast with other places, or who you are through a contrast with other people.'

Tourism, representation and race

It is well established that marketers select and utilise particular images and aspects of society and discard others (Williamson 1978) and all representations (including those in tourism) are created, filtered and mediated through cultural and ideological structures. Nixon (1997: 211) has commented that 'the kinds of gender, "racial" and ethnic identities or scripts that are sanctioned' in the media needs further investigation and although it is beyond the scope of this paper to assess the composition of advertising agencies, it is possible to examine their output to discern the nature of their scripts and their underlying meanings. Whilst text and images may convey many potential meanings, one meaning tends to be privileged over others (Denzin 1995: 200) and such is the power of this dominant ideology that it often blinds consumers to other interpretations (Mellinger 1994: 775). The images portrayed by the travel media assume a particular kind of tourist - white, western, male and heterosexual - privileging this gaze over others (Urry 1990, Pritchard and Morgan 2000b) - not surprising, perhaps, given that most marketers are white, western and male. Despite the growing economic power of African-American tourists (Real 1996), for instance, there are few black advertising agencies in the USA whilst the national tourism organisations of developing countries overwhelmingly employ Western agencies (Richter 1995: 80, Morgan and Pritchard 1998).

Racialised tourism representations and power

Race has received significant attention in the social sciences, demonstrating how racism 'has long structured socio-structural relations' and has 'been woven into a range of power differentiated regimes ... into the present' (Anderson 1996: 198). In tourism, however, this human status characteristic has been marginalised (Richter 1995) although its interplay with other status characteristics creates new dimensions to inequalities - space, place and power have different implications for men and women of different races, even of the same social class (Enloe 1989: 40). Extant research also suggests that touristic representations portray and reinforce existing power structures and reflect a masculine and 'Western desire for an exotic "other"' (Cohen 1995: 418), indicating that the relationship between the West and the Other is expressed through racialised and gendered exchanges. MacCannell (1984: 377) has argued that mass tourism is a powerful shaper of identity which produces 'new and more highly deterministic ethnic forms than those produced during the colonial phase because 'Westerners continue to write the true story of the existence of other peoples.' Thus, images of the developing world or ethnic minority groups within societies tend to reflect a western, male, colonial perspective of the 'Other' and defend white racial advantage by marginalising and excluding non-whites. The body is perhaps the ultimate site of racialised representation and different races have been 'seen' and described differently throughout history - their bodies being inscribed with particular meanings and constrained or empowered in particular ways (Rose 1993: 9). Moreover, since the media constructs and interprets 'reality', the ways in which tourism marketing materials portray and describe peoples has implications not only for how they are seen and how they act, but also how they perceive themselves (Wood 1984: 366). In such ways is cultural domination maintained '...as much by consent as by direct and crude economic pressure' (Said 1978: 324).

The role of stereotyping in representation

Stereotypes and clichés (classifying people and places according to particular traits and roles) are pivotal to racialised representations. They reduce people to certain traits, exaggerating and simplifying them, producing caricatures which are resistant to change. In such ways stereotyping 'sets up a symbolic frontier between the "normal" and the "deviant" ... the "acceptable" and the "unacceptable", what "belongs" and what does not or is "Other", between "insiders" and "outsiders", Us and Them' (Hall 1997: 258). Stereotyping is a manifestation of the power of one to label or define another and dominant groups and perspectives 'attempt to fashion the whole of society according to their own world view, value system, sensibility and ideology ... they make it appear as "natural" and "inevitable" ... [and] in so far as they succeed, they establish their hegemony' (Dyer 1997 in Hall 1997: 259). Stereotypes abound in the tourism image and it is not enough to dismiss them as evidence of lazy thinking, rather such 'Clichés are the common-sense, everyday articulations of the dominant ideology' (Fiske 1989: 118).

This ability of powerful groups to manage and manipulate cultural power has resulted in the production of what Said (1978: 260) has described as a 'racialised knowledge of the Other ... [which is] deeply implicated in the operations of power'. This is a radicalised knowledge of the Other seen in images of the Orient, Africa (McClintock 1995) and the USA (Fredrikson 1987, Mellinger 1994) which make no attempt to communicate the rich diversity of other cultures. This radicalised knowledge, in which the west has labelled and defined Others could largely be described as the product of three ages - of slavery, empire and (in the post-war period) the age of migration from the 'third world' into the west (Hall 1997: 239). In many ways, however, contemporary representations are more insidious in that they are less overt. Morgan and Pritchard (1998: 216-7) observe how the language of tourism mediates the exotic, often juxtaposing the Other with the familiar and marking the difference between 'them' and 'us.' Thus, on a *Thomas Cook* holiday British tourists can enjoy 'an Oriental Journey beyond the wildest dreams of Marco Polo', where they can visit: Bangkok ('the Venice of the East'); Hong Kong, ('where Britain meets China'); and Macau, ('the oldest European settlement in Asia'). Alternatively, they can visit Delhi, (the 'Paris of India') and even closer to home culturally: 'South Africa is, in many ways, more European than African', a destination where 'visitors will find a measure of sophistication and a good standard of accommodation, food, shopping and entertainment.'

The significance of such imagery is far wider than the impact of seeing a photograph in a brochure since the selection process conveys messages both to visitors and to visited. MacCannell (1984: 385-6) has argued that certain ethnic identities are maintained and promoted over others in order to entertain the tourist and the Other continues to be described in the terms highlighted by Spivak (1988):

> *People of colour are seen but do not see, are represented but do not represent, and are photographed but do not photograph.... This racist regime of representation preserved and defended the racial privilege of European Americans.*

Hall (1997: 236) has commented that 'The marking of "difference" is thus the basis of that symbolic order we call culture.' People who differ from the majority (them as opposed to us) have traditionally tended to be represented in binary terms, such as good or bad, civilised or primitive; and ugly or attractive. This racialised knowledge of the Other frequently makes use of binary representations which label and define the world in terms of us and them, superiority and inferiority, intellect and instinct. Peoples and places are assigned key characteristics which conform to this two-dimensional or oppositional world view. These binary representations between the primitive, sexual and violent blacks and the civilised, cerebral and restrained whites are, according to Segal (1990: 179), 'internalised by Black people themselves' because of the essentially white dominated culture in which they live. Wrapped up in these stereotypes are certain notions of black sexuality - black men as 'studs' and black women 'whores'. In this gaze black sexuality has been constructed as masculine, animalistic, elemental and unrestrained; and Oriental sexuality as feminine, sophisticated and decadent. Despite the binary depiction of others, it is important, however, to note that 'relationships between dominant and minoritised groups are crossed not only by discursive fields but also by multiple *positionings* that are not reducible to the binary division of 'us' and 'them' (Anderson 1996: 199). In this sense, racism often draws on gender as a form of oppression, an intersection of power relations which needs to be understood to fully appreciate the 'wider discursive network' which structure racism, sexism and homophobia.

In this polarised gaze, we can see how the West 'set Africa up as a foil to Europe', (Achebe in Segal 1990: 173). In the same way as Said argued that Western conceptions of the Orient continue to structure how the West sees the East, Segal (1990: 174) comments that 'The image of Africa as dark and malevolent, primitive and unchanging is with us still ... increasingly the idea grew that Africa was not simply unchanged, but unchangeable.' The legacy of colonialism continues to dominate western thinking - as Jablow and Hammond (1970: 108) concluded in their study of four centuries of British writing about Africa: 'The liquidation of empire by no means bankrupted the traditional messages. On the contrary, the new situation has been as much a stimulus for proliferation of the tradition as had been the growth of empire.'

This 'racial grammar of representation' is well documented, not only in nineteenth century colonialism but also in modern popular culture (Hall 1997: 251). For example, Denzin (1995) has analysed Hollywood's manipulations of class, race and gender, arguing that:

> *the cinematic apparatus operated as a technology of gender (and race) which reproduced the structure of patriarchy (and racism) by implementing a concept of looking and spectatorship which often made women (and non-whites) the objects of the male (white) gaze...*

Similarly, in contemporary tourism Others continue to be described as simple, dependent, mischievous, primitive, and fixed in a paternalistic relationship with the first world (Cohen 1995). The racial grammar can be seen in how tourism marketers represent 'women of colour', particularly in view of Hall's (1997: 263) comment that racialised knowledge is as much about fantasy as perceived reality, about *'what is not being said, but is being fantasised, what is implied but cannot be shown.'* Since difference is 'powerful, strangely attractive, precisely because it is forbidden, taboo, threatening to cultural order' (Hall 1997: 237) race is never neutered but interwoven with sexuality. Racial hierarchies are maintained 'through fantasies which reinforce those differences through references to gender. Thus fantasies of threatening Asian men, emasculated eunuchs, alluring Asian "dragon ladies", and submissive female slaves all work together to rationalise white, male domination' (Marchetti 1991: 289). This linkage is apparent in contemporary tourism imagery, and just as Denzin (1995: 93) describes the portrayal of the Asian film detectives Charlie Chan, Mr Moto and Mr Wong as 'feminised Asian men, even eunuchs,' never sexually threatening to the white majority, so the same portrayals of Asian males appear in tourism images - either as the young Buddhist monk or the aged, wise, even stoic, Oriental.

A methodology for measuring racialised representations

Whilst there is a need for a critique of racialised representations in tourism marketing, analyses of visual material are highly problematic and a number of researchers have discussed the reading and analysis of visual data, visual culture and visual design (Ball and Smith 1992, Jenks 1995). Kress and Van Leeuwen (1996: 12) emphasise that the analysis of visual communication should be an important element of critical disciplines encompassing both the system and use of visual communication. Methodologies include semiotic and discourse approaches which provide a critical framework for understanding how 'visual structures realise meaning' (Kress and Van Leeuwen 1996: 2). This paper combines content analysis with a critical, discourse framework. Content analysis is a research tool ideally suited to systematically quantifying and classifying the content of media messages (Kress and Van Leeuwen 1990) and, as Hornig Priest (1996: 83) points out: 'Where media content itself is the object of study, content analysis - whether quantitative or ... qualitative - is the logical choice'.

Content analysis (together with semiotics and discourse analysis) is a technique which has been used to provide a consistent interpretation of what are difficult, contentious and usually subjective cultural objects. Slater (1998: 234) highlights how content analysis and semiotics are both:

> *forms of textual analysis, aiming to provide convincing readings of cultural texts, and to draw various conclusions from them, by looking at the texts themselves rather than at the ways in which people actually consume the texts.*

Content analysis has a long history in communication studies and as a research technique in tourism it has been frequently used in destination image studies and rather less frequently in examinations of gendered and racialised representations (Pritchard and Morgan 2000a). It involves taking a sample which is representative but small enough to allow for substantive analysis - it is rarely random because of the nature of the investigation and the materials involved (Slater 1998: 235). Critical to successful content analyses are the development of appropriate classifications which are independently verifiable and reliable: this is usually resolved by using more than one coder (as was the case here). Although content analysis has its roots in positivism, when it is utilised in conjunction with other forms of textual investigation - such as discourse analysis - it creates more critical, richer and complex interpretations of representations.

Discourse analysis involves investigating cultural texts to understand how they help to create and reproduce meanings which in turn shape our knowledge of the social world. These texts are viewed not as neutral vehicles for communication (precisely because language involves classifying and stereotyping), instead they are sites in which social meanings are created and reproduced and social identities are formed (Tonkiss 1998: 246). Discourse refers to any text or language which 'draws on a particular terminology and encodes specific forms of knowledge' (Tonkiss 1998: 248). Particularly relevant to discourse analysis is its tendency to discuss cultural texts within an analysis which refers to external social relations. Commonalties do exist in the sense that in the analysis, the researcher looks for key themes and patterns of emphasis but equally significant are the silences and omissions which become apparent when the researcher reads *against* the text.

Clearly research tools need to be developed to facilitate in-depth, critical analyses of tourism representations - in particular there is a need to develop tools which can be used quantitatively to complement extant qualitative analyses (Uzzell, 1984; Selwyn, 1992; Dann, 1996). These could then be used longitudinally to establish the degree of continuity in representations. The research tool demonstrated below adapts a content analysis technique developed by Butler-Paisley and Paisley-Butler (1974) known as the consciousness scale. Originally developed to evaluate gendered representations in magazine advertising, the consciousness scale is based on an ordinal as opposed to a nominal classification which enables the analysis to focus not only on the measurement but also on the comparison of media representations. Images can thus be placed in relation to each other, as opposed to being merely enumerated as racist or non-racist. The scale has been applied to gendered advertisements in magazines or television commercials (Pingree *et al.*, 1976; Skelly and

Lundstrom, 1981) but this study seeks to establish the extent to which it can be applied to tourism brochures and adapted to an analysis of race.

Figure 1   a scale for measuring racism in tourism representations

Level V

Hosts and Guests as Equals

Level IV

Hosts Serving Guests

Level III

Hosts as 'Tourism Attractions'
(depicted as dancers etc)

Level II

Hosts as the 'Backdrop' to Tourist Experiences

Level I

Hosts as a one Dimensional Sexual Object or 'Decoration'

The current application of the scale incorporates a number of refinements to the original, including the weighting of images according to size, a methodology used by Dilley (1986) in his analysis of tourism brochure imagery. Another refinement is in the implementation of the scale, since although the consciousness scale has been successfully applied in a variety of situations, its usefulness and validity as a measure of media content is dependent on its ease of application and the accuracy and reliability of its coding. Since the coding of images can be criticised as subjective, here each image was assigned to one of six size categories by two independent coders, ranging from A3 to an eighth of a page, with values of six to one used to weight the overall significance of the images. A key methodological point is the multi-layered nature of the images and since the photographs in these brochures may depict more than one representation, the analysis evaluated each separate image.

The scale has five levels of representation. The first level is 'the other' as decorative and welcoming. Here images of indigenous peoples have no context and are simply seen as attractive individuals. The second level is where local peoples are purely the 'canvas' on which the tourism marketers paint a more detailed picture. Here indigenous peoples appear merely to provide a backdrop to set the scene - in an 'exotic' marketplace or as tea-pickers in the distance. Level three in the scale presents people as a tourist attraction in themselves, maybe as an elephant herder or performing a dance. Arguably, in these three levels other peoples are seen as part of the destination itself. In the last two levels this changes. In level four local people remain part of the product but in ways which directly serve the tourist, appearing as employees or in some serving capacity. This category is dominated by waiters and waitresses, kitchen staff and chefs. The final category is where the locals are seen as the equals of the tourists, maybe in conversation or having a drink or meal with them. The following exploratory case study analysed a total of 752 images of host populations in four long haul UK tourism brochures (the same sample of short haul brochures portrayed virtually no local people, an interesting comment on how tourism marketers 'use' indigenous peoples - in more 'exotic' locales).

Tourism marketing representations of 'others': a case study

The dominant adult male representations show hosts as the 'backdrop' to the scene (half of all adult male images); 'attractions' (a quarter) and employees (just under a quarter). It is interesting that 75 per cent of all the employees we see are male, and just under a fifth of all images show local people in some serving capacity. Perhaps the most interesting statistic is that in only one per cent of images are they other depicted as the equal of the tourist and these images come from a handful of photographs where the local inhabitants appeared as wedding guests. The nature of the representations would seem to confirm that hosts and tourists occupy largely oppositional roles and the host overwhelmingly appears as a backdrop to the tourist's experiences.

Table 1   Representations of adult hosts in long haul brochures

Level	description	female %	male %	total %
I	decorative	4	0	2
II	'backdrop'	56	51	53
III	attractions	26	25	26
IV	servants	12	23	19
V	equals	1	1	1
weighted totals		100	100	100
Base figures		225	382	607

Source: Thomas Cook Holidays, Worldwide Faraway Collection, Kuoni Worldwide Holidays; BA Holidays Worldwide brochures.

Whilst just under a fifth of all images are of children, child-like images predominate in the category of decorative/welcoming imagery, since 88 per cent of these images are of children. Moreover, of the decorative images two-thirds are female (both women and girls) and it is particularly interesting that there are no adult male welcoming images. The most dominant images for children, however, are decorative (exactly a half) and 'background' (almost a half of all children).

Table 2   Representations of child hosts in long haul brochures

Level	description	female %	male %	total %
I	decorative	61	38	50
II	'backdrop'	31	62	49
III	attractions	8	0	1
IV	servants	0	0	0
V	equals	0	0	0
weighted totals		100	100	100
Base figures		64	81	145

Source: Thomas Cook Holidays, Worldwide Faraway Collection, Kuoni Worldwide Holidays; BA Holidays Worldwide brochures.

Whilst the levels at which local peoples are presented is remarkably similar across the 'exotic destinations' featured in the four brochures, the numbers in which people occur are strikingly different. The Orient and Latin America are seen as highly populated regions, where the exoticism and the traditions of the local peoples are integral to the tourism experience. In the brochure pages promoting these destinations, photographs of local people appear, on average, every one and a half pages. In stark contrast, in black destinations the local people rarely figure and, if they do, it is largely in a service capacity (level IV) or as an attraction (level III). Africa provides a wild, empty and untamed landscape, seemingly devoid of human inhabitants, populated instead by wild animals. In contrast, the Caribbean appears as an almost exclusive white, heterosexual playground similarly devoid of local inhabitants. Indeed, images of local people appear in these countries, on average, only once every seven pages. The huge discrepancies in the host-guest images revealed by the scale analysis demands more detailed examination and is thus contextualised below by a discursive reading of brochure texts focusing on the Caribbean, Africa and the Far East.

Ways of seeing the Caribbean

The key marketing theme which characterises the Caribbean is that of a 'playground', but one from which local people are virtually absent. Jamaica is marketed as a 'Playground of the Rich and Famous' which tourists are invited to join:

> *With so many of the rich and famous choosing to work and play in Jamaica's technicolor splendor, how can you not have a wonderful and memorable vacation on this picture-perfect island?* (Jamaica Hotel and Tourist Association 1996: 27)

The island is one giant playground - '...the Magic Kingdom of the Caribbean' where tourists are invited to 'Hop on a magic carpet and take a look at this king-size amusement park' (Jamaica Hotel and Tourist Association 1996: 29-30).' This paradise of celebrities and royalty, is, however, one where exclusivity is based not just on affluence but on race and tourists enjoy a playground populated by a clientele consisting almost entirely of white, young, beautiful couples. Jamaica is not unique in this, as Dann and Potter (1994: 22) comment of an advertisement for Barbados, 'The young couple might as well have stayed at home in an all Caucasian setting bereft of Bajans.' Indigenous African-Caribbeans hardly feature at all in this white Garden of Eden of beaches, swimming pools and luxury hotels and, when they do appear, they are only there to service the white holidaymakers, whether as waiters, masseurs, beauty therapists or bar staff.

Analysis of representations of the Caribbean not only highlight the theme of play and the absence of local people, but also the reconstruction of Caribbean identity as: 'Caribbean locales [are] fabricated into a pastiche of Polynesian architecture, exotic voodoo and Creole cuisine, which becomes more real than reality' (Dann and Potter 1994: 20). Caribbean destinations therefore appear to be 'identically unique', grounded in some sort of universal, marketed and reconstructed Polynesian mythic image - perhaps because Polynesia poses a less problematic identity for marketers than that of the Caribbean which was built on slavery and black African Caribbean identities. The few representations of Caribbean peoples which appear in the tourism literature severely limit local identities and acceptable spheres of action. They also combine to rewrite the Caribbean's history of plantations, slavery and brutality to sanitise Western consumption of the Caribbean. In this scenario, local peoples become a 'spectacle' which tourists consume nightly:

> *Dancers wearing spectacular costumes twirl across the stage to the rhythm of Caribbean sounds. Talented singers entertain.... Limbo dancers challenge the flames as they slide across the floor. Fire dancers jump to the front, lighting up the night* (Jamaica Hotel and Tourist Association 1996: 29-30).

As spectacles, representations of people echo representations of nature, reflecting Hall's racialised grammar of representation. The rhythms of the Caribbean seem like the rhythms of the night, frenzied dances and fire rituals take the local people much closer to nature, in contrast to their technological, rational Western audience. Constructed images thus distort the reality of people's lives, heritage and culture and in so doing transform and reconstruct historical relationships. As Dann and Potter (1994: 23) write: 'The plantation, once the scene of iniquitous black slavery, has now been transformed into a carnival of entertainment.' Plantation life has been rehabilitated, denying the existence of the oppressed majority. *Destination Jamaica* (1996: 25) proclaims that 'The English turned the island into one vast sugar plantation. Sugar became "king". Everyone prospered'. In this sense, tourists consume and gaze upon a Jamaican history bearing more resemblance to a fairy-tale or a swashbuckling Hollywood movie script - Disneyfication seems almost complete:

> *From pirates to sugar barons, the island's history is a tapestry of colorful characters and events. Jamaica's history is a turbulent story of sugar and slaves, Spaniards against Englishmen, fragrant tropical evenings, howling hurricanes, crushing earthquakes, pirate and naval heroes* (Jamaica Hotel and Tourist Association 1996: 24).

Just as Caribbean history has been recreated and remade to entertain the Western tourist, so to have power relationships been reproduced. Arguably, slavery has to all intents and purposes been replaced by or exchanged for another form of exploitation which recreates identity and history. Reality is eschewed in favour of a represented myth which ignores issues of poverty, low wages and illiteracy and Caucasian power is once again reaffirmed, only this time instead of by slave chains, disenfranchisement is characterised by sequinned costumes. Westerners have exchanged their 'mission to educate' with one to be entertained and the tourist is confirmed in his or her economic, cultural and historical superiority. As MacCannell (1984: 389) points out:

> *tourism has helped in getting beyond the phase of ethnic relations where minorities are kept in place with light salaries, heavy prison terms and redneck cruelty. But one may have come full circle ... one is only doing with admiration what he earlier did with dogs and guns.*

Ways of seeing Africa

In the marketing construction of Africa colonialism frames the gaze. The *South African Airways Holidays* brochure (1996/97: 20) offers, as one of its special interest tours, 'Young Winston', a tour which mediates the African experience whilst reaffirming former colonial links. Here, working with Churchill's granddaughter, South African Airways Holidays 'has created a unique tour celebrating the exploits of young Winston's life as a war correspondent during the Boer War in 1899.' In Africa, as elsewhere, the old world links are strongly evident in the text and imagery of tourism: 'In 1855 explorer David Livingstone stumbled upon the magnificent Victoria Falls which he was to name after the Queen...' (The Cape to Victoria Falls, Journeys through southern Africa, Airwaves, 1997).

Perhaps the most significant feature of the representations of African, however, is that in the tour operator marketing and in travel writing, Africa is a destination populated almost exclusively by wild animals. Not only are there very few tourists but there are virtually no inhabitants - a significant silence in the text. Tourists are sold images of the continent as a wild, untamed and unexplored land and the few black faces which are seen in brochures promoting sub-Saharan Africa are usually presented as local 'spectacle' wearing tribal dress or in occupations servicing white tourists. The *South African Airways Holidays 1996/97* brochure is typical of those marketing the continent: 35 per cent of its imagery is devoted to empty landscapes; 30 per cent to both wild animals and tourist facilities (e.g. hotels), and only five per cent to images of the indigenous black population (Morgan and Pritchard 1998: 224).

Ways of seeing the Orient

Representations of the Far East (or what Said terms the Orient) have long been defined as oppositional to the West. The latter has been instrumental in developing a discourse in which the Oriental is portrayed as 'irrational, depraved, childlike and different', whilst the Occidental is seen as 'rational, virtuous, mature and normal.' (Said 1978: 40) In popular culture images of this Oriental discourse revolve around daydreams of 'harems, princesses, princes, slaves, veils, dancing girls and boys...' (Said 1978: 109) These fantasies continue to shape contemporary tourism marketing and represent a constructed reality in which tourists can escape from Western morality and such daydreams are not merely the preserve of the individual but are 'socially organised .... through television, advertising, literature, cinema, photography and so on' (Urry 1990: 83). Pritchard and Morgan (2000b) have discussed how this discourse is reflected in contemporary constructions of Eastern landscapes which are construed as feminine and sexual, inviting exploration by white, western, male tourists. In this sense, Said's Orient of harems, sultans and legends, can still be visited today - for instance in Marrakech, where 'Few visitors will resist the appeal of ... its singers, sorcerers, herbalists, acrobats, preachers and snake-charmers' (British Airways Holidays brochure: 48). It can also be found:

> *On the eastern part of the Arabian peninsula, [where] the Sultanate of Oman is the legendary home of the Queen of Sheba and said to be the inspiration of such explorers as Marco Polo and Sinbad the Sailor* (British Airways Holidays brochure: 117).

Such images and daydreams of the East are more about Western fantasies than Eastern realities and even where the modern Orient cannot be repressed, it is tempered by an Occidental view of the East. Thus, it is acknowledged that Singapore 'is now a thriving modern community with a dynamic cosmopolitan life.' Yet, we are told, it was 'Once the haunt of tigers, crocodiles and pirates,' and even now 'the mysterious East is ever-present, whether in the lush vegetation sweeping down to the harbour or in the thronged bazaars of Chinatown' (Airwaves Worldwide Holidays 1997: 52).

Interestingly, in the context of the above discussions of the Caribbean and Africa, there are substantially more photographs of indigenous people featured in the pages of the tour operators' brochures devoted to India, the Far and the Middle East. Not only do the local people form a major part of the tourism 'product', but they also feature in particular ways. The scenes portray 'traditional' as opposed to technological ways of life - markets, rural landscapes, agricultural life and religious worship are common themes and male Buddhist monks and female Balinese dancers (often young) are the key icons of Eastern destinations. Whilst there emerges a common way of seeing the Orient, there are clear differences between specific regions. The Middle East is largely populated by men, usually as employees in tourism or as 'local colour', often astride camels or trading in souks. Images of Indians and Sri Lankans are also dominated by tradition - traditional dress and activities abound - we see snake charmers, tea pickers, fishermen and elephant handlers, usually in rural landscapes. There are no references to the modern, economic powerhouses which constitute today's Asia and as the tourist gaze moves further east, into Hong Kong, Vietnam, Thailand and Indonesia, markets and agricultural scenes continue to predominate but images of the local population become more clearly *the focus* of the gaze. Particularly dominant are images of the Thai hill tribes, Buddhist monks, and Balinese dancers. Thus when people are seen in brochure images of Hong Kong, aside from one or two city scenes, they are depicted in very traditional pursuits: taking part in dragon boat races, worshipping in temples, and shopping in floating markets; the urban inhabitants of modern Hong Kong - one of the world's most important financial centres - are totally absent.

Perhaps the most significant feature of the touristic construction of the Orient is its child-like portrayal. More than in any other continent (where children very rarely feature), there are many images of smiling young children in tourism promotional literature and in travel articles devoted to the East. They are often seen in traditional dress, and particularly in the case of young boys, as Buddhist monks. Adult and child images in the Orient are interchangeable - even the adults have a childlike quality, a feature previously highlighted by Selwyn (1992). Such representations are by no means innocent of meaning or value, and as Mellinger (1994) has discussed, in historical representations black children had a rascally and mischievous quality which signified an underlying belief in American society that blacks themselves were merely grown up children who should be treated as such.

Conclusion

The representations which appear in the tourism media are by no means neutral or mere reflections of reality - they are drawn from a stock of cultural knowledge which is highly ideological and selective. As O'Barr (1994: 157) comments: 'Contemporary advertising does not constitute a single global discourse but rather a set of discourses that operates within the boundaries of nations and languages.' Tourism advertising (as all other) is instrumental in constructing systems of meaning and assists in defining and describing and even limiting its audience. In tourism's case it presents and represents others for a particular audience's consumption:

> ...*peoples... [and] cultures have been freely appropriated by twentieth-century ...* *advertising in its promotion of goods and services in the marketplace - a* *marketplace that also includes ideologies in its offerings* (O'Barr 1994: 158).

This paper has argued that for too long tourism imagery has remained divorced from discussions of power which have been articulated elsewhere. The cultural power of tourism and the discourse of tourism imagery, as evidenced by the oppositional nature of representations, their mythical qualities and timelessness, demand more attention. Similarly, just as these cultural issues deserve examination, so too do historical perspectives, as these have shaped contemporary realities but rarely figure in analyses of tourism processes. Tourism representations, in fact, are more concerned to distort historical, social and economic relations in marketing destinations and contemporary tourism images are actively re-shaping how we see the past as well as the present. Indeed, it could be argued that many marketers are engaged in presenting us with a touristic vision of the future based on a careful and selective orchestration of the past. The distortion is particularly acute in former settler countries since colonialism continues to exert cultural power in terms of how marketers construct peoples and places in an ethnocentric and androcentric pastiche of history, events and identities.

This misrepresentation of historical relationships is just one facet of a much more complex, multi-dimensional power reality in which powerful white worlds dominate and define black worlds; in which male dominates female; and a dynamic first world contrasts itself with a static, timeless and unchanging third world. This is not power confined to international politics and global players - this is the power and politics of everyday life. The same discourses - the powerful, male, white, heterosexual axis - construct history, heritage and tourism through the representation of others - 'a particular cultural politics of discursive production' in which one set of truths 'acquire the status of truth and normalcy' (Anderson 196: 200). We are witnessing what Urry (1990: 143) identified as the selective touristification of 'certain ethnic groups [which] have come to be constructed as part of the "attraction"' of some places - a process which this paper suggests is most common in the Far East where the Other is feminised and made child-like.

The view of tourism destinations as timeless and immutable to the forces of change could also be said to be related to the so-called search for authenticity and the sacred. In our industrialised, urbanised, fragmented world some of us search for the sacred to compensate for our own alienated existence. This search for the sacred is itself an outcome of nineteenth-century (white, male, heterosexual) anthropology - a social science constructed around binary concepts: savage and civilised; primitive and developed; them and us. In tourism we can see the same opposition between the 'noble savage', the 'happy peasant', the tribal dancer and the technologically sophisticated, camera-totting, 'civilised' tourist. What the West once documented with pseudo-science, now it documents with 'a Kodak moment'. Unfortunately, in their search for 'authentic' cultures, anthropology and tourism often both deny the reality of external and indigenous change. This is not to deny the abilities of local people to negotiate, resist or even locally exploit the terms of the tourism exchange. Nor does this analysis deny that Caucasian power is to some extent mediated through indigenous elites who are themselves exploiters participating in the re-creation of identity and reality. Points of resistance develop, and power relationships may shift or destabilise, thereby fracturing specific dominant discourses. Power is by no means monolithic and it is not merely exercised from above, but within societies. When examining the wider power structures which inform and underpin tourism marketing, it would be a mistake to see those structures and relationships as static or immutable.

It would also be a mistake to see the formation of representations as linear or one-way - in the 'circuit of representation' tourists are not passive recipients of marketed images but are themselves products of particular socio-economic and cultural systems and share common ontologies with the tourism marketers. It is also simplistic (not to say patronising) to portray ethnic minorities and indigenous peoples, as helpless in the face of the power of the representers. They may well attempt to subvert and resist marketed images, however, their ability to do so is often severely constrained because the powerful tourist organisations often control the terms and the boundaries of the encounter. What is produced, therefore, is a consensual framework for seeing, albeit one grounded in an unequal, multi-dimensional relationship of domination and subordination. As Clegg (1989: 151-2) has argued, whilst 'there is no reason to expect that representations will remain contextually and historically stable', it is equally apparent that power will be exercised to attempt to maintain the representations or to manage the change. In such ways '...knowledge that is used to structure and fix representations in historical forms is the accomplishment of power.'

References

advertisement placed in the *Conde Nast Traveler,* July 1997: 52.

Anderson, K. (1996), *'Engendering Race Research: Unsettling the self-Other dichotomy'* 197-211 in Duncan, N. (ed.), *Bodyspace: destabilising geographies of gender and sexuality,* Routledge, London.

Ball, M. and Smith, G. W. H. (1992), *Analysing Visual Data*, Sage: London.

Berger, J. (1983), *Ways of Seeing*, BBC and Penguin, London and Harmondsworth.

British Airways Holidays Worldwide 1995.

Britton, R. (1979), 'The Image of Third World Tourism in Marketing', *Annals of Tourism Research* 6 318-329.

Butler-Paisley, M., and Paisley-Butler W. J. (1974*), 'Sexism in the Media: Frameworks for Research'*, a paper presented to the annual meeting of the Association for Education and Journalism, San Diego, August.

Cohen, C. (1995), 'Marketing Paradise, Making Nation, *Annals of Tourism Research* 22 404-21.

Clegg, S. R. (1989), *Frameworks of Power*, Sage, London.

Dann, G. (1996), *The People of Tourist Brochures*, 61-82 in The Tourist Image: Myths and Myth Making in Tourism, T. Selwyn, (ed.) Chichester: John Wiley and Sons.

Dann, G. and Potter, R., (1994), Tourism and postmodernity in a Caribbean setting', *Cahiers du Tourisme*, Serie C no. 185.

Denzin, N. K., (1995), The Cinematic Society. The Voyeur's Gaze, Sage, London.

Dilley R. S. (1986), 'Tourist Brochures and Tourist Images', *The Canadian Geographer* 30 (1) 59-65.

Dyer, R. (1977), Gays and Film. British Film Institute, London, quoted in Hall S., (1997) *'The Spectacle of the "Other"* 223-90 in Hall, S. (ed.) Representation. Cultural Representation and Signifying Practice, Sage and the Open University, London.

Enloe, C. (1989), *Bananas, Beaches and Bases. Making Feminist Sense of International Politics*, Pandora, London.

Evans-Pritchard, D. (1989), "How "They" See "Us"", *Annals of Tourism Research* (16) 89-105.

Fiske, J. (1989), *Understanding Popular Culture*, Routledge, London.

Foucault, M. (1980), *Power/*Knowledge, Harvester, Brighton.

Fredrikson, G. (1987), *The Black Image in the White Mind*, Wesleyan University Press, Hanover, NJ.

Hall, C. M. (1994), *Tourism and Politics: Policy, Power and Place,* John Wiley, Chichester.

Hall, S. (1997), *The Spectacle of the "Other"* 223-90 in Hall, S. (ed.) Representation. Cultural Representation and Signifying Practice, Sage and the Open University, London.

Hornig Priest, S. (1996), *Doing Media Research. An Introduction. Sage*: Thousand Oaks.

Jablow, A., and Hammond, D., (1970), *The Africa That Never Was: Four Centuries of British Writing About Africa*, Twayne Press, New York.

Jenks, C. (1995), (ed.) *Visual Culture*. Routledge: London.

Kuoni Worldwide Holidays (1995).

Kress, G. and Van Leeuwen, T. (1996) Reading Images: The Grammar of Visual Design. Routledge: London.

Kress, G. and Van Leeuwen, T. (1990), *Reading Images* Geelang, Australia, Deakin University Press.

Laxson, (1991), Tourism and Native Americans, *Annals of Tourism Research* (18) 365-391.

Marchetti, G. (1991), *'Ethnicity, the Cinema, and Cultural Studies,'* 277-309 in Friedman, L. D., (ed.) Unspeakable Images: Ethnicity and the American Cinema, Urbana: University of Illinois Press.

Mellinger, W. M. (1994), 'Towards A Critical Analysis of Tourism Representations', *Annals of Tourism Research* 21 (4) 756-775.

MacCannell, D. (1984), 'Reconstructing Ethnicity, Tourism and Cultural Identity in Third World Communities', *Annals of Tourism Research* 11 375-391.

McClintock, A. (1995), Imperial Leather, Routledge, London.

Morgan, N. J. and Pritchard, A. (1999), *Power and Politics at the Seaside. The development of Devon's resorts in the twentieth century*, Exeter University Press, Exeter.

Morgan, N. J. and Pritchard, A. (1998), *Tourism Promotion and Power. Creating Images, Creating identities*, John Wiley & Sons, Chichester.

Nixon, S. (1997), *'Circulating Culture'* 179-234 in Du Gay P. (ed.) The Production of Culture/Culture of Production, Sage, London.

O'Barr, W. (1994), *Culture and the Ad. Exploring Otherness in Advertising*, Westview Press, Boulder, Colorado.

Pingree, S. *et al*. (1976), 'A Scale for Sexism'. *Journal of Communication*. Autumn 193-200.

Pritchard, A. and Morgan, N. J. (2000a), 'Constructing Tourism Landscapes. Gender, Sexuality and Space.' *Tourism Geographies*, 2 (1) forthcoming.

Pritchard, A. and Morgan, N. J. (2000b), 'Privileging the Male Gaze. Gendered Tourism Landscapes.' *Annals of Tourism Research* 27 (3), forthcoming.

Real, T. (1996), *'Looking Good. How Cultural Tourism Has Changed the Face of North American Travel Destinations,* 171-184 in Robinson M. *et al.* (eds.) Tourism and Culture, Image, Identity and Marketing. The Centre for Travel and Tourism, Sunderland.

Richter, L. K. (1995), *'Gender and Race. Neglected Variables in Tourism Research'* 71-91 in Butler R. and Pearce D. (eds.) Change in Tourism. People, Places, Processes, Routledge, London.

Rose, G. (1993), *Feminism and Geography. The Limits of Geographical Knowledge*, Polity Press, Cambridge.

Said, E. (1978, 1991), *Orientalism. Western Conceptions of the Orient*, Penguin, Harmondsworth.

Segal, L. (1990), *Slow Motion. Changing Masculinities, Changing Men*, Virago, London.

Selwyn, T. (1992), *'Peter Pan in South East Asia. Views from the brochures'*, 117-37 in Hitchcock, M., et al. (eds.), *Tourism in South East Asia*, Routledge, London.

Silver, I. (1993), 'Marketing Authenticity in Third World Countries', *Annals of Tourism Research* 20 302-318.

Skelly, G. V. and Lundstrom, W. J. (1981), 'Male Sex Roles in Magazine Advertising, 1959-79' in *Journal of Communication* Autumn 52-6.

Slater, D. (1998), *'Analysing cultural objects: content analysis and semiotics'*, 233-244 in Seale, C. (ed.), *Researching Society and Culture*, Sage, London.

Spivak, G. C. (1988), *'Can subaltern speak?'* in Nelson, C. and Grossberg, L. (eds.), *Marxism and the Interpretation of Culture*, University of Illinois Press, Chicago.

South African Airways Holidays, (1996/97: 20).

The Jamaica Hotel and Tourist Association Official Guide, Destination Jamaica, (1996).

The Cape to Victoria Falls, Journeys Through Southern Africa, Airwaves, (1997), Thomas Cook Holidays brochure.

Tonkiss, F. (1998), *'Analysing discourse'* 245-260 in Seale, C. (ed.), *Researching Society and Culture*, Sage, London.

Urry, J. (1990), *The Tourist Gaze. Leisure and Travel in Contemporary Societies*, Sage, London.

Uzzell, D. (1984), 'An Alternative Structuralist Approach to the Psychology of Tourism Marketing', *Annals of Tourism Research* 11 (1): 79-100.

Williamson, J. (1978), *Decoding Advertisements. Ideology and Meaning in Advertising.* Marion Boyars, London.

Wood, R. E. (1984), 'Ethnic Tourism. The State and Cultural Change in South-East Asia', *Annals of Tourism Research*, 11 353-374.

WorldWide Faraway Collection brochure, (1995).

Whose festival? whose place? An insight into the production of cultural meanings in arts festivals turned visitor attractions

Bernadette Quinn

Dublin Institute of Technology, Ireland

Festivals as settings of 'cultural drama'

Festivals are known to exist in virtually all human cultures (Falassi 1987) and to have a history that spans many centuries. In medieval times they represented a 'fundamental ritual order of Western culture', involving most sectors of society (Stallybrass and White 1986). Their immense cultural and social significance has attracted the interest of numerous scholars from the social sciences and humanities. Geographers, for instance, have construed festivals as one of the many practices that humans evolve in the process of connecting with their places, making homes for themselves and carving out landscapes in their own likeness. Anthropologists, sociologists and folklorists, among others, have explored the drama enacted in festival sites to gain insights into how groups of people view their place in society and interact together to variously contest and reproduce the social structures and value systems that bind them together.

Festivals represent a means of forging communal identity and of perpetuating a sense of commitment to a community and to its officially held values. They represent arenas where local knowledge is reproduced, where the history, cultural inheritance and social structures that distinguish one place from another are revised, rejected or reproduced. There is, however, little that is natural or spontaneous about this process. A significant amount of literature makes the case that the production of cultural meanings in the festival site is closely bound up with issues of power and control. Farber (1983: 40) has interpreted the festival as 'a symbolic representation of the asserted, believed and controlled community identity'. Elsewhere, individuals and groups have been shown to use the festival as a forum to promote particular sets of values, seek to extend control over a set of real or imaginary spaces and variously attempt to contest and reproduce hegemonic meanings (Cohen 1982; Jackson 1988; Marston 1989; Stokes 1994). Festivals are thus one example of a setting within which people struggle to assert their ownership to a place, and to claim their right to produce particular sets of cultural values and practices.

When the festivals at issue are arts festivals, as in the current paper, an additional focus of interest lies in understanding how the arts, in the festival setting, acquire meaning in people's lives. Recent geographic literature on the arts, for example, has explored a diverse range of themes associated with how people connect with their place and with other people through their arts practices. It has further begun to address the ability of festivals to transform ordinary landscapes into spaces of cultural discourse, altering and challenging the meanings that a place usually holds for its population.

The significance of the festival as a cultural phenomenon is enhanced by the role that it plays in displaying a constructed mythology to the outside world. If at the heart of every festival are a place and a place-based community actively reproducing its shared values and belief systems, there is an important sense in which these cultural meanings are intentionally produced to be read by the outside world. Festivals are forum where people can make statements about who they are and about how and where they live. They are thus characterised by a pronounced outward orientation. The open nature of the festival setting is exaggerated by the fact that its very existence is premised on movement, interaction and exchange, with flows of people, ideas, money, skills, etc., continuously circulating between the festival site and elsewhere. Festivals can thus be said to be characterised more by interrelations than by autonomy of place.

Globalising cultural meanings - festivals and tourism

Such a characterisation is not unique to festivals. In a much broader context Clifford (1988) has contended that the extensive movement and contact which characterise contemporary society have created a situation where the differences between the experiences of dwelling and of travelling are becoming less distinct. Sack (1997) similarly argues that that the effect of cultural interaction and exchange is to create sameness, a familiarity about places such that people feel increasingly at home when away from the place in which they dwell. These contentions raise a whole series of interesting and complex questions about how place, the people who live in a place and the cultural processes in which they engage, are affected as local – extra-local interrelations develop. Festival settings constitute one case in which to examine these changing meanings. How, for instance, in the context of globalisation, can a festival continue to fulfil its role as a forum for local people to interpret and reproduce cultural meanings based on their sense of place, or on their sense of community. Can place retain its position at the heart of the festival while a particular constellation of internal/external linkages are being forged over time? Or is it perhaps that a festival's claim to distinctiveness may come to rest on a constellation of inter-relationships, rather than on any set of 'indigenous characteristics'?

The linkages and interactions which globalise cultural processes in the festival site are multiple and varied. One significant and inevitable globalising variable is the flow of visitors passing through the festival landscape. In recent times this has become increasingly important, promoted by the contemporary widespread and pronounced tendency to commodify cultural forms in the interests of economics. As part of this process, festivals everywhere have become key elements in the place-selling strategies adopted by places, large and small. Undoubtedly, the globalising force of tourism complicates the 'cultural drama' enacted in festival sites.

To date, the effect which tourism has on the production of cultural meanings in the festival setting has not concerned the growing literature on tourism and festivals. The bulk of this work has conceptualised festivals in the context of event tourism. It has focused on festivals not because they are interesting as cultural phenomena in and of themselves, but largely because they generate impacts of varying kinds. In general, tourism researchers have appeared disinterested in the cultural significance of festivals and have avoided seeking to unravel the complex issues surrounding the contested nature of cultural meanings, the production of local knowledge, and the negotiation of communal identity that lie at the heart of festival activity.

Attempts to unravel these issues can begin by revisiting the basic conceptualisation of festivals as contested spaces. Several studies interpret the festival as a forum through which individuals and/or groups seek to assert control and the right to claim ownership over space, beliefs and practices. Implicit in this work is the recognition that populations are not homogeneous groups but are socially structured in such a way that access to power is a constant source of struggle. In a tourism context, the question that emerges is: how does the arrival of tourists complicate the power dynamics and the heterogeneity of the place-based population? Can the emergence of tourist audiences alter the balance of power in a way that serves to variously marginalise or strengthen certain groups? Sack (1997:13) has written about home as 'a locus of control'. He suggests that one feels at home when one is in a position to control, within reason, what goes on there. Might the arrival of tourists cause local people to sense a loss of control and to feel excluded from the production of cultural meanings in the festival site? Does the answer to this question depend on the extent to which the generation of tourist flows compliments prevailing hegemonic meanings?

The debate about whether globalisation promotes cultural homogenisation or creates new, reconstituted differences, is another important avenue of enquiry. Rather than promoting sameness between places, tourism as a globalising variable may be more responsible for inverting difference, by introducing the exotic into the local and confusing an understanding of what constitutes a 'dwelling place' and a 'visited place'. Sampath (1998), for example, in an analysis of carnival in Trinidad has discussed how the arrival of tourists can change the meanings which carnival holds for local people. The outcome here would be one example of what several researchers (Massey 1991, Smith 1994, Thrift 1997) consider a general consequence of globalisation, i.e. the continuous emergence of new, recreated and hybrid forms of difference. However, many important questions remain unanswered. In the festival as visitor attraction context, for example, one has to ask: who is now producing the dominant meanings? How are these being received and by whom? Can we accurately define a group to be labelled 'tourists' and another to be labelled 'local residents'? Or is this terminology now too simplistic?

This paper seeks answers to some of these questions within an arts festival setting. Its arguments draw upon the findings of case study research conducted during the years 1996-1997 in Wexford in the Republic of Ireland.

The case of Wexford

Wexford (current population 15,000) is a medium-sized county town located some 100 miles south of Dublin on the south-east coast. In 1951, when the newly independent Irish state was engrossed in the weighty task of modernising itself, the town ambitiously launched an opera festival dedicated to a repertoire of 'rare and unjustly neglected opera'. The individuals behind the venture came from among the town's middle classes and specifically comprised a group of local opera devotees accustomed to gathering in each others' drawing rooms to enjoy opera, and to travelling to the UK and further afield for the opera seasons.

The successful establishment and subsequent development of the festival over the ensuing decades represents a classic example of the well-known tendency for local elites to appropriate the organs of community participation for their own benefit (Brohman 1996). Initially, the process necessitated persuading a broad section of the local population that this was a venture that the townspeople as a community should pursue. The early decades of the festival attest to the accomplishment of this challenge as local people eagerly supported the founders' very ambitious plans to make Wexford 'the outstanding centre in Ireland for music and the arts' (Wexford Festival Opera, 1952). Their willing support manifests itself in the form of avid attendance, generous funding, and a broad spectrum of vital in-kind involvement spanning performance, production and administration. Wexford in the 1950s was a town steeped in musical and cultural tradition. The tremendous excitement generated by the emergence of the opera festival must be viewed in this context, as must the extensive interest expressed by local people in becoming actively involved in the festival in the guise of choristers and more widely as audience members. By 1953, the active engagement of townspeople in the festival was very extensive, if perhaps not quite as complete as some of the national newspaper commentary suggested at the time:

'The 1953 festival is above all, a product of voluntary effort on the part of the Wexford man on the street, his wife and family, and his fellow workers and friends. Shop-keepers large and small, and the householders in the fashionable and humbler quarters alike....have come out in a spontaneous drive to give these narrow streets a look of gaiety and colour they never had before' (*Irish Press*, 26/10/1953).

Constructing the myth of the 'Wexford people's festival'

However, as the 1950s wore on, the tensions inherent in balancing a festival simultaneously intended to function as the 'Wexford people's festival', 'the great social event of these islands' and a leading European elite arts festival were coming ever closer to the surface. Local newspapers began reporting that 'such was the demand for seats that hundreds (of local people) were unable to gain admission' (*The Wexford People* 8/11/52). The following year, the same newspaper wrote of the need to extend the season 'so that local people can still share in a thing that many travel to see from foreign parts' (*The Wexford People* 17/10/53). Very quickly, it became apparent that the festival could not accommodate local demand for opera seats.

The early failure to accommodate local demand for opera tickets should not be read solely as an indicator of demand exceeding supply. Satisfying local demand for tickets was not a priority. It was demand from outside of Wexford that the festival organisation preferred to stimulate. The Festival Council's ambitions to create an international reputation for their festival meant engaging international artists and this in turn required high ticket prices. Prioritising a local audience would have exerted a downward pressure on ticket prices and would have impeded the organisation in its pursuit of ambitious artistic objectives. More generally, the policy of privileging 'outsiders' in preference to locals was attractive from several perspectives. At the local level, it served a broad range of interest groups including the business community, politicians, and opera devotees themselves. Crucially, it also furthered national interests. Bord Fáilte (the state Tourism Agency), for example, was very keen to see overseas tourism promoted. The Arts Council of Ireland was equally favourably disposed towards the festival because it represented an arts initiative devoted to the pursuit of excellence in the 'high' arts. Furthermore, the idea that an Irish initiative should be aspiring to produce to an international standard, one of the most intellectually demanding of all high art forms, was immediately attractive in a country which was at the time struggling to define its own cultural identity. Thus, while at no point did the festival organisation espouse tourism objectives, visitors have always been privileged in the dominant vision shaping the Wexford Festival.

There was, of course, a significant place for the local population in this vision. There had to be. The realisation that local people were not being encouraged to fill the seats of the Theatre Royal had led to a decline in local interest, and between 1958 and 1964 the number of festival subscribers fell dramatically from 800 to 250. This had serious financial implications for the venture's sustainability. Furthermore, local people's in-kind support represented an immense subvention without which the festival might not have survived. The roles created for local participation revolved largely around producing the festival that was to be subsequently enjoyed by 'others'. Somewhat ironically, communicating this vision and constructing the process began by inculcating a sense of local ownership of the festival. From its earliest days, the Wexford Festival was publicly constructed as a festival which was 'owned' by the local people. In 1952, for instance, Festival Council members espoused aspirations such as that which follows: 'everybody connected with the organisation of the festival would feel very badly if the Wexford people did not look upon it as their festival (*The Wexford People*, 25/10/52). Without any hint of the complications involved, the Council member went on to speak about how visitors to the festival must be 'looked upon as friends' and that a 'spirit of friendliness and homeliness is expected of the Wexford people'. Sustaining a widespread sense of both goodwill and local ownership while simultaneously limiting access to audience engagement with the festival was a task that required considerable skill. It was largely achieved by creating a number of roles in which locals could stake a claim to the festival.

From the outset, the Festival Council sought and found financial support in the local community. The economic possibilities of the festival were emphasised and it was presented as a venture which 'was going to put Wexford on the map not alone from the point of view of art and music, but also from the trade it would bring to the town' (*The Wexford People*, 3/1/51). Also from the outset, the Festival Council successfully sought to engage a broad spectrum of in-kind support from a cross section of the local community. In addition to choral singing, local energies were avidly channelled into administration roles and into multiple production roles that included wardrobe, make-up, lighting, set construction, stage management and interior decoration. It was in this behind-the-scenes capacity that local

Wexford people's creative energies were given the most freedom to flourish in uncontested fashion. Here, they invested something of themselves in making the festival happen and developed a deep sense of their stakeholder status. In return, they earned the right to purchase tickets for dress rehearsal performances but more importantly they could bask in the glory of seeing 'their' festival put Wexford on the map, draw thousands of national and international visitors and achieve both national and international critical acclaim.

Local people could also sense involvement in the guise of spectator. Spectators are a vital element in any spectacle and local people happily fulfilled this role, emerging to indulge in the glamorous and exotic atmosphere created by the foreign singers, producers, directors, and visiting dignitaries attending the festival. As the decades wore on, diminishing local access to opera performances was partially compensated by unproblematic access to an additional programme of fringe arts events that initially could justifiably claim to be creative and innovative. In the late 1990s, the contemporary festival officially comprises the main opera programme. However, an unofficial fringe programme[1], loosely administered by the town's Chamber of Commerce runs concurrently.

Sustaining the roles – the locals behind-the-scenes, the visitors front-of – house

A historical analysis of the landscape reveals a complex series of structures and actions which the festival architects devised and produced both to deepen the festival's penetration of the international opera world of gatekeepers, artists and audiences and to simultaneously maintain the critical goodwill and behind-the-scenes support of local people. It shows Wexford to be an undisputedly elitist arts festival. Yet one which actively publicises its voluntary foundations[2] and portrays the 'welcoming and friendly' local people as a key signifier of what Wexford, in its invented state as a festival town, represents. It is not alone in presenting itself as an elitist venture. Waterman (1998:66) asserts that there is little doubt that highbrow arts festivals still explicitly prefer to present themselves as elitist. He cites the case of the Israel Festival as one which is unashamedly elitist, directing itself at the few who can afford to attend and believing that it should not be denigrated for this.

Its commitment over time to privileging visitors in the festival audience has been both consistent and successful. As early as 1959, 60% of audiences came from outside of Wexford, with some 25% coming from outside of Ireland. By 1989, 85% of audiences came from outside of Wexford, with 30% – 35% coming from abroad (O'Hagan et al. 1989). During festival time, the patterns of engagement exhibited by visitors and locals are sharply divided. Locals participate freely and extensively in both the day-time and night-time fringe programmes, in contrast to their engagement in the main opera programme which is much more partial, especially at night-time. A survey undertaken during the 1996 festival (N=166) found that while almost 60% of local people engaged in fringe activities, just 7% attended an evening opera performance. Equivalent figures emanating from the visitor survey (N=94) undertaken at the same time were 36% and 55%. An in-depth analysis of engagement in the festival found that, in their capacity as festival-goers, the worlds of locals and of visitors were quite distinct. It revealed the festival landscape to be spatially and temporally ordered into distinct, relatively bounded spaces. The main opera programme unfolds within a well-defined set of temporal and spatial boundaries, the fringe programme within a different, equally well defined set. This ordering serves a number of functions: the reproduction of hierarchical understandings of 'high' and 'low' arts, the reproduction of social difference through engagement in the arts; and the perpetuation of the specific local-visitor interaction dynamic that construes the local as the host, producing a festival to be enjoyed by other people.

Over time local people have shown little inclination to challenge the dominant position held by visitors or to resist the cultural meanings being reproduced through the festival process. Survey findings portray a local population that clearly understands that their possibilities for engaging in the festival have been purposefully constrained and that they have been, in effect, marginalised and excluded. Reactions to this status range from stoical acceptance to extreme anger but overall, protest actions have been subdued and have centred on a quiet yielding of space to the visiting audience. Local voluntary involvement in performance and productive capacities have declined over time while local attendance at the main opera festival has declined greatly, relative to audience capacity since the early years of the festival. That there has been little sense of any radical dissension is readily explained by reference to the historically embedded structures shaping people's engagement in the festival. If one fundamental force was to deter local people from entering the front spaces of the main opera landscape, another was to render local compliance, sustain local support and generously compensate them for their consent. The rewards for acquiescing to the hegemony of the festival and for yielding space to visitors are many. In their stakeholder capacity local people derive very significant benefits associated with the deep and widespread sense of pride that they feel in the festival. More quantifiably, in consistently generating sizeable flows[3] of very high yielding tourists in the off-season, the festival brings significant economic benefits to the town. At the same time, the introduction of the fringe festival created welcome opportunities to socialise, while the prevailing view of opera as a 'high' art form that exists only for the enjoyment of a minority excuses the festival organisation from any obligation to broaden its artistic remit.

Enlisting tourism to promote hegemonic meanings

A number of researchers have debated the relative merits of the arts-tourism relationship (e.g. Hughes, 1989). A general comment on the debate is that while it seems to be relatively unproblematic to produce arguments pointing to outcomes that favour tourism interests (Myerscough 1988) it is much more difficult to decisively comment on how outcomes weigh in respect of the arts. The foregoing analysis of the Wexford Festival attests to one instance of how an arts organisation can beneficially employ tourism to pursue artistic aims. At all times, the artistic vision propelling the festival forward has remained dominant and tourism has been employed merely as a means of achieving the over-riding artistic goals. There is no evidence to suggest that the organisation has ever bowed to pressure to popularise the repertoire or to adapt its artistic policy to pander to tourist demands. Rather, the reverse is the case. The organisation's tourism strategy has greatly facilitated its sustained dedication to producing 'rare and unjustly neglected opera'. The Wexford Festival Opera is a highly successful tourist attraction. It is, in fact, a model tourism event because it generates significant flows of high yielding tourists and it does so in the off season. However, it is suggested that replicating this success may not be easy. In Wexford, specific factors were responsible for maintaining the balance of power in favour of the festival organisation and for producing this particular outcome.

The most obvious factor is that tourism served as an effective vehicle for reproducing the cultural meanings promoted by the festival organisation. A second critical factor is that the scale of the tourism activity concerned has been sufficiently small-scale for the festival organisation to be able to maintain strict control over its development through time. It achieves this by controlling the distribution channels through which access to the festival as a tourism product is made available. The tourism activity generated by the festival has also been very specialised in terms of the type of tourists attracted and the timing of their arrival. Thus, the generation of extra-local visitor flows can be said to have unproblematically served the interests of the local festival organisation.

If at this point we revisit the conceptualisation of festivals as forum through which individuals and groups seek to assert control over the production of local knowledge and to reproduce certain cultural meanings, the issue as to where tourists fit into this process in the Wexford case now arises. Clearly, the festival initiative came from one specific socio-cultural group within the town. The festival served as a vehicle to communicate and promote particular sets of values and beliefs about, for example, the arts and social engagement in the arts, as well as about what Wexford represents as a society and as a place. As already discussed, an early challenge facing the festival founders was to encourage other sectors of the local community to adopt and support their priorities. Allying their position with more powerful tourism interests was one critical factor in broadening their support base to include a wider section of the middle class and business community. The tourism potential of the festival also strengthened the ease with which it connected with powerful gatekeepers in the form of the national media, major sponsors and the state tourism agency. As tourism flows began arriving, the festival organisation's position became increasingly secure. Thus, from this position of strength, it became increasingly easy to withstand oppositional voices seeking to render prevailing ideals and values more inclusive of other positions. Instances of unheard voices include early appeals for a more inclusive approach to favour local audience development (as voiced in early newspaper commentaries), arts critics critiquing the festival for apparently failing to adequately contribute to the development of Irish opera (especially in 1970s) and approaches from the Arts Council to more closely pursue national opera objectives (in the 1990s).

Thus, visitors did not introduce any new perspectives on the cultural meanings being promoted in the festival setting. Rather, they simply allied, very strongly, with the powerful group commanding the process. The effect that the emergence of visiting audiences had was to greatly reinforce the status of the existing hegemony and to virtually eliminate the possibility that this position would ever be successfully challenged. It must be noted that the drive to create in Wexford a festival of international standing did not derive externally. It came out of the local milieu within which the dominant vision driving the festival took shape. The skill of the locally derived festival organisation was to demonstrate an ability to connect with extra-local forces and to generate sufficient flows of externally derived visitors, which in turn yielded income, reputation and international status.

Distinguishing the 'visitor' from the 'visited', a case of inverted difference

A distinguishing trait of the Wexford Festival is that from its earliest days it determinedly sought to eliminate its status as a 'local' festival. Forging connections, extending its reputation and elevating its standing in international spheres was a fundamental preoccupation driving it forward. Hence it engaged international artists, invited socially prominent people to open each festival, timed the hosting of the festival to coincide with an opening in the European opera calendar, forged sponsorship deals with national and international companies and targeted overseas audiences. Its outward orientation was such that its place-based identity was continuously being reinvented through its ever-expanding international connections. The shifting identities of the flows of people circulating around the festival landscape serves to illustrate the point.

As already discussed, the possibilities for engaging in the Wexford festival serve to continuously assert difference between locals and visitors. Both groups surveyed during the 1996 festival exhibited quite different spatial and temporal patterns of movement around the festival landscape. Relatively little interaction between the two groups was identified. Yet, despite this emphasis on difference, there are times when the roles played by the two groups call into question basic conceptualisations of what constitutes both a 'local' and a 'visitor'. The earliest instance of this confusion occurs in the earliest years of the festival when local newspaper accounts of the festival describe how at festival time the town of Wexford became a spectacle to be gazed on by local dwellers. The opening night of the inaugural festival was thus described:

> 'a night the likes of which has never before been experienced in Wexford town...From an early hour, spectators gathered around the vicinity of the Theatre Royal to witness the arrivals of the principals[4] and the audience, and to admire the dresses of the ladies' (The Wexford People, 3/11/51).

The dramatic power of the festival to transform the small coastal town is well captured in this quote. The ordinary streetscape, transformed by the presence of glamorous individuals, many of them visitors to the town, acquired an unprecedented novelty for its dwellers. In contemporary festivals, the presence of visitors no longer represents the spectacle that it once did, the novelty having gradually worn off. Nevertheless, 75% of the local people surveyed during the 1996 festival sensed an air of difference about their place and the key variable transforming the ordinary landscape into an extraordinary one was identified as the presence of visitors. Furthermore, in terms of participating in festival events, some local survey respondents explained their absence from the main opera landscape on the basis of not knowing anybody in the audience.

Thus it is that visitors can introduce an exoticism into a place, and transform the banal into a veritable tourist attraction for local dwellers. Equally, they can disguise the familiar such that local residents feel uncomfortable or ill at ease circulating within their own place. Conversely, in-depth assessments of audience movements around the festival landscape revealed the distinct probability of visiting audience members coming into contact, either deliberately or accidentally, with very many friends and acquaintances from their home place, be it Dublin, London, or elsewhere. Hence for those who travel to Wexford, the difference and the attraction which inspired the journey, can come to assume the trappings of familiarity. There is therefore some justification in querying who is the tourist.

To return to Geertz' (1988) observation, these case findings suggest that the experiences of dwelling and travelling can indeed become blurred. Wexford, during festival time, can seem to be a place where it is tourists who feel at home while local people can feel excluded or at least disinterested in the major cultural performance that is transforming their place. Not only that, but it is this mythological 'Wexford, the festival town' that is being sold to the world in television coverage, international newspaper reports, etc, as the Wexford people's place. However, it is not a question of sameness being promoted. Instead one could argue that it is an inversion of difference, as locals play the role of visitors and visitors the role of locals. Yet, this is only a partial inversion, as respective visitors and locals can be seen to move in and out of their conventional roles. It might therefore be more appropriate to think of the roles of tourist and local as having an ambiguous quality.

This paper undoubtedly raises more questions than it answers. Immense research possibilities remain to be explored. The hope is that these research findings will serve to interest other tourism researchers in the cultural significance of festivals and to draw some attention to the effects which tourism has on the production of cultural meanings in the festival setting.

Endnotes

1. The fringe programme has no artistic direction.

2. In the late 1990s, the festival enjoys the support of some 300 volunteers

3. The main opera festival attracts audiences of approximately 30,000.

4. The Theatre Royal had no dressing room and so the principal singers, who came from UK opera companies, had to arrive in costume.

References

Brohman, J. (1996), New directions in Third World development, *Annals of Tourism Research*, 23 (1): 48-70.

Clifford, J. (1988), *The Predicament of Culture: Twentieth Century Ethnography, Literature and Art*, Harvard University Press, Cambridge, Massachusetts.

Cohen, A. (1982), A polyethnic London carnival as a contested cultural performance, *Ethnic and Racial Studies*, 5 (1): 23-41.

Falassi, A. (1987), *Time out of Time: Essays on the Festival*, University of New Mexico, Albuquerque.

Farber, C. (1983), High, healthy and happy: Ontario mythology on parade, in Manning, F. E. (editor), *The Celebration of Society: Perspectives on Contemporary Cultural Performance*, Bowling Green University Press, Bowling Green, Ohio, pp. 33-49.

Hughes, H. L. (1989), Tourism and the arts: a potentially destructive relationship? *Tourism Management*, 10 (2): 97-99.

Irish Press, (1953).

Jackson, P. (1988), Street life: the politics of carnival, *Environment and Planning D: Society and Space*, 6, pp.213-227.

Marston, S. (1989), Public rituals and community power: St. Patrick's parades in Lowell, Massachusetts, 1841-1874, *Political Geography Quarterly*, 8 (3): 255-269.

Myerscough, J. (1988), *The Economic Importance of the Arts in Britain*, Policy Studies Institute, London

O'Hagan, J. et al. (1989), The Economic and Social Contribution of the Wexford Opera Festival, Department of Economics, Trinity College, Dublin.

Sack, R. D. (1997), Homo Geographicus. *A Framework for Action, Awareness and Moral Concern*, The John Hopkins University Press, Baltimore, Maryland.

Sampath, N. (1998), Mas'identity: tourism and global and local aspects of Trinidad carnival, in Abram, S. et al. (editors) *Tourists and Tourism: Identifying with People and Places*, Berg, Oxford, pp. 149-172.

Smith, S. (1994), Soundscape, *Area*, 29 (4): 232-240.

Stallybrass, P. and White, A. (1986), *The Politics and Poetics of Transgression*, Methuen, London.

Stokes, M. (ed.) (1994*), Ethnicity, Identity and Music: the Musical Construction of Place*, Berg, Oxford.

Thrift, N. (1997), Cities without modernity, cities with magic, *Scottish Geographical Magazine*, 113 (3): 138- 149.

Wexford Festival Opera, (1952), Submission for funding to Arts Council, File 14 of first accession of Arts Council files, archived in the National Archives, Dublin.

Wexford People, (1951 – 1953).

Is mass tourism bad for us?: Socio-cultural impacts of tourism development in Siófok, Hungary

Tamara Rátz and László Puczkó

Budapest University of Economic Sciences, Hungary

Introduction

Tourism has become one of the most significant industries around the world, having transported 635 million people internationally (WTO 2000). It is a major economic force, generating directly and indirectly 11% of GDP in 1999 and creating employment for 8% of the global workforce (WTTC 2000). Tourism's physical, social and economic impacts pay an ever-increasing role in determining the quality of life of hundreds of millions of people world-wide. In Hungary, most studies on the impacts of tourism have so far been restricted to economic analysis, and the subject of socio-cultural impacts of tourism has been under-researched.

Lake Balaton is the second most important tourist destination in the country, but the region is also the home of app. 130,000 people. Research in the area has concentrated mainly on environmental, ecological or on economic issues. Ecological research focusing on the quality of the water has been given priority since the lake itself is the major attraction of the region, it is the basis of tourism development. The importance of the economic issues, on the other hand, comes from the monocultural economic structure of the area (and in the socialist system, international tourism at the Lake was the source of much needed hard currency). However, as Lengyel said (1995:51), "The main actors of tourism are the residents – it cannot be developed without them and it is useless if they do not benefit from it". The ultimate goal of tourism development is to improve the quality of life of local people, and this goal cannot be achieved without knowing their perceptions on the changes that tourism development brings about.

In Hungary this has been the first research on the socio-cultural impacts of tourism based on a complex methodology (including surveys of experts, residents and tourists). The objectives of the research project were to study residents' perceptions of the socio-cultural impacts of tourism development in Siófok, a well-known holiday resort at Lake Balaton, and to understand the process of tourism development in the Balaton region.

The socio-cultural impacts of tourism

The socio-cultural impacts of tourism are basically the consequences of either the development of the tourism industry or the presence of the tourists (and the characteristics of the tourist-host relationship) (Sharpley, 1994). Table 1 contains a comprehensive list of these impacts, following the classification adapted from Figuerola (1976, in Pirillis, 1991) and Burdge (1994).

Table 1   The Socio-cultural Impacts of Tourism

Positive	Negative
Impacts on population	
Population increase *(immigration, no emigration)*	
Immigration of seasonal workforce *(positive in case of lack of labour - negative in case of unemployment)*	
Presence of second home owners *(positive if involved in community life - negative if not involved)*	
Changes in population distribution (by age, sex, race, ethnicity)	
Urbanisation of population	
Changes in labour market	
New jobs	Seasonal jobs
New types of jobs in tourism	Unskilled jobs
Increased value of knowledge, language skills	Lack of labour in traditional sectors
Economic diversification	Increased economic inequality
Stimulation of underdeveloped regions	
Changes in community structure, characteristics	
Income from tourism	Increase in the number of temporary residents *(not very committed)*
Growing importance of service sector	Conflicts with second home owners
Stimulation of social, cultural life	Difficulties in acquiring real estate
Increase in the value of land	Increase in real estate prices
Development of infrastructure	Increase in prices, inflation
Wider opportunity for shopping	Loss of cultural identity
Improvement in the destination image	Transformation of value systems
Increase in residents' pride in their settlement	Religious conflicts *(with second home owners, with tourists)*
Decrease of prejudices, disappearance of stereotypes, increase in tolerance	Overdependence on tourism
	Congestion
	Traffic problems
Transformation of social stratification *(owners of tourist resources rise, owners of traditional resources fell)*	
Impacts on individual and family level	
Increase in social mobility *(especially among the young and women)*	Disruption of social networks
Improvement in leisure opportunities	Changes in the rhythm of life
Meeting new people, wider social contacts	Loss of importance of friendship

Improvement in the quality of life	Increase in perception of danger *(due to increased criminality)*
Language skills	Xenophobia
Income from tourism	Commercialised hospitality
Improvement in attitudes toward work, politeness, manners	Deviant behaviours *(alcoholism, prostitution, gambling, drug abuse, vandalism)*
	Local language suppressed
	Increased sexual permissiveness
Transformation of family structure	
Transformation of consumer habits	
Changes in housing conditions	
Transformation of behaviour (demonstration effect)	
Impacts on cultural and natural resources	
Protection of rare resources of outstanding beauty	Disappearance of local habits, traditions
Revival of local arts, crafts, cultural events	Commercialisation of culture
Revival of local architectural traditions	Littering, pollution

Methodology

The methodology used in the project included both secondary and primary methods. Secondary research focused on the following main topics: (a) literature on tourism development in the Lake Balaton region, (b) literature on the history, development and present social, economic and environmental characteristics of Siófok, and (c) literature on tourism development in the city. Newspaper and periodical articles, books and unpublished research papers were all used.

Empirical research methods included:

- A Delphi survey on the positive and negative socio-cultural impacts of tourism in Siófok;

- A mail survey of local residents concerning their perceptions of tourism's socio-cultural impacts in the town; and,

- A tourist survey studying tourists' characteristics (types, motivations, activities, socio-economic background, etc.) and their perceptions of tourism's socio-cultural impacts in Siófok.

Tourism development at Lake Balaton

Tourism development in the Lake Balaton area (not only in Siófok, due to the lack of comprehensive and comparable statistical data) was studied in the framework of two theoretical models: Doxey's Irridex (Doxey, 1975) and the destination life-cycle (Butler, 1980).

The Irridex model (Doxey, 1975) represents the connection between the development of tourism and the local residents' attitudes toward tourists and tourism. The model assumes that the presence of tourists creates tension for locals, and as this tension accelerates due to the continuous presence of tourists, locals' attitudes toward tourists become more and more negative (Doxey, 1975; Glasson et al, 1995). Though tolerance levels are destination-specific, a model can present the general phases of attitudinal changes. Figure 1 shows the four levels of residents' attitudes. The temporal position of each phase depends on various economic, social, cultural, natural and psychological factors.

Figure 1   Irridex

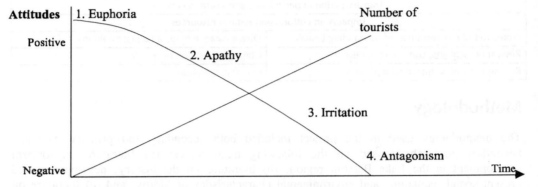

The research proved that the development of tourism resulted in profound social and attitudinal changes in the Lake Balaton region indeed. However, the direction of the changes differed from that proposed by the Irridex model.

The arrival of the first tourists at Lake Balaton did not bring about particular changes for the local people - mainly fisherman and peasants - for a while. The guests belonged to higher classes, their interactions with the locals were rather limited, dues to their different social positions. Consequently, the arrival of the first tourists did not elicit euphoria among local residents, their early attitude was most probably neutral. The further development of tourism stimulated local involvement which, together with an increase in contacts between tourists and residents, resulted in a more positive - euphoric - attitude. However, first the social differences between hosts and guests, then, after 1945, the rapidly increasing demand led to the emergence of the typical tourist-host inequality, so the locals' attitudes became more negative again and reached in general the Irritation phase of Doxey' model, but in some cases even Antagonism might have been occurred. The political changes in 1989 transformed the characteristics of tourism in the region once more, the demand-oriented market became supply-oriented, a higher level of professionalism started to characterise the planning and the operation of the sector, so locals' attitudes became more positive - i.e. neutral, apathetic - again. Residents had to learn to live together with tourism and to accept that in order to benefit of tourism' positive impacts, they should cope with at least some negative changes. Figure 2 shows the modified Irridex model in the Lake Balaton region.

Figure 2   Hypothetical Irridex in the Lake Balaton region

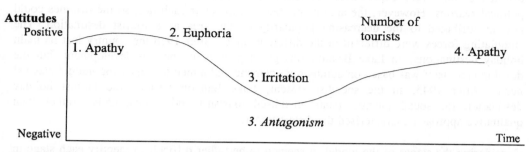

The other theoretical model analysed in this research was Butler's destination lifecycle model (Butler, 1980). The model assumes that the lifecycle of tourist destinations follow a specific pattern that can be divided into six consecutive stages (Figure 3). During this process, the number and characteristics of tourists change, together with the characteristics of the tourism industry, and the impacts of tourism development.

Figure 3   The tourist destination lifecycle

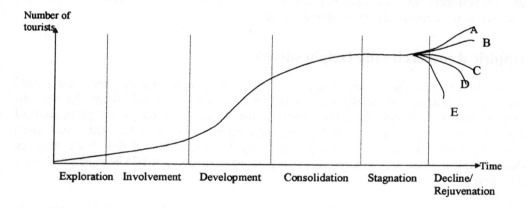

The major problem in the practical application of the model was the lack of reliable and comparable statistical data (as it was also experienced by other researchers abroad). In my research, I used data on visitor arrivals and on the capacity of commercial accommodation (the latter served as an indicator of the expansion of the industry). Besides statistical data sources, I also used qualitative information that proved to be particularly useful in the identification and description of the lifecycle stages (Eötvös 1900, 1909; Lóczy, 1921; Pálos, 1974a, 1974b; Zákonyi, 1974; Gertig, 1985; Lengyel, 1995; Virág, 1997).

Overall the analysis of the development of tourism in the Lake Balaton region showed that the lifecycle of the destination followed a pattern quite similar to that proposed by Butler (1980). However, some major differences were also experienced which seemed to prove other researchers' argument that the lifecycle curve is destination-specific (e.g. Haywood, 1986; Cooper and Jackson, 1989; Getz, 1992: Agarwal 1997).

The main difference between Lake Balaton and the model was that at Lake Balaton two distinctive falls were experienced (between 1914-1918 and between 1942-1945), due to political reasons. However, the area continued to grow after each fall, so the declines could not be attributed to the decreasing popularity of the area as a tourist destination. The stimulating forces were different in the different stages: after 1918 the country lost its main holiday destinations, so Lake Balaton was given priority in tourism development, but the development itself was based on commercial demand and aimed to satisfy the middle classes' needs. After 1945, in the socialist system, Lake Balaton became the largest holiday destination for social tourism (state-subsidised tourism) and a quantitative rather than qualitative approach characterised the development.

Considering the stages of the model, it seemed to be rather difficult to identify each stage in time, since the development process was influence by destination-specific factors. An interesting fact that the early development of tourism in the area was not initiated by today's major attraction, the Lake itself, but by the thermal springs found nearby. In some stages the types of tourists differed from those in the model (e.g. in the Exploration stage and in the Consolidation/Stagnation stage). Though tourism's negative impacts appeared earlier than in the model, these unfavourable changes did not actually effect the tourism demand, due to the demand-oriented market. Tourism is highly seasonal in the region, which - in addition to obvious political constraints - partly explains why no major international companies have got involved in the industry (as opposed to the model).

Empirical research - the Delphi survey

As the first step of the research project, an expert mail survey (in the form of a Delphi survey) was carried out among various representatives of the local community and the tourism industry in Siófok. As it is suggested in the Delphi methodology, the participants of the survey were selected by nomination: one local expert and one national expert were asked to nominate panel members. As the aim of the project was specific to Siófok, it was assumed that a relatively small and, to a certain extent, homogenous group would be most suitable for this survey.

After evaluating the potential respondents, 26 persons were selected to participate who were considered to be able to present a significantly broad view on the survey topic, the socio-cultural impacts of tourism in the destination. The respondents represented the local community, civil groups, the local authorities, the tourism industry in Siófok and tourism in Lake Balaton. Based on their field of expertise and residence, it was assumed that they would be motivated to contribute to this survey.

In the first round, the selected persons were asked to provide a list of the positive and negative socio-cultural impacts of tourism development in Siófok. 19 responses were received from the panel members with a 73% response rate. Altogether 57 positive and 52 negative impacts were mentioned (with serious overlaps in the participants' answers) which proves one of the project's original hypothesis that tourism has both positive and negative socio-cultural impacts in the studied area.

In the second stage in the survey, respondents were asked to identify, on the basis of the first round lists, the 10 most important positive and negative impacts of tourism development.

Altogether 30 positive and 35 negative impacts were selected again. The relatively high number of most important impacts proves that there was no real consensus between respondents (this observation is also supported by the fact that standard deviation was higher than 2.00 in 23 cases out of 54 - the remaining impacts were only selected by one respondent each).

Based on this result, a third round of the survey was considered to be appropriate in order to bring expert opinions closer and to try to reach a higher level of consensus. In this round, respondents once more were asked to evaluate the importance of tourism's positive and negative impacts in the settlement. Furthermore, they were also asked to identify if the listed changes were only seasonal or could be experienced throughout the year. As the final result of this survey, respondents identified the a number of changes as the most positive and the most negative impacts of tourism development in Siófok:

Table 2   The most Positive and the most Negative Impacts of Tourism Development in Siófok

Most positive	Most negative
• Development of settlement, regional development	• Organised crime (prostitution, car theft)
• Income generation	• Environmental damage, due to temporal pressure on the infrastructure
• Higher quality of life	• Economic dependence on tourism, monocultural economic structure
• Employment creation	• Short-term way of thinking

Of the above listed impacts, income generation, organised crime, and environmental damage due to seasonal pressure were considered as seasonal changes by the experts, all the other impacts are effective throughout the year.

Empirical research - resident survey

As the second part of the research work, a mail questionnaire survey of local residents was carried out in Siófok, concerning residents' perceptions of tourism's impacts on various socio-cultural factors. In accordance with the research plan, the survey sample was set on the basis of the population size of the city. The original plan was to set the sample at 10% of the population, i.e. in this case 1.900 questionnaires. In the moment of the draft project design it was not decided yet which settlement would be involved in the project, and as Siófok proved to be smaller than the other considered alternatives, the research budget made it possible to use a larger sample, i.e. 3.500 questionnaires. However, it was considered to be more appropriate to send out the questionnaires in two stages, so that no unforeseen event decreases the response rate.

The preliminary version of the questionnaire was tested in Siófok by the assistance of the staff and that of the students of the Tourism Department, Kodolányi János College. Their comments and suggestions on contents, language usage and structure proved to be very useful in creating the final version of the questionnaire.

In selecting the survey sample, a combined method of cluster sampling and systematic sampling was used. The data source was the city's voters' list, as only respondents older than 18 years were intended to involve in the survey. As the city is divided to 22 electoral districts, first 11 of these districts were selected (using systematic sampling, thus selecting every second district), then systematic sampling was used again to select the respondents themselves (every fifth person on the remaining list was chosen).

In the resident survey, 3,492 questionnaires were sent out and 1,088 completed ones were received with a 31.1% response rate (in addition, 85 questionnaires were received back empty, so the overall response rate was 33.6%). This response rate can be considered as very good, given the lack of financial motivation for the respondents.

Empirical research - tourist survey

The third empirical method used in the research was a tourist survey in the summer of 1999 in Siófok. The sample size proposed in the original research plan was 1,000, considering the relatively high costs of interviews. According to the data of the Siófok Tourinform (1999), the city had approximately 100,000 guests in commercial accommodation, so this sample size means app. 10% of the statistically registered tourists (there are no any other data available on the overall number of visitors). However, in the survey Hungarian respondents were over-represented (47,2% instead of 25%), because experts estimate that about half of the city's visitors are Hungarians (the majority of whom stay with friends or in their own summer houses and do not use commercial accommodation).

The preliminary version of the questionnaire was tested in Siófok by a student of the Budapest University of Economic Sciences. Both her suggestions and the comments of the tourists interviewed proved to be very useful in creating the final version of the questionnaire.

The interviews were conducted by five students of the Budapest University of Economic Sciences. The questionnaires were printed in three languages, Hungarian, German and English, but later an Italian version was also produced. Since there were no detailed reliable data on the distribution of the tourists, a combination of cluster sampling (based on nationality) and convenience sampling was used (the students were allowed to interview any tourist who belonged to a given nationality group). Altogether 907 questionnaires were fully completed.

The distribution of the sample is quite complex: tourists of 14 nationality were interviewed (the majority being Hungarian, German, Austrian, Italian and Dutch). 50.2% of the respondents were male, 49.8% female. According to profession, most respondents were employees (27.9%), students (23.5%), professionals (14.3%), physical workers (15.2%) and entrepreneurs (6.7%). 55.8% of the respondents belonged to the youngest age group (15-29 years) which is not surprising, since Siófok is the most popular holiday destination among young people in the southern part of Lake Balaton (the city is the site of the Coca-Cola Beach House, a summer-long series of concerts and other events). Older respondents were under-represented in the sample (1.9% over 60 years) which might be the result of their lower willingness to participate or the interviewers bias. However, since there are no data on the age distribution of the tourists, it cannot be analysed whether the sample is representative in this respect.

Main findings of the empirical research

The impacts of tourism

All the surveys supported the original hypothesis that tourism has both positive and negative impacts in the area. In the Delphi research, the experts identified altogether 57 positive and 52 negative impacts (the majority of these impacts were mentioned by more than one respondent) and even on the list of the most important impacts there remained 30 positive and 35 negative impacts. Residents also perceive tourism's impacts in a complex way: the changes attributed to tourism development vary from significant improvement (e.g. employment opportunities or income) and significant increase (e.g. in congestion or in noise) to significant worsening (e.g. traffic conditions or public security) and significant decrease (e.g. in honesty or in unemployment). Though the tourists obviously have a limited knowledge of tourism' impacts in the area, they showed a relatively strong consensus in listing both positive and negative changes. The main difference between tourists' and residents' perceptions is that the changes tourists mentioned are mainly of those kind that affect the holiday experience, while residents' perceptions covered all areas of their own quality of life.

Tables 3 and 4 present the perceptions of Siófok residents on the impacts of tourism development on 40 socio-cultural variables. Residents had to evaluate pre-defined variables, but also had the opportunity to add anything if they wished to do so.

Table 3   Residents' mean response to tourism's effect on the region+

	Variable	Mean	Std.dev.
1.	Employment opportunities	4.03	1.46
2.	Income and standard of living	3.76	1.46
3.	Language skills	3.76	1.58
4.	Opportunity for learning more about other nations	3.70	1.59
5.	Opportunity for shopping	3.57	1.59
6.	Cultural facilities (theatres, cinemas, museums, etc.)	3.46	1.54
7.	Opportunity for meeting interesting people	3.40	1.54
8.	Quality of life	3.33	1.47
9.	General infrastructure	3.26	1.57
10	Leisure facilities	3.21	1.50
11.	Tolerance toward difference	3.03	1.49
12	Sports facilities	2.98	1.44
13	Attitude toward work	2.91	1.48
14.	Cultural identity	2.85	1.51
15.	Conservation of old buildings	2.78	1.48
16.	Relationship of generations	2.65	1.33
17.	Housing conditions	2.52	1.42
18.	Public security	2.05	1.33
19.	Availability of real estate	2.04	1.29
20.	Traffic conditions	1.77	1.15

+ - Response range was 1 to 5
1 = Significantly worsen   2 = Worsen somewhat   3 = Not make any difference   4 = Improve somewhat
5 = Significantly improve

Table 4   Residents' mean response to tourism's effect on the region++

	Variable	Mean	Std.dev.
21.	Congestion	4.12	1.59
22.	Noise	4.05	1.57
23.	Prostitution	4.01	1.64
24.	Settlement's overall tax revenue	3.99	1.57
25.	Crime	3.99	1.62
26.	General prices for goods and services	3.95	1.57
27.	Cost of land and real estate	3.84	1.67
28.	Littering	3.78	1.58
29.	Vandalism	3.78	1.61
30.	Drug abuse	3.78	1.71
31.	Residents' concern for material gain	3.74	3.12
32.	Costs of living	3.72	1.60
33.	Gambling	3.58	1.69
34.	Hospitality and courtesy toward strangers	3.37	1.48
35.	Residents' pride in their settlement	3.26	1.50
36.	Alcoholism	3.18	1.48
37.	Politeness and good manners	3.02	1.43
38.	Mutual confidence among people	2.56	1.33
39.	Honesty	2.44	1.36
40.	Unemployment	2.04	1.29

++ - Response range was 1 to 5
1 = Significantly decrease   2 = Decrease somewhat   3 = Not make any difference   4 = Increase somewhat
5 = Significantly increase

As Tables 3 and 4 illustrate, standard deviation values for all but one studied variables are between 1 and 2 (on a 1-5 scale) which does not prove particularly high differences in perceptions (so the respondents seem to have a certain consensus on the nature of the studied impacts). Expert opinions are more complex, both the means and the standard deviation values of the impacts and the respondents' comments on various factors show higher disagreement. It is surprising to notice that there is a significant difference between expert opinions and residents' perceptions in various cases: for example, as it can be seen in Table 3, residents unanimously perceive that traffic conditions worsened significantly due to tourism development, while only one of the experts mentioned bad traffic conditions as a relatively important problem (with an importance rate of 5 on a 1-10 scale).

Since cultural differences between tourists and residents are not significant, it was assumed that residents perceive tourism's socio-economic impacts more strongly and more positively than tourism's cultural impacts. Though it is not possible to separate tourism's socio-economic and socio-cultural impacts, certain impacts are more based on economic or cultural factors than others. In this respect, the findings at first glance show a complex picture again.

Employment and income created by tourism are perceived very strongly by the respondents ("employment opportunities" is considered to be the most significantly improved variable and "unemployment" as the most significantly decreased one), and so are tax income and prices, but the general infrastructure is not perceived to be considerably improved because of tourism development. Variables related to quality of life are perceived very strongly (like congestion, public security, noise and criminal activities). Among mainly cultural variables, language learning is perceived to be the most beneficial consequence of tourism, followed by the opportunity to get to know other nations and the appreciation of the city's cultural facilities and services. On the other hand, tourism does not seem to affect the locals' cultural identity and does not create pride in residents. Experts again are more ambivalent about this issue: though they also rate income - a socio-economic variable - as tourism development's most significant (and obviously positive) impact, they form different opinions on the interrelationship of tourism and culture, being concerned about the commercialisation of local culture and appreciating its role in attracting tourists.

Tourists in general did not feel that their trip to Siófok affected the environment in the city in a negative way (mean$=1.63^1$, std. dev.$=1.08$). On the other hand, 31.2% believed that their travel positively affected the environment (mean$=2.70^2$, std. dev.$=1.53$).

As Table 5 shows, the tourists who visit Siófok cannot be considered particularly environment-conscious, so it is rather unlikely that they would make efforts to diminish their impact on the environment (including both the physical and the cultural environment). The comfort factor most respondents would have been willing to give up was air conditioning and the use of a swimming pool, the least frequently used services on the list (since the Lake is freshwater and the climate is continental). Altogether only 25.2% of the tourists would consider to buy a publication on how to travel in a more environmentally friendly way, but almost 50% would not spend money for this purpose.

Table 5   Environmental consciousness of tourists

Willingness to give up.........[3]	Mean	Std. dev.
• air conditioning	3.30	1.57
• using own car/tourist coach	2.71	1.47
• unlimited consumption of water and electricity	2.68	1.37
• swimming pool	3.26	1.60
Willingness to.........		
• choose more environment conscious services even if at higher prices	2.67	1.42
• read a publication on how to become a more environment conscious tourist	3.20	1.51
• buy a publication on how to become a more environment conscious tourist	2.46	1.47

Attitudes of tourists and local people

The model created by Bjorklund and Philbrick (1972) and adapted to tourism by Butler (1974) present residents attitudes toward tourism and their behaviour related to tourists and tourism . According to these factors, residents can actively or passively support or oppose the presence of tourists and tourism development.

36.6% of the resident survey respondents answered that they had done something in order to help tourism development (their efforts range from being polite and helpful to tourists to setting up tourist services), while only 3.1% of the respondents had done anything to prevent it. Respondents also have favourable attitudes toward tourism: more than 80% believe that tourism has a positive impact on the image of Siófok and 71% are pleased with the presence of tourists in the city. Since the success of tourism depends very much on the human factor, i.e. the attitudes and behaviour of the residents of a destination towards tourists, this seems to be an encouraging result for the future of tourism development. Almost one third of the respondents rent out rooms to tourists (which is one form of active tourism support) and more than one fifth work in tourism.

App. 56% of the respondents in the resident survey believe that the number of tourists in the city should further increase and only less than 9% would like to see tourist numbers decrease. However, 57% of the respondents stated that the presence of tourists disturb them in certain activities (particularly in transportation, in shopping and in rest and relaxation) which shows that - at least during the main season - the region's social carrying capacity is exceeded (the psychological carrying capacity can be assessed from the tourist survey). One possible explanation for this contradiction is tourism's seasonal nature and the locals' awareness of its economic significance.

Tourists did not seem to perceive unacceptable levels of congestion (Table 6) anywhere in the city, though the relatively high standard deviation values show that their perceptions significantly differed. Nor did their perception of congestion highly affect their overall evaluation of Siófok (with a mean of 3.07 - on a 1-5 scale -, they considered the problem of personal inconveniences as moderately important).

Table 6   Congestion perceived by tourists

Variable	Mean+	Std.dev.
Beach	3.60	1.14
Roads	3.78	1.10
Restaurants	3.21	1.02
Night clubs	3.81	1.07
Trains	3.57	1.12
Buses	3.69	1.05
Other	3.51	1.42

+ - assessed on a scale from 1-5 (1 - not congested at all, 5 - very congested)

Tourists acknowledged that their own presence caused most of the crowding on the beaches (67.2% put the blame other tourists) and in the restaurants (82.8%)[4]. However, in the night clubs and on the roads they perceived that both they and the local people increased the congestion (58.2% and 55.4% blamed the tourists, respectively). Concerning the trains and the buses, tourists thought that crowding was mainly caused by local people (and partly by tourists).

Altogether the findings do not prove that the number of tourists in the city would reach the social or psychological carrying capacity of the settlement, even though the opposite would not be very surprising, given the mass tourism nature of the industry and the high seasonality of demand.

It was assumed that those residents who work in tourism or who have family members who work in tourism evaluate tourism's socio-cultural impacts more positively than those who do not belong to these categories (this hypothesis was verified e.g. by Pizam, 1978; Brougham and Butler, 1981; Gergely, 1989; Long, Perdue and Allen, 1990). However, there was no significant relation between being (or having a family member) employed in tourism and the overall satisfaction with the situation of tourism in the city ($\chi^2=6.135$, p=0.189). The only variables affected by employment in tourism were the following: income ($\chi^2=19.507$, p=0.001), the quality of life ($\chi^2=21.994$, p=0.000), the opportunity to meet interesting people ($\chi^2=13.360$, p=0.010), language skills ($\chi^2=13.169$, p=0.010), the price of land and real estate ($\chi^2=9.488$, p=0.050), politeness and good manners ($\chi^2=11.388$, p=0.023), gambling ($\chi^2=11.254$, p=0.024) and congestion ($\chi^2=11.419$, p=0.022). However, the results of the λ tests showed no causal relationship between employment in tourism and any of these variables which means that the hypothesis assuming that those residents who work in tourism or who have family members employed in tourism evaluate tourism's socio-cultural impacts more positively than those who do not belong to these categories must be rejected.

Conclusions

Tourism in Siófok is typical mass tourism in many aspects (Shaw and Williams 1994): the relatively high number of tourists (in season) results in mass produced services which are generally difficult to distinguish. The tourist product of Siófok is based on the Lake, the sunshine, and the night clubs and other entertainment facilities. This product is rather similar to the Mediterranean seaside holidays, though the shallow, freshwater beach can be an advantage for families. The tourists visiting the region are quite price-sensitive and arrive mainly from Hungary or from Central-Eastern Europe (i.e. travel relatively short distances). During the last decades, tourism in the region has been blamed for many environmental and socio-cultural problems, both by local residents and experts.

The results of this survey show that residents are aware of the negative consequences of tourism development, but they are also aware of the benefits tourism brings about. Tourists evaluated most elements of the destination as of medium quality (entertainment, shopping and sports facilities were most appreciated, and the quality of folk traditions and museums proved to be the lowest). However, almost 80% of the tourist respondents were returning guests at Lake Balaton and more than 70% in Siófok, and app. 30% were prompted to select the area as their holiday destination by previous pleasant experiences.

The impacts of tourism are complex, both positive and negative in the town (and in the whole Balaton region). Residents seem to have been accustomed to the negative - mainly seasonal - consequences and seem to be ready to accept these inconveniences in return for important benefits such as employment opportunities, income or a lively atmosphere in the summer.

Though tourists only spend a limited time in the town, the majority (78.2%) of the survey respondents were able to identify some kind of socio-cultural impact of tourism development: the most frequently mentioned positive examples were general development and income, while crime and price increase were the most perceived negative impacts. A major difference between residents' and tourists' opinions is that tourists in general did not mention those negative changes that residents attributed to tourists' presence or behaviour, like congestion, noise, littering or traffic problems (see Tables 3 and 4).

The research showed that on annual level the overall balance of impacts in Siófok is perceived by residents as more positive than negative. Due to the high seasonality of tourist demand, most planning and development efforts focus on improving the services and increasing the attractiveness of the town out of season (in addition to the crucial issues of water quality and environmental protection). These efforts could also improve residents' quality of life: higher demand would most probably produce more income (so the most positively perceived impact of tourism would become even stronger), and a demand more dispersed in time would result in less seasonal stress. However, as the quality of life depends on many social and cultural factors, hopefully in the future socio-cultural issues get even more attention in local and regional decision-making.

[1]Measurement of agreement with the following statement on a 1-5 Likert scale: "My current trip has negative impact on the environment" (1 - totally disagree, 5 - totally agree).

[2]Measurement of agreement with the following statement on a 1-5 Likert scale: "My current trip has positive impact on the environment" (1 - totally disagree, 5 - totally agree).

[3]Measurement of agreement with the following statement on a 1-5 Likert scale: " When I travel, I would be willing to choose more environment conscious services even if I had to give up.... " (1 - totally disagree, 5 - totally agree).

[4]The percentages apply to those tourists only who perceived the given variable as congested.

References

Agarwal, S. (1997), The Resort Cycle and Seaside Tourism: An Assessment of Its Applicability and Validity, *Tourism Management*, 18 (2): 65-73

Bjorklund, E. M and Philbrick, A.K. (1972), Spatial Configurations of Mental Processes, Unpublished paper, Department of Geography, University of Western Ontario, London, Ontario, Canada.

Brougham, J. E and Butler, R. W. (1981), A Segmentation Analysis of Residents' Attitudes to the Social Impact of Tourism, *Annals of Tourism Research*, 8 (4): 569-590.

Burdge, R. J. (1994), The Social Impact Assessment Model and the Planning Process, in Burdge, R.J, *A Conceptual Approach to Social Impact Assessment. Collection of Writings by Rabel J. Burdge and Colleagues*, Social Ecology Press, Middleton, Wisconsin, USA, pp.41-49.

Butler, R. W. (1972), Social Implications of Tourist Development, *Annals of Tourism Research*, 1, pp.100-111.

Butler, R. W. (1980), The Concept of a Tourist Area Cycle of Evolution: Implications for Management of Resources, *Canadian Geographer*, 24 (1): 5-12.

Cooper, C.P and Jackson, S. (1989), Destination Life-Cycle: The Isle of Man Case Study, *Annals of Tourism Research*, 16 (3): 377-398

Doxey, G. V. (1975), *A Causation Theory of Visitor-Resident Irritants*, Paper given at San Diego, California, The Travel Research Association Conference no.6. TTRA pp.195-198.

Eötvös, K. (1900), *Utazás a Balaton körül*, I-II. kötet, 2. kiadás, Révai Testvérek, Budapest.

Eötvös, K. (1909), *A Balatoni utazás vége*, in Utazás a Balaton körül. A Balatoni utazás vége, Révai Irodalmi Intézet, Budapest.

Gergely, R. (1989), Social Impacts of Tourism in Hungary, in J. Bystrzanowski (Editor), *Tourism as a Factor of Change. National Case Studies*, The Vienna Centre, Vienna, Austria, pp.9-31.

Gertig, B. (1985), A Balaton üdülőkörzet idegenforgalmának néhány gazdaságföldrajzi jellemzője, különös tekintettel a természeti adottságok és a társadalmi-gazdasági szerkezet kapcsolatrendszerének kialakulására, in Gertig, B and Lehmann, A. (Editors), *A Balaton és az idegenforgalom*, Pécsi Janus Pannonius Tudományegyetem Tanárképző Kar, Pécs, pp.47-101.

Getz, D. (1992), Tourism Planning and Destination Life Cycle, *Annals of Tourism Research*, 19 (4): 752-770.

Glasson, J. et al (1995), *Towards Visitor Impact Management*, Avebury, Aldershot, UK

Haywood, M. K. (1986), Can the Tourist Area Cycle of Evolution Be Made Operational ?, *Tourism Management*, 7 (3): 154-167.

Lengyel, M. (1995), *A balatoni turizmus fejlesztési koncepciója*, KIT Képzőmûvészeti Kiadó, Budapest.

Lóczy, L. (1921), *A Balaton földrajzi és társadalmi állapotainak leírása*, Hornyánszky Viktor m. kir. udvari könyvnyomdája, Budapest.

Long, P. T, Perdue, R. R. and Allen, L. (1990), Rural Resident Tourism Perceptions and Attitudes by Community Level of Tourism, *Journal of Travel Research*, 28 (3): 3-9.

Pálos, I. (1974a), Népesség, településhálózat, ipar, kereskedelem és mezＤgazdaság, in Tóth. K. (Editor), *Balaton monográfia*, Panoráma, Budapest, pp.127-161.

Pálos, I. (1974b), A balatoni üdülés és idegenforgalom. Az üdülＤforgalom fejlＤdése a számok tükrében, in Tóth, K. (Editor), *Balaton monográfia*, Panoráma, Budapest, pp.430-471.

Pirillis, D.A. (1991), *Impact of Tourism on the Paralimni and Ayia Napa Areas of Cyprus*, Unpublished M.Sc. Dissertation, University of Surrey, Guildford, UK.

Pizam, A. (1978), Tourism's Impacts: The Social Costs to the Destination Community as Perceived by Its Residents, *Journal of Travel Research*, 16, (4), pp.8-12.

Sharpley, R. (1994), *Tourism, Tourists and Society*, ELM Publications, Huntingdon, UK.

Shaw, G. and Williams, A. (1992), Tourism, Development and the Environment: the Eternal Triangle, in Cooper, C. and Lockwood, A. (Editors), *Progress in Tourism, Recreation and Hospitality Management; Vol. 4.*, Belhaven Press, London, UK, pp. 47-60.

Virág, Á. (1997), *A Balaton múltja és jelene*, Egri Nyomda Kft, Eger.

Zákonyi, F. (1974), A balatoni üdülés, üdültetés és idegenforgalom története, in Tóth, K. (Editor), *Balaton monográfia*, Panoráma, Budapest, pp.482-493.

WTO (2000), *Report of the Secretary-General on the Preliminary Results of World Tourism Activity in 1999*, WTO, Madrid.

WTTC (2000), *http://www.wttc.org/economic_research/keystats.htm*.

Tourism, culture, heritage, and shopping in the United States: Fruitful new linkages at the dawning of the 21st century

Tamara Real

Get Real! Communications, Michigan, USA

Introduction

Recognition of the value of cultural/heritage tourism in the United States has been slow in coming. Similarly, recognition of the importance of shopping as a travel activity has taken time to develop. Today, travel professionals acknowledge shopping as the #1 pastime of tourists, followed closely by visiting museums and/or historic sites (the third top choice of travellers) (TIA, 2000). The profitable connection between cultural/heritage tourism and shopping, however, is just starting to be understood. This paper will explore the rise of cultural/heritage tourism in the United States, the growth of the shopping-tourism connection, and will report on recent studies that provide important new information about the characteristics and behaviour of cultural/heritage tourists in this country, particularly in relationship to shopping. This paper will then go on to profile three examples of innovative cultural tourism/shopping partnerships in the United States. These partnerships, which range from the high-tech to the homespun, reflect an evolution of attitude among cultural leaders and retailers, as the diverse groups recognise that they can work together for their mutual benefit. The partnerships, by their very composition, also reflect the distinctly different values and perspectives of their organisers.

Definition of cultural/heritage tourism

Although many people feel they "know" what cultural/heritage tourism means, many different definitions exist. One of the most focused and concise comes from the Virginia Department of Historic Resources:

> "*Cultural or heritage tourism is travel directed toward experiencing the heritage, arts, and special character of a place in an exciting, informative way.*"

This definition captures several of the key points of cultural/heritage tourism. This tourism is oriented toward encountering those components of a destination that make it unique. These components could be largely historical, in which case people typically use the term "heritage tourism," or they could be more arts-focused, hence prompting the term "cultural tourism." (For ease of reading, the term "cultural tourism" will be used throughout this paper to refer to tourism that includes visiting cultural and/or heritage attractions or events.) But art and history aren't the only elements that make a place special. Many cultural tourism practitioners today recognise that such features as the built environment, ethnic traditions, food and culinary heritage, farming patterns, sporting traditions, and even industrial complexes can all contribute to the essence of an area and are valid parts of the "cultural tourism product."

Another important part of this cultural tourism definition lies in the phrase "experiencing the heritage, arts, and special character of a place in an exciting and informative way." Cultural tourism is not simply about witnessing something new and different; rather, it encourages interactions that will be meaningful and even educational. For cultural tourism practitioners, these interactions become significant and meaningful when they involve engagement with authentic objects, stories, songs, foods, traditional performances, etc. Authenticity is at the root of cultural tourism and it is these authentic experiences that provide the visitor with a new understanding of the destination or "a sense of place."

Growth of cultural tourism activities

Although today it is generally accepted among travel industry professionals in the United States that people travel to *see* or to *do* something, for many years, tourism leaders dismissed the importance of attractions, cultural and otherwise, within the travel industry. The focus of many travel professionals' energies went to filling the rooms in hotels and motels, and the mantra repeated over and over again by tourism promotion agencies such as state travel bureaus and convention and visitors bureaus was "heads in beds." What motivated the traveller was of less interest than tracking room occupancy rates. In part, this can be explained by the fact that many convention and visitors bureaus are funded by special taxes or assessments levied on overnight guests in commercial lodging establishments. Many other convention and visitor bureaus also count the membership fees paid by lodging facilities as a critical part of their operating budgets. Thus, the higher the occupancy rate, the higher the funding for the "destination marketing organisations," the collective term for agencies such as state travel bureaus and convention and visitors bureaus.

As the cultural community grew and gained cohesion in the 1970s (a result in part of the formation of the National Endowment for the Arts in 1965), some arts leaders began to realise that little was being done to attract tourist audiences to U.S. cultural institutions. They recognised that cultural icons such as the Louvre and the Sistine Chapel, and indeed culture in general, were a key selling points in European tourism marketing, and yet culture in America was not even on the tourist's radar screen.

As a result, in October 1980, the American Council for the Arts (an arts service organisation now known as Americans for the Arts), the Ontario Ministry of Culture, and the Ontario Ministry of Industry and Tourism convened a three-day conference, "The Arts and Tourism: A Profitable Partnership," in Toronto, Canada, to explore the potential for co-operative ventures. Attended by both cultural and tourism leaders, the conference examined European models, such as the Holland Culture Card, and considered ways in which the two industries could best work together (American Council for the Arts, 1981). The seed was planted.

Throughout the 1980s and into the 1990s, efforts began at the local and national levels to build awareness of and interest in cultural tourism. The National Trust for Historic Preservation, with support from the credit card company American Express, became a leader in this area, developing the first widely disseminated informational material on cultural tourism. States such as New York and New Jersey sponsored state-wide conferences on cultural tourism while cities as diverse as Austin, Texas and New Haven, Connecticut also explored possibilities.

By the time the 1995 White House Conference on Travel and Tourism was held in Washington, D.C., arts leaders were well energised to claim a seat at the tourism table. In preparation, a position paper entitled *Cultural Tourism in the United States* was developed by a consortium of organisations led by the National Endowment for the Arts, National Endowment for the Humanities, the Institute of Museum Services (now known as Institute of Museum and Library Services), and President's Committee on the Arts and the Humanities (NEA, n.d.). Garrison Keillor, host of the popular radio program, "A Prairie Home Companion," delighted the 1800 conference attendees with a luncheon speech that asserted, "All tourism is cultural tourism." Although only a handful of conference attendees represented non-profit cultural attractions, the resulting ten-point national travel and tourism strategy included the directive "The National Council of State Travel Directors should convene a series of regional Natural and Cultural Tourism Summits to identify conservation and management strategies to meet the unique needs of each region of the country," as its ninth priority action step. (Withers, 1995)

A series of five regional forums were held in 1996 and 1997 throughout the United States, co-ordinated by the American Association of Museums working with a consortium of other organisations known as "Partners in Tourism: Culture and Commerce." These forums brought together heads of state travel bureaus, convention and visitors bureaus, state arts and humanities councils, and individual arts organisations to examine how partnerships could be established.

Profile of the domestic cultural tourist

Although the potential of cultural tourism had captured the interest of some arts and tourism leaders, many were still not convinced of the significance of this market. Seeking to better understand these travellers, the Travel Industry Association of America (TIA), a trade association that represents the travel industry as a whole in the United States, directed its research department, the U.S. Travel Data Centre, to conduct a study in 1997 to identify cultural tourists. Their findings produced the first nation-wide profile of the domestic traveller who took part in a cultural activity or festival, or visited a museum or historic site as part of his/her trip (TIA, 1997).

For the first time, reliable statistics were available that compared the demographics and behaviours of travellers partaking in cultural activities with U.S. travellers in general. The findings confirmed previous "hunches" and provided important new insights as well. For example, the study provided a sense of the size of the cultural tourism market: in 1996, one-third of U.S. adults (a total of 65.9 million adults) reported taking a trip that included visiting a historic place or museum, or participating in a cultural event or festival. The report notes that "Of these [65.9 million] travellers, 10 million (5% of U.S. adults) said that interest in an historic place or museum prompted their travel, that is, was the primary reason for the trip. Similarly, 12.3 million travellers (6% of U.S. adults) said that interest in a cultural event or festival prompted their trip" (TIA, 1997).

The demographics of cultural tourists versus general tourists (see Table 1) show some slight differences. Cultural tourists tend to be slightly older, less likely to have children at home, better educated, and more apt to be retired. The demographic differences between the two groups, however, are not great. This seemingly innocuous finding is important because it negates the notion that arts- or heritage-oriented tourists are somehow a breed apart from the general tourist market. Tourism professionals could no longer dismiss cultural tourists as a peculiar group, intrinsically different from the markets they ordinarily serve.

Table 1   Historic/Cultural Travellers Compared to Total US Travellers Demographics of Head of Household

	Total US Travellers	Historic/Cultural Travellers
Average age	46 years	48 years
Children in Household	45%	41%
Completed College	52%	54%
Postgraduate Education	18%	21%
Employed Full-time	75%	72%
Managerial/Professional Occupation	41%	42%
Annual Household Income (Median)	$41,455	$42,133
Retired	15%	18%
Own Personal Computer	42%	44%

Source: Travel Industry Assn. of America, *Profile of Travellers Who Participate in Historic and Cultural Activities*, 1997

The TIA study examines cultural tourists' behaviours, and it is here that their differences with other travellers becomes striking (see Table 2). Pleasure is more likely to be the primary purpose of their trip, and on this trip, they will spend more money ($180 more per trip) and will stay longer (1.4 nights longer) than their general traveller counterparts. Further, this group is significantly more inclined to stay in a commercial establishment (14% more likely), and most importantly for this paper, the study shows that cultural tourists are 12% more likely to shop during their trip than are U.S. travellers in general.

Table 2   Historic/Cultural Travellers Compared to Total US Travellers

	Total US Travellers	Historic/Cultural Travellers
Primary Purpose of Tri		
Pleasure	67%	72%
Business	21%	17%
Other	12%	11%
Average Travel Party Size	1.9 people	2.0 people
Child on Trip	20%	21%
Group Tour	3%	7%
Average Length of Trip	3.3 nights	4.7 nights
Average Spent on Trip	$425	$615
Lodging Used (multiple responses)		
Hotel/Motel/B&B	42%	56%
Private home	33%	33%
Other	18%	17%
No overnight	18%	11%
Nights in hotel/Motel/B&B		
(average based on those answering)	3.3 nights	4.0 nights
Nights in Private Home		
(average based on those answering)	4.3 nights	5.6 nights
Shopping as trip activity	33%	45%
Average # of trip activities	1.8 activities	2.5 activities

Source: Travel Industry Assn. of America, *Profile of Travellers Who Participate in Historic and Cultural Activities*, 1997

Recognition of shopping as a tourism activity

Tourists love to shop, but in the United States the largest retailers have not always recognised this, and tourism professionals have been slow to capitalise on this propensity. For many years, retailers (except those in resorts or other tourism-dependent communities) viewed tourist shopping as "icing on the cake," a nice addition to the bottom line, but not an important part of their revenue mix. Similarly, destination promotion organisations were careful to mention the shopping opportunities their destinations offered, but shopping was not viewed as a prime attraction. Few tour operators specifically focused on shopping: perhaps the first shopping-specific tours were those organised in the 1980s to visit the outlet clothing stores in Reading, Pennsylvania where participants could shop for deeply discounted coats, dresses, shoes, lingerie items and more.

A major change came, however, when the 4.2 million square foot Mall of America opened in 1992 in Bloomington, Minnesota with more than 500 speciality retail shops, 49 restaurants and food outlets, eight night-clubs, a 14-screen movie theatre, and a seven-acre amusement park featuring 28 rides and attractions. Located in a state with a population of only 4.5 million people, the Mall needed to attract 40 million shoppers annually. The shopping centre clearly recognised that its success would lie in not only attracting a local market, but also in luring tourists to its shops.

Although the shops at the Mall of America were not unique, the convenience of finding so many desirable retailers was appealing – as was the novelty of the experience. (This emphasis on the "experience" of shopping would become increasingly important in the shopping centre industry, and indeed, Joseph Pine and James Gilmore argue in their book *The Experience Economy* that in the future, the most successful businesses will be those that create engaging experiences for their customers.) To lure tourists, the Mall developed an attractively priced, one-day shopping package program with Northwest Airlines in 1995 that included round-trip airfare from Detroit, Michigan to Minneapolis, Minnesota (a 1½ hour's flight), transportation between the airport and the Mall of America (only a trip of five minutes), and discount offers to a number of the Mall's shops.

Shopping as an integral part of the travel experience and as a travel motivator in and of its own right, however, still did not exist within the tourism industry, as demonstrated by the fact that only one shopping industry representative was invited to attend the historic 1995 White House Conference on Travel and Tourism. Shopping centre executives, however, were starting to recognise the value of tourist audiences. For example, The Taubman Company, owner/operator of some 25 premier shopping centres around the country began to create tourism packages in 1995 that featured overnight accommodations and special shopping offers. These packages were offered by five Taubman malls (Beverly Centre in Los Angeles; Cherry Creek in Denver; Biltmore Fashion Park in Phoenix, Arizona; Woodfield in Chicago; and The Mall at Short Hills in Short Hills, New Jersey) and marketed under the title "World Class Shopping" both to tour operators and individuals.

The shopping industry leaders who appreciated the potential of the shopping-tourism link began to recognise that they could reach tourist audiences more effectively by working collaboratively. Just as communities established destination marketing organisations, groups of shopping centre leaders banded together to form organisations to promote regional shopping. "Shop Arizona" was the first such shopping/tourism promotion agency, formed with the goal of promoting participating Arizona shopping centres to tour operators nationally and internationally. By 1998, a national organisation, "Shop America Alliance," had formed and held its first shopping and dining tourism summit outside of San Francisco, California. A tourism marketing co-operative organisation, Shop America Alliance serves its members by participating in many of the world's major travel trade marketplaces, producing promotional materials, and hosting educational programs.

Profile of the international cultural tourist/shopper

Seeking to learn more about the link between cultural tourism and shopping, The Taubman Company formed a Memorandum of Understanding in 1997 with the U.S. Department of Commerce, Tourism Industries office to formally engage in a custom analysis of the special characteristics of overseas travellers who engaged in shopping during their visit to the U.S. and also took part in cultural tourism and/or ethnic heritage tourism as part of their activities while in the United States (U.S. Department of Commerce, 1999).

According to the study, 24,194,000 overseas travellers whose residencies were outside the US visited the United States in 1997 for leisure or business purposes. Of these, 89% or 21,533,000 travellers, engaged in shopping as part of their visit experience. Within this group, the study researchers identified three sub-sets who took part in both shopping and cultural and/or ethnic heritage tourism activities during their U.S. visit: the "American Culturalist Shopper," the "Cultural Shopper," and the "Ethnic Shopper."

The "American Culturalist Shopper" was defined by the researchers as an overseas traveller who both shopped *and* participated in one of the following activities during his/her visit to the United States:

- Visited a Cultural Heritage Site

- Visited an Ethnic Heritage Site

- Visited at least two of the following:

    * Art gallery/museum

    * Concert/play/musical performance

    * American Indian community

    * Historical place

    * National park

The study found that one in three overseas visitors to the US in 1997, or 7,852,000 individuals, met this criteria.

The "Cultural Shopper" segment represents overseas travellers who shopped and visited a cultural heritage site during their visit. In 1997, this totalled 4,477,000 or 19% of overseas visitors to the United States.

The "Ethnic Shopper" sub-set includes travellers who took part in both shopping and visiting an ethnic heritage site during a U.S. visit. In 1997, this segment represented 1,190,000 or 5% of the overseas visitors to the United States.

The *Shopping and Cultural/Heritage Tourism* report findings are summarised below (see Table 3) and offer significant information about the behaviour of overseas travellers to the United States who shop and those who shop and take part in cultural/heritage tourism activities. The culturally inclined travellers (American Culturalist Shoppers, Cultural Shoppers, and Ethnic Shoppers) are much more likely to be visiting the United States on a vacation or holiday and tend to stay appreciably longer (5.4 to 6.1 nights longer) than do other shoppers. Like their domestic counterparts, international cultural tourists stay longer in commercial lodging establishments (1.2 to 1.7 nights longer) and spend more money during their trip ($36 to $191 more) than do other international shoppers. In terms of categories of spending, culturally oriented shoppers outspend other shoppers in every virtually every category except gift and souvenir purchases. (Although even here, culturally inclined tourists spent only $11 to $48 less than their more shopping oriented compatriots.)

Table 3   Shopping and Cultural/Heritage Tourism

	Shoppers	American Culturalist Shoppers	Cultural Shoppers	Ethnic Shoppers
Size of Shopping Markets				
to the US in 1997 (in thousands)	21533	7852	4477	1190
Trip Purpose: Vacation/Holiday	69%	80%	82%	84%
Trip Purpose: Business	27%	18%	17%	15%
Trip Purpose: Visiting Friends and Family	33%	41%	40%	35%
Travelled with Spouse	27%	33%	35%	40%
Travelled Alone	31%	29%	27%	24%
Travelled with Business Associates	10%	5%	6%	5%
Select Activities:				
Visit Cultural Heritage Site	21%	57%	100%	65%
Visit Historical Places	35%	75%	75%	69%
Visit an Art Gallery/Museum	20%	48%	45%	45%
Attend a Concert/Play/Musical	15%	32%	28%	24%
Visit National Parks	21%	47%	45%	47%
Sightseeing in Cities	47%	67%	69%	74%
Average Number of Destinations Visited	2.3	2.9	2.9	2.8
Average Number of Nights in US	15.2	21.3	20.6	21.2
Average Number of Nights in Hotel/Motel	7.7	9.4	9.0	8.9
Average Number of Nights				
in Private Home	17.7	21.0	19.2	25.3
Average Expenditures in US				
Per Visitor Per Trip	$1,593	$1,784	$1,629	$1,771
Expenditures Per Visitor Per Trip				
Lodging	$380	$433	$361	$526
Gifts and Souvenirs	$407	$396	$359	$360
Food and Beverage	$290	$357	$337	$374
Transportation	$219	$267	$257	$230

Source: U.S. Dept. of Commerce and The Taubman Company, *Shopping and Cultural/Heritage Tourism*, 1999

Linking cultural tourism and shopping

The findings of the TIA and the Department of Commerce/Taubman Company studies clearly show that culturally oriented travellers represent an appealing market for retailers. Other studies, conducted in conjunction with specific museum exhibitions, further reinforce this finding. For example, an economic impact study produced after "The Age of Rubens" exhibition held at The Toledo (Ohio) Museum of Art in 1994 report that 38% of the 126,327 non-tour group out-of-town visitors planned to go shopping as part of their visit experience. According to the report, these travellers spent an estimated $283,968 shopping outside the Museum during the three month (February through April) run of the exhibition (Brunner, 1994).

Similarly, the "Van Gogh's Van Goghs" exhibition, which took place at the Los Angeles County Museum of Art from January 17 through May 16, 1999, dramatically revealed the propensity of cultural tourists to shop. According a report on the economic impact of the exhibition, residents of the area who visited "Van Gogh's Van Goghs" spent $38.20 shopping while non-resident visitors spent $48.50, or 27% more. (These figures include expenditures made at the Museum as well as those made shopping elsewhere.) In all, exhibition attendees (both resident and non-resident) spent $14.2 million shopping. This represents 30% of all expenditures made in conjunction with the exhibition, the largest single category of expenditures (see Table 4). (Morey, 1999)

Table 4   Visitor Expenditures During the Van Gogh Exhibition

Total Expenditures	$48.5 million	100%
Shopping	$14,174,827	30%
Entertainment	$12,724,056	26%
Restaurants	$10,627,546	22%
Accommodations	$ 6,416,691	13%
Gasoline	$ 2,426,827	5%
Car Rental	$ 1,575,522	3%
Groceries	$ 527,707	1%

Source: Morey and Associates, Economic Impact Analysis of the Los Angeles County Museum of Art and the Van Gogh Exhibition, 1999

World class shopping, The Taubman Company

With figures such as these, it was hard to overlook the potential offered by linking cultural attractions and shopping. The Taubman Company already had a sense of this potential, as evidenced by its willingness to co-sponsor the *Shopping and Cultural/Heritage Tourism* study with the U.S. Department of Commerce, Tourism Industries office. By 1997, the shopping centre giant had become the first in its industry to actively incorporate cultural attractions into its shopping tourism packages. Biltmore Fashion Park, The Taubman Company shopping centre in Phoenix, Arizona offered a World Class Shopping package that included overnight accommodations in a nearby deluxe hotel, discounted admission tickets to the Heard Museum (an institution focusing on Native American culture), and a handsome shopping tote bag filled with special offers for discounts and gifts at a number of the mall stores. In Denver, The Taubman shopping centre Cherry Creek offered a holiday shopping package in 1998 that featured "the best that Denver has to offer." "The best" included complimentary tickets to the Denver Zoo, Denver Museum of Natural History, the Denver Botanical Gardens and the Denver Art Museum. To sweeten the pot even further, Beverly Centre, The Taubman Company mall in Los Angeles, negotiated a special relationship with the nearby Los Angeles County Museum of Art for its "Picasso: Masterworks from The Museum of Modern Art" exhibition in 1998. In this World Class Shopping package, the purchaser received special VIP tickets to the exhibition that provided immediate entry into the exhibit, thereby avoiding the sometimes lengthy wait to enter that ordinary ticket holders faced.

By 1999, The Taubman Company was starting to build a seamless connection between some of its centres and their local cultural attractions through its promotional activities on the Internet. The web site for its Norfolk, Virginia mall, MacArthur Centre, (www.shopmacarthur.com) includes listings for more than 50 area attractions (virtually all cultural) in Norfolk and the neighbouring communities of Hampton, Newport News, Portsmouth, Virginia Beach, and Williamsburg. These cultural attraction listings, for such organisations as the Virginia Stage Company, the Virginia Symphony, Virginia Ballet, and Hampton Roads Naval Museum, appear in a special "Tourist Information" section of the web site and include hyperlinks to obtain additional information about each attraction.

Two interesting points emerge from The Taubman Company's World Class Shopping packages and its Internet promotional activities. The first is that the promotion of cultural attractions by The Taubman Company represented an emerging new attitude among shopping centre managers. Traditionally, retailers have single-mindedly focused on promoting themselves and their merchandise. The Taubman Company, however, recognised that although shopping was the number one activity of tourists, it was not their only activity. Travellers like to visit attractions (cultural and otherwise) and see the "sights" as well as shop. Thus, by actively promoting non-mall-related attractions as part of its marketing strategy, The Taubman Company demonstrated a keen understanding of its target market and a new sensibility among shopping centre operators. Interestingly, the cultural attractions listed in The Taubman Company websites do not seem to have achieved the same level of marketing sophistication for their websites contain no links back to The Taubman Company shopping centre sites.

The second point reflects the basic contention of this article that combining culture and shopping with tourism represents a profitable connection. The Taubman Company clearly recognised that the affiliation with cultural attractions was to its benefit. Given all the tourism attractions available for partnership, The Taubman Company strategically chose to partner with cultural attractions in its World Class Shopping packages. The increasing number of World Class Shopping packages offered by The Taubman Company shopping centres testifies to the success of the program.

Spree – ultimate shopping excursions, urban retail properties

In 1998, Urban Retail Properties, another major shopping centre owner/operator, introduced an exciting new shopping/culture/tourism product that utilises state-of-the-art technology to provide users with shopping, lodging, dining and entertainment discounts as well customised tourism itineraries. The goal of the Spree – Ultimate Shopping Excursions program is to drive shopper/tourists to ten Urban Retail Properties in prime tourism destinations (Boston, Chicago, Memphis, San Francisco, Tampa, and Orange County, CA).

The centrepiece of the program is the Spree card, a credit card-like vehicle with a magnetic strip that enables users to obtain discounts in the participating Urban Retail Properties malls along with discounts at a dizzying array of participating hotels, restaurants and attractions. To obtain the card, shopper/tourists need to visit the Spree website (www.myspree.com), where all ten participating shopping centres are listed. Upon selecting a city or shopping centre, the site functions as a virtual travel advisor, providing the shopper/tourist with maps and activity information that can be used to build a personalised itinerary.

The Spree – Ultimate Shopping Excursions program is impressive because of its scale and the multitude of discounted tourism opportunities it offers users. For example, for Water Tower Place in Chicago, the website provides special offers for 27 mall shops and 21 other tourism facilities (hotels, restaurants, museums, and other attractions) along with visitor information about 12 area hotels, 52 restaurants, 14 museums, and 20 attractions. Among the offers available to Spree users are 10% off purchases made at the Chicago Historical Society store, 20% off a ticket purchase for a Chicago Neighbourhood Tour, and two-for-the-price-of-one tickets to the Adler Planetarium.

The program is also impressive because of the accountability it offers Urban Retail Properties. Each Spree card is registered to a specific user and as the shopper/tourist claims a discount or special offer, the card is "swiped" and the transaction is recorded by the merchant or tourism partner. This enables Urban Retail Properties and its tourism partners to reliably track the success of the program and the preferences of the shopper/tourists. This information will enable Urban Retail Properties to build an impressive database that can be used for highly sophisticated targeted marketing in the future.

For the purposes of this paper, the Spree program is interesting because of its customisable itinerary component. Urban Retail Properties, like The Taubman Company, recognised that travellers want to partake in a variety of experiences, sightseeing and dining for example, as well as shopping, and so for each participating shopping centre, the Spree program provides a wealth of entertainment information. In this way, the Spree program differs from the World Class Shopping program because it demonstrates no preference for cultural attractions. But, by enabling its shopper/tourists to create their own itineraries, the Spree program is subtly encouraging these travellers to go out and experience Chicago – to discover what makes this city unique and gives it a sense of place. For some, that sense of place may come from going to a White Sox baseball game or visiting the Chicago Mercantile Exchange. For others, taking a Chicago Neighbourhood Tour or visiting the Chicago Art Institute may provide a sense of place. By supporting these explorations, the Spree – Ultimate Shopping Excursions program is actually encouraging cultural tourism.

The craft heritage trails of Western North Carolina, HandMade in America

In sharp contrast to the high-tech sophistication of the Spree program is the tourism initiative undertaken by HandMade in America, a non-profit organisation dedicated to preserving the quality of life in the western region of North Carolina while broadening its economic base. Although much of North Carolina experienced explosive growth and economic expansion in 1980s and 1990s, the western part of the state, dominated by the hills and hollows of the Smokey and Blue Ridge Mountains and the area's numerous waterfalls and cascades, was economically depressed. Looking for strategies to reverse the dismal economic situation, regional leaders took stock of their strengths. The area had a long, proud tradition of creating handcrafted items – pottery, paper, textiles, and furniture. In the mid-1990s, the region was home to some 4,000 full- or part-time artisans, along with some the nation's finest craft schools. Furthermore, an economic impact study conducted in 1994 revealed that craft-related activities generated in excess of $122 million in North Carolina. The decision was made to face the future by returning to the past: HandMade in America would work to revitalise the economy by establishing western North Carolina as the geographic centre for handmade objects in America (Anderson, 1996).

Among its strategies to do this, HandMade in America turned to tourism. The dollars spent by tourists in purchasing handcrafted items, as well on accommodations and dining, could significantly stimulate the local economy and provide an important source of new jobs. Working with representatives from over 20 counties, HandMade in America co-ordinated an effort to establish craft heritage trails throughout the mountains and valleys of the area. These figurative "trails" led through towns and villages where a visitor could discover the heritage of the area, as represented by its handcrafted traditions. To attract the public to the area, HandMade in America published a guidebook in 1996 entitled *The Craft Heritage Trails of Western North Carolina.* This handsomely, yet simply, designed handbook laid out seven self-guided driving tours throughout the region that offer much more than an opportunity to shop for quality craft objects. As the introduction says,

> "This is more than a simple guidebook to craft. It is the story of people. People whose lives are coloured by their art and whose art colours the lives of anyone who comes to know their work. And where are these people? They're 'down the road a piece' or 'round the bend' or 'within shoutin' distance.' And they're in this book."

Each tour in the book has a theme – "High Country Ramble" and "Farm to Market," for example – and each tour includes not only shops where authentic American and North Carolinian craft items are sold, but also restaurants and accommodations that continue the focus on an authentic experience. The criteria for inclusion in the guide state that:

- Studios have dependable times for guests to visit

- Galleries have a focus on objects made in the U.S.A., particularly North Carolina

- Restaurants have a reputation for fine food and feature dishes indigenous to the region

- Inns and bed and breakfasts have a historical underpinning and an architecture that, in and of itself, bespeaks craft

- Scores of photos of hand-woven mats, homespun textiles, imaginative pottery, whimsical and functional furniture, and other craft items enliven the guide's pages and whet a tourist's acquisitive interest while folksily written sidebars provide insights into the folklore and history of this creative region. Brief essays provide a deeper look into certain aspects of the area, such as "The Blue Ridge Parkway, The First Rural Parkway in the U.S." and Penland School, an internationally renowned crafts center. The profile of 80+ year-old Floyd Rose, custodian of the 1915 Climax steam train at the Cradle of Forestry, prompts a desire to "set a spell" and chat.

The Craft Heritage Trails of Western North Carolina fulfilled its mission. As the pace of technology quickened in the waning years of the 20th century, the appeal for a simpler life, a handmade –not mass-produced – object, and an authentic – not virtual – experience became greater. The book received extensive media coverage in such media outlets as *USA Today*, *The Wall Street Journal*, and the *Sunday Morning* television program on CBS, among many other outlets. Its initial print run of 25,000 copies sold out in less than 2 years and a second edition of the guide was printed in 1998.

In this instance, the shopping/culture/tourism connection was initiated by people as concerned with maintaining a way of life as with increasing earned income. The founders of the craft heritage trails worked diligently with community members to identify those attractions and businesses (shops, restaurants, etc.) they wished to share with the travelling public and those they did not want to promote to tourists, but rather keep privately to themselves. The basic tenets of cultural tourism – the emphasis on authenticity and the quality of the experience – formed the foundation of HandMade in America's tourism marketing product, *The Craft Heritage Trails of Western North Carolina*. The result was a program that perhaps did not sell as much merchandise as a retail marketing professional might have liked, but that preserved the integrity of the region and heritage of its residents.

Conclusion

Although cultural attractions and shopping were for many years not recognised as important components in the tourism industry, today their status is clear. Recent studies have demonstrated that cultural tourists are a particularly appealing target market for retailers and some shopping centre executives have acted upon this knowledge to create travel packages that carry great appeal for culturally oriented travellers. The participation of cultural organisations in these packages reflects a significant evolution in the thinking of both retailers and cultural leaders. Both were formerly self-focused in their marketing endeavours, but increasingly, both sectors are realising that they share target markets and can enhance their success by working together.

The shopping/culture/tourism programs noted above all reflect the values and perspectives of their creators. The Taubman Company's World Class Shopping program features packages with pre-determined components. The non-mall elements include cultural attractions because cultural tourists have a demonstrated propensity to shop and shopping is clearly the focus of the program. Spree – Ultimate Shopping Excursions was designed to drive quantities of travellers to participating Urban Retail Properties and hence, it features the most sophisticated marketing system and offers a wide variety of entertainment opportunities, of which cultural attractions are a part. Although shopping is clearly the goal of this initiative, the Spree program emphasises marketing the destination and encouraging an exploration of it. HandMade in America's tourism program, on the other hand, reflects the sensibilities of an organisation committed equally to preserving a way of life as to economic development. While shopping, dining, and staying overnight are certainly goals of HandMade in America's tourism initiative, sharing a taste of the history and heritage of the Blue Ridge and Smokey Mountain area is also a fundamental goal.

The examples cited in this paper could be considered as points along a continuum. One continuum that comes to mind is that of implementation: the programs described here range from the extremely simple to the incredibly complex. At one end is the Taubman Company World Class Shopping package, with its basic discounted hotel, attraction, and shopping components. At the other end is the Urban Retail Properties Spree program, with personalised, bar-coded cards and a highly sophisticated Internet presence. Another way of viewing these examples is along a continuum of character. At one end is the Mall of America, an artificially created attraction with shopping as the focus. At the other end is HandMade in America's guidebook, which reveals and markets an authentic community, using heritage and shopping as the gateway experiences. All the various options along these continuums should be considered as retail, cultural, and tourism professionals continue to create new shopping/culture/tourism products.

References

Books

American Council for the Arts (1981), *The Arts & Tourism: A Profitable Partnership*, American Council for the Arts, New York, NY.

Brunner, J. (1994), *The Age of Rubens: A Study of the Exhibition's Economic Impact and the Characteristics of Its Visitors*, University of Toledo, Toledo.

Fields, J. and Campbell, B. (1996), *The Craft Heritage Trails of Western North Carolina*, HandMade in America, Asheville, NC.

Pine II, B. J. and Gilmore, J. (1999), *The Experience Economy: Work is Theatre & Every Business A Stage*, Harvard Business School Press, Boston, MA.

Travel Industry Association of America [TIA](1997), *Profile of Travellers Who Participate in Historic and Cultural Activities*, Travel Industry Association of America, Washington, D.C.

U.S. Department of Commerce and The Taubman Company (1999), *Shopping and Cultural/Heritage Tourism: A Special Study of Overseas Travellers to the United States*, U.S. Department of Commerce, Washington, D.C.

Articles

Anderson, B. (1996), A Profile of HandMade in America, *Building Social Trust*, Spring, pp. 6 – 11.

Other

Morey and Associates (1999), *Economic Impact Analysis of the Los Angeles County Museum of Art and the Van Gogh Exhibition*, (unpublished report).

National Endowment for the Arts [NEA], National Endowment for the Humanities, Institute of Museum Services, President's Committee on the Arts and the Humanities (n.d.), *Cultural Tourism in the United States: A Position Paper for the White House Conference on Travel and Tourism*, American Association of Museums, Washington, D.C. (pamphlet).

Virginia Department of Historic Resources (n.d.), *Tourism Handbook: Putting Virginia's History to Work*, Virginia Department of Historic Resources, Richmond, VA (pamphlet).

Travel Industry Association of America [TIA] (2000), *Fast Facts*, www.tia.org/press/fastfacts3.stm (website).

Withers, P., editor (1995), *National Travel and Tourism Strategy: White House Conference on Travel and Tourism*, Washington, D.C. (pamphlet).

Conservation, authenticity and tourism: Syria's emerging problems

Barry G Rowney

Adelaide University, Australia

Heritage conservation and tourism are allied disciplines in the preservation and presentation of both ancient and recent cultures. The concept of authenticity is essential to both if the correct identity of the culture and its physical evidence is to be manifest. Syria, as a country emerging into the world of tourism is taken as an example, illustrating current problems in both conservation and tourism, and how these disciplines can be mutually compatible, and be the vehicle for the understanding and promotion of authentic culture and its built environment.[1]

Introduction

Syria, as a country of considerable antiquity, has a significant collection of archaeological sites and ancient and traditional urban centres, so it could be expected that it would attract the interest of archaeologists, conservation experts and tourism companies. (Figure. 1) Archaeologists have been attracted, and there has been almost continual archaeological activity during the 20th C. The conservation of it's archaeological sites and historic urban centres has been slower to gain acceptance. Although the country has always been open to tourists, organised tourism on a large scale has only gathered momentum since the beginning of the 1990s. This has given rise to several factors: that major tourist sites are relatively free from exploitation which can arise from tourist activity (such as that of Egypt), and that the culture of Syria has seemingly remained intact without the pressures and influences of both tourism and conservation.

Figure 1   Map of Syria

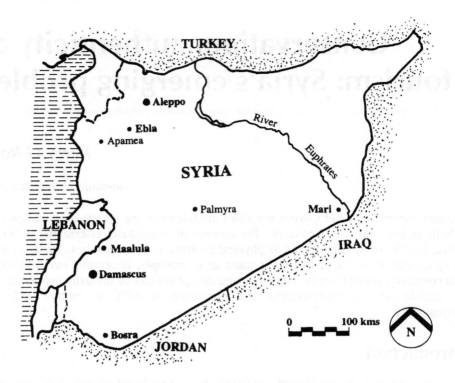

Heritage conservation and tourism are closely allied in several respects – they both have an interest in the understanding and presentation of past and present cultures, through the retention and presentation of the historic environment and artefacts. More importantly, both attempt to present the true understanding of these cultures through the authenticity of the displayed evidence.

In this paper two specific areas of concern are canvassed: in the case of archaeological sites – the over-emphasis of the visual aspects of a site to the exclusion of it's real significance; and in the case of present-day urban centres – the desire to present a predetermined historical image, resulting in the presentation of their heritage as a museum production, thereby denying the inhabitants the necessary opportunity of normal cultural development.

Authenticity has been chosen as a pivotal point in this discussion, even though it's use and understanding is complex. Recognised as an essentially western concept (the Arabic language has no equivalent word for authenticity) and specifically Eurocentric,[2] it has formed the basis of conservation philosophy and action, even though its acceptance has often been taken for granted (Jokilehto, 1995. p.17). It has been an important concept in conservation, from the exhortations of John Ruskin to its codification in the various conservation charters, e.g. the Venice Charter. With the increasing realisation of cultural differences, the conservation charters have been criticised for their approach which place great emphasis on the authenticity of the physical historic fabric, and often ignoring other significant cultural aspects, such as the intangible processes associated in a traditional, functional technical, and artisanal context.

Authenticity in archaeology

Authenticity in relation to archaeology has its own specific problems. As a scientific discipline, archaeology is concerned with the collection of information which will reveal the secrets of an ancient site and lead to the understanding of the society and it's culture. There is generally no problem with the authenticity of the physical fabric of the site, except that gaining this information also has the potential to destroy it. Also, if the evidence is of considerable artifactual significance, it will be removed to a museum storage for possible later presentation under controlled conditions. Conservation of the remaining site evidence then presents physical as well as philosophical problems in the authenticity of the final product. To this must be added the presentation of the site to the public in conveying the correct message, and thereby imposing further difficulties in the understanding of its authenticity.

Syria's archaeological sites

Syria has been the arena for the life and death of many ancient civilisations reaching back over 6000 years. From early biblical times when it formed a vital part in the political life of the "fertile crescent" which stretched from Ur in present-day Iraq, north into Turkey, and swept down to present day Israel, this land rich in minerals, agriculture and timber, was strategically placed to house several major centres of political power reaching throughout the whole Middle East. Syria has also played a major role in the formation of two of the world's largest religions, Christianity and Islam, and hence it is not surprising that it has a wealth of archaeological and cultural sites as well as major historical urban centres and buildings.

The lack of conservation (or its mismanagement) of archaeological sites has brought it's own problems, but it is only in the latter half of the twentieth century. that conservation has been considered an essential adjunct to normal archaeological activity. The earlier practice of ignoring conservation during the course of an archaeological dig points to the philosophical attitude of archaeologists that once the site was fully excavated and all the information recorded, there was no longer any reason to retain the evidence. With the acceptance by present day archaeologists that the gathering of all information cannot be assured, conservation of the site is now accepted. But even-so, the method of conservation may not be in accordance with tourism objectives.

In the following examples, it will be seen that there are concerns regarding both conservation action and tourism expectations, both in the manner in which they interact and occasionally when their objectives clash.

Mari   (Tell Hariri)

The present-day far-flung position of Mari be-lies it's original pivotal significance as the political centre of Mesopotamia and upper Syria during the Early to Middle Bronze Age. Beginning c.2900 BCE, it went through a series of upheavals and periods of power, until it's final demise in 1757 BCE. It's significance lies in its substantial archive of Babylonian cuneiform tablets (Burns, 1992. p.150), supplying a major source of political, economic and social information.

Today, Mari is known mainly through its widely published plan of the so-called Palace of Zimri-Lim (Figure 2). This was one of the most impressive and best preserved palaces of the Early Bronze Age to be unearthed in Syria, constructed mostly of mud-brick. It was not only extensive in plan but impressively tall, some remaining walls reaching 5 metres in height (Bahnassi, 1989. p.227).

Figure 2   The Usually published Palace of Zimri-Lim at Mari showing the myriad of rooms – 90% of which no longer exist

0   50 m

Excavations began in 1933 under the French archaeologist André Parrot and continued under his direction until his death in 1974. Excavations have been continued by the French since that time. Sadly, and contrary to the descriptions given in the several popular tourist books, only a small group of rooms - approximately 10 rooms of the formerly extensive 275 rooms - exist under an open shelter of metal framing and pyramidal plastic roofing. The rest of the extensive remains are now gone. Burns claims that the mud-brick remains, which ". . . have been successively peeled off to expose the preceding layers beneath, are difficult to appreciate" (Burns, 1992. p.149). However, an official opinion is that the ruins have been lost to the ravages of wind and rain (Bahnassi, 1989. p.227). The remaining 10 rooms are impressive in their height and material (the mud brick construction can be easily appreciated), but, with the exception of Bahnassi, the information given in the tourist books refers only to the original extensive palace, and the visitor is not prepared for the much depleted exhibit. Nevertheless the site is still a tourist destination, even though most of the expected palace ruins can no longer be appreciated.

Ebla (Tell Mardikh)

Excavations began at Ebla in 1964 by an Italian team headed by Paolo Matthiae, but it was not until 1975 and again in 1978 that the major archives were found which rocketed Ebla into world recognition and controversy. The archives produced in excess of 14000 clay tablets recorded in Akkadian cuneiform writing in a hitherto unknown language now referred to as Eblaite (Matthiae, 1997. p.151).[3] The translation of these tablets has progressed slowly, but the early translations, amounting only to approximately 600 tablets, identified Ebla as a major centre in the Early Bronze Age period, reaching it's peak c2400 - 2250 BCE, and revealed it's inter-relationships with other kingdoms and city states in this notable area of the fertile crescent. The present-day significance of Ebla now focuses on the translation of these tablets, as their information has already changed the previously accepted Bronze Age history of the Middle East, and Syria in particular (Burns, 1992. p.119. See also Matthiae, 1997. Bermant et al. 1979. and Wilson, 1979).

The controversy centres around the interpretation of the tablets as "proving" certain Biblical stories, particularly the Genesis tales concerning Abraham and Ishmael, and referring to, and therefore vindicating, the existence of the "Five Cities of the Plain" including the infamous towns of Sodom and Gomorra (Wilson, 1979. p.36). Although Matthiae has gone to great pains to refute these assumptions, the arguments and counter-arguments have never been resolved. However, in spite of this notoriety there is little on the ground to illustrate this aspect of Ebla's significance. Burns (1992) states that "This may be one of the most important Bronze Age sites discovered since the Second World War but it yields few of it's secrets to the naked eye." The mud-brick ruins, although extensive and interesting in their sculptural forms cannot convey to the viewer the sites true significance. Bahnassi does not refer to either the controversial interpretations of the tablets, nor does he comment on the ruins of the site or their condition. Never-the-less, the site is included on tourist routes, and draws many visitors. Perhaps this gives some indication of the interest which can be engendered in associated evidence - to see the very place where the physical traces relating to the ephemeral arguments were found (if the arguments are known).

The Italian team has implemented a conservation program aimed at preventing the mud-brick walls from deteriorating by rendering them in weak plaster. In one way, weak plaster is a good choice, as it allows easy removal should further investigation become necessary, and, being weaker than the mud-brick, will not present the danger of structural incompatibility. However, although re-presenting a similar finish to the walls as the original finish - and some remnants of the original plaster can be seen under a protective roof, the lack of interpretation information confuses the understanding of these original buildings. Some believe that this new plaster is the original plaster, and others expect to see the mud-brick construction, even though the construction and finishes are not specifically described in the guide books.[4] The current presentation is a picturesque vernacular style hand-plastered finish, which unfortunately has areas of plaster now spalling off due to it's weak mix, and hence negating it's purpose. This program will require constant maintenance - a situation which, unless the Italian team continues in the future, the Syrian authorities will find a constant drain on their resources.

Discussion on Mari and Ebla

Apart from the obvious problems with conservation on both these sites, presentation to the tourist can also be called into question. The desire for authenticity in conservation has moved into the sphere of cultural tourism, where the demand for an authentic experience is becoming paramount in both archaeological sites and present-day sites. The desire for the understanding of ancient civilisations draws the tourist to experience first hand the evidence of ancient cities. But it becomes apparent in the case of Ebla or Mari that tourist visitation is based on visual qualities and that the less tangible form of the real significance is not conveyed. The fascination of experiencing the very place of the major steps in the history of the expanding culture of the human race, such as the evolution of writing systems as shown in the logographic system of both Mari and Ebla could transcend merely visual interest if presented in an imaginative way.

But criticism should also be aimed at the conservation industry. What experiences and information can be gained from the mish-mash of remaining evidence following excavation and the clumsy attempts at conservation? The deterioration of the palace at Mari has not only destroyed the chance of further study of four and a half thousand years evidence, but has depleted a significant site for the better understanding of this palace and its context by the tourist.

The answer to the conservation problems of both Mari and Ebla is back-filling. This has a double advantage: first the deterioration of the fabric would be arrested and would require no maintenance, and second, the evidence of the fabric would be retained for further study should archaeological techniques improve in the future. However, back-filling is not considered an option by the tourist industry,[5] as there appears to be a perceived desire by tourists to visit these sites even though the realisation of the full extent of their significance is not presented nor appreciated. This may be due simply to the desire to see ancient ruins for their own sake, or it may be that the tourist promoters require such sites for a viable tourist industry, whether or not a reliable and correct account of the significance of the site is presented. In either or any case the deterioration of these sites should not be allowed to continue simply because of the tourist dollar. Rather, the tourist industry should attempt to convey the correct message of the sites' significance, and also take some of the responsibility for the conservation of these sites or leave them well alone so that correct remedial action can be taken.

Cultural authenticity

In the above examples authenticity is only concerned with the physical remains, and the ancient society no longer exists. The problems of authenticity are greatly compounded when the site is a continuing traditional urban centre with a vital living society, and where the ever-changing and developing culture is a necessary factor for its dynamic continuance. It is this living dynamism which is largely responsible for the existence of the present-day society, and should ensure that this society will continue to develop and not stagnate. It has been recognised that this continuing development, as an essential ingredient of historic towns and centres throughout the world, renders the assessment of their authenticity more difficult (van Droste et al, 1995. p.5). But nevertheless it is this very dynamism which brings the mantel of authenticity to the life of the society and its culture, and consequently to its built environment.

Culture must develop, and the built environment will develop with it. This brings the paradox, that development could lead to a loss of historic fabric, being the evidence of this continuing growth and development and hence the need for conservation, which in the eyes of many would mean freezing the historic environment and restricting development. The danger lies in the desire to retain all of the former historic fabric and seeing new development as being anachronistic, spoiling the history and its accepted aesthetics, and thereby stultifying the genuine development process. Conservation is not just preservation but includes development, and hence is a delicate balancing act. In addition, continual creation and development of new forms is the fundamental essence of the evolutionary process and vital for the continuing growth of a living culture. But, as stated by Jokilehto at the NARA Conference on Authenticity (1995), "...even in countries where the physical cultural heritage acquires importance, the non-physical heritage remains the essence of the quality of life, as a basis for the understanding and appreciation of the physical patrimony, and for the continuation of traditional crafts and technologies required for it's maintenance and care."

Maintaining the authenticity of the culture should be the first objective of conservation, for when this is achieved the conservation of its built environment will be assured. The reverse is not necessarily true - that conserving the built environment will ensure the continuation of the culture - for unless the inhabitants are integrated into the decision making processes throughout the full course of the project the built environment will not be the true reflection of the culture and hence will not be authentic.

Tourism and urban conservation

Cultural tourism presents the tourist with an understanding of cultural life in both ancient and present-day exotic places, and therefore relies on authentic experiences for its credibility. But the interaction of tourism and urban conservation has in the past resulted in an uneasy alliance. The growing interest in cultural tourism has long been recognised by conservationists, but earlier concerns regarding it's adverse affects on heritage sites tended to obscure it's potential benefits.

The impact of tourism on fragile historic and traditional centres was cautioned as early as 1978, when ICOMOS (International Council on Monuments and Sites) initiated its International Specialised Committee on Tourism for action and the eventual production of it's Charter of Cultural Tourism. The concerns expressed at that time were that tourism, as "... an irrefutable social, human, economic and cultural fact" was likely to "... exert significant influence on Man's environment in general and on monuments and sites in particular, "and that"... as a result of widespread uncontrolled misuse of monuments and sites, exploitative and destructive effects [could] not be disassociated from it." Further comments referred to "..tourism's anarchical growth which would result in the denial of it's own objectives." The positive impact of tourism was conceded in-so-far as it contributed to the maintenance and protection of monuments and sites, even though it was thus seen to satisfy it's own ends. The Charter concluded that the intention was to respect the authenticity and diversity of the cultural values in developing regions and countries.

The most recent charter issued by ICOMOS on cultural tourism approaches the conservation/tourism alliance with much greater optimism. It shows a clear attempt to accept tourism for it's benefits and recognises the need for mutual co-operation. For such an approach to be successful it is imperative that conservation and tourism have mutually agreed aims and objectives. However, the emphasis lies towards tourism to the extent that it almost implies that the reason for conservation is tourism. The principle that conservation should facilitate personal access and interpretation programmes engenders the feeling that conservation is only appropriate for tourism purposes. The danger in this charter is that tourism may become the *raison d'être* for conservation. Although the charter presents principles for the protection of cultural heritage characteristics the following warnings sounded by Cantacuzino (1997) at the Sofia Symposium should be heeded: "It is a truism that an excess of cultural tourism becomes a threat to the cultural heritage....Much of this heritage, especially the vernacular, is fragile and will not stand up to mass tourism over a long time. So tourism must be adapted to the heritage and not the other way round."

In line with similar developments around the world, particularly in those countries wishing to reaffirm their national identity in the face of increasing globalisation, the conservation of the traditional built environment has become a priority. In similar fashion the conservation of vernacular villages has been widely recognised as an expression of true national identity (Oliver, 1997. p.xxiii). Conservation is seen in this context to be not only the means of preserving the physical evidence of this identity but also ensuring the continuing life and development of the society and its culture.

Bosra

Bosra is situated 140 km. south of Damascus close to the Jordanian border. It contains extensive remains of the Nabatean, Roman, Byzantine and Arabic civilisations. It's greatest relic is the Roman theatre, being one of the most well preserved theatres from the Roman period, and of further importance as it is encapsulated within an Arabic fortress. The rest of the Roman ruins are quite extensive, and their condition varies from good to incomprehensible. Within the Roman wall which bounds the site lie several significant Byzantine church ruins and even more significant very early Islamic mosques.

Tourist books devote several pages to this site, carefully detailing the many and varied sites. However, what has failed to be recorded is the current lifestyle of a small group of the Bosra population. Many families live among the Roman ruins along the main axis road. Steps from the original road surface to the upper "footpath" still overlaid with column drums and capitals, lead to humble houses tucked among the Roman walls. The local people are still using the ancient structures as the foundation for their habitation. This, however, has not caught the imagination of the various travel book writers, who tend to concentrate on the recognisable ruins and antiquities. The local residents and their culture are ignored.

The continuation of the occupation of a Roman site is a fascinating phenomenon. In other such sites any incidence of "squatter" occupation would be cleaned out in order to present an archaeologically "pure" Roman site. Syria already has several excellent Roman sites: Palmyra – one of the most extensive sites in the ancient Roman world – and Apamea – another extensive and well presented example of ancient Roman ruins. But Bosra has the potential to present a site with two significant factors beyond the usual Roman ruins presentation: one - a Roman theatre encapsulated in a mediaeval fortress, and the other - a Roman site still in continuing occupation.

And speaking of continual occupation brings us to the next example:

Maalula

Maalula is a small village 60 km north of Damascus. Burns (1992. p.145) states that "though rich in historical associations, Maalula preserves only a few remains of it's past." This illustrates the bias of the writer towards perceived tourist and archaeological interests in ancient sites.

The significance of this vernacular village lies in it's cultural roots reaching back to Pre-Christian times which is manifest in the inhabitants still speaking Aramaic - the common language of Biblical times. They remain one of the very few groups (a few communities in the north-east of Syria also speak a form of neo-Aramaic, descendant from Persia or Iraq) which have continued with this language, showing a tenacity to their early Aramaean/Christian culture in the face of an overwhelming Arabic culture and language.

In the case of their built heritage, the houses are equally fascinating, illustrating the community's troglodytic beginnings by forming their houses in caves in the steep limestone cliffs. The development of these dwellings took the form of flat facades being constructed on the front of these caves, and as time moved on, further extensions were built to the front of these facades. Today many of these dwellings remain, still retaining their early cave rooms deep in the confines of these houses. Some of the early cave houses are more easily recognised than others from the exterior.

Having visited Maalula in 1966 and again in 1995 and 1999, the extent of the retention of these houses is quite apparent. But since 1966 the old Greek Orthodox Monastery of *Mar Taqla* (St Thecla) and several churches and chapels, all illustrating the strong Christian commitment of the community, have completely gained the attention of the tourist industry. That specific part of the culture of the inhabitants, their language and their houses, has slipped into unspoken oblivion. The unseen significance of the continued use of the Aramaic language is given passing mention in a few tourist books, whereas the continuing traditional development of the ancient housing system of caves with their built facades ranks no mention at all. Recognising that this retention of the language and the housing system exemplifies a continuing culture reaching back 2000 years, it's omission from the tourist guides is unforgivable.

It is rumoured that the use of the Aramaic language is declining in Maalula,[6] and this may well be the attitude of the younger generation being influenced by what the tourist industry, as representing outside and hence "modern" opinion, sees as not being important. Whatever the reason, it is interesting to note that the decline in the use of the language is in parallel with the development of new housing in the form of large modern apartment blocks on the edges of the village, indicating the change in the traditional built culture is concomitant with the change of the traditional spoken culture.

Discussion of Bosra and Maalula

An issue confronting the conservationist when studying a site is identifying just what *is* considered to be significant. On this issue hangs the whole approach to the conservation action. Suffice to say that in the past a great deal of important information and historical evidence has been lost to the world because those responsible for recording and implementing conservation action have failed to appreciate the real significance of the site. This is a matter of opinion residing in the attitude and opinion of the assessor. The presentation of sites in the tourist guides is formed by what the writer considers will be of interest to the tourist. This is clearly shown in the examples of Bosra and Maalula. Surely the understanding of a society and it's culture is an essential element in the understanding of an authentic cultural experience.

An excellent example of this exists in Maalula, where the decline of the Aramaic language and the growth of new housing could be presented to the tourist which would highlight the significance of the old language and place it in context with the evolving culture. This developing cultural experience would be of greater impact than merely visiting the monastery of *Mar Taqla*.

Damascus and Aleppo

In traditional urban areas such as Damascus and Aleppo, one can see (if one has the eyes) the continuing traditions and culture and the concomitant evidence in the built environment. These centres have been in residential and commercial use for over several thousand years, and their on-going legacy has been assured by their placement in the geography of the country, and their ability to develop as necessary to meet new requirements. That the physical means of change have been comparatively slow and always steeped in traditional methods of construction has meant that the changes have maintained a solid character which denotes the particular city. Both traditional centres contain ancient monuments, but more importantly they continue to house their dynamic societies with their distinctive cultures, dramatically illustrated by their well-knit building fabric. It is only in the last half of this century that development has assumed Western forms of design and construction, and some at such speed that is shown in alarming changes to the traditional fabric and character.

Damascus lays claim to being the oldest continuously inhabited city in the world. Situated on a large oasis the settlement has a history reaching back to at least the fourth millennium BCE. Much of the ancient city walls remain together with their seven Roman gates, and two Arabic gates. The city was consolidated into a coherent town plan during the Hellenistic period, and it is remarkable that this basic plan exists to the present day, despite the many wars and civil upheavals the city has suffered. Each layer of history has left it's mark on the city, and the expansion of modern Damascus outside the walls has ensured to some extent the integrity of the old city's fabric.

There are current attempts to restore the walls and older buildings in the city - a formidable task given the extent and condition of the historic fabric. The control of the conservation of monuments is the responsibility of several controlling bodies - major monuments may come under the control of the Department of Antiquities or may be delegated to specific authorities such as the Umayyad Mosque Restoration Committee. Conservation work to private properties is the responsibility of the Committee for the Preservation of Old Damascus.

The old City of Aleppo claims, with Damascus, to be the oldest continuously inhabited city in the world. Portions of the old walls exist, although not to the same extent as those of Damascus. The notable feature of Aleppo is the Citadel. It's commanding position has assured it's central role as a fortification within the city walls. Excavations have revealed evidence of it's existence since the 10c BCE, and since that time it has had a history of continuous destruction and reconstruction.

Aleppo's fortunes have followed in similar vein to it's Citadel's history. It no longer commands the significant strategic and commercial role that it did in previous centuries, and it is this factor which has ensured it's better preservation than that of Damascus. Burns (1992) states: "...it's very lack of a modern economic boom has encouraged Aleppo in it's old habits of turning in on itself, to preserve it's traditional methods of operation and it's architecture. Untouched as yet by the contemporary tourism surge, the rediscovery of Aleppo may come in an age when it's past will be more sympathetically preserved. Meanwhile Aleppo remains one of the treasures of the Middle East that should be savoured carefully lest it's dignity and fragility be lost."

It seems the time of sympathetic preservation is nigh, as a series of rehabilitation projects is beginning in the Old City of Aleppo, through a collaboration between the Syrian and German Governments. The total scheme is being organised through 16 Action Areas, with the first currently being initiated.

Discussion of Damascus and Aleppo

One of the most significant documents produced for urban conservation was the *Recommendation concerning the safeguarding and contemporary rôle of historic areas* adopted by the UNESCO General Conference in Nairobi, 26 November 1976. The two most notable points about this document are: the constant reference of the document to social and cultural requirements; and the recognition, even in the heading of the document, for the necessity for an historic area to have a contemporary role in today's world. The document commences by recognising the vital need for the conservation of historic areas and then extensively covers the practical implementation of conservation action by considering all the associated factors: legal, social, cultural, economic, administrative, technical, education and information. This *Recommendation* was followed by the *ICOMOS Charter for the Conservation of Historic Towns and Areas,* in 1987. This latter 16 point document codifies the *Recommendation* to a set of broad principles, and in doing so significantly loses a lot of the social, cultural and even economic objectives which had so strongly formed the original basis. I fear that the new charter is so broadly concerned with the practicalities of urban conservation methods, that it promulgates western attitudes to conservation, which, whilst not denying non-western cultural attitudes, does not specifically focus attention on the necessity of recognising differing cultural factors.

This can be seen in the current approach to the urban conservation guidelines for both Damascus and Aleppo. In Damascus, the official conservation document for the city has been drafted by conservation experts trained in Europe, and in Aleppo, the current Project for the Rehabilitation of Old Aleppo, is being implemented with the assistance of the German Government. That such projects will be greatly influenced by western methods and standards is not surprising, in fact it is probably inevitable. The experience of moving through a city of great antiquity like Damascus is only fulfilled with the knowledge that the very fabric of the city is authentic. The problem is that often western urban conservation standards lead no further than the presentation of the façade of the buildings and their environment in the desire to present an historic "face", and the result is an empty charade of both the culture and it's buildings. Where now will be the authenticity of the culture and the city for both heritage conservation and tourism purposes?

Returning to the *Recommendation,* its emphasis on the contemporary role indicates the concern recognised over twenty years ago for the necessity for a society to grow and develop in a natural way. The problem with both conservation and tourism is that the desire to present a culture in contrast to the globalised view, has the strong potential to freeze that culture into a museum presentation. This is in contrast to the deliberate presentation of an open-air museum – where a collection of heritage buildings from a number of regions in a country are brought together as a museum collection promulgated no doubt by the perceived ease of presentation to the tourist of a variety of cultural differences within the country without the drudgery of extended travel. In this form of presentation the real living culture cannot be experienced except as a performance, but at least the architecture can be appreciated as a museum artefact without the culture. In the case of an urban centre such as Damascus and Aleppo the historic environment is presented as the real and continuing culture, even though, given the conservation approach, this culture may become more and more a façade as may the architecture.

Conclusion

Maintaining the authenticity of the culture should be the first objective of conservation, and when this is achieved the conservation of it's built environment will be assured. The reverse is not necessarily true – that conserving the built environment will ensure the continuation of the culture. This is particularly so if conservation only extends to the maintenance of a façade, where the resultant presentation will reflect nothing of the culture or the real architecture that lies behind it.

It is time that both the conservation and the tourism industries changed their attitude towards heritage, and saw present day cultures, not as a piece of history frozen in time, but part of, and maybe in contrast to, the historic development of that society and its culture. In this way the true and authentic culture could be presented and appreciated, and as a true and authentic culture, the buildings and their development would be a true and authentic reflection of that culture.

Perhaps this is too much to expect, as there are far greater influences on societies today than merely respecting their heritage or it's presentation to tourists. But the tourism industry does have a unrivalled opportunity to present an authentic picture to the world public of the vast panorama of cultural differences that make up the collective global patrimony. That this seems too formidable task should not be the reason for either the tourism or conservation industries to renege on their responsibilities to this most necessary part of cultural understanding throughout the world.

Endnotes

1. This paper has been developed from a previous publication by the author. See "Conservation : the Question of Authenticity - Ideals and Realities," in *Preservation of the Vernacular Built Environment in Development Projects,* IASTE Working Paper Series Vol. 114, 1998, University of California, Berkeley, USA.

2. As expressed by a number of participants at the NARA Conference on Authenticity held in Nara, Japan, 1- 6 November 1994.

3. Wilson, (1997), claims 15000 tablets with a further 1600 having been found later.

4. Personal comments made to the author in Jordan and Syria.

5. The Director of Antiquities in the Damascus Museum is fully aware of the problems of conservation to archaeological sites, but is also aware of the requirements of the tourist industry. His answer to the suggestion of back-filling was: "The Minister of Tourism would kill us".

6. Personal comment made to the author during his last visit.

References

Bahnassi, A. (1989), *Guide to Syria,* Al Salhani, Damascus.

Bermant, C., and Weitzman, M. (1979), *Ebla: an Archaeological Enigma,* Weidenfeld and Nicolson, London.

Burns, R. (1992), *Monuments of Syria,* I. B. Tauris and Co Ltd., London.

Cantacuzino, S. (1997), The Heritage and Social Changes, *ICOMOS NEWS,* Vol.7, (1), pp.19-24.

Committee for the Conservation of the Old City of Aleppo. (no date), *The Old City of Aleppo: a Changing Process Influenced.*

ICOMOS International Specialised Committee on Cultural Tourism, (1978), *ICOMOS Bulletin,* German Democratic Republic.

ICOMOS Scientific Committee on Cultural Tourism, (1998), *International Cultural Tourism Charter* (7th Draft), ICOMOS.

Jokilehto, J. (1995), Authenticity: a General Framework for the Concept, *NARA Conference on Authenticity,* Conference Proceedings, UNESCO.

Matthiae, P. (1997), *Ebla,* Hodder and Stoughton, London.

Oliver, P. (Ed) (1997), *Encyclopaedia of Vernacular Architecture of the World,* Cambridge University Press.

van Droste, B. and Bertilsson, U. (1995), *NARA Conference on Authenticity,* UNESCO.

Wilson, C. (1979). *Ebla Tablets: Secrets of a Forgotten City,* Master Books, San Diego.

The worst of journeys, the best of journeys: Travel and the concept of the periphery in European culture

A V Seaton

University of Luton, UK

Introduction

This paper explores the concept of the periphery in culture and myth, and its impact upon European travel and tourism from the Middle Ages to the present day. The periphery may be seen as a concept comparable to those "keywords", explored by the late Raymond Williams (1976), the evolution of whose meanings illuminate cultural transformation and changing social attitudes. Like "nature", "the city" (to which Williams later devoted a whole book (Williams, 1973), and the word "culture" itself, the concept of the periphery has an embedded history that has given it a potent influence on travel practices, and also travel inhibitions, for more than seven centuries. This paper sketches out some of the evolving notions of the periphery and suggests the sedimented weight of connotation and denotation that make it both a manifest and latent force in tourism choice and behaviour. To adapt a distinction used by Saussure and Barthes, this is a study of the periphery as both langue and parole, as a linguistic concept, and a field of usages (Barthes, 1973).

Inquiries into the historical shifts and connotations of ideas cannot be undertaken with recourse to a discrete, readily identifiable sample of texts, within a unitary disciplinary focus. Some ideas, often the ones most potent within culture like those Williams engaged with, do not circulate in bounded, disciplinary fields, nor are they accessed from texts that can be neatly chased down in the demarcated categories of Dewey decimal library systems and subject bibliographies. This is partly because ideas are mediated and transformed within a range of different kinds of textual and human practices, so that they are as much to be understood from what people say and do, as how they are more formally and systematically reported between the covers of books. The second and related problem is that an idea may be active, even when it is not named. The concept of periphery existed long before it had a name, and the first part of this analysis seeks to illuminate discourses about it. The paper adopts an eclectic socio-historical line of inquiry which draws on anthropology, literature, travel writing, and the history of aesthetics to illustrate the complex and contradictory resonances of the concept of periphery. In addition to the model of Raymond Williams' linguistic studies, the paper owes something to the metaphorical approaches of Foucault's

"Archaeology of knowledge" in which he argued that ideas and concepts are promoted to historical effectivity, through the ways in which they are constituted and articulated within temporally specific, discursive networks that can be uncovered and recovered through excavation of the layers of textual practices and social and institutional relationships that mediated them (Foucault, 1973). Since this can never be an exact process, in that the data necessary for tracking ideas does not have the same unambiguous, material substance as archaeological evidence, but must always be a problematic field, moderated by the choices and interpretative frameworks of the investigator this paper is offered as an exploratory "dig", rather than an excavation that completely lays bare the field of study that is its focus.

Where and what is the periphery?

The first citation of "periphery" in the OED is as a mathematical concept in 1666, meaning *"a line that forms the boundary or surface of any space or body"* (e.g. the perimeter of a circle or sphere). By the nineteenth century the word had acquired a broader spatial dimension, as it developed from a mathematical to a geographical meaning, defined as, *"a surrounding area, not at the centre"* (OED, 1979).

In the twentieth century the meaning of the word fissioned into several directions, partly retaining its physical associations, but acquiring other social and metaphorical ones. Firstly its spatial denotations intensified but narrowed, assuming a more politico-technical character, as "peripheral" regions came to be defined as those which social scientists, politicians and other public prescribers implicitly contrasted with core regions not just on spatial, but on economic dimensions. This quasi-technical usage, as the authors of a recent text note, "was a product of development studies and became part of dependency theory." (Brown and Hall, 1999, p. 8). Within this developmental tradition peripheries have also been characterised as, "remote, marginal, and sparsely settled" (Hohl and Tisdell, 1995, p. 518). "Peripheral" has also been widely used in a figurative sense as a perjorative term for irrelevant elements presented in an argument (e.g. "Your last point is peripheral to this particular debate"). Finally, the term has been applied to people, as when someone is said to have played a "peripheral role" or part in a project. So far had the meaning slipped from a spatial to a social one that the anthropologist Kroeber observed that some "retarded cultures" were often spoken of as peripheral, "whether their situation be on the edges or in the interiors of land masses." (Webster, 1976, p.1681). Gowers has suggested that these more metaphorical and social meanings had made "peripheral" a "vogue word" by the late 1960s and early 1970s (Gowers, 1973).

This paper focuses on the periphery as a spatial and social concept, and its impact on travel behaviour, so it is worth trying to bring out some of the key aspects of the definitional discussion so far. Firstly, the concept of periphery is inherently about boundaries and margins dividing a putative centrally-located collectivity (place, community, society) from others at a distance from it. Secondly, as a word, the periphery was a late coinage even though the ideas it denoted and connoted, were not. Boundaries and margins, and the places and peoples perceived to be located at them, have always existed. Thirdly this geographical and social conception of periphery is an inherently dyadic, relativistic one, predicated upon explicit or implicit, binary contrasts between two constructed spheres of contrasted spatial and social difference. Moreover these spheres of spatial difference have normally been constructed and defined by agents deriving their perspectives, self-definition, and not infrequently, their power and authority, from membership of the constructed core sphere, rather than membership of the constructed, peripheral one. Another way of saying this is to note that nobody lives, sui generis, in a periphery, because the periphery is always defined as an entity that exists, like suffering in Auden's famous poem, "Musee des beaux arts", somewhere else, away at the margin of, and beyond, where one happens to be. One can live in a cold country or a rich country, but not a peripheral one, because where one lives is by definition a centre or core. When peoples or societies are typified as peripheral and accept the categorisation, it often means they have become subjects, willingly or unwillingly, of the discursive, classifying systems of others, or at least have been profoundly influenced by them. It is at this point that Foucault's ideas about the relationship between discourse, power and regimes of truth becomes relevant. From a Foucaultian perspective the changing meanings of the word "periphery" are not just linguistic issues, but are connected with prescriptive networks of social power and, ultimately, with agencies of action. Once the concept of a peripheral region as a problematic has been accepted, it almost inevitably authorises members of the groups who have generated, promoted and legitimated the discursive field – or their ideological supporters- to take action as a result of the classification. In short a peripheral area is not just a verbal signifier of a physical location, but a social agenda; not just a designation, but a call to arms. Later in this paper we shall see how travel agendas arise from this. Lastly, since the concept of periphery is, as we have argued, a relative one, driven as much by perceptions as physical realities, its location is inherently and irredeemably elastic. The periphery may exist in other countries, but it may also be in domestic regions away from imputed core places and collectivities in a single country, or even in a single city:

> "The increase of population (in London) in the past decade was entirely peripheral" (OED, p. 701, 1979).

Though core/periphery as a spatial distinction has in recent years, largely been annexed to the discursive practices of social scientists, politicians and planners, it represents a conceptual distinction that, freed of these more recent politico-technical connotations is of universal relevance, precisely because everyone unavoidably has their origin and current existence in specific places, in relation to which there are always inevitably boundaries and elsewhere beyond them that are likely to be experienced, at the level of subjective perception, as peripheries. Core/periphery may therefore be seen as a binary, spatial contrast that is fundamental to all culture and one which closely relates to a number of other binary oppositions in culture: here/there; home/away; near/far; close/distant; familiar/unfamiliar.

The purpose of this paper is to provide a historical excavation of the discursive fields within which peripheral locations have been constructed within European culture and to suggest how these have constrained, liberated and shaped the general propensity to travel to them.

The four discourses

Within Foucault's archaeological analogy the concept of the periphery can be viewed as a historical site constituted and configured by four main discursive strata, each of which accumulated, through time, upon the previous one, but never to an extent that did not allow residual sedimentations from earlier periods to project and intermingle with later accretions. The periods during which these four discursive strata developed were not discrete, equal in length and neatly sequential; they overlapped, broke off and returned (like glacial periods or hot summers), so that cross-sectionally the strata looked, not like parallel layers distributed vertically one upon another, but more like veined marbles in which veins of colour that were their constant features, twisted and commingled, and sometimes doubled back upon themselves. The four strata of the periphery, its layered meanings, may be designated as follows:

- the periphery as the discursive site of fabulation, salutary myth and sacred truth;

- the periphery as the discursive site of observational physical and social science, and prescriptive social engineering;

- the periphery as the discursive site for the spiritual raptures, archaic identifications, physical retreats and challenges of the romanticism;

- the periphery as the discursive site of imperial mission and adventure.

Fabulation, salutary myth and sacred truth

Once upon a time, elsewhere - the regions that lay at, or beyond, the margins of the familiar world and which came to be known as "peripheral"- had no name but were mysterious regions symbolically understood through, often multiple, layers of discursive myth. During the Middle Ages and for many centuries after most traditional societies, those in Europe included, tended to see their own physical and social environments as the measure of all. They existed in a world that was ethnocentric before the term was invented, secure in the primacy of their own religious and social practices. At the margins and beyond this familiar world strangeness increased in an almost linear manner as one advanced towards peripheral locations, and it was here that the mythical world blossomed.

One of these myths was that peripheries were inhabited by people and animals quite unlike those that existed at home:

> *"For centuries people satisfied themselves with outrageous tales, told as fact, of lands where there existed griffons and men without heads, dog headed simmians and birds that glowed in the dark."* (Wilford 1981, p. 344)

Early maps offer one kind of textual evidence of this . What was at the margins of the known, "terra incognita" in early cartography, was almost routinely filled in with rubrics that characterised the regions in terms of fabulous fauna and flora ("here be dragons"). Swift satirised this tendency in relation to Africa, one of the main subjects of peripheral discourse, before the great 19th century European explorations, of myth making:

> *"Geographers, on Afric maps*
> *With savage drawings fill their gaps,*
> *And o'er unhabitable downs*
> *Draw elephants for want of towns."*
> (Swift, quoted, Gardner, 1969, p. 10)

In Mornes' 1761 map of Africa the following rubric occurs:

> *"It is true that the centre of the continent is filled with burning sands, savage beasts, and almost uninhabitable deserts. The scarcity of water forces the different animals to come together to the same place to drink. Finding themselves together at a time when they are in heat, they have intercourse with one another, without paying regard to the differences between species. Thus are produced monsters which are to be found there in greater numbers than in any other part of the world"* (Wilford, 1981, p. 35).

Even people who had travelled tended to subscribe to the mythological characterisation of peripheral regions. Thus Marignolli, who had travelled widely in the east between 1338-1353 and admitted he had never seen the kind of wonders common to the mythology of distant places added:

> *"Yet giants, monstrous serpents, and certain animals with countenances almost like that of man do exist"* (Baker, 1937, p. 53).

In addition to its physical differences the periphery was also mythologised as the site of moral and metaphysical disorder and danger. The quotation from Mornes suggests that Africa was not just thought to be inhabited by strange animals, but that sexual disorder characterised their relations. Cannibalism was widely believed to be practised among peripheral tribes in Africa.

The periphery was also seen as the potential source not just of physical invasion (a well founded assumption) but also of moral invasion. The Biblical demons, Gog and Magog, were predicted to swarm in hoardes from the north to come south and pillage in the literature of Judaism, Islam and Christianity (Wilford, p. 40).

A key historical text that exemplifies many of the attitudes to peripheries in the Middle Ages, and for some time after, is Mandeville's Travels. This book was presented as the memoirs of an English knight, Sir John Mandeville, and his experiences in the Holy Land, Africa and the Orient over 33 years from 1322 to 1355. Now known to be spurious, a compilation from existing texts, it was written in French on the continent, probably not by an Englishman, about 1357. (Seymour, 1967, p. xiii). Its content was most likely translations from French originals, the most important of which was a series of genuine itineraries by a monk from St Omer, Jean Long, known as the "Hakluyt of the Middle Ages", in 1351. (Seymour, p. xiv). Mandeville's Travels achieved great popularity and currency, representing the "epitome of the later Middle Ages" and came to overshadow Marco Polo's travels (Seymour, 1967, p. xiv). It was a popular, literary classic, much reprinted and published in chapbook form until the nineteenth century (Ashton, 1887). Its accounts of the wonders of peripheral countries corresponded with other contemporary representations, including some of the fabulous features of the Hereford Mappa Mundi (Ashton, 1888) including details of one eyed men, those with their heads in their breasts, and the big footed one-legged man. The book's influence was great:

> *"More than any other work, it popularised many of the facts and fictions of our classical inheritance- the representation of the True Cross in the banana, the*

weeping crocodile, 'the men whose heads grow beneath their shoulders', and a hundred other colourings of popular imagination, draw their strength from Mandeville's Travels..(It) fertilised the minds and kindled the hearts of generations of poets and playwrights" (Seymour, 1967,p. xx).

A copy of Mandeville and Marco Polo's travels accompanied Columbus to America.

The Middle Ages were followed by the age of exploration beginning with the European voyages of the fifteenth and sixteenth centuries. These provided eye witness accounts that began to supplant the myth and legend of the previous thousand years. However the tradition of investing peripheries with positive and negative wonders persisted for reasons that Bucher (1981), among others, has addressed in her study of the illustrations to Bry's "Great Voyages". These volumes, published between 1590 and 1634, were accounts of the New World with copperplate engravings by Dutch Protestant engravers. Bucher's semiotic analysis of their imagery demonstrates how the visual strategies and conventions deployed served to impose European conceptions of sin and virtue on representations of peripheral habits and customs. She shows, for instance, how representations of old women depicted them as witch-like hags with sagging breasts, thus framing them within a cosmological stereotype of wickedness and depravity. Of another illustration Bucher writes:

"Here (the depicted Amerio-Indians) .. break another European taboo, idolatry, which, along with cannibalism and nudity, is part and parcel of the concept of savagery and barbarism in the Christian consciousness of the period. In these idols it is easy to recognise Europeans' fantasies of the devil, zoomorphic and androgynous, familiar in medieval and Renaissance iconography" (Bucher,1981, p. 69).

One final text in this tradition of fabulation is Wanleys' "Wonders". Nathaniel Wanley was a Vicar of Coventry who, in 1678 published "The Wonders of the little world: or, A general History of Man in six books displaying the various faculties, capacities, powers and defects of the human body and mind forming a complete system of the mental and corporeal powers and defects of human nature". It thus claimed the verisimilitude of anthropology in setting out to present truths about the human condition derived from the evidence of "historians, philosophers and physicians, of all ages and countries". Its author's introduction specifically cited Bacon's experimental approach and the methodology of empirical research in scientific inquiry:

"That the only way to investigate the nature of any object whatever, is to collect together and compare all the observations and experiments that have been made of its properties" (Wanley, 1688, p. 6).

In practice the book was a vast compilation of several thousand facts, cut and pasted from many classical texts and a smaller number of more recent ones, that constituted exemplary and curious anecdotes about the vices, virtues, physical and mental accomplishments of people past and present. Today it reads like something between Trivial Pursuit, the Guinness Books of Records, and Casaubon's key to all the mysteries in George Eliot's *Middlemarch*. A few chapter titles may be cited to convey the flavour of the whole: "Of the strange constitution, and properties of some bodies"; "Of persons recovering, after being thought dead"; "Strange ways by which murders have been discovered"; "Of the deep dissimulation and hypocrisy of some men"; "Instances of entire friendship"; "Of cheats and the extraordinary boldness of some of their thefts"; "What hath befallen some men through error and mistake"; "Of incredible strength of mind under tortures and hardship"; "Of the longevity or length of life in some persons". The book was an enormously successful epitome and was still being published, in an abridged form, a hundred years later on the eve of the Industrial Revolution. The book reinforced the image of peripheries as locations of the strange and wonderful. One section provided a catalogue of the peculiar dietary practices of peoples in distant countries, including: diets of locusts, scorpions, worms bread on "rotten and putrescent stuff", maggots, horses blood, lice, tortoises, ape flesh, acorns, hens dung, lizards, leaves, and "filthy spittle and snot";. The book also detailed outrageous religious practices that included: devil worship, the worship among the Javanese of whatever they first encounter in the morning whether "a hog, or any other animal or reptile", the worship of jewels, and worship of oxes, cats, crocodiles and falcons. (Manley, 1788, pp. 609-619).

Yet this othering was not entirely negative. The periphery was from the outset a contradictory space that could simultaneously connote the fabulously good and the fabulously evil. Alongside the legend of Gog and Magog, peripheries were also the putative location of the sacred. The four great rivers of Paradise and Paradise itself were thought to lie in the East. Africa was thought to be the realm of Prester John, a legendary Christian leader, first described in the 1145, and whose land was depicted by Ortelius in 1573 (Ross, 1926, Wilford, 42-43) and the subject of a novel by John Buchan in the early twentieth century.

In summary, early European representations of places at the edge of, or beyond, the known world were commonly invested with features of extreme difference, that process of "othering" that has largely been presented as a modern, imperialistic phenomenon. Peripheries were presented as geographical freak shows, imagined zones of physical monsters and fabulous beasts, as well as lands of social and moral turpitude. Yet they were also sites of the divine and holy, where gods and heroes existed beyond the everyday world. It was these contradictory perceptions that paved the way for peripheries to become the fictitious locations of both dystopias and utopias.

Observational physical and social science, and prescriptive social engineering

From the 17th century onwards discourses about peripheries began to change under the growing impact of experimental and observational science, and that phase in European culture that has been called the Enlightenment . Though the earliest wave of science was focused on chemistry, physics, mechanics and medicine, all of which could be studied in laboratories, theatres and settings for controlled experiments, other sciences required travel. Geology, geography and all forms of natural history were comparative sciences in which much of the data were abroad, outside Europe. The Enlightenment sought to extend the study of the known world, to dispel spatial myths and superstitions of the past, and to bring the entire natural and social order under the empirical and imperial gaze of the scientist. Study of the natural world was exemplified in the classifying works of such figures as Linnaeus and Buffon; study of the social order in the project that came to be named anthropology. The concept of the scientific expedition arose, which in the main meant voyages to peripheries.

As a result by the end of the eighteenth century locations of scientific endeavour were not just concentrated in anatomy theatres, laboratories and public auditoria in core cities like London, Birmingham, Edinburgh and Glasgow but had come to diversify into observational field work in countries abroad. For members of scientific and learned societies there was considerable academic and public kudos in going further and further outward from Europe to make scientific observations. Cook in the Pacific, Banks is Iceland and the South Seas, Waterston in South America and Darwin in the Galapagos, are only among the more celebrated of dozens of scientific expeditions taken to peripheries which created a glamour for travel with a scientific purpose. Many of the participants in these voyages were publically feted on their return for their contributions to science.

Science is virtually never just descriptive. People who claim to anatomise and diagnose the nature of the world almost invariably end up prescribing for it, or becoming the tools of those whose interests are served by doing so. This universal tendency came to impact upon notions of the periphery. In the late nineteenth and early twentieth century the rapid development of the social sciences and particularly anthropology, made the periphery the location for the systematic study of people and the social world as well as fauna, flora and the inanimate. In Foucaultian terms scientific discourse was increasingly implicated into regimes of observation, inspection, classification and, as will be discussed in the next section, with administrative policies of imperialists. One social scientific effect of travel to the periphery was the anthropological project of trying to systematise a hierarchy of races and racial types. The peripheral world became a human specimen cabinet, and later a theatre for reform (aided by missionaries), and social control. It was scientists who became empowered to identify problematics that established agendas to be acted upon by policy makers. A standard history of anthropology published as recently as 1970 reflects the tone of patronising superiority that accompanied many of these developments in peripheral social science:

> *"It is easier and safer to study a primitive people; easier because there is not as a rule so vast an amount to study, and novelty makes the outlines clearer and more interesting, and safer because the majority of men do not so much care what they say about savages who live at a distance, so long as they can keep a good conceit of themselves and not upset any respectable and well-established prejudices"* (Penniman, 1970, p.18).

Though many of the overt attitudes of racial superiority have been purged from it, anthropology is still mainly a one-way flow of white, western academics from developed countries observing, describing and prescribing for peripheral dwellers. One still waits the seikh, the aborigine or the native American Indian on a research grant, taking field notes on the customs and habits of white westerners, in a shopping mall or bank in Huddersfield or Minnesota.

In summary, scientific discourses about peripheries created the role of the scientific traveller - the plant collector, the field biologist, the geographical surveyor, the social and cultural anthropologist - all of them, pursuing knowledge that would improve understanding of the physical and social worlds, and demystify all manner of traditional myths about far away places. In the last analysis, they deemed themselves superior to all that they surveyed.

The spiritual raptures, archaic identifications, and physical retreats and challenges of romanticism

But the progress of science did not succeed in demystifying and dismantling myths about peripheries as realms of the marvellous, because at the end of the eighteenth century a powerful, new set of discourses remythologised the social imaginary of distant places, in ways that at once resuscitated pre-scientific attitudes, and provided radical extensions to them. These discourses were the product of the movement known as Romanticism. Romanticism is a much debated phenomenon. In general it refers to changes in modes of aesthetic apprehension, thought and expression that happened between 1770 and 1830 and which affected all the arts, particularly literature, painting, music and philosophy. What these changes amounted to, and even, if and when they took place, has provided a fertile soil for academic argument and counter-argument. Among the elements of Romanticism were : a greater emphasis on feeling and emotional response in life and art; a reaction against the formality of eighteenth century neo-classicism; a greater awareness and, in some instances, near-worship of nature as a form of spiritual communion; reverence for a non-classical past, particularly the Middle Ages; the cult of the child as a paradisial innocent whose perceptions were superior to those of worldly adults; an interest in mystery and abnormality (Newton, 1962) ; and an extreme belief in individuality, often at odds with society.[1]

Peripheries occupied an important place in the "structures of feeling"[2], produced by Romanticism. Romantics would have agreed with the modern psychologist who has proclaimed that, "Everything that is interesting in nature happens at the boundaries" (Nicholas Humphrey, quoted Burnside, 1996, p. 202). Nature was a purifying force, according to Rouseau, a seminal figure in Romanticism, and virtue resided among simple people and "noble savages" in rural and mountain settings. The themes were taken up by other major figures including Wordsworth, Coleridge, and Heine (Babbitt, 1919; Green 1955). Primitivism, solitary communion, and extremes of feeling were found in peripheral regions. They were places where fresh starts could be made away from industrial pollution and urban corruption. Coleridge, one of the first great theorists of Romanticism, envisaged a Pantisocracy in native American territories on the banks of the Sesquahaa in the 1790s where property would not exist, and all would live in harmony with nature (Holmes, 1985). Instead of being beyond the pale of civilisation and morality, as the fabulations of earlier times had suggested, peripheral communities were perceived as centres of spiritual growth and revealed truth. One of the achievements of Romanticism was to turn on its head the adverse evaluation implicit in previous connotations of peripheral locations as barbarous, marginal and disordered. Instead they became psychological core regions, offering visions of inspirational and nurturing nature, freedom, and re-creation. Backwardness was seen as progressive. Native simplicity and spontaneity were seen as superior to the artifices of conventional conduct.

However in one major respect Romanticism kept alive peripheral myths of an earlier period, in its perpetuation of the tales of the marvellous that existed in distant places, as part of its commitment to imagination and the naïve emotional responses of wonder, expressed by and admired in, children. The word "romance" itself originally meant tales of wonders and, for the growing middle class reading public that developed in the first century of Romanticism, books like *The Arabian Knights, Baron Munchausen's travels* and *Gullivers Travels* were much loved best sellers that implicitly perpetuated the association between peripheral travel and the marvellous.

Finally, and less emphasised in the vast body of exegetical works on the movement, many of the seminal Romantics - Shelley, Byron, Heine, Goethe, Hazlitt, Stendhal, Chateaubriand- were great tourists and sang the praises of abroad, not just of peripheries, but in some cases, of classical core regions like Italy and Greece.

Two of the key ideologies of Romanticism in relation to place and peripheries were the aesthetic discourses of the Picturesque and Sublime. The first was a set of ideas about place as landscape, a subject for the painter's gaze, which had the effect of turning locations into "views", a spectator aesthetic under the controlling imagining of the visitor, often a tourist with sketchbook in hand, designating worthy sights like a hunter picking off prime game targets (Andrews, 1989 and 1994: Hussey 1912), The Sublime was a theory, seminally formulated in an influential dissertation by Edmind Burke published in 1757, *Philosophical Inquiry into the Origin of Our Ideas of the Sublime and Beautiful*, about the aesthetic appeal of those phenomena - places, events, literature- that induced horror, awe and majestic meditations on the infinite (Burke, 1958):

> "*Born from the oxymoron of agreeable horror, Romanticism was nursed on calamity. ...Edmund Burke set himself up as the priest of obscurity, of darkness. To be profound was to plumb the depths. So it would be in shadow and darkness and dread and trembling, in caves and chasms, at the edge of the precipice, in the shroud of a cloud, in the fissures of the earth, that, he insisted in his* Inquiry, *the sublime would be discovered*" (Schama, 1995, p. 450).

The two aesthetic ideologies had a crucial impact in the re-evaluation of peripheries. Burke's book helped to turn the Alps from a "horrid" obstruction in the eyes of earlier travellers like Addison, into a setting of majestic beauty. Northern peripheries both within the UK, notably the Lake District and Scotland , and those outside it in Scandinavia, began to rival the classical core regions of Europe (France, Italy, Greece) as attractions for some travellers (Hodge, 1957; Nicholson, 1972; Butenschon, 1960; Seaton 1998).

One of the effects of this new romantic attachment to peripheries was an intensified interest in polar travel .The story of polar exploration is too well known to require detailed restatement (Stefansson, 1921; Victor, 1964; Mountfield, 1974). For three hundred years before Romanticism polar travel had been pursued for instrumental reasons, a quest for trade routes, particularly for a north west passage from Europe to the East Indies. From the Romantic Period onwards the poles became an imaginative and aesthetic stimulus rather than a mercantile focus. The aesthetic attractions of northern peripheries were exemplified by the traveller, Acerbi, who journeyed through Finland to the North Cape in the late 1790s. This Italian's account perfectly expresses the positive, binary contrasts that northern peripheries were seen to offer to the beaten tracks of central and southern Europe:

> "*It may possibly excite curiosity to know, why a native of Italy, a country abounding in all the beauties of nature, and the finest productions of art, should voluntarily undergo the danger and fatigue of visiting the regions of the Arctic Circle. He promised to himself, and he was not disappointed, much gratification*

from contrasting the wild grandeur *and* simplicity *of the North, with the luxuriance, the smiling aspect, and the refinements of his own country. He was willing to exchange, for a time, the beauties of nature and art, for the novelty, the* sublimity, *and the* rude magnificence *of the northern climates"* (Acerbi, Vol 1, p. 8, 1802, my italics).

Iceland, although hardly a polar region, rapidly achieved popularity as a destination among a young, middle class intelligenstia during the nineteenth century (Seaton, 1989). Little regarded or described in English before 1779 Iceland was the subject of more than 80 published, first-hand accounts in English over the next century, by writers who included : Lord Dufferin, Anthony Trollope, William Morris, Rider Haggard and Richard Burton (the latter, exaggerating the growing popularity of the country to tourists by the 1870s, acidly branded it a "cockney" route).

There was one major exception to the predominantly benign othering of peripheries in romantic mythology. Romanticism also created the gothic novel, a textual form in which peripheries were often the settings of horror and evil[3]. The attraction of the gothic genre with its spectres, phantoms, ghosts, violence and horror was another manifestation of the reaction against the secular rationality of classicism and the Enlightenment (Summers n.d., Davenport-Hines, 1998).

Some of the most celebrated gothic novels were set in peripheries, including the most famous, *Frankenstein*. This was conceived at the Villa Diodati in Switzerland where its author, Mary Shelley, was staying with Byron, the poet Shelley and their companion, Polidori in 1816. A month before she and Shelley had been enjoying the Sublime in the Alps and climbed to see the intimidating Mer de Glace (Grylls, p. 62-63, 1938). Her book, she later said, had been the product of "habits of fancy" forged in another northern periphery, "the dreary shores of the Tay near Dundee" in Scotland, and part of its action is in the Orkneys. But its most resonant image is of the monster adrift on an iceberg in the polar sea, where he had his last resting place.

Other Romantic works used polar settings. Eugene Sue's gothic best seller, *The Wandering Jew* opened with doomed lovers at opposite poles of the earth, helplessly contemplating each other through an optical refraction of image across wastes of ice. The subject of Melville's *Moby Dick* is whale fishing in the arctic. And in Coleridge's *Ancient Mariner* the fate of its ghastly hero is set in polar seas. Appearances of the ghost ship in *Flying Dutchman* legends were also often in northern oceans. In short there was an association between gothic horror and peripheries. *Dracula* took place in two peripheries; in Transylvania, a non-polar, region whose obscurity in the eyes of most Europeans was one of the reasons that Bram Stoker chose it as a setting; and Whitby, a remote fishing village in England.[4]

But, like peripheral discourses of the Middle Ages, those about polar peripheries in the age of Romanticism had contradictory connotations. They were seen as settings of horror and the abnormal, but also as spiritually grand and sublime. Here are two passages that embody the contradictory visions. The first is an early passage from *Frankenstein*.

"I am already far north of London; and as I walk in the streets of Peterborough, I feel a cold northern breeze play upon my cheeks, which braces my nerves and

fills me with delight. Do you understand this feeling? This breeze, which has travelled from the regions towards which I am advancing, gives me a foretaste of those icy climes. Inspirited by this wind of promise, *my daydreams become more fervent and vivid. I try in vain to be persuaded that the pole is the seat of frost and desolation; it ever presents itself* to my imagination as the region of beauty and delight. *There..the sun is forever visible, its broad disk just skirting the horizon and diffusing a perpetual splendour. There..snow and frost are banished; and sailing over a calm sea, we may be wafted to a land surpassing in wonders and in beauty every region hitherto discovered on the habitable globe. Its productions and features may be without example, as the phenomena of the heavenly bodies undoubtedly are in those* undiscovered solitudes. *What may not be expected of a country of* eternal light? *I may there discover the* wondrous power *which attracts the needle and may regulate a thousand celestial observations that require only this voyage to render their seeming eccentricities consistent forever. I shall satiate my ardent curiosity with the sight of a part of the world never visited, and may tread land never before imprinted by the foot of man. These are my enticements, and they are sufficient to conquer all fear of danger or death and to induce me to commence this laborious voyage with the joy a child feels when he embarks in a little boat, with his holiday mates, on an expedition of discovery up his native river"* (Shelley, Penguin, 1978, pp. 269-270, my italics).

The passage, and the italicised words within it, suggest how the north pole could be viewed as an intimidating, freezing wilderness, dangerous to seek out, but at the same time as an imaginative and spiritual stimulus.

The second extract comes from one of the great classic accounts of polar travel, Cherry-Garrard's *Worst journey in the world (1922)*. In the introduction the author acknowledges the horrors and privations of polar journeys ("Polar exploration is at once the cleanest and most isolated way of having a bad time which has been devised"), yet then rhapsodises:

> *"Even now the Antarctic is to the rest of the earth as the Abode of the Gods was to the ancient Chaldees, a precipitous and mammoth land lying far beyond the sea which encircled man's habitation, and nothing is more striking about the exploration of the Southern Polar regions than its absence, for when King Alfred reigned in England the Vikings were navigating the ice-fields of the North; yet when Wellington fought the battle of Waterloo there was still an undiscovered continent in the South"* (Apsley-Garrard, 1924, xvii).

Both these extracts combine an interdiscursive mix of science, fabulation, and Romanticism.

A tourism innovation that emerged from the peripheral discourses of Romanticism and science in the mid-nineteenth century was mountaineering as a leisure activity. Mountains, until the advent of flying, were peripheries in the air, which had formerly been seen as objects to navigate around, rather than seek to ascend for pleasure. By the second half of the century many educated, middle class Englishmen, were testing themselves on ascents of ever higher, more difficult and more distant mountains (Irving, 1955).

At the opposite extreme from poles – and Romantic discourse often dealt in extremes- the other peripheries that generated a great volume of discursive representation were in Africa and Arabia . What they shared with the poles as Nicholson has noted was, "an asymmetry that violated all classical canons of regularity". (Nicholson, 1959, p. 32). The interest in Arabia was a secular one that augmented its traditional place as the landscape of the Bible. From Niehbuhr onwards a succession of European travellers brought back literary and artistic representations that created the mystique attached to the Orient, and was later extended into India and other parts of Asia . The appeal of Arabia is caught in a recent history:

> *"Desert, nomad, bedouin, oasis - Arabia.. The words drop into our understanding with a disturbing resonance. The echoes they create seem to contain a complicated message - a message that hints at an unattainable nobility, at freedom and an ancient honour, at the grandeur of simplicity and the cleanliness of distance"* (Brent, p. 9, 1979).

Arabia, and particularly its most peripheral regions such as the Hadhramaut, held an imaginative fascination for a long line of English intellectuals and writer travellers whose ranks included: Sir Richard Burton, C. M. Doughty, Gertrude Bell, T. E. Lawrence, St. J. B. Philby, Freya Stark, Bertram Thomas, Wilfred Thesiger, as well as lesser known figures working as administrators in the Middle East for the British government. The attractions of Arabia symptomised the paradigmatic contradictions that characterised romantic attitudes to peripheries. On the one hand "peoples of the Desert" were seen as carriers of archaic values of stoic nobility, loyalty and bravery; on the other, they were deemed to be treacherous and barbaric. This duality is typified in the comments of one of the lesser known figures in Arabian hagiography, Wyman Bury, whose obsession with the region led him adopt the Arab pen name of Abdullah Mansur:

> *"I choose this opportunity of making public some ten years' intimate experience of a people whose country will ever exercise a great fascination for me as the gateway of an unknown land. There one may step straight from this modern age of bustle and chicanery into an era of elemental conditions; where faithful friendship is jostled by the blackest treachery, and the crude facts of a semi- barbaric life are encountered at every turn; while the glamour of an early civilisation and a mighty creed gives one the impression of having stepped back in the pages of history to mediaeval (sic) times. The illusion is further enhanced by ancestral castles and a working feudal system"* (Bury, 1911, p. xxi,).

Many of the discourses of Romanticism came to act, not just as a counterbalance to those of science, but complemented them. For a brief period - roughly the first half of the nineteenth century - scientific interests and a Romantic sensibility could coexist, mainly among the young, middleclass male, intelligentsias that filled the memberships of learned societies, literary and philosophical institutions and academia. In the 1830s, for example, it was possible for a young scientist to inventory geological and ornithological specimens in Iceland, and quote Byron and Felicia Hemans at the same time in his journal of the expedition (Seaton, 1989). The attraction of peripheral places and landscapes to visitors could thus be simultaneously picturesque, sublime, literary and scientific. The "two cultures" as C.P. Snow later designated the cultural divide between the arts and sciences as two mutually exclusive fields, only began to develop in the second half of the nineteenth century, and to solidify in the twentieth.

Though the Romantic period can now be seen, less as a total revolution than one of ruptures and continuities, some of the ruptures were deep and radical, and some of the continuities small. The special place that peripheries, as spaces on the horizon and beyond, came to hold within Romanticism can perhaps best be summarised by a comment from one of it's greatest apologists, William Hazlitt.

> *"Distant objects please, because, in the first place, they imply an idea of space and magnitude, and because not being obtruded too close to the eye, we clothe them with the indistinct and airy colours of fancy"* (Hazlitt, 1944, p. 127).

The Middle Ages had built explanatory fictions about peripheries as a way of accommodating the unknown securely within the certainties and self-satisfactions of their own preferred world view, a medieval cosmology grounded in an overarching Christianity. For the Romantics peripheral discourses were the reverse, a set of oppositional readings that made peripheries an imaginative and spiritual stimulus in an alternative cosmology that offered a critique of, and compensation for, the deficiencies of that of their own societies. This Romantic response to peripheries is alive and well today, and the implicit ideological basis of many kinds of tourism practice and representation.

Imperial mission and adventure

The final discourse relating to peripheries affected only a few European countries, particularly Britain and, to a lesser extent, France. It was that of Imperialism.

Distance from administrative core centres has always made peripheries a problem of control for empires. Maintaining imperial hegemony at spatial margins was as much an issue for the British in the eighteenth and nineteenth centuries, as for the Romans more than a thousand years earlier. Imperial peripheries were often seen as barbaric locations where the maintenance of the hegemonic order was most contested by the subjugated people themselves, and by groups competing from outside to challenge the existing colonial power.

One of the prime discourses that affected peripheral travel from Britain was an evolving mythology regarding "outposts of Empire" and the "white man's burden". Attached to it were jingoistic forms of display that revolved round representations of Queen, country and military might. Though the Victorian era has commonly been regarded as a peaceful one, hardly a year went by that there were not expeditionary forces, punitive expeditions or "little wars" whose function was the subduing of insurrections or the defence of borders. On an everyday basis holding an Empire meant the permanent presence of significant numbers of British administrators and military in those countries that were part of that sixth of the world that was marked red on maps of the world.

Imperial interests thus came to affect travel agendas by mythologising peripheral locations that formed " the outposts of Empire", particularly in Africa and the East, with a glamour as playing fields of colourful adventure in an empire on which "the sun never set". Images supporting this version of the geography of imperialism were widely dispersed in childrens books, boys stories (particularly the works of Henty), film, music hall, popular song and other kinds of popular culture (Mackenzie, 1986).

Imperialism also affected travel to peripheral regions that were not within the Empire, but which were seen as uncharted territories, ripe for discovery and inventory. The association between imperialism and exploration was fanned by a press-fuelled mania for stories about Africa and the Poles in the second half of the nineteenth century and the first half of the twentieth:

> *"In the last great age of terrestial discovery, such areas were more than merely interesting; they were at first paradoxes, then unacceptable, and finally national insults. By the 1850s subjugating nature and filling in the blank spaces had become the aim of numerous organisations, including the Royal Geographical Society and the American Geographical Society"* (Riffenburgh, 1994).

In Britain the "romance of exploration and adventure", provided material that filled travel memoirs, boys books and comics, film and the early days of TV (Mackenzie, 1986). Its final high point in Britain was less than 50 years ago when the ascent of Everest was hailed as a fanfare to a new Elizabethan Age at the time of the Coronation of 1953.

Peripheries in modern times came to connote adventure of a more general kind. Zweig has described the fate of the adventurer in the modern world through an analysis of the work of a number of important, post romantic writers and noted how peripheries became synonymous with adventure in both fact and fiction.

> *"Poe, Melville, Conrad, T.E. Lawrence, Malraux, Genet, all found their subject matter in the margins of culture..Behind the elaborate fiction of such writers as Melville, Malraux, T.E Lawrence, and Genet lies the splendour of ancient figures: Gilgamesh, Odysseus, Herakles, Beowulf, Sir Gawaine: characters for whom life declared itself in the energy of their exploits, as they explored the margins of the human world, where men and gods, the known and the unknown, the human and the monstrous were mingled"* (Zweig, 1974, p. 15, my italics*).*

Imperialism, like Romanticism, also affected the development of the social sciences by providing vaste new fields of human data among colonised populations. One historian of anthropology has camouflaged the reasons behind this process in terms of masterly neutrality:

> *"..the spread of European and American power over so much of the earth has brought us into close contact with a greater number of races and customs alien to our own, and the necessity for dealing with this enormous amount of new material has preoccupied the attention of anthropologists faced with the practical problems raised when peoples of very different cultures must live in the same territory."* (Penniman, 1970, p. 18).

The observation silences questions of power and choice, under a preferred rhetoric of passive, impersonal necessity. More active forms might have been found for some of its ideas: "has brought us into close contact" (*has forced our contact on, and with, distant races?*); "necessity for dealing" (*the need to deal and rule?*);"practical problems" (*the dangers of resistance and dissent?*); "must live" (*are forced to live*).

Other writers have explored the links between the development of anthropology and colonial administration, including contemporary observers (Hailey, 1946), and the modern historian, Kuper, who qualifies the supposition that anthropology played a key role in allowing colonial administrators to manage other cultures. He argues that anthropologists were often fairly marginal to the imperial project and tended to magnify their functional role as a means of gaining travel funds for their fieldwork (Kuper, 1983, pp. 99-120). The same author also suggests that anthropologists were often seen as ideologically different from mainstream administrators

> "..*the anthropologist was regarded as a romantic reactionary, who wanted to preserve 'his tribe' from any outside contacts, and to keep them as museum exhibits in splendid isolation from trade, government, and Christianity*" (Kuper, 1983, p.114).

This view of the anthropologist bears resemblance to that of Dennison Nash in his celebrated essay on the "Ethnologist as Stranger" when quoting Budney (1953) he depicts the ethnologist as manifesting "a romantic cultural pluralism". (Nash, 1963).

The binary contrasts of core/peripheral discourses

On the basis of the discussion so far it is possible to divide the attributes of Cores and Peripheries into three different domains that can be compared on an axis of binary contrasts : the physical, politico-economic and psycho-cultural.

Physical contrasts

The most obvious peripheral domain in the discourses examined relates to their physical characteristics. The principal peripheries were in Africa, the East and at the Poles. They can be characterised by 4 main differences from core regions.

Core /Periphery: Physical Contrasts	
Core	**Periphery**
Climatically temperate	Climatically extreme (heat/ cold)
Close	Distant
Peopled	Sparsely populated
Same language	Linguistic rites of passage required

Politico-economic contrasts

The second set of contrasts are those implicit within the politico-economic discourses of the social scientist, discussed at the start of this paper. The contrasts allude to economic and developmental differences between core and peripheral regions. Some of their main contrasts have been usefully summarised by Owen et al, 1999.

Core/ Periphery: Politico-Economic Contrasts	
Core	**Periphery**
High levels of economic vitality and a diverse economic base	Low levels of economic vitality and dependent on traditional industries
Metropolitan in character. Rising population through in-migration with a relatively young age structure	More rural and remote- often with high scenic values. Population falling through out-migration, with an ageing structure
Innovative, pioneering and enjoys good information flows	Reliant on imported technologies and ideas, and suffers from poor information flows
Focus of major political, economic and social decisions	Remote from decision making- leading to a sense of alienation and lack of power
Good infrastructure and amenities	Poor infrastructure and amenities
Modern, fulfilling lifestyle	Traditional deprived lifestyle

The striking thing about these contrasts is how one-sidedly positive they are in their typification of core regions, and how inferior the periphery looks by comparison. There is no indication of the mythic plentitude and connotative richness that have emerged in our earlier analysis of the four discourses. The deficit is however, more than compensated for in the final set of contrasts.

Psycho-cultural contrasts

This final set of contrasts presupposes that peripheries can only partially be understood, in the context of travel propensity, as physical and politico-economic domains. The periphery is also a psychological and cultural phenomenon as this article seeks to show. The psycho-cultural domain produces a quite different set of evaluative associations from those of the previous two.

Core/Periphery: Psycho-Cultural Contrasts	
Core	**Periphery**
Spaces of mundane comfort	Spaces of extraordinary hardship or ease
Sites of safety and the familiar	Sites of danger and adventure
Classic spaces	Romantic spaces
Profane spaces	Sacred spaces
Space appeals to common sense and reason	Spaces appealing to heart/passion
Level spaces	Space involves ascents/descents
Spaces of ordered cultivation	Spaces of disordered wilderness or paradisial abundance
Social uniformity/similarity	Social/physical diversity/difference/Other*R
Inhabitants ego controlled and "civilised"	Inhabitants id/superego driven and "natural"
Town-dominated spaces	Country-dominated spaces
Societies product of culture	Societies product of Nature
Governance = moral mean + reality principle	Governance = Extremes of virtue or barbarism = Dystopias and Utopias

Peripheries and tourism propensity

How do these discursive contrasts of the periphery relate to travel and tourism behaviour? A generation ago MacCannell observed:

> *"The tourist world has also been established beyond the frontiers of existing society, or at least the edges of the Third World. A paradise is a traditional type of tourist community, a kind of last resort, which has as its defining characteristic its location not merely outside the physical borders of urban industrial society, but just beyond the borders of peasant and plantation society as well"* (MacCannell, 1975, p. 183).

Our discussion of peripheral discourses suggests that it is not just the tourist world that has been established beyond the frontiers of existing society, but many other discursive worlds. Tourism may be said merely to appropriate, or at least to promote, cultural myths, already embedded in notions of the periphery. The deep structure of many kinds of tourism representation is nothing more than reconstitution and reactivation of a complex, discursive mythos about faraway places that has accreted historically in culture, and sedimented in the minds of individuals in that culture. Semiologists and anthropologists often deconstruct the rhetoric of tourism promotion, for instance, as if to show it as an original fabrication, a primal force newly invented by commodifying agents, out of sheer bad faith to seduce innocent subjects into particular forms of travel. The truth is that promotion of peripheral travel (and other forms) attempts to mine a mythos that already exists in consumers' minds, indeed must exist, for it to have any impact. People are already constituted ideological subjects, moulded by cultural discourses, whose sedimented effects they have assimilated, long before they are exposed to tourism promotion.

Secondly, it is not, as the MacCannell extract implies, just paradises that are thought to lie and attract tourists as "last resorts". This analysis has demonstrated that paradise is only one kind of discourse within the mythos of peripheries; many other values - adventure, spiritual insight, enactment of the roles of scientist, survivor or explorer – are also inscribed into peripheral discourses.

Further it should be apparent that the arguments in this paper shift the problematic of tourism choice and behaviour from the realm of individual motivation to that of culture. It is still common to find peripheral behaviour being seen as an individual matter:

> *"The peripheral destination may possess symptoms of peripherality, but relies upon subjective interpretation of these symptoms by the tourist, while simultaneously the tourist will not perceive an area as peripheral without certain symbols of peripherality being present"* (Sorensen, 1998, quoted Brown and Hall, 1999, p. 9).

Soren's view has, of course limited truth, but this analysis suggests that it is cultural factors lying in processes of historical representation that make the "symptoms of peripherality" at destinations recognisable "for subjective interpretation". A destination achieves meaning through its resemblance to, and fit with, previously established notions of the generic properties of destinations to which it appears to belong. Thus, for instance, a barren landscape with ice and snow may be classified as polar and spark off a specific set of cultural, mythological associations even when, as in the case of Iceland, it is not in fact mainly polar.

> *Brown and Hall have recently argued that, "the attributes of peripherality, long viewed as disadvantageous, are now being seen as opportunities. Isolation and remoteness represent peace, difference, even exoticism"* (Brown and Hall, 1999, p. 9).

Again this paper suggests some revision to perspectives like this one. This historical inquiry has attempted to show that there were always positive elements in the mythos of peripheries, and that their cultural meanings were always to an extent contradictory. The Romantic movement, in particular, multiplied the positive discourses about peripheries in ways that have made them continuously attractive to fractions of educated, middleclass travellers for almost two centuries (not least, to travel and tourism lecturers with special interests in anthropological and environmental aspects of tourism!)[5].

Yet peripheral travel comprises the seeds of its own demise. Tourism domesticates the periphery. All peripheries start out as mysterious nowheres and end up as beaten tracks. Once a periphery starts to become well known, more visited and populous, it loses the mythic connotations of its peripheral status. Tourism tends to turn peripheries not into "pleasure peripheries", but pleasure cores, mini-versions of the profane regions from which they drew their visitors. Their problem is to preserve their symbolic identity to travellers and tourists, after the physical and social otherness that once constituted their imagined potency, has begun to weaken. Norway is a good case in point. In the first half of the nineteenth century it was perceived as a romantic wilderness (Butenschon, 1960) but by the end of the century, tourism had begun to turn it into something much tamer, as this cosy travel memoir by three girls in 1888 suggests:

> *"I have written to Mudies, to ask him to send me books on Norway; as, like all the world, we mean to be in fashion, and go there this autumn; and I can't get any. I said in my note, nothing scientific, not a treatise on fishing, or a guide-book; but something to tell me what to see, where to go, what clothes to take, and more particularly, what other people have done when they got there. Either there are no books such as I want, or they are all being read, and are "out""* (p. vi).

It is hardly surprising that, once they arrived, they found that the Lapps were charging threepence for being photographed and sixpence if their dog was included, and that they were also selling tourist pin cases, spoons made of reindeer horn, boxes, fur shoes, skins, and photographs. The disappointed peripheral adventurers concluded:

> *"They (the Lapps) seem to have been quite spoilt by the number of tourists coming to see them, and are dreadfully mercenary"* ("Three girls, 1888, pp. 51-53).

Nevertheless, though peripheral contacts may sometimes disappoint, the periphery remains a powerful force in travel and tourism by virtue of the historical weight of discursive myth that has been attached to it. The tourist is a culturally constituted subject, whose motives are affected by his/her history of exposure to the representations and discursive features attached to particular kinds of destinations and specific forms of travels. The tourist may therefore be, to varying degrees, a watered down fabulist, scientist, romantic or imperialist. Many specialist forms of modern peripheral travel are a product of the discourses in this paper. Backpacking – the traveller as romantic seeker of the sublime and picturesque ; eco-tourism - the tourist as quasi scientific expeditionary ; the trek and safari tour - the tourist as post-imperialist explorer; the guided archaeological tour - the tourist as orientalist scholar. Even the forms of peripheral travel may be a product of discourse- camping for example, is a form that owes its original popularity, not just to romantic notions of "sleeping under the stars", but to the glamour and adventure of military life under canvas (the Scout Movement, the first kind of organised mass camping, was designed with a military model behind it by Baden Powell).

Finally the link between peripheries and tourism is, in Germany, a country even more influenced by Romanticism than Britain, embedded in colloquial speech. When they need a holiday they use a phrase that translates as, "I'm ready for the island".

Conclusion

This paper has provided a historical sketch of four main discourses attached to the concept of periphery and suggested their effect on travel and tourism from Europe. Though they had their origins in different periods, they shared some similarities (Romanticism reinvigorated and reinflected the Medieval notion that peripheries could be the site of the marvellous; Imperialism and science both tended to envision peripheries as sites of adventure, but for different reasons). Elements of all four discourses have survived over time but in constantly varying mixes and proportions. It is the weighting and balance of each of the elements of each discourse in the interdiscursive whole at any given time that provides part of the cultural dynamics behind travel and tourism propensity.

All the discourses reflect a process of othering, since they constitute the imposition of finite provinces of constructed meaning and imagining on spaces and societies, brought within the classifying gaze and action perspectives of those from societies outside them. Even discursive elements of Romanticism, perhaps the most benign of the four primary discourses, represents a radical othering, as anyone who has seen the amazement (and delight) of Italian peasants at the commercial worth of old derelict casa colonicas, long since abandoned by their indigenous owners, to Germans and British weaned on notions of Romanticism and the Picturesque. The discourse of science reflected in the development of Anthropolgy was also established, and continues to operate, on a basis of othering that assumes difference between core regions (where the subjects of anthropology operate from) and peripheries (where the objects of anthropology are acted upon), Whatever its modern attempt to liberate itself from binary contrasts between native savages/ and civilised Europeans to this day the anthropologist predominantly sees the ambit of anthropology, including tourism anthropology, as one where people from developed core regions of the world go abroad to observe, classify and prescribe for those from developing peripheries, a regime of truth that Foucault would have appreciated.

However, far from being a distinctively modern process, condemned by writers like Edward Said and other post-imperial critics as monolithic, racist, and an ideological pillar of hegemonic domination, othering may be seen as a culturally universal process by which all indigenous populations invest societies and places at the edge of their known world, and beyond, with meaning that almost invariably assumes difference, rather than similarity. The main issue is not whether othering will operate, but what forms it will take and who, if any, has the power to act, prescribe and rule on the basis of the perceptions it produces - in the places they are produced about.

Moreover the othering of peripheries is, as has been shown, contradictory, rather than monolithic. The adverse discursive evaluations of peripheries are still marginalisation, fringe status and all the connotations that reside in phrases like "backwater", "out in the sticks", "beyond the pale", "middle of nowhere" and so on. But equally, as we have seen, peripheral discourses can invest distant regions with nobility, spirituality, scientific interest, and anticipations of adventure, as well as with all the favourable tourism attributes implicit in notions of "getting away from it all", "peace and quiet", "another world". Like the famous optical illusion of the simultaneous picture of the old and young woman in figure-and-ground sections of perceptual psychology texts, it is possible to be aware of both evaluations, though never to respond to them equally. The periphery is a cultural paradox- at once an inferior place, a joke location beyond the pale, but also an exotic outer limit where the body is tested or indulged, the mind exercised and the spirit sublimated.

Finally the implicit structural basis of this paper suggests how motivation may be envisaged, less as a psychological process, than as a cultural construct to be approached through the analysis of interdiscursive myth that people inhabit as a product of largely unrecognised forms of historical representation. Individual motivation is primed by cultural influences of such pervasiveness that they go unnoticed. The social imaginary relating to peripheries and faraway places, elements of which surround every member of a society, is not just a present force but, as Gramsci has suggested of ideology a historical legacy that sediments in common sense, collective aspiration, and subjective perceptions of individual choice. Every society carries its own stores of travel myths which cause its travellers to set out with different role models, different interests, different relationships to the past that are formed through historical representations, not just of places, but of travel itself. There are always culturally approved ways of going and approved places to go to. In European culture the periphery has been, and continues to be a potent travel goal.

Endnotes

1. A more detailed discussion of the elements of Romanticism, with a good sample of opposing views in the debate about its origins and meanings, can be found in Halsted, 1965.

2. The phrase is Raymond Williams from his seminal analysis, "Culture and Society", 1958, Chatto and Windus, London.

3. It would be more than half a century before the detective story and the thriller domesticated murder and horror in the confines of core cities, traditional market towns, and country vicarages.

4. Bram Stoker had never visited Transylvania and based his account on descriptions in Baedeker and other travel books.

5. For reasons of space a section on the selective class bias of travel to the peripheries had to be omitted. This issue will be separately examined in a later paper.

References

Acerbi, Joseph (1802), *"Travels through Sweden, Finland and Lapland to the North Cape in the years 1798 and 1799"*, 2 vols, Mawman, London.

Andrews, Malcolm (1989), *"The search for the Picturesque: landscape aesthetics and Tourism in Britain"*, Scolar Press, Aldershot.

Andrew, Malcom (1994), *"The picturesque: Literary sources and documents"*, 3 vols., Helm Information, Robertsbridge.

Ashton, John , ed. (1887), *"The voiage and travayle of Sir John Maunderville Knight"*, Pickering and Chatto, London.

Babbitt, Irving (1919), *"Rousseau and Romanticism"*, Houghton Mifflin, Boston.

Baker, J. N. L. (1937), *"A history of geographical discovery and exploration"*, Harrap, London.

Barthes, Roland (1982), "Introduction to the structural analysis of narratives" in, ed, Susan Sontag, *A Barthes Reader*, pp. 251-295, Jonathan Cape, London.

Brent, Peter (1979), *"Far Arabia"*, Quartet, London.

Brown, Frances and Derek Hall (1999), *"Case studies of tourism in peripheral areas"*, Bornholm Research Centre, Denmark.

Bucher, Bernadette (1981), *"Icon and conquest: A structural analysis of the illustrations of de Bry's Great Voyages"*, University of Chicago, Chicago and London.

Burke, Edmund (1958), ed. J. T. Bolton, *"A philosophical enquiry into the origin of our ideas of the Sublime and Beautiful"*, Routledge and Kegan Paul, London.

Burnside, John (1997), "Poetry and a sense of place", in, *Nordlit*, Nummer 1, *Proceedings of the Writing and a Sense of Place Symposium*, Tromso, 15-18 August, 1996, pp. 201-222..

Bury, Wyman ("Abdullah Mansur"), *"The land of Uz"*, Macmillan, London. (1911) Chatwin

Butenschon, B. (1960), *"Discovering Norway in the nineteenth century"*, London.

Cherry- Garrard, Apsley (1937, 1st ed. 1922*), "The worst journey in the world Antarctic 1910-1913"*, Chatto and Windus, London.

Davenport-Hines, Richard (1998), *"Gothic, 400 years of excess, horror, evil and ruin"*, Fourth Estate, London.

Foucault, Michel (1974*), "The archaeology of knowledge"*, Tavistock, London.

Gardner, Brian (1969), *"The quest for Timbuctoo"*, Cassell, 1969.

Green, F. C. (1955), *"Jean-Jacques Rousseau , A study of his life and writings"*, Cambridge University Press.

Grylls, R. Glynn (1938), *"Mary Shelley"*, Oxford University Press, London.

Hailey Rt Hon Lord (1944), "The role of anthropology in colonial development", *Man*, 5, Jan-Feb.

Halsted, John B. (1965), *"Romanticism, Problems of Definition, Explanation and Evaluation"*, Heath and Co., Boston.

Hazlitt, William (1944), *"Selected essays of William Hazlitt"*, ed. Geoffrey Keynes, Nonesuch Press, London.

Hodge, Edmund W. (1957), *"Enjoying the Lakes, From post chaise to National Park"*, Oliver and Boyd, Edinburgh.

Hohl, Andreas E. and Clem A. Tisdell (1995), "Peripheral tourism Development and Management", *Annals of Tourism Research*, Vol 22, No. 3, pp. 517-534.

Holmes, Richard (1989), *"Coleridge Early Visions"*, Harper-Collins, London.

Hussey, C (1912/1927), *"The Picturesque, Studies in a point of view"*, Frank Cass, London

Irving, R.L. G. (1955), *"A history of British mountaineering"*, Batsford, London.

Izzard, Molly (1993), *"Freya Stark, A biography"*, Sceptre, London.

Kingslake, Alexander (1982), *"Eothen"*, Oxford University Press, Oxford and New York.

Mackenzie, John M. (1986), *"Imperialism and popular culture"*, Manchester University Press.

Manley , Nathaniel (1788), *"Wonders of the little world, or, A general history of man"*, C. Taylor, Thornton and Jeffery, London.

Mountfield, David (1974), *"A history of polar exploration"*, Hamlyn, 1974.

Newton, A. P. (1926); *"Travellers' tales of wonder and imagination"*, in, A. P. Newton, "Travel and travellers of the Middle Ages", pp. 159-1173, Kegan Paul, Trench, Trubner, London

Newton, Eric (1962), *"The romantic rebellion"*, Longmans, London.

Nash, Dennison (1972, originally published 1963), "The ethnologist as stranger", in, ed. Curtis, J. E. and John W. Petras, *The sociology of Knowledge, A reader*, pp. 468-487, Duckworth, London.

Nicholson, M. H. (1959*), "Mountain gloom and mountain glory, the development of the aesthetics of the infinite"*, Cornell University Press, Ithaca, New York.

Nicholson, Norman (1972, 2nd ed), *"The Lakers The First Tourists"*, Robert Hale, London.

Oxford English Dictionary, compact edition (1977).

Owen, Elwyn R., Botterill, D., Emmanuel, L, Foster, N., Gale, T., Nelson, C. and Martin Selby (1999), *"Perceptions from the periphery- the experience of Wales"*, in, Brown, Frances and Derek Hall, *"Case studies of tourism in peripheral areas"*, pp. 15-48, Bornholm Research Centre, Denmark.

Penniman T. K. (1970 revised version of 1935), *"A hundred years of anthropology"*, Duckworth, London.

Riffenburgh, Beau (1994), *"The myth of the explorer"*, OUP, Oxford and New York.

Ross, Sir E. Dennison (1926), *"Prester John and the Empire of Ethiopia"*, in, ed, A. P. Newton, *"Travel and travellers of the Middle Ages"*, pp. 174-194, Kegan Paul, Trench, Trubner, Londonn

Ryall, Anka (1997), "A Vindication of Struggling Nature, Mary Wolstonecraft's Scandinavia", *Nordlit*, Nummer 1, *Proceedings of the Writing and a Sense of Place Symposium*, Tromso, 15-18 August, 1996, pp. 127-150.

Said, Edward (1978), *"Orientalism"*, Routledge and Kegan Paul, London.

Schama, Simon (1995), *"Landscape and Memory"*, Harper-Collins, London.

Seaton, A. V. (1989, ed), *" Journal of an expedition to the Feroe and Westman Islands and Iceland 1833 by George Clayton Atkinson"*, Bewick-Beaufort Press, Newcastle on Tyne.

Seaton, A. V. (1998), The history of tourism in Scotland, approaches, sources and issues", in, ed. MacLellan, R. and R. Smith, *Tourism in Scotland*, pp. 1-41, Thomson Business Press, London.

Seymour, M. C. (1967) ed, *"Mandeville's Travels"*, Oxford University Press, London.

Shelley, Mary (1978), *"Frankenstein"*, Penguin, London.

Stefansson, V. (1921), *"The friendly Arctic"*, London.

Summers, Montague (n.d..), *"The Gothic Quest"*, Fortune Press, London.

"Three girls" (1888), *"A jubilee jaunt to Norway by Three Girls"*, Griffin Farran, Okeden and Welsh, London and Sydney.

Victor, Paul-Emile (1964), *"Man and the conquest of the poles"*, Collins, London.

Webster (1976), *"Webster's Third New International Dictionary of the English Language"*, Encyclopaedia Britannica Inc., Chicago.

Wilford, John Noble (1981), *"The mapmakers"*, Junction Books, London.

Williams, Raymond (1973), *"The country and the city"*, Chatto and Windus, London.

Williams, Raymond (1976), *"Keywords, A vocabulary of culture and society"*, Fontana Paperbacks, London.

Zweig, Paul (1974), *"The adventurer, The fate of adventure in the western world"*, Dent, London.

The Odyssey in 2001: Representations of travel in space and time

Steve Shaw and Jackie Mulligan

University of North London, UK

Abstract

This paper explores the use of *travel* as a metaphor for Progress into the twenty-first century. In European and other cultures, the idea of the epic journey recurs as a motif to represent the intellectual and spiritual progress of a man. The idea of a collective journey may also be used to represent the communal achievements of humankind: a narrative recently retold in the 'Journey Zone' exhibition at the Millennium Dome, Greenwich. It is argued by the authors, however, that there is also a darker side of the journey-myth which is far from inclusive, for it may be used to sustain the image of one ideology to the exclusion of others. The latter may be 'vanquished' and subdued by those who master the technology of movement, especially where this facilitates superior motive power, speed and elevation. The vehicle may itself become a potent icon of modernity: the ship, the locomotive, the sportscar, the jet airliner, the spacecraft. The paper discusses the atavistic Ulysses with reference to the astronaut-heroes of Apollo 11, and how the lunar landing of 1969 has been mythologised as a critical event in the history of 'Mankind'.

Introduction

The idea of *life-as-a-journey* is an enduring metaphor, which in Europe can be found in the earliest literature. Around 700 BC, the poet Homer articulated a story of heroism and cunning which reaches even further back into oral tradition. In *The Odyssey*, the mortal favoured by the goddess Athena begins his nineteen year voyage after the defeat of Troy. The adventures of the resourceful Ulysses include amorous liaisons, encounters with the Underworld, as well as the mastery of elemental forces, sorcery and monsters before he returns to Ithaca to defeat the suitors of the faithful wife and queen Penelope. The ship which he commanded is a strong motif which features on Greek drinking vessels, frescoes and coins. As Roppen and Sommer (1964) emphasise, the epic 'journey' and progress of an individual is a recurring image and literary device used by writers as diverse as Dante, Mendoza,

Cervantes, Bunyan and Fielding. The extended metaphor thus spans five millennia of European culture.

The collective *journey-of-humanity* is also used as an analogue for communal achievements as Progress. The 'Journey Zone' of the Millennium Dome, contributes to the celebration of the year 2000 with a remarkable exposition of this idea. Sponsored by Ford, the exhibition identifies significant phases in world history from dug-out canoes and invention of the wheel. Sailing vessels and horse-drawn vehicles yield to steam power in the nineteenth century. The innovation of the horseless carriage and powered flight marks the turn of the twentieth, and the development of space travel leads us into the twenty-first. Through human ingenuity, the tyranny of distance is gradually overcome. Developments in technology facilitate a universal and liberating growth in personal mobility. The exhibition encourages the visitor to view a diversity of vehicle prototypes, and to consider the future as a range of travel possibilities.

It is argued by the authors, however, that there is another, more sinister and hidden aspect of the myth: a darker side of journeying, which is far from inclusive, for it may be used to sustain the image of one ideology to the exclusion of others. The latter may be 'vanquished' and subdued by those who master the technology of movement, especially where this facilitates superior motive power, speed and elevation. There may be an increasing gap between the travel-rich who enjoy the freedom of personal mobility and the travel-poor who increasingly feel imprisoned. The vehicle may itself become a potent icon of modernity: the ship, the locomotive, the sportscar, the jet airliner, the spacecraft. The paper discusses the atavistic Ulysses with reference to the astronaut-heroes of Apollo 11, and how the lunar landing of 1969 has been mythologised as a critical event in the history of 'Mankind'.

Of travaile and ravel

As Wallace (1993) comments, it is difficult for those of us living in comparative affluence in developed countries to dissociate the idea of travel with the prospect of fun and recreation. To someone undertaking travel just three or four centuries ago, however, the idea of taking pleasure in the journey itself would have seemed strange indeed. Today, it is not easy to appreciate the difficulties and dangers encountered by people making journeys which now seem comparatively short, but the old spelling of *travaile* - used by some authors until the early 1700s - makes a telling association between movement, hard work and physical discomfort. The vast majority of people spent their lives confined within the perimeter of a day's walk from home. Those who tramped the roads were generally treated with suspicion. The poor wayfarer was a marginal figure, a potential thief or social parasite. In times of economic hardship, many 'masterless men' took to the road seeking work: itinerants whose movement late medieval rulers tried to control by statute through the requirement to carry a licence and identity papers (Heal, 1990).

Those who could apply for a licence to travel included students and pilgrims. In England, the Reformation introduced a radical new Protestant theology which *inter alia* brought an abrupt end to Catholic pilgrimages. The Tudor monarchs and their successors nevertheless licenced a secular journey which came to be known as the 'Grand Tour'. The state needed an educated governing class of noblemen and gentlemen, endowed with knowledge of international politics, as well as an appreciation of the languages and customs of the European mainland. This 'moving academy' consequently became an important source of prestige, but it was rightly recognised that such travel might encourage more worldly distractions. Furthermore, visits to foreign countries by wealthy young men in their formative years, entailed the risk of religious indoctrination. Bacon's (1625) essay *Of Travaile*, emphasised the need for a tutor or 'grave servant' to act as a moral guardian. Bacon provides instruction on appropriate during and on returning home, especially the need to maintain one's cultural identity and superiority as an Englishman:

"'...and let his travaile appear rather in his discourse than in his apparel or gesture... and let it appear that he doth not change his country manners for those foreign parts; but only prick some flowers that he hath learned abroad into the customs of his own country."

Cartographers were mapping out a new geography of commerce, warfare and diplomacy. The medieval Mappa Mundi had shown a flat Earth represented by a circle centred on Jerusalem. Now, the Renaissance world view held sway. European explorers had reached China, colonisation of the New World had begun and the British Isles were no longer on the world's periphery. As yet, travel on home ground was not particularly fashionable. Some graduates of the two to three year Grand Tour might spend a month or so exploring the British Isles, but in general this lacked the status, intellectual stimulation, and excitement of foreign travel. It was also hard, dangerous and slow, even for those increasing number of 'well mounted horsemen' who rode post (Webb and Webb, 1913: 63-4). For such travellers, cartographers were beginning to produce folios of strip-maps enabling riders to plan their route, and by the early eighteenth century there were more portable road books for use on the journey itself. Ousby (1990: 14-18) comments on the significance of these developments in the material culture of travel:

"The road itself is emphasised at the expense of natural features like hills and rivers, which, unless they constitute an impediment to the journey, are relegated to the same category as country houses or churches marked along the margins of the route, as sights or features of interest falling within the traveller's view."

Between 1700 and 1800 important new relationships were to develop between the idea of landscape and the emerging notion of travel for pleasure. *Landskip* had first entered the English language in the late sixteenth century from the Dutch as a painterly word to describe the pictorial representation of a piece of countryside as a subject in its own right or as the background scenery behind a portrait (Barrel, 1972). Once regarded as an inferior art, over the first half of the eighteenth century landscape art became respectable. The genre was deeply influenced by Renaissance Italy where the innovation of linear perspective froze reality at a specific moment 'removed from the flux of time and change, and rendered the property of the observer' (Cosgrove, 1998: 22). A fine collection of landscape paintings evinced affluence as well as good taste, and those attributed to Claude Lorraine were especially prized. These evoked the pastoral idylls of the Augustan poets: nostalgic views of the Roman campagna in a Golden Age.

The Picturesque gaze required detached observation to visualise the harmonious whole, an abstraction which was made easier by the Claude glass. In origin an optical device used by painters to assist composition, typically it comprised a portable convex mirror about four inches across, mounted on black foil and in a convenient travelling case. The viewer sat with his or her back to the true landscape, observing its modified reflection in the mirror. The miniaturised, reflected image gave detailed definition only in the foreground and distorted the background so that its features shrank away into the distance (Bell, 1993). This had the effect of superimposing on the reality of landscape, effects corresponding to a Claudian type: Neo-Classical in form, composition, colour and tone (Andrews, 1989). For the leisured classes, the aestheticisation of landscape was thus promoted through Picturesque travel, and the perusal of landscape engravings of places which could be visited. 'Looking over prints' became a genteel afternoon pastime for the drawing room, sketching an outdoor activity for the well-mannered. An appreciation of scenic beauty in reality, as well as in art, was an important social accomplishment, rather like the ability to sing well or to compose a polite letter (Barrell, 1972).

In the last quarter of the eighteenth century, the aesthetic of the Picturesque thus became a fashionable way of contemplating the actuality of scenery, consciously derived from painters' compositions. Hitherto, art could imitate a landscape. Now, a landscape could imitate art, and in the British Isles influences from mainland Europe were naturalised. The quintessentially English landscapes of Gainsborough, such as *The Woodcutter's Return* (1773) and *The Watering Place* (1777), portrayed rustic scenes of Albion's own Golden Age: a countryside untouched by the reality of agricultural improvement and enclosure. There was a preference for the asymmetric, for rough and rocky terrain, winding lanes and watercourses, shady trees and natural vegetation, broken gates, well-worn stiles and dilapidated and derelict buildings. Viewed from a distance, figures in the landscape could also be Picturesque: low life characters poignantly adorned with tattered and ragged clothes going about their daily lives, or in repose watching over livestock, their posture deferential (Bermingham, 1986).

By the time that mainstream bourgeois culture was so readily absorbing Picturesque taste, the sensibility of the intellectual avant-garde was, however, moving in a new direction. In reaction to the Enlightenment, with its emphasis on Reason and Progress, Romantics were inspired by the philosophy of Rousseau and Goethe, the mysticism of Blake. Their discourse renounced the anaesthetising comforts of urban life and modern travel. Wallace, (1993) examines the origins of walking long distances to refresh the body, mind and soul. The virtues of 'excursive walking' were advocated by Wordsworth and those who formed the vanguard of artistic taste. Roaming on foot had previously been associated with impoverished wayfarers who had no alternative. Now, the idea of walking purposefully but with no practical aim was becoming the recreation of those with access to other means of transport had they wished to use it. Through the 1800s, as travel became less physically demanding and faster with a wider choice of modes, the practice of the Romantics became a leisure pursuit enjoyed by those in society's highest echelons.

Annihilating time and distance

Britain was leading the world in a 'transport revolution' (Bagwell, 1974). Industrialisation and the market economy for farm produce required improvements to the trunk thoroughfares across the country and by 1800 Parliament had authorised over 1,600 turnpike trusts to raise capital, upgrade roads, install bars or gates, and charge regulated tolls. Many remote areas were still poorly served by local roads, but there was now a compelling economic rationale to link smaller settlements to market towns and hence to regional centres and the metropolis.

Barrell (1972: 89) suggests that these developments should be understood as part of a wider movement to explain the countryside, and make each particular place more available to those outside it. There is therefore a concurrence between this process and the Picturesque way of seeing the landscape, with its desire to fix and appropriate the scene:

> *"The concern to be always moving through a place, to see it never primarily as a place-in-itself, but always as mediated by its connection to one place in the east, and another to the west, produces a sense of space which is always defined by this linear movement, so that to stop at a place is still to be in a state of potential motion."*

This way of seeing landscape was also a significant feature of the work of Turner, whose paintings could be interpreted as a meeting of the everyday and the epic. As Daniels (1993) comments, thoroughfares and intersections of route-ways, including rivers, canals and sea lanes, turnpikes, drove-roads, and later railways, are prominent elements. Development of the nation's industry, transport infrastructure, and the increasing bustle of traffic could be viewed with pride by the ascendant middle classes, and engravings of work by Turner and other less celebrated painters were reproduced singly or in bound volumes: a kind of vicarious tourism which also offered access to the greatness of the nation. In *Rain, Steam and Speed* (1844), a broad gauge express seems to glide above the Thames on the newly-built bridge at Maidenhead. Following the style of railway promotional prints, the heroic qualities of the civil engineering feat are dramatised, and contrasts emphasised: the old bridge and the new; speeding train and drifting boat; steam-driven locomotive and horse-drawn plough; straight track and meandering river.

The ideology of those with wealth and power thus tended to reinforce the notion that such circulation or touring remained their prerogative, whereas the immobility of the poor confirmed their subordination. To the rising middle classes of the nineteenth century, journeying to places which came to symbolise the nation and its heritage conferred inclusion and 'possession'. The itinerary - or surrogate journey through the perusal of landscape prints - could express patriotism and identification with the interests of the state (Helsinger, 1994). By the mid nineteenth century, however, the distinction between the mobile and immobile population was challenged by a revolution in travel technology which brought a sharp fall in cost, as well as some spectacular improvements in speed and convenience (Bagwell, 1974). Remote regions, once visited with difficulty and discomfort by the few, became accessible to the many.

The development of rail transport had far-reaching implications for leisure activities across a broad social spectrum. From the 1830s, cheap travel to the coast, countryside, festivals and sporting events was facilitated by charter trains and excursions. The locomotive became an emblem of modern times. Granville (1841), introducing his comprehensive guide to spas and seaside resorts, hailed it as a means of conveyance which seemed to level all topographical distinctions, 'annihilating time and distance'. In 1851, visitors by the million were brought to London to celebrate the nation's industrial prowess at the Great Exhibition. Limited purchasing power and free time remained, nevertheless, significant constraints for many, including women and children whose leisure was generally confined to the street and local neighbourhood (Walvin, 1978). And, those who could afford to exercise this new-found mobility disturbed the sensibility of some among the leisured elite. Wordsworth, now an ageing member of the Establishment, railed against the anticipated impact of mass tourism on the Lake: an assault by 'artisans, labourers and the humbler classes of shopkeepers' who should not be tempted to 'ramble at a distance' from their urban dwellings (quoted in Stephenson, 1989: 58).

The cultural implications of rail transport were fundamental: a profound reappraisal of relationships between society, nature, time and space. The very building of the railways flattened and subdued the landscape. The traveller, propelled through space, was separated as never before from the moving scenery which 'came to be viewed as a swiftly passing series of framed panoramas' (Urry, 1995: 119). Schivelbusch (1986) argues that rail travel put an end to the intense experience of traversed space characteristic of the pre-industrial age, and highlights contemporary use of the word 'projectile' to describe the rapid movement of the train. To the passengers, hurled forward at speeds of up to seventy-five miles per hour, the track, cuttings and tunnels appeared as the barrel through which the missile was fired. The view from the carriages was neither to the front nor back, but to the side, an evanescent landscape to which they were no longer connected. As velocity dissolved the foreground, train travellers felt as if they no longer belonged to the same space as the perceived objects which passed by so quickly.

Coinciding with the early development of rail transport, photography soon established its position as a creator of the picturable scene. In the nineteenth century, this was the exclusive domain of professional 'art' photographers and highly committed amateurs. Their picture views of the 'ideal scene' allowed the viewer to gain admission to the nation's heritage, tapping a market for surrogate travel which had already been established through the mass reproduction of engravings. As Taylor (1990) notes, however, by the early 1900s photography could be enjoyed by amateur snap-shooters of modest means, for Kodak had pioneered the mass production of cheap hand-held cameras, along with the industrialisation of film processing and printing. Sontag (1973: 9) comments on the association between photography and tourism:

> *"It seems positively unnatural to travel for pleasure without taking a camera along. Photographs will offer indisputable evidence that the trip was made ...that fun was had."*

Through its 'realistic' representation of places near and far, captured at a specific moment, photography also played its part in the transformation of people's consciousness of time and space. The linear view of the camera lens thus emulated the Claude glass. For, as Cosgrove (1998: 257-8) comments, it enabled 'the conventional landscape way of seeing, the visual appropriation of nature as a commodity, to be sustained and disseminated among a population far broader than that which landscape painting had addressed'.

By the turn of the century, mass-produced bicycles had also become available to artisans and the lower middle classes. With improvements to roads leading out of urban areas, a cycling craze caught on in Britain, France, Germany, Italy and other countries (Rubinstein, 1977). Cycling provided freedom from the constraints of public transport routes and timetables, a liberating feature which foreshadowed the invention and subsequent mass production of motorcycles and motorcars. Throughout Europe, roads were soon to be upgraded in response to the increasing volume and speed of motor traffic. And, with the development of powered flight, the technology of travel promised an unprecedented freedom of personal mobility. Marinetti's (1914) Futurist Manifesto eulogised the exhilaration of this new era:

> "*...adventurous steamers that sniff the horizon; deep-chested locomotives whose wheels paw the tracks like hooves of enormous steel horses bridled by tubing; and the sleek flight of planes whose propellers chatter in the wind like banners and seem to cheer like an enthusiastic crowd.*"

Flights of fancy?

The development of photography into cinema made it possible, not only to project visions of landscapes onto a screen, but to convey the sensation of moving through it. Such scenes could be set in the past, present or future. Cosgrove (1998: 263) discusses the futuristic scenes in the film of Wells' *Things to Come* (1936) in which the city is dominated by Modernist architecture and the rapid movement of vehicles. In contrast, the countryside is designed for 'relaxation and aesthetic pleasure, to be viewed from afar, from above, or from the window of a fast-moving machine'. By the time the film was first seen, the seductive appeal of the touring car on the open road had become a key theme in the motor industry's advertising campaigns. Modernity and speed were also features of the luxury train and ocean liner, while the novel sensation of even faster travel by airship or aeroplane was promoted to a wealthy clientele.

In post-war western Europe, the motorcar became personal transport for the affluent majority, following a similar growth curve to that experienced in pre-war North America. The construction of motorways flattened the landscape as the railways had done in the previous century. In Britain, as in other countries, the national motorway programme was hailed as a great public project. Wright (1985) notes how Shell encouraged the 'citizen motorist' to explore their common heritage of countryside and historic towns through three minute travelogues *Discovering Britain,* broadcast through the relatively novel medium of commercial television. With the development of wide-bodied jets, air travel was also to become citizens' transport, while the popular television programme *Tomorrow's World* demonstrated how science fiction fantasies would soon be made real through a technology which could propel humanity into space.

Pichel's Oscar-winning film *Destination Moon* (1950) had already captured the public's imagination. To coincide with its release, tour operator Thomas Cook had produced a leaflet advising customers that they were now taking reservations for holidays on the moon and elsewhere in the solar system. Thus began the 'moon register' of all those interested in booking a place on their inaugural lunar tour, whenever it might take place, a list which included 10,000 names when it finally closed in 1996. Clearly smitten with this idea, in 1950 Thomas Cook's marketing department had decorated a window of their London headquarters with a diorama depicting the possibilities of space travel, and an accompanying text:

> "*Already the restless mind of man is reaching beyond this little planet, out to the stars. Soon the cold surface of the moon may bear the print of his feet.*"

When footprints finally did mark the lunar landscape, the event was presented to the world by astronaut Neil Armstrong (1969) as an epic journey symbolising Progress: 'That's one small step for a man, one giant leap for Mankind.' The NASA space mission was, nevertheless, at the same time, an explicit propaganda exercise to fulfil President Kennedy's ambition of landing an American on the moon by 1970. The earlier triumphs of the Soviet Union through its sputnik technology and the achievements of her cosmonauts could be outdone, American confidence and pride restored. It has long been argued that the United States was thus asserting its claim, not only on physical space, but on the geography of the imagination; that the moon landing was as much about the advancement of an ideology as it was about the advancement of science.

Only recently has the gender dimension of the space mission been raised as a matter of concern in the media. In 'I'd Prefer to Send a Monkey into Space than a Bunch of Women', *Sunday Times Magazine* (15/01/98) commented on NASA's non-selection of female astronauts, and John Glenn's dismissive rationale that this was simply 'a fact of our social order'. Not until 1983, nearly twenty years after the Civil Rights Act had been passed, did NASA allow a woman into space. The fact remains that in 1969 a man stepped on the moon, a woman did not. But, in the United States and elsewhere there is now a growing awareness of the unanswered case of Wally Funk and six other female astronauts who were denied the opportunity to fly, despite out-achieving their male colleagues in training. Over three decades on, they are beginning to gain recognition as, for example, T-shirts emblazoned with their names and the words 'Women Fly' become available on the internet.

In contrast to the near-invisibility of Wally Funk and her female colleagues, astronauts' wives soon became celebrities, the object of popular adoration. In 'Apollo's Giant Leap to the Moon' *LIFE* magazine (04/08/69) portrayed them supporting their men, patient and faithful as Penelope to Ulysses. In one photograph, Jan Armstrong clutches a handkerchief to her tear-stained face, in a statuesque, submissive pose eerily suggesting the image of the Virgin Mary. Even today, representations of the space mission demonstrate a reinforcement of gender stereotypes which may seem inappropriate in the twenty-first century. In the 'Exploration of Space' gallery of the Science Museum, Kensington, for example, the only image of a real-life woman is a small photograph of Soviet cosmonaut Valentina Tereshkova, the 'first woman in space' (1963). Unlike her male counterparts, the caption tells the visitor her age, and little else. The only other image of a woman in the exhibition is a nameless mannequin, apparently engaged in women's work in the galley of a spacecraft.

In the new millennium, some predict another space race, this time unashamedly commercial in character. As Thomas Cook anticipated half a century ago, we are now entering the era of space tourism. Zegrahm Space Voyages is pioneering the opportunity for 'Adventure Travel in Space', and significantly, perhaps, the would-be astronaut Wally Funk is among those who have already booked. And, as global capitalism goes universal, the moon and planets of the solar system may also offer opportunities as real estate. As with landscapes on Earth, these may be commercially exploited, less for their physical resources than as fantasy-objects of post-modern consumer demand. Caidin *et al* (1998) discuss the prospects for exploiting Mars as NASA sells the right to name prominent areas of its geography, and global brands rush to associate themselves with the leading edge of space technology.

Conclusion: The Odyssey in 2001

References to travel and the means of propulsion to signify the idea of 'moving forward' - physically, intellectually and spiritually - are deeply ingrained. The metaphor of a journey to represent Progress of an individual, or of humanity towards a common purpose, is so commonplace that it is sometimes used unconsciously. The idea of 'travel for travel's sake' is, however, a fairly recent notion, facilitated by developments in transport and communications: a social construct with wealth and leisure time as prerequisites for participation. The experience of passing through an ever-changing landscape enables the leisured traveller to catch passing views of places to which he or she has no lasting commitment. The journey can be regarded not simply as a means to an end, but as a source of pleasure derived from a sense of freedom through movement. Those who are excluded through their poverty and immobility are merely gazed upon.

The restless joys of such travel can now be represented with spectacular realism through the moving images of cinema, television, video and multimedia. Feifer (1985) discusses the McLuhanesque global village: a network of communications from which it is possible to gain a little knowledge of a great many places and times. Such images are consumed, free from the context of any universally-held world view. For some years, then, it has been possible to experience the passive seeing function of tourism without the need to travel. Now, as microelectronics-based telecommunications merge with digital computer and media developments, the barriers of space-time are transcended with even greater ease. Multimedia technology offers the prospect of virtual travel: a 'vehicle' on which to roam around the world and accumulate tourist experience without ever boarding a mechanism of physical transport (Rojek, 1998).

The paradox of the armchair itinerary has thus reached a new stage of sophistication as the illusion of travelling through distant landscapes - and even backwards or forwards in time - is enjoyed as home entertainment. The new or post-(mass) tourist is, however, far more than a passive consumer of images. He or she derives pleasure from comparing image with reality, self-consciously playing the role of outsider-tourist (Urry, 1990). The actuality of landscape is to be anticipated, encountered and then relived through reminiscence. Developments in communications and media technology have seldom dampened the demand for travel. Indeed, for those who enjoy the privilege of social and physical freedom of movement, such technologies seem to offer stimulation by heightening awareness of the possibilities and creating the desire to experience places and pleasures of the journey at first hand.

Urry (1995: 144) argues that movement is central to the very idea of modernity, since it is 'responsible for altering how people experience the modern world, changing both their forms of subjectivity and sociability and their aesthetic appreciation of nature, landscapes, townscapes and other societies'. It is argued by the authors that this argument needs to be developed further to explore the relationships between freedom of movement, social mobility and power. Those who are prosperous and travel-rich may now enjoy complex lifestyles that blur the boundaries of work and non-work, liberated from dull routines and constraints of physical space which are the lot of the travel-poor. And, as the Futurist Manifesto presaged, fast-moving vehicles, from which scenery is briefly glimpsed, have become important cultural icons which make an explicit association between pleasure and power, not only in its literal sense of exerting mechanical force, but also in its broader allusions to sexual potency, social superiority and the capacity to control. As we enter a new millennium which offers the prospect of space tourism, the moon rocket and spacecraft may be added to the list.

References

Andrews, M. (1989), *The Search for the Picturesque*, Aldershot: Scholar.

Bacon, F. (1625), *On Travaile*, reprinted (1906) in Francis Bacon's Essays, London: Everyman.

Bagwell, P. (1974), *The Transport Revolution*, London: Batsford.

Barrell, J. (1972), *The Idea of Landscape and the Sense of Place, 1730-1840, An approach to the poetry of John Clare*, Cambridge: Cambridge University Press.

Bell, D. (1993), Framing Nature: First Steps into the Wilderness for a Sociology of Landscape, in *Irish Journal of Sociology*, 3, 1-22.

Bermingham, A. (1986), *Landscape and Ideology: the English rustic tradition 1740-1860, Berkley*, Los Angeles and London: University of California Press.

Caiden, M., Barbee, J. and Wright, S. (1998), *Destination Mars in Art, Myth and Science*, Harmondsworth: Penguin.

Cosgrove, D. (1998), *Social Formation and Symbolic Landscape*, Wisconsin and London: University of Wisconsin Press.

Daniels, S. (1993), *Fields of Vision: Landscape imagery and national identity in England and the United States*, Cambridge: Polity Press.

Granville, A. (1841), *The Spas of England, and Principal Sea-Bathing Places*, reprinted (1971), Bath: Adams and Dart.

Heal, F. (1990), *Hospitality in Early Modern England*, Oxford: Clarendon.

Helsinger, E. (1994), Turner and the Representation of England, in Mitchell, W. (Ed) *Landscape and Power*, Chicago and London: University of Chicago Press.

Marinetti, F. (1914), *Manifesti del Futurismo*, Florence.

Moir, E. (1964), *The Discovery of Britain: The English Tourists 1540-1840*, London: Routledge and Kegan Paul.

Ousby, I. (1990), *The Englishman's England: Taste, travel and the rise of tourism*, Cambridge: Cambridge University Press.

Feifer, M. (1985), *Going Places: the ways of the tourist from imperial Rome to the present day*, London: MacMillan.

Rojek, C. (1998), Cybertourism and the phantasmagoria of place in Ringer, G. (Ed) *Destinations: cultural landscapes of tourism*, London and New York: Routledge.

Roppen, G. and Sommer R. (1964), *Strangers and Pilgrims: an essay on the metaphor of journey*, New York: Humanities Press.

Rubinstein, D. (1977), Cycling in the 1890s in *Victorian Studies*, 1, number 1.

Schivelbusch, W. (1986), *The Railway Journey: Trains and Travel in the nineteenth century*, Oxford: Blackwell.

Sontag, S. (1973), *On Photography*, Harmondsworth: Penguin.

Stephenson, T. (1989), *Forbidden Land: the struggle for access to mountain and moorland*, Hold, A. Ed), Manchester and New York: Manchester University Press.

Taylor, J. (1990), The Alphabetic Universe: photography and the picturesque landscape, in Pugh, S.(ed) *Reading Landscape: country-city-capital*, Manchester and New York: Manchester University Press.

Urry, J. (1990), *The Tourist Gaze: Leisure and Travel in Contemporary Societies*, London: Sage.

Urry, J. (1995), *Consuming Places*, London and New York: Routledge.

Wallace, A. (1993), *Walking Literature and English culture: the origins and uses of peripatetic in the nineteenth century*, Oxford: Clarendon Press.

Walvin, J. (1973), *Leisure and Society 1830-1950*, London and New York: Longman.

Webb, B. And Webb, S. (1913), *English Local Government: the story of the King's Highway*, London: Longmans, Green and Company.

Wright, P. (1985), *On Living in an Old Country: the national past in contemporary Britain*. London: Verso.

Nazareth 2000: Time for celebration?

Noam Shoval

The Hebrew University of Jerusalem, Israel

The angel Gabriel was sent from God to a city of Galilee named Nazareth, to a virgin.... and the virgin's name was Mary.... And he came to her and said, "Hail, O favoured one, the Lord is with you! ....And behold, you will conceive in your womb and bear a son, and you shall call his name Jesus." — Luke I

Introduction

Nazareth is first mentioned in the New Testament as the place where Joseph and Mary – Jesus' parents – reside. In Nazareth Mary learns of her pregnancy (the Annunciation) and Nazareth is the place where Jesus grew up and was educated; the town also served as his base as he wandered through the Galilee. Consequently, since the very early days of Christian history, Nazareth became a focal point of Christian pilgrimage. In the past 150 years, Nazareth also became a magnet for other forms of tourism, following the initial development of modern tourism in the Eastern Mediterranean Basin (Ben-Arieh 1984). Today, in addition to its being a main focal point for tourism and pilgrimage to Israel, Nazareth is also the largest Arab city in Israel (more than 60,000 residents) and serves as an economical centre for the Arab population of Northern Israel (Hamdan and Jabarin 1997). Much like other small historical towns that are located in proximity to large cities (especially in a small country like Israel), Nazareth suffers from the fact that most visitors to the city arrive for a short visit of only several hours and then tend to leave the city, practically without making any economic contribution.

Nazareth annually receives approximately 700,000 incoming tourists to Israel and several hundred thousand visitors from the local Israeli population. However, since no more than 7% of these visitors remain to spend the night (Central Bureau of Statistics 1999), the city enjoys practically none of the economic benefits that originate from its being an important tourist attraction, while it suffers from negative impacts such as traffic and parking problems. Despite the poor performance of the tourist industry, this would nevertheless appear to be the city's best available direction of economic development since it is precisely in this area that the city enjoys a relative potential advantage.

For the past ten years, the Nazareth Municipality has striven to change this situation altogether. Accordingly, in the early 90s, the Municipality set the year 2000 as a leverage for attaining various goals such as the renovation of the city center and the development of tourism infrastructure that will render possible the desired transformation. However, it is already evident that despite the comprehensive actions that were initiated in the city in conjunction with the national government in anticipation of the year 2000 – the realization of the goals remains distant at this stage.

Background

In 1991, the "Art Cities and Visitors Flow" project was launched by the University of Venice Ca' Foscari and the UNESCO Venice Office (UVO-ROSTE). The objective of this project was to undertake interdisciplinary research on the management of tourism flows in art cities. In co-operation with international experts and local institutions, comparative studies were carried out in a number of selected art cities (including Aix-en-Provence, Amsterdam, Bath, Bruges, Oxford, Salzburg and Venice). The results of such studies were presented at the International Meeting held in Venice in 1991 and published in the UVO-ROSTE Technical Report No. 20. The International Seminar on Alternative Tourism Routes in Cities of Art was held from 24 to 25 June 1995 in Venice in order to gather further knowledge on the alternative tourism routes as one of the effective management tools for controlled tourism in art cities. In-depth analyses relating to the alternative tourism routes were presented for the cases of Genoa, Ferrara, Prague, Venice, etc.

In recent years, UNESCO Member States have requested strongly for appropriate guidelines and strategies to deal with new complex issues relating to culture, tourism and sustainable development. A new stage of co-operation was therefore launched with the first international seminar of the "Network for Tourism Management in Heritage Cities", held in Venice, 18-19 December 1998 (van der Borg and Russo 1999).

As a result of this seminar, Nazareth was selected to be one of four cities wherein pilot studies will be carried out during 1999. The pilot research in Nazareth began in April 1999 and was carried out until December 1999. The research was co-funded by UNESCO (Venice) and the City of Nazareth. The research may be divided into three main parts:

- The first stage focused on collecting data relating to tourism to Nazareth, both aspects concerning the "supply" of tourist services in the city, such as land use distribution in the historical core, as well as aspects concerning the "demand", such as the spending patterns of tourists in the city. The field work was conducted primarily in three cycles of concentrated field work, each lasting three days, with the participation of students from Bar-Ilan University (April 1999) and the Hebrew University of Jerusalem (September1999, November 1999). The following surveys were completed during the different field work sessions:

  1. Existing land uses in the historical core of Nazareth.

  2. Forty in-depth interview with shop owners in the historical core.

3. Surveys among "consumers" of the historical core:

    *Questionnaires to tourists/daytrippers.

    *Telephone survey of local citizens and residents of Arab villages around Nazareth.

    *Questionnaires to residents of Nazareth Illit and other Jewish settlements around Nazareth Illit.

-   The purpose of the second stage of the pilot research was to establish guidelines for creating a change in the character of the current tourist activity in Nazareth.

-   The third stage of the research was dedicated to an evaluation of the specific impact of different tools of tourism management that were considered for implementation in the second stage of the research.

This paper will present the major findings of the pilot study, which will serve as the foundation for the preparation of the municipal economic development plan of the historical core.

The urban decline of the historical core of Nazareth

The historical core of Nazareth has, for a considerable time, suffered from symptoms of physical, economic and social decline. This gradual process, which peaked in the mid 1990's, began decades ago following the process of modernization which took place in the region and led to the more well-established, Christian population abandoning the town's historic, crowded core for the newer, more spacious neighborhoods on the hill-tops overlooking the old city (Chad 1995). This process accelerated after the 1948 war, bringing a wave of refugees to the town from villages in the vicinity which had been destroyed during the war. The process of urban decline in city centers in general and in historic cores in particular is well known and has been documented in academic studies in many locations around the world and is the result of similar processes - the more comfortable sectors of the population leave the historic city centers for newer areas, with more spacious housing and modern infrastructure. As in Nazareth, it is the weaker population, both socially and economically, which usually remains behind in the city center and which is unable to maintain the historic buildings, some of which are hundreds of years old.

This emigration of the wealthier populace to the suburbs together with improved access resulting from the increasing use of private cars, has also led to a considerable share of the commerce, which had previously been concentrated almost entirely in the old city, moving out to the newer areas, as well as to the neighboring town of Nazareth Illit, which now possesses a large and modern shopping mall. Commercial centers have also developed in the Arab villages around Nazareth so that some of the customers no longer come to the town to purchase basic items. As a result of the commercial decline, more than one third of the businesses in Nazareth's historic core no longer function (see Figure 1), and those which do still operate, usually close their doors during the afternoon due to low demand.

A land use survey carried out for the entire historic core area, found that there were dozens of abandoned buildings, one to four stories in height, in which there is no activity. Another survey which examined all forms of land use in the historic core at street level (some 500 in number), also found that a third of all the stores in the historic core are inactive, and that a fair proportion of these had been closed due to renovations being carried out as part of the Nazareth 2000 project. In certain cases the stores were closed for several months of renovation and in many cases, the owners of the business, who in any case saw very little income, decided not to reopen the store. A further prominent fact is that the character of the area is not tourist oriented - less than 2% of the businesses are suited to tourists, and a fair share of other land uses are not attractive to visits by tourists or local residents in their leisure hours.

The processes described above create a vicious circle which sustains the physical, social and economic decline within the historic core.

Figure 1   Land use distribution in the historic core of Nazareth

Type of Land Use	% of Total
Offices used by self-employed professionals or other private firms	5.2
Light handicrafts (carpentry, metal work, etc.)	15.2
Fruit and vegetables	2.3
Food and light drinks (restaurants, bakeries .... processed foods)	5.5
Unprocessed foods (grocery store, spices, butchers, etc.)	7.4
Jewelry and cosmetics	5.1
Shops designed especially for tourists and day-visitors	**1.6**
Household goods (toys, stationers, etc.)	6.1
Clothing	14.3
Inactive business	**32.7**
Municipal or government offices, as well as medical services	1.5
Other	3.1
	100

The Problematic character of "tourism" to Nazareth

The second problem pertaining to the historical core of Nazareth and to Nazareth in general is that of tourism in the city. Despite the town's importance with respect to religion and tourism, this is not reflected economically. The main reasons for this are:

- The relationship between tourists and day-trippers: Only a small proportion of the total number of visitors actually lodge in the city (Ministry of Tourism and Israel Airport Authority 1988; Taskir1995; Midgam 1996), and this is due to the fact that in recent decades there has been no development of large, modern hotels in Nazareth capable of hosting large-scale tourism. This is in part due to political reasons of the central government, since unlike other towns in the area such as Tiberias and Netanya, Nazareth did not enjoy preferential status with regard to tourist development.

- Room occupancy as compared with Tiberias and the national average is low, and even in 1995, which was a record year for tourism in Israel, room occupancy in Nazareth hotels was far lower than in Tiberias or as compared with the national average (Central Bureau of Statistics 1999).

- Patterns of activity in time and space of day-trippers to the town – Much like other small historical towns that are located in proximity to large cities (especially in a small country like Israel), Nazareth suffers from the fact that most visitors to the city arrive for a short visit of only several hours and then tend to leave the city, practically without making any economic contribution. It is therefore no wonder that tourism occupies such a small share of land use, as noted above (Shoval 1999).

- Spending patterns of tourists and day-trippers in Nazareth:
  The small segment that spend the night in town spends an average of $39.7 in Nazareth. Net of the spending on accommodation, this segment spends an average of $8.35. The remaining visitors spend an average of just $4.2. Half of this group does not even spend one single cent in Nazareth and this group account for more than 90% of the visitors to the city. Both groups are spending relatively small amounts of money in the city. And only a negligible proportion of this sum involves economic activity in the historic core. Since there are no accommodation facilities in the historical core, contributions to churches do not usually make their way to the municipal economy, and most of the food services in the town - both tourism and non-tourism related – are not located in the historical core.

- Another problem is the development of hotels and tourist attractions outside the historic core due to greater availability of land. This further weakens the historic core. An example is the case of *Nazareth Village* (Shoval 2000). Many Christian tourists that visit Nazareth expect to find the calm and peaceful village where Jesus was brought up, but after experiencing the town's environment, they are frequently disappointed. In addition, a huge Catholic cathedral overshadows the historic core and actually serves to "drive out" believers, mainly from the various Protestant denominations, for example, that were hoping to experience natural or "authentic looking" sites. An initiative by Protestant groups both locally and from abroad sought to solve this situation by reconstructing an "authentic" first century village simulating the time when Jesus lived. To date, approximately $2 million out of a planned total of 30 million US$ have been invested in this project (Kesselman 1997a, 7; Kesselman 1997b).

It was claimed that tourists do not spend the night in Nazareth or remain for a more extended visit as there is nothing to do there in the evening, that the town does not offer the visitor sufficient experiences apart from the main churches (see Programatic plan, p.18), and in general there is no touristic atmosphere in the town. Although these claims should not be rejected outright, the fact is that the tourist routes taken by incoming tour operators in Israel since 1967 have led to a situation where it is not profitable to create such activity as there is no demand for it, while there obviously can be no demand if there is no activity. This situation is self-perpetuating and results in a vicious circle from which it is not easy to escape.

It should be noted that the urban decline of the historic core and the understandable problems in the town are interrelated and reciprocal, so that instead of tourism helping to rehabilitate the historic core as occurs in many other places, the situation simply deteriorates due to the state of the tourism industry in the town.

Critical evaluation of the Nazareth 2000 project

The concept of the "Nazareth 2000" project was initiated by the municipality in 1991. The aim of the project was to transform the city into a tourist city by building urban and tourist infrastructure such as new hotels, improving access to the city, renovating the old bazaar, the conservation of historic monuments, the dramatic lighting of monuments and the creation of tourist sign-posting.

In 1993, The Labour Party government took up the challenge and decided to lend financial support to the project. Since 1993, the different Israeli governments allocated an estimated sum of $100 million and have also classified the city as a "Type A" Development Area (1993). This classification enabled hotels and other tourist facilities to enjoy the benefits of being classified as an "Approved Enterprise" (eligible for government grants, government-guaranteed loans and tax benefits).

The government budgets were used primarily for two main purposes: The first was to solve the traffic problems concerning the access to Nazareth and especially the movement within Nazareth itself. The second concerned taking care of the infrastructure (electricity, water, gas etc.) in the historical core of the city that lies beneath its two major attractions – the Basilica of Annunciation and the Greek Orthodox St. Gabriel Church (see map no. 1).

Private investment as a result of the project lay mainly in the accommodation sector, as three large hotels were built: the Marriott (250 rooms) located outside the municipal boundary of Nazareth, the Howard Johnson – located in proximity to the historical core (246 rooms) and the Renaissance near the Mt. of the Precipice tourism complex (270 rooms). A total of 750 new hotel rooms joined the existing inventory of 600 hotel rooms in all categories (300 hotel rooms and 300 more rooms in Christian hospices).

The project which is now nearing completion should be credited with several major achievements:

- The physical rehabilitation of the historical core, which was carried out during the course of the project, represents an essential part of the current dealing with tourism management.

- There has been an improvement in the quality of life for some of the residents in the historical core, due to the work carried out in upgrading the various infrastructures.

- The project has resulted in positive exposure for Nazareth in the local and international media.

The first half of the 1990s, when the project took shape, was an excellent period for Israeli tourism. Incoming tourism expanded rapidly with a record 2.5 million tourists, including sea passengers, in 1995. This was largely the result of progress made on the political front between Israel and the Palestinians (1993 and thereafter) and the signing of the peace agreement between Israel and Jordan (1995).

At the same time, following these processes, international hotel chains began entering the Israeli market, taking over the management of many hotels. These developments, while the Nazareth 2000 project was being consolidated, led to extremely high expectations (Israeli Ministry of Tourism 1997). However, during the second half of the 1990s , at the phase in which the private sector was supposed to become involved in the project by investing in the construction of hotels and tourist attractions, several events took place which adversely affected the tourist industry in Israel both financially and in terms of image, and caused a number of investors (not just in Nazareth) to reconsider their intentions to invest in tourist infrastructure in Israel at the time. I refer to the assassination of Prime Minister Rabin in 1995, followed by a series of Hamas terrorist attacks in 1996 and the election of Benjamin Netanyahu to power which served to slow down the peace process and led to an outbreak of violence between the Palestinians and Israel (the Western Wall Tunnel incidents in Sebtember 1997).

Notwithstanding these mitigating circumstances, several points may definitely be credited to the project:

- The project was planned and carried out initially as a physical infrastructure project and as such it did nothing to change the activities of visitors to the town, either spatially or economically. Thus, due to the fact that only a small number of the planned hotels were actually built, and that even these were built far away from the historic core, the relationship between tourists and day-trippers and those who stay in the town did not change significantly and had no substantial impact upon the historical core. Moreover, no change was discerned in the visiting patterns of day-trippers to the town.

- The local population was not involved in planning the Nazareth 2000 project and no extensive information campaigns were therefore carried out on this subject. The feeling was also created that the project was designed to give precedence to visiting tourists over local residents, most of whom do not make a living from tourism. One example of this was the plan to turn Pope Paul VI Street, which is the town's main artery, into a one-way street for private cars and a two-way street exclusively for buses. Consequently, and particularly as the initial stages of the project severely disrupted the daily routine of local residents and owners of businesses, large sectors of the population were alienated and the project did not gain the political support of local residents.

- As a result of the infrastructure work in and around the historical core, various businesses were forced to shut down for several months, and in some cases even for a year. A fair proportion of these businesses did not resume their activities either in their old format or in a new format adapted to the new plan. In this instance, the project accelerated the processes of decline which the historical core is undergoing.

- According to the plan, preference was to be given to tourist traffic so as to reduce the time wasted by tourists in traffic congestion so common in Pope Paul Street. This was to take the form of loosening the traffic congestion in the city and especially in the city's main artery, Pope Paul VI street, by turning it into a one-way boulevard with two-way traffic being permitted only for buses. These improvements had the opposite effects in terms of keeping tourists longer in the city, and from the following quotation it appears that the planners had no idea of the outcome of the changes in accessibility in a city like Nazareth: *"... In any event, it is much more advisable to offer free parking if tourism is to be seriously encouraged".* (Rachamimof 1995, 29).

- The location of the hotels which were planned and built as part of the project: Little land is available in the city center or in the historical core, and the cost of existing plots is extremely high. On the other hand, there are dozens of abandoned buildings in the historical core, some of which could be converted to lodging facilities of various sizes. Moreover, in and around the core there are several historic buildings with conversion potential.

There is no doubt that bringing the lodging services into the actual core could have had a positive impact on economic activity in the entire core. In practice, two of the three hotels were built on the outskirts of the town's built-up area, at a considerable distance from the historic core (the Marriott is even outside the municipal area, and it pays local taxes to a different municipality). The main area designated for hotels is at the southern entrance to Nazareth, close to the mount of the precipice, that is traditionally identified as the "brow of the hill" to which Jesus was led by an angry crowd (Luke 4:29). This compound in the southern entrance to Nazareth comprises 2500 planned hotel rooms (in 8 hotels). Since the beginning of 1996, the tenders for hotel construction have been published several times but no bids were submitted by developers probably because of their location and the sum requested for the plots. In our opinion and the present situation lends credence to that, the decision to establish a huge tourism complex in the southern entrance to Nazareth was basically faulty - even tough it was perhaps the only large area of government land that was available for such a complex.

First of all, the large distance between the complex and the historic core, coupled with the fact that the complex was planned in such a way that it could support itself in terms of shopping and dining - would have led this complex even if it had been built not to contribute to the revitalization of the historic core of Nazareth.

Strategies for changing the nature of tourism in Nazareth and its impact on the historic core

The current approach to tourism management in Nazareth as reflected in the Nazareth 2000 Project:

Figure no. 2 presents this approach to tourism management, pursuant to which, as a result of the creation of sites to be visited in the core and the creation of infrastructure aimed at directing some of the commerce toward tourism, there will be changes in the spatial patterns of tourists visiting Nazareth. They will stay in the town for a longer duration and will reach areas much further out than the Basilica of the Annunciation. As a result, consumption patterns in the town will also change and those tourists who stay longer may also wish to eat in the town, buy souvenirs, etc., although all this without active steps being taken to bring about such change. The Nazareth 2000 project proposed the creation of a certain order in organized tourist traffic by suggesting that buses would let the tourists off at St. Mary's Well, from where the buses would travel to the parking lot in the garage area close to the Basilica of the Annunciation, where they would wait for the tourists until these have completed their tour of the church (Rachamimof 1998). In practice the plan has never been implemented. A parking lot for the buses as part of the commercial area was not constructed in the garage area and this concept has not been proven in practice.

Figure 2

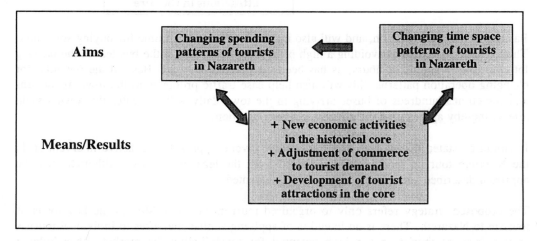

An alternative approach to tourism management in Nazareth:

Figure no.3 reflects the approach that active measures must be taken in order to bring about the desired change in tourism in Nazareth. Accordingly, and contrary to the previous diagram, the use of various measures to cause tourists to spend more money during their visit to the historic core will in turn bring about changes in the time and spatial patterns of tourism in the town (and not the reverse as in Figure no. 2). These measures will help break the vicious circle of tourism in Nazareth and provide reasonable conditions for the operation of the reciprocal system described in the diagram.

The key means of changing the patterns of tourism in Nazareth is to force tourist buses to park only at organized parking lots, fully supervised by the municipality. Payment at such parking areas will be progressive, that is in theory, a relatively high amount will be charged for entry to the parking area, and the longer the bus remains parked, the lower the payment. The idea behind this approach is to cause tour operators to change their routes for the day on which the tourists plan to travel to Nazareth, so that the visit to the town will include other sites besides the

Figure 3

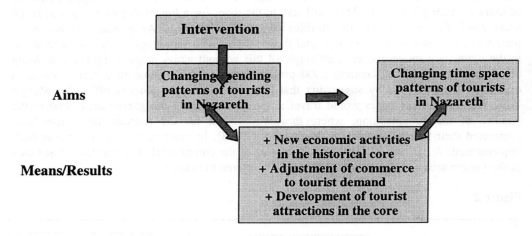

Basilica of the Annunciation, and will also include lunch and even time for buying souvenirs. This is naturally aimed at avoiding a high price from being paid if the bus leaves the parking lot after only a couple of hours, as has been the practice thus far. Beyond the potential for changing operation patterns, this will also help ease traffic problems in the town as the tens and sometimes hundreds of buses arriving in the town daily will not enter the town's main artery, thereby aggravating the already severe congestion.

It should be stated that as part of a pilot study, several approaches to active intervention in the Nazareth tourism models were reviewed from the legal perspective, although only the approach described above can be lawfully implemented.

The proposed strategy refers only to organised tourism which constitutes the key focus of tourism to Nazareth. There is no intention of applying similar measures to individual tourists as this form of tourism has a high potential for rehabilitating the market, since lodging services such as pensions, hostels, and the like, could be established for these tourists in the historic core. Municipal by-laws must naturally be implemented with regard to tourist transport and other drivers.

Reaction of tourists to restrictions: Imposing an entrance fee on the historical core

It could be claimed that such drastic measures will push tourists away from Nàzareth - that is, they will have a negative effect. However, the study assumes that since Nazareth is a holy site par excellence, tourists and pilgrims alike will continue to visit the town even if this entails payment, as is the case at many other tourist attractions which have sufficient powers of attraction or which are unique and have no substitute. The following shows an empirical study carried out in Nazareth during 1999 the purpose of which was, in part, to examine the subject of restrictions on the tourist (payment for visiting the town) and his/her willingness to visit the town.

The degree to which tourists are willing to pay for their visit to Nazareth's historical core and their reaction to the possibility of payment being imposed, are extremely important factors in assessing the "inflexible nature of the demand" for visits to the town by various groups of visitors. This issue is particularly important in estimating the impact that any type of policy would have on tourism to the town.

Foremost in importance rests the question of whether the demand for the product is inflexible by nature. In other words, this means that the hardships surrounding a visit to the city are of no consequence, as the tourists will continue to come because of the religious significance of the place. If this holds true, it may allow for the implementation of "extreme measures" in managing the tourism to the city. It is important to understand whether the demand for Nazareth is inflexible, in the sense that the tourism product that the city offers simply cannot be found elsewhere and that most of the tourists that visit the city today will continue to do so in spite of any difficulties they will incur.

Below are three Figures which present the findings with reference to the three questions that tourists were asked:

- In your view, should the municipality charge a payment for a visit to the historical core?

- In your view, what should the charge be for visiting the historical core?

- If payment is imposed on a visit to the historical core, would you still visit Nazareth?

A review of the three tables shows that there is indeed a basis for the claim that demand for visit to Nazareth is inflexible. Although it is clear from the figures, that most of the tourists would prefer not to be charged, half of them are willing to pay any amount and three quarters would visit the town in any event, even if a fee was charged for their visit.

Figure 4   In Your opinion, should the municipality impose an entrance fee to the historical core

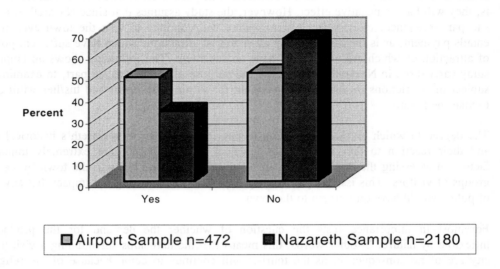

□ Airport Sample n=472   ■ Nazareth Sample n=2180

Figure 5   The amount of money ($), tourists are willing to pay for visiting the historical core of Nazareth

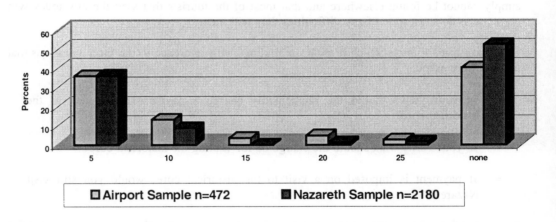

□ Airport Sample n=472   ■ Nazareth Sample n=2180

Figure 6   If an entrance fee will be imposed would you still visit Nazareth?

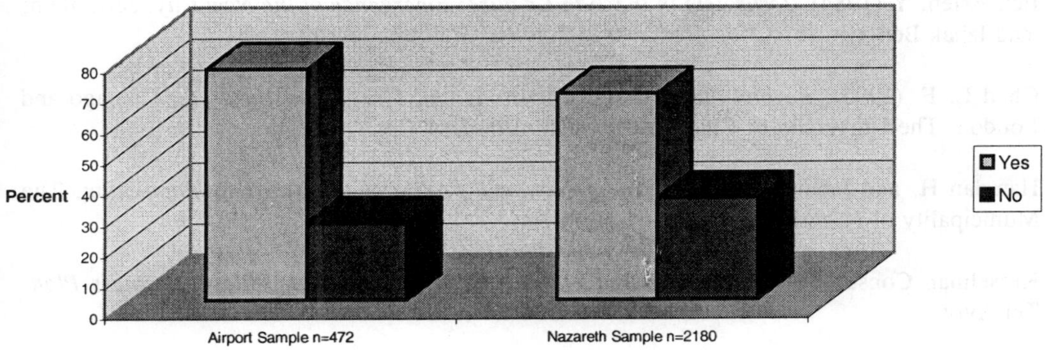

Conclusion

The first phase of the pilot study focused on collecting the relevant data and presenting the prevailing situation in Nazareth's historical core, particularly from the tourist and urban perspectives. In the second phase, an attempt was made to propose new thought patterns and a variety of tools for changing the patterns of incoming tourism visiting Nazareth in the coming years. This, by encouraging tourists to spend more time in the town and to consume more goods. It is proposed that at least in the first stage this should be done by implementing certain hard measures to "force" tour operators and visitors to consider increasing their visiting time to Nazareth.

The objective is that these processes will encourage the local economy, which in response will create additional tourist services, thereby creating the initial conditions to break the vicious circle which currently exists in the town with respect to tourism.

Acknowledgements

The author wishes to thank the following persons for their assistance during the different stages of the research: Mr. Abdallah Jubran, Director General of the Municipality; Mr. Ehab Sabbah, Director of the Strategic Planning Unit and Mr. Tareq Shehada, the Director of the Tourism Unit, at the municipality of Nazareth.

References

Ben-Arieh, Y.(1984), *Jerusalem in the 19th Century: Emergence of the New City*. Jerusalem: Yad Izhak Ben-zvi

Chad E. F. (1995), *Beyond the Basilica: Christians and Muslims in Nazareth*. Chicago and London: The University of Chicago University Press.

Hamdan H. and Jabarin J. (1997), *Socio-economic profile of the Nazareth Population*. The Municipality of Nazareth: Nazareth (In Hebrew).

Kesselman Consulting and Coopers and Lybrand (1997a), *Nazareth Village Business Plan*. Tel Aviv.

Kesselman Consulting and Coopers and Lybrand (1997b), *Nazareth Village* Market Study: Final Report. Tel Aviv.

Midgam – Consulting and Research Ltd. (1996), *Tourist's Survey: March 1995 – February 1996*. Jerusalem: Ministry of Tourism.

Ministry of Tourism and Israel Airport Authority (1988*), Survey of Tourists and Residents Departing by Air 1986/7*. Jerusalem: Dahaf Research Institute.

Rachamimof A. (1995), *Nazareth 2000*. Ministry of Tourism: Jerusalem. (In Hebrew).

Rachamimof A. (1998), *Master Plan for Nazareth: Final Draft*. Tel-Aviv. (In Hebrew).

Shoval, N. (1999), "The Challenge of Urban Tourism Management in a Historic City and a Pilgrimage Center: Nazareth as a Case Study," in J. van der Borg and A. P. Russo (eds.), *Tourism Management in Heritage Cities* . Technical Report no. 28: UNESCO, Regional Office for Science and Technology for Europe (ROSTE).

Shoval, N. (Forthcoming, Spring 2000), 'Commodification and Theming of the Sacred: Changing Patterns of Tourist Consumption in The "HoLand", in M. Gottdiener (ed.), *New Forms of Consumption: Consumers, Media and Commercial Spaces*. Boulder, Colorado: Rowman and Littlefield.

State of Israel, Central Bureau of Statistics and the Ministry of Tourism (Various editions), *Tourism and Hotel Services Statistics Quarterly*.

Taskir – Survey and Research Ltd. (1995), *Survey of Tourists Departing from Israel* 1994. Jerusalem: Ministry of Tourism.

The Israeli Ministry of Tourism (1994), *Programmatic plan for developing the tourist industry: Nazareth and Kefar Qana region*. Jerusalem (In Hebrew).

The Israeli Ministry of Tourism (1997), *Israel 2000*: Final account. Jerusalem (In Hebrew).

van der Borg, J. and Russo, A. P. (eds.), *Tourism Management in Heritage Cities*. Technical Report no. 28: UNESCO, Regional Office for Science and Technology for Europe (ROSTE).

Sustaining tourism and culture in the Donegal Gaeltacht

Jayne Stocks

University of Derby, UK

Sustainability, heritage and community involvement have all been 'buzz words' in tourism in the 1990s. It is important not only to expound these principles at the academic, and sometimes ideological, level but also to examine their practical implementation. A case study approach has been used to research the issues encountered by a community in the Republic of Ireland (hereafter Ireland) endeavouring to develop a sustainable form of tourism, sensitive to the cultural and natural environment of the area.

From a national perspective, culture and heritage have been integral to the development of tourism in Ireland. Between 1989 and 1993 almost £50million of the £131.4 million spent on product development under the Operational Programme for Tourism was designated to culture and heritage attractions. Between 1994 and 1999 the 2nd Operational Programme allocated a further £98 million to the same area (Department of Tourism and Trade, 1994). A Visitor Attitude Survey conducted for Bord Failte in 1997 put culture and history as the third main advantage of Ireland as a holiday destination after the friendly hospitable people and scenery. It would therefore appear that the tourists place as much importance on this facet of the Irish holiday experience as do the government bodies.

In the Bord Failte Development Plan, 1994 –1999, the need to attract an 'optimum' number of tourists, rather than maximisation of tourist numbers previously desired in earlier strategies, was seen to be the sustainable way forward (Stocks, 1996). This strategy implies maintaining acceptable carrying capacities throughout the country to ensure a sustainable tourism product. Thus, the importance of encouraging a geographical as well as seasonal spread, so as not to exceed the proposed but vague optimum number of tourists, is expounded, in theory, by government agencies (Bord Failte, 1994).

Research into the allocation of the funding mentioned indicates that a large proportion has, in the past, been concentrated on Dublin and the South West, areas which already enjoy the benefits of large numbers of tourists. The North West of the country, in which Donegal is situated, currently attracts the fewest numbers of tourists and creates the lowest revenue of any of the regions in Ireland. In fact these numbers have been falling from 1,456,000 tourists in 1996 to 1,397,000 in 1998. Similarly the revenue from tourism has decreased from Ir£201.8m in 1996 to Ir£200.6m in 1998. In the same periods tourist numbers to Dublin, for example, have increased from 3,470,000 to 4,095,000 and revenue increased from Ir£529.1m to Ir£627.8 Overall, the figures of both tourists and revenue to Ireland have shown a marked increase. (Bord Failte, 1997 and 1999). These disappointing figures for the North West are from an area which has outstanding natural beauty and is steeped in culture and heritage – the prime tourist attractions Ireland markets to the world. Rather than creating a greater geographical spread of tourism it would appear that the regional disparities have been increased.

This paper considers how a specific community has used tourism as an aid towards economic redevelopment and at the same time attempted to maintain the social fabric and cultural integrity of the area with little external assistance. This lack of external aid, or interference, will be assessed as to whether this has actually benefited or created problems for the community in the long term. The sustainability of the existing product, particularly relating to the social and cultural aspects of the area, into the 21st century will also be evaluated. The specific case study to be examined in this paper is Glencolumbkille (Gleann Cholm Cille) a small, remote, Gaeltacht community in Donegal. Richards and Hall (2000) discuss the changing concept of the term community from the traditional place-based notion of community through challenges to this based on rationalisation, global communications and increased mobility of society. However, the postmodern concept of a community "as a vehicle for rooting individuals and societies in a climate of economic restructuring and growing social, cultural and political uncertainty" (Richards and Hall, 2000:2) is relevant to this case study. The fact that this is also a community contained within a specific topographical location should also be acknowledged.

The Gaeltacht

The meaning of the term 'Gaeltacht' must first be established in order to understand the context of this case study. 'Gaeltacht' is the term given to those areas of Ireland, designated by Government order, where Irish is still spoken as the community language. There are seven specific Gaeltacht regions. These are Donegal, Mayo, Galway, Kerry, Cork, Waterford and Meath. The areas of the Gaeltacht are not necessarily contiguous and the regions are not specific to any county boundaries or cover any particular counties in their entirety. They are made even more difficult to distinguish due to the fact that do not appear on the standard, or more commonly used tourist maps of Ireland and there is no clear signposting to establish the fact that you are entering a Gaeltacht region. The majority of these areas are on the periphery of Ireland and have suffered from lack of accessibility combined with poor agricultural land and a less favoured climate. In many cases this has led to financial uncertainty or even poverty. It can be argued that their peripherality and difficult social circumstances has allowed the strength of culture, in terms of language, music, story telling and dance to survive. In addition, many of these areas, including the Donegal Gaeltacht, are characterised by their spectacular scenery. The 1991 census monitored just over 81,000 people living in these regions (Udaras na Gaeltachta, 1995) with their traditional forms of employment being in the primary industries of farming and fishing. However, there has been more recent growth, supported by government initiatives, in textiles, engineering, electronics, aquaculture, media and tourism.

There are agencies in place which have specific responsibilities for the Gaeltacht regions. Udaras na Gaeltachta is a Government agency given the task to develop the economy of the Gaeltacht so as to facilitate the preservation and extension of the Irish language as the principal language of the regions. Although they are involved with many areas of economic development and tools for regeneration, tourism plays a significant part within their strategy. They state that these areas present an opportunity to naturally maintain the continuation of Irish tradition and language and to provide an environment where other people can learn Irish (Udaras na Gaeltachta, 1995).

Meithal Forbatha na Gaeltachta (MFG) has the responsibility for operating the LEADER programme in rural development in the Gaeltacht. LEADER, sponsored through the EU, identifies four different types of projects: promotion of regional identity, exploitation of cultural heritage, creation of permanent cultural infrastructures and organisation of specific cultural activities. They state:

> *"affirming the local cultural identity and the improvement in the quality of life brought about by these activities strengthens pride of rural populations and their sense of belonging to a territory – which mean guaranteed survival and development".*(European Commission, 1997:1)

MFG poetically, but quite accurately describe the Gaeltacht areas as follows:

> *"The Gaeltacht is many things – a physical space, a state of mind, a symbol, the residuary legatee of an ancient civilisation, a metaphor for a central strand of national identity. But, for the residents it is also a space in which to earn a living, in a place and time where such is difficult to achieve."* (MFG, 1994:1)

This quote emphasises the importance of the heritage and culture of these regions, which alone could be criticised as ideological or an attempt at museumification, but also considers the reality of the communities living in these areas. The current dilemma is further acknowledged in the following quote:

> *"The very achievement of even a modest prosperity demands a level of interaction with the 'outside world' which threatens the existence of linguistic and cultural identity."* (MFG, 1994:1)

MFG commissioned the Tourism Research Unit at University College Dublin, in association with University College Galway to produce a strategy for the Gaeltacht regions. The resulting paper, From the Bottom Up, examined the strengths and weaknesses of all the Gaeltacht regions and proposed several strategies that should be considered. As the name implies, the strategies heavily involve the local communities and suggest that the communities should determine the priorities for each area and that they should be the primary beneficiaries (MFG,1994:3). The key strategies identified as the way forward for these areas include the desire to maintain quality and increase revenue, with careful monitoring of carrying capacities; developing accommodation provider's associations who could collectively link in with touring agents offering holidays such as cultural tours; giving support to tourism related operators committed to the use of the Irish language; and strengthening the marketing of the regions as a 'place apart'. They also suggest that local empowerment should be developed by extending the 'block grant' scheme so that real devolution could take place, rather than relying on central government approval on a project by project basis (Stocks, 2000). Although the full range of the strategies is not discussed it can be seen that the community approach to the development of tourism in these areas is expounded as being the optimum strategy for sustainable cultural development. It is also important to note that agencies exist which aim to regenerate the Gaeltacht in conjunction with maintaining the social and cultural fabric of the regions.

The Donegal Gaeltacht

The Donegal Gaeltacht is a particularly remote and sparsely populated area where traditional industries such as hill sheep farming, in-shore fishing and turf cutting have tended to be subsidised by social welfare allowances (O Gallachoir, 1995). With the decline of many of these traditional industries the Donegal region generally has suffered steady out migration, although research indicates that people would rather stay if employment were available.

The report conducted for MFG (1994:130) identified a variety of strengths and weaknesses relating to this region which are still applicable today. Amongst the strengths, the important points to note which are relevant to the case study site include the reputation of the Donegal Gaeltacht for 'spectacular scenery and high quality unspoiled environment', summer colleges based on the language and culture of the region, strong Irish musical tradition and friendly, hospitable people. On the negative side the requirement for better accommodation, access and infrastructural difficulties, seasonality, depopulation leading to a lack of local craft providers and the need to strengthen poor local marketing skills through information and training have all been recognised. It is acknowledged that improvements have been, and are being, made in the Donegal Gaeltacht but that different areas within this region require specific strategies for their development based on their particular circumstances.

The case study examined within the Donegal Gaeltacht is that of Glencolumbkille. Primary research has been conducted over a period of four years. Some of the research stems from specific secondary sources, which are referenced, but much of the information is taken from semi structured interviews and informal discussions with many of the key players and local community who were all very generous of their time and knowledge.

Glencolumbkille

Glencolumbkille, the area for this case study, is situated on the Slieve League Peninsula at the South West point of Donegal. It is set on the coast, within a beautiful but wild and rugged landscape. The area has a strong tradition of culture and heritage. Evidence of settlers as far back as the Stone Age with their ancient tombs, through the Celtic period and on to early Christianity are all to be found within the many archaeological sites of the area, and annual pilgrimages to the Stations of the Cross still take place in June each year. As a Gaeltacht area the continuation of the use of the Irish language is also important to the community. Glencolumbkille epitomises the earlier suggestion given that remoteness has helped to preserve the rich heritage of this area. However, it is this same remoteness which led to almost catastrophic problems in the 1950s. Emigration, no industry, no electricity, no water supply and few tarred roads were leading to a dying community (McDyer, 1984).

It is acknowledged that it was the work of one man, Father James McDyer, and his ceaseless work and inspirational attitude that was to change the situation. This does not intend to become a testimonial to a Parish Priest, although when visiting the community his importance and inheritance after his death in 1987 can not be escaped. However, his vision and actions towards developing tourism as one of the means of sustaining the community has to be recognised.

Fr. McDyer was obsessed with the idea that strangers would come in and destroy the character of the community by instigating a type of tourism development out of character with the environment. His idea was that the benefits of tourism should be for the local people to the greatest possible extent. Although the term was not in popular use in the 1960s it must be acknowledged that he was intent on developing tourism with a 'bottom up' approach. This involved developing tourism from within the local community, maximising the economic benefits to them and creating a type of tourism which would work with, and enhance, the natural beauty and culture of the area.

The folk museum

His first idea, to instigate the establishment of 60 'mini-hotel' farm holidays failed due to lack of community interest. However, visits to the Bunratty Folk Museum and the Ulster museum inspired him to build the West Donegal Folk Museum. In 1967 a site was chosen, a local factory owner sold him the land and the local Lord Moyne gave a substantial donation. The initial four buildings were erected within 3 months, many of the local community giving a free day's labour to complete the project. All the locals then gave old utensils, furniture and artefacts to create cottages depicting various periods of history over the last three centuries. In fact a mangle donated from a nearby hospital is the only artefact not to come from Glencolumbkille itself. This vision was made a reality for the village with outline planning permission only. Dublin finally assented to the full planning permission and this was received the day after the folk village was formally opened by the Minister for Transport and Tourism in 1967 (McDyer, 1984).

Since that time the village has expanded considerably with a craft shop selling as much locally made produce as possible, a shebeen – not selling the traditional poteen but homemade wines, cake and marmalade, and replica lime kiln, mass rock, sweat house and round tower. There is also a large building which is used for a café during the open season and can be used for evening concerts. A new small museum and interpretation centre has also recently opened portraying the archaeological, social and cultural heritage of the area. All the exhibits are explained in Irish and English and there is also a video tape of Fr. McDyer demonstrating his work and love for the area. Fr. McDyer conveyed the idea for the interpretation centre to the current manager some years ago and he was determined to complete the project in his memory.

Originally the folk museum was set up as a charitable trust with the profits being made over to the community

> *"For the advancement of traditional culture and for higher education of their more needy children, in perpetuity"* (McDyer, 1984, p93)

Today the folk village is held in trust by four local people and still only employs local workers, thus keeping alive the vision of a community run tourism development for the direct benefit of those same local people. In 1998 the number of visitors per annum was approximately 30,000.

Oideas Gael

In 1984 Oideas Gael was founded in Glencolumbkille by Dr. Watson, a Presbyterian from Belfast and Liam Cunningham, a Catholic from the local community. Originally it was run on a part time basis with just 34 students attending classes in a local school. Oideas Gael now has a permanent base created with funding from the International Fund for Ireland (IFI), Udaras na Gaeltachta and bank borrowing. This organisation aims to promote the Irish language and foster Irish culture by offering language courses to adults as well as bilingual courses in subjects such as archaeology, hill walking, set dancing and painting. The idea that the centre has is that young and old can come to the centre, bringing people together from Irish, other Celtic and alternative backgrounds to participate in the culture of the area as well as everyday Gaeltacht life.

> *"Our programme is one of total immersion in the language, not just in classes, and that is what is attracting people"* (Liam Cunningham, 1995)

In 1997 Oideas Gael had over 2,000 participants from over 26 countries with over 50% of the participants of these programmes from overseas. There is also an estimated 40% – 50% return rate of students, which demonstrates its popularity once discovered. The belief is that this is also keeping the use of Irish alive for those who come to the classes and for the local community to interact with the participants. As well as creating this cultural benefit each participant gives economic benefit to the area by their spend on local accommodation, provided by Oideas Gael or local Bed and Breakfast establishments, food, drink and souvenirs. In 1994, with far less visitors than today, research indicated that visitors to Oideas brought in £250,000 per year to the Irish community, of which the local community received £150,000 (O'Hara, S. 1994). Whilst this does not solve the economic problems of Glencolumbkille it is a significant income to a small community which was in danger of collapse only forty years ago. Oideas Gael is still growing, offering a wider range of courses in 1999 to include landscape and culture, Celtic pottery, flute and bodhran playing, with some courses beginning in April and available until October.

> *"We are not developing a mass tourism product but a specific product that is compatible to the region."* (Liam Cunningham, 1995)

Tapies Gael

In 1993 another initiative was developed based primarily on cultural continuity and revival, but also on tourism. This is Tapies Gael. Weaving is a traditional industry to the area, but it had fallen into decline since the late 1940s. Udaras na Gaeltachta gave a grant to a group, known as Tapies Gael, for older members of the community to train six young people in the traditional crafts of dying, spinning and weaving. Four members of this team survive, producing tapestries influenced by their Gaelic culture, music, archaeology, folklore and social history. The tapestries vary from traditional to contemporary and may be commissioned by private or corporate sponsorship. They have been successful in exhibiting their work in Ireland and overseas and have continued their own work and developed short courses to encourage staying visitors using premises within the Oideas Gael buildings. This again demonstrates a community based initiative which has been developed to maintain the cultural heritage of the area and encourage tourists to visit, and stay in the area to provide much needed employment and income.

Current Issues and initiatives

The community based cultural tourism initiatives outlined appear to be very positive. To date this has generally been the case and, whilst they do not address all the problems of peripherality and lack of revenue in the area, they have made a significant contribution to retaining and reviving various aspects of the cultural heritage of the community and to stemming the out migration of many of the inhabitants.

However, the local people still perceive there to be some problems with the development of tourism in the area. The manager of the Folk Museum commented that many people are coming to the Glen but few are staying. As well as this being negative in terms of maximising revenue this also means that the tourists do not fully appreciate the culture.

> *"If you don't come and meet the people and talk to the people and them talk to you then you haven't visited."* Shane Gillespie (1998)

There is a wide selection of accommodation available in the Glen, supporting many livelihoods, including a hotel, self-catering cottages, chalets, bungalows and houses, hostel, and numerous bed and breakfasts. Therefore there is the infrastructure in place to meet the demand of a limited number of tourists, and it is established that the Glen is not trying to attract mass tourism. The aim is to maximise the occupancy of these establishments and possibly see some limited growth. In order to attract more staying visitors the area is likely to require a more proactive marketing strategy. The community does not want to attract mass, low spending, day visitors and therefore specific expertise must be used when developing the strategy. However, there is little money for marketing within a small community such as this and outside assistance, for finance and training, and co-operations with other similar areas could be required to facilitate a targeted marketing strategy.

The loss of Fr. McDyer has had a negative effect on the motivation and management of tourism. Since his death Glencolumbkille has not sent any delegates to trade fairs and has relied greatly on word of mouth marketing. The Father was seen as a leader and thinker and the current situation is described as a 'famine of leadership'. A parish council exists where ideas are heard, but there is no focus of one person to co-ordinate and manage tourism in the community. In much of the literature on community based tourism the emphasis is placed on the involvement and consultation with the locals. However, rarely is the need for a leader and motivating force within this group examined. In this case study it was the actions of the community inspired by the vision and determination of one individual that instigated these developments. The story of a community, Port, a few miles away with a similar situation to Glencolumbkille some fifty years ago was related by a local of the Glen. There, there was no guiding force. A visit to examine this site of Port revealed a poor, single track, dirt road leading down through beautiful scenery to a spectacular rocky bay. The only evidence that this had once been a community were the remains of several deserted cottages along the hillside. The feeling created was not specifically frightening, but one of isolation and unease. Either side of the same headland were so dramatically different sites which had such similar resources and opportunities a relatively short time ago. Quickly, and almost relieved to be leaving the beautiful but troubled site of Port before darkness fell, it was a marked contrast to enter the warmth of Glencolumbkille, complete with fiddle players at every turn who were attending a week long festival. The comparison is being made to stress the fact that many felt a similar fate was to befall Glencolumbkille in the 1950s, until the active fight for its survival was championed by this local priest. The issue of leadership and motivation in community based initiatives, including tourism, is one that is often neglected. This case study serves to illustrate its importance.

Another problem raised was that some members of the community felt that government bodies were overlooking the area, both regionally and on a community basis. Shane Gillespie, manager of the folk museum, termed the North West of Ireland as the 'forgotten counties'. Udaras have identified a small number of specific locations, which includes South-West Donegal (the region surrounding this case study), where special emphasis will be placed on sourcing suitable projects during 2000. The remit of such projects is intended to be through small industry development and the promotion of the social economy, natural resource and cultural tourism initiatives (http://www.udaras.ie/releases/yearend.html). This would appear to be positive news for the Glen, although locally the reservation was raised that although Udaras do good work for Gaeltacht areas too much emphasis was given to 'lame duck' enterprises rather than to 'developed' projects which still required assistance.

Mr. Gillespie also felt that devolved responsibilities to the regions were required and that there was a danger that tourism in the future may not be 'appropriate' to the community. This concern reflects the MFG strategy for devolving block grants which was mentioned earlier. This issue is of particular importance when considering the implementation of the strategies proposed by the Donegal Employment Initiative Task Force (http://www.donegal.ie/dei/establish.htm). Within this strategy devolved responsibility has been given to Donegal from Dublin with a £732m budget to be allocated over seven years. The important strategies that relate to the issues concerned in this paper are access and the potential growth in tourism. In relation to access it is estimated that £138.5m should be spent on the roads within Donegal, a further £320m on the roads leading to the County from the Republic and a similar amount on access roads from Northern Ireland. Proposals are also made for investment in Donegal airport and nearby Derry airport. Whilst it can not be denied that significant improvements are required on the roads in Donegal improved access to the Glen will have repercussions on tourism in the Glen. This could be viewed as an opportunity for the area to attract the desired staying market, possibly as a cultural hub from which to act as a base for exploration of other attractions in the Donegal region. Pessimists may believe this will open the way for more day trippers, detracting from the heritage of the small community and inputting little to its economic regeneration.

The same Task Force document recommends that targets should be set for the growth of tourism with incentives such as grants and 'soft loans' given to projects which provide or upgrade accommodation and visitor facilities, activity based and special interest attractions. Particular note is made of rural tourism initiatives and those related to the 'unique language, musical and cultural heritage of the County'. This could prove to be very beneficial to the Glen as it fulfills many of the criteria specified in the Task Force document. However, the strategies also focus on the development of 'clusters' of attractions to create a critical mass. It is at this point that it would seem appropriate to consult the local community. The critical mass defined by a centralised government agency may be different to that considered by a small Gaeltacht community. The inclusion of incentives should benefit local people, but this could also lead to external entrepreneurs moving to the area to profit from the new initiatives. The amount of consultation planned in relation to the implementation of these strategies is unclear and it is impossible to speculate. Within the devolvement of responsibilities to the regions as suggested by Mr. Gillespie it could be that further devolvement could be required to maintain 'appropriate' tourism development for the Glen. It is planned that further research will explore this current scenario further.

Conclusion

Glencolumbkille is a spectacular scenic area with a rich heritage and living culture. To date it has successfully maintained its environment, social fabric and cultural integrity, facing numerous obstacles, using tourism as one of its key tools of regeneration. There has been some external assistance in the past but the motivation for its success has come from within the community generally and the late Fr. McDyer specifically. Today it could be facing obstacles of a very different nature which a single strong minded leader may, or may not, be able to challenge or manage. The importance of tourism as a means of economic regeneration has been high on the agenda of the Irish government over the last decade and the focus now appears to have shifted to the more peripheral regions. The Donegal Task Force strategy is to encourage regeneration and the development of jobs to the County of Donegal. The danger may lie in the fact that money could be allocated without adequate consultation with the local community, and that the hard work and slow, but steady, growth of a sustainable form of cultural tourism could be jeopardised by a desire to exploit the sensitive cultural resources upon which the tourism is based. This could be an over critical supposition and the new initiatives could actually be the impetus the Glen requires to maintain the products it has struggled to develop and to move forward with their vision of a strong, economically sound community firmly dedicated to the preservation of their heritage and ability to keep their culture thriving into the 21st century. It is hoped that the latter is the case and that other such peripheral, culturally strong communities in various parts of the world can gain ideas and confidence from the success of Glencolumbkille.

Acknowledgements

The author would like to thank all the people in Glencolumbkille who generously gave their time, impressions and knowledge. Specific thanks go to Shane Gillespie, the manager of the Folk Museum, Liam Cunningham, joint founder and Language Director of Oideas Gael and all staff at Tapies Gael. I would also like to thank Udaras na Gaeltachta and Meithal Forbatha na Gaeltachta for their support and supplying me with specialised information and reports.

References

Bord Failte, (1994), *Developing Sustainable Tourism – Tourism Development Plan 1994 – 1999*, Dublin.

Bord Failte, (1997), *Tourism Facts 1996*, Dublin.

Bord Failte, (1999), *Tourism Facts* 1998, Dublin.

Cunningham, L (1995), *Foreign students lap up the Gaeltacht culture*, Donegal People's Press, 26.07.95.

Department of Tourism and Trade, (1994), *Operational Programme for Tourism 1994 /1999*, Government of Ireland Stationary Office, Dublin.

Donegal Employment Initiative, (1999), *Establishing Donegal as a Prime, Competitive and Attractive Location for Job Creation : Priorities for Action*, http://www.donegal.ie/dei/establish.htm.

European Commission, (1997), *Culture and Rural Development*, www.rural-europe.aeidl.be/rural-en/biblio/culture/art05.htm.

McDyer, P. (1984), *Fr. McDyer of Glencolumbkille – an autobiography*, Brandon, Dingle, Co. Kerry.

Meithal Forbatha na Gaeltachta, (1994), *From the Bottom Up – A Tourism Strategy for the Gaeltacht*.

O Gallachoir, C. (1995), *Culture as an Economic Resource with special reference to the Donegal Gaeltacht*, Unpublished Masters Dissertation, University College Galway.

O'Hara, S. (1994), *Ireland of the Welcomes – The marketing of tourism and the alternative holiday venues*, Irish Press, 25.04.94.

Richards, G. and Hall, D. (2000), *Tourism and Sustainable Community Development*, Routledge, London.

Stocks, J (1996), Heritage and Tourism in the Irish Republic – Towards a Giant Theme Park? In Robinson et al, *Tourism and Culture: Image, Identity and Marketing*, Centre for travel and tourism in association with Business Education Publishers Limited, pp251-260.

Stocks, J. (2000), Cultural Tourism and the Community in Rural Ireland in Richards,G. and Hall, D. eds., *Tourism and Sustainable Community Development*, Routledge, London, pp.233-241.

Udaras na Gaeltachta (1995), *Tuarascail agus Cuntais 1995*, Co. Donegal.

Political instability and tourism: A cross-cultural examination

A L Theocharous, M W Nuttall, H R Seddighi

University of Sunderland, UK

Background and scope of the study

Tourism is considered to be one of the world's most important economic activity and fastest growing elements of the global trade. In the last years we have witnessed a dramatic growth of the international tourism market. At a global scale, tourism's rate of growth has been phenomenal with worldwide international arrivals rising from 25 million in 1950 to 670 million by the end of 1999 (WTO, 1999). According to official forecasts by World Tourism Organisation by the year 2020 the international tourism trips will be trebled to 1.6 billion with an estimated worth of $2 trillion annually (Robinson, 1999).

Despite its economic importance and significance, tourism is a highly vulnerable industry and is particularly sensitive to exogenous factors that are able to distract and obstruct the sensitive equilibrium and balance under which the tourism industry is functioning. An exogenous factor that can have negative effects on the tourism industry is political instability. There are various examples where the adverse and catastrophic effects of political instability led many tourist destinations to decline and total disappearance from the tourism map. (Ryan, 1991; Sonmez, 1998a; Hall, 1992; Mansfield, 1994; Richter and Waugh, 1986; Bar-On, 1996).

Political instability is characterised by a multifaceted and complex character and its existence and impact in various countries worldwide is multilevel and multidimensional (Gupta, 1990; Sanders, 1981; Andriole and Hopple, 1984). The need for assessment, evaluation and analysis of the various interrelationships of political instability and the tourism industry is essential considering the sensitive nature of the tourism industry, the ever-increasing competition, and the very narrow profit margins. However, the review of the extant literature revealed that this particular research field suffers from lack of research direction, and absence of systematic, detailed and thorough analysis. The limited number of studies that have been conducted so far follow different conceptualisations, and they offer different empirical or theoretical frameworks for the evaluation of the impact of political instability on the tourism industry (Pizam, 1999; Sonmez, 1998; Ryan, 1991; Hall and O'Sullivan, 1996; Clements and Georgiou, 1998; Ioannides and Apostolopoulos, 1999). Furthermore the total absence of cross-cultural examination of the tourism and political instability relationship was pinpointed. The location of this research gap consisted the inaugural point for the conceptual beginning of this paper.

This study attempts to build on the foregoing insights by developing an ingrained theoretical and empirical framework for the examination of a neglected but key issue in the study of international tourism: the cross-culturally perceived impact of political instability on tourism.

The consideration of cultural particularity and singularity is taken seriously into consideration when tourism policy makers are designing and developing tourism-marketing strategies. For every tourism generating country, special consideration must be given to develop a marketing strategy that is compatible with its special characteristics and socio-cultural beliefs and values. Such tourism policy measures enhance the probability of success of a tourism-marketing plan. For tourism destinations that suffer from any type and extent of political instability, the consideration of this cultural factor becomes imperative. However although this need is acknowledged, the tourism policy maker is faced with questions which are impose insuperable obstacles: *How and in what extent the public from a tourism generating country perceives the impact of the various types of political instability? Are these views common among all the tourism-generating countries?*

The aim of this study is to provide answers to the above questions by examining the relationship between political instability and tourism on a cross-cultural basis. The focus of the study is to determine how the impact of political instability as perceived by travel agents varies among six European tourism generating countries.

To accomplish the aim a survey of 2,000 travel agents from the six major European tourism-generating countries was carried out. Travel agent's perceptions were examined using a multiple item 'political instability on tourism' impact scale. The motive behind the development of this research instrument was the need for the measurement of the attitudes and perceptions of tourists and tourism professionals towards the impact of political instability on tourism. The methodological considerations for the development of the composite index of political instability indicators are also discussed in this paper.

Unquestionably the perceptions and attitudes of tourists for a tourist destination play an important role in the final choice of their holidays. The policymakers from every tourist destination have a critical need to be aware of how tourists from the major tourism generating countries perceive the relative degree of political instability that exists at the tourist destination, and how sensitive are tourists to political instability. The more sensitive the tourists are to political instability, the more aggressive the marketing and promotional strategies, of a tourist destination which is experiencing any degree of political instability, should be in order to counterbalance the adverse and devastating consequences of an situation of instability.

Definitions of 'culture' in cross-cultural research

The definition and analysis of the concepts, which are involved in this paper, are essential in order to derive to ingrained research propositions and to develop a conceptual basis for the development of the analytical framework that is necessary in order to successfully meet the aims and objectives that were set for this study.

Although the type of this study is not culture-bounded, the need for definition and conceptualisation of culture is central in order to create a nomological framework that is both capable of defining and analysing attitudinal phenomena and at the same time providing a basis for hypothesis generation and testing.

It has to be pointed out that the detailed and in depth analysis and explanation of the various theoretical properties and conceptual approaches of culture is beyond the scope of this paper. The objective is to develop a strong theoretical framework on which the research propositions will be based. This does not mean that the conceptualisation and theoretical investigation of culture is ignored in this study. On the contrary, emphasis is given to the identification and measurement of the cultural variations among travel agents in relation to the impact of various types of political instability on the tourism industry.

What is culture?

The research approach of this chapter involves the examination of the relationship between tourism and political instability on a cross-cultural basis. In this regard a discussion will follow on the theoretical and conceptual properties of the term 'culture'.

More specifically the emphasis at this point is to suggest that before engaging in a study where the word 'culture' is involved, a theoretical explanation of the word has to be provided. The next step involves the rationality behind the meaning that the word 'culture' is taking for the purposes of this study and the explanation of the relationship of the definition of 'culture' as used in this research context with the other research parameters of this paper, namely tourism and political instability.

A starting point for any examination or analysis of the term culture has to consider the nature, character and meaning of the multiple, coexisting and closely interacting concepts of culture that can be found in the literature. On a first examination it is easy to observe terminological and conceptual anarchy, which inhibits the researcher in understanding the internal complexities and the notional associations, which characterise the definition of culture. Perhaps the best description of the terminological anarchy around the concept was given by Triandis et al. (1986, p.258) who defined culture as a "fuzzy, difficult to define construct".

"Culture" in general terms can be defined as the amalgam of attitudes that determine the perceptions of a person or a group of persons. Culture as a concept is transferred and transmuted from generation to generation. Through culture, frameworks for social behaviour are shaped, values are determined and models of social canons and institutions are conventionalised. Culture defined in this way, is the determinant of the type, kind and extent of actions, reactions and interactions in a social system.

It is helpful for reasons of conceptual clarity to consider culture as a kind of map of the above cultural forms. Viewing culture in this way, makes it more easier to be conceived as a concept and facilitates its empirical and theoretical application since it becomes a more simple and easy-to-use concept. According to Hartley and Hawkes who first suggested this approach "just as a map is not the thing that it represents, but an abstract version of it, so culture can be seen as an abstraction of the concrete business of everyday existence. Again, just as a map is a pattern of symbols, by means of which we can interpret a real landscape, so culture can be seen as a system of symbols and signs which mediates between the social 'mind' and reality: it suggests-in fact requires-a certain way of looking at life" (1975, p.11).

By viewing culture in this way makes it is possible to see the culture of a society as rooted in its social structure, and it logically follows that the shape of that culture is inevitably determined by the nature of the class antagonisms characteristic of the social structure (Hartley and Hawkes, 1975).

After considering the research aims and objectives the term "culture" was defined in the most suitable but theoretically correct way so as to serve the conceptual and methodological requirements of the study. Hartley and Hawkes' definition of culture is adopted, which satisfies the methodological requirements of this research. Therefore when we refer to the national cultural background of a society the term 'society' is considered to mean the 'totality of the individuals living in interdependent relationships in a social community'. Therefore conceiving society with the definition that was given above, 'culture' of a society could be taken to be the 'culture' of the whole society (Hartley and Hawkes, 1975, p.20). This view of culture was expressed by Eliot in 1945 who suggested, that "the culture of the individual is dependent upon the culture of a group or class, and that the culture of the group or class is dependent upon the culture of the whole society to which that group or class belongs. Therefore it is the culture of the society that is fundamental, and it is the meaning of the term 'culture' in relation to the whole society that should be examined first". (Eliot, 1945, p.21)

A final concluding point that has to be noted is that there is non one right 'meaning' of culture, and that anyone of its meanings can be 'invaded' by the further complication of the pervasive 'culture as scale of values'. (Hartley and Hawkes, 1975, p.72)

The nature and development of cross cultural studies

According to Berry et al (1992, p.220) "a cross-cultural study usually starts with a psychologically interesting difference in behaviour between two or more cultural groups". With the localisation of the difference, a theoretical explanation has to be formulated, and for this reason a study must be designed and data has to be collected from various cultures.

For the purposes of the current study the 'difference' in need for theoretical explanation concerns the perceptions of travel agents from different cultural backgrounds concerning the impact of political instability on tourism. Therefore cultural populations had to be examined against a set of political instability variables.

Verma and Mallick (1988, p.96) suggested that the use of the term 'cross-cultural' presents problems of definition as to what is implied operationally "since it is used interchangeably with terms such as 'inter-culture', 'cross-ethnic', 'multi-cultural' and 'race research'". It is obvious that there is not a clear agreement of the definition of cross-cultural studies and it can be simply suggested that are the type of studies which look at similarities and differences among nations in terms of limited sets of phenomena.

A theoretical approach on the relationship between political instability, tourism and culture

Before beginning an investigation of the relationship between tourism, culture and political instability it should be made clear that the theoretical framework and empirical application of the term "culture" as used in this study is not directly related with the cultural tourism perspective.

In the tourism research field the term 'culture' is treated on a multidimensional and multilevel basis, and attention has to be given for the clear definition of the concept in relation to the research topic under examination, prior to its theoretical and empirical investigation.

For the purposes of this analysis, culture is seen as the concept which taxonomises the travel agents from different cultural backgrounds into groups. The term encompasses the characteristics, social norms and patterns which distinguish cultures from each other. However, for reasons of theoretical sufficiency and explicitness a review of the diverse and multiple relationships between culture and tourism will be carried out. Where it is appropriate the concept of political instability (or elements of the concept) will be discussed in connection to tourism and culture.

Back in 1978 Greenwood masterfully pinpointed the relationship of culture to tourism. In his words "culture is being packaged, priced and sold like building lots, rights of way, fast food, and room service, as the tourism industry inexorably extend its grasp. For the moneyed tourist, the tourism industry promises that the world is his/her to use. All the 'natural resources', including cultural traditions, have their price, and if you have the money in hand, it is your right to see whatever you wish.... Treating culture as a natural resource or a commodity over which tourists have rights is not simply perverse, it is a violation of the people's cultural rights (Greenwood, 1978, p.136-137 after Crick, 1989, p.336)

The literature on tourism is characterised by contradictory views and approaches as concerning the overall contribution of tourism development. The possessiveness or negativity of the approach is highly dependent at a great extent from how authors approach their studies. As Crick (1989, p.336-337) pointed out for almost any effect of tourism that is discovered (positive or negative), a counter example can be found. In essence the contradiction about the positive and negative consequences of tourism development and growth can be explained in that "international tourism sets in motion, or at least reinforces, different and even antithetical patterns of change".

Conceiving tourism as a source of antithetical patterns of change it can be safely said that it can be simultaneously a source of social divisiveness and conflict over the exploitation, over-usage and contested use of the environment for touristic purposes. (Crick, 1989; Robinson, 1999).

Robinson offers a 'rarefied definition' of cultural tourism which "is unfortunately dogged by the dominant perspective of culture in the high-arts sense". In this context cultural tourism is conceived as a "form in which the focus is upon an experience of museums, theatre, architecture and the like" (Robinson, 1999, p.4).

This conception of culture treats the term as a construct for the development of new forms of tourism. The saturation of the forms of tourism which are offered by the majority of the tourism destinations and the similarity of their tourist products, created the need for diversification for the offering of new types and forms of tourism, sufficiently distinctive so as to create the competitive advantage which is important and vital for a tourist destination in order to survive in the fierce and extremely competitive environment of the tourism industry.

Within this context in the last decade a significant market trend was generated which resulted in the emergence of a new form of tourism: "cultural tourism". Furthermore, the market mechanisms of the tourism industry, which are controlled and manipulated by the national tourism authorities, tourist organisations and agents, shifted steadily the consumer tastes towards more 'meaningful' (and at the same time profitable and promising) travel experiences by offering traditional tourism products or more formally defined 'cultural tourism packages'. This has led into a situation where the number of tourist destinations worldwide is increasing in response to the need for 'new' experiences and for serving larger markets (Boniface, 1999)

Under these parameters tourism can be largely seen as the "marketing of culture as a commodity to strangers" (Moutinho and Witt, 1995, p.382).

For the Australian Department of Communications and Arts "cultural policy is an economic policy", because it creates wealth, employment, economic benefits and it is essential for the national economic success. This materialistic and one-sided view of culture is widespread among tourism professionals and policy makers. For them culture is conceived as an "attraction that it serves the vital position of keeping the attention of a wide and novelty-seeking audience" and the reason behind its maintenance and preservation by the hosts is for putting it on show at destinations. (Boniface, 1999, p.287). The crucial role that culture plays in the tourism industry can be attributed to the fact that the cultural differences of various destinations offer the possibility for tourist destinations to differentiate their products and in this way to gain a competitive advantage over their competitors (Craik 1997, after Boniface 1999)

Tribe (1997, p.159) viewed culture from a different perspective defining it as "the dominant beliefs, values and attitudes of society, or a subgrouping in society". He related this definition to tourism by suggesting that the beliefs, values and attitudes of people (seen as potential tourists) are the determinants of how they "perceive, demand and use leisure and tourism products". An interesting association that is pinpointed from Tribe's conceptualisation is the relationship of crime with culture. Tribe explained this association by contending that as crime is increasing, and the associated fear of crime, the attitudes of tourists for a certain destination are creating an uncertain situation for the future of a destination. This conceptualisation is important for the current study because the rationale for the theoretical development of this analysis is based on a similar causal relationship: that of political instability and tourism.

An interesting and vivid investigation of the dimensions of cultural conflicts in tourism is offered by Robinson (1999) who investigated extensively the various and contradictory interrelationships of culture and tourism. He conceptualised tourism as an agent of cultural conflict (but not the sole mechanism for conflict) since "tourism as a form of intercultural interaction is bearing the effects of the associated risks of intercultural conflicts which is explained as the incompatibility between individuals, societies and cultures". (Robinson, 1999, p.6)

Based on the above conceptual approximation of culture, Robinson defined four dimensions of cultural conflict:

1.   Conflict between tourist and hosts;

2.   The interface between the tourism industry and the host community;

3.   Cultural conflicts between the tourism industry and tourists;

4.   Cultural conflicts within host-communities.

There is no need for engaging into an examination and analysis of the above dimensions since their general meaning and rationale behind their interaction is straightforward. However the only point where particular emphasis and attention will be given is Robinson's fourth dimension of 'cultural conflict within host communities'. The rationale behind this decision is twofold. First this dimension as expressed by Robinson acts as a linchpin for the development of a conceptual basis where tourism, culture and political instability (as a specific and empirically tested concept) can be simultaneously examined under a common conceptual and empirical framework. Secondly, cultural conflict within host communities although it is independent from tourism, its results and impacts on the tourism industry are devastating. As Robinson correctly points out this dimension (host-host conflict) is largely overlooked in the extant literature. Therefore this research gap substantiates the research context of the current analysis, since the purpose of this research is to examine how travel agents from different cultural backgrounds are evaluating/perceiving the impact of political instability (as a theoretically and empirically tested term for conflict).

Research design and methods

The central purpose of this study is to determine the cross-cultural differences in the perceptions of travel agents concerning the impact of political instability on tourism. Before the juxtaposition of the methodological considerations of the study, some general issues concerning the study design are addressed.

Although the study focuses on the perceptions of travel agents, the study assumes that the interpretation of the views, opinions and perceptions of travel agents, which are considered to be the experts of the tourism industry, can be generalised so as to cover the whole national population from which travel agents are coming from. This approach also known as Delphi method was considered as the most appropriate since the perceptions and opinions of travel agents are considered to be more reliable and valid and moreover can be generalised to the whole population (Heuer, 1978; Carter and Beaulieu, 1992; Lang, 1997; Helmer, 1983; Feierabend and Feierabend, 1966).

In order to investigate the perceptions of travel agents from different cultural backgrounds, it was essential to identify the countries from where the subjects were to be drawn. Based on statistics provided by World Tourism Organisation (WTO) and from National Tourism Organisations (NTO's) the countries from where the subjects were to be drawn were identified. Based on the percentage of total arrivals accounting for each country the corresponding number of subjects was randomly selected.

The sampling frame of travel agents, was obtained from the official members catalogue of the association of travel agents from each country. Because of the international focus of the study, it was decided to draw the sample from the six major European tourist-generating countries. Using a systematic random sample technique the final samples from each tourism generating country were determined.

An initial sample of 2000 was deemed necessary in order to ensure reliable and valid statistical procedures. The sample was drawn from each population proportionally to the number of outbound tourists that each tourism generating country had during the 1998 tourism statistical year. The sample was allocated as follows: Germany (n=742), United Kingdom (n=514); France (n=328), Italy (n=207); Netherlands (n=124); and Switzerland (n=85).

Development of the research instrument

The process of moving from abstract concepts to the point where we can develop questionnaire items (indicators) to tap the concept is called 'descending the ladder of abstraction'. This process involved moving from the broad to the specific, from the abstract to the concrete. In this stage there were three general problems to deal with: a.) how many indicators to use, b.) how to develop the indicators and c.) how to form items into questionnaires (research instrument for the measurement of political instability).

An initial pilot study was carried out between academic staff from 30 universities from the United Kingdom and USA, as well as to students from the University of Sunderland. With the assistance of this pilot study the initial set of 42 indicators of political instability that was defined from the literature review was reduced to 24. Following the initial pilot study, a research instrument was developed which was distributed to 704 travel agents from UK (n=400) and Cyprus (n=304). The purpose of this extensive pilot study was to minimise the 'inferential gap' between the indicators and the concept and secondly, and most important, to ensure that the key concept of political instability was thoroughly measured by the selected indicators. The second pilot study identified a number of four indicators that were initially omitted and were finally included in the final version of the research instrument.

As a form of communication, it was decided to use mail interviews. This decision was mainly suited by the nature of the research sample, since mail surveys allow for wider geographical coverage (Nachmias and Nachmias, 1992; De Vaus, 1991; Crano and Brewer, 1986).

The overall response rate of the survey reached a level of 36.1%. This is considered to be satisfactory since the expected response rate to mail surveys normally varies between 20-40 percent (Nachmias and Nachmias 1992, p.277; Bourque and Fielder 1995, p.14). The serious difficulty of securing acceptable response rates was overcome by using various strategies like cover letters, and follow up procedures as suggested by Dillman's Total Design Method (Dillman, 1978).

Before analysing the survey data, the instrument reliability and validity was examined in order to ensure that the study was on the right track and was measuring what it was intended to measure (Rossi et al, 1983).

As Litwin suggested (1996, p.27) when a new survey is developed it is important to test its internal consistency before using it to collect data from which inference will be drawn. Cronbach's Alpha coefficient was used and revealed a satisfactory internal consistency for the research instrument ($a=0.89$). This is surpassing by far the cut off limit of 0.75 that is generally considered as acceptable (Crano and Brewer 1986, p.44).

The canons of scientific investigation demand that once a measurement instrument is proposed it must be validated as a theoretical concept having a meaningful role in a theoretical system. Measurement validity refers to the extent to which an operationalisation measures a theoretical concept (Litwin, 1996, p.33). Content and construct validity was assessed for this study. To carry out a reliable and objective content validity assessment the two major standards that Nunnally (1970, p.136) has suggested were carefully considered:

(a)   a representative collection of items

(b)   sensible methods of test construction

The scale showed high internal consistency reliability ($a=0.89$). It has been suggested by Parasuraman (1986) that if internal consistency reliability is high construct validity is also supported.

Respondents were asked to indicate the extent of the perceived impact that each type of political instability event had on the tourism industry. The questionnaire scale ranged from "very important" to "unimportant" for the 50% of the sample, and from "unimportant" to "important" for the rest, by using a five-point Likert scale. The reason for changing the direction from important to unimportant and opposite was to minimise the chance of bias that can be caused from the direction of weighting. This procedure was suggested by Nachmias (1994, p.436) who suggested that the direction of weighting is being determined by the favourableness or unfavourableness of the item, which for the case of this time had to remain strictly neutral.

A particularity of the scaling procedure that was employed in this study was the decision to offer verbal tags between the two extreme anchors of the scale so as to assist the respondents in avoiding any misinterpretation or confusion that should have resulted from the scale. Another particularity of the questionnaire layout was the decision to change the order of the questionnaire items. The rationale behind this decision was that the bias resulting from the ordering of the questionnaire items was going to be minimised. With the assistance of a table of random numbers six different versions of the questionnaire were produced. As Kinnear and Taylor (1996) suggested, the sequencing of questions can influence the nature of the respondent's answers and can be the cause of serious errors that can affect, to a great extent the survey findings.

The last characteristic of the research instrument scale was the inclusion of the "I don't know" option in order to avoid forced answer bias which is introduced when this response category is omitted. Thus forced choice scale offers potential for misinterpretation of responses and the provision of the "no opinion" option appears advisable. (Tsan, 1999, p.99)

The research instrument was translated into five languages besides English so as to assist and motivate the respondents to answer and return back the questionnaires. The translation was made by professional translators who were fluent in both the original and target language. Furthermore the method of back-translation was employed for all the translations. (Brislin, Lonner and Thorndike, 1973), and the 'translation equivalence' of the research instrument was tested in order to ensure that "verbal items and instructions could be used cross-culturally" (Berry et all, 1992, p.239). The research instrument was also examined and, where necessary, amended by bilingual nationals of each of the countries under examination.

Development and statement of the research hypotheses

Cross-cultural comparisons of attitudes and perceptions towards the impact of various types of political instability in the tourism industry, is an area that has remained largely neglected and unexamined.

The first issue at stake is whether the perceptions of travel agents concerning the impact of the various types of political instability in the tourism industry are affected by their cultural background. The term 'initial' in front of the hypotheses indicates that these hypotheses are going to be redefined during the Repeated Measures ANOVA Procedure since during that process each hypothesis is going to be broken down into three sub-hypotheses.

> *Initial Hypothesis H$_A$: The opinions/perceptions of travel agents from the six leading European tourist generating countries concerning the impact of various types of political instability incidents on the tourism industry are not affected from their national cultural background.*

The subjects of this survey were also asked to rate the relative degree of instability for eight selected Mediterranean destinations. The subjects were asked to rate the countries taking into consideration the types of political instability events included in the first part of the survey. Therefore the hypothesis was shaped as follows.

> *Initial Hypothesis H$_B$: The relative degree of political instability for eight selected Mediterranean destinations as perceived by travel agents is not determined/influenced by their cultural background.*

Data analysis and results

The statistical procedure of Repeated Measures Analysis of Variance (RM-ANOVA) was used first to test both hypothesis H_1 and H_2 to discern if any significant differences exist between the perceived impact of each type of political instability incidents between subjects from the same national cultural background and to identify if the perceived level of instability of selected Mediterranean destinations is affected by the cultural background of the respondents.

The GLM Repeated Measures ANOVA procedure is a method, which allows the analysis of variance when the measurement is performed several times on each subject (SPSS Advanced Statistics, 1997, p.27). Under this method the equality of means is tested and is used when all the subjects of a random sample are measured under a number of different conditions.

According to Marascuillo and Serlin (1988, p.563) repeated measures design are those "in which the same subjects are observed in a before-after paradigm or across a series of similar experimental trials". More simply defined, is a study where a "single sample of individuals is tested more than once on the dependent variable and the same subjects are used for every treatment condition. (Graveter and Wallnau, 1985, p.362)

For this study, the research goals and objectives were considered carefully and the following research hypotheses were formulated:

Test of Initial Hypothesis H_A

Within Subjects Main Effect Hypothesis

Do the types of political instability influence the perceptions of travel agents for the impact of political instability on tourism? (Does mean 'perceptions for the impact f political instability' change across the trials of types of political instability?). For this study this s the test for a within-subjects main effect of types of political instability (polinst).

Between Subjects Main Effect Hypothesis

Does the national cultural background influence the perceptions of travel agents for the impact of political instability on tourism? (Do Germans have different perceptions for the impact of political instability on tourism than the British? And so forth for all the possible cross-cultural combinations of the study).

Within-Subjects by Between-Subjects Interaction Effect Hypothesis

Does the influence of the national cultural background on the perceptions of travel agents for the impact of political instability on tourism depend upon the rating of the types of political instability? (Does the pattern of differences between mean 'perceptions of travel agents for the impact of political instability' for national cultural background groups change at each political instability trial?)

This is the hypothesis for a between-subjects by within-subjects interaction of travel agents' national cultural background by perceived impact of types of political instability.

A decision has to be made on the alpha level that is acceptable for the current analysis. If the *p* value, which appears on the SPSS output, is larger than the alpha level which is adopted for the research, then the null hypothesis should be rejected. By convention the alpha level is usually set at 0.05.

Table 1 shows the results of the Mauchly's tests for the current analysis. As can be seen Maucly's W is significant, $W(377)=0.000$, $p<0.005$, so it can be concluded that the sphericity assumption has not been met. Having obtained these results two options can be employed. For the current analysis both options will be utilised. The first option suggests ignoring the averaged F-tests, and reporting instead the multivariate tests of significance. An alternative to the use of the multivariate approach is the adjustment of the univariate test-statistic degrees of freedom (both the effect *df* and error *df*) by one of the epsilons which are provided by the Mauchly's Test of Sphericity. By default SPSS prints two different correlation factors: the Greenhouse-Geisser and Huynh-Feldt. The most commonly used is the Huynh-Feldt because Greenhouse-Geisser correction factor is conservative in that some times fails to detect a true difference between group means.

The first option, as was already mentioned, suggests overlooking the average F-tests and reporting the multivariate tests of significance.

Table 1   Mauchly's Test of Sphericity

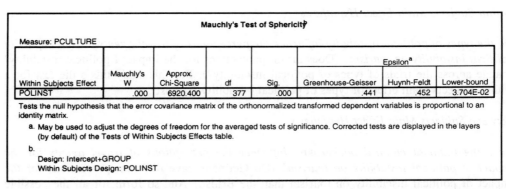

The second test entails a relatively more complicated procedure. One of the epsilons (Huynh-Feldt) is used to correct both degrees of freedom for the time main effect and then look up the F value using the new degrees of freedom. To carry out this corrective procedure the *df* for the effect is multiplied by the epsilon value and the *df* for the error term by the epsilon value. The significance of the F value is then determined by the corrected *df*. (see Table 2)

The univariate approach output of the POLINST within-subject effect is shown in Table 2. The Sphericity assumed notation indicates that the statistics have not been adjusted by any of the epsilons. It is not appropriate for this analysis since the sphericity assumption was violated, and corrections were made to the data. Therefore values from Huynh-Feldt correction factor are used.

The results of the tests of the within-subject effects indicate significant effects for both the

POLINST main effect F (27, 19332) = 228.699, p<0.0005, and the POLINST by national cultural background interaction (GROUP), F (135,19332)=16,427, p<0.0005. The figure that is more important for interpretative purposes is the interaction effect (POLINST * GROUP). The hypothesis to be investigated behind this interaction is where the change in the mean of the perceived impact of political instability across the types of political instability (28 levels) depends upon the cultural background of the respondents.

Table 2   Within Subjects Effect Output

Tests of Within-Subjects Effects

Measure: PCULTURE

Source		Type III Sum of Squares	df	Mean Square	F	Sig.	Eta Squared
POLINST	Sphericity Assumed	5344.383	27	197.940	228.699	.000	.242
	Greenhouse-Geisser	5344.383	11.894	449.324	228.699	.000	.242
	Huynh-Feldt	5344.383	12.194	438.290	228.699	.000	.242
	Lower-bound	5344.383	1.000	5344.383	228.699	.000	.242
POLINST * GROUP	Sphericity Assumed	1919.356	135	14.217	16.427	.000	.103
	Greenhouse-Geisser	1919.356	59.471	32.274	16.427	.000	.103
	Huynh-Feldt	1919.356	60.969	31.481	16.427	.000	.103
	Lower-bound	1919.356	5.000	383.871	16.427	.000	.103
Error(POLINST)	Sphericity Assumed	16731.919	19332	.866			
	Greenhouse-Geisser	16731.919	8516.297	1.965			
	Huynh-Feldt	16731.919	8730.698	1.916			
	Lower-bound	16731.919	716.000	23.369			

Table 3 shows the output for the Between-subjects effects. The Group test is nonsignificant F(5,716)=1.201, p=0.307. From this result it can be concluded that the country of origin (cultural background) has no statistically significant effect on overall mean perceptions of travel agents as concern the impact of political instability on tourism. However this result is not meaningful for the purposes of this study since between-subjects effects as the above are based on the average of the within-subjects trials. For the current analysis the average rating of all the types of political instability is computed, and then this mean political instability rate for Germans is compared to the mean of British, then to the mean of French and so forth for all the possible combinations for all the country groups. As such, these tests do not provide any information for the within subjects effects. If important differences in the rating of political instability across the levels of the within-subjects factor are expected (as in the case of this research) the between-subjects main-effect output is providing results which are not meaningful for the purposes of the study (Stevens 1996, SPSS Advanced Statistics 1997).

Table 3   Tests of Between Subjects Effects

Tests of Between-Subjects Effects

Measure: PCULTURE

Transformed Variable: Average

Source	Type III Sum of Squares	df	Mean Square	F	Sig.	Eta Squared
Intercept	2476.603	1	2476.603	8077.709	.000	.919
GROUP	1.842	5	.368	1.201	.307	.008
Error	219.524	716	.307			

GLM-Repeated Measures ANOVA also displays a multivariate output table (see Table 4). As was already noted even if the sphericity assumption is not met, the multivariate output is still valid. SPSS prints four separate lines, with each one reporting a multivariate test statistic (Pillai's trace, Wilks' lambda, Hotelling's trace, Roy's largest root. The Wilks' Lambda is the test which is most commonly used.

Table 4   Mutivariate tests

Multivariate Tests^c

Effect		Value	F	Hypothesis df	Error df	Sig.	Eta Squared
POLINST	Pillai's Trace	.832	126.368^a	27.000	690.000	.000	.832
	Wilks' Lambda	.168	126.368^a	27.000	690.000	.000	.832
	Hotelling's Trace	4.945	126.368^a	27.000	690.000	.000	.832
	Roy's Largest Root	4.945	126.368^a	27.000	690.000	.000	.832
POLINST * GROUP	Pillai's Trace	1.207	8.183	135.000	3470.000	.000	.241
	Wilks' Lambda	.239	8.512	135.000	3408.271	.000	.249
	Hotelling's Trace	1.730	8.821	135.000	3442.000	.000	.257
	Roy's Largest Root	.667	17.143^b	27.000	694.000	.000	.400

a. Exact statistic

b. The statistic is an upper bound on F that yields a lower bound on the significance level.

c.

Design: Intercept+GROUP

Within Subjects Design: POLINST

Table 4 shows the test for the null hypothesis that the mean perceived impact of political instability does not change across different types of political instability. To recall, this is the within –subjects main effect hypothesis. Since the *p* value for this hypothesis is small [F $(27,000,690,000)=$ 126.368, $p < 0.0005$] the null hypothesis can be rejected with confidence and it can be concluded that the perceived rate of political instability changes with the types of political instability, in the population from which the sample was drawn.

The last hypothesis to be investigated is the Within-subjects by Between-Subjects Interaction Effects Hypothesis. The null hypothesis tests whether the country of origin (national cultural background) is not interacting with the levels of political instability to produce different perceptions for the impact of political instability on tourism.

From an examination of the Wilks' value for this test (.239) and its associated F value and p value [F (135,000, 3408,271)=8,512, p=. 000] it can be concluded that differences between the perceptions of the travel agents for the impact of political instability across the different levels of political instability, depends upon the cultural background of the respondents.

Test of Initial Hypothesis H$_B$

To provide an answer to the last research problem Repeated Measures ANOVA was employed again.

The sample of subjects which was used to carry out the analysis for Hypothesis A was asked to rate the relative degree of instability in eight selected Mediterranean destinations having in mind the 28 types of political instability. The purpose of this research question is to examine how travel agents from different cultural backgrounds perceive the degree of instability of tourist destinations. Ultimately the answer of this research question is expected to show clearly the degree of sensitiveness of travel agents from different cultural backgrounds to various events of instability that are taking place at different destinations, and to demonstrate once again (but in this time with real data and examples) that the perceived level of instability between travel agents from different countries for different tourists destinations differs significantly.

To investigate these issues, the same sample of subjects (n=722) was selected and again was grouped according to their national cultural background (between-subjects-factor) into six groups.

The within-subjects factor that was included was the rating of the relative degree of instability for eight selected Mediterranean destinations. To simplify, each subject was measured for his/her perceived instability against eight Mediterranean destinations. Thus, the country differentiation is the within-subjects factor for this design.

The research goals that are going to be investigated are the following:

Within subjects Main effect:

Does the country differentiation influences the perceived level of instability for selected Mediterranean destinations? (Does mean perceived level of instability change across the trials for country differentiation?)

Between subjects main effect:

Does the national cultural background of travel agents influence their perceived level of political instability for selected Mediterranean destinations? (For example do Germans have different perceptions about the relative degree of instability for the selected countries than British?)

Within-subjects by Between subjects Interaction effects:

Does the influence of the cultural background of the respondents on the perceived level of instability of the selected Mediterranean destinations depend upon the country differentiation? (Does the pattern of differences between mean perceived levels of political instability for travel agents from different cultural backgrounds changes at each country trial?)

It has to be reiterated that for all the hypotheses that are stated above the null hypothesis that is tested assumes no differences between population means. Also the alpha level adopted for this analysis is again set at 0.05.

The perceived impact of travel agents for the relative degree of instability of selected Mediterranean destinations is measured at 8 trials, and these 28 variables appear in SPSS dataset as PARTBCYP (Cyprus), PARTBEGY (Egypt), PARTBGRE (Greece), PARTBTUN (Tunisia),PARTBTUR (Turkey),PARTBISR (Israel), PATRTBMOR (Morocco), PARTBMLT (Malta). The variable 'COUNTRY' is the between-subjects factor, and it denotes the cultural background of the respondents, with values of 1 for Germany, 2 for United Kingdom, 3 for France, 4 for Italy, 5 for Netherlands and 6 for Switzerland.

Table 5 shows the results for Machley's test of sphericity. Mauchly's W is significant, $W(27) = p < 0$, and this leads to the conclusion that the spherisity assumption is violated. To tackle this problem both available options are going to be employed and thus Multivariate tests of significance as well as correction of the averaged F-tests is going to be reported.

Table 5   Mauchley's Test of Sphericity

	Mauchly's Test of Sphericity[b]							
Measure: MEDPOL								
						Epsilon[a]		
Within Subjects Effect	Mauchly's W	Approx. Chi-Square	df	Sig.		Greenhouse-Geisser	Huynh-Feldt	Lower-bound
COUNDIFF	.170	1265.042	27	.000		.638	.647	.143

Tests the null hypothesis that the error covariance matrix of the orthonormalized transformed dependent variables is proportional to an identity matrix.

a. May be used to adjust the degrees of freedom for the averaged tests of significance. Corrected tests are displayed in the layers (by default) of the Tests of Within Subjects Effects table.

b.
Design: Intercept+GROUP
Within Subjects Design: COUNDIFF

The corrected averaged F-tests are reported on table 6 which is the univariate approach output of the COUNDIFF within subject effect. The sphericity assumed notation shows that the statistics have not been adjusted by any of the epsilons. In light of this values from Huynh-Feldt correction factor are used.

Table 6   Univariate Approach Within-Subjects Effects Output

Tests of Within-Subjects Effects

Measure: MEDPOL

Source		Type III Sum of Squares	df	Mean Square	F	Sig.
COUNDIFF	Sphericity Assumed	1499.870	7	214.267	203.529	.000
	Greenhouse-Geisser	1499.870	4.466	335.850	203.529	.000
	Huynh-Feldt	1499.870	4.529	331.188	203.529	.000
	Lower-bound	1499.870	1.000	1499.870	203.529	.000
COUNDIFF * GROUP	Sphericity Assumed	177.296	35	5.066	4.812	.000
	Greenhouse-Geisser	177.296	22.329	7.940	4.812	.000
	Huynh-Feldt	177.296	22.644	7.830	4.812	.000
	Lower-bound	177.296	5.000	35.459	4.812	.000
Error(COUNDIFF)	Sphericity Assumed	5276.434	5012	1.053		
	Greenhouse-Geisser	5276.434	3197.574	1.650		
	Huynh-Feldt	5276.434	3242.594	1.627		
	Lower-bound	5276.434	716.000	7.369		

The results of the table indicate that there are significant effects for both the COUNDIFF main effect [F (7, 5,012)=203.529, $p < 0.0005$], and the COUNDIFF by GROUP interaction, F (35, 5,012)=4,812, $p < .0005$. The hypotheses that are tested with the above univariate output are the within subjects main effect hypothesis and the within subject by between subjects interaction hypothesis. The results indicate that the null hypotheses for both tests have to be rejected. This means that there are significant differences between the means of the perceived level of political instability at each level of the COUNTDIFF within subjects factor. To simplify, each selected Mediterranean country appears to have different perceived level of instability in relation to the other selected countries. The second hypothesis which is tested examined if the pattern of differences between mean perceived levels of political instability for travel agents from different cultural backgrounds changes at each country trial. The null hypotheses was rejected again for this case and this is explained as the existence of differences in the perceived level of political instability from travel agents from different cultural backgrounds for each of the selected Mediterranean countries.

The between-subjects effects are reported in table 7. As can be seen the GROUP test is significant [F (5,716)=4950.986, $p = .0000$]. It can be therefore concluded that the cultural background of the respondents has a statistically significant effect on overall mean perceptions of travel agents as concern the level of instability in the selected Mediterranean destinations.

Table 7   Tests of Between-Subjects Effects

Tests of Between-Subjects Effects

Measure: MEDPOL
Transformed Variable: Average

Source	Type III Sum of Squares	df	Mean Square	F	Sig.
Intercept	23130.109	1	23130.109	4950.986	.000
GROUP	183.010	5	36.602	7.835	.000
Error	3345.022	716	4.672		

The Multivariate output of the GLM RM analysis is reported in table 8. As was already noted even if the sphericity assumption is violated, the validity of the multivariate output is not affected. Table 8 shows the test for the null hypothesis that the mean perceived level of instability does not change across the different trials (countries) of the COUNTDIFF factor. This is the within-subjects main effect test. By examining the results provided give a p value for Wilks' test lower than 0.05 [F $(7.000, 710.000) = .543$, p $= .000$]. The results lead to the conclusion that the differences in the perceived level of instability for selected Mediterranean countries changes with different countries in the population from which the sample was drawn.

The next hypothesis that is to be tested from the multivariate output of table 8 is the within by between subjects hypothesis. It may be recalled that this hypothesis tests whether the cultural background of the respondents interacts with the country differentiation. As can be seen from the reported Wilks statistic is high; therefore the associated p value is low [F $(35.000, 3570.000) = 5.097$, p $= .000$]. With these results the null hypothesis can be confidently rejected and the conclusion can be drawn that change in mean perceptions of the relative instability of selected Mediterranean destinations depends upon the country differentiation.

Table 8   Multivariate Test Output

				Hypothesis		
Multivariate Tests^c						
Effect		Value	F	df	Error df	Sig.
COUNDIFF	Pillai's Trace	.457	85.474^a	7.000	710.000	.000
	Wilks' Lambda	.543	85.474^a	7.000	710.000	.000
	Hotelling's Trace	.843	85.474^a	7.000	710.000	.000
	Roy's Largest Root	.843	85.474^a	7.000	710.000	.000
COUNDIFF * GROUP	Pillai's Trace	.234	5.002	35.000	3570.000	.000
	Wilks' Lambda	.784	5.097	35.000	2989.130	.000
	Hotelling's Trace	.255	5.157	35.000	3542.000	.000
	Roy's Largest Root	.134	13.666^b	7.000	714.000	.000

a. Exact statistic

b. The statistic is an upper bound on F that yields a lower bound on the significance level.

c.
   Design: Intercept+GROUP
   Within Subjects Design: COUNDIFF

Discussion and interpretation of the results of hypothesis H$_A$ and H$_B$

To interpret a significant interaction, an examination of the cell means and standard deviations is needed. By plotting the cell means it is obvious that the mean perceptions for the impact of political instability increases and decreases across trials: this is the within-subject effect. Another important observation is that the Germans have different average perceptions for the impact of political instability than British at every trial, the British with the French at every trial (and so forth for all the possible combinations). A closer examination reveals that the difference is different at each level (trial). This is the result of the national cultural background by types of political instability interaction.

As the subjects (travel agents) are rating different types of political instability, the average perceived impact of political instability of the Germans is increasing/decreasing at different pattern than that of British (this applies for all the other possible combinations).

Figure 1   Estimated Marginal Means

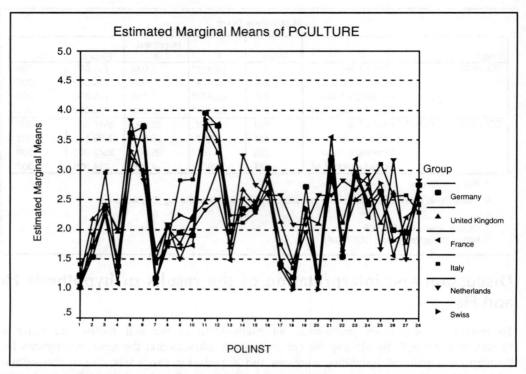

Figure 1 represents the interaction between the treatments. If the interaction term is not statistically significant, then the effects of the treatments are independent. In the case where the interaction term is significant (as in the case of this study), the type of interaction must be determined. There are two general types of interaction which are referred to as ordinal and disordinal. An ordinal interaction occurs when the effects of a treatment are not equal across all levels of another treatment, but the magnitude is always the same direction. In a disordinal interaction, as in the case of this study, the effects of one treatment are positive for some levels and negative for other levels of the other treatment. As can be seen from figure 2 the differences in the type of political instability vary not only in magnitude but also in direction. This is shown by lines that are not parallel and that cross between levels. It is suggested that when the significant interaction is disordinal the main effects of the treatment cannot be interpreted and the have to be redesigned since in disordinal interactions the effects vary not only across treatment levels but also in direction (positive or negative). (Hair et al., 1998, p.344) However, in the case of this research the direction of the levels of the treatment are unavoidably appearing with various positive and negative directions since the rating of the types of political instability is expected to be fluctuating.

As can be seen from figure 2 the mean perceived impact of political instability is displayed on the Y-axis labelled "Estimated Marginal Means". The types of Political Instability define the X-axis labelled Polinst (within-subjects factor). Six lines are shown which are representing the six national cultural backgrounds.

Figure 2   Estimated Marginal Means for four levels of POLINST (simplified structure)

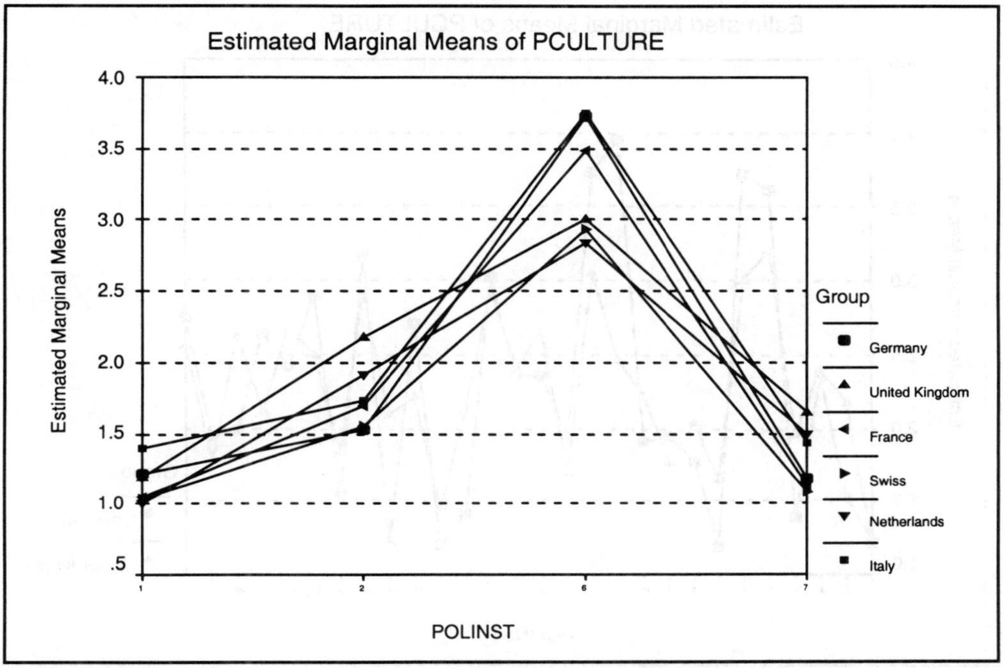

In Figure 2 only four levels of Polinst within-subjects factor are shown and this is done in order to make the discussion and analysis more illustrative. Figure 3 shows clearly that the main effect for the types of political instability is significant since the perceived impact of political instability increases/decreases across trials. For example for all the six national cultures the mean perceived impact for trial 1 increased by an average of 0.6 for trial 2 and the mean perceived impact for trial 6 decreased by an average of 2 points for trial 7.

The main effect for the national cultural background is interpretable since it can be seen that the average perceptions for the impact of political instability are different between the countries at every trial. For example the Germans have a mean perceived level for the impact of trial 10 (Kidnappings) on the tourism industry which is almost 1.5 points higher than British travel agents. (see figure 3)

Figure 3   Estimated Marginal Means for two groups (simplified structure)

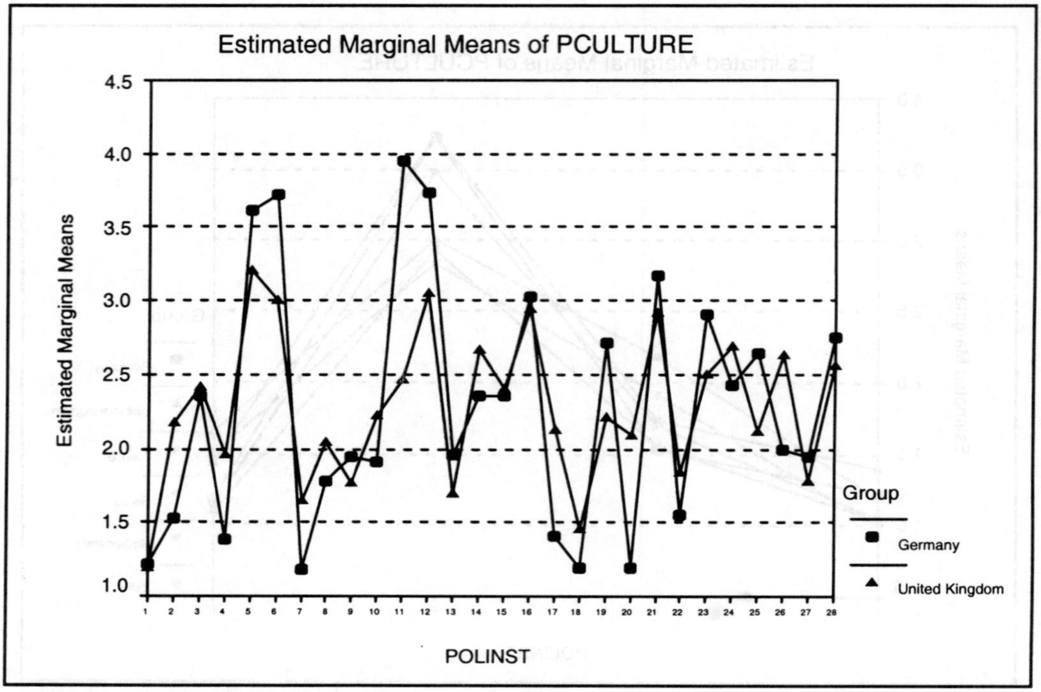

Estimated Marginal Means of PCULTURE

The interactions as illustrated in figure 2 show that differences between Germans, British, French, Italians, Dutch and Swiss change under different types of political instability. All the above observations lead to the conclusion that the effects for the types of political instability and national cultural background as well as the interaction between the two variables are practically and statistically significant.

Figure 4 illustrates data for the obtained means for the national cultural backgrounds and country differentiation factors. The graph shows clearly that the relative perceived level of instability of a destination depends on the cultural background of the respondents. Translating this into statistical terminology it can be said that there is interaction between country differentiation and national cultural background of the respondents.

Figure 4   Estimated Marginal Means – Interaction Effects

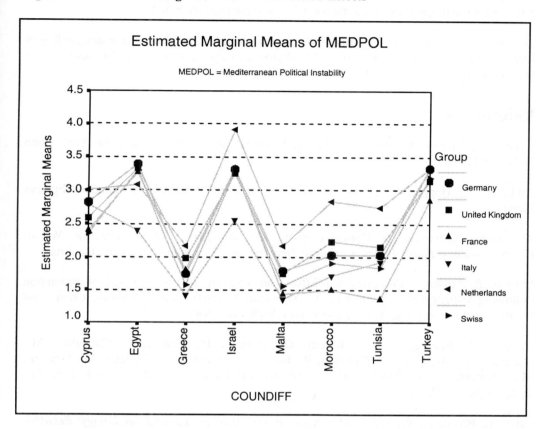

Concluding remarks

The major purpose of this study was to provide answers to two fundamental research problems examined in this thesis. The results suggest in general that travel agents from different cultural backgrounds have different perceptions for the impact of political instability on the tourism industry.

The significant interaction between national cultural background and types of political instability suggests that are some degrees of variance between travel agents from the six European tourism generating countries for this trend.

The finding of significant interactions between national cultural backgrounds and perceived stability of selected Mediterranean destinations indicate that cultural differences in attitudes towards tourism destinations exist for all the tourism generating countries.

Although the results of the present study might be limited by the size and representativeness of the samples with regard to the tourism generating countries and tourist destinations, the results are valuable. Not only did the study examine and compare the presence of political instability perceptions in the context of six different cultural backgrounds, but it also provided a clear insight into how, and in what way, perceptions of political instability can affect the normal operation and sensitive balance of the tourism industry.

Tourism is one of the most important industries worldwide. Therefore, the understanding of tourists attitudes from different cultural backgrounds may serve as a valuable resource for tourists policymakers from different tourist destination countries.

References

Aaker, D., Kumar, V., Day, G. (1995), *Marketing Research*. 1st ed. New York: John Willey and Sons.

Andriole, S., Hopple, G. (1984), *Revolution and Political Instability*. London: Frances Pinter.

Australian Department of Communications and the Arts. (1994), *Creative Nation: Commonwealth Cultural Policy*. Canberra: Department of Communications and the Arts.

Bar-On, R. (1996), "Measuring the Effects on Tourism of Violence and of Promotion Following Violent Acts". In: Pizam, A., Mansfeld, Y. (eds) (1996) *"Tourism, Crime, and International Security Issues*. Chichester: John Willey and Sons.

Bennett, T., Blumer, J., Boyd-Barrett, O., Braham, P., Curran, J., Gallagher, M., Gurevitch, M., Halloran, J., Hamilton, P., Hartley, J., Hawkes, T., Graham, M., Graham, M., Triesman, S., Woollacott, J. (1977), *The Study of Culture 1*. 1st ed. Milton Keynes: The Open University Press.

Berry, J., Poortinga, Y., Segall, M., Dasen, P. (1993), *Cross-cultural psychology: Research and applications*. 3rd ed. United States: Cambridge University Press.

Boniface, P. (1999), "Tourism and Cultures: Consensus in the Making?". In: Robinson, M., Boniface, P. (eds) (1999), *Tourism and Cultural Conflicts*, Wallingford: CABI Publishing.

Bourque, L., Fielder, P. (1995) *How to Conduct self-Administrated and mail surveys*. 1st ed. London: SAGE Publications.

Brunt, P., Courtney, P. (1999), "Host Perceptions of Sociocultural Impacts", *Annals of Tourism Research,* 26 (3): 493-515.

Carter, K., Beaulieu, L. (1992), "Conducting A Community Needs Assessment: Primary Data Collection Techniques". *Florida Cooperative Extension Service*. University of Florida.

Clements, M., Georgiou, A. (1998), "The Impact of Political Instability on a Fragile Tourism Product", *Tourism Management*, 19 (3): 283-288.

Crano, W., Brewer, M., (1986), *Principles and Methods of Social Research*. 1st ed. Boston: Allyn and Bacon.

Crick, M. (1989), "Representations of International Tourism in the Social Sciences: Sun, Sex, Sights, Savings, and Servility", *Annual Review of Anthropology*, 18, pp. 307-344.

De Vaus, D. (1991), *Surveys in Social Research*. 3rd ed. London: UCL Press Limited.

Dilman, A. (1978), *Mail and Telephone Surveys: The Total Design Method*. London: Wiley.

Doney, P., Cannon, J., Mullen, M. (1998), "Understanding the Influence of National Culture on the Development of Trust", *Academy of Management Review*, 23 (3): 601-620.

Edwards, A. (1985), *Multiple Regression and the Analysis of Variance and Covariance*. 2nd ed. New York: W.H. Freeman and Company.

Eliot, T. (1948), *Notes towards the Definition of Culture*. 1st ed. London: Faber and Faber Limited.

Enders, W. (1991), "Causality Between Transnational Terrorism and Tourism: The Case of Spain", *Terrorism*, 14, pp. 49-58.

Feierabend, I., Feierabend, R., Gurr, T. (eds) (1972), *Anger, Violence and Politics – Theories and Research*. Englewood Cliffs: Prentice Hall.

Gravetter, F., Wallnau, L. (1985), *Statistics for the Behavioral Sciences*. 1st ed. St. Paul: West Publishing Company.

Gupta, D., (1990), *The Economics of Political Instability: The Effect of Political Instability on Economic Growth*. New York: Praeger.

Hair, J., Anderson, R., Tatham, R., Black, W. (1998), *Multivariate Data Analysis*. 5th ed. Upper Saddle River: Prentice Hall.

Hall, C., O'Sullivan, V. (1996), "Tourism, Political Stability and Violence". In: Pizam, A., Mansfeld, Y. (eds) (1996) "*Tourism, Crime, and International Security Issues*. Chichester: John Willey and Sons.

Helmer, O. (1983), *Looking Forward: A Guide to Futures Research*. Beverly Hills: Sage Publications.

Heuer, R. (1978), *Quantitative Approaches to Political Behaviour: The CIA Experience*. United States: Central Intelligence Agency.

Ioannides, D., Apostolopoulos, Y. (1999), "Political Instability, War, and Tourism in Cyprus: Effects, Management, and Prospects for Recovery". *Journal of Travel Research*. 38 (1): 51-56.

Javalgi, R., Thomas, E., Rao, R. (1992), "US Pleasure Travellers' Perceptions of Selected European Destinations", *European Journal of Marketing*, 26 (7): 45-64.

Kerlinger, F. (1973), *Foundations of Behavioral Research.* 2nd ed. New York: Holt, Rinehart and Winston Inc.

Kinnear, P., Gray, C. (1997), *SPSS for Windows.* 2nd ed. Wiltshire: Psychology Press.

Kinnear, T., Taylor, J. (1996), *Marketing Research: An Applied Approach.* 5th ed. New York: McGraw-Hill Inc.

Lang, T. (1995), "An Overview of Four Futures Methodologies". *Manoa Journal,* 7, pp. 1-43.

Lankford, S., Howard, R. (1994), "Developing a Tourism Impact Attitude Scale", *Annals of Tourism Research*, 21, pp. 121-139.

Lindman, H. (1974), *Analysis of Variance in Complex Experimental Designs.* 1st ed. San Francisco: W.H. Freeman and Company.

Litwin, M. S. (1995), *How to Increase Measure Survey Reliability and Validity.* London: Sage Publications.

Mansfeld, Y. (1994), "The Middle East Conflict and Tourism to Israel, 1967-90". *Middle Eastern Studies.* 30 (3): 646-667

Mansfeld, Y. (1996), "Wars, tourism and the "Middle East" Factor". In: Pizam, A., Mansfeld, Y. (eds) (1996) *"Tourism, Crime, and International Security Issues.* Chichester: John Willey and Sons.

Marascuilo, L., Serlin, R. (1988), *Statistical Methods for the Social and Behavioural Sciences.* 1st ed. New York: W.H. Freeman Company.

McKercher, B. (1995), "The Destination-Market Matrix: A Tourism Market Portfolio Analysis Model", *Journal of Travel and Tourism Marketing*, 4 (2), pp. 23-40.

Miliken, G., Johnson, D. (1997), *Analysis of Messy Data.* 2nd ed. London: Chapman and Hall.

Money, B., Gilly, M., Graham, J. (1998), "Explorations of National Culture and Word-of-Mouth Referral Behaviour in the Purchase of Industrial Services in the United States and Japan", *Journal of Marketing*, 62, pp. 76-87.

Moser, C., Kalton, G. (1993), *Survey Methods in Social Investigation.* 2nd ed. London: Darmouth Publishing

Nachmias, C., Nachmias, D. (1992), *Research Methods in the Social Sciences.* 1st ed. London: Edward Arnold.

Nash, D. (1981), "Tourism as an Anthropological Subject", *Current Anthropology,* 22 (5): 461-481.

Nunnally, J., (1970), *Introduction to Psychological Measurement*. 1st ed. New York: McGraw-Hill.

Parasuraman, A. (1986), *Marketing Research*. Reading, MA: Addison and Wesley.

Pizam, A. (1996), "Does Tourism Promote Peace and Understanding Between Unfriendly Nations?". In: Pizam, A., Mansfeld, Y. (eds) (1996) *"Tourism, Crime, and International Security Issues*. Chichester: John Willey and Sons.

Pizam, A. (1999), "A Comprehensive Approach to Classifying Acts of Crime and Violence at Tourism Destinations", *Journal of Travel Research,* 38 (1): 5-12.

Pizam, A., Mansfeld, Y. (eds) (1996), *"Tourism, Crime, and International Security Issues*. Chichester: John Willey and Sons.

Ralston, D., Holt, D. (1997), "The Impact of National Culture and Economic Ideology on Managerial Work Values: A Study of the United States, Russia, Japan and China", *Journal Of International Business Studies*, 28 (1), pp. 177-207.

Richter, L.K., Waugh, W.L. (1986), "Terrorism and Tourism as Logical Companions". *Tourism Management*. 7 (4): 230-238.

Ritchie, B., Goeldner, C. (1994), *Travel and Tourism, and Hospitality Research: A Handbook for Managers and Researchers*. 2nd ed. New York: John Willey and Sons.

Robinson, M. (1999), "Cultural Conflicts in Tourism: Inevitability and Inequality". In: Robinson, M., Boniface, P. (eds) (1999) *Tourism and Cultural Conflicts*, Wallingford: CABI Publishing.

Robinson, M., Boniface, P. (eds), (1999), *Tourism and Cultural Conflicts*, Wallingford: CABI Publishing.

Ryan, C. (1991), *Tourism, Terrorism and Violence: The Risks of Wider World Travel*. London: Research Institute for the Study of Conflict and Terrorism.

Sanders, D. (1981), *Patterns of Political Instability*. London: MacMillan.

Scheffe, H. (1967), *The Analysis of Variance*. 5th ed. New York: John Willey and Sons.

Smith, P., Dugan, S. (1996), "National Culture and the Values of Organisational Employees", *Journal of Cross-Cultural Psychology*, 27 (2): 231-263.

Sonmez, S. (1998), "Tourism, Terrorism, and Political Instability", *Annals of Tourism Research,* 25 (2): 416-456.

Sonmez, S., Graefe, A. (1998), "Influence of Terrorism Risk on Foreign Tourism Decisions", *Annals of Tourism Research*, 25 (1): 112-144.

Sparrow, P., Pei-Chuan Wu, (1998), "Does National Culture really matter? Predicting HRM preferences of Taiwanese employees", *Employee Relations*, 20 (1): 26-56.

SPSS Inc. (1997), *SPSS Advanced Statistics 7.5*. Chicago: SPSS Inc.

SPSS Inc. (1997), *SPSS Base 7.5 Applications Guide*. Chicago: SPSS Inc.

Stevens, J. (1996), *Applied Multivariate Statistics for the Social Sciences*. 3rd ed. New Jersey: Lawrence Erlbaum Associates.

Triandis, H., Bontempo, R., Leung, K., Harry Hui C. (1990), "A Method for Determining Cultural, Demographic, and Personal Constructs", *Journal of Cross Cultural Psychology*, 21, pp. 302-318.

Tribe, J. (1997), *The Economics of Leisure and Tourism*. 1st ed. Oxford: Butterworth-Heinemann.

Tsan, C. (1999), *Measuring Service Quality of Professional Sports Events: An Empirical Study of Newcastle Ice-Hockey Club*. Ph.D. Thesis. University of Sunderland.

Verma, G., Bagley, C. (eds) (1988), *Cross-Cultural Studies of Personality, Attitudes and Cognition*. 1st ed. London: Macmillan Press.

Verma, K. G., Mallick, K. (1988), "Problems in Cross-cultural Resaearch". In: Verma, G., Bagley, C. (eds) (1988) *Cross-Cultural Studies of Personality, Attitudes and Cognition*. 1st ed. London: Macmillan Press.

Voich, D., Stepina, L. (eds) (1994), *Cross-Cultural Analysis of Values and Political Economy Issues*. 1st ed. Westport: Praeger Publishers.

Wahab, S. (1996), "Tourism and Terrorism: Synthesis of the Problem with Emphasis on Egypt". In: Pizam, A., Mansfeld, Y. (eds) (1996) *"Tourism, Crime, and International Security Issues*. Chichester: John Willey and Sons.

Witt, S., Moutinho, L. (eds) (1995), *Tourism Marketing and Management Handbook*. 1st ed. London: Prentice Hall.

World Tourism Organisation. (1998), *Tourism Economic Report*. 1st ed. Spain: World Tourism Organisation.

World Tourism Organisation. (ed.) (1994), *National and Regional Tourism Planning: Methodologies and Case Studies*. 1st ed. London: Routledge.

Zikmund, W. (1997), *Exploring Marketing Research*. 6th ed. Forth Worth: The Dryden Press.

Explaining the blandness of popular travel journalism: Narrative, cliché and the structure of meaning

Richard Voase

University of Lincolnshire and Humberside, UK

Introduction

This paper is about the language used in popular travel journalism. Specifically, it is about the role of cliché in the language surrounding tourism, as it appears in popular televisual travel programmes. It shall be argued that an analysis of this discourse in terms of its narrative structure and the meanings intended to be conveyed, when combined with an detailed understanding of what really constitutes the 'tourist product', reveals that messages about travel opportunities addressed to a mass market cannot be adequately expressed in any way other than cliché. First, the author offers some background comments on the ways in which cliché appears in the discourse surrounding tourism. Second, a particular example of televisual travel journalism will be used to expose further insights into the role of cliché. Third, the author shall analyse the discourse in terms of various theoretical paradigms, coupled with insights into the real nature of the 'tourist product'. The paper will conclude by suggesting that cliché is an indispensable linguistic device in popular travel journalism.

Background

The author proposes to establish the background for the investigation by looking at ways in which cliché appears in the discourse of tourism. More shall be said about 'discourse' later, but for the present the author will use 'discourse' to mean a set of messages which relate to social practices, which are embedded in language-use, and which appear across a range of texts (Barker and Brooks, 1998: 109, 115). Strictly speaking, a content analysis of various linguistic constructs within forms of tourism discourse should be conducted in order to document cliché as a significant motif. For the present, it is suggested that a certain body of clichés surfaces regularly in certain forms of tourism discourse. In particular the author has in mind mass-market televised travel shows, promotional brochures, and conversation. Such clichés are also apt to surface in level 1 student essays, as we shall see shortly. The author shall now clarify the meaning of the word 'cliché' and offer incidental examples of how they might appear in forms of tourism discourse.

'Cliché' is a word of French origin. In French, a cliché is an object: it is a plate of lead type which is used in the now-obsolete, or obsolescent, technique of letterpress printing. The English word for this object is 'stereotype'. Both words are both used in English to convey purely metaphorical meanings: a 'cliché' is an overworked and overfamiliar phrase; to 'stereotype' is to create an image or impression which is fixed. In contemporary parlance, 'stereotyping' carries additional and negative connotations of oversimplification and misrepresentation.

To illustrate this point, the author cites a sentence from a level 1 student essay which he marked recently. This was work from a reasonably promising student, but for the fact that she borrowed, at one point, a phrase from the lexicon of tourist clichés:

> *'...there are growing numbers of people with incomes sufficient to be able to afford to go on holiday. Due to factors such as guaranteed weather, these people choose to go on holiday abroad...'* (my emphasis).

The author pointed out to her that if the presence of one thing was guaranteed over every square inch of God's earth, it was the weather. What she actually meant was something different: that some overseas destinations offer an increased likelihood of fine, warm and sunny weather (which nevertheless cannot, even in favoured climes, be absolutely guaranteed). Rather than think through her point and express it in an articulate way, she had reached for an often-heard off-the-peg expression, faulty as deployed in context. Whether its faultiness emptied the term of meaning is a different matter, which will be discussed later.

There are three so-called 'moments of truth' which gave rise to the authors personal interest in this topic, and he believes it will help establish the background for the authors case he permits himself to relate these. The first occurred during an edition of a popular television travel show. Owing to the fact that the author did not record its provenance, it will remain anonymous. He was watching casually, while undertaking some other activity. One feature in the programme concerned a visit by a seasoned female travel journalist to an expensive hotel on an island in the South Pacific. The author glanced at the television to see, momentarily, the travel journalist reclining on a sun lounger in the grounds of the hotel, cocktail in hand, announcing that 'There's something here for everyone'. This is a common enough cliché in the lexicon of tourism promotion. What became obvious to me, after a moment's reflection, was that it was, in that context, a very strange thing to say. In terms of access, expense, and probably in terms of available activities, this island and its hotel could never be anything other than a niche opportunity for a very particular kind of visitor. But what for me constituted the 'moment of truth' was not so much that she said it, but *that the author needed a moment's reflection* to perceive that the comment was, in any literal sense, nonsense. He had to think and reflect, in order to perceive the nonsense.

The second 'moment of truth' occurred when reading a newspaper review of an edition of a popular TV holiday programme (Sweeting, 1997). This show had featured visits to destinations by a celebrity as guest presenter; a comedy actor called Martin Clunes, infamous for being both forthright and facetious. This formula had, in the opinion of the reviewer, created a successful programme. However, the show was introduced by its regular presenter who, 'surrounded by cocktail, beach and palm tree', was, in the opinion of the reviewer and in contrast with Martin Clunes, in need of 'something interesting to say'. The dilemma seemed to be this: should TV travel shows be tour operator propaganda, or attempt to offer 'a real flavour of the place'.

The third moment of truth is also anecdotal, and concerns an incident in the life of the author. Having spent two days on the beach of a well-known English seaside resort during a period of fine summer weather, the author walked from the beach into a seafront restaurant, during the late afternoon, to reserve a table for the evening. The sun outside was still shining vigorously. A waitress greeted me:

> Waitress: *My, you do look brown, have you been abroad?*

> Author: *No, I have been out there on the beach.*

His reply was delivered in a factual tone with no hint of sarcasm, but the waitress seemed surprised and a little offended. 'Who is this smart alec?' was the message of the look she gave him. The presence within conversational discourse that suntans are signifiers of having taken a foreign holiday is in my experience ubiquitous, and, of course, thoroughly irrational. Despite the most compelling and self-evident domestic context - consistent fine weather, the beach - that waitress effortlessly ascribed the authors suntan to having accomplished an overseas vacational trip. His articulation of the self-evident truth verged on causing offence. Whatever the game was, he was not playing it.

Based on these experiences, the author formulated three propositions for investigation:

- first, that clichés are deployed when the sender of a message feels able to assume in advance the agreement of the receiver;

- second, that the sender has reasons to avoid a full articulation of the meaning intended by the cliché, and assumes the compliance of the receiver;

- third, to deploy a cliché is to assume that its premise will not be challenged.

If these propositions are valid, then the cliché is much more than a simple overworked or overfamiliar phrase. This indeed will be argued to be the case in the discussion later in the paper. For the present, the author wishes to use a particular example of televisual travel journalism to expose further insights into the role of cliché.

Exposition

The example of televisual travel journalism is taken from one of three features contained within an episode of the BBC1 travel programme, *Holiday,* broadcast on 1st July 1997. The author had this episode recorded at random by engineers at my place of work, with the intention of seeking to investigate my propositions using its content as a basis. The author wishes to add that, although reflection on the linguistic constructs deployed in the examples which he has selected offers scope for amusement, the author does not intend this as a mockery of the skills of the presenters. To say nothing, without the audience noticing that nothing has been said, is an artform and demands an intelligent use of language. Like purposely playing a piano out of tune, it is very difficult to do deliberately. The particular feature within the programme which the author has chosen as a vehicle for exposing my argument involves a short stay in a castle converted into tourist accommodation on the west coast of Ireland: the travel journalist presenting this particular piece is Craig Doyle. The presenter of the programme is the late Jill Dando. Of particular interest are two sequences: Jill Dando's introduction to the piece, and an excerpt for which Craig Doyle uses the coast of western Ireland as a setting.

First, we examine Jill Dando's introduction:

> *Craig Doyle was suitably chuffed when we sent him away to rattle around in a fabulously huge 15th century castle, the pride of County Clare. Knappogue Castle is one of Ireland's classiest estates, and has in its past been fit for a number of kings.*

If we examine this introduction in the terms which we have established, the text appears to be structured around four clichés. Craig Doyle is to *rattle around* in a *classy* destination, describable as the *pride of County Clare* and *fit for a king*. We shall consider each one in a little more detail in the order in which they appear.

1   Craig Doyle will *rattle around*. The usual deployment of this verb is to refer metaphorically to the way in which ghosts occupy castles: rattling, presumably, because they expired in chains in the dungeons, or wear suits of armour. Ghosts go with castles as chips with fish, as every tourist knows.

2   The destination is one of the *classiest*. Class, strictly speaking, is a neutral term of categorisation; but when deployed in common discourse in its adjectival form, it normally indicates a certain consciousness of category. High class accommodation - *classy* - suggests physical and symbolic comfort for people for are *classy*, and commensurate discomfort for those who are not.

3   The castle is the *pride of County Clare*. This epithet would make a suitable name for a railway locomotive. The deployment of this phrase vaguely positions the castle as a major visitor attraction within the region: civic pride, we know, chooses old and valued structures as its emblems of self-worth.

4   The accommodation is *fit for a king*. The deployment of this cliché achieves two objectives: the 'classiness' of the destination is further emphasised by invoking regal standards; and as every tourist knows, kings go with castles just as surely as fish with chips.

If we reflect on this material in terms of the three propositions outlined earlier, it becomes apparent that to structure this introduction around cliché is to establish a context in which the advance agreement of the reader can be assumed: kings accompany castles, ghosts rattle around, major buildings of ancient origin are the object of civic pride. The presenter assumes, probably correctly, that to avoid a more detailed articulation will be acceptable to the reader, the reasons for which we shall discuss shortly. What is particularly interesting, though, is the forgettability of the clichés as constructs: mixed metaphors always jar, but in this piece, Craig Doyle mutates metaphorically from a ghost to a king in the space of two sentences, without us noticing. As the author will suggest later, there are very good reasons for this.

The second sequence is taken from the piece itself. The setting is the cliffs of Moher overlooking the sea: the camera shows the impressive coastline, and in the foreground is young woman, with red hear, wearing a green dress, playing a harp and singing some kind of Irish song. Craig Doyle's voice, off-camera intones:

> *Street entertaining takes on a whole new meaning on the cliffs of Moher, one of County Clare's most popular attractions...*

He then, on camera, immediately abandons the initial scene and its voice-over in favour of offering practical advice on walking the cliff-top path.

This, the author suggests, is a combination of a visual and verbal cliché to enliven the otherwise stark sight of a line of cliffs, whose undoubted attractiveness does not transfer well to the two-dimensional television screen. The young woman, placed there for the purpose out of context, is a cliché in the English translation: a stereotype. The red wavy hair, the green dress, the harp, the choice of song, are all signifiers which point in syntagmatic relationship to a common signified: this girl is Irish. The problem arises when the presenter has to choose a voice-over to complement the already self-evident message from the visual image: 'Street entertaining takes on a whole new meaning...' This particular cliché is interesting in that it diverts attention from the fact that there is no meaning to articulate beyond that which is evident in the visual image.

Just as a politician, when challenged by an interviewer on a point of policy which is uncertain, always responds along the lines of 'our position on this has always been absolutely clear', the mention of a 'whole new meaning' masks the central point: that there is no meaning: at least, there is no meaning beyond the obviousness of the image before us. And in a literal sense, the image as anchored by Craig Doyle's voice-over creates a stark improbability: a street entertainer, hoping to attract revenues from passers-by, is unlikely to choose an isolated clifftop as a location to perform.

Discussion

The discussion begins with an examination of what is meant by the term, 'narrative'. This is arguably the essence of a travel programme: it is an account of a set of facts and comments recited in the first person by an author or narrator. In this case, therefore, authors/narrators were Jill Dando and Craig Doyle: or, if we wish to delineate their roles, Jill Dando's function was more of a narrator, and Craig Doyle was the author of the account of his particular visit to western Ireland; but the difference, the author suggests, is of little importance for our present purpose. It is also possible to speak of 'narratives' in other contexts. A colleague of the author, Kevin Meethan, has written about the historic built environment of the City of York, in England, in terms of constituting sets of 'spatial narratives' to be 'read' by tourists (1996: 324). In such a case there is no specific author, but there is still something which can be 'read' and from which meaning can be generated.

In order to gain insights into the workings of narrative the author looked at the understanding of the concept as expressed in writings concerned with the analysis of cinematic film. One useful perspective comes from an American author Seymour Chatman, who suggested that a narrative is composed of two components: a *story*, and a *discourse*. The story is the content of the narrative, and the discourse is the vehicle by which the story is communicated (1978: 9). Arising from this are two points to note: first, the independence of the two components means that a story is transposable from one medium to another: for example, a novel can appear as a stage play or a film. Second, there is the need to posit the existence of both an author and an audience, either real or implied (1978: 28). The fact that a story such as *Sleeping Beauty* can and does appear as a book, a pantomime, a film, a ballet and a theme park attraction are viewed by Chatman as powerful evidence for his essentially structuralist approach to understanding narrative (1978: 20). However, a problem arises when we turn to the question of authorship: it is fairly easy to identify the original authors of a story and their contributory authorship of those who adapt a novel for stage or screen. But who authors the 'spatial narratives' of the city of York? The historic environment of such a city was not 'written' over two thousand years as a coherent narrative to be read by tourists. Indeed, mediaeval walls, timbered houses and other structures were not intended to tell any particular story at their point to construction, with the very obvious exception of the cathedral. City walls and timbered houses were not designed as narratives to be read by tourists, but in the present-day, or as some say, postmodern cultural condition, in which inspiration is so often sought in the past rather than in the present or anticipated future, they become vehicles to generate meaning.

And this is the point: when a tourist 'reads' the spatial narratives of York, he or she is simultaneously the author and the audience. Whatever meanings are generated by reading such narratives are produced in the mind of the tourist by the sights, architectural styles and objects which, by their antiquity and style, facilitate the generation of such meanings. This is the essence of the poststructuralist approach to understanding narrative: as Derrida observed, 'There is nothing outside of the text' (1998: 158); that is to say, a text does not of itself retain meaning: meaning is generated in the mind of the reader at the point of reading. In this sense the 'author' of the spatial narratives of the City of York is the tourist him/herself.

Interestingly, a later writer on narrative in cinematic film, David Bordwell, with the benefit of a growing climate of poststructuralist thought, offers an analytic model which differs somewhat from that of Chatman. While he accepts, as the author does, the usefulness of Chatman's structured story+discourse model, he observes that is a mistake to 'impute a fundamental passivity to the spectator' (Bordwell, 1985: xiii). Bordwell sees the reader as the final author of the narrative, and analyses the authoring role of the reader as a 'dynamic psychological process' in which perceptual capacities, prior learned knowledge and experience, and the facilitating role of the perceived content and structure of the narrative, combine to generate meaning (Bordwell, 1985: 32-3).

So in other words, the visitor to York deploys perceptual capacities (which may vary from individual to individual), pre-learned knowledge (which will also vary), and use the object of his/her gaze to create a self-authored narrative. The tourist will be assisted, of course, by the inevitable markers in terms of tourist information, signs on buildings, visitor centres and other paraphernalia which compensate for the perceptual and experiential inadequacies of the visitors (MacCannell, 1976: 41-2). However, the author sees the marking-and-signing industry not as full attempts at authoring, but as adapting the spatial narratives to the demands of the particular discourse and the particular readership: in much the same way as the story of *Sleeping Beauty* must be linguistically adapted to a young audience if produced as a pantomime.

What, then, do these insights tell us about analysing the narrative of a televisual holiday programme? First, the discourse, quite clearly, is televisual travel journalism; the reader is the viewer, who is intended to construct meaning in his or her mind, deploying perceptual capacities and prior experience, facilitated by watching the programme. What, though, is the story? Or to put it another way, what is the content? 'Street entertaining takes on a whole new meaning', we are told. What meaning? What is the story? And the answer is, for very good reasons which I shall now argue, is that *there is no story*. This kind of mass-market travel journalism works, because it is narrative without a story. It is pure discourse. And to understand why that should be, we need to examine what is known about the nature of the tourist product, and the ways in which it is the object of motivations and the generator of satisfactions.

We tend to use the term 'tourist product' rather loosely. While we can talk of a destination as a 'product', and a particular kind of holiday as a 'product', we have to admit in the end that the tourist product is, in the words of Christopher Holloway, 'largely psychological in its attractions' (1989: 11). Seaton & Bennett suggest that 'tourism provision is as much about the management of illusion as the supply of physical goods' (1996: 113). And as the present author has argued, 'the true definition of the tourist product is in the mind of the tourist. By implication, there can be as many definitions of the tourist product as there are tourists' (Voase, 1995: 91). If we define the tourist product in the terms outlined by these authors, we find ourselves confronting what is effectively a product of the mind, synonymous with the self-authored narrative.

Proceeding further with this line of argument, we must now consider what is known about the particular motivations and satisfactions which accompany tourist experience. There are two structural features of the consumption of the tourist product which differentiate it from other forms of consumption: first, temporal delay between decision to consume and actual consumption; and second, spatial differentiation between decision to consume and actual consumption. This temporal and spatial differentiation gives rise to three qualitative features of tourist consumption: first, the temporal differentiation creates copious potential for pleasurable anticipation of the consumption of the product through the process of daydreaming. In this respect, tourism is a form of 'imaginative hedonism' (Campbell, 1994: 510-11, 1995: 117-119). Second, the whole point of a tourist trip is to consume a set of experiences which contrast with the everyday. Whether this is a search for a mythical 'other' (Selwyn 1996: 2) or simply an intensification of pleasurable activities associated with the home environment, the tourist experience is expected to be extraordinary in some way, and thus binarily opposed to the everyday (Urry, 1990: 11). Third, and crucially, research has revealed ample evidence that the actual *satisfactions* of tourist experience may differ significantly from the advance *motivations* (Crompton, 1979: 421; Dann, 1981: 203; Mannell and Iso-Ahola, 1987: 322). As Philip Pearce concluded, 'When travellers reflect on their holiday experiences the fulfilment of self-actualisation needs is frequently recalled because they reflect *largely unplanned spontaneous and personal interests*' (Pearce, 1982: 129, my emphasis). Crompton observes that the tourism industry seems to operate on the assumption that people go on holiday to do and see things: research suggested this to be challengable, at the very least (Crompton, 1979: 421). So, the argument thus far is as follows: first, that tourists themselves are the authors of the tourist product; second, that the product is configured in the mind, in advance, by imaginative daydreaming; but third, that actual *post-hoc* satisfactions may differ radically from advance motivations. At this point we return to the question of the televisual travel show, and subsequently, to the apparently salient role of the cliché as a narrative device in such shows.

It was suggested earlier that the mass-market travel show is a discourse without a story. Why? The reason, the author suggests, is that its very form demands such an approach, for the following reasons. First, if as has been suggested the tourist product is self-authored in the mind of the tourist, and is characterised in advance of consumption by daydreaming, then an explicit story would usurp the existential prerogative of the consumer. For example, for Craig Doyle to actually author a story about how he felt returning to his country of origin, using the full potential of the English language to produce an articulate summary of what it was like to visit the west of Ireland with a film crew, would be fine for viewers who wished to travel vicariously with him. For similar reasons, Noyce's *South Col* was a book on the thoughts and feelings generated by mountaineering experience, and held in greater regard than Hunt's more accomplishment-oriented *Ascent of Everest* (Hamilton-Smith, 1987: 340). So, a mass-market travel show which adopted an authentically narrative approach would risk engaging some viewers, and alienating many others. However, to produce a simple framework onto which the viewer can, by means of daydreaming, weave their own projected experience, would be much more suited to the needs of the tourist as we now understand them. The travel show becomes a televisual version of a brochure: visual images things to see and do, accompanied by a verbal commentary which is remarkably reliant on the deployment of cliché. What, then, is the role of the cliché?

The author suggested earlier that clichés are deployed when the sender feels that the advance agreement of the receiver can be assumed; that the sender wishes to avoid a full articulation of an intended meaning, and deploys the cliché to accomplish the task; and that to deploy a cliché is to assume that its premise will not be challenged. If these propositions are valid, then the cliché cannot be quite as devoid of meaning as it appears. In the paragraphs which follow the author will offer an explanation as to the linguistic function of the cliché.

He suggests that the cliché is the bearer of one of the most fundamental embedded elements of discourse, ideology. Ideology itself needs some explanation: it has been understood as 'meaning in the service of power' and is detectable in all communicative forms, from everyday conversation to complex texts. Crucially, in particular contexts it serves to 'establish and sustain relations of domination' (Thompson, 1990: 7). Alternatively, ideologies may be understood as 'forms of consciousness'; 'discourse' and 'ideologies' are separate concepts but which exist in symbiosis: an ideology is a concept, a discourse is its vehicle (Purvis & Hunt, 1993: 476). Following this suggestion, we can suppose that the cliché in travel shows has two functions: to invoke relations of domination without articulating the same. For example, to describe the Irish Castle as 'one of the classiest places around' is tantamount to saying, 'If you are riff-raff, you will not enjoy yourself here, nor will you be particularly welcome'. Or alternatively, 'If you fancy yourself, take a second look at this'. These are two alternative meanings, self-authored from the apparently meaningless. Facilitated by the cliché, you author your own meaning. Cliché offers, quite simply, 'something for everyone'. In this sense there is a compliance between author and reader, termed by Hall a process of encoding and decoding, by which the cliché offers scope for interpretation in accordance with a wide range of ideological positions:

> *The level of connotation...is the point where* already coded *signs intersect with the deep semantic codes of a culture and take on additional, more active ideological dimensions*. (Hall, 1980: 133, Hall's emphasis)

What is interesting, though, is that the cliché, unlike the deployment of articulate language, achieves the effect of connotation without alerting us to the fact. It succeeds in occluding not only its role in sustaining specific relations of domination, but in numbing our minds to its own role in sustaining these relations and, to boot, masks its own inherent nonsensicality.

In this respect, the workings of cliché coincide well with the workings of ideology as theorised by Louis Althusser in the 1970s (1992). His proposition is that ideologies are all around us, and 'interpellate' us when we least expect it. The effect is comparable with hearing our name called in the street: we hear a greeting, and we instinctively turn around and respond in terms of established protocol. When we consider that we are least affected by ideology, that is the time when we are most affected by it. Its working also assumes a two-fold category of the subject: the subject in terms of a Cartesian subject who is hailed and can decide whether and how to respond; and the 'interpellated' subject who, in responding to the hail, is *subjected* to the workings of ideology. It is worth quoting Althusser on this topic:

> *It is indeed a peculiarity of ideology that it imposes (without appearing to do so, since these are 'obviousnesses') obviousnesses as obviousnesses, which we cannot fail to recognise and before which we have the inevitable and natural reaction of crying out (aloud, or in the 'still small voice of conscience'): 'That's obvious! That's right! That's true!* (Althusser, 1992: 54)

So, presented with a girl with red hair in a green dress playing a harp on a coastline redolent of what we know of the celtic seaboard, accompanied by the comment 'Street entertaining takes on a whole new meaning', the visual and verbal clichés presented thus in syntagmatic relationship leave no room for doubting the obviousness of the mental image which we are intended to construct: we can expect to encounter Irishness in Ireland. The mention of the 'whole new meaning' serves to occlude the fact that there is no meaning, save obviousness as obviousness. As subjects, we cheerfully submit to our subjection (Althusser, 1992: 57).

In some ways, clichés are part of the armoury of what Jean-François Lyotard called 'performative language'. This Lyotard regarded as increasingly symptomatic of the postmodern condition as the proliferation of information demanded linguistic adaptations to 'position' receivers more forcefully into subjection. For example, the BBC management under John Birt produced a report about itself in 1993 entitled *Turning Promises into Reality*. In 1996, the Church of England produced a report about itself entitled *Working as One Body*. By enquiring further, you are already subjected by the (wishful) thinking embodied in these titles. The idea of these language games, says Lyotard, is to 'displace' your 'opponent' and use language in a way which, at the point of debate, subjects the receiver to passive acceptance of the central point of your argument before debate has opened (Lyotard, 1984: 9, 16-17).

The point of performative language as exposed by Lyotard is that it is a *deliberate* linguistic construct. By contrast, the cliché is a pre-prepared linguistic construct used in an off-the-peg manner to achieve similar ends. So, for example, on that sunny afternoon on the esplanade of an English resort, when the author entered a restaurant to reserve a table, the waitress took one look at him, and reached for the nearest device which would facilitate conversation on the basis of an ideology which she believed we had in common. First, the suntan is an indicator of having the good sense to take a holiday abroad; and second, she wished to greet me as a person of good sense. Hence, the author was invited to confirm his good sense by admitting to a holiday abroad. He denies his subjection, and responds as a free subject. But the easiest option is to be subjected. So, cliché is performative in its deployment, rather than in its construction.

Before concluding, we have to ask ourselves whether the deployment of cliché in mass-market travel shows is a deliberate use of the device. The author would speculate that it *is* deliberate, though not necessarily through an understanding of the kind of theoretical route which he has charted. He speculates that the clichéd format of the travel show exists in binary opposition to the investigative documentary. Typically the latter, and the topics chosen as objects of investigation, involve intrigue, outrage, and discomfort for the viewer. Quite obviously, a travel show needs to achieve opposite ends, for the simple reason that travel shows *are* tourism propaganda produced with the co-operation of tourism organisations. This, coupled with some awareness of the power of the cliché to facilitate self-authored meaning without engendering contestation, the author suggests to be the likely explanation.

Conclusion

Given the complexity of this argument, the author proposes to offer a summary in terms of eight discrete points:

1.   To deploy cliché is to assume the advance agreement of the reader, that the reader shares the author's reason to avoid a full articulation, and to assume that the premise of the cliché will not be challenged.

2.   Two examples of mass-market televisual travel journalism discussed in this paper are constructed around cliché, of both verbal and visual kinds.

3.   The tourist product is self-authored in the mind of the tourist: and there are potentially as many tourist products as there are tourists.

4.   The temporal and spatial differentiation between decision to consume and actual consumption encourages the advance configuration of the product in the mind of the tourist, through daydreaming.

5.   To offer an authentic narrative in a travel show is to usurp the prerogative of the tourist to configure the product in their minds through daydreaming: for this reason, travel shows are discourse without story.

6. Cliché is deployed because of its capacity to achieve connotation, without alerting the reader to the fact. Cliché is thus a vehicle for the most fundamental (and invisible) of ideological positions.

7. The concept of 'interpellation' as advanced by Althusser is a useful model for understanding the workings of cliché: at the very point when the subject perceives no meaning, he or she is subjected by meaning.

8. Cliché is therefore a feature of performative language, but in deployment rather than in construction: its use is to subject the reader into the interpretive options contained within a certain reading position, and assumes their consent and compliance.

As Althusser suggested, our natural reaction is to cry out, aloud or in our minds, 'That's obvious'. It is the obviousness which we recognise, but which when cleverly deployed, remains unnoticed.

References

Althusser, L. (1992), from 'Ideology and Ideological State Apparatuses (1970) in Easthope, A and McGowan, K: *A Critical and Cultural Theory Reader,* Open University Press, Milton Keynes, pp 50-58.

Barker, M. and Brooks, K. (1998), *Knowing Audiences: Judge Dredd: Its Friends, Fans and Foes,* University of Luton Press, Luton.

Bordwell, D. (1985), *Narration in the Fiction Film,* Methuen, London.

Campbell, C. (1994), Consuming goods and the good of consuming, *Critical Review*, 8, (4), pp 503-520.

Campbell, C. (1995), The Sociology of Consumption, in Miller, D (editor): *Acknowledging Consumption: a review of new studies,* Routledge, London, pp 96-126.

Chatman, S. (1978), Story and Discourse: Narrative Structure in Fiction and Film, Cornell University Press, London.

Crompton, J. (1979), Motivations for pleasure vacation, Annals of Tourism Research, 6 (4): 408-424.

Dann, G. (1981), Tourist motivation: an appraisal, Annals of Tourism Research, 8 (2): 187-219.

Derrida, J. (1998), Of Grammatology, (corrected edition), John Hopkins Press, London.

Hall, S. (1980), Encoding/decoding, in Hall, S *et al* (editors): *Culture, Media, Language,* Routledge (1992 reprint), London, pp 128-138.

Hamilton-Smith, E. (1987), Four Kinds of Tourism? *Annals of Tourism Research,* vol 14, pp 332-344.

Holloway, C. (1989), *The Business of Tourism,* Third Edition, Pitman, London.

Lyotard, J-F. (1984), *The Postmodern Condition: a report on knowledge,* Manchester University Press, Manchester.

Mannell, R. and Iso-Ahola, S. (1987), The psychological nature of leisure and tourism experience, *Annals of Tourism Research,* vol 14, pp 314-331.

MacCannell, D. (1976), *The Tourist: a New Theory of the Leisure Class,* Schocken Books, New York.

Meethan, K. (1996), Consuming (in) the civilised city, *Annals of Tourism Research,* 23 (2): 322-340.

Pearce, P. (1982), The Social Psychology of Tourist Behaviour, Pergamon Press, Oxford.

Purvis, T. and Hunt, A. (1993), Discourse, ideology, discourse, ideology, discourse, ideology...British Journal of Sociology, 44 (3): 473-499.

Seaton, A. and Bennett, M. (1996), Marketing Tourism Products: concepts, issues, cases, International Thomson, London.

Sweeting, A. (1997), Fly me to Freebie, The Guardian, 23 April.

Thompson, J. (1990), Ideology and Modern Culture, Polity Press, Cambridge.

Urry, J. (1990), The Tourist Gaze: leisure and travel in contemporary societies, Sage, London.

Voase, R. N. (1995), *Tourism: the human perspective,* Hodder and Stoughton, London.

A century of indigenous images: The world according to the tourist postcard

Elvi Whittaker

University of British Columbia, Canada

Postcards are much more than a medium for the retention of timely images. They also fall within several familiar intersecting intellectual frames: colonialism, romanticism, liberal humanism, realism, Social Darwinism, capitalism, the bourgeoise, postmodernism and, over-riding all, the culture of the tourist industry. These theoretical concerns serve as both subtexts and pretexts to a myriad of images throughout the century, each image clearly an ephemeral testimonial, intentionally or not, to its theoretical roots. Captured images of the indigenous person remain suspended in complex intellectual webs which make it possible to interpret their fate throughout the twentieth century - from the apex of colonial might, itself the legacy of several previous centuries, through the fading days of empire and finally to a relentless postmodern presence. For the hundred years of change, I envision four major periods: (1) from the *belle epoque* to the Great War, (2) between the two World Wars, (3) after World War II and, finally, (4) the final decades of the twentieth century. Since its arrival on the world scene the postcard has come to constitute an historical text of popular attitudes. Through historical shifts it has changed, often dramatically, with each era, as well as fostering some enduring conventions.

Conventions of the postcard

Clearly the physical presence of the postcard would not have been possible without dramatic technological advances in the nineteenth century, namely the invention of photography by Fox Talbot in 1839, the perfecting of the printing process and the emergence of stamps. There were the growing advantages afforded the middle class - wide literacy in some parts of the world and, ironically, not in others - a wider reading public than ever before, and an early glimmer of the existence of what came to be called in the later decades of the century, the global village. These technological advances and social changes were widely celebrated in a series of world exhibitions, which not only extolled the latest of marvels drawing large crowds to view them, but also bore witness to the other offered curiosity: the lives of indigenous and exotic people. Such world fairs made clear statements about the advances of technology contrasted with the "primitive." Inevitably, the industrial age brought with it a consumerism such as had never existed before, not only for the goods produced at home or in other industrialized nations, but also for knowledge of that exotic other, the indigenous person. The popular preoccupation with the latter in particular came to centre on the picture postcard, helping to make it an ubiquitous mode of communication, but perhaps even more influential than the letter before it. Beginning with the first such missive in Austria in 1869 (Schor, 1994:261), postcards had become an unprecedented commercial success by the early years of the twentieth century. Postcard albums in the parlors of middle class families served as entertainment, education and as tacit ways to claim status and identity. Despite such popularity, it is still very surprising to learn of its actual proliferation, that in the years 1909-10, 866 million postcards were posted in Britain alone (Staff, 1966:91).

The early postcard depicting non-European subjects, whether actually sold in Europe or sent from the colonies, was produced through four distinct steps.[1] Firstly, European (or American) photographers, on journeys to the far-flung parts of the colonized world, captured on film those images which caught their attention. Thus the choice of subject, situation, the style of depiction, positioning were according to current European idioms of representation. In the second step the photographs were taken back to the home country and manufactured into postcards by one of the very successful new postcard production firms located principally in Germany, Switzerland, Great Britain and, a little later, in America. Thirdly, come cards were exported back to the colonies where they were purchased by those Europeans who were there under the auspices of imperialism in one of its many forms - government officers, entrepreneurs and missionaries. Included, at this early time, were a much smaller number of special sojourners we now know as tourists. Lastly, in the fourth step, the cards were dispatched once again to Europe or America to assume the postcard's status as testimonies of presence, exotic curiosities, collectible objects and comforting reassurances about who were privileged to view and who were destined to be viewed.[2] Clearly early postcards were a Europeanization, a figment of white mythologies and their claimed right to exhibit and view. As products of the eye of the camera and the mind's eye of its producer, buyer and receiver, cards reinforced the accepted conventions about race and power.

Postcards are characterized by an existential poverty. They depict a body, a face, a scene, all contextually removed. The indigenous person is often posed in a nondescript background, without cultural accoutrements of any kind, occasionally identified only by costume or perhaps a single cultural artifact. As often as not, foreign props are imposed by the photographer. Thus the card takes what is essentially a stranger and domesticates that person for the viewer. It is this scarcity of context that allows interpretations to be mapped onto the image. At the very minimum the photographer facilitates interpretation when positioning the figure, supplying an ecological background (not always geographically or culturally relevant to the subject), dictating the pose to be struck and the facial expression to be assumed. The stance, more often than not, is a familiar one, taking its form from European paintings, such as the reclining portraits of the women painted by Ingres, David or Manet. Thus native women pose like odalisques langerously stretched out on divans, enwrapped in the flimsy and revealing draperies that the proprieties of the age suggested. On occasion, as if in deference to the Old Masters, one breast is nude. This, in an age when the photographic semi-nudity was permitted for indigenous images and was completely unthinkable for white women. Sometimes the conventions of studio portraiture are used as in photographs of European aristocracy or affluent middle class figures posing for a *carte de visite* or a *cabinet* photograph. In yet other cards the rigours of anthropometrism are evoked in full frontal perspectives as if in preparation to be compared to others using the scientific measurements developed by anthropologists.

Postcarding is a peculiar act of abstraction. Essential strangers are brought within the purview of the consumer. The social distance may be reduced. On the other hand, however, the indigenous person is now actually visibly shown to be stranger, more exotic and even further removed from the middle class viewer than in any previous imaginings. As these sparse images are without auditory, visual or tactile accompaniments, no observations over time are possible - all the kinds of contacts that would permit the normality of persons to emerge. Such restricted access, together with the offered abstractions, created cultural markers which were to endure and to become reality. The Australian Aboriginal male becomes associated with a spear which is either raised or held resting on the ground (Plate 1), the North American appears beside a teepee, the Mexican sleeps in a sitting position with sombrero tipped over his face (Albers and James, 1987). The image is reduced even further to where the figures are recognizable even in reductionist cartoon form. Such minimalism is the required essential for stereotyping, which in turn becomes the benchmark for Aboriginality, Indianness, Mexicanness (see also Handy, 1998). Stereotypes are disengaged from time, place and individuality and everything else is not only omitted, but becomes and remains irrelevant. It could be said of such stark simplicity that "the individuality of the stranger is dissolved in the category; it is the category, not its individual members, which is set and seen as the genuine supra-personal carrier of cultural difference" (Bauman, 1989:16).

Plate 1   Woomera Spearsman, North Queensland. The Edco Series No. 1157, printed in Germany, ca. 1906. Private Collection

Postcards are narratives and ways of looking, standing as the relationship between the actual object of the photograph and the world. As I suggest in this essay, as long as postcards endure as historical texts, they are continually linked to whatever the current narrative and, hence, always in the process of becoming. The lack of identifying attributes make them fertile fields for interpretation. They picture unknown individuals, are produced by unknown photographers, sent by unknown purchasers, received by unknown viewers, collected somewhere by unknown persons and brought to whatever their final destination. This in itself is a very curious situation, and one rife with possibility. The possible interpretations at each stage are a challenge to contemplate. At every historical turn, the everyday epistemology of the viewer, whatever that particular cultural literacy happens to be, is mapped onto the image.

From the Belle Epoque to the Great War: Realism, social Darwinism, "the disappearing peoples" and other calamities

The first decade of the century saw the postcard craze, both in supply and demand, reach its zenith. The craze responded to several forces, each a demanding dictum of the enlightenment - realism, romanticism, Social Darwinism. These forces put their mark on the early twentieth century as they had on the nineteenth and culminated in the World War that was to destroy many carefully ordered views of the world. Colonialism was at its apex, bolstered by technology and the almost boundless supply of labour and resources in European and American colonies overseas. This situation provided innumerable indigenous images ready for the taking. Postcards reflected this economic privilege and millions of cards documented the success of colonization. It should be remembered, of course, that at this time, the industry of tourism was in a relatively fledgling state compared to its future as a global enterprise.

The world's indigenous people provided a limitless reservoir for a traffic in images. The myth of the time was that there is a world of types, a veritable smorgasbord of racial, ethnic and indigenous people. Deeply-rooted beliefs about colonial entitlements, sanctified by science and its closest lieutenants, truth and reality, kept these types prisoners of the roving camera. The task of scientist and layperson alike was to document and preserve the huge variety of peoples, surely a global mission to record each and every "type" and "species" and "culture". This was a powerful universal racial/racist discourse proclaiming the need for categorizing. The identifying print on many cards addressed this very idea, describing images as *Types jaunes*, *Types noirs* (Plate 2), or as *Scene et Types*. At the same time, Social Darwinist predictions deemed that indigenous people were a "disappearing people." There was, of course, enough physical evidence of this in far-flung sites of empire. Thus it was the duty of scientists and even of all Europeans and Americans to provide testimonials and keep records of the existence of these "dying races." A project such as this, with its encyclopedic goals, undoubtedly found a willing conspirator in every viewer and collector. It was also an undertaking of some urgency for the holy arm of colonialism to bring salvation to those colonized souls deemed to be in dire need of it (see Mathur, 1996-97).

Plate 2   Types Noirs. ca. 1908. Private Collection

There were reminders enough of the remnants of a disappearing world in postcard images. A 1907 photograph showed a dejected and obviously deprived "Old Casca Indian deserted by his tribe." The Church Missionary Society "Picture and Fact" postcard depicted "Some young Arabians" on a donkey cart and informed the viewer that "Only one in 20,000 of the children of Mesopotamia has ever heard of Christ's love from the lips of a Christian teacher." The tattered Western clothing and dishevelled hair of two women entitled only "Deux sauvages. Gaspe, Que." (1905) was clearly intended to be read as proof of the miserable, heathen condition of colonized people.

Such cards served several ends: they satisfied the commitments to realism, evoked the full sentiments of humanism and, perhaps even more importantly, helped to draw the boundaries between the "civilized" and the "uncivilized." Images were put to use even in the European world itself, serving old political conflicts and declaring stigmatized identities. A card, produced both in England and in New York (1906), hiding behind a supposed veneer of humour, entitled "My Irish Molly," depicted an unattractive Irish woman in a state of moral depravity, sporting a black eye, smoking a clay pipe, seated on a broken chair besides an empty grate, wearing down-at-heel boots, *but* in clear possession of three bottles of whiskey.[3] Such derogatory images were perpetuated by most world fairs, where native people were relegated to the edges of the technological marvels which received star exposure, to Shantyvilles, to marginal venues where they appeared as the Wild Man of Borneo or Fijian man-eaters (Hinsley, 1991:345). Obviously the moral and rational superiority of the viewing world remained intact.

Classification verified by photography added immensely to colonial control. It was evident that "taking pictures was indeed another means of taking possession of native peoples and their lands" (Corbey, 1993:362). Not only was ownership obviously there for the photographer and his people, but the certainties of racial polarities were installed. The major lesson of the enlightenment was served - that the supposed laws of nature were, after all, the reality of the world. The commitment to such supposed laws kept racialism alive. If there was still any doubt about the superiority of the European, there were postcards enough which insisted upon it as truth.

Almost as if embarrassed by such derogatory images and spurred on by the prevailing cults of romanticism and liberal humanism, a different tack was sometimes taken (see also Peterson, 1985). These were the kind of sentiments that, in a slightly earlier era, had made *Uncle Tom's Cabin* the most popular novel in America. In a familiar switch the "savages" of the racist version became imbued with their proverbial nobility. The ghosts of Rousseau, Thoreau and Kipling reigned unchallenged in these images. The usual romantic agenda about the authenticity of the natural and untamed, about exaggerated mysteries and everything exotic and about the basic goodness of humanity were clearly admired. This moved readily to seeing the heroic in the indigenous condition. The script is familiar not only in popular ideas, but in scientific and academic imagination as well. The males on the postcard became noble warriors and hunters. Proud North American chiefs sat astride their steeds wearing flowing ceremonial headdresses (Albers, 1998). Full-bearded patriarchs were honoured in pensive poses. Rickshaw operators became exotic and dignified in full Zulu regalia.

For women, the western romantic idiom produced visions fixated on attributes of beauty (beauty being the female equivalent of male power). The woman on the postcard was endowed with ethereal qualities, a combination of sensuality, innocence and delicacy, sometimes tinged with a demure spirituality and a promise of self-sacrifice - qualities already evoked in postcards of western women of that period. For example, a card which had several versions and was widely circulated from Niagara falls in the first decade of the century depicted the "myth of an Indian maiden" going over the falls to her death (Plate 3). A two-part version depicted first, a naked young woman cresting over the falls in her canoe, under a title that read "The Red Man's Fact: the Maiden Sacrifice." The second version showed her rising with gossamer wings from the base of the falls, while a caption informed that "The White Man's Fancy: Niagara Falls." If there were doubts about the innocence and spirituality of native women, cards presented them in flower-encircled portraits and titled them "Princesses", Hindu women in prayer, Filipino women demurely holding the skirts of national costumes. Everywhere faces assumed the much admired romantic melancholy . Children appeared in a series of poses meant to endear them to the viewer: as shyly smiling, innocently cuddling up to their mothers, or as newborns in the laps of medical missionaries (in one, ironically called "A Batch of Babies").

Plate 3 **The Red Man's Fact: "The Maiden's Sacrifice"/The White Man's Fancy: Niagara Falls. Made in Germany, ca. 1908. Private Collection.**

Other romantic depictions of women showed the more overt sexual attributes not sanctioned in popular depictions of respectable white women: bare-breasted island women, comely dancers, "ladies" with arms seductively behind their heads, women with direct bold gazes, "girls" clad in revealing European draperies. In the early years of the century, full nudity was known to be the practice of "savages," but not permitted in photographs of them, and altogether unthinkable for white women (aside from the proverbial "dirty French postcard"). This was not the case for bare-breastedness, however, and many postcards took advantage of this opportunity when showing indigenous women. Equally clearly as every feminist will argue, these are images produced by men especially for the titillation of a supposed male audience and for the shock value of everyone else.

Between the World Wars: Emerging equalities and "a camera in every hand"

A notable characteristic of the period after the Great War which had engaged most of Europe was that many of the polarities that had made earlier imagery possible were becoming fuzzier. White views of the world, separating the "them" from the "us," previously supported by Social Darwinism and the notions of value-free science, were being placed in question. Arrogance and subjugation, strangeness and familiarity, colonial power and colonies - once seen as the polar rules of existence - moved towards each other, lost some of their cultural isolation. The intensity of the postcard era had passed and cards no longer fed the innocent desire to know the world. The prosperity and peace of the 1920s offered a greater grasp of the incipient global village. The visual metaphors and cherished fictions of the *belle epoch* and the years before the war were no longer viable. They carried a morality fast becoming unfashionable. The boom of more technology placed a camera in almost every middle class home; telegraphy, the radio, motion pictures and telephone, as well as new publications, made a new immediacy possible. The powerful new media connected individual persons not only to others but also to strangers in strange places.

The mail was no longer delivered three times a day as it had been in many big cities and the postcard, a large part of that mail, slumped in popularity and came to be attached almost solely to the activity known as tourism. This change in function explains why there are more cards in museums and private collections from the first years of the century than there are from the period between the wars. No longer a treasured collectible, the card became an item of ephemera.

Tourism itself assumed unprecedented popularity. Along with the decline of the powers of the aristocracy associated with the end of the war, the one preoccupation once almost solely enjoyed by them, the Grand Tour, became the pastime of the affluent middle class. Moreover, the sense of entitlement to holidays became available to all but the impoverished. In this new atmosphere, tourism became more than a simple commodity, the tourist more than a consumer, and the cultures and persons consumed more than mere consumer goods. These new awarenesses led to a modification in postcard images.

The decrease in social distance brought a growing sense of relativity to what had been a seemingly preordained social world. Enfranchised citizens were emerging in the European and American world, and women already were making such gains. Colonialism, which eventually was to endure culturally long past its simple geographical manifestations, had become more aware of its own effects. More pointed attention was directed to the horrors wrought by war, famine, disease, natural disaster and, most importantly, by colonialism's own excesses.

The postcard image ceased to denigrate. Gone were the photographs which could in any way be interpreted as hardships or scarcities imposed by colonial status. There were no cards of indigenous people in tattered western cast-off clothing, performing demeaning occupations which were well-mechanized elsewhere (e.g. Mexican water carriers, Asian rickshaw pullers). The missionary photographic postcard had disappeared. In the United States earlier images such as Afro-Americans scrambling for tossed coins, black children eating watermelon (the quintessential demeaning stereotype for young Afro-Americans), were no longer visible. Instead people were pictured in their usual occupations. For example, cards showed southern black work crews on tobacco plantations. The messages on the back of these sociological cards informed the receiver of industrial practices. Postmarked 1940, one such card sender writes: "Here's the way cotton was picked in 1940...We do have a machine for it but it isn't perfect - and it would throw 1000's (sic) out of employment."

The possibilities for making indigenous images narrowed down to four standard scripts: their occupations, their costumes, the romantic poses of earlier years - heroes (nomads who resembled Rudolph Valentino), noble chiefs (magnificent in headdress) or sexually appealing females (demure but usually no longer bare-breasted), and the undeniable charm of young children. Certain stereotypes established earlier endured: the Aboriginal spear-thrower, the dozing Mexican, the hula dancer, the attractive child. Yet cards still continued to convey, more subtley to be sure, the degradation and poverty of the subject cultures. Although crassly exploitative depictions were scare, enough imagery remained to reflect ongoing attitudes. Hiding behind humour, for the comedic card was popular, cards shouted underlying biases. One such tableau from Mexico showed a search for head lice and bore the title "'Round Up' on the Frontier" (Plate 4). This particular image, curiously, was also found in cards from other parts of the world.

Plate 4   **"Round Up" on the Frontier. T C Chicago, 2003 H.S. B., C. T. American Art Coloured, dated 1936. Private Collection**

After World War II: constructivism, ethnologizing and the vertigo of relativism

The aftermath of World War Two, a war that took many years from the normal life of most of the nations on earth, heralded more radical changes, unthinkable even twenty-five years before. Western imperialism was gasping its last and self-government was the only viable alternative. Not only geographical boundaries but also the boundaries of race, class, ethnicity were called into question, although it would take the next fifty years to deconstruct and modify these centuries' old social classifications. While Social Darwinism still retained a presence, it was under continual attack. Existentialism, phenomenology and later the inevitable notion that there was not just one reality but many, forced the growing acceptance that everything was, perhaps after all, a social construction. Notions of absolute truth, whether in science or in the describing humankind, were robustly challenged.

While the postcards of architectural landmarks and the splendors of landscape remained essentially unchanged through the century, this was not true of those showing people and cultures. By the 1950s not only were independent countries producing their own postcards, but they were also vying for their own foreign and domestic tourists. The centrality of the human body as a representational medium for culture began to fade. Certainly some of the previously established stereotypes endured. The nobility of the Aboriginal elder, the Aboriginal hunter with spear, the romanticism of the Japanese woman in traditional kimono and the grass-skirted women of the South Pacific remained. In North America, Indian chiefs, resplendent in feathered headgear, remained institutionalized. In Canada, this icon was strengthened with the chiefs now joined by that other national icon, the red-coated officer of the Royal Canadian Mounted Police. In the United States cards make even stronger declarations. For example, the Indian chief is photographed with Mount Rushmore in the distance, thus equating his portrait with that of four presidents.

The codes of depiction, however, imposed strict new boundaries. The only cards deemed acceptable were set around traditional occupations, artistic productions, costumes, traditional dwellings, ceremonies and the performances developed for tourists. The gaze could focus on Saami herders positioned amidst their reindeer, Aboriginal men demonstrating fire-making, Brunei fishermen making nets, Inuit children at play, Navaho women weaving, Mexican potters decorating their work, and so on. This touristic idiom, limited to what was public and hence viewable, heralded the new order. As if to enforce this rule a new type of card made its appearance - photographs of cultural theme parks with people in native dress assembled in front of western reproductions of their dwellings and villages, museum displays and diaramas. Card titles and commentaries became ethnologized. The caption on a card using a photograph from a museum diarama of the North American Sun Dance with the central male figure suspended by hooks through the flesh of his chest - a disturbing and, of course, biased choice of display - reads "The Sun Dance was the most important annual ceremonial gathering of the Plains Indian. Some men endured self-torture in fulfillment of a vow made previously during a time of severe crisis." The images had assumed a performative function, a theatricality, as if the figures therein had stepped out of their lives and, as actors, had instructed the tourists about their culture.

Nowhere were the tourist connections stronger than in Hawaiian postcards. Hawaiians were depicted in typical tourist situations such as lifting pineapples from the field for the visitor to view, teaching rows of guests how to do the hula, sitting around luau tables with them, paddling canoes together, making leis and placing these around the necks of new arrivals. Ironically this did not stop the proliferation of seductive maidens in sarongs or grass skirts, flowers behind their left ear, holding two pineapples or reclining invitingly against a background of tropical island flora.

A new individualism was afoot. Indian chiefs and Aboriginal elders, two perpetuated and acceptable images of individuals, were often identified by their actual names. Young women never are. Tribal affiliations were given, e.g. "The Bamyili dancers are members of the Ngalpun, Maiali, Rembarrnga and Djuana tribes living 250 miles south of Darwin." Added to this was a new enthusiasm for archival material, leading to old photographs and paintings being reproduced on cards, citing either library or museum sources, and correctly describing the subject matter in ethnological style. Reproductions of the art works of indigenous artists became common, particularly those of Australian artists whose works now sell in the six figure range in New York and London.

Last decades: representational crisis, postmodernism, "whose culture is it anyway?"

The representational crisis is completed in the last decades of the century. Cultural autonomy is the name of the movement. Postmodernism has questioned essences, made race into a nineteenth century fiction, deconstructed all images presented heretofore, and blurred the line between reality and parody. It had no time for old certainties. Parallel to this new sensibility, old identity references such as Indians, natives, Eskimos, Lapps, Aborigines have been corrected to First Peoples, First Nations, Inuit, Saami and hyphenated nationalities. It should be noted that the word "indigenous", though currently acceptable, may eventually be associated with at present unforeseen historical or political embarrassments.

While the performative functions and the stereotypical photographs of the previous period endure, perhaps as kitch or camp, a new element is added. Indigenous people are not resources for tradition-making but as the rightful owners and makers of tradition. It is also obvious that individuality and privacy have reappeared and the person is sacrosanct. Similarly, it is also clear that intellectual property and ownership of resources are of paramount significance (Whittaker, 1999; see also Hollinshead, 1996), as is the control of cultural property and even of major geographical tourist sites like Uluru (Ayers Rock) in Australia (Whittaker, 1994) and specific abandoned village sites in Haida Gwaii (Queen Charlotte Islands) in British Columbia. Indigenous people have assumed the construction their own past, their own ethnology and their own narratives. This includes new imperatives such as projecting the diversity and multiple identities hitherto denied them.

In keeping with the dominant discourses of the indigenous communities, postcards have taken a new tack. There are still tourist industry cards with carefully controlled imagery. But now there are also self-produced cards (in the Australian case by Aboriginal councils and associations), indigenous tourist guides and guide books. A card of social protest, featuring the figure of a woman, hands defiantly on her hips, reminds the viewer that "You are on Aboriginal Land." Another card claiming to celebrate "Two Hundred Years of Post Cards" positions an Aboriginal woman against an Uluru/Ayers Rock background painted in the colours of the Aboriginal national flag - orange, red and black. Other cards inform the buyer that the proceeds of the sale go to some indigenous institution or are being returned by an non-indigenous photographer to the community photographed. That this movement is in its early stages is clear. One can still find postcards with embarrassingly biased depictions - indigenous people posed in a gallery of images with fauna, seemingly as invitations to view the "natural" exotica of regions. Bare-breasted native women with come-hither looks are still to be found. These cards, however, are increasingly understood by a more sensitized public to be the unacceptable examples of a time lag in social change.

At the turn of the newest century, therefore, the images of one hundred years ago are excursions into a now painful historical past. The transnational culture of tourism has proclaimed a new recognition of cultures becoming decolonized. Whatever image a card assumes, it is now interpreted as a political act. The voice of prohibition that speaks in each head warns against image vulgarities, against old insensitivities. It promotes honouring new codes of representation and appropriation and, above all, consulting when in doubt.

Endnotes

Acknowledgements: This paper is part of an ongoing project on the imagery of indigenous people in the tourist industry. A partial earlier version was read at Tourism section of the Annual Meeting of the Popular Culture Association, April 1999, San Diego, California. Thanks are due to Carl Whittaker, Neil Eaton and to Michael Robinson for encouraging me to present part of this work. Earlier parts of this work were supported by a grant from the Social Sciences and Humanities Council of Canada.

1. Credit is due to Frank Staff who made this circular production visible in his attention to the history of the postcard (1966).

2. Although little is known about this particular area, it would be surprising if any "colonized person" entered into the postcard craze, collected or even cherished photographs of themselves. Despite this, a few indigenous photographers are known to have recorded their own cultures, but this area is also poorly researched. See, however, the special case of George Hunt (Jacknis, 1992).

3. The denigration of the Irish in popular images and in identity politics is a popular theme on both sides of the Atlantic from the nineteenth and earlier twentieth century. For an analysis of the early racist image of the Irish, as projected in cartoons, in periodicals and in the press, see L. Perry Curtis, Jr. (1971) *Apes and Angels: The Irishman in Victorian Caricature*. Smithsonian Institution Press, Washington.

References

Albers, P.C. (1998), Symbols, souvenirs and sentiments: postcard imagery of Plains Indians, 1898-1918. In: Geary, C.M. and Webb, V. (eds) *Delivering Views: Distant cultures in early postcards*, Smithsonian Institution Press, Washington, D.C., pp.65-89.

Albers, P. C. and James, W. R. (1987), Tourism and the Changing Image of Mexico. Paper given at the Annual Meetings of the Society for Applied Anthropology, Oaxaca, Mexico.

Bauman, Z. (1988-89), Strangers: The social construction of universality and particularity, *Telos*, 78, pp. 7-42.

Corbey, R. (1993), Ethnographic showcases 1870-1930, *Cultural Anthropology*, 8 (3): 338-369.

Handy, E. (1998), Japonisme and American postcard visions of Japan. In: Geary, C. M. and Webb, V. (eds) *Delivering Views: Distant cultures in early postcards*, Smithsonian Institution Press, Washington, D.C., pp.91-113.

Hinsley, C. M. (1991), The world as marketplace: Commodification of the exotic at the World's Columbia Exposition, Chicago, 1893. In: Karp, I and Lavine, S. D. (eds) *Exhibiting Cultures: The poetics and politics of museum display*, Smithsonian Institution Press, Washington, D.C., pp. 344-365.

Hollinshead, K. (1996), Marketing in the twilight of time: Tourism as a regenerative force for aboriginal culture. In: Robinson, M., Evans, N. and P. Callaghan (eds), *Tourism and Culture: Towards the 21st century*, University of Northumbria, Newcastle, pp.97-108.

Jacknis, I. (1992), George Hunt, Kwakiutl Photographer. In Edwards, E (ed.) *Anthropology and Photography 1860-1920*, Yale University Press, New Haven, pp.143-151.

Mathur, S. (1996-97), Re-visualising the missionary subject: history, modernity and Indian women, *Third Text*, 37, pp.53-61.

Peterson, N. (1985), The popular image. In: Donaldson, I. and Donaldson, T. (eds) *Seeing the First Australians*, George Allen and Unwin, Sydney, pp. 164-180.

Schor, N. (1994), Collecting Paris. In: Elsner, J. and Cardinal, R. (eds) *The Cultures of Collecting*, Harvard University Press, Cambridge, Mass. pp.252-274.

Staff, F. (1966, 1979), *The Picture Postcard and its Origins*, Frederick A. Praeger Publishers, New York.

Whittaker, E. (1994), Public discourse on sacredness: the transfer of Ayers Rock to Aboriginal ownership, *American Ethnologist*, 21, pp. 310-334.

Whittaker, E. (1999), Indigenous tourism: reclaiming knowledge, culture and intellectual property in Australia. In: Robinson, R. and Boniface, P. (eds) *Tourism and Cultural Conflicts*, CAB International Publishing, Oxon, pp. 33-46.